WORLD OF

IRVING HOWE

with the assistance of Kenneth Libo

OUR FATHERS

Galahad Books · New York

Copyright © 1976 by Irving Howe

All rights reserved. No part of this work may be reproduced or transmitted
in any form or by any means, electronic or mechanical, including photocopying,
recording, or any information storage and retrieval system, without permission in
writing from the publisher. All requests for permission to reproduce material
from this work should be directed to Harcourt, Brace & Company,
6277 Sea Harbor Drive, Orlando, Florida 32887.

The author wishes to thank the following publishers for permission to quote from the
sources listed:

Alfred A. Knopf, Inc., for *A Lost Paradise* by Samuel Chotzinoff, copyright 1953, ©
1955 by Samuel Chotzinoff; American Jewish Historical Society, Waltham, Mass., for
"A Portrait of Ethnic Politics" by Arthur Gorenstein [Aryeh Goren], and "The
Polarity of Jewish Attitudes Toward Immigration" by Esther Panitz, both published
in *American Jewish Historical Quarterly*; *American Political Science Review* for
"American Jews and the Presidential Vote" by Lawrence Fuchs; Bloch Publishing
Company for *Out of Endless Yearnings: A Memoir of Israel Davidson* by C. Davidson;
Cambridge University Press for *The Class Struggle in the Pale* by Ezra Mendelsohn;
Central Yiddish Culture Organization for *Dertsayler un romanistn* by S. Niger; *Com-
mentary* for "The Golden Age of Thomashefsky" and "The Politicians" by S. L.
Blumenson, "Toward a History of the Holocaust" by Lucy Dawidowicz, "Suburban
Jewish Sunday School" by Theodore Fraenkel, "Progress of a Suburban Jewish Com-
munity" by Herbert Gans, "The Comedy of Lenny Bruce" by Albert Goldman,
"The Lost Young Intellectual" by Irving Howe, "CCNY—a Memoir" by Meyer Liben,
"The Vanishing Jew of Our Popular Culture" by Henry Popkin, and "Is There a
Jewish Art?" by Harold Rosenberg; Conference on Jewish Social Studies for "The
Jewish World: A Study in Contrasts" by Lucy Dawidowicz, published in *Jewish
Social Studies*; Doubleday & Co., Inc., for *A Bintel Brief*, translation copyright © 1971
by Isaac Metzker; *Esquire* for "The Yiddishization of American Humor" by Wallace
Markfield, © 1965 by Esquire, Inc.; Farlag Unser Tsait for *Di yidishe sotsialistishe
bavegung* by J. S. Hertz; Harper & Row, Publishers, Inc., for *My Life Is in Your
Hands* by Eddie Cantor, *An American in the Making* by Marcus Ravage, and *The
Downtown Jews* by Ronald Sanders; Herzl Press for *Nachman Syrkin, Socialist Zion-
ist* by Marie Syrkin; Holt, Rinehart and Winston, Publishers, for *A Treasury of
Yiddish Poetry* edited by Irving Howe and Eliezer Greenberg, copyright © 1969 by
Irving Howe and Eliezer Greenberg; *Jewish Daily Morning Freiheit* for *Teg fun
mayne teg* by Moshe Nadir; *Jewish Frontier* for "Old-Timers and Newcomers" by
Will Herberg; The Jewish Publication Society of America for "The Jewish Labor

(Continued on page 694)

Published in 1994 by

Galahad Books
A division of Budget Book Service, Inc.
386 Park Avenue South
New York, NY 10016

Galahad Books is a registered trademark of Budget Book Service, Inc.

Published by arrangement with Harcourt, Brace & Company.

Library of Congress Catalog Card Number: 75-16342

ISBN: 0-88365-882-8

Printed in the United States of America.

For Arien

Contents

Illustrations

The drawings that appear throughout the text are by Jacob Epstein.
The cartoon strip on page 534 is from *Zagat Drawings and Paintings: Jewish Life on New York's Lower East Side, 1912-1962,* edited by Ida R. Zagat.

Preface

This book tells the story of those east European Jews who, for several decades starting in the 1880's, undertook a massive migration to the United States. There were two million of them, and they settled mostly in the large American cities, where they attempted to maintain their own Yiddish culture; then, as a result of both external pressures and their own desires, they made their way into American society. Among the Jews settling in America, the east Europeans were by far the largest component and thus the most influential. To tell their story is, to a considerable extent, to tell the story of twentieth-century American Jews. Nevertheless, this book is not a history of the American Jews as a whole, nor a history of American Jewish institutions, religious or secular. The German Jews, who arrived earlier and whose status and prospects were better, do appear repeatedly in these pages, but mostly insofar as they enter relations with those from eastern Europe. The Sephardic Jews as a group hardly figure at all. In 1870 there were probably about 60,000 Jews in New York. By 1880 the estimate had risen to approximately 80,000; by 1910, there were about 1,100,000 Jews in the city.

   This book is a work of social and cultural history and thereby lays claim, with all the notorious pitfalls besetting any such work, to being an accurate record. I have used as major sources the vast memoir literature in both English and Yiddish; an accumulating secondary scholarship which deals with various aspects of immigrant experience; the rich materials of the Yiddish press; accounts in American newspapers, journals, and historical studies; a range of personal interviews; and, to a lesser extent, works of fiction that touch upon this aspect of American life. In addition to the materials used in the social portraits I have drawn, some of them necessarily composites, there are numerous further citations that could have been brought to bear. In fact—heaven forbid!—it would have been easy to make this book twice as long simply by piling up further evidence. But I have used materials that I judged to be representative.

   Problems of space have also prevented me from including as much material as I should have liked about the immigrant Jews in cities other than New York. While there were, of course, significant differences between the experiences of immigrant Jews in Chicago or Philadelphia and those in New York, I have gone on the assumption—which the available evidence largely supports—that in crucial respects what is shown here regarding the immigrants of the East Side of New York also holds for those in other large cities. As for the relatively small number of Jews who settled in small towns or became farmers, that is another story.

All documentation appears in the Reference Notes at the end, grouped according to the subsections of each chapter. Footnotes at the bottom of pages are meant to be read as illustrations of or comments on or, sometimes, diversions from the main text.

Where a Yiddish word or phrase is used only once or twice, a translation is immediately provided. Where a Yiddish word is used frequently, a translation will appear with the first use and, if the word recurs over a number of chapters, also at later points. A glossary at the back of the book contains translations of all Yiddish words and phrases. But you don't have to be Jewish, or know Yiddish, to read this book.

Transliterating Yiddish presents some problems, which I have tried to solve mainly with an eye toward helping the reader. YIVO, the Yiddish scholarly center, has provided a standard system of transliteration, meant mostly for scholarly purposes. It thereby comes into conflict, at some points, with the liberalities of customary usage. For example, the guttural sound in Yiddish is rendered by YIVO as *kh,* while customary usage in the United States has been *ch.* It seems mere hindrance to the reader to insist upon Sholom Alei*kh*em rather than Sholom Alei*ch*em. So, while following the YIVO system as closely as possible, I have made some concessions to customary usage. In this book our great writer remains Sholom Aleichem, and I use *Yiddishkeit* rather than *Yiddishkayt.* For the measure of inconsistency in my transliterating, I hope my friends at YIVO will forgive me.

WORLD OF OUR FATHERS

TOWARD

1

AMERICA

Origins

T

HE YEAR 1881 marks a turning point in the history of the Jews as decisive as that of 70 A.D., when Titus's legions burned the Temple at Jerusalem, or 1492, when Ferdinand and Isabella decreed the expulsion from Spain. On March 1, 1881, Alexander II, czar of Russia, was assassinated by revolutionary terrorists; the modest liberalism of his regime came to an end; and within several weeks a wave of pogroms, inspired mostly by agents of the new government, spread across Russia. For the Jews packed into the Pale* and overflowing its boundaries, the accession of Alexander III signified not only immediate disaster but also the need for a gradual reordering of both their inner life and their relationship to a country in which Jews had been living for hundreds of years. The question had now to be asked: should the east European Jews continue to regard themselves as permanent residents of the Russian empire or should they seriously consider the possibility of a new exodus?

> * The Pale of Settlement comprised that area of czarist Russia in which the Jews were legally authorized to settle. The Pale covered an area of about 386,000 square miles, from the Baltic Sea to the Black Sea. By 1897, slightly less than 4,900,000 Jews lived there, forming 94 percent of the total Jewish population of Russia and about 12 percent of the population of the area.

There had already been a trickle of Jewish emigration to America—
7,500 in the years between 1820 and 1870 and somewhat more than 40,000 in
the 1870's. But the idea of America as a possible locale for collective renewal
had not yet sunk deeply into the consciousness of the east European Jews.
During the reign of Alexander II many of them had experienced modest
hopes of winning equal rights as citizens. Others hoped to persuade the less
benighted agents of Russian autocracy that the Jews merited a share in its
prospective enlightenment. By the 1880's that hope was badly shaken, perhaps destroyed.

At no time could the life of the Jews in Russia have been described as
comfortable. With the caprice of absolutism, the monarchs had alternated
between prolonged repression and intervals of relaxation. They had frequently believed that toleration of other religions might bring a risk of
disloyalty to the supreme truth of Christianity, and the more fanatical
among them had tried to "convert" the Jews through coercion and force.
Rarely were the Jews able to ease their guard against blows from above and
below, bureaucrats and folk, and never could they see themselves as citizens
like all others. Their role as pariahs, the stiff-necked enemies of Christ, was
fixed both in official doctrine and popular legend. Repression took the forms
of economic harassment and legal humiliation, sometimes pogroms and accusations of ritual blood murder. At intervals these policies would be eased a
little, and the Jews would be allowed, as part of a tendency toward West-
ernization, to settle in outlying southern and western districts. With the
conquest of new territories in the south during the middle of the eighteenth
century and the partition of Poland a few decades later, the number of Jews
under Russian domination greatly increased. For a time Catherine II welcomed them as merchants and traders who might stimulate the economy,
but soon—in what seems a constant alternation between tightening and
loosening of the chains of power—her exercise in tolerance came to an
end.

Once the Holy Alliance sealed the defeat of Napoleon and stabilized
Europe as a concert of reaction, the conditions of the Russian Jews, as
indeed of almost all Russians, sadly deteriorated. The reign of Nicholas I,
from 1825 to 1855, proved to be a nightmare. Over six hundred anti-Jewish
decrees were enacted, ranging from expulsions from villages in which Jews
had traditionally resided to a heavy censorship of Yiddish and Hebrew
books; from meddling with the curriculums of Jewish schools to a conscription that tore Jewish children away from parents, often at ages between
twelve and eighteen, for periods of up to twenty-five years. In his memoirs
Alexander Herzen has unforgettably portrayed a convoy of conscripted
Jewish children:

> "You see, they have collected a crowd of cursed little Jewish boys of eight or
> nine years old" [a Russian officer tells Herzen in a village in the province of
> Vyatka]. ". . . they just die off like flies. A Jew boy, you know, is such a
> frail, weakly creature . . . he is not used to tramping in the mud for ten

hours a day and eating biscuit . . . being among strangers, no father nor mother nor petting; well, they cough and cough until they cough themselves into their graves."

. . . it was one of the most awful sights I have ever seen, those poor, poor children! Boys of twelve or thirteen might somehow have survived it, but little fellows of eight and ten. . . .

Pale, exhausted, with frightened faces, they stood in thick, clumsy, soldiers' overcoats, with stand-up collars, fixing helpless, pitiful eyes on the garrison soldiers who were roughly getting them into ranks. . . . And these sick children, without care or kindness, exposed to the icy wind that blows unobstructed from the Arctic Ocean, were going to their graves.

The acknowledged aim of Nicholas's measures was the destruction of the Jewish community as a social and religious body. One of his secret decrees explained, "The purpose in educating Jews is to bring about their gradual merging with the Christian nationalities and to uproot those superstitious and harmful prejudices which are instilled by the teachings of the Talmud." Through the following century, at least until a more scientific precision was developed in the art of murder, the Nicolaitan persecutions would leave a shudder vibrating in the minds of the Jews, with stories passed from generation to generation, even to children of immigrants in America, about little boys forcibly converted by Russian officers or accepting a death of martyrdom rather than yield to such conversion.

No wonder that Alexander II, whom Disraeli called "the kindliest prince who has ever ruled Russia," aroused enthusiasm among the Jews. Alexander II reduced the period of military service to five years; opened the doors of the universities to some Jews; permitted Jewish businessmen to travel in parts of Russia from which they had been barred. Under his reign the forty million serfs of Russia were freed, though the economic consequences for both the peasants and that narrow stratum of Jews who had occupied a precarious position between landowner and peasants were by no means completely advantageous. But once this weak effort at official liberalism collapsed and the pogroms of 1881 left the Jews stunned and bleeding, it was no longer possible, even for the Russified middle-class Jewish intellectuals, to hold out much hope for Fabian solutions. Though not as bestial as Nicholas, Alexander III pursued a steady anti-Jewish policy. Neither stability nor peace, well-being nor equality, was possible for the Jews of Russia.

The World of the Shtetl

For several hundred years this culture had flourished in eastern Europe. Bound together by firm spiritual ties, by a common language, and by a sense of destiny that often meant a sharing of martyrdom, the Jews of eastern

Europe were a kind of nation yet without recognized nationhood. Theirs was both a community and a society: internally a community, a ragged kingdom of the spirit, and externally a society, impoverished and imperiled.

The central trait of this culture was an orientation toward otherworldly values—though this may be too simple a way of describing it. For the world of the east European Jews, at least in its most serious and "ideal" manifestations, did not accept the Western distinction between worldly and otherworldly. Kierkegaard's dictum that "between God and man there is an infinite, yawning, qualitative difference" might have struck them as a reasonable account of their actual condition, but not as a statement of necessary or inescapable limits. In order to survive, the east European Jews had to abide by the distinction between worldly and otherworldly, but they refused to recognize it as just or inevitable. In their celebration of the Sabbath and in the sharp line they drew between the Sabbath and the rest of the week, they tacitly acknowledged that they had to live by the ways of the world; this was the price of exile and dispersion. Ideally, however, the worldly and otherworldly should be one—here on earth. Every Jew would have recognized immediately the symbolic rightness in the refusal of Reb Shloyme, a character in Peretz's drama *Di goldene keyt* ("The Golden Chain"), to accept "the week," those six mundane days that lie scattered beneath the glory of the Sabbath.

The life of the east European Jews was anything but an idyl. Given the pressures from without and a slow stagnation within, this world was bound to contain large portions of the ignorant, provincial, and even corrupt. One of the motivating forces behind the communal and political movements that sprang up during the last two decades of the nineteenth century, as well as of the Yiddish poetry and fiction written at the same time, was a desire to stir the blood of a society that had gone sluggish, to cleanse the life of a people that had suffered too long from isolation, poverty, and violence.

Locked into a backward economy, the Jews of eastern Europe continued to act and think primarily in premodern, prebourgeois terms. The struggle for livelihood, unending and rarely successful, occupied much time—it had to. But never was it regarded by the acknowledged spokesmen of the Jews as the primary reason for existence. Scholarship was, above all else, honored among the Jews—scholarship not as "pure" activity, not as intellectual release, but as the pathway, sometimes treacherous, to God. A man's prestige, authority, and position depended to a considerable extent on his learning. Those who were learned sat at the eastern wall of the synagogue, near the Holy Ark. Women often became breadwinners so that their husbands could devote themselves to study, while householders thought it their duty, indeed privilege, to support precocious sons-in-law studying the Holy Word.

There was another side, of course. Scholarship often degenerated into abysmal scholasticism. Intellect could be reduced to a barren exercise in distinctions that had long ago lost their reality. Manual labor was frequently regarded as a mark of social disgrace. Among the more orthodox, modern thought met with furious resistance: how could the works of man measure against the Word of God? Secular books, by the early or mid-nineteenth century, began to be smuggled into the yeshivas and read on the sly, their forbidden contents eagerly examined by students as they chanted the Talmudic singsong. A few rabbis were ready to receive the new learning of the West, but in the main the rabbinate felt that any large infiltration of Western thought would be its undoing; and it was right.

The traditional world is lovingly summoned by a nineteenth-century Jewish writer as he describes a visit to a *heder* (school):

> Soon a poorly clad couple entered, the man carrying in his arms a young boy of about six, wrapped in a *talit* [prayer shawl]. Both father and mother were weeping with joy, grateful to God who had preserved them that they might witness this beautiful moment. Having extended a cordial welcome to the newcomers, the *melamed* [teacher] took the hero of the celebration into his arms and stood him upon a table. Afterwards the boy was seated on a bench and was the first to receive cake, nuts, raisins and dainties of which the happy mother had brought along an apron-full. The teacher then sat down near the youngster, placed a card with a printed alphabet before him and, taking a long pointer, began the first lesson by blessing his newly-initiated pupil that he may be raised for the study of Torah, marriage, and good deeds.

And here, in quite another voice, is a report, written in 1894, of a Jewish school in Vitebsk:

> Our Talmud Torahs are filthy rooms, crowded from nine in the morning until nine in the evening with pale, starved children. These remain in this contaminated atmosphere for twelve hours at a time and see only their bent, exhausted teachers. . . . Their faces are pale and sickly, and their bodies evidently not strong. In parties of twenty or thirty, and at times more, they all repeat some lesson aloud after their instructor. He who has not listened to the almost absurd commentaries of the ignorant *melamed* cannot even imagine how little the children gain from such instruction.

Which of these accounts is the truth, which can we believe? There is no simple answer, for each summons a portion and only a portion of the truth, so that the two qualify and complement one another.

The world of the east European Jews was colored throughout by religious emotion, yet it was not a theocracy: by no means were the rabbis undisputed rulers. It was a world dominated by an uneasy alliance between a caste of the learned and the somewhat wealthier merchants. In their formal value system, the Jews gave precedence to the learned, but as with any other formal system, this precedence was honored at least as much in the breach as in the observance. The closer this world came to modern life, the more did wealth challenge and usurp the position of learning. There was never, it is true, a formal dispossession of learning, but often enough there smoldered a subterranean rivalry between learning and wealth that could suddenly flare into the open. What preserved a degree of social fluidity was that learning, at least potentially, was open to everyone and not the exclusive property of any group or caste.

Socially this world had not yet split into sharply defined and antagonistic classes. By the 1880's some Jews had settled in the larger cities, such as Warsaw and Lodz; within the next few decades the number of Jews moving from the *shtetl* to urban concentrations increased sharply. The beginnings of a Jewish proletariat started to appear in the cities, though in the main it consisted not of factory workers but of artisans employed in small shops. Strikes broke out, class feeling hardened. But in the *shtetl* one could hardly speak of fully formed rival classes, since few Jews owned any massive means of production and fewer still sold their labor power. Often the relations between the social strata of the *shtetl* came to little more than a difference between the poor and the hopelessly poor. Only if the pressures of the external world had been suddenly removed would the suppressed economic conflicts within the *shtetl* have reached full expression. As it was, the *shtetl* nestled in the crevices of a backward agricultural economy where Jews, often prohibited from ownership of land, had to live by trading, artisanship, and their wits. But if, strictly speaking, the *shtetl* did not have articulated social classes, it was still far from what we would now regard as a democratic community. Distinctions of caste were urgently maintained, through learning, economic position, and the concept of *yikhes*, which pertains to family status and pride.

Gross misapprehensions about the nature of the *shtetl* have flourished since its destruction by modern totalitarianism. The *shtetl* was not a village—the term east European Jews used for a village was *dorf*. The *shtetl* was a town, usually a small one; it sometimes had cobbled streets; it occasionally had imposing structures; and it rarely was picturesque. It consisted, writes a portraitist, of

> a jumble of wooden houses clustered higgledy-piggledy about a market-place . . . as crowded as a slum. . . . The streets . . . are as tortuous as a Talmudic argument. They are bent into question marks and folded into parentheses. They run into culs-de-sac like a theory arrested by a fact; they ooze off into lanes, alleys, back yards. . . . [At the center is] the market-place, with its shops, booths, tables, stands, butchers' blocks. Hither come daily, except during the winter, the peasants and peasant women from many miles around, bringing their live-stock and vegetables, their fish and hides, their wagonloads of grain, melons, parsley, radishes, and garlic. They buy, in exchange, the city produce which the Jews import, dry goods, hats, shoes, boots, lamps, oil, spades, mattocks, and shirts. The tumult of the market-place . . . is one of the wonders of the world.

Because the *shtetl* lived in constant expectation of external attack, all the inner tendencies making for disintegration were kept in check. The outer world, the world of the gentiles and the worldlings, meant hostility, sacrilege, brute force: the threat of the fist against the defenseless Word. This condition of permanent precariousness gave the east European Jews a conscious sense of being at a distance from history, from history as such and history as a conception of the Western world. Living in an almost timeless proximity with the mythical past and the redeeming future, with Abraham's sacrifice of his beloved son to a still more beloved God and the certain appearance of a cleansing Messiah*—for heaven was *real*, not a useful myth, and each passing day brought one nearer to redemption—the Jews could not help feeling that history was a little ridiculous, an often troublesome trifling of the gentile era. Once the *shtetl* began to crumble under alien pressures, the sense of history, suddenly rising to acute consciousness, became an obsession; or more accurately, the modern idea of time as the very stuff of life which can never be held or held back, was absorbed into a faith that had always been addressed to eternity, so that certain of the political movements among the east European Jews, notably Zionism and socialism, received nutriment from the very faith they had begun to displace.

The world of the east European Jews was a world in which God was a living force, a Presence, more than a name or a desire. He did not rule from on high; He was not a God of magnificence; nor was He an aesthetic God. The Jews had no beautiful churches, they had wooden synagogues. Beauty was a quality, not a form; a content, not an arrangement. The Jews would have been deeply puzzled by the idea that the aesthetic and the moral are distinct realms. One spoke not of a beautiful thing but of a beautiful deed. Only later did Jewish intellectuals discover that, even in the usual Western terms, there was an innocent beauty in Jewish liturgical music, the carving of the Holy Arks, the embroidery of prayer shawls, the calligraphy of the Holy Scripts. But where intellectuals saw these as objects or qualities to be isolated for aesthetic inspection, their ancestors had seen them as integral elements in the cultivation of God's Word.

It was the word that counted most. Yiddish culture was a culture of speech, and its God a God who spoke. He was a plebeian God, perhaps immanent but hardly transcendent. Toward Him the Jews could feel a peculiar sense of intimacy: had they not suffered enough in His behalf? In prayer His name could not be spoken, yet in or out of prayer He could always be spoken to. Because the east European Jew felt so close to God he could complain to Him freely, and complain about Him too. The relation between God and man was social, intimate, critical, seeming at times to follow like a series of rationalistic deductions from the premise of the

* In a lovely phrase, Maurice Samuel writes that for *shtetl* inhabitants, "the Bible was a daily newspaper."

Chosen People. The Jewish God, to whom one prayed in Hebrew and with whom one pleaded in Yiddish, had been humanized through experience with His people. He had been taught the uses of mercy. The despair with which a Kafka knocks on the door of the Lord suggests that he does not expect the door ever to be opened, whereas the rasping impatience with which Yiddish folk writers of the Hasidic period appealed to the Lord leaves no doubt that they knew He would respond.

"There is a sense," writes Isaiah Berlin, "in which no social problem arose for the Jews as long as rigid religious orthodoxy insulated them from the external world. Until then, poor, downtrodden, and oppressed as they might be, and clinging to each other for warmth and shelter, the Jews of eastern Europe put all their faith in God and concentrated all their hope either upon individual salvation—immortality in the sight of God—or upon the coming of the Messiah."

Together with a living God went a holy language, Hebrew, known by the educated and admired by the ignorant. The events of Jewish life were divided into two endless days, the Biblical yesterday and the exile of today. History was seen less as a vertical movement through time than as a horizontal simultaneity, and Jewish history as the emanation of a pure idea, the idea of the Chosen People. In a sense, history did not even exist: there was only an endless expectation until the Messiah came, and until that moment there would be the glory of Hebrew, a language not unaffected by the passage of time but meant ultimately to stake out a defiance of time.

Near and beneath Hebrew flowed another language, Yiddish. Elbowed away from the place of honor, it grew freely and richly. Based originally on a mixture of Middle High German dialects, it soon acquired an international scope, borrowing freely from almost every European language. Neither set nor formalized, always in rapid process of growth and dissolution, Yiddish was a language intimately reflecting the travail of wandering, exile, dispersion; it came, in the long history of the Jews, like a late and beloved, if not fully honored, son.

The moral and psychological burdens this world took upon itself were very great. Nature is not a frequent presence in Yiddish thought or writing; it hardly could be in a culture so desperately besieged and so thoroughly committed to the exploration of moral order; but when it does appear, as in the writings of Mendele Mokher Sforim, the first major Yiddish novelist, it is often used self-consciously as a counterpoise to that deadening of appetites which long years of study in the yeshivas might entail.

In other respects, the Jews did make their peace with natural impulse. The view that sexual activity is impure or at least suspect, so often an accompaniment of Christianity, was seldom entertained in the *shtetl.* Paul's remark that it is better to marry than to burn would have seemed strange, if not downright impious, to the Jews, who believed that marriage and procreation, far from being a lesser evil, were a positive good. The modern idea of sexuality as a form of play sufficient unto itself could hardly flourish in the east European Jewish world. But this was still very far from the puritan notion that the human body is inherently suspect. Similarly, the idea of asceticism, a kind of programmatic withdrawal from communal life, played only a minor part among the east European Jews, partly because a society of deprivation is not likely to be tempted by the luxury of self-deprivation. As for romantic love, that appears during the twilight of the *shtetl*, when the values of the West have begun to undercut its foundations. Traditionally, marriages were arranged by families, with the wealth and rank of the groom counting for more than personal feelings. In Sholom Aleichem's writings, romantic love comes to signify the breakup of traditional forms and values.

At the peak of its development the *shtetl* was a highly formalized society. It had to be. Living in the shadow of lawlessness, it felt a need to mold its life into lawfulness. It survived by the disciplines of ritual. The 613 *mitzvot*, or commandments, that a pious Jew must obey, which dictate such things as the precise way in which a chicken is to be slaughtered; the singsong in which the Talmud is to be read; the kinds of food to serve during the Sabbath; the way in which shoes should be put on each morning; the shattering of a glass by the groom during a marriage ceremony—these were the outer signs of an inner discipline. In so heavily ritualized a world there was little room for individuality as we have come to understand it, since the community was the manifestation of God's covenant with Israel, as the family was the living core of the community. The world of the east European Jews clung to its ways, and to nothing more fiercely than the myth of the Chosen People, the full irony of which it was the first to recognize, above all in the network of humor it threw up against the alien world.

No simple response is possible, no unambiguous one adequate, to this lost world of the east European Jews. There is truth, even if idealized and sublimated, in the elegiac memoir of Abraham Heschel:

> A blazing passion permeated all activities. . . . Immersed in complicated legal discussions, they could at the same time feel the anguish of the Divine Presence that abides in exile. In endeavouring to unravel some perplexity raised by a seventeenth-century commentary on a commentary on the Talmud, they were able in the same breath to throb with sympathy for Israel and all afflicted people. Study was a technique for sublimating feeling into thought, for transposing dreams into syllogisms, for expressing grief in difficult theoretical formulations. . . . To contrive an answer to gnawing doubts was the highest joy. Indeed, there was a whole world of subdued gaiety and sober frolic in the playful subtleties of their *pilpul* [dialectic]. . . . Carried away by the mellow, melting chant of Talmud-reading, one's mind soared high in the pure realm of thought, away from this world of facts and worries, away from the boundaries of the here and now, to a region where the Divine Presence listens to what Jews create in the study of His word.

And there is truth, more acrid and bitter, in the words of Ba'al Makh-shoves, the pioneer Yiddish literary critic, who in a study of Mendele Mokher Sforim writes about the *shtetl:*

Jewish poverty is a kind of marvel to Mendele, for no parallel to it can be found anywhere. This is not the poverty of the great European cities, nor is it the poverty of the Russian peasant. . . . Jewish poverty has no idea what a factory looks like, for it exists in the *shtetl* where it has its origins in fathers and grandfathers who have been wretchedly poor since time immemorial. The Russian peasant, poor as he may be, is the proprietor of a small piece of land. And his condition is not hopeless—one feels that sooner or later it will improve. But Jewish poverty is utterly without a cure; the Jew has no available means for improving his condition, which will remain abject as long as he lives among alien peoples. In villages where life should have brought him closer to the earth, he lives as though he were in the city. . . .

This Jewish community has a remarkable past. It walks around with two thousand years of history on its back. . . . It is separated from the outside world as though it were an island in the middle of an ocean, and what goes on in that world is like a splashing of surf that never reaches higher than the ankles. The members of this community are bound and shackled to one another, and should one of them wish to break away, he has no choice but to cast himself into the waves, which will carry him apart from the Jewish world forever.

The Jews live in constant fear lest they stray out of the narrow cage into which their forefathers had directed them, heaven forbid, and they tend even to forsake whatever pleasures Jewish law allows them. They are constantly placing new yokes upon themselves. They hide their natural impulses. They renounce the darker elements in their nature. They have ears only for the reading of the law, eyes only for scrutinizing sacred texts, voices only for crying, "Hear, O Israel."

They regard themselves as a chosen people, and they live worse than dogs; they believe in an eternal life after death, and yet it is a sufficient ideal to them to see marriage as only for making children. . . . The Eternal People in Mendele's world who live by plucking chicken feathers and furnishing holy items for the religious institutions of Glupsk, die three times a day from hunger. . . .

But long before the world began to percieve this, the Jew, with his sharp intelligence, had sensed it himself. He then realized there were only two ways of expressing himself If his senses had still been fresh, he could have tried, in his bitter disillusionment, to make something better of his life. . . . But among his atrophied senses there remained vivid only the sixth one: an overly sharp intelligence which tended to laugh and jeer at the contradictions of the life he was leading. . . .

A sharply critical intelligence that hangs suspended over a dead body feels the agonies of life as though in a dream; they pass through the dust-covered sense and reach the mind like some distant flicker of lightning without thunder. . . . In Jewish wit one can hear the voice of self-contempt, of a people who have lost touch with the ebb and flow of life. In Jewish mockery one can hear . . . the sick despair of a people whose existence has become an endless array of contradictions, a permanent witticism.

Ferment and Enlightenment

The picture sketched here of east European Jewish life is necessarily a static one; the reality was of course full of internal conflict and change. Jewish life in east Europe, it can reasonably be said, had been stagnant for centuries, in the sense, first, that the rabbinate had maintained its power and become more rigid in outlook and, second, that the relationship of the *shtetl* to the Russian empire remained one of weakness and dependency. Yet there had been upheavals and convulsions too. In the seventeenth century the false messianism of Sabbatai Zevi had shaken the Jews in a paroxysm of antinomian desire, which the Yiddish writer Hayim Greenberg has described as "the absolute negation of the *Galut* [Diaspora] and all its manifestations, the revulsion against continued passive waiting for redemption, the stubborn refusal to be reconciled to the hobbled reality of Jewish life." In the late eighteenth and early nineteenth centuries, Hasidism, a movement of pietistic enthusiasm drawing upon the aspirations of plebeian Jews, swept across eastern Europe to brighten its spiritual life. And in the nineteenth century the Haskala, or Enlightenment, brought modern thought to at least the middle-class segments of the Jewish population. The greatest ferment came, however, in the last third of the nineteenth century. A phalanx of new political and cultural movements, all competing for intellectual hegemony in the Jewish world; a generation of thoughtful and, in some instances, distinguished intellectuals; an upsurge of the Jewish masses to social awareness, revolt, and self-education; the blossoming of a secular Yiddish literature which, at its very beginning, thrust out such major figures as Sholom Aleichem and I. L. Peretz; above all, the widespread feeling in both the *shtetl* and city that Jewish culture had again come alive—all these were signs of renascence.

As long as the authority of the rabbis was supreme and east European Jewry remained self-sufficient in its religious life, a secular culture could not flourish. It could hardly be envisaged. But under the impact of the European Enlightenment, especially that of Germany; after the internal fissures produced by competing movements for Jewish revival, including some within the tradition itself, such as *Musar*, an effort at ethical purification within the limits of orthodoxy; through the appearance of such worldly movements as Zionism, socialism, and various blends of the two; in short, as a result of the confluence of these and other forces, the east European Jews turned to the *idea* of secular expression. Turned, one might say, with religious intensity to the idea of secular expression.

Through the last third of the nineteenth century and into our own time, first in eastern Europe and then in the immigrant centers of America, there came into being the culture of *Yiddishkeit*.* This is a period in which the opposing impulses of faith and skepticism stand poised, one fiercely opposed to the other yet both sharing a community of values. It is a period in which Jewish intellectuals find themselves torn by conflicting claims: those of the alien world, whether in the guise of accomplished cultures or revolutionary movements, and those of their native tradition, as it tugs upon their loyalties and hopes for renewal. It is a period of extreme restlessness, feverish collective dreaming, pretentious ideological effort. The sufferings of an oppressed people rub against and contribute to utopian expectation and secularized messianic fervor.

In the first decade of our century, the life of east European Jewry boils over with movements, parties, associations, many of them feeble and short-lived, but others—like socialism, Zionism, Yiddishism—soon to become major forces in Jewish public life. We make distinctions between religious and secular ideologies, and we are right to make them; but in the heated actuality of east European Jewish life the two had a way of becoming intertwined, with the imagery of religious aspiration finding a strange hospitality in secular speech. (The word *herem*, for instance, signifying in its religious context "excommunication," comes to be employed by Jewish socialists to mean a boycott of employers.) Religious Jews reluctantly entering political life sometimes borrow the rhetoric of militancy from their secular opponents. Jewish socialists celebrate the rising proletariat of Warsaw and Lodz as a reincarnation of ancient Jewish heroism. Polemics grow fierce and differences of opinion acute; but from the vantage point of time, it seems clear that the energies of collective resurgence holding the Jews together were more important than the vocabularies of political sectarianism driving them apart.

There had been a considerable history in Jewish life of movements that came to the Yiddish language through expedient motives, usually a wish to reach the masses who could read nothing else, and then remained with the

---

* Like other important terms in cultural discourse, *Yiddishkeit* has no single, agreed-upon meaning. No one has a monopoly on the term, and, naturally enough, different groupings of opinion within the Jewish world have used it in different ways. Yet there may be the possibility of some common, minimal usage.

As I use the term here, *Yiddishkeit* refers to that phase of Jewish history during the past two centuries which is marked by the prevalence of Yiddish as the language of the east European Jews and by the growth among them of a culture resting mainly on that language. The culture of *Yiddishkeit* is no longer strictly that of traditional Orthodoxy, yet it retains strong ties to the religious past. It takes on an increasingly secular character yet is by no means confined to the secularist elements among Yiddish-speaking Jews. It refers to a way of life, a shared experience, which goes beyond opinion or ideology.

language out of love. Only Hasidism, arising from the depths of folk experience, had never shown condescension to Yiddish or supposed that God cared in which language men offered devotion. The *maskilim* (enlighteners) of the Haskala had at first looked down on Yiddish and had themselves often written it badly, with heavy admixtures of Hebrew and adulterations of German; yet they had been driven by necessity to employ Yiddish—otherwise how enlighten the unenlightened? The early Jewish socialists, as if to validate their revolutionary credentials, were hostile not merely to Yiddish as a language but to everything having to do with Jewish tradition. The major Jewish socialist movement, the Bund, at first showed little concern for the cultural resources of Yiddish, using the language only because it was the natural medium for speaking to the Jewish proletariat; but after a time the Bundists recognized that their task was not merely economic and political but cultural as well, so that despite their radical secularism they could not avoid an uneasy relationship to traditional Jewishness. For them, too, Yiddish became a language to be loved, the very marrow of their experience. By contrast Zionism, at least before it became a mass movement, was hostile both to traditional Jewish ways and to those who sought to build a lasting Jewish culture within the Diaspora.

> Zionists [Lucy Dawidowicz remarks] chose to revolutionize their own Jewish society, to "normalize" the Jewish people, make it like all other peoples, and, above all, to repudiate Israel's chosenness . . . they came to loathe the Jewish Diaspora, the good and bad without distinction: the inflexibility of religious tradition, the Yiddish language and its folk culture, the Jewish gift of accommodation and nonviolent resistance. . . . The philosophical concept of the negation of the *galut* became, among many Zionists, a negation of Jewish creativity in the Diaspora.

The spokesmen and artists of *Yiddishkeit*, while always aware of its precarious condition and trained to sharpen their gift for irony on the stones of this awareness, had nevertheless to assume that the survival of Yiddish culture was not in question. The cultural milieu they created was one in which all the competing tendencies of Jewish life were brought together under maximum pressure. That the centuries-long reign of the rabbis had been challenged with some success, to the point where the more vital rabbis began themselves to search for new modes of belief—this led to a release of intellectual energies. That this release nevertheless occurred under conditions both economically cramped and socially humiliating—this gave the work of the Yiddish writers an occasional touch of unreality and led to a suspicion that they were no more than scribbling *luftmenshn* who dealt in ideas without substance.

Today we know that the survival of Yiddish culture was very much in question. For insofar as the Yiddish intellectuals continued in the path of their own tradition, they could not open themselves sufficiently to the surrounding cultures of Europe and America, nor engage themselves suffi-

ciently with the values of modernity to which they now and again aspired.
Yet insofar as they accepted the secular cultures of their time, they risked
the loss of historical identity, a rupture with that sacred past which could
stir the skeptics almost as much as the believers. The culture of *Yiddishkeit*
—at once deep-rooted and precarious, brilliant and short-breathed—had
always to accept dilemma as the ground of its existence. It had always to
accept the burden of being at home neither entirely with its past nor
entirely with the surrounding nations. Out of its marginality it made a
premise for humaneness.

One condition for the rise of a Yiddish culture was that to the rising
young intelligentsia of Warsaw, Lodz, Vilna, and the numerous peripheral
shtetlakh the traditional religious system should remain a powerful force yet
seem more and more inadequate. The winds of the Enlightenment, sweeping
across the airless streets of the Pale, promised secular freedom—but were
not strong enough to bring it. The past remained vivid, even beautiful, to
those who found themselves attacking it as obsolete, while the future en-
ticed, almost against their will, those who declared themselves defenders of
the past. You could denounce religion as superstition and worse, but the
Yom Kippur service shook the heart, and the voices of the Talmud lured the
mind. You could decry the secular writers as apostates and worse, but no
one with a scrap of Yiddish could resist Mendele's satires or Sholom Aleichem's ironic monologues.

It was a condition of east European Jewish life that every idea emerging
from it be brought to absolute extreme, even while—and no doubt because
—few of its ideas could be realized in actuality. And while the thrust of
historical energy that *Yiddishkeit* represented for the east European Jews
would in the long run be exhausted in mid-twentieth-century America, the
immigrant Jews of the East Side and other such settlements would for some
decades continue to act upon the vision of an indigenous Yiddish culture,
one retaining its ties with the national-religious past of the Jews yet dedicated to a humanitarian, perhaps even universalist present.

The rhetoric of this period seems at times a little overblown, a little
grandiose, but deep down the Yiddish writers and intellectuals knew perfectly well how precarious their culture, their very existence, really was.
Abraham Reisen, a Yiddish poet, once wrote a lovely little quatrain reflecting the dominant mood among his contemporaries:

> My life I would compare
> To a lamp with a bit of kerosene:
> The lamp continues to flicker,
> But it hasn't the strength to flare.

At the center of this culture was a loving attachment to Yiddish as a
language. In the east European milieu Yiddish had been treated as both
spoiled darling and neglected stepchild; it had been loved for its pithiness

and folk strength yet regarded as unworthy when compared with the sacred tongue of Hebrew or the learned one of German. Yiddish was the language that sprang first to a Jew's lips, a language crackling with cleverness and turmoil, ironic to its bones; yet decades of struggle were required before the learned, somewhat modernized Jews could be convinced—some never would be—that this mere *zhargon*, this street tongue, this disheveled creature wearing the apron of the Jewish week, this harum-scarum of a language recklessly mixing up bits of German, Hebrew, Russian, Polish, Provençal, English, and God alone knows what, could become the vehicle of a literature through which Jewish life would regain its bearing.*

One ideology behind *Yiddishkeit*, never very elaborate, was developed in the 1890's by the historian Simon Dubnow. He saw the Jewish people as a spiritual community held together by historical, cultural, and religious ties, despite the absence of a common homeland or territory, and he urged the Jews to struggle for cultural and religious autonomy in whichever country they happened to find themselves. In opposition to the Bundists, he stressed the unity of the Jewish people, and in opposition to the Zionists, he desired the preservation of Jewish identity in the Diaspora. The ultimate experience of Yiddish culture, as distinct from its momentary ideological tendencies, would in fact come close to Dubnow's prescription:

> perennial struggle for communal autonomy—autonomy of the cells that make up the body of the nation—in a form that is appropriate to the conditions of the time; a struggle for national education at home and in schools established for this purpose—education in the ancient national language and the vernacular languages developed in the Diaspora which unites the entire people or large sections of it; a struggle for the cultivation of all basic national possessions and their adaptation to universal culture without damaging their own individuality.

For Yiddish secular culture, all roads led to the home in Warsaw of I. L. Peretz, one of the founding figures of modern Yiddish literature. Peretz lacked the brilliance of Sholom Aleichem or the corrosive wit of Mendele Mokher Sforim, the two other masters of the literature; but insofar as the culture of *Yiddishkeit* took on intellectual coherence, Peretz stood at the center. He opened his house and his heart to the younger Yiddish writers and intellectuals, often the sons of rabbis and learned men, often themselves *yeshiva bokhurim* (religious students) in both physical and cultural flight from their youth. He was familiar with the thought of the West, for one strand of his creative self would always be cosmopolitan and skeptical. In a

---

* Today it seems almost impossible to imagine that there was a time when in both eastern Europe and America the lovers of Yiddish had to create a *movement* for its defense within the Jewish world. Calling themselves *Yidishistn*, they organized a conference in Czernowitz, Romania, in 1908, at which writers, intellectuals, and public figures came together to declare a programmatic adherence to Yiddish, not merely as a language meriting its quotient of respect and pedagogic rights but as the agent of a national-cultural idea.

passionate little essay, "Hope and Fear," he composed a remarkable warning that the gods of secular progress might fail, long before leading European writers would announce that their god had indeed failed. At the same time Peretz turned back lovingly to the half-buried cultural past of the east European Jews, discovering a treasure of legend in folk and Hasidic sources.

What Peretz did, remarked Jacob Glatstein, himself a major Yiddish poet, was to create "single-handed a Jewish nineteenth century." By this phrase Glatstein meant that Peretz succeeded in yoking together the worldly culture of Europe with the religious traditions of the Jews, or, more precisely, that Peretz rediscovered and refined the Jewish tradition so that on its own it could enter the era of intellectual modernism that began in the nineteenth century. It was an achievement that signified the coming-of-age of the Yiddish-speaking intelligentsia in both eastern Europe and, soon enough, the United States.

The Start of Social Change

For several centuries the rabbis, intent upon preserving "the ancient Jewish faith," had "served as an armor for the Jewish people in their struggle for national existence." Not many rabbis would have acknowledged so mundane an end, but there is historical evidence that they did have some awareness of their distinctive social role. When, for example, Jewish reformers under Haskala influence proposed changes in the schooling of the young, the rabbis resisted such schemes on the grounds that even a partially secularized education would deprive Jewish youth of traditional ways of life without really enabling them to find a place in the gentile world. Motives apart, the rabbis were speaking to a reality.

Seen from a distance, the forms of Jewish family life in eastern Europe can be judged as harshly as the encrusted rabbinate, since both had been hobbled by an excess of ritual and regulation. Yet it was the ferocious loyalty of the Jews to the idea of the family as they knew it, the family both as locus of experience and as fulfillment of their obligation to perpetuate their line, that enabled them to survive. So too did the tradition of communal self-help and solidarity, soon to become one of the most powerful forces in secularized Jewish life. Often, it seems, the Jews aroused the anger of Russian authorities precisely because of the inner discipline with which they bore oppression.

By the mid-nineteenth century, however, the agencies of communal survival were visibly weakening. The rabbis had been seriously challenged; the family had begun to buckle under the weight of alien ideas and economic distress; and no communal solidarity could cope with the growing pauperization. All through the last third of the century, the economic situation of the east European Jews kept growing worse. In a four-year period, 1894–1898, the number of Jewish paupers increased by almost 30 percent. "In many communities," writes the historian Salo Baron,

> fully 50 percent of the Jewish population depended on charity, particularly during the Passover week. . . . In Russia, as in other countries going through the early stages of modern capitalism, the rich grew richer while the poor became more and more indigent. . . . It has been estimated that in many communities up to 40 percent of the entire Jewish population consisted of families of so-called *luftmenshn*, that is, persons without any particular skills, capital, or specific occupations.

All these troubles were further aggravated by the legal restrictions placed on Jewish residential and occupational rights.

The emancipation of the serfs had a damaging effect on those Jews, not large in number but still important in the Jewish economy, who had worked as agents of the nobility or as economic middlemen disposing of the peasants' produce. Jewish petty officials and traders tended to be squeezed out, and as a result many rural Jews were compelled to seek employment in the cities.

Inevitably, as the *shtetl* began to empty a portion of its youth into the slums of Warsaw, Vilna, Lodz, Minsk, Bialystok, and other cities, the first blurred signs of a Jewish proletariat began to be seen—that proletariat Karl Kautsky would declare in 1901 to be "still more oppressed, exploited, and ill-treated than all others, a pariah among pariahs." How terrible were the conditions of these Jewish workers, really more artisans than proletarians, can be glimpsed in a petition sent to the governor of Vilna province in 1892: ". . . work in the shop lasts from 7:00 A.M. to 11:00 P.M. or 12:00 P.M., and before holidays the employer makes us work all night." A report submitted by the Bund to the International Socialist Congress of 1896 estimates that the average working day of a Jewish artisan was between fourteen and sixteen hours, with the pay as low as two to three rubles a week. If such conditions were everywhere characteristic of nascent capitalist economy, they had a special source in the Pale: a generalized poverty forcing upon small employers intensive exploitation of labor, as well as the technological backwardness of the handful of "Jewish industries."

All through the 1880's and 1890's bitter strikes kept breaking out, often led by Bundists or Bundists-to-be and celebrated by them as evidence that the class struggle was deepening within the Jewish community. *"In di gasn, tsu di masn"* ("Into the streets, to the masses"), went a popular Vilna song of the 1890's. Yet even as these strikes would occasionally bring some relief to Jewish workers, it soon became clear that their effect could only be marginal. Courageous and brilliant in strikes, the Jewish workers often lacked the discipline that comes from factory structure; they would allow their organizations to disintegrate in "normal" times, and only a tiny portion of them managed to elbow their way past the barriers of discrimination that kept them out of the larger and better-paying industries. Abraham Liessen, the Yiddish poet, acutely remarked that among the Jews the class struggle could be little more than "pauper against pauper." In western Europe and in the great Russian factory centers, "workers struggle against capitalists who are very wealthy, while in our Jewish towns and cities the workers struggle against paupers like themselves." Ber Borokhov, the left-Zionist theoretician who believed that a significant Jewish proletariat could be created only beyond the Pale, argued that the class struggle within the Jewish community was bankrupt from the very start, since the Jewish craft industries were in decline and their artisans becoming more and more obsolete. Even the Bund, committed as it was to political work within the Pale, had to recognize at least the partial validity of what Liessen, Borokhov, and others were saying. The Bundist leaders,

> Kremer and Gozhanskii, conceded that . . . the socialists were operating under severe handicaps. Kremer admitted that since many Jewish artisans might in time become employers who could operate independently within their own shops, "a worker regards his situation as temporary and agrees to put up with a certain amount of sacrifice." Gozhanskii even questioned whether one could hope to improve the living conditions of the Jewish artisan masses when, as he said, "some masters are so poverty-stricken that an increase in wages will force them to close down the shops."

Yet by a final historical reckoning the nascent labor and socialist movements achieved something of great consequence for the Jews. In these early struggles there began to emerge a new social type who would become the carrier, and often the pride, of Yiddish culture: the self-educated worker-intellectual, still bearing the benchmarks of the Talmud Torah, forced to struggle into his maturity for those elements of learning that his grandsons would accept as their birthright, yet fired by a vision of a universal humanist culture and eager to absorb the words of Marx, Tolstoy, and the other masters of the nineteenth century. A certain Moses "the Binder"

> read everything he could get his hands on. Yet in the course of time he developed a feeling for good books . . . he would read only those which enriched him spiritually, which satisfied his need to learn. He loved literature, and was especially interested in the classics. His favorites were works of the great satirist Saltykov-Shchedrin, and those of Turgenev and Tolstoy, Zola and Dickens.

A young artisan describes his socialist "teacher":

> I remember as if it were today with what a remarkable feeling of fear and awe I and other students sat on a wooden bench near a large brick oven that was hardly warm. Opposite us, at a table, sat a young man of twenty-seven or twenty-eight [Arkady Kremer, one of the founders of the Bund, whose lectures created the feeling that] a new soul had entered me.

The rise of early Jewish socialism was a key factor in stirring the masses of both city and *shtetl* to a new awareness of their condition, their possibilities, their unused powers. But insofar as objective conditions imposed severe limits upon social revolt within the Jewish community—for such revolt had always to face the feebleness of its victory, the bitterness of its handful of fruits—the very release of insurgent energies led to frustration and despair, sometimes to the abandonment of the Jewish world entirely. One labor militant, writing from Minsk, shrewdly remarked that "in fact we were only preparing socialists for America." His point could have been generalized. Except for the religious and cultural movements, which by their nature were self-sufficient, all the new energies within the Jewish world of eastern Europe were doomed to failure. Neither communal growth nor political gradualism, neither socialist aggressiveness nor Zionist preparations could break, or break out of, the limits of the Pale. If nothing else, the cultural-political revival of these years made the Jews painfully aware of how intolerable their life remained.

Some of the younger Jewish radicals, convinced that the Bund was locked in parochial impotence, decided to join their Russian comrades to build a revolutionary movement that would encompass and then destroy the empire. This represented a personal solution that in relation to Jewishness was not very different from assimilation or conversion. Just as the distinguished orientalist Daniel Khwolson could explain his conversion by a witticism that won admiration even from those who despised him as an apostate —"Yes, I was *convinced* that it is better to be a Christian professor in Saint Petersburg than a Jewish *melamed* in a *shtetl*"—so the young Jewish intellectuals taking up the banners of populism and Marxism could declare that making the revolution among gentiles was better than leading petty strikes among Jewish brushmakers. But even as they tried to don the mask of racial anonymity, many young Jewish radicals met with rebuff. Lev Daitch, an early Marxist, would recall affecting the dress and speech of a *muzhik* to "go to the people." One day a peasant asked him point-blank, "Are you not a *zhid* [Jew]?" and Daitch could only keep silent. Another Jewish socialist, Shalom Levin, would recall his difficulties, all too characteristic, in approaching gentile workers:

> Someone would send along a bottle of "monopolke" [whisky]. They would pour it into tea glasses and drink it down like a glass of water. I had to drink along with them, otherwise I would not have been a "good brother." I hoped that by becoming their "good brother" I would be able to make them class conscious. In the end neither of us achieved anything. They could not make me a drunkard, and I could not make them class conscious.

Still more troubling to at least some of the radical Jewish youth was the position taken by the populist groups, especially Narodnaya Volya, defending pogroms against Jews on the grounds that such outbursts expressed the legitimate resentments of the peasants against their exploiters. The dilemma in which the more sensitive Jewish revolutionists felt themselves has been described by Lev Daitch:

> A revolutionary can indeed give no practical answer now to the Jewish question. What should he do, for instance, in Balta where they beat Jews? Take their part? This would mean . . . bringing down the wrath of the peasants on the revolutionaries: "Not enough they have murdered the Tsar but they also defend the *zhids!*" The revolutionaries thus find themselves on the horns of a dilemma: this is a simple cul-de-sac for both the Jews and the revolutionaries.

The Prospect of America

Had the persecution and poverty of the late nineteenth century occurred at a time of cultural stagnation or even stability, it would probably have led to the sort of internal convulsions that had previously broken out among the east European Jews: perhaps a new version of the orgiastic false messianism of the seventeenth and eighteenth centuries, perhaps a new phase in the ecstatic pietism of Hasidism, perhaps some unforeseeable religious outburst. Had the cultural renewal of the east European Jews occurred in relatively "normal" circumstances, without the wounds of external assault and internal hunger, *Yiddishkeit* might have established itself as the stable culture of a minority people slowly undergoing that process of assimilation that would later occur in the United States. But what now uniquely characterized the east European Jews was the explosive mixture of mounting wretchedness and increasing hope, physical suffering and spiritual exaltation. And what was new in their experience was that for the first time they could suppose there was someplace else to go, a new world perceived as radically different from the one in which they lived. The spiraling energy, strength, hope, dream of the European Jews enabled many of their sons and daughters to make their escape to America, sometimes for mere personal relief, often with the wish for a fulfillment of those collective aspirations which had been nurtured but could not be realized in the old country. America, even as it drained millions of Jews from *shtetl* and city, helped the Jews of eastern Europe to survive and for intervals even flourish as a community. America was safety valve and haven, place for renewal and source of support.

Serious debates were bound to arise as to whether emigration should now become a communal policy. As early as 1882 a conference of "Jewish notables" met in Saint Petersburg to discuss this question. The majority of the delegates feared that mass emigration, officially encouraged by the Jewish community, would appear unpatriotic and might undermine the struggle for emancipation. *Russky Evrei,* a Russian-language weekly edited by Jews, wrote:

> Pogroms are a result of rightlessness and when that has been obviated the attendant evils will vanish with it. By supporting mass emigration the Jews would be playing into the hands of their enemies, who hope they will flee from the field of battle.

The views of the minority at the Saint Petersburg conference were expressed by a delegate from Kiev, Max Mandelstam:

> Either we get civil rights or we emigrate. Our human dignity is being tramped upon, our wives and daughters are being dishonored, we are looted and pillaged; either we get decent human rights or else let us go wherever our eyes may lead us.

Among the Jewish intellectuals of various persuasions there grew up the conviction that anti-Semitism, as they experienced it in Russia, was a disease beyond cure in the foreseeable future. Leon Pinsker, in a famous essay, declared Judeophobia to be

> a form of demonopathy, with the difference that the Jewish ghost has become known to the whole race of mankind . . . and that it is not disembodied like other ghosts. . . . Judeophobia is a psychic disorder. As such it is hereditary and, as a disease transmitted for two thousand years, it is incurable.

No matter what the more Russified Jewish intelligentsia said by way of caution or how the handful of wealthy Jewish merchants hesitated, the masses made their own decision. Millions would soon tear themselves away from the land that held the dust of their ancestors; millions would leave the *shtetlakh* and cities in which they had built their life, their Houses of Study and burial societies, their wooden synagogues and paintless houses, their feeble economy and thriving culture. Obsolete artisans, socialist firebrands, bewildered wives, religious fanatics, virtuosos of the violin, illiterate butchers, scribblers of poetry, cobblers, students, *luftmenshn*—above all, the numberless ordinary Jews, the *folksmasn* for whom being a Jew was not an idea or a problem but the vibrant substance of their lives—now began to ready themselves. And not merely because their life in common was weak, but because as Jews they knew themselves to be strong.

CHAPTER TWO

Departure and Arrival

IN THE thirty-three years between the assassination of Alexander II and the outbreak of the First World War, approximately one third of the east European Jews left their homelands—a migration comparable in modern Jewish history only to the flight from the Spanish Inquisition. Some, with the blood of the pogroms barely dry, fled in fear for their lives; others chose to leave in organized groups searching for a new soil in which to replant Jewish life; most went for personal reasons, to ease lives that had become intolerable and release ambitions long suppressed. Yet, in its deepest significance, the migration of the east European Jews constituted a spontaneous and collective impulse, perhaps even decision, by a people that had come to recognize the need for new modes and possibilities of life.

Circumstances often made it unavoidable that the Jews flee from Russia, Poland, and Romania; circumstances sometimes made it convenient for them to leave; but the impetus and the desire were their own. They moved westward not only because life was hard under the czar, but because elements of strength had been forged in the Jewish communities and flashes of hope sent back by brothers who had already completed the journey. They moved westward because they clung to the dream of national fulfillment while hoping individually to gain some decencies of survival.

To separate, for any but analytical reasons, the most exalted motives for the migration from the most self-centered is probably a mistake. What Maldwyn Jones says in his history of immigration holds for the Jews quite as much as for other national groups: "The motives have been very similar from first to last: a mixture of yearnings for riches, for land, for change, for tranquility, for freedom, and for something not definable in words . . . a readiness to pull up stakes in order to seek a new life."

Only a tiny minority undertook the journey with ideological intent. The national pioneers of Am Olam (Eternal People), marching off to the trains with Torah in one hand and *Das Kapital* in the other, neither expected nor desired that the masses of ordinary Jews follow in their footsteps; but these idealistic settlers were greatly admired among ordinary Jews, less for their vision of setting up agricultural communes than for their determination to break with *shtetl* lassitude. One Jewish immigrant, Dr. George Price, kept a diary during 1882, the year he left for America, and what he wrote can stand as representative of what millions felt:

> Sympathy for Russia? How ironical it sounds! Am I not despised? Am I not urged to leave? Do I not hear the word *zhid* constantly? Can I even think that someone considers me a human being capable of thinking and feeling like others? Do I not rise daily with the fear lest the hungry mob attack me? . . . It is impossible . . . that a Jew should regret leaving Russia.

The other half of the story is told by Mary Antin, who came to the United States nine years after Price:

> America was in everybody's mouth. Businessmen talked of it over their accounts; the market women made up their quarrels that they might discuss it from stall to stall; people who had relatives in the famous land went around reading their letters for the enlightenment of less fortunate folk . . . children played at emigrating; old folks shook their sage heads over the evening fire, and prophesied no good for those who braved the terrors of the sea and the foreign goal beyond it; all talked of it, but scarcely anyone knew one true fact about this magic land.

There was strong resistance to the idea of migration. In the eighties and nineties it was the orthodox Jews who were most skeptical: they had little faith in any mundane solution to their problems and they foresaw that America would mean a weakening of the faith. "Where do you travel and wherefore do you travel?" wrote one of them. "You are heading for a corrupt and sinful land where the Sabbath is no Sabbath. Even on Yom Kippur they don't fast. And for what purpose are you going there? So you can eat meat every day? . . . But their meat is *treyf* [unkosher]. No good Jew would touch such meat." There were other, more personal reasons. Older Jews were often unprepared for the hazards of the journey; the small class of prosperous Jews had a stake in remaining where it was; letters from those who had emigrated sometimes painted a bleak picture of "the golden land"; and then, of course, there was that natural conservatism which causes human beings to cling to what they can for as long as they can.

The departure from Russia, Poland, Romania, and Austro-Hungary can be traced along four main routes:
1. Jews coming from the Ukraine and southern Russia would usually cross the Austro-Hungarian border illegally, travel by train to Vienna or Berlin, and regroup themselves for the journey to one of the major ports of embarkation: Hamburg and Bremen in Germany, Rotterdam and Amsterdam in Holland, and Antwerp in Belgium.
2. Jews emigrating from western or northwestern Russia would surreptitiously cross the German border and proceed to Berlin and then the northern ports.
3. Jews from the Austro-Hungarian empire would legally cross the German border, journey to Berlin, and there join with the mass of Jews from Russia to proceed to the ports.
4. Jews from Romania, whose mass migration first began in 1899, traveled mostly through Vienna, Frankfurt am Main, and then the Holland ports, though a few took the sea voyage from Trieste or Fiume.
These paths of migration were seldom direct. Theoretically, Jews from the Ukraine might have embarked from Odessa, going through the Black and Mediterranean seas to the Atlantic. Or they might have crossed the Romanian border, which was considerably closer to them than the Austrian town of Brody, where most of the Ukrainian Jews in fact gathered. The Jews of northern Russia might have gone from Libau, the Baltic port, rather than undertake the illegal and sometimes dangerous trip across the German border. In both north and south, however, the roundabout routes were used for quite sensible reasons. A sea journey from Odessa was rarely practical, since it meant a longer and costlier trip than would be involved in the combination of rail travel across Europe and embarkation from a north European port. More important, Brody was preferred to the Romanian border because the Romanian authorities were feared as particularly savage anti-Semites while the Austro-Hungarian empire seemed mildly benevolent. As for the north, Libau was for a few years a popular port of embarkation, more than 21,000 Jews sailing from there in 1904 alone; but the Russian passport required at Libau was not only expensive, it also raised the fear, especially among draft-age men, of becoming entangled with czarist authorities. By all accounts, it seemed safer to sneak across the Russo-German border, even if that meant the risk of theft and rough treatment. With systematic perversity, the czarist regime made it hard for Jews to get legal passports yet tolerated illegal border crossings.
The mass of Jews moving westward included thousands of refugees in

direct flight from pogroms, a small number of would-be settlers intent upon creating "normal" modes of Jewish life through agricultural co-operatives (notably the Am Olam, or Eternal People, movement), and the masses of ordinary immigrants traveling as individuals or in family units. The refugees appeared as waves of victims first after the outrages of 1881–1882, then again in 1891, when Jews were driven out of Moscow and other Russian cities, and still again after the Kishinev massacre of 1903. (Another group came after the defeat of the 1905 Russian Revolution, though these were political rather than strictly Jewish refugees.) Of settlers with programs there were a mere handful, not a significant factor in the over-all migration. The mass of Jews leaving eastern Europe were simply the *folksmasn* in an upheaval at once desperate and purposeful, people determined to escape conditions of misery.

Crossing into Europe

The first major exodus began during the summer of 1881, when thousands of refugees, in flight from pogroms that had spread across the whole of the Ukraine, poured into Brody. Starving and homeless, sometimes forced to sleep on the streets, and treated far less well by the Austrian authorities than the legends about Franz-Josef had led them to expect, these refugees presented a problem not merely for the Jewish community of Brody, obviously unable to care for them, but for the entire Jewish population of Europe. Clinging to their acrid pride even in wretchedness, the east European Jews had harsh things to say about their more prosperous west European brothers. Yet the west European Jewish communities, through such agencies as the Baron de Hirsch Fund and the Alliance Israelite Universelle, did help. Their responses were inadequate and, given the scope of the migration from the east, could hardly be anything but inadequate. But relief poured into Brody, refugees were enabled to travel to Hamburg and Bremen, quarters were set up—often miserable, but set up—in the ports. In Paris a committee headed by Victor Hugo organized a public protest against the pogroms, and liberal newspapers undertook subscriptions to aid the refugees. The world, or at least a few decent portions of it, could still be moved by the sight of thousands of victims, perhaps because it had not yet become hardened to the sight of millions.

In the spring of 1882, after renewed pogroms in Russia, fresh streams of victims poured into Brody, which had now become a magnet for all the helpless who had heard of the relief and emigration depots in that town. During the early months of 1882, there were perhaps twenty thousand refugees clustered in Brody, which normally had a population of no more than fifteen thousand; and what had at first been envisaged as a limited relief operation by the Alliance now began to confront the Jews of Europe as the task of coping with a mass exodus. During the next few years permanent agencies, especially, after 1900, the Hilfsverein der Deutschen Juden, were created to help the east Europeans on their way. In view of the strained relations that would continue for decades between German and east European Jews, it is only fair to record that the German Jews worked hard and often well in behalf of the thousands pouring in from the east. They established information bureaus to help the travelers; they negotiated special rates with railway companies and steamship lines; they set up precautions against the hordes of scoundrels, both Jewish and gentile, who tried to fleece the immigrants; they negotiated with governments to ease the journeys. In the peak decade of immigration, 1905–1914, some 700,000 east European Jews passed through Germany, and 210,000 of these were directly helped by the Hilfsverein. Mark Wischnitzer, a historian of immigration close to the institutions created by east European Jewish immigrants, acknowledges that "the German Jewish community always bore the brunt of the tidal wave of emigration from eastern Europe." Before 1900 its work was inadequate: "Orderly migration requires a long and thorough preparation by experts in the field. . . . The voluntary committees of the 19th century, created *ad hoc,* were simply unable to perform this work." Later, things improved—but the problem grew larger. Between 1901 and 1914 the number of Jews who left Europe, almost all of them from Russia, Romania, and Galicia, came to 1,602,441. A leader of the German effort to help the emigrant Jews, Dr. Paul Nathan, came to the conclusion that in the period of 1900–1903 90 percent of them "went forth each year on their own initiative and at their own risk."

In the earlier years some efforts were made by the Alliance Israelite Universelle to repatriate the Russian Jews, or, more accurately, to persuade them to attempt repatriation. In late 1881, Charles Netter, an official of the Alliance who had been dispatched to Brody, wrote his home office in Paris: "The emigrants must be checked, otherwise we shall receive here all the beggars of the Russian empire." Netter issued an appeal to the Jewish press in Russia saying that no new emigrants would be received in Brody, but, as the Alliance ruefully admitted, this met "with scant results." It reveals the magnitude of feeling that had overcome the refugees that, no matter how wretched they were in Brody, they rejected the idea of returning to the land of the czars. In 1882 Netter wrote to his Paris headquarters: "They [the refugees] will get along with or without our help, as shown by the fact that they are already beginning to do so." A group of Jewish emigrants sent the Alliance a touching declaration in October 1881: America, they said, "is the most civilized region, and offers the most guarantees of individual freedom, freedom of conscience, and security of all property . . . and endows every one of her inhabitants with both civil and political rights." And when the Alliance, in response to heavy pressure from the Board of Delegates of American Israelites, proposed to send only males to New York, a group of refugees wired Paris: "Impossible accept. Spirits broken, hope lost. Even more unhappy than in Russia. Would rather starve than leave families." Recognizing how stiff-necked these east European Jews could be, the Alliance gave up the idea of repatriation. Its efforts, through circulars and correspondence, to persuade the Russian Jews to remain where they were had about as much effect on them as, in the words of a Yiddish saying, "last year's snow."

"Strangely enough," writes Wischnitzer, "American Jewry [in 1881], a quarter of a million strong, was at first indifferent, apathetic and unfriendly, to say the least" toward the prospect of hordes of immigrants from eastern Europe. Why "strangely enough"? The Jewish organizations in America had been set up by the German Jews; their life was reasonably comfortable, sometimes prosperous; what benefits could they foresee, what but certain embarrassment and probable burden, from a descent of thousands of penniless Jews whom they supposed to be steeped in medieval superstition when not possessed by wild radicalism?

During the 1870's and 1880's the general feeling in America was receptive to immigration, though the Jewish community tended to favor a mildly restrictionist approach. Myer S. Isaacs, a leader of the German Jews, reported to the Board of Delegates of American Israelites: "The dispatch of poor emigrants to America has long constituted a burden and unjust tax upon our large cities. . . . It is habitual with benevolent organizations in certain cities in Europe to dispatch utterly helpless Jewish families to America—only to become a burden upon our charities."

The records, inner correspondence, and public statements of the American Jewish organizations all through the 1880's bristle with anxieties concerning an influx of debilitated and pauperized east European Jews. All insist that only skilled workers, healthy and young, be encouraged to come. All plead that the American Jewish community, expected to take care of "its own," lacks the resources to do so. All charge that the Jews of western Europe are not carrying a fair share of the costs.

If we are now inclined to regard such attitudes as unfeeling, we must remember that the security of the Jews already settled in the United States was neither long-standing nor well established. The depressions of the time had done damage to many Jewish businesses, and by the mid-1880's there was already a sizable body of poor Jewish immigrants in the urban ghettos.

> A statistical account of expenditures during those years lent some credence to the complaints that funds [among American Jews] were lacking. Although only a small proportion of the many thousands of newcomers who settled in New York City applied for aid to the United Hebrew Charities, from 1881 to 1889 that society expended over $500,000 annually for immigrant welfare. An additional $500,000 was spent each year for general relief. But the amount

consigned for immigrant use . . . proved insufficient. Three-fourths of the needy immigrants looked for help to charitable institutions, but only one-tenth of those seeking such aid received any. . . . The relatively wealthy of New York's established Jewry found it difficult to sustain an increase of 200,000 Jews in one decade, about 80,000 of whom arrived in New York City from 1885 to 1889.

That the Jews in America should respond at first with anxiety, even hostility, is therefore not at all surprising. What is remarkable is that the German Jews in America soon began systematically to help the immigrants; by 1891 Dr. Julius Goldman, representing the United Hebrew Charities at a conference of European Jewish societies, could say that, yes, America *was* the best destination for the Russian-Jewish refugees; and by the early 1900's the German-Jewish leaders had not only organized effective relief in the larger American cities but also were engaged in a subterranean struggle against efforts to restrict immigration. Their sense of solidarity, their moderate but firm liberal principles, their growing ease in America—whatever the reason, they were now committed, especially through the work of such figures as Jacob Schiff and Louis Marshall, to supporting the masses of Jews pouring in from eastern Europe.

They came, these masses, in several mounting waves: first in the eighties from Russia, then at the turn of the century from Romania, and after 1905 from Russia again. The departure from Romania was especially dramatic. In 1878 the Treaty of Berlin, which Romania had signed with the European powers, had guaranteed Jews full civil and political rights, but venal Romanian governments had systematically violated this treaty, sometimes through decrees reducing thousands of Jews to pauperdom, such as one in 1884 that prohibited them from peddling in the cities. In 1899, when economic depression led to famine, a pogrom was organized in the city of Jassy by its police chief, violent denunciations of Jews were delivered in the parliament, and Jews were expelled from entire districts. There followed a remarkable episode in which Jews, acting through improvised committees, began to leave the country as *fusgeyer* (walkers, wayfarers) who tramped hundreds of miles across the country.

> In towns and townships [writes Joseph Kissman, a historian of the Romanian Jews], bands of emigrants organized for the purpose of journeying on foot to Hamburg and thence to America.
>
> The wayfarers of 1899 were different from the earlier emigrants. In the first place, the human material consisted not of poor, worn out, exhausted peddlers, but of young, healthy people, mostly artisans and workers. . . . The very manner in which these groups were organized testified to their idealism and youthful romanticism. . . .
>
> The members sold all their belongings, saved their meager pennies, trained themselves in marching long distances, and strengthened their spirit of brotherhood. Some groups, before departing, went to the synagogue and

took a solemn oath to share with one another their last morsel of bread. . . .

The *fusgeyer* established a "press" of their own. In these newspapers we find appeals for aid, articles in which they say farewell to their old home, and sometimes a bit of verse. Dozens of such papers came out, but apparently no more than one issue of each. . . . The authorities were surprised at the attitude of the non-Jewish peasantry toward the *fusgeyer*. Impoverished peasants stood on the dusty roads waiting for them and bringing water, bread, and milk.

One *fusgeyer* would later remember a contingent "in double file, clad in brown khaki, military leggings, and broad-brimmed canvas hats, each with an army knapsack on his back and a water-bottle slung jauntily over his shoulder." Another, in a Yiddish reminiscence composed in old age, recalled the first contingent that set out from Barlad in April 1900, singing a recently composed "Song of the *Fusgeyer*": *"Geyt, yidelekh, in der vayter velt; in kanade vet ir ferdinen gelt."* ("Go, little Jews, into the wide world; in Canada you will earn a living.") The group of seventy-five men and three girls set off from the center of town:

> After the speeches, our captain gave a signal on his cornet, and our march began. The order of our ranks was the following: first the captain, then two men with flags, one the Romanian and the other the blue and white, and then we following, ordinary foot soldiers, four in a row, and finally a wagon with our baggage. . . . At the outskirts of the city we began saying farewell in earnest to our parents, sisters, and brothers. It was painful to wrench ourselves from the arms of our relatives.

Offering amateur theatricals as a way of raising funds, the Barlad *fusgeyer* met with fervent receptions in town after town; Jewish communities greeted them as pioneers, and ordinary Romanian folk were often friendly too. Our memoirist, honest to the bone, records that as his group was zigzagging to the Hungarian border, it discovered that one of its leaders had absconded with the funds it had painfully accumulated; but to avoid giving their Romanian enemies a chance to crow, they decided to hush up the incident, "bite our lips," and sell the wagon for money with which to proceed.

In the thirty-four years between 1881 and the First World War, 75,043 Romanian Jews entered the United States, approximately 30 percent of the total Jewish population of Romania. An additional small number went to other countries. The *fusgeyer* were only the most exuberant strand of the Jewish emigration from Romania, those young people who wanted not merely to escape but to display their feelings while escaping. Though many of their expeditions disintegrated and they never came to more than a tiny percentage of the entire emigration, the *fusgeyer* help to sustain our contention that the departure of the east European Jews must be seen not merely as a sum of individual responses but also as a collective enterprise, not merely as a reaction to material need but also as a sign of moral yearning, not merely as a consequence of despair but also as a token of morale.

The Lure of America

"Even an imaginative American," writes a Jewish memoirist, "must find it very hard to form anything like a just idea of the tremendous adventure involved in the act of immigration." Tremendous adventure, yes, but only if that term comprehends a rich share of misery and trauma. The misery of journeying to America is by now a familiar story, but the trauma of undertaking the journey is often suppressed. The purposefulness of Am Olam, the bravado of the *fusgeyer* are exhilarating, but far more frequent were the wrenchings of personal ties, the tearing away of sons from distraught mothers and grim fathers. Young men eager to escape, but shaken by the thought of a lifelong separation, would cultivate a secret ally, mother against father or father against mother, appealing to hopes that both shared but one was readier to act upon than the other. "My father," remembered Stanislaw Mozrowski, a Jew from Montenegro,

> would not even let me talk to him about my hopes. My place, he said emphatically, was at home. Once in a while my mother would feel that he was in a good mood—wives can sense these things—and she would look at him, put her finger over her mouth as if to say, "don't say anything, let me do the talking," and start by remarking about something I had done well, and of course he would agree. Then she would begin to talk about my future. He would immediately stiffen, but sometimes she would continue until he would pound on the table and yell, "Silence! No more, do you hear?"

More characteristic, perhaps, was the experience of Marcus Ravage:

> In the evening when we were alone together my mother would make me sit on her footstool, and while her deft fingers manipulated the knitting-needles she would gaze into my eyes as if she tried to absorb enough of me to last her for the coming months of absence. "You will write us, dear?" she kept asking continually. "And if I should die when you are gone, you will remember me in your prayers." . . .
>
> At the moment of departure, when the train drew into the station, she lost control of her feelings. As she embraced me for the last time her sobs became violent and father had to separate us. There was a despair in her way of clinging to me which I could not then understand. I understand it now. I never saw her again.

Trapped in the *shtetl*, seldom familiar with the experience or idea of travel, and sensing in their bones that, whatever the ultimate benefit, the immediate loss was certain to be irreparable, many of the fathers bitterly resisted the demands of their sons. The fathers were trapped. They could not make out a persuasive case for keeping their sons at home, to be drafted into the army or becoming herring salesmen at town fairs, but neither could they overcome their own sense of despair at the falling apart of their families. For who really knew what this America was like, and who could be sure that, with or without streets of gold, one could remain a Jew there? Let us not suppose for a moment that they were all naïve and narrow-minded, these stubborn Jewish fathers. "A person gone to America," recalls Marcus Ravage, "was exactly like a person dead . . . the whole community turned out, and marched in slow time to the station, and wept loudly and copiously, and remembered the unfortunates in its prayer on the next Saturday." If most communities were less demonstrative than Ravage's Vaslui, all shared its underlying feeling.

Yet the inducements seemed overwhelming. Letters from America often vibrated with optimism, sometimes falsely so. The occasional emigrant who came back with the insignia of success—the others never came back—could not always keep from spreading misinformation, like the wonderful Couza, who returned to Marcus Ravage's home town dressed in frock coat and silk hat, bringing gifts of razors, pen holders, and music boxes, donating 125 francs to the *shul* (synagogue), and telling everyone "there were many ways of getting rich in America. People paid, it seemed, even for voting." (Later it turned out that poor Couza, with frock coat and silk hat, lived in a tenement on Attorney Street, and his wife took in piecework.) Steamship agents, spreading Yiddish leaflets, were shameless in their deceptions. Little brochures in Yiddish and Hebrew tempted the Jews with stories of riches and freedom. "I remember having read a book, *Paris in America*," writes Gregory Weinstein, which "thrilled me with its description of the blessed life where all men were equal before the law, where manual labor was held in high esteem."

Such Hebrew periodicals as *Hamelits* and *Hatsfira*, published in Saint Petersburg and Warsaw, were more cautious, reporting for instance that "there is no land which devours its lazy inhabitants and those not suited to physical labor like the land of America" and that the "lot of Jewish peddlers" was "toil of flesh and weariness of soul." But even such publications, read in any case by a mere handful of Russian Jews, gave glowing pictures of American opportunity (as well as angrily reporting a banquet of the Hebrew Union College at which shrimp cocktails were served—food as *treyf* [unkosher] as *treyf* can be.) In these papers there regularly appeared a little advertisement, "*Bank Wechsel und Passage Geschäft*" ("Money Exchange and Steamship Passage Office"), which probably had more impact than any quantity of reporting. Even those who wrote soberly, like George Price in his booklet *Yidn in amerika* (1891), could not resist the enticements of myth: the journey across the Atlantic, he told people back home, was "a kind of hell that cleanses a man of his sins before coming to the land of Columbus." If so, there would be no lack of opportunity for cleansing.

From Border to Port

For those without legal passports, the first major crisis along the journey was the border crossing into Austria or Germany. Bands of smugglers, increasingly expert, worked on the fears of the emigrants. The imagination of these Jews was stirred and disordered; removed from the small circle of space in which they had spent their lives, they became easy prey to rapacious peasants and heartless fellow Jews. Only when they came under the guidance of the German-Jewish organizations in Berlin, Hamburg, and Bremen could they be shielded from sharpers and thieves. Abraham Cahan's account of his 1882 crossing of the Austrian border is classic:

> We were to leave the train at Dubno where we were to take a wagon through the region around Radzivil on our way to the Austrian border. That would be our last city in Russia; across the border was . . . Brody.
>
> In the evening we followed two young Ukrainian peasants to a small, freshly plastered hut. One of the peasants was tall and barefooted and carried a small cask at his side. In Austria, there was no tax on brandy, so he smuggled it into Russia; on his return trip, he carried tobacco, more expensive in Austria, out of Russia.
>
> We waited a long time in the hut before realizing we were being held for more money. Having paid, we moved on. We made a strange group going across fields and meadows in the night, halted suddenly every few minutes by the tall peasant holding up his finger and pausing to listen for God-knows-what disaster. . . .
>
> We stumbled on endlessly. It seemed as if the border were miles away. Then the peasant straightened up and announced we were already well inside Austria.

Another emigrant, writing about himself in the third person, adds a touch of excitement:

> The crowd was told that in the dead of night they would be permitted to slink across the border provided they paid for the privilege. This they had expected, but what they were not prepared for was the fording of a stream. They were also told to be very cautious, to make no noise, and get over as quietly as possible. Terror lent impetus to swift movement and Alter made a dash for the opposite bank. But to his dismay, the tin cup inside the coffee pot began to rattle. This would surely give the alarm to the guards who would not hesitate to shoot. There was no alternative. . . . He opened his bundle and threw away the can—his first step on the "downward path."

Legal travelers stumbled upon other hurdles. The German authorities, fearful of plague during the 1880's and 1890's, conducted inspections—rigorous, impersonal, but worst of all, incomprehensible—of every trainload of emigrants:

> In a great lonely field, opposite a solitary house within a large yard, our train pulled up at last, and a conductor . . . hurried us into the one large room. . . . Here a great many men and women, dressed in white, received us. . . .
>
> Another scene of bewildering confusion, parents losing their children, and little ones crying . . . those white-clad Germans shouting commands, always accompanied with "Quick! Quick!"—the confused passengers obeying all orders like meek children. . . . Our things were taken away, our friends separated from us; a man came to inspect us, as if to ascertain our full value; strange-looking people driving us about like dumb animals . . . children we could not see crying in a way that suggested terrible things; ourselves driven into a little room where a great kettle was boiling on a little stove; our clothes taken off, our bodies rubbed with a slippery substance . . . a shower of warm water let down on us without warning . . . we see only a cloud of steam, and hear the women's orders to dress ourselves—"Quick! Quick!" or else we'll miss—something we can't hear.

In Hamburg, more questioning, disinfecting, labeling, pushing, money taken, money stolen, and a strange imprisonment called quarantine:

> Two weeks within high brick walls, several hundred of us herded in half a dozen compartments . . . sleeping in rows . . . with roll-calls morning and night . . . with never a sign of the free world beyond our barren windows . . . and in our ears the unfamiliar voice of the invisible ocean, which drew and repelled us at the same time.

But discomfort, hunger, humiliation, were as nothing to the one absolute fear gripping all emigrants: that one of their family might be sent back or kept off the boat after the dockside inspection.* In a sketch that comes from the very center of Jewish experience, Sholom Aleichem describes a family waiting in Antwerp:

---

* The increasing strictness of these inspections had a direct economic motive: steamship companies were required to take excluded immigrants back to Europe at their own expense. In a 1903 report, Henry Diedrich, the U.S. consul at Bremen, wrote:

"The large German steamship lines have had so much expense in returning emigrants from the United States who have been excluded under our laws that they have entered into an arrangement with the Prussian railway authorities under which the latter companies refuse transportation to persons from Austria and Russia who fail to meet certain requirements. Accordingly, Russian emigrants must have passports, steamer tickets to an American port, and a certain sum of money. . . . On the day before each departing steamer every one of these emigrants, who have already undergone the sifting process twice—on the border of their native country and again at Ruhleben—are most carefully inspected for the third time here under the supervision of the United States consul."

People tell them that they should take a walk to the doctor. So they go to the doctor. The doctor examines them and finds they are all hale and hearty and can go to America, but she, Goldele, cannot go, because she has trachomas on her eyes. At first her family did not understand. Only later did they realize it. That meant they could all go to America but she, Goldele, would have to remain here, in Antwerp. So there begins a wailing, a weeping, a moaning. Three times her mama fainted. Her papa wanted to stay here, but he couldn't. All the ship tickets would be lost. So they had to go off to America and leave her, Goldele, here until the trachomas would go away from her eyes.

Port cities were especially dangerous because there "a whole array of vocations existed to fleece the emigrant . . . keepers of hostels, railroad employees, ships' officers and crews, and preeminently, ticket agents. Many of these dealers were Jews who spoke Yiddish, and exploited their victims' trust in them. Stolen baggage, exorbitant lodging rates . . . tickets sold to the wrong destination by unscrupulous agents." Con men, cheap-Jacks, sharpers, white slavers, thieves, money changers, thugs: a rich assortment of villains drawn from all races worked the ports of the north Atlantic. The Alter whom we encountered fording a stream at the Russian border would later become a prosperous businessman who frequently traveled in Europe, but he always refused to return to Hamburg:

> This unsophisticated young man was the easy prey of all kinds of advisers. . . . They told him to stock up on herring and potatoes and bread for the ocean voyage, which he did. He also took the advice of some mean practical joker who told him that if he bought a bottle of whisky and drank the complete contents as soon as he got aboard, he would not be seasick. He did that too. He was not exactly seasick but dead drunk. . . . The voyage lasted seventeen days so he had plenty of time in which to recover.

Once the west European Jewish agencies started to supervise at least some of the land journey of the Russian emigrants, things became better.* The more spectacular cheating was stamped out. There were times when corporate good will thawed into warm generosity. One group of emigrants before the turn of the century was welcomed in Breslau "as though for a wedding feast. Rich ladies and gentlemen acted as waiters; even Jewish military officers waited on us. Physicians were also on hand . . . and it goes without saying that they were kept very busy, for is there a time when a Jew is not in need of a doctor?" With time the emigrants grew more worldly, learning from the experiences of those who had already gone and heeding the cautions of the Jewish organizations. And since it also became a

* The magnitude of the problem is suggested by the fact that between 1882 and 1902 the number of emigrants departing from Bremen alone was 2,173,919. We do not know how many of these were Jewish, but even if we assume no more than a sizable minority, it becomes evident that the German Jewish agencies simply lacked the resources to handle such vast numbers.

custom for steamship tickets to be sent in advance by relatives in America, the emigrants could be cheated only in relatively small ways.

The expense of the journey from Romania or the Ukraine can be estimated with fair precision; what that expense signified is harder to say. In 1903 steerage from Bremen to New York was $33.50 and from Antwerp $34, though the rates were increased the following year. The cost of getting to one of the ports, together with the expense incurred while crossing borders and paying off officials, was perhaps half again as much. Somehow, vast numbers of Jews in eastern Europe scraped together the money, often by selling their last few possessions and arriving penniless in New York. If an emigrant wanted to bring his wife and children, he had to lay out what for him was a small fortune. Often it was necessary for husbands to go first and bring their families later. Some husbands never did bring their families later.

The Ordeal of Steerage

Was the Atlantic crossing really as dreadful as memoirists and legend have made it out to be? Was the food as rotten, the treatment as harsh, the steerage as sickening? One thing seems certain: to have asked such questions of a representative portion of Jews who came to America between 1881 and 1914 would have elicited stares of disbelief, suspicions as to motive, perhaps worse. The imagery of the journey as ordeal was deeply imprinted in the Jewish folk mind—admittedly, a mind with a rich training in the imagery of ordeal.

Of the hundreds of published and unpublished accounts Jewish immigrants have left us, the overwhelming bulk can still communicate a shudder of dismay when they recall the journey by sea and the disembarkation at Castle Garden or Ellis Island. Only a historian sophisticated to the point of foolishness would dismiss such accounts as mere tokens of folk bewilderment before the presence of technology, or of psychic disorientation following uprooting, journey, and resettlement. Tokens of bewilderment and disorientation there are, certainly, and these contributed to rhetorical exaggeration about the ordeal of the Atlantic crossing. But the suffering was real, it was persistent, and it has been thoroughly documented.

By the time they reached the Atlantic, many immigrants had been reduced to a state of helpless passivity, unable to make out what was happening to them or why. An acute description of this experience has been provided by Oscar Handlin:

> The crossing involved a startling reversal of roles, a radical shift in attitudes. The qualities that were desirable in the good peasant [and, we might add, in

nonpeasant Jews also] were not those conducive to success in the transition. Neighborliness, obedience, respect, and status were valueless among the masses that struggled for space on the way. They succeeded who put aside the old preconceptions, pushed in, and took care of themselves. . . . Thus uprooted, they found themselves in a prolonged state of crisis. . . .

As a result they reached their new homes exhausted—worn out physically by lack of rest, by poor food, by the constant strain of close, cramped quarters, worn out emotionally by the succession of new situations that had crowded in upon them. At the end was only the dead weariness of an excess of novel sensations.

Let us sample a few memoirists, of widely varying sensibilities, as they recall the Atlantic journey. Morris Raphael Cohen, a philosopher distinguished for acute skepticism, wrote:

> We were huddled together in the steerage [of the ship *Darmstadt*] literally like cattle—my mother, my sister and I sleeping in the middle tier, people being above us and below us. . . . We could not eat the food of the ship, since it was not kosher. We only asked for hot water into which my mother used to put a little brandy and sugar to give it a taste. Towards the end of the [fourteen-day] trip when our bread was beginning to give out we applied to the ship's steward for bread, but the kind he gave us was unbearably soggy. . . .
>
> More than the physical hardships, my imagination was occupied with the terrors of ships colliding, especially when the fog horn blew its plaintive note. . . . One morning we saw a ship passing at what seemed to me a considerable distance, but our neighbor said that we were lucky, that at night we escaped a crash only by a hair's breadth.

Here is a passage from an unpublished memoir by a barely literate woman writing in Yiddish more than fifty years after her arrival in 1891:

> The sky was blue—the stars shining. But in my heart it was dark when I went up on the ship. . . . We rode three weeks on a freight train so I had plenty of time to think things over. My future . . . where am I going? to whom? what will I do? In Grodno I was at least someone in the store. But in America, without language, with only a bit of education. . . . Young people laughed and joked even though in my heart it was like the storm at sea. . . . And then a real storm broke out. The ship heaved and turned. People threw up, dishes fell, women screamed . . . but in my heart I didn't care what happened.

And here is the voice of a self-educated immigrant whose sense of life's indignities recalls the English novelist Smollett:

> On board the ship we became utterly dejected. We were all herded together in a dark, filthy compartment in the steerage. . . . Wooden bunks had been put up in two tiers. . . . Seasickness broke out among us. Hundreds of

people had vomiting fits, throwing up even their mother's milk. . . . As all were crossing the ocean for the first time, they thought their end had come. The confusion of cries became unbearable. . . . I wanted to escape from that inferno but no sooner had I thrust my head forward from the lower bunk than someone above me vomited straight upon my head. I wiped the vomit away, dragged myself onto the deck, leaned against the railing and vomited my share into the sea, and lay down half-dead upon the deck.

In all such recollections, the force of trauma overcomes differences of personality and cultivation. Steerage could reduce people to a common misery, and insofar as it did, their reactions were likely to be the same whether they were illiterate or students of the Talmud. We may suspect that the shock of being uprooted led some memoirists to overstate, we may have ironic reservations about the Jewish appetite for remembered woe; but there is plenty of dispassionate evidence, ranging from government reports to acounts by journalists who themselves took the trip in steerage, that supports the dominant immigrant memory. Edward Steiner, an Iowa clergyman, wrote a book in 1906 called *On the Trail of the Immigrant*, sober in content yet full of passages like this one:

> The steerage never changes, neither its location nor its furnishings. It lies over the stirring screws, sleeps to the staccato of trembling steel railings and hawsers. Narrow, steep and slippery stairways lead to it.
>
> Crowds everywhere, ill smelling bunks, uninviting washrooms—this is steerage. The odors of scattered orange peelings, tobacco, garlic and disinfectants meeting but not blending. No lounge or chairs for comfort, and a continual babel of tongues—this is steerage.
>
> The food, which is miserable, is dealt out of huge kettles into the dinner pails provided by the steamship company. When it is distributed, the stronger push and crowd. . . .
>
> On many ships, even drinking water is grudgingly given, and on the steamship *Staatendam* . . . we had literally to steal water for the steerage from the second cabin, and that of course at night. On many journeys, particularly on the *Fürst Bismarck* . . . the bread was absolutely uneatable, and was thrown into the water by the irate emigrants.

By the turn of the century conditions had in some cases improved. The German lines offered a modified steerage on their newer ships, a sort of separate stateroom containing two to eight berths and with improved sanitary conditions. The lucky ones came on these ships, some of which, like the *Kaiser Wilhelm*, could now make the trip from Hamburg to New York in a bit less than six days. And even the gloomiest of accounts speak about the upsurge of hope and animal spirits among the younger immigrants: there was often music, cardplaying, even dancing when the weather eased and the decks could be used. Sometimes, the more ambitious younger emigrants brought along Russian-English dictionaries and tried to master a few words for the moment of their arrival. Above all there was talk: the Jewish immigrants' burgeoning nostalgia for the old country and curiosity about the new.

A congressional committee investigating steerage conditions in 1910 offered an enormously detailed report which, in bureaucratic prose, substantiates the recollections of the immigrants themselves. In the old-type steerage, it reported, "filth and stench . . . added to inadequate means of ventilation," creating an atmosphere that was "almost unendurable. . . . In many instances persons, after recovering from seasickness, continue to lie in their berths in a sort of stupor, due to breathing air whose oxygen has been mostly replaced by foul gases." A woman investigator, disguising herself as a Bohemian peasant, gave vivid details:

> . . . one wash room, about 7 by 9 feet, contained 10 faucets of cold salt water, 5 along either of its two walls, and as many basins. . . . This same basin served as a dishpan for greasy tins, as a laundry tub for soiled handkerchiefs and clothing, and as a basin for shampoos without receiving any special cleaning. It was the only receptacle to be found for use in the case of seasickness.
>
> The toilets for women were six in number. . . . They baffle description as much as they did use. Each room or space was exceedingly narrow and short, and instead of a seat there was an open trough, in front of which was an iron step and back of it a sheet of iron slanting forward. . . . The toilets were filthy and difficult of use and were apparently not cleaned at all in the first few days.
>
> . . . Everything was dirty, sticky and disagreeable to the touch. Every impression was offensive. Worse than this was the general air of immorality. For 15 hours each day I witnessed all around me this . . . indecent and forced mingling of men and women who were total strangers and often did not understand a word of the same language.

If a certain prissiness creeps into this report, a tone we will encounter even in the most warmhearted of native responses, it does not finally matter. For about a crucial moment of the immigrant experience, this investigator offered a good portion of the truth.

At Ellis Island

"The day of the emigrants' arrival in New York was the nearest earthly likeness to the final Day of Judgment, when we have to prove our fitness to enter Heaven." So remarked one of those admirable journalists who in the early 1900's exposed themselves to the experience of the immigrants and came to share many of their feelings. No previous difficulties roused such overflowing anxiety, sometimes self-destructive panic, as the anticipated test of Ellis Island.* Nervous chatter, foolish rumors spread through each cluster of immigrants:

> "There is Ellis Island!" shouted an immigrant who had already been in the United States and knew of its alien laws. The name acted like magic. Faces grew taut, eyes narrowed. There, in those red buildings, fate awaited them. Were they ready to enter? Or were they to be sent back?
>
> "Only God knows," shouted an elderly man, his withered hand gripping the railing.

Numbered and lettered before debarking, in groups corresponding to entries on the ship's manifest, the immigrants are herded onto the Customs Wharf. "Quick! Run! Hurry!" shout officials in half a dozen languages.

On Ellis Island they pile into the massive hall that occupies the entire width of the building. They break into dozens of lines, divided by metal railings, where they file past the first doctor. Men whose breathing is heavy, women trying to hide a limp or deformity behind a large bundle—these are marked with chalk, for later inspection. Children over the age of two must walk by themselves, since it turns out that not all can. (A veteran inspector recalls: "Whenever a case aroused suspicion, the alien was set aside in a cage apart from the rest . . . and his coat lapel or shirt marked with colored chalk, the color indicating why he had been isolated.") One out of five or six needs further medical checking—H chalked for heart, K for hernia, Sc for scalp, X for mental defects.

An interpreter asks each immigrant a question or two: can he respond with reasonable alertness? Is he dull-witted? A question also to each child: make sure he's not deaf or dumb. A check for TB, regarded as "the Jewish disease."

* Ellis Island was opened as an immigration center in 1892, shortly after the federal government took over the supervision of incoming aliens. Until 1890 the matter had been in the hands of the states, and in New York, starting in 1855, immigrants were received at Castle Garden, a massive structure built in 1807 as a fort on a small island close to the west side of the Battery (later attached to it through landfill). During the early 1850's Castle Garden had been used as a concert hall; Jenny Lind and Lola Montez performed there.

By the 1880's it became clear that Castle Garden could not possibly take care of the thousands of immigrants arriving each week. In the late 1880's several government investigations were held into conditions at Castle Garden, at which missionaries testified that immigrants were forced to sleep on hard floors, some were made to pay twice for shipment of their baggage, and others were cheated by money-changers who hung about the Battery like leeches. One of the New York state commissioners testified that the Castle Garden operation was "a perfect farce."

These scandals were compounded in regard to immigrants detained for medical examination, who were sent to Ward's Island in the East River. Here, writes Edward Corsi, a commissioner of immigration for the New York district at a later time, "riots occurred frequently. Many immigrants escaped by swimming to the Manhattan shore [an exaggeration —I.H.], asking to be arrested and confined in the New York jails, rather than remain there with the insane and, as some charged, in a state of starvation. An investigation on one occasion revealed the startling fact that the bodies of dead immigrants were being used for purposes of dissection."

Then a sharp turn to the right, where the second doctor waits, a specialist in "contagious and loathsome diseases." Leprosy? Venereal disease? Fauvus, "a contagious disease of the skin, especially of the scalp, due to a parasitic fungus, marked by the formation of yellow flattened scabs and baldness"?

Then to the third doctor, often feared the most. He

> stands directly in the path of the immigrant, holding a little stick in his hand. By a quick movement and the force of his own compelling gaze, he catches the eyes of his subject and holds them. You will see the immigrant stop short, lift his head with a quick jerk, and open his eyes very wide. The inspector reaches with a swift movement, catches the eyelash with his thumb and finger, turns it back, and peers under it. If all is well, the immigrant is passed on. . . . Most of those detained by the physician are Jews.

The eye examination hurts a little. It terrifies the children. Nurses wait with towels and basins filled with disinfectant. They watch for trachoma, cause of more than half the medical detentions. It is a torment hard to understand, this first taste of America, with its poking of flesh and prying into private parts and mysterious chalking of clothes.*

Again into lines, this time according to nationality. They are led to stalls at which multilingual inspectors ask about character, anarchism, polygamy, insanity, crime, money, relatives, work. You have a job waiting? Who paid your passage? Anyone meeting you? Can you read and write? Ever in prison? Where's your money?

For Jewish immigrants, especially during the years before agencies like the Hebrew Immigrant Aid Society (HIAS) could give them advice, these questions pose a dilemma: to be honest or to lie? Is it good to have money or not? Can you bribe these fellows, as back home, or is it a mistake to try? Some are so accustomed to bend and evade and slip a ruble into a waiting hand that they get themselves into trouble with needless lies. "Our Jews," writes a Yiddish paper,

> love to get tangled up with dishonest answers, so that the officials have no choice but to send them to the detention area. A Jew who had money in his pocket decided to lie and said he didn't have a penny. . . . A woman with four children and pregnant with a fifth, said her husband had been in America

---

* Years later a scrupulous British ambassador, A. C. Geddes, visited Ellis Island and reported back to his government. By 1922, when he wrote, the high point of immigration had been passed, yet conditions struck him as bad:

"The line of male immigrants approached the first medical officer with their trousers open. The doctor examined their external genitalia for signs of venereal infection. Next he examined inguinal canals for hernia. The doctor wore rubber gloves. I saw him 'do' nine or ten men. His gloves were not cleansed between cases. I saw one nice, clean-looking Irish boy examined immediately after a very unpleasant-looking individual . . . I saw the boy shudder. I did not wonder. The doctor's rubber gloves were with hardly a second's interval in contact with his private parts after having been soiled, in the surgical sense at least, by contact with those of the unpleasant-looking individual."

fourteen years. . . . The HIAS man learned that her husband had recently arrived, but she thought fourteen years would make a better impression. The officials are sympathetic. They know the Jewish immigrants get "confused" and tell them to sit down and "remember." Then they let them in.

Especially bewildering is the idea that if you say you have a job waiting for you in the United States, you are liable to deportation—because an 1885 law prohibits the importation of contract labor. But doesn't it "look better" to say a job is waiting for you? No, the HIAS man patiently explains, it doesn't. Still, how can you be sure *he* knows what he's talking about? Just because he wears a little cap with those four letters embroidered on it?

Except when the flow of immigrants was simply beyond the staff's capacity to handle it, the average person passed through Ellis Island in about a day. Ferries ran twenty-four hours a day between the island and both the Battery and points in New Jersey. As for the unfortunates detained for medical or other reasons, they usually had to stay at Ellis Island for one or two weeks. Boards of special inquiry, as many as four at a time, would sit in permanent session, taking up cases where questions had been raised as to the admissibility of an immigrant, and it was here, in the legal infighting and appeals to sentiment, that HIAS proved especially valuable.

The number of those detained at the island or sent back to Europe during a given period of time varied according to the immigration laws then in effect (see pp. 53–54) and, more important, according to the strictness with which they were enforced. It is a sad irony, though familiar to students of democratic politics, that under relatively lax administrations at Ellis Island, which sometimes allowed rough handling of immigrants and even closed an eye to corruption, immigrants had a better chance of getting past the inspectors than when the commissioner was a public-spirited Yankee intent upon literal adherence to the law.

Two strands of opinion concerning Ellis Island have come down to us, among both historians and the immigrant masses themselves: first, that the newcomers were needlessly subjected to bad treatment, and second, that most of the men who worked there were scrupulous and fair, though often overwhelmed by the magnitude of their task.

The standard defense of Ellis Island is offered by an influential historian of immigration, Henry Pratt Fairchild:

During the year 1907 five thousand was fixed as the maximum number of immigrants who could be examined at Ellis Island in one day; yet during the spring of that year more than fifteen thousand immigrants arrived at the port of New York in a single day.

As to the physical handling of the immigrants, this is [caused] by the need for haste. . . . The conditions of the voyage are not calculated to land the immigrant in an alert and clear-headed state. The bustle, confusion, rush and size of Ellis Island complete the work, and leave the average alien in a state of stupor. . . . He is in no condition to understand a carefully-worded explanation of what he must do, or why he must do it, even if the inspector had the time to give it. The one suggestion which is immediately comprehensible to him is a pull or a push; if this is not administered with actual violence, there is no unkindness in it.

Reasonable as it may seem, this analysis meshed Yankee elitism with a defense of the bureaucratic mind. Immigrants *were* disoriented by the time they reached Ellis Island, but they remained human beings with all the sensibilities of human beings; the problem of numbers *was* a real one, yet it was always better when interpreters offered a word of explanation than when they resorted to "a pull or a push." Against the view expressed by Fairchild, we must weigh the massive testimony of the immigrants themselves, the equally large body of material gathered by congressional investigations, and such admissions, all the more telling because casual in intent, as that of Commissioner Corsi: "Our immigration officials have not always been as humane as they might have been." The Ellis Island staff was often badly overworked, and day after day it had to put up with an atmosphere of fearful anxiety which required a certain deadening of response, if only by way of self-defense. But it is also true that many of the people who worked there were rather simple fellows who lacked the imagination to respect cultural styles radically different from their own.*

One interpreter who possessed that imagination richly was a young Italo-American named Fiorello La Guardia, later to become an insurgent mayor of New York. "I never managed during the years I worked there to become callous to the mental anguish, the disappointment and the despair I witnessed almost daily. . . . At best the work was an ordeal." For those who cared to see, and those able to feel, there could finally be no other verdict.

A Work of Goodness

Whatever could be eased in the trauma of arrival, the Jewish community tried to ease. When the immigrants reached Ellis Island, they found waiting for them not only the authorities with their unnerving questions,

---

* Nor were such limitations confined to the lower ranks of immigration officials. The Immigration Commission of 1910, created by Congress, published a *Dictionary of Races or Peoples,* which, together with elementary anthropological material, could announce that "the Jewish nose, and to a less degree other facial characteristics, are found well-nigh everywhere throughout the race, although the form of the head seems to have become quite the reverse of the Semitic type. . . . Taking all factors into account, and especially their type of civilization, the Jews of today are more truly European than Asiatic or Semitic."

It would probably be a mistake to regard such passages as evidence of deliberate anti-Semitism; they indicate, however, that notions were afloat that hardly encouraged a warm-spirited response to alien peoples.

but also the friendlier faces of HIAS representatives. HIAS is one of the few Jewish agencies that over the decades has been praised by almost every segment of the American Jewish world—no small feat in a community that has been notoriously contentious. It was also one of the first major institutions in America set up and administered by east European Jews on their own.

There had been Jewish immigrant aid societies as far back as the 1870's. In 1881 the Hebrew Emigrant Aid Society (HEAS) was founded, and eight years later, the Hakhnosas Orkhim, a sheltering home for penniless immigrants. A makeshift group, the HEAS was utterly unprepared for the flood of immigration. In 1882 it sent east European Jews to farm colonies in Connecticut, New Jersey, and Colorado, but without sufficient training or funds; the colonies quickly collapsed. In October 1882 some four hundred immigrants housed by HEAS on Ward's Island to await medical inspection rioted, charging, the New York *Times* reported, that they were being "brutally treated by HEAS officers, who fed them decayed food and beat both men and women on the least provocation." The riot was quelled and the rioters placated, but the incident left a feeling of dismay on the East Side. Shadowed by these failures, HEAS dissolved in 1883. It took another nine years before HIAS, as it came to be known throughout the world, was formed in New York City, as the result of a meeting called in an East Side store by a *landsmanshaft** anxious to provide burial for Jews who had died on Ellis Island.

One of the first things HIAS did was to station on the island a representative who could mediate between the immigration officials and the flow of incoming Jews. Between 1904 and 1909, when immigration came to a peak, this representative was Alexander Harkavy, whose name is still remembered as the compiler of a Yiddish-English dictionary. Both their ignorance of legal formalities and their language handicaps made it hard for immigrants to cope with Ellis Island officials; the presence of Harkavy and his successor, a shrewd lawyer named Irving Lipsitch, acted as a strong restraining hand upon authorities who might otherwise have been inclined to dispose of cases a shade too rapidly.

HIAS representatives were sent to the shipping lines of Britain and Germany to protest steerage conditions. The Hamburg-American line was pressured into posting Yiddish notices explaining its ship regulations. On shore, HIAS worked out a system of placing immigrants with their relatives —not as easy as it might seem, since the relatives often knew only a bit more about American ways than did the immigrants. And as soon as they were checked out at Ellis Island, the newcomers would be steered by HIAS agents past the numerous sharpers, some posing as pious Jews, who waited on shore. These swindlers would remain a constant disgrace to the East Side;

* An association of people who had emigrated from the same town or district.

in March 1912 HIAS reported that it was prosecuting Hyman Eskins and
David Teffit for cheating immigrants.

All immigrants received at Ellis Island a Yiddish bulletin issued by
HIAS, full of hardheaded advice—an English translation was issued in 1912
under the happy auspices of the Connecticut Daughters of the American
Revolution:

> The immigrant who needs assistance from [HIAS] agents should hold in his
> hand or have pinned upon his coat . . . the card of identification which has
> been given out by the ship's doctor. . . . The agent will come to meet the
> immigrants and, when necessary, will act as their interpreter in the examina-
> tion that is necessary before admission.
>
> The immigrants who have been admitted, but have neither relatives nor
> friends to receive them, are taken by these same agents to the office of HIAS.
> . . . They will be accompanied, together with their baggage, either to their
> respective destinations in other parts of the city, or to the railway station to
> continue their journey. The agents who undertake this duty are entirely
> worthy of confidence, and their services are rendered without any charge
> whatever. . . .
>
> The home of HIAS is open day and night. . . . Accommodations are
> provided for men, women and children. There is an interpreter for Oriental
> Jews. . . . Pen, ink and paper are supplied free, as are also newspapers.
> Immigrants may use this Society as a forwarding address for letters. There
> are excellent baths, always at the free disposal of guests.

HIAS also ran an employment bureau, which, said its *First Annual
Report*, "was kept open every night, except Friday." City editions of the
papers would be rushed over from Park Row, and the staff would remain
until morning, trying to match immigrant to want ad.

In 1908 HIAS began to issue a bilingual monthly, *The Jewish Immigrant*, mostly in Yiddish, which was circulated widely in Russia, providing
reliable information on who could and could not be admitted in the United
States. Alexander Harkavy conducted a homely Yiddish column explaining
immigration laws and giving advice on proper behavior at Ellis Island. Such
bits of help proved extremely valuable, since it gave the immigrants not
merely practical guidance but a sense that there were friends and brothers
waiting for them.*

* A piquant incident is described by Mark Wischnitzer:
"HIAS maintained the American Jewish tradition of nonsectarian philanthropy. A group of 54 Russian peasants landed in New York . . . in 1905. Having
no relatives in the U.S. to act as guarantors, and lacking the $25 required in lieu of
a guarantee, the men in the group were detained for deportation. Harkavy remon-
strated with Commissioner Williams, pointing out that the Russians were hale and
hearty farmers who were not likely to become public charges. When he was unsuccessful in his representations, Harkavy signed a guarantee for the men, who were
then found lodgings at HIAS expense. . . . All of the men obtained work after a
while, with the exception of one hospitalized in Philadelphia (HIAS met the bill of
about $100).
"The peasants wrote home that no Russian representative had met them . . .

By 1914 HIAS had grown from a modest welfare society with a budget of less than ten thousand dollars to an organization with a nationwide membership, offices in Washington, D.C., and a number of port cities, and affiliations throughout the world. During 1912 there were more than 150,000 callers at its information bureau at 229 East Broadway. New immigrants helped at its home that year numbered 14,992, of whom over 3,000 were given shelter. Its naturalization aid meetings were attended by nearly 12,000 at different periods during the year; Sabbath afternoon classes by 4,000 children; at times space had to be bought elsewhere to shelter the overflow of immigrants.

Gradually—and as an early indication of the ability of east European Jews to adapt themselves to the American political structure—HIAS learned to function as a pressure group working to beat back nativist and/or bureaucratic attempts to reduce the flow of immigration. When a committee of the New York State Legislature proposed in 1911 to deport aliens suffering from mental disorders, HIAS attorneys persuaded the committee that immigrants afflicted with such disorders within three years after their arrival should not be liable for deportation if it could be shown that their ailment had been caused by some event after they had reached American shores—which was virtually to remove the possibility of deportation on mental grounds. In 1913 HIAS fought hard against the Burnett bill, previously vetoed by President Taft, which would have required a literacy test for immigrants. Such campaigns brought the east European Jews who ran HIAS into effective alliance with the German Jews who had more experience and skill at lobbying. Superbly energetic and persistent,* HIAS learned to play the bureaucratic game at least as well as the government's bureau-

---

but that a Jewish society had intervened in their behalf. . . . When it learned of this, the Russian government . . . offered the HIAS an annual subsidy of six thousand rubles for assistance to Russian subjects.

"John Bernstein [an early HIAS leader] recounted years later how the offer came up for discussion at a special meeting of the Board of Directors. Some favored accepting the money; others argued that since immigrants often left Russia illegally, there was a danger that the Russian government might try to get information about them from the Society. Then, too, Jewish public opinion would strongly oppose the acceptance of any subsidy from the Tsarist government. The offer was rejected on the grounds that the HIAS . . . did not wish to limit its independence by accepting government support."

* An illustration of HIAS's doggedness in fighting for the rights, sometimes more than the rights, of immigrants: In 1914 Joseph Aronoff, in the United States for a year and earning ten to twelve dollars a week, was notified that his wife and four children, who had arrived on the S.S. *Königin Luise* at Baltimore, were to be returned to Europe because two of the children, Rachel, ten, and Kazia, eight, had contracted *tinea tonsurans* (ringworm of scalp), a loathsome, contagious disease requiring an indefinite period to effect a cure. HIAS followed up this case for two years, arranging for prolonged and difficult treatment, warding off attempts by the authorities to declare the children incurable and thereby deportable. The family struggled to pay the hospital bills, enormous for the time; a private benefactor, one Mr. X, was recruited by HIAS to cover part of the cost; the children were cured and remained in America.

crats, maintaining with them an amiable relationship, yet prepared, when
necessary, to fight their rulings.

In later years it became fashionable to sneer at the tendency of American Jews to create a bureaucratic plethora of organizations. No doubt there
was a point to such criticism—but not with regard to HIAS. Thousands of
sons and daughters, as also their sons and daughters, would find life a little
easier, a little more comfortable because of the men who waited at Ellis
Island with those blue caps on which the Yiddish letters for HIAS had been
embroidered.

"Hordes" of Aliens

The sheer magnitude of immigration from Europe during the last third
of the nineteenth century made it certain that old-stock Americans, even if
favoring in principle an open door for aliens, would begin to feel uncomfortable. From the vantage point of distance, what seems remarkable is not
the extent of antiforeign sentiment that swept the country but the fact that
until the First World War it did not seriously impede the flow of immigration.

'We are the heirs of all time," wrote Herman Melville in the 1840's,
"and with all nations we divide our inheritance. On this Western Hemi-
sphere all tribes and peoples are forming into one federated whole; and there
is a future which shall see the estranged children of Adam restored as to the
old hearth-stone in Eden. . . . The seed is sown, and the harvest must
come." Forty or fifty years after Melville wrote these classically patriotic
lines, the "harvest" had turned sour for many Americans, both the fastidious
patricians and embattled plebeians.

In the 1860's and 1870's, when cheap labor was needed by the railroads
and both western and southern states were eager to absorb white settlers,
American business interests sent special agents to Europe in order to attract
immigrants. Popular sentiment remained attached to the notion that
America was uniquely the land of refuge from tyranny and a country where
fixed class lines gradually softened. Jews, to be sure, were already encountering social discrimination in the 1870's, some of it due to a feeling that the
recent immigrants from Germany, unlike their refined Sephardic cousins
who had been here for a long time, were too "loud" and "pushy" in their
social ascent. For the most part, however, there was not yet any large-scale
articulation of anti-Semitic prejudice, if only because the Jews did not yet
figure in the popular imagination as a major force in American life. Only
during the last two decades of the century did the multiplication of aliens
come to seem a national problem. Historians of immigration have distin-

guished, with rough usefulness, between "old" and "new" immigrants, the former mostly from northern and the latter from southern and eastern Europe. Close in cultural style to Protestant Americans, the "old" immigrants seemed more easily assimilable and thereby less threatening than the "new." By the eighties and nineties the mass influx consisted largely of "new" immigrants, ill-educated and often illiterate peasants whose manner could unnerve native Americans. And most immigrant Jews were regarded as among the "new."

Nativism as a movement taking the "immigrant hordes" as a target for attack began to make itself felt during the eighties; in its rudimentary forms it emerged as a xenophobia bristling with contempt for unfamiliar speech, dress, food, and values. Much of the hostility toward immigrants was stoked by the fear of radicalism which swept the country during the late eighties, partly as a result of the Haymarket Affair of 1886, in which six immigrants were sentenced to death after a bomb explosion at an anarchist rally in Chicago, and partly as a result of fierce labor struggles across the country, which could be attributed conveniently to foreign agitators. Second only to antiradicalism as a nativist motif was a virulent hatred of Catholicism. The Roman Church was feared as a vessel of medieval superstition, dripping with European decadence; and by the last years of the century public warnings began to be heard, not for the first or last time, that "*they* are taking over."

It would be an error to suppose that anti-immigrant feelings were confined to a single social class or political outlook. Brahmins and rednecks, bourgeois and proletarians, reactionaries and populists—all joined the outcry against the intruders. The one constant was that the outbreak of a depression, something that occurred with distressing frequency during the eighties and nineties, meant both a drop in the number of immigrants and a rise in sentiment against them. These were hard years in American society: unsettled by the consequences of rapid industrialization and uncontrolled urbanization, tormented by incomprehensible economic collapses, haunted by the fear that the country, as it moved away from the age of the independent farmer, might come to take on the social bitterness of Europe. The "new" immigrants, helpless in urban slums, seemed to many native Americans both symptom and cause of a spreading social malaise. Could they be expected to honor the democratic outlook of the Founding Fathers? Would they not disdain the traditions of individualism on which the nation had thrived? Were they not hopelessly marred by ignorance, dependence, superstition? If so enlightened a public figure as Henry George could write in 1883, "What in a few years more, are we to do for a dumping-ground? Will it make our difficulty the less that our human garbage can vote?"—if so humane an intellectual could speak in this way, it need come as no surprise that mere editorialists and common folk began to look upon the alien "hordes" as a threat to their well-being.

Some liberal academicians joined the cry for restricting immigration, though with arguments more subtle than those of the newspapers or the streets. They saw the immigrant masses as a threat to democratic survival, their presence as making still harder the solution of already difficult social problems. As John Higham, the historian of nativism, has remarked:

> It was not difficult for this early generation of urbanized reformers—full of dark forebodings and ill-experienced in realistic social analysis—to fix upon the immigrants as a major source of current disorders. Nor was it entirely unreasonable for men who feared a decline of opportunity and mobility to lose confidence in the process of assimilation. In discovering an immigrant *problem,* the social critics of the eighties might not indulge in the characteristically nativist assault on the newcomer as a foreign enemy of the American way of life. . . . But they raised the question of assimilation in a broadly significant way by connecting it with the issues of the day. They gave intellectual respectability to anti-immigrant feelings.

Other segments of the population joined the attack. Influential figures in the Brahmin elite of New England warned that the millions of immigrants were a threat to political controls and cultural authority; they feared, with reason, that an America bustling with foreigners would mean an end to their caste pre-eminence. In 1894 a small group of Bostonians formed the Immigration Restriction League, which proved to be a skillful propaganda agency for the campaign against aliens. Equally skillful in his own way was the Congregational clergyman Josiah Strong, who thundered against the massing of aliens in the cities, where they would spawn crime, immorality, radicalism, and Catholicism. The Republican party, protector of Anglo-Saxon respectability, served as the political home for the restrictionists, though in a while some of the party's more sharp-eyed leaders noticed that votes of foreign-born citizens were every bit as good as those of natives. Even the reform movements that kept cropping up in the nineties—temperance, women's rights, clean government—saw the immigrants as besotted and benighted.

For the unions, the problem was especially hard. Many native-born workers looked upon aliens as unfair competition, ready to work for wages that no respectable American would accept—and it would be foolish to deny that this complaint had some validity.* Unionists often saw the immigrants as a mass of potential strikebreakers, again with some validity. Jewish immigrants seldom came into direct conflict with unionized American workers, first because they usually worked in trades that had barely been touched by native unionism, and second because some of them brought over

---

* "The tremendous immigration influx of 1882, followed by the industrial depression of 1883–1886, persuaded many wage-earners that the whole incoming stream directly threatened their livelihood. In New York City an Independent Labor Party petitioned Congress to impose a head tax of $100 on each entrant. Philadelphia saw the appearance of a National Home Labor League, aiming 'to preserve the American labor market for American workingmen.'"

a tradition of class solidarity that would have made it seem shameful to become a scab. Yet during the eighties and nineties Jewish immigrants were occasionally tricked into brief service as strikebreakers—one immigrant who arrived in the early eighties, I. Kopeloff, has left a recollection of being taken directly from Castle Garden to the New York waterfront, put to work at heavy labor, and then suddenly pounced upon by an enraged mob. Only later did Kopeloff and his fellow immigrants discover they had been used to replace striking workers; they immediately left in indignation.

Some unions clung to sentiments of internationalism, and, more important, large segments of union membership were themselves foreign-born and therefore inclined to be unsympathetic to restrictionist agitation. The unions were largely responsible for the passage in 1885 of the Alien Contract Labor Law, which brought to a halt the practice of importing European labor under contract to work for wages below union scales. For a few years during the late eighties and early nineties, such union leaders as Samuel Gompers, himself a Jewish immigrant who had worked as a cigar maker in New York, tried to check the restrictionist wing in the AFL. Only during the mid-nineties, when the country was struck by a very harsh depression in which millions of workers found themselves jobless, did the unions come out in favor of restricting immigration.

Open Door—and Closed

All through the several decades between the early eighties and the First World War, a struggle took place in American society between the partisans of free immigration and the advocates of restriction. Partly to regulate but also to limit immigration, a series of acts was passed by Congress—though, more important from the standpoint of those who wished to enable the Jews to find refuge in the United States, most of the proposals for radically cutting down the number of immigrants were beaten back. Let us note, as pertinent to our story, a few of the acts that were passed:

1882—an act extending the category of "excluded classes" to include lunatics, idiots, and "any person unable to take care of himself or herself without becoming a public charge." This last clause would become a major cause of dispute between immigration authorities and HIAS, since the vagueness of its language opened the possibility for arbitrary rulings. The act also stipulated that aliens excluded upon arrival were to be returned to Europe at the expense of the shipowners—which meant that more stringent physical tests would now be given at the European ports.

1885—the Alien Contract Labor Law, already described, which did not seriously affect Jewish immigration.

1891—an act that added to the "excluded classes" paupers, polygamists, persons suffering from "a loathsome or dangerous contagious disease," and persons whose tickets had been paid for by someone else, unless it was shown that they were not otherwise objectionable. The last two provisions, even if not malicious in intent, led to hardships for Jewish immigrants.

1891—the most comprehensive act yet passed on immigration, transferring entirely the inspection of immigrants from the states to the federal government, prohibiting the encouragement of immigration by advertisement, and extending the principle of deportation to "public charges." This last provision led to some harassment of immigrants, as fearful stories spread among them about the danger of being sent back to Europe after a year in the United States if they could not support themselves. An unintended consequence, however, may have been strengthened arrangements in the Jewish community for self-help.

1903—an act tightening immigration and especially fulfilling the wish of President Theodore Roosevelt that "we should aim to exclude absolutely not only all persons who are known to be believers in anarchistic principles . . . but also all persons who are of a low moral tendency or of unsavory reputation."

Irksome as such laws were from the point of view of the immigrants and their defenders, none constituted nearly so great a threat as the recurrent proposal that persons unable to read or write their own language be barred. Such a law would have been a severe blow to free immigration, and each time it was proposed in Congress, all the resources of the various ethnic communities had to be mobilized in opposition. By the turn of the century, these resources were considerable, for the foreign-language press had grown into a powerful institution, the economic strength of the immigrant communities had increased, and in a number of states immigrants had become citizens in sufficient numbers to swing crucial elections. Three times literacy proposals passed the Congress, three times they were vetoed by presidents—Cleveland in 1897, Taft in 1913, Wilson in 1915.

In the struggle against restrictionism, the German Jews developed notable skill at employing the kinds of quiet pressures that have played a crucial role in American politics. The single most effective publicist in behalf of free immigration was Louis Marshall, a brilliant lawyer of German-Jewish descent and for many years head of the American Jewish Committee. Though a formidable speaker ready to take on restrictionists in public debate, Marshall worked best behind the scenes, through well-argued and well-mannered appeals to public officials. He kept pointing out that illiteracy was not itself a ground for regarding an immigrant (or anyone else) as "undesirable" and that "men able, sometimes, to speak fluently five or six languages" may nevertheless be "degenerates, forgers, blackmailers." Quite free of illusions as to the mental breadth of the politicians he wished to influence,

Marshall was on occasion prepared to tap their antiradical prejudices—as in a 1907 letter to Governor Page of Vermont in which he remarked that "an educated immigrant is not ordinarily the most beneficial. The ranks of the anarchists and the violent socialists are recruited from the educated classes, frequently from among those who read and write several languages."

The Jewish socialists, favoring mass pressure rather than private persuasion, were always dubious, often scornful of Marshall's methods—though it must be admitted that their hostility was partly the result of a refusal to adapt themselves to the workings of American politics. On the level of expediency, Marshall understood the politics of America far better than they did. The best chance for maintaining a free flow of immigration, he felt, was to keep the issue out of the public arena; he had no wish to rouse the deep, almost unconscious sentiments which he knew to lie waiting in the most kindly of gentile souls. In 1905 he wrote to a friend,

> I consider a public discussion of [the immigration] question at this time by any Jewish organization, an extremely unfortunate step. It serves to attract the attention of Congress and of the various labor unions, to the fact that we expect a large influx of Jewish immigrants from Russia. It is a subject which can only be handled with the greatest delicacy.

In sharpest contrast to Marshall's tactics—indeed, as part of a prolonged debate within the Jewish community—was the approach of the labor and socialist groups that believed in public militancy and mass demonstrations. Some historians have suggested that in fact there occurred a tacit division between polite lobbyists and rude protesters; if so, neither would have admitted it.

In the spring and summer of 1909 the East Side was deeply shaken by a conflict between many of its leading spokesmen and the New York commissioner of immigration, William Williams. The commissioner had decreed that an immigrant would need twenty-five dollars in order to be admitted, a sum that for most arrivals from eastern Europe represented a small fortune quite beyond their ability to secure. Appointed by President Theodore Roosevelt, Williams had introduced desirable reforms at Ellis Island, even posting signs reminding officials to be courteous to aliens. Intractable, public-spirited, honest, Williams believed in a "strict" interpretation of the immigration laws; privately, in correspondence with Roosevelt, he had expressed the view that "all below a certain physical and economic standard" should be excluded. Precisely his righteousness kept him from bending to humaneness—a rigidity not unknown among American reformers—and made him come to seem an enemy of the immigrants. HIAS agents found him much harder to deal with than his predecessors.

Directly after the edict requiring a twenty-five-dollar fee, the *Jewish Daily Forward*, by 1909 a considerable power in the East Side and even, for that matter, in New York, began a fierce campaign against Williams. Day after day it hammered at his cruelty, his prejudice; the support of leading liberals was enlisted; angry mass meetings were held. On July 7 the *Forward* printed a letter from one hundred immigrants detained at Ellis Island plead-ing that when breaking up their homes in Europe they had known nothing about the twenty-five-dollar requirement. "Most of the immigrants working in factories today," thundered the *Forward*, "came to these shores without a penny. But they are the ones who have built up the palaces, machines, food and clothing which America enjoys. Williams's new ruling has no common sense and no fair play."

Surprised by this outcry, Williams retreated in part, saying that only "some" immigrants would be required to have twenty-five dollars; yet he continued to direct his staff toward a harsher series of examinations, and the result was a sharp increase in the number of immigrants sent back from Ellis Island. On July 14 the *Forward* reported that some of those detained had gone on a hunger strike, led by Alexander Rudenief, son of a Russian army doctor, who had made a flaming speech in the mess hall that the food "is suitable for hogs. We are treated like wild beasts. We sleep on a wet floor." Continued the *Forward* reporter: "The officials were afraid that a revolu-tion would break out and an inspector ran into the room with a revolver. The immigrants looked at him scornfully—it had not occurred to them to use violence."

Secretary of Commerce and Labor Charles Nagel, himself a second-generation American, rushed to New York to investigate the scandal. "The twenty-five dollars is not important," he said; "the immigrant must prove he is healthy and has a trade." But again, the seeming reasonableness of this remark could be turned against the immigrants, many of whom, never in a position to learn a trade, had been forced to live by their wits. The *Forward* did not let up, even after the twenty-five-dollar provision was relaxed. On August 2 it reported that during the month of July 1,333 immigrants had been sent back from Ellis Island, twice the usual number. A month later it carried a report from its Russian correspondent, A. Litwin:

> You can't imagine the chaos that Williams's twenty-five-dollar edict has created in the towns and villages of Russia. Thousands of emigrants on the eve of departure don't know what to do. Those who had a few extra rubles, though not the entire fifty, decided to take a chance and embark . . . while cabling to their friends in America.

The *Forward* kept denouncing the treatment of immigrants at Ellis Island, and when Williams left his post a few years later, it ran a headline, "The Haman of Ellis Island Resigns." But such victories were only tempo-rary, perhaps illusory, since the basic trend in American politics was by now toward restricting immigration. A forty-volume congressional report issued in late 1910 prepared the way; the First World War brought immigration entirely to a stop; and by 1924, after a brief postwar rise in the number of

European Jews accepted in the United States, restrictionism gained a seemingly permanent victory.

The Jews Who Came

The most difficult questions remain: who came? Which Jews? Rich or poor, city or *shtetl*, old or young, religious or secular? Are there verifiable distinctions of character, sensibility, opinion, and condition to be observed between those who remained and those who left? And were there differences between the kinds of Jews who came to America in the 1880's and those who came in the first decade of the twentieth century?

Like most truly interesting historical questions, these do not lend themselves to convenient answers. Few statistics, and those usually inadequate, were kept among the east European Jews. (Many evaded legal registration in order to save their sons from the draft; others drifted about so much they were probably never counted.) In the United States, immigration statistics prior to 1899 were classified by country of nativity, not by race, religion, or nationality, so that with regard to the last two decades of the century students of Jewish immigration such as Samuel Joseph and Liebmann Hersch could do no more than work up estimates. Even the statistics for the years after 1899 do not provide answers to many questions one would like to ask—and in regard to the replies Jewish immigrants gave about their occupations, a decided skepticism is in order. (A portion of those innumerable "tailors" surely had less than expert acquaintance with needle and thread.)

The enormous memoir literature provides some clues, but not enough: the habit of sociological scrutiny was not yet strongly developed among east European Jews, nor were the necessary conditions of leisure and detachment available. Besides, to those who came to the United States the need for flight seemed so overwhelming that they rarely supposed their journey required elaborate explanation. The statements one finds in the memoir literature are persuasive through their very repetition.* We came because we were hungry; we came because we were persecuted; we came because life in Russia or Poland had grown insufferable. These are the answers one gets over and over again, and there is not the slightest reason to doubt them. But

---

* In 1891 the Department of the Treasury sent two special commissioners, John B. Weber and Dr. Walter Kempster, to investigate the causes of emigration from Europe to the United States. They spent several months touring the major concentrations of Jewish settlement in Russia. Their conclusion seems classically precise: "Aside from a small proportion of Jews who look longingly and hopefully toward Palestine, next to their religion and their persistent eagerness for education, America is the present hope and goal of their ambition, toward which their gaze is directed as earnestly as that of their ancestors toward the promised land."

what they do not, perhaps cannot, explain is why some Jews acted on these urgent motives and others did not.

The statistics give some clues, not why people came but which people came. Between 1881 and 1914 close to two million Jews arrived in America, the overwhelming bulk of them either directly or indirectly from eastern Europe. A migration of such magnitude must have drawn upon all segments of the Jewish population, though in varying proportions at different points in time:

The Jewish migration was much more a movement of families than that of other European nationalities and groups.

> That the Jewish movement is essentially a family movement is shown by the great proportion of females and children in it. From 1899 to 1910, out of a total immigration of 1,074,442 Jews, 607,822 or 56.6 percent were males, and 466,620 or 43.4 percent were females.
>
> Between 1899 and 1910, 267,656 or practically one-fourth of all the Jewish immigrants were children under fourteen years.
>
> For the entire period the percentage of females in the Jewish population was much higher than in the total immigration, 43.4 percent of the Jewish immigration being females as compared with 30.5 percent of the total.
>
> The proportion of children under fourteen years of age was 24.8 percent, while that in the total immigration was only 12.3 percent.

The Jewish migration, like that of all other groups, was overwhelmingly a movement of young people.

Between 1899 and 1909 the percentage of Jewish immigrants in the age group fourteen to forty-four was 69.8, while that of every other immigrant group was decidedly higher, the Greek reaching 94.6. There is a plausible explanation for this difference. Because the Jews brought more young children, came as families (either all at once or in sequence), and also brought a somewhat higher percentage of older people, than most of the immigrant groups, the percentage of those between fourteen and forty-four had necessarily to be lower among them. Nevertheless, the immigration was, as it had to be, overwhelmingly a movement of young people.

The Jewish immigration was directed much more toward permanent settlement in the United States than was that of other European groups.

While only two thirds of the total number of immigrants to the United States in the years between 1908 and 1924 were to remain here permanently, 94.8 percent of the Jews remained permanently. In the crucial year of 1908, only 2 percent of the Jewish immigrants returned to the old country. Neither legal impediments, nor hardships upon arrival, nor recurrent depressions could drive the Jews back to Europe. A study of the immigration statistics shows that in the years directly after a depression the total number of immigrants declined but that the decline among Jewish immigrants was both slower and less precipitous.

The Jewish migration contained a higher proportion of skilled workers, many of them from urban or semiurban environments, than that of any other group; correspondingly, it contained a much smaller proportion of unskilled laborers.

> Before the [First World] War one-fifth of all immigrants, but two-thirds of the Jews specifying occupation, were skilled laborers. . . . The percentage of Jews among the skilled laborers coming into the United States was three times as high as their proportion among all immigrants with occupations.

Of these skilled Jewish workers, clothing workers embraced 60 percent—or 40 percent of the entire Jewish immigration—in the years between 1899 and 1914.

> . . . the Jews coming to the United States, 1899–1914, included about 80,000 workers on buildings and furnishing, 50,000 workers on machines and metals, and 40,000 workers in the food industry.
>
> One can say, broadly, that out of three Jewish migrants specifying occupation, there is one *luftmensh* and one tailor.

If one does speak "broadly," it ought to be suggested that some of those "tailors" and "building workers" were also *luftmenshn* who assigned themselves occupations in order to get past Ellis Island. And the category of "skilled laborer" employed by U.S. immigration authorities had only the haziest relevance to the Jewish workers who came over, since many of them were small craftsmen and artisans without industrial experience. Nevertheless, the statistics do indicate that the Jews coming to the United States had a considerably better preparation for urban life than did most of the other immigrants from eastern and southern Europe.

We do not have statistics as to how many Jewish immigrants came directly from Russian and Polish cities and how many from the *shtetl*. But it is known that in the last two decades of the nineteenth and the first decade of the twentieth century there was a large population movement out of the *shtetl* and into the Russian and Polish cities, so that many of the Jewish immigrants would have had a brief—though only brief—urban experience on the other side.

We may conclude that the Jewish immigration constituted, among other things, an extension or final step in the profound dislocation that was occurring in eastern European Jewish life—from *shtetl* to Russian or Polish city, and then to New York, as a series of steps in the breakup of a traditional society.

The Jewish migration changed in character between the 1880's and the 1900's, with a greater number of intellectuals, relatively educated persons, and skilled workers coming in the later period.

In part, this merely reflected changes in the social structure of the east European Jewish community during those years—the trend toward urbanization already mentioned. The proportion of teachers, rabbis, engineers, musicians, and physicians among the Jewish immigrants did not change radically in the years between 1899 and 1908, but the number of such persons did go up sharply (91 Jewish teachers in 1899, 269 in 1907; 197 "other professionals" in 1899, 1,045 in 1907). The character of the immigrant communities in New York and elsewhere was crucially affected.

Here is a statement by an ordinary Jewish immigrant who, still sharp-witted at the age of eighty-two, was interviewed in an old-age home:

> I am a tailor and I was working piecework on Russian officers' uniforms. I saved up a few dollars and figured the best thing was to go to the U.S.A. Those days everybody's dream in the old country was to go to America. We heard people were free and we heard about better living. I was seventeen when I came in 1905. I was the first to leave from my family. My father didn't want me to go . . . I figured, I have a trade, I have a chance more or less to see the world. I was young.

A few phrases ring out: "everybody's dream . . . was to go to America" and "I have a chance more or less to see the world," the first characteristic but the second not. Strictly speaking, not everyone did want to go to America, but as hyperbole, the statement touches upon a central truth.* As for "a chance more or less to see the world," it is not the kind of phrase that appears frequently in Jewish memoirs, perhaps because their authors, by the time they came to write, did not look upon such a confession as weighty enough. But to read these memoirs extensively is to grow convinced that "adventure" did play a role—if not in the sense of *Treasure Island*, then in the sense of *Kim:* if not fun for the devil, then journey for a breakthrough. Even in those airless Talmud Torahs, even in those claustrophobic *shtetlakh* there were Jewish boys panting for a chance to get out and stretch their legs. A few may have resembled the youngster later to become Darwin Hecht, M.D., who began running away from home before he was ten and decided to leave for America at the age of eleven:

> When Mother saw me copying the addresses she asked me where I was going this time. I told her I was going to America. To my surprise, she said, "Very well, you can go." She looked over the addresses I had copied to make sure they were correct. The next day she assembled a few items, such as a change of underwear and some food, and tied it all in a large multi-colored handkerchief. She gave me 40 *groshn* [ten cents] and a post card with my home address on it, and she told me to mail it as soon as I crossed the Russian-German border. She took me to the railroad station, kissed me goodbye, and put me on the train with no railroad ticket, no ship ticket, no passport. She

---

* The *Forward's* Russian correspondent, A. Litwin, wrote in 1909: "If they could afford it, half the Jewish workers in the big cities and all in the small towns would emigrate. They save up the hundred rubles for the ticket for years, adding a groschen to a groschen, going half-naked, borrowing and pawning."

probably thought this would be another escapade and that I would be back home as usual, though what was really in her thoughts I will never know. Thus my venturesome journey to America began.

As he made his way across Europe, this Jewish Roderick Random hid under railroad seats, was arrested as a vagrant in Hamburg, smuggled himself under a woman's skirt to get on board ship, and, that failing, clambered up the side of the ship to stow away. Discovered, he became the ship's darling and told the captain a yarn about "going to look for my father who had deserted my mother." Surely there were always a few such Jewish boys, unspoiled by their environment for the risks and pleasures of adventure.

At least for the 1880's and 1890's, if somewhat less so for the later years, there is truth in the remark of a Jewish historian that "the Jewish immigrants . . . constituted in great part the 'dissenters,' the poor and under-privileged, the unlearned and less learned, and those who were influenced by secularism." This estimate conforms to the observation frequently made by Yiddish memoirists and historians that the immigrants of the 1880's tended, socially speaking, to be the flotsam and jetsam of the old country, the *luftmenshn* without trades or roots driven to take a chance across the sea.

At some points, such as after the 1881 pogroms or the 1903 Kishinev massacre, there were large-scale movements of Jews from regions of eastern Europe that were closer in character to mass flights than to ordered migrations. When these occurred almost everyone left who could leave—though here too the sick and the old remained because they had no choice, while those who rejected immigration often clung to shattered homes and businesses. But in the years when conditions in Russia reached a measure of stability, people were able to make choices. Clearly, age was a decisive factor: the young were always a large portion of the immigrants, grown restive precisely through the stimulus created by the Yiddish cultural-political upsurge, or stirred to personal hope by reports from relatives already in America. In part, the Jewish migration was a function of the intellectual and spiritual turmoil within the Jewish community of eastern Europe; and some, if not the majority, of those who left would have wanted to get away even if there had been no hunger or persecution.

At least before 1905 Jews who held strong religious or political convictions were less likely to emigrate than those who did not. The socialists of the Bund believed they should stay in Russia and Poland in order to organize the Jewish working class; the Zionists, that America was a false hope, no more than the Diaspora aglitter, and that preparations for leaving should be directed toward the Holy Land; and the Orthodox Jews, that America was a jungle of worldliness in which the faith might be destroyed. Once the Russian Revolution of 1905 failed, some Bundists fled to avoid imprisonment; others concluded they had exhausted their possibilities in the old country, so they too joined the trek to America; but many Bundists remained, to rebuild their movement into the powerful force it would become during the twenties and thirties. The number of Orthodox Jews entering the migration also increased, not out of ideological decision but because the postrevolutionary reaction in Russia was deeply discouraging to Jewish life.

As for the vast majority of ordinary Jews, the *folksmasn* who responded more to the urgencies of their experience than to any fixed ideas, they had no "principled" reason whatever for remaining under the czar. Many stayed; there were ties of sentiment, family obligations, personal fears, all the elements of psyche and will that shape our lives. But by 1905 those who decided to leave the old world were no longer merely the displaced and declassed but increasingly the energetic, the vigorous, the ambitious. "The happy and powerful," De Tocqueville has written, "do not go into exile." Yes, but sometimes the aroused and determined do.

Most historians of the Jewish immigration have agreed that the social and cultural characteristics of the Jewish immigrants in the 1905–1914 period were notably different from those who came during the last two decades of the nineteenth century. By and large, the later immigrants brought with them a somewhat higher cultural level than those who had come twenty-five or thirty years earlier: first because there had occurred in the interim a resurgence of Jewish consciousness in eastern Europe (the Bund, Zionism, Yiddish literature, a range of political and religious movements), and second because important segments of the Jewish intelligentsia now felt that the time had come to leave. That some progress had meanwhile been made among the Jews in New York caused the journey to seem less fearful; an immigrant in 1905 was not quite the pioneer he would have been in 1882.

The point should not be exaggerated. Given the sheer magnitude of the migration, there were bound to be large numbers of ignorant or barely educated Jews arriving in any year between 1881 and 1914. And even in the 1880's there were already the thin beginnings of a Yiddish-speaking intelligentsia in New York. By the turn of the century, however, such notable figures of Yiddish culture as Abraham Reisen, the poet, and Abraham Liessen, the poet and publicist, were coming to America, men who represented a distinctly higher level of cultural sophistication than the New York "sweatshop poets" of a few years earlier.

Finally, it would be a mistake to suppose that the regional, class, and social distinctions that can be applied to, say, the Italians who came to America will help very much in explaining the east European Jewish immigration. The Italians came from their own independent nation, in which they had developed a far more stratified and internally diverse society than had the Jews; and this fact was strongly reflected in the regional, class, and cultural character of the Italian immigration. Individual Italians might be in flight, but not the Italians as a people. Of the Jews, however, it can almost be said that a whole people was in flight. So cautious a historian of Jewish immigration as Liebmann Hersch makes this point:

On the average, of 1,000 Jews in the Russian Empire, 13 came annually [between 1899 and 1914] to the United States and 15.6 emigrated annually from Russia. This is one of the highest rates of emigration recorded in the history of modern migrations. As it is an average rate for a period of 16 years and as 95 percent of the emigrants remained abroad, we must go back to the great Irish emigration in the middle of the nineteenth century to find an exodus of equal magnitude.

It is best to turn back to the folk voices themselves. An unpublished Yiddish memoirist writes, "They pushed me into America"—"they" being all those forces of oppression he encountered in his youth. Another unpublished Yiddish memoirist recalls still more vividly, "A powerful storm-wind ripped us out of our place and carried us to America." No one in the path of that "storm-wind" was left untouched.

THE

2

EAST SIDE

CHAPTER THREE

The Early Years,
1881-1900

WHERE WAS I to go? An awkward, unkempt, timid youth of sixteen, with the inevitable bundles, I dumbly inquired my way from the Battery to the slums. . . . The only vantage point I had was an address on the letter my uncle had given me to deliver to a friend of his. I showed this to an officer who sent me in the direction of the East Side. I probably could have done it without an address, for where else did immigrant Jews congregate?

It was a long walk, especially on a hot summer's day . . . Orchard Street. The crush and the stench were enough to suffocate one: dirty children were playing in the street, and perspiring Jews were pushing carts and uttering wild shrieks. A far from pleasant first impression. . . . Was this the America we had sought? Or was it only, after all, a circle that we had traveled, with a Jewish ghetto at its beginning and its end . . . Division Street, Bayard Street, Canal Street, Allen, Ludlow, and Essex streets with their dark tenements, filthy sidewalks; saloons on nearly every corner; sinister red lights in the vestibules of many small frame houses—all these shattered my illusions of America and made me feel terribly homesick for the beautiful green hills of my native Vilna. . . .

In the late afternoon I walked along East Broadway. Old, white-bearded men sat on some of the stoops, and the skullcaps on their heads made me feel at home. . . .

On the way I encountered a familiar figure, one who was anathema in his home town. There I would have scorned even to notice him. It was Shmuel, the son of a horse thief, who had probably followed in his father's footsteps. But here! What a joy it was to have Shmuel greet me effusively with "Why are you here? What crime did *you* commit?" He assumed that the only people that emigrated were those who had run afoul of the law and wished to avoid punishment. . . . At any rate, he proved a friend in need and directed me to the house where I was supposed to find a welcome. But alas, the man I expected to find was already on his way home—an American failure. . . .

The landlady, observing my dismay, invited me to partake of a cup of coffee with cake. I was amazed. Cake for breakfast! . . . My first full meal was an object lesson of much variety. There were several kinds of food, ready to eat, without cooking, from little tin cans that had printing all over them. Someone attempted to introduce me to a queer, slippery kind of fruit which he called "panana," but I had to forgo it for the time being. After the meal I had better luck with a curious piece of furniture on runners, called a "rocking chair." There were five of us newcomers in the room, and we found five different ways of getting into this American machine of perpetual motion. . . .

I was given the privilege of leaving my bundle while I went through the swarming streets to try to find work, as well as a place to sleep, since all the "corners" in the place I had just left were already leased.

The first English expression that struck my foreign ear as I walked through the ghetto that day and which I set down in my American vocabulary were "sharrap" (shut up) and "garrarrehere" (get out of here). It took me a little while to learn that the English tongue was not restricted to these two terms. . . .

A job was offered me on the waterfront as a laborer if I could get to work immediately. Since it was a Jewish holiday I could not accept. Then someone told me of a job in a grocery store. I had no idea what this was, but I rushed back to search for my diploma from the yeshiva. Finally I found the grocer and exhibited my credentials. The grocer handled it gingerly and remarked, "I guess you can chop wood all right without that." Well, at least it didn't prevent me from getting the job, for which I was to receive board and lodging. . . .

And while the bed linen wasn't particularly white or clean (the sheets were decorated with little blood stains), we gladly surrendered ourselves to sleep and the American fleas, who were the first to enjoy our blood—until we went to work in the factories.

Loneliness, weariness, and, at last, night under the roof of a stranger who shared his home with me. Thus closed my first day in the United States.

This composite of recollections could be duplicated by hundreds of similar ones, for the experience of immigrants was so unsettling there was at first little possibility for variation of response. Only a bit later, after the opening weeks of panic, could they begin to look about them and take the measure of this new world.

The First Shock

In the early eighties the Jewish quarter was still small, with much of the East Side under the control of Irish and German immigrants.

> A few Jewish families had moved into houses along East Broadway at Clinton and Montgomery Streets. Only a few years earlier this had been a purely native American section. . . . The number of Jewish families diminished as one moved away from East Broadway toward Henry to Madison, Monroe and finally to Cherry Street where there were no Jews at all. In the other direction, the Jewish quarter . . . extended north to Delancey Street.

East Broadway, in those days an imposing avenue with wide sidewalks and distinguished homes, was often called *ulitza* (the Russian word for street) because the Jewish intellectuals who made it their center felt it was more cultivated to speak Russian than Yiddish. By 1883 "we hear of great overcrowding in Essex and York Streets among Russian and Polish Jews. It was said that in one house of 16 apartments, of two rooms each, about 200 people were quartered. . . . On the East Side the Jews have pressed up through the [whole area] driving the Germans before them."

Within a few years, the Lower East Side became the most densely populated area in the city. By 1890 it had 522 inhabitants per acre, by 1900 more than 700. The density of the Tenth Ward, reported the University Settlement Society shortly after the turn of the century, was greater than that of the worst sections of Bombay. And since many small shops were crammed into this area, the crowding by day was scarcely less extreme than by night. One of the worst spots was "the Pig Market," as the Jews called it, on Hester near Ludlow, where everything but pig could be bought off pushcarts—peaches at a penny a quart, "damaged" eggs, eyeglasses for thirty-five cents, old coats for fifty cents—and where greenhorns would bunch up in the morning to wait for employers looking for cheap labor.

In 1890, within the small space bounded by the Bowery on the west, the river and its warehouses on the east, Houston on the north, and Monroe on

the south, there were some two dozen Christian churches, a dozen synagogues (most Jewish congregations were storefronts or in tenements), about
fifty factories and shops (exclusive of garment establishments, most of
which were west of the Bowery or hidden away in cellars and flats), ten
large public buildings, twenty public and parochial schools—and one tiny
park, on Grand and East Broadway. Gangs of German boys pressed down
from the north, Irish from the south. A dominant impression of the Jewish
quarter, shared by immigrants and visitors alike, was of fierce congestion, a
place in which the bodily pressures of other people, their motions and smells
and noises, seemed always to be assaulting one. Of space for privacy and
solitude there was none.

"Curse you, emigration," cried Abraham Cahan in a letter written for a
Russian newspaper in 1882. "Accursed are the conditions that have brought
you forth! How many lives have you broken, how many brave and mighty
have you rubbed out like dust!" Such sentiments were not at all unusual in
the eighties and nineties. Coming to America with inflamed hopes, some of
the immigrants became demoralized and others permanently undone. Not
only was their physical situation wretched—that, after all, they had long
been accustomed to. Far worse was the spiritual confusion that enclosed
their lives.

No controlling norms or institutions, neither rabbinical nor communal,
could now be accepted as once they had been; no myths of tradition or even
slogans of revolt. Those who wanted to remain faithful to traditional Judaism—and in these years many did—had now to make a special effort. Pressures of the city, the shop, the slum, all made it terribly hard to stay with
the old religious ethic. The styles and rituals of traditional Judaism had been
premised on a time scheme far more leisurely, a life far less harried than
urban America demanded. As for the new ethic of materialist individualism,
what could this mean to a garment worker who spent sixty hours a week in
a sweatshop, physically present in America yet barely touched by its language, its traditions, its privileges? Those immigrants who stood fast by
religion found whatever solace it could offer, those who turned to secularism gained the consolations of new theory. But the masses of immigrants,
who rarely thought to call religion into question yet found it harder and
harder to regard it as a system illuminating the totality of existence—what
was left to them? Fragments of a culture, a parochialism bred by centuries
of isolation, and a heritage of fear, withdrawal, insularity. Except for those
who clung to faith or grappled toward ideology, the early immigrants consisted of people who were stranded—stranded socially, morally, psychologically. That all this was happening at the very time Jewish life in eastern
Europe had begun to experience a secular renewal did not change things
very much. Few immigrants in America had a close knowledge of the east
European renewal; it was too far away to brighten or sustain their lives. All
they could bring to their experience in America—and after the first shatter-

ing years, it would prove to be a great deal—was that shared tenacity with which Jews had always clung to life.

"A Gray, Stone World"

Over the centuries they had accumulated a rich experience in living as a minority within a hostile culture.

> The need to adjust to conditions of life in a strange country first became a problem for other groups only in America; but for Jews it was a problem they had had to face for many centuries. Others came to their new country with one culture; the Jews came with two, and frequently more than two, cultures. One culture they carried deep *within* themselves, within their spiritual and psychic being. The other they bore *upon* themselves, like an outer garment.

Given this training in the strategies of the pariah, the Jews were "able [in America] to skip the whole period of accustoming themselves to minority status which demanded so much energy . . . from other groups."

True enough for the Jewish immigrant experience as a whole, this observation needs qualification in regard to the eighties and nineties. For the Jews who came during these years often were not able to carry "deep within themselves" the heritage of their past; many were so shaken by the ordeal of flight and arrival that for a time they seemed all but culturally dispossessed. It would take at least a quarter of a century before they could regain the culture they had left behind. As the Yiddish writer B. Rivkin has observed: "The first immigrant generation . . . were Jews without Jewish memories or traditions. . . . They shook them off in the boat when they came across the seas. They emptied out their memories. If you would speak with disrespect, they were no more than a mob. If you would speak with respect, they were a vigorous people."

Lost in the cities of America, the immigrant Jews succumbed to waves of nostalgia for the old world. "I am overcome with longing," wrote an early immigrant, "not only for my Jewish world, which I have lost, but also for Russia." Both the handful of intellectuals and the unlettered masses were now inclined to re-create the life of the old country in their imaginations, so that with time, distance and suffering, the past they had fled took on an attractive glow, coming to seem a way of rightness and order. Not that they forgot the pogroms, not that they forgot the poverty, but that they remembered with growing fondness the inner decorums of *shtetl* life. Desperation induced homesickness, and homesickness coursed through their days like a ribbon of sadness. In Russia "there is more poetry, more music, more feeling, even if our people do suffer appalling persecution. . . . One enjoys life in Russia better than here. . . . There is too much materialism here, too much hurry and too much prose—and yes, too much machinery." Even in the work of so sophisticated a Yiddish poet as Moshe Leib Halpern, who began to write after the turn of the century, dissatisfaction with the new world becomes so obsessive that he "forgets that his place of birth was very far indeed from being a paradise." "On strange earth I wander as a stranger," wrote Halpern about America, "while strangeness stares at me from every eye."

Yet, for all their homesickness and desperation, the early immigrants chose overwhelmingly to remain in America. We have no reliable statistics concerning re-emigration during the late nineteenth century, but we do know that in the first decade of the twentieth century the Jews had the second lowest rate of return among all immigrant groups. The Yiddish historian Elias Tcherikower estimates that in 1882 re-emigration came to 29 percent; "more than 3,000 Russian-Jewish immigrants were returned to Europe through the United Hebrew Charities. Later the rate of reemigration declined. But in 1886–87 there was a depression in the United States— and in 1888 an increase in the rate of re-emigration among the Russian Jews." For the vast majority, however, there seemed no choice: neither suffering nor nostalgia could induce them to go back to the country of the czars. They gritted their teeth; they called upon those reserves of stoicism which form so essential a part of *Yiddishkeit;* they settled down, often with savage self-denial, to the task of survival.

The Lower East Side of the nineties, said the Yiddish writer Leon Kobrin, was

> a gray, stone world of tall tenements, where even on the loveliest spring day there was not a blade of grass. The streets are enveloped in an undefinable atmosphere, which reflects the unique light, or shadow, of its Jewish inhabitants. The air itself seems to have absorbed the unique Jewish sorrow and pain, an emanation of its thousands of years of exile. The sun, gray and depressed; the men and women clustered around the pushcarts; the gray walls of the tenements—all looks sad.

It was as if the whole immigrant community, stunned by the ordeal of the sweatshop, tense before the hostilities of surrounding ethnic communities, irritated by the condescension of the prosperous German Jews, were reeling from the shock of adaptation.

> The new and alien people who came across the sea to this unimaginable city [wrote the Yiddish novelist David Ignatow] felt themselves caught up in a terrible storm that would soon tear them limb from limb. Buses and trolleys rushed through the streets with devilish force. Waves of people pounded the streets, their faces like foam. The immigrants came to feel a sense of fright before the weight of these massed streets. It was all wild, all inconceivable.

All wild, all inconceivable: the way people walked, the rhythms of the streets, the division of the day into strict units of time, the disposal of waste, the relations among members of the family, the exchange of goods and money. One early immigrant, I. Benequit, remembered that the first time his mother went shopping for food in New York, at a grocery store on Essex Street, "she brought back twenty pounds of black bread and several white *hallas* [white bread used for the Sabbath]," thinking that as in Europe you had to lay in a supply for the whole week. "As a result, fifteen pounds of the bread got moldy and had to be discarded." A larger confusion occurred when the Baron de Hirsch Fund made an informal census of the Lower East Side in 1890. "The Jewish neighborhood was excited . . . paupers began to build castles in the air. It was rumored that the Baron had to know how many immigrants there were in New York because he planned to give $100 to each person and, according to another source, $500."

These were innocent confusions resulting from the pain and absurdity of adapting to a new life. Other confusions were due to the force of social memory as it led the immigrants to misconstrue what was happening about them. All through the nineties they were subjected to a campaign of prose-lytizing by Christian missionaries who set up headquarters and held rallies on the East Side. The likelihood of conversion being what it was, this could hardly be considered a serious problem, yet the immigrants reacted to it with rage, even violence. Missionary soapboxing fanned memories of forced conversions in Russia, and it seemed, on top of all the other burdens of America, a gratuitous provocation. One of the first missionaries to appear, during the late eighties, was the Reverend Jacob Freshman, a *meshumed*, or convert from Judaism, fairly benevolent and totally ineffectual. More flam-boyant was Hermann Warszawiak, son of a Polish rabbi, who used his oratorical gifts to capture the imagination and tap the funds of old-family Protestants. Warszawiak was cordially hated in the Jewish streets, the Yid-dish press frequently sneering that his converts were mere flotsam bought off by petty bribes. Something of a confidence man, Warszawiak built models for a large structure, "Christ's Synagogue and Jewish Missionary Training School," for which he kept collecting money; the building itself he never began. Least bearable of these missionaries was Wilson Dunlop, a gentile paralytic, who spoke in the late nineties from a large wagon on Orchard and Rivington streets. Dunlop's preaching carried a streak of fa-naticism which his listeners were quick to catch out, and while he himself was never hurt, his followers were frequently roughhoused.

Nor was it only the street Jews who reacted so violently to the mission-aries. The banker Jacob Schiff, a refined Jewish gentleman who mingled easily with Christian gentlemen, privately subsidized Adolph Benjamin, a one-man crusader who kept a merciless check on the finances and morals of the missionaries. The Christian agencies supporting these missions failed to realize how deeply they offended the feelings of immigrant Jews—or perhaps, with the arrogance of wealth and place, they did not care. As late as 1899 the *Forward* printed a scare story, based on no visible evidence, that "doctors are revealing the fact that parents bring in children with a cross scratched or burned on their arms. Missionaries lure the children to their building with sweets or pennies and then scratch the cross." Only with time did the East Side learn to brush aside, or ignore, or even find amusement in the clamor of the missionaries.

A New Tempo, a New Way

During these early years, the nerves of the immigrant community were constantly exacerbated, frequently to breaking point. What might seem the most trivial problems signaled a need for major adjustments. A common theme in immigrant memoirs is the way family life suffered disruption because wives, daughters, husbands, and sons went to work at different times of the day, making it impossible for members of a family to eat together. Generalizing about such matters, Hillel Rogoff, later an editor of the *Forward*, remarked:

> Physical exhaustion was aggravated [during the eighties and nineties] by moral and spiritual anguish. . . . The safe old moorings of Jewish family life loosened, the privacy of the home was invaded and its sanctity frequently profaned by boarders, the minds of the children were often poisoned against their parents by the ridicule of the gutter.

The tempo of life in America, its "intensity and hurry," struck Morris Raphael Cohen as one of the major forces shattering traditional Jewish decorum. "At six o'clock in the morning," remembered Cohen, "the alarm would wake us all up." His mother would prepare breakfast, his father say the morning prayers after snatching a bit of food, and then both father and older brother leave so as to be in the shop by seven. Alarm clocks were simple, even useful objects, yet they signified an entirely new world outlook. Once, continued Cohen,

> I had occasion to visit my father's shop, and I was impressed with the tremendous drive which infiltrated and animated the entire establishment—nothing like the leisurely air in Minsk where my Uncle Abraham had worked and where the men would sing occasionally. Sometimes my father and another presser would start a competitive drive to see who could press the largest number of jackets during the day.

For immigrants who remained Orthodox in religious belief and custom, these early years were especially hard. Their expectations of status collapsed

in mockery, their sense of self faltered into shame. A Hebraist named
E. Lisitsky has left a recollection:

> I had only one friend in my loneliness, one whom I met every day in the
> synagogue and to whom I poured out my heart—the Talmud.
>
> I was alone in the synagogue, sitting at the table and swaying over the
> open Talmud, chanting in the old country tone. Loud sounds burst in from
> the street—the sounds of the new life into which I had been cast. . . . The
> cries reproached me mockingly: what are you doing among us, you un-
> worldly idler?

Like many others in the eighties and nineties, Lisitsky wandered from
job to job, at ease with none, fearful he would lose his spiritual balance in the
scramble for bread. In a cigar factory, where "workers with gaunt, jaun-
diced faces and eyes the color of cigar ash bent over the tables," he listened
to their vulgar talk and it made his "heart turn over: that's what I would be
like." At one point he met a Hebrew poet Menakhem Dolitsky, who had
also stumbled into America and to whom he showed a poem he had written
in Hebrew. "Stop it!" cried Dolitsky:

> The devil with poetry! Don't be a fool poetaster! You know what happens
> to Hebrew poets in this country: First stage—Hebrew poet. Second stage—
> Hebrew teacher—or rather herder, with the children as unwilling cattle.
> Third stage—you write trashy novels for servant maids. . . . Do anything,
> be anything, peddle candles and matches—sell windbags and bubbles. . . .
> Be a tailor, a shoemaker, a cobbler—anything but a Hebrew poet in America.

Few of the rabbis and learned men who came to America during the
eighties and nineties were ever able to make a bearable life for themselves—
unless they were among those who adapted only too well to the new world,
becoming businessmen of the synagogue. One Hebrew writer wrote to a
Yiddish newspaper in Poland: "For God's sake, do not come here. . . .
America is good only for the boors and the ignorant. . . . The Jewish
community in America is deceived by its leaders and misleaders, the
makhers and *knakers* [operators and big wheels]." Helpless and repelled,
such men took a revenge of sorts in little-known parodies mocking America,
the land of *ama reka*, or hollow people, the *treyfene medine*, or unkosher
country, where Judaism would find its ultimate burial in the pits of freedom. One of these parodies, mimicking Talmudic style, begins:

> The New World stands on three things: money and money and again money.
> All the people of this country worship the Golden Calf.

Imitating the Psalms, a parodist writes:

> Blessed is the man that walketh not in the counsel of scholars, nor standeth
> in the way of the enlightened, nor sitteth in the seat of the learned. But his
> delight is money, and in the accumulation of wealth does he meditate day
> and night. . . . For money answereth all things, but the poor man's wisdom
> is despised.

Another parodist remarks:

> Akabiah the son of Charlie said: Consider three things and you will be able to exist in America: forget who you are, wear a mask before those who know you, and do anything you can.

Here is one assuming the tone of *pilpul*, or dialectic:

> Rabbi Saphra said: A peddler has four characteristics. He is like a sponge, a funnel, a strainer, and a sieve. Like a sponge he absorbs all kinds of merchandise from the storekeeper, like a funnel he throws everything at his customers, like a strainer he lets the merchandise pass through his hands and retains only the debts, and like a sieve his pockets are never benefited by what he retains.

Some of these parodists indicate they have already had a taste of the new world's blessings:

> The Presser said: "Be submissive to thy boss, for he is thy God. The machine is thy Law, and the table at which thou workest is the altar upon which thou sacrificest thy blood and sweat to the money God."
>
> This is the way to live in America. Bread and salt shall be thy food, water from the hydrant thy drink, the floor in the shop thy bed, and eighteen hours a day shalt thou work.

And what these parodists intimated the Hebrew poet Dolitsky wrote directly:

> Let us deal wisely and become drawers of water,
> Load the peddler's pack and knock on the doors,
> Sit bent on the workbench,
> Bore with the awl or sew breeches—
> But of what avail is here the wisdom of Israel?

Had the ordinary immigrants been able to read such compositions, they would have relished their sarcasm; but few even knew about the work of these isolated Hebraists. The masses had their own emotions, and these came out in their own ways. How they felt about their first years in the new land has been classically expressed by Marcus Ravage, who after painful efforts learned to write in the new tongue:

> The immigrant is almost invariably disappointed in America. . . . The alien who comes here from Europe brings with him a deep-rooted tradition, a system of culture and tastes and habits—a point of view which is as ancient as his national experience and which has been engendered in him by his race and his environment. And it is this thing—this entire Old World soul of his—that comes in conflict with America as soon as he has landed. . . .
>
> With every day that passed I became more and more overwhelmed at the degeneration of my fellow-countrymen in this new home of theirs. . . .
>
> Cut adrift suddenly from their ancient moorings, they were floundering in a sort of moral void. Good manners and good conduct, reverence and religion, had all gone by the board. . . . The ancient racial respect for elders

had completely disappeared. . . . Tottering grandfathers had snipped off their white beards and laid aside their skull-caps and their snuff-boxes and paraded around the streets of a Saturday afternoon with cigarettes in their mouths, when they should have been lamenting the loss of the Holy City.

One reason for this demoralization was noticed by David Blaustein, perhaps the most gifted Jewish community worker on the East Side. The immigrants' struggle for existence, at least during the first few years, "becomes to them more severe than it was in their native lands." In Europe they were oppressed collectively, while in America economic pressure weighed most heavily on the individual. Jews trapped in a *shtetl* or a Polish city could feel they were martyrs for a sacred cause, and thereby take a kind of comfort in their misery, but in America "they could find no political explanation of their suffering" and were therefore inclined to blame themselves. Blaustein, whether he knew it or not, was providing an East Side variation on a theme by De Tocqueville.

The immigrants who came after 1905 would call those of the eighties and nineties *farloyrene menshn*, lost souls. And many *were* lost souls. How many? It is not really possible to say. Thousands must have succumbed quietly to the wretchedness of the East Side, overcome by exhaustion and prepared to end their days quietly and without fuss, over an iron or a sewing machine. What did they wrest out of their lives? A few moments of pleasure now and then at the Yiddish theatre; an occasional bitter strike, usually doomed to defeat yet signifying their will to dignity; whatever visions of the good life might come from hearing the socialist oratory of an Abraham Cahan or a Morris Hillquit; and the persuasion, surely the firmest of all, that, no matter what else, they had escaped the czars and the Cossacks and that here they might yet see their sons and daughters move on to something better. But they themselves were lost, victims of the immigrant world's pinched re-enactment of primitive accumulation—as if nature had given them no voice, or history no claims. They felt they were repeating a familiar Jewish fate; they could hardly have known they were also victims of a recurrent American condition. "In this republican country, amid the fluctuating waves of our social life," Nathaniel Hawthorne had written a few decades earlier, "somebody is always at the drowning-point." A good many of the early Jewish immigrants went under, nameless and unremembered.

Peddling and Sewing

"What does one do here for a livelihood?" asked an immigrant in the eighties who had been a *maskil*, or learned man, in Russia. "You do what everyone does," came the reply, "you become a peddler." With a pack on his back and a "garland of tinware hanging from my shoulders, I began crawling up and down the stairs."

Peddling had behind it an old American tradition: the Yankee wandering through the midwestern states, the German Jew penetrating the South and striking up a relation of sorts with the blacks whom local storekeepers refused to deal with. For German Jews, peddling in the mid-nineteenth century often served as a path to advancement: the country was expanding, agents of trade were needed in outlying places, and the "Jew peddler" was generally regarded as fair and square. Once the east European Jews started coming, some of them also took to peddling in the countryside and occasionally settling down in a small town.*

In the soft glow of retrospect there has been a tendency among American Jews to endow peddling with a certain glamour. Sometimes, perhaps, with reason: as in the stories that have come down to us of Jews wandering into small southern towns and being treated as if they had just stepped out of the Old Testament. But in the cities of the North, during the years of industrial expansion, peddling was backbreaking and soul-destroying work. There was only one reason to become a peddler: you had no skill and wanted to stay out of the shops. A popular Yiddish writer of the late nineteenth century, Oyzer Blaustein, wrote in one of his sketches:

> Those who cannot work, or do not want to work [in the garment industry] take to peddling. You need no more than to know the names of a few items in English and to have been blessed by heaven with a special gift—shamelessness, so that you don't become depressed when you are turned away or are taunted by strangers. By now America is sated with peddlers. . . . Before the big emigration from Russia, peddling wasn't a bad way to earn a living; when a peddler went out to the country with his goods people greeted him with pleasure.

Bernard Weinstein, later a mainstay of the Jewish unions, recalled that "there was no article that wasn't being peddled" by Jews in New York during the eighties and nineties. "Apart from notions, they sold fish, bread,

---

* Morris Witcowsky, who began peddling in the South during the late 1890's, has remembered that "for the first four years I peddled with a pack on my back. This pack when full of merchandise weighed about a hundred and twenty pounds, eighty pounds strapped to the back and a forty-pound 'balancer' in the front. It is not as serious as it sounds. You get used to it. Anyway, it gives you tremendous shoulder and arm and leg muscles. . . .

"Many times a customer on my route, Negro or white, would ask me questions about the Bible. I would come to a farmhouse and see the farmer walk across the field to meet me and the wife come out of the house. As I went toward the farmer, he would say to me, 'We had a big argument at the prayer meeting. . . .' The farmer would tell me the argument was something about Daniel in the lion's den, or maybe it was about Jonah, and he would ask me to settle the argument, because I was a Jew and they all looked at me as an authority.

"Selling on credit to the Negro was called 'having a book on the *shvartses*,' which meant carrying a ledger sheet for a Negro customer. Do not misunderstand me. '*Shvartses*,' which means 'the blacks,' was not a sign of disrespect."

The weary round

fruit, milk, tin and copper hardware. . . . Every peddler had his own tune; the glazers, for example, who were Orthodox Jews, cried out their wares with a depressed sort of tune."

With time, peddling would become a bit more sophisticated, but in these early decades it was simply a matter of going from house to house, up and down the stairs, knocking on doors, and hoping to cajole a housewife. House-to-house peddling was not merely exhausting, it often had its humiliations—Irish boys seemed to take special delight in taunting Jewish peddlers.

> The next day I made up my mind to knock at every door. I went and I knocked, but many refused to open the door, shouting that they did not need anything. Some did buy a couple of cents worth of goods, but with the air of one giving alms, as though to pity a poor immigrant. . . . My face burned with shame but I dragged myself along.

> Abraham the butcher became a peddler on the advice of his *landslayt.* They said it was no disgrace, almost all the millionaires in America had started out that way. But Abraham felt that carrying the basket was degrading. People insulted him, thinking he had no soul. . . . Still, at night when he came home and saw his empty dwelling full of little children, he forgot the insults. He still had hopes of becoming a butcher again. America is young, Jews are coming from all corners of the earth.

It was precisely such hopes that enabled the peddlers to keep going:

> Later on I made six dollars on a Saturday. I advised my uncle to become a
> peddler; he was not very smart but he managed to eke out five dollars a week.
> In seven weeks I saved up sixty-five dollars apart from what I paid my mother
> every week for food. Then I borrowed a few more dollars from my mother
> —and became the "boss" of a shirt factory.

That was the path upward, at least for a moment—many of these
"bosses" would fail and drop back into the ranks of the peddlers and
workers. What drew some immigrants to peddling—a minority, but an especially vigorous one—was the possibility that through intensive self-exploitation they might save up a little money, start some sort of petty business, and
thereby avoid becoming garment workers.

The majority of Jewish immigrants, both in the eighties and nineties
and in the early years of the twentieth century, could not hope to escape the
traumas of proletarianization. For the nineties we have two sources of statistical data, admittedly imprecise. The Baron de Hirsch Fund polled 111,690
of the approximately 200,000 Jews living in New York in 1890. More than
half were children. The number of gainfully employed came to 22,393;
shopworkers in the needle trades to 13,437, or 60 percent, and shopworkers
in other industries to 1,540, or 6.9 percent. Only 2,440 of those polled, or
about 10 percent, listed themselves as peddlers. Our second source is the
U.S. census of 1890, which did not specify "Jews" as an immigrant category
but did list "Russians." Students of Jewish immigration have worked out a
rough estimate according to which it seems plausible that about 80 percent
of these "Russians" were Jews and have thereby concluded from the 1890
census that about half the Jews employed in American industry were clothing workers.

The garment industries formed an ideal setting for superexploitation:
seasonal in setting; capricious in product; requiring labor both disciplined
and, for the most part, semiskilled; encouraging the sudden rise of new
manufacturers and contractors with only a petty capital investment; and
peculiarly open to such social evils as homework, child labor, the contract
system, and various refinements of cutthroat competition. The labor historian John R. Commons wrote a definitive analysis of the industry for the
U.S. Industrial Commission:

> The Jewish contractor was not a mere middleman; he was necessarily a tailor
> and an organizer of labor, for his work was done by a system of division of
> labor calling for various grades and forms of skill. . . .
>   The man best fitted to be a contractor is the man who is well acquainted
> with his neighbors, who is able to speak the language of several classes of
> immigrants . . . and can obtain the cheapest help. . . .
>   The contractor in the clothing trade is largely responsible for the primi-
> tive modes of production; for the foot-power sewing machine; for the shops

in the alleys, in the attics, on top floors, above stables, and in some cases, in the homes of the people. . . . Usually it is not necessary to have more than $50 to start a shop with foot-power machines. . . .

The unlimited hours of work, often seven days in the week, is a feature of the contracting system. The contractor himself works unlimited hours. . . . He deals with people who have no knowledge of regular hours. He keeps them in the dark with regard to prevailing number of hours that other people work.

Take the Second Avenue Elevated, wrote Jacob Riis, "and ride up half a mile through the sweaters' district. Every open window of the big tenements, that stand like a continuous brick wall on both sides of the way, give you a glimpse of one of these shops. . . . Men and women bending over their machines or ironing clothes at the window, half-naked. . . . Morning, noon, or night, it makes no difference." Nor was it unusual, reported a New York state factory inspector in 1893, "when the weather permits, to see the balconies of the fire escapes occupied by two to four busy workmen. The halls and roofs are also utilized for workshop purposes very frequently."

Bernard Weinstein, who came to America in 1882, describes a garment shop in the late nineteenth century:

The boss of the shop lived there with his entire family. The front room and kitchen were used as workrooms. The whole family would sleep in one dark bedroom. The sewing machines for the operators were near the windows of the front room. The basters would sit on stools near the walls, and in the center of the room, amid the dirt and dust, were heaped great piles of materials. On top of the sofas several finishers would be working. . . . Old people . . . using gaslight for illumination, would stand and keep the irons hot and press the finished coats, jackets, pants and other clothes on special boards.

Max Pine, a leading figure in the Jewish unions, recalls how he became a tailor in his youth:

The contractor approached me, looked me up and down, and a satisfied little smile appeared on the heavy lip under his thick, yellow mustache.

"A healthy specimen," he declared, "red cheeks, clearly a good eater. You'll do all right in America!"

So we arranged our "bargain," standing right there. I was to pay him $25 and work unpaid for three weeks. And after I had finished my apprenticeship, I would be on my own.

In this atmosphere, remarked Lillian Wald of the Henry Street Settlement, "tuberculosis seems the disease most to be dreaded. . . . We see so much of it that we call it the tailor's disease." And an unusually reflective factory inspector found himself wondering in 1899 about the relation of family life to work, of women staying home to women going to the shops:

On the one hand, we have the 3-year-old child helping its mother [to fix trimmings on women's dresses] in the home—never out of sight—always where the mother could attend to its wants and allay its fears and sufferings. While, on the other hand, we see the mother compelled to desert her three little ones of very tender years, going out to the shop to work, because the law prohibits her bringing the work into her home. As a result, these unfortunate little ones . . . are left alone in a tenement, shut up in a fireless room with no one to attend to their wants.

An overwhelming number of immigrant Jews nevertheless flocked to the needle trades. Why? Because those who had already become workers in eastern Europe brought with them a little experience as tailors. Because the garment shops were located close to the familiar East Side streets (or equivalent slums in other cities) and an immigrant just off the boat needed no English in order to reach them. Because some garment bosses were willing to let religious Jews keep the Sabbath and work instead on Sundays. Because the industry had been expanded ever since the Civil War, through the use of machinery and the manufacture of ready-made clothing, so that large numbers of new hands were needed. Because it took only a little time to learn how to run a sewing machine or press a garment. And because many employers were themselves Jews, at first mainly German but by the turn of the century increasingly east European, and therefore inclined to hire greenhorns whom they could exploit with familial rapacity.

The conflicts between German and east European Jews have been traced to a variety of cultural causes, but one brute fact should be kept in mind: the relations between German and east European Jews in the garment industry during the eighties and nineties were often those of class enemies. Of the 241 garment factories in New York City in 1885, 234 were owned by Jews, or more than 97 percent, and of these the great majority were unquestionably German Jews. An early trade-union leader put the matter with complete realism: "The early class struggles in the modern clothing industry in New York were *Jewish* class struggles; both masters and men were of the Hebrew race."

Working hours in the sweatshops, especially during busy seasons, were indefinite at both ends of the day. "In the 'inside' shops [manufacturers], as a rule, the hours [during the eighties and nineties] were sixty a week, the work day beginning at seven or eight in the morning and ending at 6 P.M. In the 'outside' shops [contractors], the working hours were 84 a week. But besides 'regular' hours, there was overtime . . . and in addition many of the workers took material home and worked until two or three in the morning." Though most of them had never been in a shop or factory before coming to America, these immigrant Jews fell in readily with the requirements of "labor discipline." They had no choice. But also, they were psychologically prepared for extreme deprivation and self-exploitation, if only they could suppose that it had some foreseeable end, or feel that after seven years of bondage would come Rachel. Self-indulgences like liquor, whoring, and wastrelism had rarely been part of their experience; revolt would not break out until years later; the bewilderments of cultural dislocation contributed to docility; and as for sickness, whether "the tailor's disease" or some other, each boat landing at Castle Garden brought eager replacements. So they bent their backs and submitted, for a while.

One immediate effect of large-scale immigration and the mushrooming of sweatshops in the early eighties was a sharp decline in wages. The average wage of a semiskilled worker in the garment trades fell from $15 a week in 1883 to $7 a week in 1885. The New York State Bureau of Labor Statistics reported in 1885 that "the very best workers" were "getting $10 a week, while the women employed in the industry were earning from $3 to $6 a week." Continued this report: "Some even with the aid of their families and working fourteen hours a day could earn only $12 and $15 a week. Others could make only $4 by working ten hours a day." By the end of the eighties wages rose somewhat, with the income of cloakmakers in 1888 being approximately $12 a week; but then, with the depressions of the early nineties there was a good deal of seasonal unemployment and occasional lowering of wages, though a series of strikes did lead to temporary improvements. The year 1893 was especially bad, with the United Hebrew Charities forced to open soup kitchens on the East Side to feed starving workers. And then, by a cruel irony, there followed a time of more work and better pay for the garment workers because the depression of 1893 had been so severe it forced a considerable number of Americans to start buying ready-made clothes.

That many of the suddenly proletarianized immigrants deeply resented their lot, everything in their experience—their culture, their radicalism, their sufferings—makes clear. A characteristic view of early immigrant life appears in I. Raboy's touching Yiddish novel, *Iz gekumen a yid kayn amerika,* or "A Jew Came to America," especially in a chapter entitled "Dos fargrebt vern," or "Becoming Coarsened":

> Mannis was heartsick because there was no time to look into a holy book. It hurt him to watch himself gradually becoming vulgarized—outside and inside. What does he think about in America? Very early, as soon as he gets up, he thinks it's time to run to the shop. . . . At noon he thinks about taking a rest and about his stomach. After his dry lunch, sitting on a pile of rags, Mannis finds his eyes are starting to close. He would like to doze off. But that's impossible. . . . He has to rush and rush until it's dark. Then he rushes home and gulps his warm supper, and then he is so full that he sits like a dummy and can't move.
>
> All that takes care of the outside, the part you can see with your eyes. But what about the inside, the part you can't see with your eyes? All day he doesn't hear a single refined word. The machines bore holes in his brain with their clatter, and the coarse words of Dave the foreman crush the spirit. . . . Life loses its flavor and the very earth beneath your feet becomes abhorrent.

God, you say, I'm worse than the horse in the stable; he gets beaten, but at least once in a while he gets a pat on the rump, too.

Going to the Land

Was there no way for Jewish immigrants to escape both peddling and the sweatshop? A few hundred zealots, organized in Russia during the early eighties as Am Olam (Eternal People), sought a radical escape from the economic rootlessness which the centuries had imposed on the Jews. Am Olam proposed to establish farm co-operatives in America so as to "normalize" Jewish life, which meant to abandon petty trade and the role of middleman. Some wanted to build socialist agricultural communes, anticipating the Israeli *kibbutz*, while others were concerned mainly with national rehabilitation through a strengthening of the Jewish economic fabric. To the goal of founding colonies "in the spirit of Robert Owen, Fourier, and Tolstoy" the Am Olam movement brought the religious fervor that would mark so many Jewish political movements.

It was a movement characterized equally by spiritual loftiness and historical inexperience. One of its founders could write in his diary before leaving Russia: "In free America, *where many people live closely in peace and amity*, we Jews too shall find a place to lay our heads" [emphasis added]. The Vilna group of Am Olam, still more naïve, hoped to create in the United States a separate "Jewish canton." The group in Minsk showed, by contrast, a certain realism when it proposed merely to seek "an uninhabited place in which all members can gather," so as to prevent the harassed Jews "from being exposed in their new domiciles to the same trials they had previously undergone." They seem to have understood in Minsk that people coming to the new world did not necessarily escape the prejudices of the old.

Arriving in America, Am Olam found the problems of colonization staggering. "Land was free or very inexpensive, but the cultivation of that land required considerable sums of money and unusually great exertion. The available land was usually virgin and had to be cleared and prepared. Farming implements and machinery, livestock and homes were needed. Without aid, the Jewish immigrants, who were unaccustomed to this type of hard work, could not accomplish anything."

But they went ahead. A colony of about 100 settlers was set up in 1881 on Sicily Island, Louisiana, where the men labored hard to clear and plant but were overwhelmed by a flood from the Mississippi that destroyed twenty thousand dollars' worth of equipment. More disastrous was the fate of a colony set up in eastern Arkansas in 1883 by about 150 people. The land upon which they settled was virgin forest, so thick as to make farming impractical. They then tried to sustain themselves by cutting and selling staves, but only too late did they learn that this required such heavy labor that it was beyond their capacity. By July, a few months after settlement, 90 percent of the colonists were sick with malaria and yellow fever, and about twenty died. Money from the staves was slow in arriving, mosquitoes consumed them, the heat wore out spirits and bodies, starvation crept up each day. A kindhearted Jewish businessman in the neighborhood helped the settlers a little, and the Am Olam headquarters in New York sent money for food, medicine, and railroad tickets. By September the colony disbanded.

Still fired with visions of the ideal, some of the young settlers set up another colony, called Cremieux, this time in South Dakota, where they would not have to suffer the southern heat. They spent their capital lavishly on horses and household effects, only to discover that because the land they had bought was arid they would have to spend still more money on digging wells. And by then they did not have enough. Fires, freezing winters, drought, inefficient work methods—all beset the colony. Cremieux failed, only to be followed, three miles away, by Bethlehem Judea, where young and strong unmarried men—it might be easier without the burden of families—struggled for eighteen months to build a co-operative colony. In the end they sadly agreed to divide their land into small private holdings.

The last and most ambitious Am Olam colony, helped by a large gift from Jacob Schiff, was established in 1883 at New Odessa, Oregon. Learning from the mistakes of the past, the colonists put aside some capital with which to get past the inevitable early failures. New Odessa lasted five years, and, by comparison with its predecessors, thrived during some of them. A letter from one of its members, dated August 2, 1883, gives a picture of its life:

> This is our daily schedule: we work from six in the morning till half-past eight in the morning. From then to 8:45 we have breakfast. Work is resumed at ten and continued to four in the afternoon. Between four and five is dinner, followed by a rest period and intellectual activity. Monday, Tuesday, Thursday and Friday are devoted to the study of mathematics, English and to William Frey's lectures on the philosophy of positivism. On Wednesday current matters are discussed and on Saturday, the problems of the "commune."
>
> On Sunday we rise at six and immediately a lively discussion begins on the subject of equal rights for women. In the beginning the women had demanded full equal rights. They had gone to work in the forest, with the men taking their turn in the kitchen and laundry. Soon, however, the women realized that they were not yet fit for that type of work and they returned to their previous tasks. Now they assure us that they have acquired the necessary physical strength and endurance for work in the forest. . . .
>
> After breakfast one member goes to survey the farm, another reads a newspaper or a book, the rest sing, shout and dance. At four dinner is served.

Two men wash the dishes, the choir sings. . . . At seven in the evening begins a session of mutual criticism.

How long this session lasted we do not know, but one reason for the difficulties at New Odessa was the moral-ideological disputes that seem unavoidable in such enterprises. Once the colony failed, some of its members went back to the East Side and set up a co-operative laundry on Henry Street, a sad outcome for people seeking "productive labor" on the land. Even the laundry failed, and its disenchanted members drifted away, a few becoming important figures in the Jewish socialist movement and others losing themselves in the routines of immigrant life.

The Jewish communes suffered from the problems all communes suffer: it is hard to remain true to fraternal principles when the group must also constitute a competitive unit in the market, it is hard to sustain moral idealism when settlers discover unanticipated wants, it is hard to find people who can combine absolute selflessness with grueling labor. But there were special reasons for the failures of Am Olam. All the colonies were poorly financed, all were too far from the centers of Jewish immigrant settlement, all were beset by a conflict between the ascetic impulse that led to their creation and the libertarian principles by means of which they tried to live. Some of the settlers, remarked Abraham Cahan, "confused communism with the concept of eating off the same plate and sleeping in the same bedroom." Most important of all, the leap from a Ukrainian *shtetl* to Oregon or South Dakota—the cultural leap, the economic leap—was simply too great. What sheer will and purity of heart could do they did, but sheer will and purity of heart were not enough. There is a manuscript diary left by Charles K. Davis, an American-born Jew who in 1882 tried to lead a group of settlers, far better acquainted with American conditions than the green youths of Am Olam, to an agricultural colony in Kansas. In one humorous paragraph Davis records the central problem of such colonizing schemes, the problem of cultural distance:

> I forgot to mention yesterday that in order to be in style here I put on my old blue suit a blue flannel shirt a broad brimmed straw hat and have dispensed with both coat and vest and together with the fact that I have not been shaved since last Wednesday I think I compare favorably with the natives excepting that I am afraid I cant get used to carrying my pistol around all the time its too heavy and beside I am afraid they might criticize it as it is only a 38 calibre. While a 44 is regulation out here.

Nothing, at first glance, could seem less similar than the experience of Jewish immigrants packed into city slums and the experience of these few hundred rural colonists. Yet both represented a common difficulty in coping with American realities. The mass of immigrants had to survive the peddler's pack and the sweatshop; to learn, if they could, how to improve their lot in a situation beyond their control; and to consider, if they cared to, whether in adapting to American society they would be paying too high a moral price. Some who sank into resignation had no choice: life was simply too hard for them. Others may have chosen to cut themselves off from the corruptions of success. All had to suffer the pain of trying to adjust to the harshness of late-nineteenth-century America. So too, despite their program and selflessness, did the settlers of Am Olam. They had to learn how ruthless were the conditions of the society into which they had plunged, and they had to learn how severe were the limits of their own will and sacrifice. The ideas they had brought to America would help them, but mostly in realizing material goals they wished to repudiate. Within a few years they had to come back to the slums and the streets, the locale in which the immigrant Jewish experience was to play itself out. And nothing—neither theory nor ideal—could alter that fact.

In the Tenements

Just north of Canal Street and extending from Mott to Elizabeth stood the "Big Flat," an enormous tenement occupying six city lots. Water was supplied to tenants from one tap on each floor, set over a sink outside the north wall. These sinks, serving as the only receptacles for refuse, were loathsome, especially in the winter, when the traps beneath them would freeze. Each apartment had three rooms and drew its light from a single window in the "living room." The two inner rooms were always dark and without ventilation, since the space allotted each resident averaged out to 428 cubic feet per head, far below the legal limit of 600. The annual death rate per 1000 for the years 1883, 1884, 1885, and the first nine months of 1886 came to 42.40, as compared with 25.72 for the city as a whole; nearly 62 percent of the deaths in the "Big Flat" were of children under five years of age, while in the city as a whole the percentage was a bit more than 42.

The Jews (also some Italians) living in the "Big Flat," reported an investigator of the New York Association for Improving the Conditions of the Poor, "are locked in the rooms like sardines in a box. . . . On the first floor are rooms for fourteen families, and they are mostly occupied by low women and street walkers. . . . While I was there I saw a family getting put out on the sidewalk. . . . The halls are about ten feet wide, and the smell is something awful."

Meticulous in accumulating detail, this investigator continued: "The rents of rooms are as follows: first floor, $9.50 per month for three rooms; second floor, $9.25; third and fourth floors, $9; fifth and sixth, $8.50 and $8.75."

The investigator visited the top floor, inhabited entirely by "Polish Jews":

> In No. 76 a peddler lives, with his wife and four small children. The rooms, like the rest of this floor, are very dirty. In a corner next to these rooms a pile of garbage about two feet high lies, right at the head of the stairs as you go up. The children on this floor are very poorly clad . . . nothing but a loose gown, and no underclothing at all.
>
> Rooms 77, 78, and 79 are crowded with men and women sewing on machines. The men generally work the machines, and the women sew the buttons on and make button-holes. They work for large clothing firms.
>
> Rooms 86, 87, and 88 are full of dirty bedding. The women were sitting out in the hallway sewing on children's knee-pants for some store, and there were no men around.
>
> In room 91 I saw five small children and the mother, but no men. The rooms were full of bedding, but I could see no bedsteads. I heard that it is a lodging-place for Jewish peddlers.

Is there any reason to suppose that the "Big Flat" was spectacularly worse than the surrounding, smaller tenements into which the immigrants were packed? Not really. Some tenements had slightly better physical appointments, and on the East Side as a whole health conditions were somewhat better during the eighties and nineties than in non-Jewish districts, perhaps because of the discipline that the Jewish family was still able to exact. From every available source—contemporary journalism, memoirs, government reports, sociological studies—the evidence seems conclusive: living conditions in the Jewish quarter during the last decades of the nineteenth century were quite as ghastly as those of early-nineteenth-century London.

An immigrant remembers a two-room apartment on Allen Street containing parents, six children, and six boarders. On Saturdays, since the father was a cantor, the apartment was turned into a synagogue. Two daughters took in dresses to sew at home. One boarder, a shoemaker, worked in the apartment. "The cantor rehearses, a train passes, the shoemaker bangs, ten brats run around like goats, the wife putters in her 'kosher restaurant.' At night we all try to get some sleep in the stifling roach-infested two rooms."

Poverty has its shadings, wretchedness its refinements:

> Not everyone was equally poor. When an immigrant family could occupy a two- or three-room apartment without several boarders, they were considered lucky. Boarders were a natural institution, particularly in the early years when most immigrants came without their families. But even the privilege of being a boarder was not enjoyed by every greenhorn. There were various categories of boarders. A star boarder slept on a folding bed. But I knew a printer who every night unscrewed a door, put it on two chairs; he couldn't pay as much as the one who had the bed.

Even an unscrewed door made into a bed could seem attractive to those who had no roof. During the nineties, especially in the summers, there were homeless immigrants who found shelter at night in the "expresses" or coaches that were left on the streets after their horses were taken to the stables.

In *Ner Hamaaravi*, a New York Hebrew periodical started in 1895, there is a story called "Breach of Promise" in which a Lithuanian Jew is shown marrying a girl for her money. "At one o'clock in the afternoon the ceremony is performed in the 'American Star Hall,' in the evening two *roomkes* [little rooms] are rented, on the following day furniture is purchased, and in the evening the couple already has three boarders and three *borderkes* [female boarders]. On the third day the husband goes back to work and the wife runs away with one of the boarders to Paterson."

Lawrence Veiller, a splendid human being who devoted himself to tenement reform, organized in 1900 an exhibit in the Sherry Building at 404 Fifth Avenue to prove that in New York "the working man is housed worse than in any other city in the civilized world, notwithstanding the fact that he pays more money for such accommodations than is paid elsewhere." At this exhibit Veiller set up a cardboard model of an entire tenement block, bounded by Chrystie, Forsyth, Canal, and Bayard streets, in the heart of the East Side. With thirty-nine tenements, the block contained 2,781 people, who among them had only 264 water closets and lacked access to even one stationary bathtub. Only forty apartments had hot running water; and on this block, over the past five years, thirty-two cases of tuberculosis had been reported. Veiller, an amateur sociologist before the age of sociology, insisted that even if the block he had chosen was somewhat worse than others, it revealed the truth about the whole of the East Side.

Throughout the eighties and nineties the New York *Times* kept sending reporters to the Jewish quarter, who sniffed about, recoiled from the clamor and stench, yet had to acknowledge the plight of its "half-starved" inhabitants. An explorer in this world "will find no richly-fed men, extravagantly attired, gleaming with diamonds, fat as Jeshurun, rubbing their hands and computing their tremendous and illicit gains with an oily satisfaction." On the contrary, he will see "attenuated creatures, clad in old, faded, greasy, often tattered clothing . . . men and youths whose cheeks are pinched and pale and hollow, whose lungs yield to the first advance of the Autumn cold and fill the air with incessant coughing; whose sad, lustrous eyes look at him pitifully, like the eyes of hunted and captured animals that press up to the bars of their cages." And then, as if to reassure his readers, the *Times* reporter added: "None of them has any jewelry."

Whatever the indignation of reformers and reporters, the problem during the eighties and nineties was less how to escape from the tenements than how to remain in them. Key terms of anxiety have survived the experience of the immigrants, echoing still in the memories of grandsons and granddaughters, and one of the most terrible among these is "dispossess." Only sickness could raise more fright than the prospect of being thrown out on the street. In the depression year ending September 1892, the district of Judge Alfred Steckler, covering the East Side, issued a total of 5,450 dispossess notices. A man of some feeling, Judge Steckler said: "Hundreds of cases full of the most pathetic disclosures are constantly cropping up in my court. . . . I rarely set the machinery of the law in motion without first making an effort to have the landlord give a little further period of grace. . . . Perhaps the granting of a week's grace will give them a chance to get on their feet, and resume their struggle against a poverty that is as hopeless as it is cruel."

The Implacability of Gentleness

No act of individual kindness could change immigrant life as it needed to be changed, yet such acts, when they occurred, were received with a warmth, almost an excess of gratitude. Lillian Wald (1867–1940), the nurse who founded the Henry Street Settlement, grew within her lifetime into a figure of legend, known and adored on every street.

She came to the East Side in 1893, a German-Jewish young woman of twenty-six who had been raised in a comfortable bourgeois family, a "spoiled child" as she later kept insisting, still largely innocent of the sufferings of life. Her father had been an optical dealer in Rochester, New York, and Lillian had gone to "Miss Cruttenden's English-French Boarding and Day School for Young Ladies." She had wanted to enter Vassar at sixteen, but someone at the college ruled that she was too young. If Vassar didn't want her, she would go elsewhere—to another life.

Several years later, Lillian Wald entered the New York Hospital's School of Nursing, learning there what she needed to learn, not least an unflinching and unsentimental capacity for living near pain. In 1893, after a frustrating interval at an orphan asylum where the children were ill-treated, she began running a class in home nursing for East Side women. One day a little girl came up to Miss Wald, asking that she visit someone sick at home. Lillian Wald followed the child to a dismal two-room apartment that housed a family of seven plus a few boarders. "Within half an hour" she had made the central decision of her life: she would move to the East Side, there to give her life as nurse, settlement-house leader, and companion to the afflicted.

There are two kinds of fastidious people, those who recoil from messes and those who stay to clean them up. Lillian Wald stayed, not out of exalted sentiments or angelic temperament, but because there was work to be done and no one else seemed likely to do it. She stayed at a time when only a handful of social workers paid any attention to the place, and long before it took on associations of glamour or nostalgia.

Together with another nurse, Mary Brewster, Lillian Wald lived and worked in a fifth-floor apartment at 27 Jefferson Street, with the single indulgence of a private bathtub. Lavinia Duck, soon to be a fellow nurse at the Henry Street Settlement, visited these tiny rooms and found the "chief solicitude" of Miss Wald and Miss Brewster to be a wish "to make their own impression as friendly souls before whom all the confidence and problems of living might be safely opened. Their nursing was their open sesame."

The two young women made themselves available to anyone asking for help; they charged a trifle to those who could afford it and gave services freely to those who could not. "I came with very little program of what could or should be done," said Lillian Wald; she kept her eyes open, saw the magnitude of need, rushed to whoever called for help, and persuaded others to join her. "I went into every room in the front and rear tenements, set the dwellers to sweeping, cleaning, and burning the refuse. In some rooms swill thrown on the floor, vessels standing unemptied after the night's use. I saw the housekeeper, who promised cooperation in keeping the place cleaner, and I impressed on her that I would repeat the rounds next day and frequently thereafter."

Her tasks were endless. Children with summer bowel complaints that sent infant mortality rates soaring; children with measles, unquarantined; children "scarred with vermin bites"; a case of "puerperal septicaemia, lying on a vermin-infested bed without sheets or pillow-cases"; a pregnant mother with a crippled child and two others living on chunks of dry bread sent in by neighbors; people "ill from organic trouble and also from poor food."

In October 1893 she was writing, "We have found several cases of typhoid fever, and in every case succeeded in overcoming hospital prejudice, accompanying patients to the hospital wards and doing what we could to satisfy their first uneasiness." Sometimes Miss Wald or Miss Brewster would stay deep into the night with patients for whom the very idea of a hospital struck terror. When patients were too sick to be moved, they would fetch surgeons to the apartment, help with operations, and then provide aftercare. It was all terrible enough during these depression years, but "we are not discouraged, and the more intimately we come to know these poor Russian Jews the more frequently we are rewarded with unexpected gleams of attractiveness."

Substantial help came from Jacob Schiff, the German-Jewish philanthropist. Between him and Lillian Wald arose a curious relationship: he helped defray costs on condition that his part be kept secret and she send him monthly letters detailing her activities. Could so intelligent a man as Schiff have thought it necessary to keep check on so selfless a woman as Lillian Wald? Perhaps; but it seems happier to suppose that he asked for these reports out of an admiring recognition that her simple sentences bore a moral substance to be treasured.

Visit and care of typhoid patient, 182 Ludlow Street. Visit to 7 Hester Street where in rooms of Nathan S. found two children with measles. After much argument succeeded in bathing these two patients and the sick baby. The first time in their experience. They insisted no water and soap could be applied to anyone with measles for seven days.

Gave tickets for Hebrew Sanitarium excursion to Mrs. Davis and three children, Mrs. Schneider and five children for Tuesday's excursion but five of the seven children are nearly naked, I am convinced, have no apparel in their possession. So we will make their decent appearance possible for the picnic.

Many of these people have kept from begging and it is not uncommon to meet families, to whom not a dollar has come in in seven months—the pawn shop tickets telling the progress of their fall, beginning some months back with the pawning of a gold watch, ending with the woman's waist.

The multitude of unemployed grows and many who had been able to live for the first few months [of 1893] are now at the end of their resources. However we are glad in one respect, that having no money to engage the midwife they allow us to furnish doctors . . . who do intelligent good work.

In a rear tenement, top floor, on Allen Street, a doctor found a woman, a Mrs. Weichert, crazy and ill with pneumonia and typhoid; cared for by her 14 year old daughter. She had been crazy for some time and the husband and child had kept it secret, fearing she would be forcibly taken to an asylum were it known. Though she died in a few days, I shall always be glad that one doctor told us in time so that she was made human and decent, bedding given and the child assisted to making her dwelling fit for habitation before her end.

Lily Klein very ill with pneumonia for whom we procured medical attention and nursed. The child died but the night before Miss Brewster had remained with the child all night. She was ineligible for hospital as she had whooping cough. Father deserted and mother worn out, was not safe to leave a child so ill with.

Annie P., 44 Allen Street, front tenement, second floor. Husband Louis P. came here three years ago and one year ago sent for wife and three children. From that time unfortunately, his trade, that of shoemaker, became less remunerative. She helped by washing and like labor, but two months ago he deserted her, though she stoutly maintains he returned to Odessa to get his old work back. The youngest, Meyer P., age five years, fell from the table and injured his hip. He lay for 7 months in the Orthopedic Hospital, 42nd Street; he was discharged as incurable and supplied with a brace. . . . The mother is absolutely tied by her pregnant condition; the cripple is in pain and cries to be carried. They had no rooms of their own but paid $3 a month to Hannah A., a decent tailoress, who allowed the family to sleep on her floor. . . . Sunday I saw them. Monday I filed application with Montefiore Home for Meyer's admission. . . . Tuesday I went to Hebrew Sheltering Guardian Society, saw Superintendent, and obtained promise of place for the two well children by Thursday. . . . Thursday afternoon we washed and dressed the two children, and I left them in the afternoon at the Asylum, leaving my address for the Superintendent so that he might know their friend in case of need. They have absolutely no one in America but their mother.

Once and for all, she gave her heart to those "poor Russian Jews" (even, with time, learning some Yiddish words and phrases). "We are full of the troubles of our neighbors," reads an early letter, and it would remain that way to the end. When the papers printed denunciations of immigrants who had joined food riots, Lillian Wald fought against these slurs upon her neighbors. When these neighbors started to form trade unions, she sided with them openly.

Some of the immigrants kept themselves apart from Miss Wald's nurses —there were rumors they were secret agents proselytizing for Christianity—but others started climbing the five flights to their apartment, asking for help, sometimes just wanting to talk. Mary Brewster had to quit: she was overworked, and her health failed. A growing number of nurses came to volunteer, some taking the fifteen-dollar-a-week salary and some quietly returning it. Miss Wald began looking for a larger place, to be used entirely by what had come to be called the Nurse's Settlement. She found a house at 265 Henry Street and moved in. For a time she kept the name Nurse's Settlement—it was really the best name—but had to give way to the pleas of a boy's athletic club attached to 265 Henry, which could no longer bear the teasing of opponents on the baseball field: "Hey, noices! Noices!" So they called the place the Henry Street Settlement.

The Settlement kept growing: by 1898, eleven full-time staff, nine of them nurses; by 1900, fifteen nurses; by 1906, twenty-seven nurses. As her work succeeded, Miss Wald's power grew, and she used it shrewdly and to keen effect. She persuaded the city to start a program of public nursing—the very phrase was hers. She persuaded the Board of Education to put nurses into the schools. She worked hard on committees opposing child labor; joined the movement for more playgrounds; badgered the mighty and wheedled the rich for money, telling them not about her theories (it is doubtful she had any) but about "little Louie, the deplorable condition of whose scalp is denying him the blessings of education"; joined the suffragettes, though not militantly; became an active pacifist in the First World War, brushing past unpopularity as if it were one of those unfortunate neighbors needing help. Ready as she was to charm millionaires for help, she never allowed that to stand in the way of her persuasions. In the 1910 cloakmakers' strike, she aligned herself firmly with the strikers—where else could she be? They were her neighbors. Within the Jewish world, she was especially skillful at creating links between the Germans and east Europeans, gaining the confidence of the former in behalf of aid to the latter.

A reporter for the New York *Press* wrote of her: "Picture to yourself a woman still in the freshness of youth: tall and well-proportioned. . . . The mouth is tender, sensitive, sympathetic. The chin says, 'I will. . . .' The would-be violator of sanitary regulations calls her 'She-Who-Must-Be-Obeyed.' . . . The poor, invalid Yiddish mother claims her as an intimate friend. . . ." Jacob Riis adds to the picture: "The poor trust her absolutely, trust her head, her judgment, and her friendship. She arbitrates in a strike, and the men listen. . . . When pushcart peddlers are blackmailed by the police, she will tell the mayor the truth, for she knows."

By 1916 the Settlement owned half a million dollars in property and had extended its activities far beyond the original task of nursing. Still, that task remained a central one, the annual budget for the Visiting Nurses Service coming to $150,000 and the more than one hundred nurses making 227,000 visits a year. Large as it now was, the Settlement kept its personal tone, run along the principles of anarchic matriarchy.

Miss Wald was the ideal Fabian. Shrewd, practical, dry-eyed, she had a genius for the concrete, seeing life as it was and wanting to make it better. There was no shrinking, no condescension, no idylizing, no sentimentalism, no preening, little theorizing, nothing but work, hard and endless and free from contaminations of self. Writing an article about the Settlement toward the end of her life, she began with a simple question: "Have you ever seen a hungry child cry?" It was a question that haunted all her years, driving her incessantly, making her into a "do-gooder"—a phrase that can never be used lightly by anyone who comes to know what Lillian Wald did for those "poor Russian Jews" stranded in America.

By some later perspectives, Lillian Wald missed a good deal in life. She never married, she seems to have had no intense personal relationships, she yielded her emotions to all about her, she showed small inclination toward self-scrutiny or introspectiveness. If these were the costs of her life, the rewards were at least as high. In the experience of thousands, she made a difference; on the consciousness of her contemporaries, she left a mark. Like the other superb women of her generation who plunged into the work they saw in front of them—women like Jane Addams, Rose Schneiderman, Lavinia Duck, Florence Kelley—she made a mockery of all the idle chatter about a "woman's place." "The subtle and persistent saintliness of these social workers was in the end more deadly than all the bluster of business. Theirs was the implacability of gentleness."

A Chaos in Hebrew

In eastern Europe the ordeal of poverty had been eased by a spiritual discipline centered on the synagogue and enclosing every department of life; in America religious authority could never be monolithic. No matter how many immigrants remained Orthodox in belief, what was now decisive was that the Jewish community as such could no longer be structured primarily along religious lines. Religion might still mean everything to individual Jews, but the Lower East Side was a secular community. It could not be otherwise.

With the mass migration there had naturally occurred an enormous growth in the number of synagogues. By 1890 there were 146 in New York City, some of which, like Ohab Zedek, the Hungarian congregation on Norfolk Street, were imposing structures; there were also reported in the same year 251 *melamdim*, or private Hebrew teachers, on the East Side. Uncounted congregations were mere storefront groups set up by rabbis desperate for livelihood and forced to improvise. During the eighties and nineties there were frequent complaints of ignorance, sacrilege, bad manners, and poor teaching; the intellectual, and sometimes the moral, level of a good many of these religious institutions was low. In 1886 Rabbi Moses Weinberger, just arrived from Hungary, caustically noted that the number of self-declared Hebrew teachers was so great, some had announced themselves ready "to teach any Jewish child, whoever he be, rich or poor, wise or foolish, for 10¢ a week." Some heads of families, continued the rabbi, failed to understand the bargain they were being offered, and hoped to drive fees down to the point where "schoolmasters will accept a penny an hour." Hebrew-school teaching was a scorned profession "which cannot support its practitioners."

In the early nineties Hirsh Masliansky, an educator and popular Yiddish preacher, announced Jewish education in New York to be utterly chaotic. Indigent *melamdim*, few of them qualified or able to cope with American children, would trudge from floor to floor, peddling Torah "like other merchandise." Invited to inspect a Talmud Torah on East Broadway, Masliansky found that

> The teachers were . . . well grounded in the Bible and Hebrew grammar, some also in Talmud; but there was no system or program of teaching. The principal was an elderly man schooled in German and Mendelssohn's translation of the Bible, and made sure that the interpretations were at least 50 percent in German.
>
> I felt so sorry for the little American *yidelekh* whose childish shoulders had to be burdened with three languages. Until three in the afternoon they studied English in the public schools; from four until eight they studied two foreign languages at once: Hebrew and half-German, jumbled together with every breath they took. To teach German to American Jewish children was a *mishegas* [madness].
>
> I examined them and found that they could read elementary Hebrew, following all the rules of vocalization. This was the pedantic trivia which occupied the youngsters for hours every day. When I asked them to explain the meaning of a section of the Torah, they replied mechanically in halting, incorrect semi-German, not even knowing what they were talking about.

Not all the schools were as bad as Masliansky said, the craze for German soon died out, and a good part of what was wrong had merely been
carried over from the old country. During these very years substantial
Jewish schools, including the Hebrew Free School Association and a variety
of yeshivas, were being set up. Nevertheless, the impression of incompetence and a partial breakdown of intellectual morale has a firm foundation in
reality. There could be no esaping the traumas of early settlement.

Dislocation and Pathology

That symptoms of social dislocation and even pathology should have
appeared under the extreme circumstances in which the early Jewish immigrants lived, seems unavoidable. There was crime, there was wife desertion,
and there were juvenile delinquency, gangsterism, and prostitution during
the eighties and nineties, as well as during the early decades of the twentieth
century—probably more than the records show or memoirists tell. How
could there not be?

Precise information on these matters is hard to come by, and the reasons
are obvious. Communities struggling for survival seldom rush to announce
their failures. The craze for sociological investigation that would overtake
America in the twentieth century was not yet very strong. And over the
centuries the Jews had developed a cultural style encouraging prudishness
and self-censorship: there were things everyone knew, had no choice but to
know, yet only rarely was it deemed proper to speak or write about them.
Life was hard enough without indulging in luxuries of revelation.

Any realistic inhabitant of the East Side could nevertheless have told
one, say, in 1890 or 1895 where prostitution flourished—mainly along Allen
Street, with its dark and smelly houses and its rattling elevated train, but also
on Houston, Rivington, Stanton, and Delancey streets. The very possibility
that some of their own might be mixed up with prostitution horrified the
immigrant Jews: it ran wholly against the values and inhibitions they had
brought across the ocean. Yet it was also true that prostitution had already
shown itself in the Jewish neighborhoods of east European cities; the subject
would soon appear in Yiddish literature, notably in Sholem Asch's popular
play *God of Vengeance*, in which the central character is a procurer trying
to keep his daughter from the path of shame; and for decades whispers
would slip through the Yiddish-speaking world about Jewish white slavers
who sent kidnaped Jewish girls from eastern Europe to brothels in Latin
America.

Describing New York immigrant life in 1903–1904 for a Russian audience, Isaac Max Rubinow reported that "the vices affected mostly the Amer-

icanized Jews, that is, those who have adopted the outward luster of so-called Americanization." By its nature, Rubinow's notion could not be verified, though it fits in with the general assumption that the spread of social pathology will be hastened by a breakdown of social structure. Dancing academies, some of them mere way stations to brothels and recruiting grounds for "cadets," as pimps were then called, began to be advertised in the Yiddish press during the late eighties. In 1899 Frederick Shackleton, pastor of a Forsyth Street church, complained that solicitation was openly practiced from the stoops of tenements near his congregation. In 1894 the Lexow Committee and in 1899 the Mazet Committee, both appointed by the New York State Legislature, dug up quantities of material concerning crime, police corruption, and prostitution on the East Side. Lists of pimps and madams compiled by these committees include a fair number of Jewish names—Joseph Klein, Charles Jacobwitz, Minnie Wiener, Louis Sugarman, Bertha Greenberg, all operated in the Jewish quarter. The same is true for the prostitutes—Lena Cohen, Ida Katz, Sadie Felman, others. A president of an Allen Street synagogue, Isaac Pearlstein, testified before the Mazet Committee that "the women of these houses stood on the street and annoyed the congregation. They . . . call to the people that are passing by. . . . It is a very bad thing for the men and children going to the church to have to pass through all the things in all the houses." An investigator for the committee, Edward Riordan, reported that "I have observed boys and young men peddling cards for disorderly houses and girls on Allen Street. . . . [Their job is] getting customers for them and warning them of the approach of enemies, and looking after the girls." Especially striking is the accumulated material showing a close relationship between vice on the East Side and the Tammany political machine, often through the organizing gifts of a Jewish "godfather" named Max Hochstim.

Newspapers and memoirs offer substantiating evidence. The New York *World*, in 1896, reported the suicide of Lena Meyers, twenty-eight, found in her room at 193 First Avenue. The young woman had sent money regularly to her parents in Cracow from her earnings as a prostitute, and two weeks before her death had received a letter in Hebrew from her mother thanking her for money received and asking, "Lena, why don't you get married? Do you want to be an old maid?" Death was thought to be the result of drinking carbolic acid. (The Mazet Committee listed other young women, mostly prostitutes, who took their lives: a sprinkling of Jewish names.) Recalling his childhood on the East Side, Michael Gold would write: "On sunshiny days the whores sat on chairs along the sidewalks. They sprawled indolently, their legs taking up half the pavement. People stumbled over a gauntlet of whores' meaty legs. The girls gossiped and chirped like a jungle of parrots. Some knitted shawls and stockings. . . . Others chewed Russian sunflower seeds."

By the turn of the century, the Yiddish press began to pay attention.

The *Forward* wrote in 1898: "It is better to stay away from Allen, Chrystie, and Forsyth streets, if you go walking with your wife, daughter, or fiancée. There is an official flesh trade in the Jewish quarter. In the windows you can see human flesh instead of shoes. Chrystie is full of saloons and prostitutes who are not afraid any more, because 'we are Tammany' "—a sardonic reference to the recent electoral victory of the Tammany machine, to which Jews had contributed and which brought a relaxation of police regulations on the East Side, as throughout the city.

Throughout these years the immigrant community was extremely sensitive, as all such communities must be, to charges that it served as a breeding ground for crime. Its standard defense was offered by Abraham Cahan in an article he wrote in 1898 for the *Atlantic Monthly:* "Jews constitute six percent of the total population of New York state [but] furnish only three percent of the prisoners of that state. . . . The ratio of foreign-born Jews to the total immigrant population is fifteen percent, yet less than five percent of the foreign-born prisoners are of the Hebrew race." True enough; yet if seen not as a problem in ethnic defense but as a problem to be confronted within the East Side itself, the subject of crime could not be so easily disposed of. Some of the "crime" was innocent. Peddlers could not avoid breaking local regulations if they were to survive; the kosher slaughter of chickens in tenements, while violating the sanitary code, was unavoidable. Immigrants still firmly Orthodox went to their rabbis for divorce and then assumed they could legally remarry; in 1890 a grand jury declared that "granting these so-called divorces should be absolutely prohibited by law." After a while, the rabbis found it wise to accept this brake on their authority.

The Jewish population, wrote William McAdoo, a New York police commissioner, "is not apt, unless under great pressure, to resort to force or to commit crimes of violence. . . . Among themselves disputes are mostly confined to wordy arguments. They argue with great vigor and earnestness, but the argument ends as it begins." McAdoo was acute enough to note that Jews fresh from Europe had "a great suspicion and fear of the police. The words 'police,' 'law,' 'prison,' conjure up dire possibilities in their minds, and for self-protection they naturally become evasive and secretive."

The most frequent crimes in the Jewish neighborhood were crimes of fraud, not violence. Studying 1898 police and municipal court records, the University Settlement Society concluded that Jews "are prominent in their commission of forgery, violation of corporation ordinances, as disorderly persons (failure to support wife or family), both grades of larceny, and of the lighter grade of assault," but were "notably little addicted to intoxication" and furnished "a very small proportion of vagrants." How poor the whole immigrant world still was is suggested by the fact that most summonses issued in these courts were for amounts below fifteen dollars! "A low criminal record, somewhat litigious, very poor, yet furnishing an extremely low contingent to the vagrant classes—these are the characteristics of the East Side Jew." Seventy years later a scholarly survey based on newspaper reports for the years 1900–1904 came to the same conclusion.

To the Jewish immigrants, the idea of physical violence among themselves seemed a little unreal, perhaps not to be taken very seriously. When the *Forward* began publishing, in 1897, it gave special attention to a murder on the Lower East Side precisely because it was so unusual an event: "Shapiro murders Liberman. All because his fiancée left him. Claims self-defense. Terrible uproar in Jewish quarter." Love, the article began, "a deeply rooted, fiery love, ended last night with an awful murder in the Jewish quarter." Closer by far to the common Jewish feeling about violence, especially violence committed by one Jew against another, was a *Forward* story a few weeks earlier: "Wants to be a hero. Hasn't got much luck. Sam wants to shoot his uncle and stepdaughter but only manages to wound his knee and his own finger."

Far more frequent during these years were *Forward* accounts of gross deceptions and pitiable swindles. "Adler's family affairs. A seventy-five-year-old man marries a twenty-five-year-old girl, steals her sixty-seven dollars, and disappears. Also has another wife." Or: "Who is the murderer? An awful tragedy with a young child. Child falls in boiling water. Mother calls *babke* [a woman 'healer'] instead of doctor; she cuts child's skin with pair of scissors. After this, child dies. *Babke* has not yet been found." Or: "Wanted to force his bride to shame. Man brought over girl from Russia, promising to marry her. When she arrived, he tried to make money through her." Or, in a Hardyesque vein: "Ten months ago Jacob Shrek sold his thirty-year-old wife for a watch and chain, worth $150, to David Saks. Saks, who lived with Mrs. Shrek, wanted his watch back and went to the police to report that Shrek had robbed him. Now all three are in prison. The wife had previously been jailed in Philadelphia on a bigamy charge."

As the possibilities of American enterprise became clearer, Jews found their way to more sophisticated crime, and some showed a talent for gambling. Arnold Rothstein, to be celebrated in the 1920's as "the J. P. Morgan of the underworld" and immortalized in *The Great Gatsby* as Meyer Wolfsheim, the man who fixed the 1919 World Series, began his career by watching games of "stuss," a New York version of faro. At sixteen Rothstein was making himself useful at the headquarters of Big Tim Sullivan, a Tammany boss of the nineties, by running errands and translating the requests of Yiddish-speaking constituents. It was at Big Tim's that Rothstein met Monk Eastman, a gangster, probably Jewish, who enjoyed some fame; later, when Rothstein went into the moneylending business, Eastman's mob provided collectors. "You're smart Jew boys," Sullivan told Rothstein and his friend Herman Rosenthal, "and you'll make out as gamblers. That business takes brains." By 1902 Rothstein was on his own, taking bets on races and fights, running crap games for large stakes; by 1906 he had a twelve-million-dollar bankroll. When he died in 1928, at the age of forty-six, Rothstein received an Orthodox Jewish funeral, in accordance with the American requirement that, no matter how brutal their lives, gangsters retain a tie of sentiment with the faith of their fathers.

Others showed a diversity of talents. Isaac Zuker headed a Jewish arson ring and ended his career with a thirty-six-year sentence. Harry Joblinski ran a school for young pickpockets and at one time was said to have employed fifteen apprentices. Somewhat earlier and into the mid-eighties, "Mother" Marm Mandelbaum acquired fame as a leading New York fence; she was estimated to have disposed of over five million dollars' worth of stolen property from her Clinton Street headquarters. "Mother" Mandelbaum employed the legal talent of Howe and Hummell for an annual five-thousand-dollar retainer and set herself up as an ambitious hostess in the criminal world.

> She is said to have been a Fagin and to have maintained a school in Grand Street, not far from Police Headquarters. . . . She also offered advanced courses in burglary and safe-blowing, and to a few of the most intimate of her associates gave postgraduate work in blackmailing and confidence schemes. The fame of this institution became widespread, but Marm Mandelbaum became alarmed and dismissed her teaching staff when the young son of a prominent police official applied for instruction.

Monk Eastman, born Edward Osterman in Williamsburg, had among his colleagues and surbordinates such accomplished hoodlums as Spanish Johnny, Sophie Lyons, Nathan Kaplan "the Kid Dropper," and Little Kishky, all of Jewish birth and some to depart this earth with Orthodox rites. Eastman enjoyed close connections with Tammany Hall, especially when floaters were needed at election time; his main contacts were "Silver Dollar" Smith, a barkeep and alderman born either Charles Solomon or Solomon Finkelstein, and Max Hochstim, an assistant to Smith, who brought together politics and prostitution. Smith's saloon, across the street from the Essex Market court, was solidly paved with silver dollars, an appropriate setting for Jews who came to gain favors and arrange for the "fixing" of summonses and tickets.* The close relationship between politics and crime

---

* When the daughter of Silver Dollar Smith, eighteen-year-old Matilda, married Izzy Dreyfuss, a reporter at the Essex Market Police Court and a link between the judicial powers there and the alderman across the street, the wedding was held at the Vienna Hall, Fifty-eighth Street and Lexington Avenue, in an atmosphere of social and political splendor. The *Herald* reported that "when Mr. Dreyfuss went to pop the question to the Alderman, he was so sure of violent treatment that he had a warrant for his arrest on charge of assault in his pocket. It turned out, however, that it was not necessary to serve it. The young man to his surprise was accepted, but on the express condition that the wedding should not take place without the family getting a full week's notice. Elopements were barred.

"Wedding presents came yesterday by the barrow load. All the principal officials of the city remembered the happy pair. Inspector McLaughlin sent a silver sugar bowl. Lawyer A. H. Hummell sent a dozen gold ice cream spoons.

"A large number of others who have had occasion to admire the courteous way in which the bridegroom administers the affairs of the police court showed practical recognition. Police Captain Dougherty gave a plush rocking chair; Chief

later served as the subject of a crude but vivid novel, Samuel Ornitz's *Haunch, Paunch and Jowl*, in which the narrator, a cheap lawyer, remembers: "I keep the political irons hot, fix the cops, do all the backing and filling in connection with the criminal cases. I split fees with court clerks . . . I take care of the boys all the way down the line from the judge on the bench to the bootblack in the criminal courts' hallway."

Crime befouled the life of the East Side during the eighties and nineties; later, as immigrants learned the devices of native enterprise, the neighborhood would export some notable graduates to New York's underworld. East Side leaders and institutions were steadily worried, more than they allowed themselves to say in public or admit to the gentiles, about the spread of prostitution among Jewish girls and thievery among Jewish boys. But in the life of the immigrant community as a whole, crime was a marginal phenomenon, a pathology discoloring the process of collective assertion and adjustment; most of the immigrants had neither training in, nor understanding of, nor appetite for, imported or native criminal methods. Crime was a source of shame, a sign that much was distraught and some diseased on the East Side; but it was never at the center of Jewish immigrant life.

Voices of the Left

Torn apart by the pressures of extreme contradiction, the culture of the East Side during the eighties and nineties was at once depressed and ebullient, shaken to its roots and clenched with a will to survive. The culture expressed itself most articulately through the writings of the sweatshop poets (see pp. 420–25), an indigenous Yiddish theatre (see pp. 460–67), and the politics of radicalism. Though the sweatshop poets affected the lives of only a minority among the immigrants, the theatre and radical politics touched the masses, bringing popular dilemmas and yearnings to the sharpest focus.

The radicalism that a tiny segment of immigrant Jews had carried across from eastern Europe was intellectually primitive and politically untried. It had more to do with a visceral reaction against religious Orthodoxy than a precise analysis of modern capitalism. It had more to do with the

---

of Police McKane of Coney Island a silver dinner set of 96 pieces; Police Justice Divver, silver dessert spoons and his compliments; Pat Keenan, a gold clock; Coroner Levy, Dresden china shepherdesses . . . Henry Eichler, a silver pitcher (for water); Judge Newburger, a silver clock; Max Steinberg, a piano lamp; Max Hochstim, a piano; and Jake Mittnacht, an iron safe."

There were four hundred guests; each of the ushers wore "massive diamond pins"; the ceremony was performed by Rabbi Bernardt Hast; and the menu was in French.

hope of self-transformation—gropings toward mild bohemianism, ethical experimentation, sexual freedom—than organizing working-class protest. The ferocity with which this early Jewish radicalism proclaimed its cosmopolitanism mirrored the ferocity with which traditional Judaism had clung to messianic separatism. In its turbulent emotions this radicalism was still strongly tied to the world it was rejecting, still deeply responsive to the fathers it meant to outrage.

In the eighties the spokesmen for Jewish radicalism were small groups of intellectuals, really semi-intellectuals soon forced by American circumstances to become workers. They knew little about the conditions of the Jewish working class in eastern Europe, still in its early stages of formation, and knew next to nothing about the conditions of the working class in America, either native or immigrant. Declamatory, impassioned, theoretic, and sectarian to the marrow, these pioneer radicals sometimes called themselves socialists and sometimes anarchists, but they really had little of any tradition to go by. They were a mixture of socialist, anarchist, positivist, village atheist, and enlightened young Jew in love with the heroic style of the Russian populists. In the meeting halls and tenements of the Lower East Side they had to work out for themselves—with little help, at first, from the masters of European socialism—the ideas they meant to bring to the oppressed and the strategies by which to stir them into action.

A good portion of the early immigrant radicals either would not or could not speak Yiddish. What was this Yiddish? A wretched jargon of *shnorers* (beggars) and *luftmenshn*, a dialect of the *shtetl* where medieval prejudice had clamped Jewish minds. No one, surely, had ever associated Yiddish with secular thought or proletarian uprising. Those looking for liberation turned to Russian as the language of grandeur, the language of poets like Pushkin and Nekrasov and rebels like the early *narodniki*. In their yearnings for culture, many of the young Jewish intellectuals in eastern Europe had come to associate Russian with "high" sentiments and Yiddish with their own backwardness. Transferred to the East Side, where the Jewish immigrants were forced to become proletarians, these attitudes came to be snobbish and self-defeating. Even before there was a radical movement, radical intellectuals were displaying an elitist condescension toward the masses they proposed to liberate, the masses in whose behalf they would make enormous sacrifices.

In the late spring of 1882 there broke out a bitter longshoremen's strike on the New York waterfront. A number of immigrants, just off the boat and still being housed at Castle Garden, were recruited as strikebreakers. One of them, I. Kopeloff, later active in the anarchist movement, recalls that a delegation of Irish and German workers came to them explaining "that we were scabs who were taking the bread out of the mouths of the strikers' families. . . . I couldn't understand what I was doing wrong or what my sin was. Why should I not be permitted to earn my piece of bread? And what was this union, or why were those for it kosher and those against it *treyf?*"

The radical Jewish intelligentsia, loosely organized as the "Propaganda Association" (full title: Propaganda Association for the Dissemination of Socialist Ideas Among Immigrant Jews), distributed handbills calling for a meeting at Eisl's Golden Rule Hall at 127 Rivington Street on July 7, 1882, with the aim of persuading Jewish immigrants not to become strikebreakers.

These handbills were printed in Yiddish: it was essential that Jewish workers be able to read them. But the speeches at the rally were delivered in Russian: it was necessary that the radicals maintain their linguistic purity. Sergius Schevitsch, a Russian socialist of elegant speech and bearing, explained why it was wrong for Jewish workers to scab on Irish longshoremen, and by all accounts his several hundred listeners, or at least those who could make something of his Russian, were persuaded. At the meeting's end a green young immigrant named Abraham Cahan rose to make a few impassioned, if stray, remarks, in Russian too, that brought him to the notice of the leaders of the association. Intoxicated by this success, Cahan challenged them by saying that if they wanted to reach Jewish workers they would have to provide Yiddish speakers. "What Jew doesn't know Russian?" snapped Mirovich, one of the leaders. Cahan's answer was decisive: "My father." Coming from Saint Petersburg, Mirovich was quite ignorant of the *shtetl* Jews whose Russian was limited to the few phrases needed to placate a peasant or policeman. "More in jest than in earnest," the association proposed that Cahan lecture in Yiddish—and thereby, it is only a slight exaggeration to say, begins the story of Yiddish-language radicalism in the United States.

Together with a teen-age friend named Bernard Weinstein, whom he had converted to socialism while the two were working in a cigarette factory and who would later become a mainstay of the Jewish trade unions, Cahan distributed five hundred Yiddish leaflets "in the Jewish streets." On August 18, 1882, he spoke for two hours "in the simplest Yiddish" to several hundred people, explaining "Karl Marx's theory of surplus value, the theory of class struggle, and the inevitability of socialism." About all of these formidable topics Cahan knew only a little more than his audience, and there is cause to marvel at the ability of this youngster—an ability, in the radical milieu, alarmingly widespread—to speak at great length out of small knowledge. His lecture, it was later recalled by Weinstein, "kindled a wave of excitement . . . as if the dumb had begun to speak"; indeed, one reason so many came was that "the greenhorns wanted a chance to experiment with 'freedom of speech.'" A few weeks later Cahan gave another lecture, this time three hours long, in which he attacked the millionaires with "elaborate Vilna curses" and urged the workers "to march on Fifth Avenue with their tools and their axes and to seize the palaces and the riches which their labor had produced." Not many Jewish workers owned tools and fewer still axes, so that Cahan's call to revolt, as he himself wrote years later, was "a boy's, not a man's, speech." It was also typical of the moment, with its mixture of Marxist approximations and anarchist bravado, its verbal radicalism at once innocent and empty.

For several years the social democratic and anarchist outlooks existed uneasily side by side in the discussion groups and lecture societies the immigrant radicals formed, split up, and re-formed. Not everyone was certain as to which he really was, or what the differences amounted to, and some, like Cahan, shifted back and forth between anarchism and socialism before coming to a halt. As the Jewish radical immigrants moved from the Propaganda Association to the Russian Workingmen's Association and then to the Jewish Workingmen's Association (107 members, and significant because for the first time there was candor in labeling), and, after that, to Section 8, the Yiddish-speaking branch of the Socialist Labor party, they kept struggling among themselves for definition, grasp, rectitude, and extreme posture. And also for contol of the library. Each group, with a membership overlapping the others, would accumulate a few radical and scientific books, and when the time for a split arrived it was over those books, visible tokens of their yearning for enlightenment, that the factions would quarrel most.

Intellectual distinctions took time to work up, but the inevitable law of sectarianism—that in the absence of mass participation and social power it is ideology that becomes the substance of politics—was fiercely at work. A former czarist officer who had renamed himself William Frey preached a "religion of humanity" garnished with vegetarianism, and for a little while this Tolstoyan ascetic, whom Cahan regarded as a "moral giant," claimed admirers in the Jewish colony. Competing with him was Dr. Felix Adler, the father of Ethical Culture, who would deliver, with pomp and circumstance, weekly lectures at Chickering Hall, on Fifth Avenue near Eighteenth Street. Far to the left of Frey and Adler thundered Johann Most, the German anarchist leader and, at that time, advocate of "propaganda of the deed," or terrorism. In 1883 Most printed in his German-language paper, the *Freiheit*, the infamous "Catechism of a Revolutionary," a defense of political amorality written by Bakunin and Nechayev. Most was not much of a thinker—Karl Marx had denounced his "idiotic secret conspiratorial plans"—yet in the Jewish radical milieu of the eighties, where fervor counted at least as much as sense, he gained a following. One immigrant would remember the "teachings of the three," Adler, Most, and Frey, as "confounded in the minds of the youth, and an ethical-anarchist-positivist hash resulting."

For a few years, during the late eighties and early nineties, it was anarchism that captured the imagination of the more radical immigrants. In the totality of its rejection, in the absolutism of its intellectual system, in the theological fervor with which it assaulted traditional theology, this anarchism mirrored the deracination of a stratum of immigrants. It spoke to their sense of being utterly adrift, without ties in the old world or new, at home nowhere but in the regions of their thought. And it provided them with a self-contained milieu in which their feelings of hurt and aspiration could burn, and burn themselves out, barely in touch with such mundane considerations as wage struggles, trade unions, and electoral contests. Their statements of internationalism notwithstanding, these early radicals wanted to keep within the familiar bounds of the immigrant culture, for even when scoffed at on the East Side, it was still the place where they felt most at home. The great world they dreamed of conquering was actually the world they were least prepared to visit.

Organized in 1886 as the Pioneers of Liberty, the anarchists held weekly forums at which several score listeners would regularly appear; in 1889, renamed the Knights of Freedom, they began publishing the weekly *Varheit*, which lasted five months; a year later they started bringing out the *Freie Arbeiter Shtime*, a weekly that would become the longest-lasting Yiddish paper in America, and would offer both political comment and a range of social and cultural material in Yiddish. At the anarchist forums doctrine was expounded, the Almighty told off, and instruction offered in the social and natural sciences. When a debate was arranged, the audience could grow to several hundred or more—the immigrant world loved these gladiatorial exercises in oratory and dialectic. Jacob Merison, a veteran of those days, has recalled one debate between Saul Yanofsky, an anarchist leader, and Louis Miller, a social democratic writer: "Quotations pour out of Miller like burning lava from a volcano. He cites Marx and Bakunin, Kropotkin and Jules Guesde, Darwin and Buckle, Spencer and Hegel, Aristotle and Spinoza, until his opponent is utterly shattered. The hall resounds with applause. Miller has emerged triumphant."

Like its European equivalents, Jewish anarchism had little concern with strategy or tactics, methods of persuasion or councils of conciliation. For a vital minority of Jewish workers, anarchism was the name of their despair. And inevitably

> the religious question was at the core of the [anarchist] struggle against the existing social order. The masses, uprooted from an integrated and tradition-bound way of life inseparable from Orthodox Judaism, and subjected to disintegrative pressures, were, although perhaps inchoately, attempting to reorder their lives. This meant dealing with the question of religion, and confronting the propaganda of the radicals in their midst. Public avowal of agnosticism, atheism, apostasy, and backsliding was no new phenomenon in Jewish life by the 1880's. The anarchists, however, went far beyond secularism or anticlericalism in the bitter extremes of their antireligious struggle.

That they might thereby put off Jewish workers ready for political radicalism yet still attached to their religious past was an argument the anarchists dismissed with scorn. For they were less interested, at least to begin with, in struggles for improving the common lot than in articulating an entirely new outlook upon life within the Jewish world. Morris Winchevsky, a leading Yiddish poet and publicist, later remembered ironically, "For me . . . disbelief and hatred toward all faiths reached a high point of fanaticism. . . . My greatest delight was to prove that Moses did not write the Pentateuch, that Joshua did not cause the heavens to stand still." The anarchist Alexander Berkman recalled a conversation:

"I do not believe in religion."

"Young man . . . when, permit me to ask, did you reach so profound a conclusion?"

"Since I wrote the essay 'There Is No God.'"

"When did you write it?"

"Three years ago."

"How old were you then?"

"Twelve."

It was a village atheism, in a reconstituted Jewish village, where faith among the masses remained strong and the mere thought of apostasy required emotional courage. That the anarchists and some of the social democrats chose to demonstrate their freedom from superstition by holding balls and parades on Yom Kippur night, the most sacred moment of the Jewish year, showed not merely insensitivity but also the extent to which traditional faith dominated those who denied it. The Pioneers of Liberty declared in 1889 that they were simply intent on celebrating in their own way "the great festival of the slaughter of the fowl," but this home-brewed anthropology fooled no one; what was ringing in their ears was not the sound of primitive ritual but the haunting melody of Kol Nidre. The parodies of the traditional prayers they printed in their papers were often clever, but also revealed how well they remembered the prayers. In 1890 the anarchists moved their ball to the Brooklyn Labor Lyceum, on Myrtle Avenue, and announced:

> Grand Yom Kippur Ball.
> With theatre.
> Arranged with the consent of all new rabbis of Liberty.
> Koll Nydre Night and Day.
> In the year 5651, after the invention of the Jewish
> idols, and 1890, after the birth of the false Messiah. . . .
> The Koll Nydre will be offered by John Most.
> Music, dancing, buffet, "Marseillaise," and other
> hymns against Satan.

The consequences of such tomfoolery were or should have been predictable. Many immigrants, although no longer Orthodox, still maintained a sense of piety toward religious occasions, and the anarchist assault came to seem a threat to their very being. Later, too late, one anarchist leader would recognize that "the war against God . . . played a great part in the decrease of anarchist influence in Jewish life."

There were moments when the anarchists could still rouse the emotions of the Jewish workers, but, as a rule, more through invocations of martyr-dom than appeals to ideological rightness. When the convicted defendants in the 1886 Haymarket case in Chicago, almost certainly victims of a frame-up, were finally put to death, the Jewish anarchists held protest rallies on the East Side, as well as in other cities with immigrant populations. This was the kind of issue Jews could quickly grasp: they had known pogroms, they now learned about legal outrage. In 1903, when Alexander Berkman, an intellectual more sophisticated than the earlier anarchists, shot H. C. Frick, the labor-hating steel magnate, this example of "propaganda of the deed" shocked a good many of the Yiddish-speaking comrades. Talking about violence, they had not really meant that anyone should actually take gun in hand and try to kill another human being!

After a bloody strike in Colorado coal mines owned by the Rocke-fellers, a young anarchist woman, Marie Ganz, decided that "one man is guiltier than all others . . . and he must no longer live." She went to the Rockefeller office and was met by a secretary, who told her, "Mr. Rocke-feller isn't in town. . . . What can I do for you?"

" 'If you're Mr. Rockefeller's secretary,' I replied, 'I want you to tell him that if he doesn't stop killing the workers in Colorado I'll shoot him down like a dog.'

" 'I will deliver your message,' returned the young man suavely, and bowed me out.

"Already the newsboys were yelling extras that Marie Ganz had tried to shoot Rockefeller. Had tried! Bah!"

Throughout the nineties, and beyond them, Emma Goldman—young, vibrant, brilliant—loomed across the immigrant milieu as a solitary heroine of emancipation, a little admired and a little feared, an astonishing sort of "Jewish daughter" to have arisen in a world still far from morally relaxed or even at ease with its secularism. Speaking for "the philosophy of a new social order based on liberty unrestrained by man-made law," she suffered constant legal assault whenever she toured the country. The East Side became for her a place to which she could retreat in relative safety, and during the depression of 1893 she found employment there as a social worker, serving the jobless bread and leaflets with equal zest. But, in truth, her notoriety in the world at large was always greater than her influence among the Jewish immigrants; she was one of the first intellectuals to "graduate" from and then move out of their milieu.

By the nineties it was becoming clear that anarchism would never win the Jewish workers, simply because it had no answers to their immediate needs and, out of an ideological willfulness, denied their intuitions as to what might be achieved in America. For all their claims to emancipation, the anarchists largely shared the feelings of lostness that were so heavy in the early immigrant world. When they denounced the ballot box as a proposed way of achieving social change, they were not merely reflecting standard anarchist doctrine; they were also speaking out of the bewilderment Jewish workers felt when confronted with American politics. Once the immigrants began to root themselves a little in native life, they quickly brushed aside the ultimatism of the anarchists—as later, they would the dogmatism of many socialists—and worked to improve their conditions of existence.

Such efforts, for a good many years, were doomed to fail. Repeated attempts were made to organize unions of Jewish immigrant workers during the eighties and nineties; sometimes they would break out into ferocious strikes ending in hunger and demoralization; sometimes reach a momentary victory soon dissipated by their inability to maintain a stable organization. What characterized the outbursts of working-class rebellion on the East Side during these years was the repeated conjuncture of heroism in strikes and ineptitude in organization. The immigrants brought with them no tradition or experience of unionism, as would the generation coming to America after 1905. These early immigrants, writes the Yiddish historian Abraham Menes,

> were obsessed by one idea: to work as hard as possible and spend as little as possible in order to save passage for the family [that had remained in Europe]. The accusation leveled against the Jewish immigrants of the eighties, that they were themselves to blame for the intolerable working conditions of the sweatshop, was not entirely unfounded. . . . The workers wished to work longer hours and thus to earn a little more, so as to hasten the day when they could bring their families to America.

Workers imbued with this outlook might, as in fact they did, erupt into desperate strikes once life came to seem unbearable; but they were not really good material for unionization, which requires persistence at least as much as heroism.

In the few stable unions that were organized, the interests of the workers and the traditions of Jewishness tended to seem all but inseparable. Union leaders understood the need for weaving Biblical references into their agitational speeches ("Moses was the first walking delegate") and to justify the heretical course they were now advocating by injunctions of Orthodox piety. Bernard Weinstein has left a charming vignette of a visit he made to one intensely Jewish union:

> Among the unions we had at the end of the nineties a few were composed of old men, like the pressers', the butchers', the ragpickers' locals. One of these that we of the United Hebrew Trades helped organize in 1894 was a union of cleaners. Its members, who had mostly been tailors in Europe, operated out of cellars and worked by hand. They'd take dirty old clothes, wash them with benzene, dye them with brushes, and then press them. Many a time their pails of kerosene would spill over and cause fires in the tenements.
>
> The union of these elderly cleaners had been started by one of its younger members, M. Segal, of the Socialist Labor party, and their meetings turned out to be quite lively—they usually arranged to have representatives of

the United Hebrew Trades in order to settle the frequent fights that would break out, fights of joy.

We couldn't really complain about this uncomradely mode of behavior since the worklife of these people was very bitter—old men, usually in *yarmulkes,* standing twelve to fifteen hours a day by long tables in dirty cellars, cleaning dirty clothes.

One day three of us from the United Hebrew Trades were invited to a meeting held on the top floor of a loft at 49 Henry Street. This time, it turned out, there'd be no fighting—apparently our presence shamed them out of it.

When we arrived, everyone was sitting around a table facing the chairman; all wore *yarmulkes* except a few younger members with hats. Most were dressed in long smocks resembling caftans. Everyone had a glass of beer in hand, and before him a plate of herring and chunks of pumpernickel.

The place was half dark from the smoke of pipes and one could have been deafened by the banging of the beer glasses. A few fellows served as waiters and would steadily put down glasses of beer with a *"l'chaim."*

The chairman stood on a platform in the middle of the room. When he noticed us—we hadn't known where to sit among the hundred or so members—he summoned us to the head of the table. As we drew near, everyone rose and as the chairman recited our "pedigree" we were resoundingly toasted with the clinking of glasses. . . .

The noise grew. Someone began a Simchat Torah melody; glasses continually refilled from a nearby barrel; also, pails of ice to keep the beer cold. Finally I asked my bearded neighbor, "What's the occasion?"

"How should I know?" he answered. "Every meeting is like this, or else we wouldn't show up. The men give a few dimes apiece, and we have a Simchat Torah. That's how we are—sometimes we kiss each other from happiness, sometimes we fight."

At the end of each of our speeches, we all cried out, "Long live the union!" as the old Jews applauded and bumped glasses. Meanwhile a few started to move aside the tables and began dancing to a Hasidic tune.

In our report to the UHT, we called this group the Simchat Torah Union.

Strikes broke out again and again during the eighties, in the garment, cigar-making, bakery, and hat-making industries; unions were improvised again and again, sometimes by workers meeting in a hall and waiting for the socialists to send over Bernard Weinstein, Abraham Cahan, or Joseph Barondess to act as speaker-organizer; but of lasting results there were few. In 1883 a strike broke out at the large Keeney Brothers tobacco plant, which employed many Jewish immigrants, but after a few weeks the men had to drift back to work. In 1885 there was a major strike by the Jewish cloakmakers, some fifteen hundred strong, who claimed they had to work from 6:00 AM to 8:00 PM in order to make from twelve to fifteen dollars a week (relatively decent wages for the time); they were demanding a rate that would allow them to make the same amount while working "only" from 7:00 AM to 6:00 PM. The *Times* reported that the strikers "also demanded that in the future they be treated with politeness and consideration." This strike ended with a written agreement, rare for those days, but again the union itself was neither firm nor durable enough to enforce it for any length of time. In 1888 a central body of Jewish unions, the United Hebrew Trades, was organized, though for some years it had more trunk than branches.

A glimpse of the Yiddish press in the years before the turn of the century reveals the heartbreaking difficulties behind even the simplest strike. Here is a characteristic report:

> The strike of the knee-pants makers in the firm of Cohen and Braun, Brooklyn, continues. The workers have been on strike for two weeks and nobody thinks of returning to work until their persecutor, the rude foreman, has been fired. Especially admirable is the attitude of the Poles in this shop. The "lovely" foreman tries to create intrigues among the workers. He tells the Poles that the Jews are on strike because they don't want to work with them, and to the Jews he tells the opposite. But all these tricks cannot help him.
>
> Yesterday he promised the Poles fifty dollars for everyone who went back to work, but that didn't help either. Until today there were no scabs. Tonight, however, they tried to frighten the geese. Somewhere they found five whole scabs. . . . Accompanied by five cops, this procession entered the factory. The pickets doubled up with laughter, that these guys, who are likely to finish one pair of knee-pants a day, should do the work of seventy workers.

Probably the workers at Cohen and Braun were not quite as sanguine as the reporter made out—the phrase about "the geese" is terribly revealing. That it was hard to persuade Jewish workers to organize lasting unions during these years, all the testimony confirms. The *Yidishe Folkstseitung,* a pioneering radical weekly put out between 1886 and 1889 by two earnest young men who had saved up five hundred dollars working in Boston garment shops, devoted issue after issue, written in broken Yiddish, to simple lessons in solidarity: "When two people establish a relationship as husband and wife, they create a family organization," and by extension that was what the Jewish workers needed. Again and again, the *Folkstseitung* came head on against the limitations, the fears, the bedraggledness of its readers. It was singularly empty of humor, colloquial ease, or any effort to describe the actualities of Jewish life in New York. (Perhaps the editors felt that their readers knew those actualities only too well.) Yet even into the impoverished pages there crept motifs that would later course through the radical Yiddish press. "Together with the cry of 'food' there is another to be heard throughout the world: 'I want more light in my darkened life.' " The word *finsternish,* darkness, recurs again and again, as the one note Yiddish readers could be expected immediately to recognize—their lives are overcome by *finsternish* and it is to escape from *finsternish* that men must learn to act.

In 1890, a more sophisticated Yiddish radical weekly began to appear, the *Arbeiter Tseitung*, published by the Yiddish-speaking section of the Socialist Labor party. Only a few years intervene between the two papers, but the gap in political culture is enormous. In the *Arbeiter Tseitung*, there is more relaxed and pithier writing; there are poems by Morris Rosenfeld, who would gain recognition as the lyricist of the sweatshop, and even one or two by Abraham Cahan ("Dos Lied fun Operator," "The Song of the Operator"); there are homely theoretical pieces by M. Hillkowitz, later to become Morris Hillquit, theorist of the Socialist party; there is a serialization of the Yiddish classic *Di Kliatche*, by Mendele Mokher Sforim; and there is the beginning of a serious effort to report back to Yiddish readers the terms of their own life. When thousands of Jewish workers marched to Union Square on May Day 1890, demanding an eight-hour day, the *Arbeiter Tseitung* came alive with a proud description; when cloakmakers went on strike, as they did almost every year, the reportage was crisp and impassioned. Behind this improvement was the guiding hand of Abraham Cahan, a master journalist of the years to come; now he was working his way toward a plain style, especially in the pieces he wrote under the by-line of *Der Proletarishker Magid*, the working-class preacher, in which he shrewdly united the manner of an old-country itinerant preacher with the stripped ideas of socialist agitation.

To readers of a later time, much of what appeared in the *Arbeiter Tseitung* may appear intellectually coarse and primitive, but far more pertinent is the response of Morris Raphael Cohen, then a youth on the Lower East Side: "For intellectual stimulus I turned every week to the *Arbeiter Tseitung*. In its columns I read translations of Flaubert's *Salammbo*. . . . I was seriously interested in the news of the week and in Abraham Cahan's articles on socialism, which were in the form of addresses like those of the old Hebrew preachers."

For all the defeats and difficulties encountered by the pioneer radicals and unionists, these were the years in which the future leadership of the Jewish labor movement was being forged. From failures in trade union organization, valuable lessons were slowly learned. From the 1886 Henry George campaign, after which the United Labor party disintegrated into its component parts and most of the radicals went back to their sectarian preoccupations, the lessons were slower to come by—it would take some time before the Jewish immigrants learned that, through unity and shrewdness, they could become a power in the political life of the city. And impressive young men began to appear: Abraham Cahan, with his intuitive grasp of the immigrant mind; Morris Hillquit, who began as a shirtmaker and became the best mind of American social democracy; Bernard Weinstein, a model of the selfless and modest union leader; and Joseph Barondess, half charismatic agitator and half charlatan.

Among all the early Jewish radicals, Cahan stands out overwhelmingly. Somehow, he managed frequently to break past the formulas of his comrades and to see that for "those gray haired, misunderstood sweatshop hands of whom the public learns every time a tailor strike is declared" there were so few joys "that their religion is to many of them the only thing that makes life worth living. In the fervor of prayer or the abandon of study they forget the poverty of their homes." Hardly a profound or original thought, but for the time an immensely valuable one. Cahan could grasp the way religious emotions slide into secular passions and how necessary it was for anyone trying to organize immigrant Jewish workers not only to avoid antagonizing but positively to draw upon their religious loyalties. He told of visiting a *mishna* class of striking vestmakers and hearing one of them declare:

> Ours is a just cause. It is for the bread of our children that we are struggling. We want our rights and we are bound to get them through the union. Saith the Law of Moses: "Thou shalt not withhold anything from thy neighbor nor rob him; there shall not abide with thee the wages of him that is hired through the night until morning." So it stands in Leviticus. So you see that your bosses who rob us and don't pay us regularly commit a sin, and that the cause of our union is a just one.

Cahan's attitude toward these matters was ruled mostly by tactical considerations, by his understanding that for the Jewish unions it would be suicidal to confront religion head on. Later, when editing the *Forward*, he wrote some notable articles that went beyond mere tactics and into the psychology of fanaticism:

> The most comical and, at the same time, saddest thing is to see an atheist turn his irreligion into a cold, dry, unfeeling, heartless religion—and this is something most of our unbelievers used to do. One must not sit at a Seder; one must extend no sympathy to the honest, ignorant mother who sheds tears over her prayer book. . . . In truth, our early unbelievers were, in their own way, just as fanatical, just as narrow-minded, just as intolerant as the religious fanatic on whom they warred.

And in one major respect that did involve subtleties of doctrine, Cahan moved far beyond the ideologues of the Jewish left. It was a standard belief among them that "we have no Jewish question in America," as an 1890 conference of Jewish workers' organizations formally declared. At that time Cahan would not have explicitly rejected this view, but the whole thrust of his mind was to see things differently, less in the set categories of Marxism and more through his own restless intelligence. Anyone with eyes to see, anyone with ears to hear, had to know that there was "a Jewish question in America," as indeed there was and would be everywhere else. Cahan used his eyes to see, his ears to hear.

If Cahan emerged as the most lucid intelligence in the early Jewish labor movement, the figure who best embodied its awkward turbulence—its pathos, its hysteria, its selflessness—was Joseph Barondess (1863–1928). His name has not survived beyond a small circle of Jewish labor veterans, for he was neither thinker nor writer and he left nothing except some achievements. But for at least twenty-five years Barondess was one of the two or three most popular figures on the East Side, as agitator and communal spokesman, genuinely a man of the people.

On and off he was a leader of the cloakmakers' union; occasionally the ally, sometimes the opponent, of the socialists; a public hero during strikes; self-appointed manager of folk celebrations and funerals ("It was almost a pleasure to die," recalls a contemporary, "knowing that Barondess would arrange the rites"); failed actor, shirtmaker, insurance agent, untiring organizational busybody. For some years he was called "King of the Cloakmakers," one of those emotionally overspilling men for whom the East Side provided the ideal outlet. Capable of complete selflessness in behalf of the garment workers, he could also behave toward them like a feudal lord bullying his serfs. When aroused, he would deal out slaps to rebellious followers and, as if to show himself evenhanded, to labor-sweating contractors. His mind was a sloppy instrument, but he could always win the hearts of the Jewish workers through his soaring voice, his gift for lacing Talmudic epigrams into radical agitation. To the cloakmakers of the nineties, it was precisely Barondess's gaudiness that made him seem the kind of man appropriate for leadership. Had he succeeded in becoming an actor, he once confided to a friend, he would have called himself Baron d'Ess.

Beginning as a cloakmaker in 1888, when he earned five dollars a week for thirteen hours a day, six days a week, Barondess catapulted himself into union leadership. The emotional channel between the workers and himself was wide if shallow, turbulent if erratic. He stressed in his speeches his essential simplicity, a simple Jew among simple Jews; but he also exploited the yearning of Jewish workers to discover some thread of distinction in their lives, a yearning that would make them forever susceptible to leaders, actors, and intellectuals affecting the "Russian style" of bohemian aristocratism: cane, flower, hauteur, rhetoric. "He talked, dressed, and behaved like an actor," recalls Joseph Rumshinsky, the theatre composer. "Barondess looked like a brother of Jacob Adler or Boris Thomashefsky. He talked like a Shakespearean actor, always very dramatically—whether he was addressing the workers, discussing a pogrom, or ordering a glass of tea. He always impressed on his brother workers that while he was with them and understood them, he was a being superior to them."

To the socialists of the nineties Barondess presented a problem. They could never fully rely on him, feeling the uneasiness intellectuals always feel toward "natural" leaders. They feared that his ability to excite the workers might turn him into a demagogue who would escape their control. As against the crusty logic of a Cahan and the quiet sense of a Hillquit, Barondess spoke to the workers with *sturm und drang*, returning to them the turmoil of feeling they had brought into immigrant life. He would abuse them with paternal intimacy, and they loved it:

> In accursed Russia, under the czar, you traded with the gentiles and earned a few kopecks a week. Only on Saturday could you enjoy a piece of meat. So you think that your wretched pay in the sweatshop, given by the cockroach bosses, is a lot. But let me tell you: these are hunger wages for America. You could earn ten times as much if you weren't such idiots. . . . You are in America now and not in Shnipishok, Tunadefka, or Blutofka [names of *shtetlakh* in the fiction of Mendele]. . . . Here you can live like human beings! If you only weren't such cows, such oxen, such jackasses!

After an especially bitter cloakmakers' strike in 1891 Barondess was arrested on a charge, probably false, of extorting money from a manufacturer. Convicted, he was sentenced to twenty-one months in Sing Sing. At a meeting of the cloakmakers after his sentencing, Barondess broke into unrestrained weeping and the hundreds of workers listening to him also wept, as if overcome by the shared outrage of their lives. A few weeks later Barondess panicked, jumped bail, and fled to Canada; only after other union leaders pleaded with him did he return to New York, demoralized, to spend some months in prison before being granted a pardon. A lion at speechmaking, he shared the common Jewish dread of the gentiles' prison. To flee during battle, however, was to violate the radical code, and Barondess's critics, neither few in numbers nor gentle in language, did not fail to notice this weakness. The United Hebrew Trades issued a troubled statement condemning Barondess as a leader yet forgiving him as a man; apparently it was one thing to judge him through the severe prism of Marxism, another to remember that he was an immigrant with wife and children whom he had to feed.

It took only a few years for Barondess to regain his popularity on the East Side. In 1904 he ran unsuccessfully as a Socialist candidate for Congress, and somewhat later, shifting his allegiance, became active in the Zionist movement. A creature of the popular imagination, he was the kind of man who usually follows the popular drift, so that his career charted the major ideological shifts and turns of the immigrant world. By nature Barondess was a *tumler*, a celebrant, a noisemaker. When nine thousand Jewish workers poured into Union Square on May Day 1890, in one of their earliest ventures beyond the streets of the East Side, Barondess rode at their head, on a white horse that did not always behave properly. (It may have been a gentile horse.) At every banquet, at every celebration, parade, ceremony, and funeral—his eloquence reached its height at funerals—Barondess was there, to speak, to arouse, to weep. In 1911 he was appointed to the Board of Education, a major sign that the East Side was gaining power in New York.

Coarse and tender, incoherent and shrewd, commonplace and theatrical, Barondess was the archetypal leader who grips the hearts of workers by mirroring in gaudy excess their yearnings for drama, storm, magnitude. As a creature of their making, he rose up above them, giving substance to their fantasies. When he died, in 1928, the Jewish unions had long since ceased having a place for him, and perhaps it was just as well. Old friends and old enemies alike came to his funeral, remarking that it would have been a far more impressive occasion had Barondess been there to deliver the eulogy.

Cahan and Barondess represented two sides of early Jewish radicalism, the logic and the turbulence, the grasp and the passion. Each was groping for ways to set the struggle of the immigrant workers in a native context, though only Cahan really understood how this might be done. Cahan saw that the greatest strength of the budding socialist movement on the East Side would be its intimate association with the workers in the shops, even though —indeed, because—this might force the radicals to modulate some of their theories and relax some of their postures. Perhaps more than anyone else, Cahan encouraged the development of the kind of quick intelligence, the mixture of idealism and pragmatic shrewdness, that would make possible the later victories. What was first necessary, he understood, was that the Jewish radicals learn to create permanent organization after heroic strikes, and then, that the Jewish community itself become persuaded of its own possibilities once it had moved past the agonies of early settlement and into a tentative morale.

What Migration Meant

The mass migration of the Jews from eastern Europe to the United States signified not only the beginning of a major change in the physical circumstances of the Jewish people; it also brought an upheaval in their social existence that was at some crucial points similar to the Industrial Revolution of about a century earlier. Masses of people being forced out of, and then choosing to flee, the land; a loss of traditional patterns of preindustrial culture; the sudden crowding of pauperized or proletarianized human beings into ghastly slums and their subjection to inhumane conditions of work; a cataclysm that leaves people broken, stunned, helpless—these elements of the Industrial Revolution were re-enacted, within a shorter time span, in the mass migration of Jews during the last two decades of the nineteenth century.

In one experience—rapid, sometimes violent, rarely understood by those who suffered it—this migration combined at least three kinds of change: first, a physical uprooting from the long-familiar setting of small-town life in eastern Europe to the wastes and possibilities of urban America;

second, a severe rupture from and sometimes grave dispossession of the moral values and cultural supports of the Jewish tradition; and third, a radical shift in class composition, mostly as a sudden enforced proletarianization. Any one of these alone would have been painful; the three together made for a culture shock from which it would take many immigrants years to recover. Some never did.

At least during the last two decades of the nineteenth century, the great majority of the east European Jewish immigrants came from the *shtetl*. There was no other place from which they could have come, since the process of urbanization among the east European Jews was just beginning. Indeed, it is essential to remember that immigration to America and a movement to the cities in Poland and Russia were closely linked, both as to cause and in time; the youth who fled the economic and cultural stagnation of the *shtetl* might go to New York or he might go to Warsaw, depending on circumstance and desire, but what mattered most was that he had to go somewhere, he felt himself stifled and without hope in the *shtetl*. Among the Jewish immigrants from eastern Europe in the years between 1900 and 1914 a growing minority would already have had some taste of city life, though not a very long or deep one; but in the first wave of immigration, most of those who came knew little about city life in any firsthand way. For the majority, the first sustained experience of modern urban life began the day after they left Castle Garden, when they could either lose themselves in the streets of the East Side or prepare to travel to one of its smaller equivalents in Chicago or Philadelphia.

The *shtetl* had been wretched enough, and every impulse to romanticize it must be resisted. But at least it was a thoroughly known place where one's ancestors lay buried, it did not loom up to terrifying heights before one's eyes, it required no special knowledge of machines in shops or on trolleys, and it seldom had much to do with the rigors of the clock. The *shtetl* encouraged that indifference to time which a true religious existence demands and a life of pauperdom enables. To many of the immigrants, when they first arrived in the United States, the sheer noise of the streets, the bulk of the buildings, the constant pushing and elbowing and rushing of daily existence, were terrifying. How painful the transition from rural to urban life can be is a familiar theme among modern historians, but consider how much more shattering it must have been when this occurred as a movement from one continent to another, from an autocratic, patriarchal, Christian culture to a democratic, egalitarian, secular culture. No matter how much more attractive the latter may have seemed in prospect, it was also, at least at first, terribly alarming. Little wonder that—like an upswell of emotion, sometimes nausea—the dominant motif in the culture of the immigrant Jews during these early decades was nostalgia, the homesickness of castaways.

The east European Jews who came to the United States in the eighties and nineties left behind them, perhaps inevitably, a good portion of their culture and religion. The rabbis, the learned institutions, the political leaders, the burial societies, the intellectuals, the wealthy: almost all the figures of moral authority remained in the old country. In the 1905 period it would be different, for then a portion of the Yiddish-speaking intelligentsia would join the workers, the paupers, the petty traders, in crossing the ocean. But now, by the common judgment and memory of the immigrants themselves, those who came were the dispossessed, the wanderers, the surplus population of the decomposing *shtetl*, those without a place in the old home or those whose homes had been destroyed. The immigrants who came were the adventurous and the adventurers; men without skills in search of elemental survival; or fugitives from the czar's armies and the *shtetl*'s barrenness. New cultural and social institutions would be created by the Jews in the American cities, and already there were present in those cities some Jews, mostly from western Europe, who helped ease the pain of adjustment and offered some continuities with traditional faith. But in the main, the Jews who risked migration during the late nineteenth century were subjected to multiple shocks. For many, the pressure to work on the Sabbath became a problem threatening the security of their souls. For others, whose religious disenchantment, begun in the old country, had been completed in the American slums, there were no longer sufficient cultural or moral guides, no longer those rules of obligation and denial which, even if one hated and cursed them, made a discipline of each day. Those who found succor in the surrogate faiths of anarchism and socialism were perhaps fortunate, since these yielded new principles by which to live. But for the mass of immigrants the effects of the transition were violently disruptive. If airless, the *shtetl* had been snug; it was a social world in which the totality of existence came under the command of religion and in which everyone knew his precise status. But here in the United States life seemed at first utterly chaotic, so much so that the idea of freedom could only gradually be apprehended and enjoyed; it was a social world in which no one quite knew where he stood and which even raised the subversive possibility that where a man stood was open to his own definition.

A very few years after the mass migration, there also began within the immigrant community that process of internal social differentiation which is characteristic of American society as a whole. The beginnings of a middle class among the east European immigrants can already be detected by, say, 1890; a decade later there are a number of Yiddish-speaking millionaires and a considerable movement outward, beyond the East Side and into Jewish neighborhoods in upper Manhattan and Brooklyn, a movement signifying the modest rise of a middle class. But when the large waves of Jewish immigration first reached the United States in the eighties and nineties, the overwhelming consequences were proletarianization, a decline in real wages over the last two decades of the nineteenth century, and then, with the period of prosperity that came to the United States during the first few years of the twentieth century, a slow rise in real wages.

The first major Jewish proletariat appeared in the United States. Physi-

cally, socially, culturally, the immigrants were poorly equipped for proletarian life. They lacked the stamina, the casual acceptance of burdens, the
roughness of manner by means of which working-class communities in
Europe and America have come to accept and ease their lot. Surely that is
one reason the immigrant Jewish workers proved to be so fiercely, if fit-
fully, rebellious, and so eager to escape the conditions of life against which
they rebelled.

CHAPTER FOUR

Disorder and Early Progress

S LOWLY and at unmeasured cost, the immigrant Jews began to get a grip on their lives. By the mid-1890's it had become clear that neither material suffering nor social uprooting would permanently break their morale, even if a good many individuals were reduced to a mute resignation. The worst moment came during the 1893 depression, which erased whatever small gains they had made in the previous decade. Hunger really did stalk the streets of the East Side in 1893 and 1894, and only the dedication of the charitable agencies prevented a debacle. "It cannot be denied," writes an authoritative Yiddish historian, "that there was a fear that the historical experiment in America might end in catastrophe. Many of the immigrants themselves, in their letters back home, warned against such a possibility."

A determination to stick it out was, nevertheless, all but universal among the immigrants. Radicals might sneer and Orthodox condescend, but the American idea had begun to take hold of the immigrant imagination. No matter how imperfectly realized in social reality, it was an idea with enough moral power to persuade them that they should persevere in the new world, and thereby it reinforced the habits of stoical endurance that the centuries had bred in eastern Europe. The success with which many German Jews had made their way into the American economy remained an example close to hand, at once inspiring and irritating. And perhaps most important, there was simply no place else to go. The slums of New York, Chicago, and Philadelphia were the last frontier: either the Jews would make a new life here or the whole experience of migration would collapse in shame.

Once the country started its slow drive back to prosperity during the years between 1898 and 1904, the immigrants were able to relax their anxieties. If wage rates did not rise significantly in "their" industries, at least they now found it easier to get work.

The signs of strengthened morale were numerous, and close observers like Abraham Cahan, David Blaustein, and Charles Bernheimer noticed them. Immigrant Jews showed a new readiness to take on their enemies—neighborhood hoodlums, bigoted politicians, or brutal policemen. Jews straightened their backs a little. The style of resignation brought over from Europe began to give way to a feeling that Jews had as much right as anyone else in America to claw and grab. The communal affairs of the East Side grew more various: an outpouring of social activities, political factions, collective programs. Even a light sprinkle of hedonism refreshed the surface of immigrant life. A middle class, still fragile but increasing in numbers and confidence, started to make its appearance, and on top of it, a few millionaires like Harry Fischel, William Fischman, and Reuben Sadowsky, who still spoke Yiddish like everyone else and were remembered as having recently been quite as bedraggled as anyone else. Poverty remained the basic condition of life, as it would be for a good many years to come, but it was a poverty that took on a livelier complexion, a firmer tone. This was not the disconsolate poverty of the eighties, nor could it, by any stretch of ideology, be called "a culture of poverty." It was the condition of a people struggling to re-establish and redefine its sense of collective worth.

Greenhorns kept streaming off the ships. The immigration from eastern Europe reached a peak in 1906, when 153,748 Jews arrived in America. From 1904 to 1907 inclusive, the years of greatest Jewish immigration, a total of 499,082 came; from 1900 to 1910 inclusive, 1,037,000. Numbers counted. They gave the East Side a sense of accumulating strength, the comfort of massed ranks.

The new immigrants often had to re-enact the grueling initiation of those who had arrived in the eighties and nineties. Within the immigrant economy they served a function somewhat like that of the immigrants as a whole (both Jewish and gentile) in the American economy of the eighties and nineties. Until they could "break in" as garment workers or at the other Jewish trades, they usually had to take the lowest-paying jobs. Still, the worst was over, the first clearings had been cut, the newcomers did not have to face a wilderness. *Landsmanshaftn* offered a corner of friendship and helped to find work. Trade unions absorbed some of the more experienced "politicals" (usually Bundists) into posts of leadership. Credit unions would

soon help immigrants open small businesses. Night schools offered instruction in English. Relatives, perhaps by now moved to Brownsville or Harlem,
taught the greenhorns how to use the streetcars, where to buy cheap clothing, and when to drop by for a meal. Jewish charities helped the destitute—
during the severe 1908 depression, relief was distributed on a larger scale and
more generously than it had been fifteen or twenty years earlier. If the new
immigrants had to undergo some of the same hardships as the first wave
from eastern Europe, they did so in circumstances less punitive and more
shielding. And in a milieu that they could quickly discern as familiar, for by
1904 or 1905 "the East Side" signified a sprawling area that had taken over
adjacent streets from other ethnic groups (notably those between Houston
and Fourteenth streets, east of Second Avenue) and had established "colonies" in Harlem, Brooklyn, and the Bronx.

Oysgrinen zikh—to cease being a greenhorn—became a favorite motif
of Yiddish culture in America, a subject for comedy and pathos in stories,
theatre, and popular songs. Also for romantic charm, as in the song about
the pretty *grine kuzine*, or greenhorn cousin: *Es iz tsu mir gekumen a
kuzine,/ Sheyn vi gold iz zi geven, di grine,/ Di bekelekh vi royte pomera-
ntsn,/ Fiselekh vos betn zikh tsum tantsn.* (A pretty cousin came to us,/
Pretty as gold, this greenhorn,/ Her cheeks were like red oranges,/ Her feet
just begging to dance.)

The newer immigrants climbed onto the shoulders of the old, building
on their sacrifices and profiting from their mistakes, while the older ones
could feel that they were veterans of early heroic days, now at ease in the
city. Among the intellectuals of the 1904–1907 immigration there was a
certain disdain, even snobbism, toward the ill-educated Jews who had come
to America fifteen or twenty years earlier, though the line of separation
between the two generations could never be as sharp as that between east
Europeans and Germans.

The social landscape of the Jewish immigrant world, until now resembling an extended flat plain with a small rise at one end, began to take on a
more complicated shape. There were more hillocks, even a few hills and
plateaus. The flood of greenhorns enabled some of the older immigrants to
push their way forward, perhaps becoming "cockroach contractors" in the
garment industry or little candy-store keepers, or owners of those clothing
stores where customers were unceremoniously "pulled in" from the street.

By the turn of the century there was also a scattering of social workers,
reformers, teachers, all those "do-gooders"—selfless Yankees, earnest German Jews, a few Americanized immigrants from eastern Europe—who
established an elite of conscience on the East Side, trying to bring the
techniques of self-improvement to a community not always receptive to
innovation. Among the native Americans were Lawrence Veiller, Robert
Weeks De Forest, Frances Perkins, Stanton Coit; among the German Jews,
Lillian Wald, Felix Adler, Louis Marshall; among the east European Jews,
David Blaustein, Boris Bogen, Paul Abelson, Henry Moskowitz. These

people—settlement-house leaders, advocates of tenement reform, community officials—could hardly begin to cope with all that was wrong in the
immigrant world; but many of them trained immigrants in the skills with
which to extract some benefits from American society. They taught immigrant fathers the value of knowing how to read and write a few lines of English. They taught immigrant mothers the sacredness of hygiene and green
salads at dinner. They taught immigrant Jews how to talk, and talk back, to
chilly school superintendents, impudent court clerks, rude police sergeants,
all those officials inclined to truculence and condescension.

At no point, however, did there really emerge a unified leadership
among the immigrant Jews—certainly not until the creation of a Kehilla, or
community organization, in 1908. Jewish garment workers might adore
Joseph Barondess when he rose to speak, the Orthodox relish Hirsh Masliansky's Yiddish sermons, and a wide range of readers follow Abraham Cahan
in the *Forward;* but all shared a disinclination to elevate anyone to the rank
of "spokesman" or "leader." The immigrant Jews were deeply suspicious of
makhers, or busybodies. They recalled with distaste the community organizations of the old country, in which rabbis and businessmen had often
weighed heavily on the backs of the poor—and wanted none of that here.
Inner competition, even a portion of chaos, might be more to their advantage. The skepticism that formed part of their moral baggage made the
whole idea of a monolithic community seem repulsive. Besides, as the experience of the Irish immigrants suggests, an airtight community could impede social mobility by making everything too cozy and self-contained.*

Because of the peculiar circumstances of their history, the east European Jews brought with them considerable experience in creating "secondary associations" that would cut through the confines, and limit the
authority, of family and synagogue. Even during the first years of the
immigration, which were marked by a quantity of social disorder, they filled
out the social spaces between family and state with a web of voluntary
organizations, the very kind that, more than half a century earlier, De
Tocqueville had seen as distinctively American but which, in this context,
were distinctively Jewish. Tacitly but shrewdly, the immigrant Jews improvised a loose pattern for their collective existence. Most wanted to maintain

* "There may be an inverse relationship," writes Stephan Thernstrom, "between the
'institutional completeness' of an ethnic community—the degree to which ethnic
organizations can perform all the services its members require, whether religious,
educational, political, recreational or economic—and the likelihood that members of
the group will be upwardly mobile in the larger society. . . . It is of course true
that a cohesive, disciplined group can act in concert to attain certain objectives—
a classic example is the Irish take-over of the big city political machines in the late
nineteenth century. But what is too often overlooked is that such a victory—winning
control of 3000 jobs in the Public Works Department, let us say—may involve
seizing one kind of opportunity at the expense of other opportunities. The success
of the Irish in the political sphere was not matched by comparable gains in the
private economy."

a distinctive Yiddish cultural life while penetrating individually into American society and economy; most wanted to insure their survival as a people while feeling free to break out of the ghetto; and most hoped for cultural and religious continuity while opting for a weak, even ramshackle, community structure. Before the term became fashionable they made their way to a sort of "pluralism"—and the later decades proved them right.

An Early Combat

On July 30, 1902, a thick shapeless procession, estimated by the police at 25,000 and by the Yiddish papers at twice that number, coiled its way through the East Side, stopping at synagogue after synagogue, to follow the coffin of Chief Rabbi Jacob Joseph. There was no music save the chanting of pupils from the Hebrew schools. A gentle soul, Rabbi Joseph had been invited in 1887 to come from Vilna and assume the post of chief rabbi, a title without clear warrant in the synagogue structure of New York. His tenure had been unhappy, and he had shown few gifts for adapting to the coarseness of New York life. Now, as if in expiation, the whole Jewish community came to mourn his death.

Passing along Grand Street, the funeral procession reached the factory of R. Hoe and Company, makers of printing presses. Suddenly, from the second floor of this building, missiles started to descend upon the tightly packed Jews. A contemporary, non-Jewish account picks up the story:

> Instead of turning up their faces to the factory windows and protesting with words and gestures, as the merry pressmakers expected, the Jews set up a mighty shout and, with a common impulse charged upon the factory. Before the clerks and workers on the ground floor knew what had happened they were surrounded by bearded men and bewigged women, jabbering excitedly and clutching at things as though intent upon wrecking the place. Meanwhile, the Jews outside had opened fire on the factory windows with bricks, stones or any other projectiles they could lay hold of. . . .
>
> The fray took its most serious turn when the police arrived. . . . They set to work at once swinging their clubs vigorously as they drove the Jews from the factory. Scores of persons were hurt, mostly by the policemen's clubs.

At no previous point in the life of the East Side had there been so free a display of Jewish fury. "This was more," wrote the *Forward*, "than even Jewish patience could take. Everybody's blood started to boil. 'Lynch them, those animals, those dogs!' we heard from all sides."

Protest meetings, at which Barondess and Cahan were among the speakers; a crude anti-Semitic statement by Inspector Cross, the official in charge of the police detail, who had allegedly told his men, "Club their brains out"; court fines for the ninety-three Jews arrested; a special investigation ordered by Mayor Low, resulting in a halfhearted apology—all followed in rapid order. For the Jews themselves, the riot had a shock, perhaps a tonic effect. The *Forward* wrote with some pungency:

> Nobody ever talked about inequality in America. Everyone tried to hide it. Not only the gentiles, but the Jews themselves, the elite of our American Jewry, tried to hide this insulting inequality. . . . They are like *heder* boys who think that if you want to stop the thunder during a storm you hide your ears in your *kapote* [long coat]. . . . But the behavior of the police, and still more the attitude of the American press, clearly prove that there is little sympathy here for the Jews. At this moment of shame not one English paper, not one important Christian voice, was raised in protest. . . . About all this, dear reader, we now have to think a little, so that we will know where we stand in the world.

Such reflections apart, what mattered most about the riot was that for the first time thousands of immigrant Jews had shown a spontaneous readiness to fight as others fought. Morally a dubious acquirement, but psychologically bracing and, on a small scale, perhaps even a turning point in the history of the East Side.*

There were other signs of this new combativeness. Some were internal, against abuses within the Jewish streets, and others external, against gentile tormentors. In early May 1902 Jewish retail butchers began a boycott against the wholesale butchers, many of them German Jews, whom they charged with ruthlessly forcing up prices. Two days later the wholesalers yielded, but when the stores reopened, many failed to pass on the lower prices. Rage swept through the East Side, with women complaining they could not afford to buy kosher meat if the price rose to seventeen or eighteen cents a pound. The "revolution," as the *Forward* excitedly called it, started on Monroe Street between Pike and Market, where Mrs. Edelson and Mrs. Levy—unremembered heroines of protest—refused to pay the new prices. Clashes occurred in front of butchershops, a "Ladies Anti-Beef Trust Association" was formed, immigrant housewives were arrested by the police, women poured kerosene over meat, and, as the *Forward* wrote, "hundreds of women, screaming and cursing the swindlers of the poor," roamed through the streets.

A scene at court:

> Rebecca Ablowitz, of 420 Cherry Street, speaks to the judge:
>   "Why do you riot?"

---

* An unpleasant side effect: the victims sometimes became victimizers. In 1905 the *Forward* deplored incidents in which "hooting Jewish boys" threw stones at a Chinese man and "Jewish boys and girls spattered mud over the snow-white dress of a little Irish girl going to confirmation. . . . We are responsible for the disgraceful things our children do. We Jews, more than others, must teach our children to respect people with different customs."

"Your Honor, we know our wounds. We see how thin our children are and that our husbands haven't strength to work. . . ."

"But you aren't allowed to riot in the street."

"We don't riot. But if all we did was to weep at home, nobody would notice it; so we have to do something to help ourselves."

"Three-dollar fine."

Together with meat strikes went rent strikes extending over several years, touching even the Galitzianer Jews (those from Galicia), who on the East Side were regarded as somewhat passive. In 1904 the rent strikes grew especially violent, spreading to Harlem and Brownsville under socialist leadership. That same year the East Side was stirred by a children's strike—125 girls, many between the ages of fourteen and sixteen, walked out at the Cohen paper-box factory on the Bowery, where they had been paid three dollars per thousand cigarette boxes and then had suffered a wage cut of 10 percent. Benefit concerts were held, the *Forward* raised a special fund, the United Hebrew Trades scraped together seven hundred dollars to see the children through a fierce struggle. "Do-gooders" were especially helpful, through the recently formed Women's Trade Union League, an alliance of women unionists and social workers led by Jane Addams and Rose Schneiderman.

Joining in the spirit of the moment, Jewish street peddlers also began to organize, holding parades and meetings to protest harassment by the police. In 1903 the city set up a market near the Williamsburg Bridge for the fish peddlers, an especially lively group, and banned the selling of fish on push-carts. It was a classic instance of officials concocting a scheme with little relation to reality—three hundred stalls were provided, and there were over a thousand peddlers of fish. The peddlers pointed out that to be fixed in a stall meant losing the business of housewives who lived far from the bridge. In July they held a parade, lined up six abreast and accompanied by brass bands: it was such a pleasure to make a bit of noise in the world! Soon they were back on the streets with their pushcarts, an indispensable part of immigrant life.

If inner wounds brought the Jews to anger, they responded still more passionately to news of disaster in the old country. The 1903 pogrom in Kishinev, a town in southern Russia, in which forty-nine people were killed and more than five hundred injured, seemed like a nightmare revisited. Relief and protest were organized on a scale the immigrants had never before undertaken. The administration of Theodore Roosevelt, though sensitive to the growing importance of Jewish votes, was not sure how to respond to Jewish demands, at first hesitating to forward a B'nai B'rith petition to the czarist government and then refusing on the ground that its wording was too sharp. In common outrage against the pogroms, German and east European Jews came together, their differences tabled for the moment; no matter how much the east Europeans may have scorned the Germans, they had to acknowledge that Louis Marshall and Jacob Schiff could mobilize financial resources and political connections beyond the reach of the East Side. What worried both the Germans and the east Europeans was that as a result of the pogroms a greater number of Jews would now be wanting to leave Russia—and how would the United States respond to a flood of penniless newcomers?

Among the immigrant Jews, Kishinev evoked a clash concerning strategies of protest that would become a recurrent problem in American Jewish life. The conservative *Tageblatt* could not quite bring itself to say that mass demonstrations were pointless, but it steadily minimized their value, charging they were used by radicals for political aggrandizement. On the other hand, "many socialists," admitted Abraham Liessen, the Yiddish poet, "say we are too hysterical about Kishinev, since it was not an event that involved class-conscious workers or labor struggle." Such socialists, Liessen said, "are Pharisees. What if some of the victims were members of the upper classes? These are our people, our blood and our pain." At least as cogent were the reflections of Abraham Cahan, who kept trying to extract from day-to-day East Side events some guiding ideas for the future: "The Americans promise not to hinder new immigration. But soon they will forget. They have pity for us, but no respect. When the tumult dies down, they will feel all the more that Jews are a degraded people. Our tree is more bent than ever."

Instinctively, Cahan found himself speaking of "we," as if he accepted in reality what he hesitated to acknowledge in theory: the existence of a Jewish community transcending class lines.* It took courage for a leader calling for mass demonstrations to acknowledge how uncertain were their probable results. A few weeks later Cahan wrote still more stringently in an editorial entitled "Are We Safe in America?":

> As the Jewish population increases, animosity grows with it. Nations love only themselves, not strangers. If we get too close to the Americans with our language and customs, they will be annoyed. The Americans can't even get along with the Germans, so imagine the chasm between *shtetl* Jews and Yankees—it's like two different worlds. When there are only a few Jews, gentiles go slumming to inspect the novelty. When the Jews fill up the streetcars and parks, we are resented.

Not many writers could have struck so fine a balance between the East Side's new assertiveness and a recognition of its likely limits. In any case, this

---

* The Yiddish writer S. Niger offers a valuable citation: "The profound effect of the Kishinev pogrom upon the minds and hearts of the radicals can be seen from the rancor with which Herz Burgin, one of those who remained true to their former extreme radicalism, speaks about it in his book about the Jewish labor movement. He writes, 'This was a veritable nationalist epidemic. . . . The radicalism of the Jewish masses practically disappeared before the nationalist wave.'" A similar response can be seen in the memoirs of I. Kopeloff, an anarchist of long standing. "The Kishinev pogrom upset me. . . . My previous cosmopolitanism, internationalism, and similar ideologies vanished at one blow, like the contents of a barrel with the bottom knocked out."

assertiveness counted more as a sign of inner feeling than as an estimate of actual strength. What it meant was that in response to an acute crisis—a pogrom thousands of miles away or an indignity on a nearby street—the immigrants could come together in a quick action, linking methods of radical protest with American styles of pressure. In the world as a whole, the gentile world, they remained of course a weak minority, unable to realize the claims of their rhetoric and still hemmed into the boundaries that all minorities find bruising.

New Tastes, New Styles

A growth of self-confidence need not stem entirely from bettered material conditions, but it is hard to imagine it occurring without them. Precisely how widespread or deep such improvements were during the opening years of the century is not easy to say. That there were, however, a good many signs of little indulgences and modest luxuries, a slow escape from the grind of mere subsistence, cannot be doubted. The *Forward*, that incorrigible student of immigrant mores, offers some useful clues. A new word, it reports in 1903, has entered the American Yiddish vocabulary: *oysesn*, eating out. This fashion, barely known among Jews either in the old country or the new, "is spreading every day, especially in New York." Vacations in the country, we read a year later, "have become a trend, a proof of status . . . though many bluff about it." "The Victrola Season Has Begun," runs the head over another piece, written with pride and irritation: "God sent us the Victrola, and you can't get away from it, unless you run to the park. As if we didn't have enough problems with cockroaches and children practicing the piano next door. . . . It's everywhere, this Victrola: in the tenements, the restaurants, the ice-cream parlors, the candy stores. You lock your door at night and are safe from burglars, but not from the Victrola." As for children pounding on pianos, it has become a craze. "There are pianos in thousands of homes, but it is hard to get a teacher. They hire a woman for Moshele or Fannele and after two years decide they need a 'bigger' teacher. But the 'bigger' teacher, listening to the child, finds it knows nothing. All the money—down the drain. Why this waste? Because Jews like to think they are experts on everything." Sad. Nevertheless, the money was there to spend.

A walk along Canal Street in 1903 or 1904 yielded similar signs of improvement. It was a street with burgeoning retail businesses, where "the powerful Louis Minsky had his store for 'peddlers' supplies,' to which all the peddlers would come for goods on credit; there too were the large men's store of Joseph Marcus (later a banker) and the Jewish banks of Yarmulowsky and others, where immigrants could buy ship's tickets for their relatives on the installment plan."

Charles Bernheimer remarked in 1905 upon "the formation of a well-to-do class in the midst of the Russian Jewish colony. . . . The sudden appearance of a dozen or more commercial banks, the well-furnished cafés of a type utterly unknown five or six years ago, the modern apartments 'with an elevator,' . . . all tell eloquently of this growth."

A *Forward* reporter described the "clerks of the East Side, those working in the fifty or so dress-goods stores on Hester, Ridge, Stanton and Rivington streets." They put in shameful hours, from 7:00 AM to 11:00 PM, yet

> they have better manners than the young men who work in other trades. At the balls and weddings they make friends, which helps their sales. . . . When they save up a few hundred dollars, two or three get together as partners and open a store. Almost all storekeepers are former clerks, and once they become bosses they have plenty of time to go to affairs. Each belongs to seven or eight societies; this helps them with business and sometimes they meet a rich girl.
>
> A clerk has to be very clever and know how to make a big sale. The liveliest time is at night, when the young shop girls come to buy fabrics for blouses and dresses. First a girl comes for a sample; the next night she brings her friends. They talk about balls, concerts, and other affairs, and the clerks find out what's going on. . . .
>
> When they decided to form a union, the clerks held their meetings after 11:00 PM, once the stores had closed.

To be an American, dress like an American, look like an American, and even, if only in fantasy, talk like an American became a collective goal, at least for the younger immigrants. "Today," remarked David Blaustein in 1905, "English is more and more the language spoken on the East Side, whereas eight years ago it was rare to hear that tongue; today American clothes are worn, whereas in years gone by persons used to go to the East Side out of curiosity to see the foreign dress." In earlier years "you could recognize a greenhorn a mile away, by his walk and behavior. Now a greenhorn looks and acts like the 'yellows' [half-Americanized immigrants]. . . . Russia is much more civilized than before and its emigrants are more educated than the 'yellow' customer peddlers and realestatenicks of earlier years." And Hutchins Hapgood observed that some of the immigrants talk not only "of the crimes of which they read in the English newspapers, of prize-fights, of budding business propositions, but they gradually quit going to synagogue, give up *heder* promptly when they are thirteen years old, avoid the Yiddish theatres, seek the up-town places of amusement, dress in the latest American fashion, and have a keen eye for the right thing in neckties."

By 1905–1906 it was no longer rare for stores in the East Side, "even on Hester Street," to be open on the Sabbath; Yiddish purists were groaning at the invasion of Americanisms into their language (*vinde, floor, job*); thousands of Jewish children, now forced to attend school regularly, besieged the Board of Health, at Fifty-fifth Street and Sixth Avenue, each summer to get "working papers." "How touching it is to see these small, pale, exhausted boys lying about their age"—only those over fourteen were legally allowed to work.

The meaning of such changes was necessarily ambiguous. In the long view, they spoke of a culture cracking apart, its most energetic offspring taking the first steps toward flight and dispersion; but at the moment, in 1903 or 1906, there was good reason to see these changes as evidence of a growing social cohesion. Whatever might happen later to its young, the Jewish immigrant world kept thickening its communal life, encasing itself in layer upon layer of protective institutions, agencies of self-help, charity, education, mutual benefit, all designed to attain for the immigrants a maximum of assurance and all premised on the wary assumption that Jews could never come close to that maximum.*

Some of these institutions were started by German Jews and then taken over by the east Europeans; others, like Beth Israel Hospital, were the work of east Europeans from the very start. By 1903 the Hebrew Free Loan Society, which lent without interest sums between $5 and $50, had a capital of almost $75,000, and during that year turned over its money four times, lending out a bit more than $320,000. A day nursery on Montgomery Street, taking without (or at minimal) fees infants of women working in factories, survived on contributions from unions, Workmen's Circle branches, charitable groups. The Romanian Jews set up their own aid association in 1898 to care for new immigrants; the Hungarian Jews had done so a few years earlier. Each year the Ladies Fuel and Aid Society held a banquet to collect funds for hospitals and provide coal for the indigent. Much East Side charity was informal, quite apart from institutions: "Mother had been collecting for a motherless bride. . . . She would come home with a large handkerchief quite heavy with money, a fitting result to her house-to-house canvass in the ghetto."

Charity was one thing, mutual aid another and better. The first legally recognized Jewish credit union was set up in Massachusetts in 1909. Weak producers' co-operatives, organized in the early years of the century by clothing, bakery, and seltzer workers, lasted awhile in New York and then faded away. In 1916 the Russell Sage Foundation put out a fifty-two-page

---

* The number and variety of institutions is astonishing. Let us name only a few: the Sheltering House for Immigrants and the Hebrew Free Loan Association, the Workmen's Circle and the HIAS, the Beth Israel Hospital and the Free Burial Society, the United Hebrew Charities and the Jewish Maternity Hospital, the Hebrew Free School Association and the Educational Alliance, the Talmud Torahs, the yeshivas, the Provident Loan Society, the Baron de Hirsch Fund and the Aguilar Free Library, the Clara de Hirsch Home for Working Girls and the Lakeview Home for unmarried Jewish mothers, the Jewish Prisoners' Aid Association, the Jewish Consumptive Association in Denver, the East Side Civic Club. And then, still more numerous, the synagogues, the *landsmanshaftn*, the trade unions.

booklet in Yiddish describing the principles of credit unions and co-operatives, and listing 107 of the former, among which some 20 or 30 were Jewish. About 1912 the small Jewish storekeepers of New York, as if emulating the Jewish workers, began to form trade associations. The German-Jewish merchants had established their own institutions as far back as 1882, but it was some thirty years before the east European Jews founded the New York Retail Grocers Union. Employers were slower to organize themselves than were workers; the Hebrew Printers Union was started in 1888 but had to wait for nineteen years before a Hebrew Printers League appeared on the scene for industry-wide collective bargaining.

Still, when a depression struck, none of these agencies, nor all of them together, could cope with the damage. In the 1908 depression, especially severe for the East Side, there were appalling scenes of hunger and destitution. On February 14 several hundred children crowded into Lorber's Restaurant, drawn by the news that it would be serving free lunch to schoolchildren; since the dining room held only two hundred people, those on the outside began to fear they would not get any food and started to push their way in, grabbing food for themselves and for parents hungry at home. That same year a People's Kitchen was established at 185 Division Street, offering a dinner for seven cents. The Yiddish writer Z. Libin described his visit:

> It is a long room with two rows of long tables; the kitchen is in the back, separated by a low wall, and anyone can go in and see what's happening.
> The waiters are serious and courteous. No tipping is allowed.
> One man wanted an extra portion of meat and wondered if he could ask the waiter to exchange his soup for meat. The waiter gave him extra meat and let him keep the soup. . . . Another man offered me his bread because he had been at a *brith* [circumcision celebration] that morning and was not very hungry. Still, he was afraid he would be hungry later, and he likes the soup in this place.

But there was never enough. The institutions providing help were themselves largely dependent on the kinds of people needing it, so that in a bad year like 1908 the Jewish tradition of self-help proved to be inadequate: the community simply did not have a large enough surplus to take care of its hungry. Yet without these charitable agencies, the years of depression would have been far worse; they prevented utter demoralization and made for a kind of order in an economy of want.

Spreading Across the City

Year by year the physical horizons of the immigrants kept expanding. The Williamsburg Bridge was opened in 1903 and the Manhattan Bridge in

1909, both enabling rapid connections with Brooklyn. In 1896 elevated cars started taking passengers by express from South Ferry to Bronx Park. In 1905 the first subway to the Bronx, through the Harlem River tunnel, began to operate; in 1908 the first subway to Brooklyn, through the East River tunnel.

By the 1890's Jewish settlements had been established in Williamsburg, across the East River, and in Brownsville, a more distant quarter of Brooklyn. By 1900 there was a large Jewish colony in Harlem, mainly between 97th and 142nd streets. A decade later the *Forward* was calling Harlem "a Jewish city, inhabited by tens of thousands of Jews . . . as busy and congested as our East Side, with the same absence of light and air." The Upper East Side, along Lexington Avenue between 72nd and 100th streets, became a "colony" for east European Jews shortly before and after the turn of the century.

The son of the great Yiddish cantor Yossele Rosenblatt recalled that when his family came to America in 1910, it settled in Harlem, "at that time the aristocratic Jewish neighborhood of New York. . . . But that was true only of the blocks between Lenox and Seventh Avenues, where the better private homes were located, not of the tenements between Fifth and Lenox Avenues, into one of which we moved."

A 1905 issue of the *Forward* has a charming report on the gradual spread of immigrant Jews throughout the city:

> The Jewish presence is strong in the New York parks: Mount Morris, Central Park, Bronx Park, and Prospect Park in Brooklyn. Fifteen years ago you seldom met Jewish strollers in most areas of Central Park; they only visited the zoo. This was because most Jewish park visitors got off there on their way back from Mount Sinai Hospital, then located at Lexington and Sixty-seventh Street, where they were either visiting a sick friend or taking treatment at the dispensary. The only thing that interested Jews in Central Park was the zoo. They were afraid to venture farther into the park lest they get lost. Even the Museum of Art on Eightieth Street was seldom visited by Jews. Immigrants couldn't find it, and didn't know enough English to ask for directions; but this summer two Jewish young men made an experiment. They sat at the museum entrance and studied the faces of the people entering—and more than 80 percent seemed Jewish.
>
> On Saturdays and Sundays you will find entire companies of immigrant boys and girls sitting in a circle listening attentively as one of them reads aloud from the finest in modern Russian literature. This is much more pleasant than sitting alone among a group of strangers, stiff and starched and silent, as the Americans usually do.

Perhaps the most traveled route out of the East Side was to Brooklyn, especially the Brownsville, New Lots, and East New York sections. Brownsville was then regarded as a pastoral village in which "Jews could live as in the old country, without any rush or excessive worries. Jews there didn't

work on the Sabbath, and they went to *shul* three times a day." By the early
1890's some four thousand Jews had settled in and near the Brownsville area;
by 1905, about fifty thousand. During the first four or five years of the
century land values rose spectacularly, and immigrant Jews owning a few
lots in Brownsville now became affluent realtors. "Only yesterday," ran a
1903 account

> everybody laughed when you mentioned Brownsville. But today business is
> booming. They are buying and selling real estate like mad. Lots are sold by
> the hundreds; houses are sold and resold every minute. You can buy a house
> for four thousand dollars with a down payment of eight hundred dollars.
> A few days later you can sell it and make a profit of a few hundred dollars.
> Brownsville will never have tenements. The houses are three stories,
> apartments have four or five rooms, with a bathtub and other conveniences,
> and a yard for the kids.

Predominantly working-class in composition, the Brownsville Jewish
community took on a distinctive character of its own, with strong religious
and socialist segments: Pitkin Avenue, its major thoroughfare, would long
be famous as a place where the Jewish socialists held street meetings and
people buzzed about discussing politics.

Tempting as it was to escape the noise, heat, and congestion of the East
Side, there were problems in moving to such outlying districts as Brownsville. Some people felt they were leaving the center of cultural life: it was
like moving from Paris to Lyons. For workers who had to count every
nickel, it brought the additional expense of carfares. Still another problem
was that "it is easier to get boarders in New York than in Brooklyn," a point
made

> by a member of a family that received $10 a month from four lodgers—three
> men and one woman—who occupied three rooms with the four members of
> the family. . . . The father earns $250 a year as a worker in the manufacture
> of smoking-pipes. The oldest daughter earns $150 as a milliner. The family
> decided to return to Manhattan, where they could get lodgers more readily
> and thus eke out their income of $400 by an addition of $120 a year. Out of
> the earnings of $520, $186—that is, $15.50 a month—had to be paid for rent.

A year or two after the trek to Brownsville, immigrant Jews started
moving to the Bronx. Visiting the Bronx in 1903, a Yiddish journalist found
it "a beautiful area . . . a suburb that could have sun and air and cheaper
rents. But the greedy landlords, knowing the workers will have to move
uptown, are putting up Hester Street tenements. Go take a look—the Bronx
is becoming our new ghetto." Only in part was this correct. Sections of the
east Bronx, especially working-class streets like Simpson and Fox, were
hardly more tolerable than the East Side, but other areas did provide better
housing, mainly because the Bronx still had quantities of unused space and
several new tenement laws restraining the greed of builders. During a visit in

1912, the English novelist Arnold Bennett found the Bronx harsh, materialistic, and enjoying an "innocent prosperity."

> The people whom I met show no trace of the influence of those older artistic
> civilizations whose charm seems subtly to pervade the internationalism of the
> East Side. In certain strata and streaks of society on the East Side things
> artistic and intellectual are comprehended with an intensity of emotion im
> possible to Anglo Saxons. . . . The Bronx is different. The Bronx is begin
> ning again, at a stage earlier than art, and beginning better. It is a place for
> those who have learnt that physical righteousness has got to be the basis for
> all future progress. It is a place to which the fit will be attracted, and where
> the fit will survive.

With his shrewd eye Bennett saw that the cultural tone of the East Side could not be imported to the other Jewish neighborhoods, even when their residents had just come from there. What remained in these new neighborhoods was a still-pulsing sense of East Side hardship and a grim urgency to banish it as quickly as possible. It was as if, in the most unlikely corner of the world, Bennett had rediscovered the social atmosphere of his Five Towns.

An Experiment in Community

In 1908, just before the great outbursts of strikes in the Jewish trades, the immigrant community underwent a test of morale that caused difficulties both in its internal life and its relation to the power structure of the city. Theodore Bingham, the police commissioner of New York City, published in the September 1908 issue of the *North American Review* an article entitled "Foreign Criminals in New York," which claimed that 50 percent of the criminals in the city were Jewish:

> It is not astonishing that with a million Hebrews, mostly Russian, in the city
> (one-quarter of the population) perhaps half of the criminals should be of
> that race when we consider that ignorance of the language, more particularly
> among men not physically fit for hard labor, is conducive to crime. . . .
> They are burglars, firebugs, pickpockets and highway robbers—when they
> have the courage; but though all crime is their province, pocket-picking is
> the one to which they take most naturally.

That so harsh an accusation should be made by a police commissioner struck all the Jewish leaders in the city as a sign of danger.* For weeks the

* A feeling reinforced by the fact that only a few months earlier they had gone through a severe conflict with the New York commissioner of immigration, William Williams, whom they also suspected of hostile sentiments toward Jews (see p. 55).

Yiddish press kept denouncing Bingham, charging anti-Semitic bias and offering an array of arguments and statistics to counter his. Statements poured out of every Jewish organization. Mass meetings of protest were held in the East Side halls. By mid-September, under severe pressure, Bingham retracted his charges "frankly and without reservation." The incident seemed now to be closed and Jewish pride vindicated, but among the more thoughtful Jews it still rankled. They knew, for one thing, that there *was* a crime problem on the East Side, not so lurid as Bingham had painted, but serious enough. And many felt that in responding to the crisis provoked by Bingham, the Jewish organizations had gone off in all directions, un-co-ordinated, often ill-spoken, and sometimes merely grabbing publicity. A number of Jewish leaders felt it was time to create a disciplined community structure or Kehilla, as it had been called in the old country.

The Kehilla, sometimes thriving, sometimes dormant in eastern Europe since the late Middle Ages, had been both necessity and burden, serving as the organ of Jewish communal self-rule and accepting the onerous task of administering decrees imposed by repressive governmental agencies. Often falling under the control of the wealthier Jews, it naturally became an object of contempt among the poorer ones. Most Jews had no very happy memories of the Kehilla as an institution, and many immigrants looked with distaste at the idea of reconstituting one in America.

Nevertheless, as a reaction to Jewish difficulties in coping with the Bingham incident, a movement grew up to create a New York Kehilla. Supporting this idea was a loose alliance of groups in the political center of the East Side, the nationalist, fraternal, and religous societies that wanted to carve out a position for themselves apart from the socialists on the left and the extreme Orthodox on the right. The German Jews, through the American Jewish Committee, also became interested—they had a taste for organization. An alliance was thereupon formed between men like Louis Marshall and Jacob Schiff from uptown and Joseph Barondess from downtown.

In 1909 a founding conference was held of representatives from synagogues, *landsmanshaftn*, Zionist branches, religious societies, and educational institutions. (The Jewish socialist and labor groups boycotted the meeting.) The Kehilla was proclaimed, with vague authorizations of power and a complicated relationship to the national office of the American Jewish Committee. It was fortunate, at the least, in finding as its leader a talented young Reform rabbi, Judah Magnes, whose energy and candor helped him to serve as a bridge between the German and the East European Jews.

Under Magnes, the Kehilla plunged into ambitious activities. A Bureau of Jewish Education was set up, which began to publish excellent modern textbooks, issue pedagogical materials, and offer aid to Hebrew teachers—this was probably the single greatest accomplishment of the Kehilla. Other bureaus were to deal with community problems, especially that of crime, and during William Gaynor's administration as mayor, the Kehilla provided confidential information about gambling and prostitution on the East Side, forcing these operations, which had been protected by the police for some years, to shut down at least temporarily.

The Kehilla flourished briefly, mostly because of Magnes's personal qualities and Jacob Schiff's financial generosity, but it never established its authority among the east European immigrants. The extreme Orthodox groups were hostile to any communal structure that claimed to transcend religion, while the socialists were hostile to any that claimed to transcend class interests. Even the sympathetic chronicler of the Kehilla, Arthur Goren, admits that "it did not fulfill its founders' goals," which, he says, were mostly "to control the unruly ghetto." Mordecai Kaplan, the leading Jewish theologian who worked for a time in the Kehilla, wrote in his journal that its essential role was that of a "Jewish social pacifier" trying to soothe the excitable East Side masses; but still far from ready to accept any sort of "social pacifier," they mostly ignored the Kehilla.

Even those East Siders who were not suspicious on ideological grounds felt the Kehilla to be something distant and aloof. Magnes, Schiff, and Marshall might be great men, but they were not one's own, not close to the streets and the shops; they might merit respect in general, but they did not need to be listened to in particular. Perhaps the lesson of this ambitious failure was that by the time it came on the scene the immigrants no longer really needed it. They had worked out agencies of their own—the unions, the *landsmanshaftn*, the Workmen's Circle—which made no claim for communal or ideological inclusiveness and for that very reason seemed more palatable.

The Failure of the Banks

A curious, if decidedly painful, sign of the gradual betterment of immigrant conditions was the rise of "private" Jewish banks. Neither the federal nor state governments were strict in the supervision of banks during the late nineteenth and early twentieth century. What is surprising is not that unscrupulous persons declared themselves bankers, but that only a rather small number did—perhaps because most immigrant Jews still held the very idea of banking in awe.

One of the earlier Jewish bankers, Joseph Marcus, began his career as owner of a clothing store at 102 East Broadway, where he opened his bank by setting up a cashier's desk and putting an advertisement in the Yiddish papers. Known as an honest man, Marcus simply announced that his word was the guarantee of his reliability. From this unimposing start grew the Public National Bank, of which Marcus was the first president, and then the

Bank of the United States, run by his sons and in the early thirties the victim of a spectacular collapse.

Other popular banks on the East Side during the years before the First World War were run by M. and L. Yarmulowsky, Adolf Mandel, and Max Kobre. The methods of these men were unorthodox by American standards: they would themselves be present almost every day at their banks, reassuring depositors and assuaging the uneasiness that many East Side immigrants felt at the thought of putting their money in someone else's hands. Sometimes, recalls a Yiddish journalist, "they would try to prevent their customers from withdrawing money. . . . A shopgirl would want to take out a hundred dollars to get married, and the banker would say, 'What's the hurry? You're still young, you can wait a few years.' " How some immigrants felt about the whole unnerving matter has been described by the Yiddish novelist I. Raboy, whose protagonist Jacob, becoming prosperous in the shirt business,

> brought his money to two banks. He brought the larger sums to the big "National," which was purely American. Every time Jacob walked in there he was filled with fear. He gives them the money, they make a record of it, and Jacob leaves with the feeling that he is making the bank rich, and yet *he* has to thank *them*. . . . Jacob loves to bring a small amount of cash into the Jewish bank on Rivington Street. The president of the bank himself stands behind the table, greets him cordially, and smiles. Jacob doesn't have as much respect for this bank, and deposits only as much as he needs to run the shop. . . . It is good to have money in two banks.

By 1912–1913 the East Side banks had accumulated considerable assets, but rumors began to spread that they were not in satisfactory condition. "Runs" were frequent, though not yet catastrophic. The outbreak of the war, however, led many Jewish depositors to withdraw their money, partly out of a general sense of alarm, and partly because they wanted to send help to relatives trapped in Europe. This time, the "runs" were uncontrollable, and on August 4, 1914, the state superintendent of banks ordered the Yarmulowsky and Mandel banks closed: they were, he said, "in an unsound and unsatisfactory condition." A day later the Kobre bank was closed. Thousands of immigrant depositors, some openly weeping, milled around the doors of the banks, trying to get their money or at least hear some reassuring word from the presidents who had always been so cordial. It was too late.

Their records showed that the banks had managed investments poorly. Too large a portion of their assets was frozen into real-estate holdings that had gone down in value and could not be liquidated without large losses. The assets of Mandel fell $1,250,000 below liabilities; the assets of Yarmulowsky were $654,000 and his liabilities $1,703,000; the assets of Kobre $3,041,000 and his liabilities $3,844,000.

For the East Side, these closings came as a shock: some fifty thousand people had put $10,000,000 of savings, mostly the fruits of working-class self-denial, into these banks. On August 5, two thousand people demonstrated in front of Yarmulowsky's bank; three days later riots broke out in front of Kobre's Brownsville branch, and one hundred policemen were called to restrain a mob of fifteen hundred enraged depositors. Kobre took out an advertisement in the *Forward* saying, "Your friend Max Kobre still lives . . . and as long as I do, no one will lose a penny. Just have patience. This misfortune will not last long." On August 30 another demonstration of five thousand people ended in a riot.

Grief, anger, a growing militancy, perhaps merely despair. On September 27, five hundred people gathered in front of M. Yarmulowsky's apartment, forcing him and his family to flee—they climbed up to the roof and escaped from an adjoining house. The next day about a thousand demonstrators massed in front of Mandel's house, and the reserves had to be called out. Three hundred depositors stormed the office of District Attorney Whitman on October 10 and were ejected by the police. At least half a dozen suicides occurred among the depositors, and both the *Forward* and the *Tageblatt* ran heart-rending accounts of suffering among depositors left penniless.

In May 1915 Mandel was convicted of having accepted a deposit after he knew the bank was insolvent; crowds of his victims stood in front of the courthouse and cheered the jury's verdict. As for Yarmulowsky and Kobre, the former received a suspended sentence and the latter committed suicide in 1916. In time, the depositors received partial payment of their money.

Burned by their experiences, immigrants soon learned to be skeptical of home-grown operators casually setting up banks. Yet this episode of the Jewish banks testified not merely to inexperience and shady dealings but also to mounting social and economic strength. Thousands of immigrants were able to put aside a few dollars in the banks; they did not accept the debacle passively, as they might have a few decades earlier; they fought back, demonstrated, rioted, made life miserable for the district attorney; in short, learned the rules, and how to go beyond the rules, of group pressure in America.

Beginnings of a Bourgeoisie

By about 1912 the East Side was still a badly overcrowded area, but, together with some economic betterment, there were the beginnings of physical improvement. Asphalt replaced rougher paving materials in the streets; along the East River, piers were built that could be used for recreation; little parks—there would never be enough of them—were opened; and new schools and libraries, some strikingly handsome in design, were erected.

How substantial was the improvement in the conditions of Jewish immigrant life? Was there a genuine rise in the standard of living, or was the easing of life mostly the result of bettered public facilities? Such questions are as difficult to answer as they are essential to ask. Comprehensive and authoritative statistical studies would be immensely comforting, but we do not have them. A scrutiny of what we do have persuades one that reliance on fragmentary statistics can be quite as misleading as the use of such "soft" data as contemporary journalism, memoirs, historical narratives, and sociological studies. In any case, there is little choice. We have to employ these materials, even as we remember the Yiddish proverb that "for example is no proof." And enough examples may approximate a proof.

All accounts of the East Side during the early 1900's stress the rise of an immigrant bourgeoisie—small, far less powerful than that of the German Jews, very distant from the centers of American wealth, yet fiercely energetic and ambitious. The classical work on this theme is Abraham Cahan's *The Rise of David Levinsky*, a novel in which the moral costs of success are measured with a stringent irony; this book is matched, at least thematically, by some hasty sketches Cahan wrote in 1906 and 1907 about the *alrightniks*, immigrants who had just become wealthy and were enjoying their ill-suited luxuries. In his memoirs, Cahan recalls searching for a word that might evoke their absurd qualities. Reminding himself of the colloquial expression, "he's all right," Cahan coined the term *alrightnik*—thereby adding a word to two languages simultaneously.

One of Cahan's sketches is entitled "Mr. Burek [Beet] Learns to Make a Speech": A real-estate operator, as he grows wealthier, finds himself invited to give more and more speeches. Alone before a mirror, he practices addressing the audience, coughing (to make the speech more of a speech), and talking about America: "It is a country where one does business, and not like in Europe, oh no, ladies and gentlemen! Europe don't come up to America in real estate and competition and pinochle. I have been in this business for only a short time but have already crushed all my competitors." Another sketch is called "He Pretends Not to Know Him," and describes a meeting between Mr. Lifshitz, skirt manufacturer, and Yoine, skirtmaker. They are *landslayt*, and in the old country their roles were quite reversed. But here, in the land of *alrightniks*, poor Yoine has to plead for a job: "For a long time his old pride struggled with his present need. Need won out." When he goes to Lifshitz's office, the latter pretends he is trying to remember who this Yoine is. "Yoine smiled to himself." A third sketch, "The Living Tunnel," ridicules the pretensions of *alrightnik* wives. Two of them meet in the street, and are dressed in what an American comedian calls the latest style: the kind of dress that resembles a mountain in the rear and juts out in front, so that if half of the woman is near you, the other half is in the next block. As they talk, two little boys pass by, pulling a wagon they pretend is a train. Suddenly one of the little boys cries out, "Look, a tunnel," and drives the wagon between the two ladies.

Cahan was reacting to the fact that a segment of immigrant manufacturers and contractors, digging itself into the garment industry, had begun to adopt a style of ostentation that evoked both the annoyance and the laughter of the East Side. By 1900 Jewish dominance of the garment industry was all but complete; over 90 percent of it was in Jewish hands. The east European Jews were taking long strides toward driving their German cousins out of the industry—this was not a milieu notable for delicacy of relations. "Several well-known [German-Jewish] firms, Meyer Jonasson & Co., Blumenthal Bros., F. Siegel & Co., Friedlander Bros. and others left the field to become bankers, wholesale cloth merchants, or department store owners. The Moths of Division Street, as the Russian contractors were called, had forced the German giants of Broadway to retreat." Between 1900 and 1912 the number of women's garment shops in New York and its environs increased from 1,856 to 5,698; the number employing up to nineteen workers, from 898 to 3,828; and there can be no question that the vast preponderance of these employers was now made up of east European Jews.

Some of the immigrants grew rich. Samuel Silverman, beginning as a sweatshop worker, became a cloak manufacturer with a fortune estimated at $500,000. Harris Mandelbaum, starting as a peddler, worked his way up to a cool million by the steady purchase of tenement houses. Harry Fischel, penniless on arriving in New York, became a millionaire through the building industry and real estate, constructing a $60,000 residence for himself a block away from Andrew Carnegie's Fifth Avenue mansion. Nathan Hurtkoff, starting with a tiny glazier's shop on Canal Street, ended as one of the largest plate-glass merchants in New York. Israel Lebowitz moved from peddling to a modest "gents furnishing shop" on Orchard Street and by 1907 was one of the largest shirt manufacturers in New York. There were dozens, perhaps scores, of other newly rich east European Jews.

Impressive as these achievements were if placed against the backdrop of immigrant life, they remained inconsequential in comparison with the wealth of either the German Jews or the American elite. The east Europeans shied away from the mainstream of American economy, or, to be more precise, had no chance to approach it. They had nothing to do with the major industries and very little with Wall Street; they were confined to light manufacturing, distributive industries, and real estate.

Of greater consequence for the East Side as a whole, though impossible to measure with exactness, was the growth of a middle class of independent businessmen, small traders, storekeepers, and the like—much of it hand-to-mouth in character. A rough indication: *Trow's Business Directory* for 1899 lists about 175 cleaning stores in Manhattan and the Bronx, a fair minority of which seem to be owned by non-Jews. By 1909 the same directory lists about 500 such stores, with the names of owners overwhelmingly Jewish.

Such pursuits having been central to the Jewish economy of eastern Europe, it was only natural that they be transported across the ocean. But it was not merely custom that led many Jews to feel that owning their own little business was better than seeking posts in larger enterprise. "The American Jew," writes Nathan Glazer, "tries to avoid getting into a situation where discrimination may seriously affect him. . . . [He] prefers a situation where his own merit receives objective confirmation, and he is not dependent on the good will or personal reaction of a person who may not happen to like Jews. This independent confirmation of merit is one of the chief characteristics of business as against corporate bureaucracy."

There was little occasion in 1905 or 1910 for Jews to worry about the problems of working in a corporate bureaucracy, yet Glazer's explanation for the attractiveness of running one's own business, no matter how burdensome, is very much to the point. To shake loose from the domination of a boss, to be free from the stares and sneers of gentiles, to take the risks of using one's own wits and gaining the rewards of one's own work—this became a commanding desire among the immigrant Jews, as indeed, among Jews everywhere and no doubt for the same reasons.

In 1904 William English Walling, then a worker at the University Settlement, wrote a fine paper entitled "What the People of the Lower East Side Do." Basing his conclusions on Census Bureau statistics, Walling found that "the favorite pursuits of the East Side after as before Americanization are, first, the professions, second, business, and third, manual labor." The second generation, he wrote, "leaves the sweatshop."

> The boys of the second generation do not work with their hands. This does not of course apply to all, but it does apply to a majority. Perhaps the principal occupations of the second generation are commercial and clerical. Especially numerous are the salesmen; many young boys under 21 are traveling all over the United States. . . .
>
> Next come the professions. The teachers are numbered by the thousand, the lawyers by the hundred and the doctors by hardly a smaller number. . . . In some of the law schools almost nine-tenths of the students are said to be Jews. In the College of the City of New York, which prepares for all sorts of professional studies, the proportion is not much less.
>
> Of those who do remain at manual labor, a considerable proportion go into the skilled trades. So we find among the plumbers, steamfitters and others of the more advanced building trades a large number of immigrant Jews. But a far greater number go directly into business—real estate, insurance and all forms of retail and wholesale trade. In the matter of preference, professional pursuits stand first and commercial second.

Walling's opening generalization that "the second generation leaves the sweatshop" requires more amendment than he provides; nevertheless, his perception of the over-all *long-range* trend was accurate. Other studies point to similar trends. In a paper entitled "Religious and Occupational

sterreichisches Staatsarchiv/Kriegsarchiv, Vienna

A *shtetl* scene: Jewish poverty in eastern Europe

Österreichisches Staatsarchiv/Kriegsarchiv, Vienna

The market place of an east European town: peasants have come
to trade; their horses and wagons stand at rest.

Roman Vishniac

An examination at a yeshiva in Carpathian Ruthenia

sterreichisches Staatsarchiv/Kriegsarchiv, Vienna

Drawing water at the village well

A group of *fusgeyer*, on their way to the United States,
pose for a picture somewhere in Romania.

Museum of the City of New York

Immigrants packed aboard
the S.S. *Westernland, c.* 1890

Steerage passengers on the
S.S. *Pennland* come up for air,
c. 1900.

The Granger Collection, New York

Courtesy of the Public Health Service

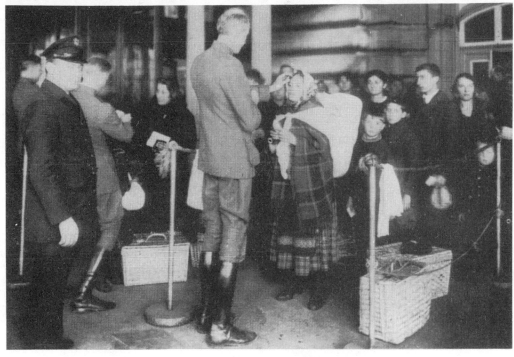

A Public Health Service officer at Ellis Island administers the eye test,
much feared by immigrants.

An immigrant girl encounters the stethoscope at Ellis Island.

Brown Brothers

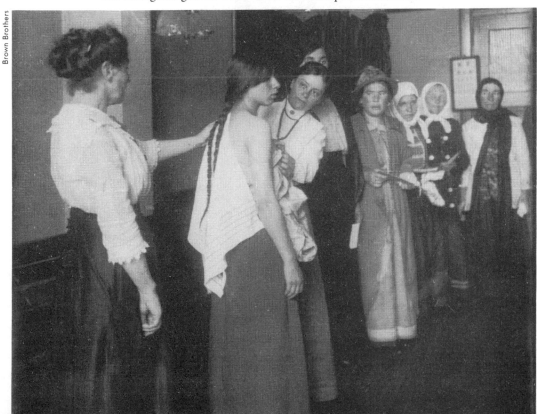

Sy Seidm

Castle Garden, the first major
reception center in New York for
arriving immigrants, in 1896

An immigrant woman
leaving Ellis Island, *c.* 1900

The Granger Collection, New York

Peddlers and customers on Hester Street, 1899

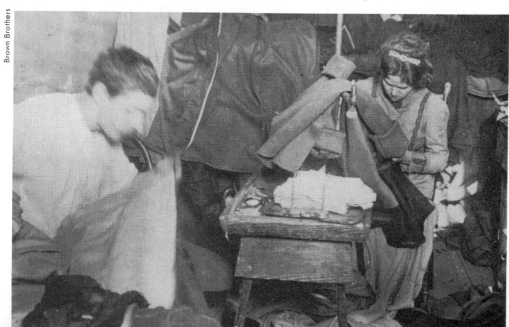

Museum of the City of New York

Sabbath eve in a coal cellar, Ludlow Street

An East Side tenement becomes a sweatshop.

Brown Brothers

The Granger Collection, New York

Children doing exercises in Seward Park, 1904

Courtesy of YIVO Institute for Jewish Research

A labor demonstration winding into Union Square, in the 1880's

Another labor rally, Union Square, 1908

Brown Brothers

Courtesy of the Visiting Nurse Service of New York

Lillian Wald,
nurse to the unfortunate

Joseph Barondess,
tribune of early Jewish unionism

Courtesy of YIVO Institute for Jewish Research

Courtesy of the Visiting Nurse Service of New York

One of Lillian Wald's nurses takes a short cut across a tenement roof,
on the way to a patient, 1908.

The Granger Collection, New York

Shopping on Hester Street, 1898

Checking out the bargains, 1898

Museum of the City of New York

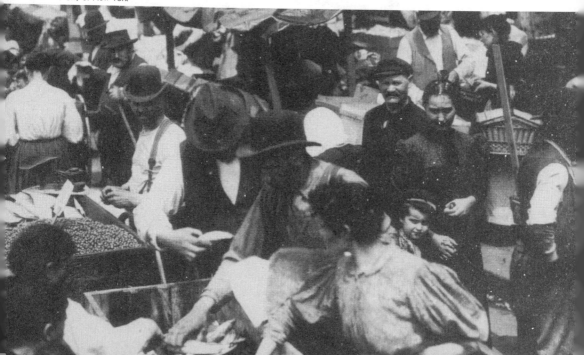

Mobility in Boston, 1880–1963," Stephan Thernstrom has drawn on a range of statistics for comparing members of the three major religious denominations in Boston with regard to occupational status and mobility. In the Jewish group for 1860–1879, most of them German Jews, 73 percent started with white-collar jobs; in the 1880–1889 Jewish group, the percentage starting to work at white-collar jobs dropped to 43, no doubt because the sample included a large number of recently arrived immigrants from eastern Europe who lacked both language and skills for clerical employment; but by the 1900–1909 group, the percentage of Jews starting with white-collar jobs had risen to 71. Thernstrom concludes:

> Popular folklore concerning the mobility achievements of the Jews is indeed well-founded. Not only did an unusually high proportion of Jewish youths in Boston start their careers in the upper reaches of the occupational structure; those who were forced to work in blue collar callings at the outset were extraordinarily successful at moving into the white collar world later. Only about half of the Jews who began their careers as laborers . . . were still employed in manual work at the time of the last job. The Jewish rate of upward mobility was double that of other groups.

As we shall see, the sparse evidence we have concerning occupational mobility of New York Jews for the same decades would seem to indicate that their social ascent was not as rapid or steep as in Boston, perhaps because the immigrant population of New York was more heavily working-class than in other cities. Nevertheless, the main elements of the picture—admittedly, a roughly drawn picture—seem clear: a very thin crust of wealthy people, the beginnings of a substantial middle class, a considerable number of petty tradesmen often no better off than shopworkers, and a majority continuing to earn their livelihood as workers, about half of them in the garment trades. These, we may say with reasonable assurance, characterize immigrant Jewish life in New York, though not perhaps in some other cities and certainly not in small towns, during the years immediately after 1900.

What the Census Shows

A social profile of the East Side immigrants emerges from a body of statistics gathered in the New York State 1905 census and sifted by Herbert Gutman and his associates. The 1905 census takers asked a number of useful questions, though it is a pity they did not ask more. All members of a household were listed, from its male or female head through its youngest members, extended relatives, and boarders. Their ages, occupations, countries of origin, and length of stay in the United States, whether as aliens or citizens, were also provided. It thereby becomes possible to gain a partial but relatively precise view of the socioeconomic conditions of some immigrant Jews at a crucial point in their history.

Sifting the data for a number of tenement houses—from 232 to 244, six houses in all—on Cherry Street, one of the poorest streets on the East Side, we have a population of about 675 people, living in three- and four-room apartments—that is, an average occupancy of 5.6 people per apartment. The occupational scale is heavily weighted toward blue-collar work. Of 118 heads of households, 52 can be categorized as garment workers, 36 as other manuals (ranging from day laborers to building-trade workers), and 15 are peddlers. This comes to a total of 103 heads of households in proletarian or sub- and semiproletarian occupations. Of the remaining 15, there are 6 small-business men, 3 rabbis, 5 housewives (widows or deserted wives), one professional (a teacher), and not a single white-collar worker. Living with these 118 families are 92 boarders, some apartments containing as many as 3. Of these 92 boarders, 75 live with families headed by garment workers and other manual workers; the boarders themselves do similar kinds of work. The overwhelming majority of wives stay at home, whether for immediate socioeconomic or received cultural reasons; only 2 out of the 118 are listed as employed (both as housekeepers).

The majority of these families in Cherry Street are young, in their twenties and thirties, and consist of immigrants who have recently arrived— the bulk within the previous six years. As a consequence they are mainly one-income families—about 60 percent of them have one income, about 40 percent more than one. Those with multiple incomes include, of course, parents in their middle and later years.

Among adults over forty, 16 are citizens while 62 remain aliens, apparently indicating that there is a considerable correlation among immigrants between economic improvement and the taking out of citizenship (a point to be confirmed later). Checking the occupations of those heads of households who have been in the United States more than five years, we find 15 garment workers, 11 other manuals, 5 peddlers, 5 businessmen, and 18 housewives—which would seem to indicate that there is no decisive correlation between length of time in the United States and economic improvement, as well as the equally suggestive conclusion that, at least in this poorer segment of the East Side, there is a persistence over the years in the blue-collar occupations.

Perhaps the most interesting figures have to do with the occupational status of the children. Those under fifteen are all listed as "At School," while almost all in their later teens work. It is a striking fact that, at this point, few children of these Jewish workers can be said to be rising economically: three are bookkeepers (a rise to white-collar status), one is a clerk, and one a hat saleslady. Some of these young people may be going to night school or college; unfortunately, the census does not tell. But as far as the information provided goes, there is no sign of the expected pattern of immigrant sons entering white-collar occupations, becoming businessmen, or going to college. Most sons continue to work in trades like those of their fathers; and there are even a few occupational changes that can be regarded as a drop in social level, the son of a teacher becoming a garment cutter and the daughter of a rabbi a garment operator (though if the teacher is a Hebrew teacher and the rabbi receives the salary most immigrant rabbis can expect, their children are probably bringing home more money than the parents).

One crucial factor in regard to the children of immigrants is whether they themselves are native or foreign born, since the former are more likely to rise socially and economically than the latter. And indeed, on Cherry Street, of the 85 children (under twenty-one) who work, mostly in blue-collar occupations, 72, or almost 85 percent, are foreign and only 13 native born.

What these figures about the Cherry Street tenements suggest, though they cannot be said conclusively to demonstrate, is that among the immigrant Jews there was forming a social segment that could be described as *a semipermanent working class:* its members did not themselves rise in economic or social level and apparently their children did not rise quite as rapidly or in as large numbers as has commonly been supposed, or as the Thernstrom study shows for Boston. Now, it is true that some of these adolescents and young people who began their work careers in blue-collar occupations probably did rise economically in later years, by becoming small-business men, finding jobs that freed them from the more onerous aspects of being a worker, or completing a part-time education so as belatedly to enter professions. But it seems safe to say that during the early years of this century any assumption of a direct and large-scale social ascent from an immigrant generation of workers to a second generation of doctors, lawyers, and teachers needs to be treated with caution. Probably it was the sons and daughters of those young people remaining in blue-collar occupations who, a quarter of a century and more later, did make the leap into the middle and professional classes.

In striking contrast to Cherry Street is East Broadway, the most prosperous thoroughfare on the East Side. In a group of buildings containing 260 people—buildings 204 through 216, or seven in all—there are 37 families. Only 18 boarders live with them, coming to a much smaller percentage of the population than on Cherry Street. The average occupancy per apartment is 7, decidedly greater than on Cherry Street, but we know the East Broadway apartments were more spacious and had more rooms than those on the surrounding streets. Of the 37 heads of families in the East Broadway houses, there are 4 garment workers, 5 other manuals, one peddler, one rabbi, one city employee, 2 retired, 2 white-collar, 7 professional, and 11 businessmen. (This last category, in regard to all streets, is very loose, since it includes both garment manufacturers and small candy-store keepers.) Living in the East Broadway houses are 12 servants, approximately one to every third apartment—clearly a sign of middle-class styles of life. Most of these servants are young girls who have recently come over from Europe; many of them will marry or find other occupations.

In the age group twenty-one to forty, among those living in these East Broadway houses, there are 55 citizens and 21 aliens; in the age group of forty and above there are 25 citizens and 10 aliens. Here, the correlation between citizenship and economic betterment seems more visible than on Cherry Street.

Most significant of all is the evidence that on East Broadway children of immigrant Jews do rise economically. Among the sons and daughters living at home with their parents are two lawyers, two typists, two nurses, two salesmen, six bookkeepers, one teacher, two doctors, two dentists, one real-estate man, two girls attending "normal schools," and five other students, three of them at CCNY. Here we do find the pattern that has come to be assumed as prevalent in immigrant Jewish life: a rather sharp social ascent within the space of two generations.

Between East Broadway and Cherry Street there is a considerable social distance; it may therefore be worth examining the statistics of streets that lie, socially, somewhere between them. A close inspection of several groups of tenement houses on Rutgers, Rivington, Madison, and Henry streets, the first three of which are the usual residential slum streets, and the last, still containing a few town houses, is a somewhat "better" street, shows a pattern fairly close to that of Cherry Street, though with a somewhat more fluid mobility from generation to generation. On Rivington Street we find a Jewish fireman with a doctor son; on Madison, a tinsmith with a pianist daughter; on Henry, several families with servants. The number of young people on these streets working in white-collar occupations is notably higher than on Cherry Street. Again, however, no evidence can be found for the commonly held notion that there occurs a sudden and massive ascent of the children of immigrants to professional and middle-class status; the process, though it will occur over the subsequent decades, seems to be more gradual and difficult than has usually been supposed.

A Slow Improvement

To what extent, we may finally ask, was there an improvement in the socioeconomic conditions of the immigrant Jewish workers during the years of the great migration? There have been two major studies of real wages in the United States for the years between 1890 and 1914, the first by Paul Douglas (1930) and the second by Albert Rees (1961). Since they diverge on crucial points, it is worth examining them in order.

According to Douglas, "until 1914 the wage earners in the clothing industry had received no increase in real wages and were on about the same footing as during the period 1890–1899." Using 100 as the base average for 1890–1899, Douglas calculated the "relative real hourly earnings" in the clothing industry as 95 in 1890, 101 in 1895, 98 in 1900, 103 in 1905, 102 in 1910. The first major increase, says Douglas, occurred in 1913, when the figure rose to 126; the next major increase came in 1920, when it rose to 166. "The relative increase in the money earnings of the clothing workers prior to 1914 was approximately the same as that obtained by employees in manufacturing as a whole." But the comparative position of clothing to other industries was poor. In 1890, weekly earnings in the clothing industry averaged $7.97, as compared with $9.78 for lumber, $10.46 for meat packing, and $15.39 for iron and steel. By 1910 weekly earnings in the clothing industry averaged $10.32, the money increase over the previous thirty years being about the same as in other industries.

Albert Rees's study, while not seriously challenging Douglas on money wages, takes issue with the assumption that "real wages from 1890 to 1914 were essentially stationary." The crucial difference between the two is in their ways of estimating the cost of living. Rees uses more refined indexes of retail prices for clothing and home furnishings than Douglas, as well as "an index of rents based on newspaper advertisements. The inclusion of rents and the correspondingly lower weight given to food account for the largest part of the differences between [the Rees] cost-of-living index and the Douglas index." Hence, "our index of the cost of living rises appreciably less than Douglas's," and in consequence, "we find that the real earnings of manufacturing workers rose 37 percent from 1890 to 1914, or at an annual compound rate of 1.3 percent." Yet Rees is careful to add that "the finding of an increase in real wages in no way denies the importance of immigration" as a factor "holding down the rate of increase in real wages during this period when compared with equivalent periods before and after."

It would be imprudent for a nonspecialist to pass judgment as to the relative merits of these two studies, though the consensus among economists appears to be that Rees's work significantly supplants that of Douglas. What seems beyond dispute is that the historical, anecdotal, and memoir literature supports the conclusion that in the years between 1890 and 1914 there occurred among immigrant Jewish workers a modest rise in the standard of living, such as Rees's study indicates.*

---

* A few additional factors, special to the clothing industry and the condition of the immigrant Jews, may be cited:

1. Douglas's statistics take into account only hourly wages, the dominant mode of payment in the garment industry; they do not consider salaried employees. In the

We may say, then, with a fair degree of probability, that in the two decades between 1890 and 1910 facilities and amenities for a good many (not all) residents of the East Side did improve slowly and moderately; that, as a result of legislation, inspection, and unionization, there was a slow and moderate improvement in conditions of work in the garment and other Jewish industries (with working hours zigzagging erratically, in some years dropping to a humane level but in the "busy" season rising to sixty per week and more—as late as 1910 the union in the women's garment trade was "demanding" a forty-nine-hour week); and that because of the strenuous efforts by Jewish immigrants to rise on the socioeconomic scale, conditions of life did improve for a good many of them, but again slowly and moderately. A

men's clothing industry alone, according to the 1914 census of manufacturers, the number of salaried employees increased from 33,245 in 1904 to 61,919 in 1914, with total salaries going up from $31,600,000 to $76,400,000. In the women's clothing industry, the number of salaried employees increased from 10,900 in 1904 to 22,200 in 1914, with total salaries going up from $9,900,000 to $26,100,000 in the same period. Even if Douglas were right about the general trend of real wages, the rise in status from wage to salaried employment for 40,000 people in the garment industry, many of them surely immigrant Jews and employed in New York, would be a significant factor in improving the socioeconomic conditions of the Jewish community.
2. Douglas's figures for real wages refer to the clothing industry as a whole and do not take into account the trend toward increased specialization within the industry —which means that there would be an increasingly wide range of earnings. Dr. Jesse Pope, in his 1905 study of the garment industry, reported that cutters, the most skilled workers in the trade, enjoyed an increase of between 20 and 42 percent in real wages between 1883 and 1902—the variation in percentages being caused by place and kind of employment. Vestmakers, a much less skilled group of needle-trade workers, earned, by contrast, about the same real wages in 1901 as in 1894, again according to Pope.
3. It seems probable, as is suggested both by the Immigration Commission Reports and by Isaac Hourwich in his 1912 study, *Immigration and Labor,* that with the influx of new immigrants, the inferior jobs fell to them while older, more experienced workers rose in skill, rank, and income. The Immigration Commission reported that with the exception of those earning less than $10 a week, there was a very general tendency for the proportion of each race earning each specified amount per week to increase with years in the United States.
4. By the turn of the century, a considerable number of Italian immigrants, many of them women, had started to work in the needle trades. Almost all of them received rock-bottom wages and performed the least skilled work. By contrast, the more skilled jobs in the industry, especially the cutters', were held by Jews. Therefore it seems reasonable to say that even if Douglas were right in his conclusion that real wages in the garment industry did not increase between 1890 and 1914, they probably did for a significant portion of Jewish garment workers.
5. For the above conclusion there is some statistical warrant. When the Immigration Commission study on wages was begun, in 1907, the average weekly wage in the garment industry for males over eighteen was $13.30. At that time only 23.9 percent of east European Jewish males resident in the United States for less than five years were earning well over the average ($15 or more), while 45.2 percent of those in the United States from five to nine years and 64.1 percent of those here for over ten years were earning more than the average in the garment industry.
     John Dyche, a leader of the garment workers' union, wrote in 1909: "There is not a cloak or a skirt shop where one cannot find one set of workers making $30 to $40 a week, while the majority makes only from $10 to $12 a week."

sharp rise in real wages did not, however, come until shortly after the First World War, due to the mutually reinforcing factors of economic boom and strengthened unionism. Until then, life for the great mass of Jewish immigrants remained hard.

CHAPTER FIVE

Slum and Shop

Even when life eased a little, even when husbands worked regularly and there was enough food on the table, the physical conditions of the slums were appalling. This was the one major element of their lives about which the immigrants could do little or nothing, at least until they had enough money to leave the East Side or, a bit later, Williamsburg and the east Bronx.

A 1908 census of 250 typical East Side families showed that fewer than a quarter of them slept two in a room; about 50 percent slept three or four in a room; and nearly 25 percent, five or more in a room. Toilet facilities, two to a floor at best and foul privies at worst, allowing neither the simplicities of nature nor the conveniences of civilization, added to the sense of people intolerably packed together. So did the clutter of buildings, the lack of ground space, the clamor of drays, refuse carts, grocery wagons. Perhaps worst was the assault of smells: the odors of human waste only intermittently carted away from back-yard privies by a careless sanitation department, the stench of fish and meat starting to rot on pushcarts, the foulness of neglected sewers and gutters. Life was abrasive, clamorous. Even if the immigrants had arrived with impeccable sanitary habits, they could not have won the battle against dirt and decay. By 1898 the Tenth Ward, only a bit more than a half square mile, bulged with a population of 82,000. As late as 1910 Manhattan had 2,500 six-story walk-ups, 14,797 basement apartments, and 25,753 tenement rooms without windows—of which the East Side had a good deal more than its share.

Only gradually did a tradition emerge in the American cities of taking public responsibility for the health of the poor. Though New York did not have a Board of Health until 1868, its first commissioner, Dr. Stephen Smith, was an admirable man who did whatever he could to alleviate suffering in the slums. He founded training schools for visiting nurses and wrote the first bill for state care of the insane; he arranged for free smallpox vaccinations; he inaugurated, in 1892, New York's first public campaign against tuberculosis. Following in his footsteps were such dedicated people as Lillian Wald, responsible for the hiring of nurses in the public schools; Nathan Strauss, instrumental in providing clean and cheap milk for children; George Waring, who from 1890 to 1898 built a street-cleaning department equipped to handle even the East Side, "a region entirely neglected in previous years."

Immigrant Jews were most susceptible to illnesses caused by overwork —neurasthenia, hysteria, breakdown. Suicide, infrequent in eastern Europe, became a serious problem in the new world, apparently an outcome, in extreme cases, of dislocation and an inability to adapt to new circumstances. On the East Side the most feared of all diseases was tuberculosis, or, as it was then called, "the white plague." Encouraged by overcrowding and lack of sanitation, tuberculosis by 1906 was afflicting twelve out of every thousand Jews living on the East Side. It came to be regarded as "a Jewish disease," or "the tailors' disease"—not only was it the disease that Jews feared most and could imagine most strongly, but the whole culture seemed to have a consumptive flush, trembling with that overwrought sensibility Thomas Mann would take to be one of the "positive" signs of the disease.

Though it would remain a serious problem until well after the First World War, tuberculosis caused fewer deaths among Jews than non-Jews. In the early 1900's, east European Jews in the United States showed a death rate from tuberculosis of about half that of the native-born population, and from half to a third of that among the non-Jewish groups immediately surrounding them. In hardly any other branch of social service was the Jewish community as active or emotionally involved as in the effort to care for its tuberculars. Early in the century there were established a number of Jewish sanitariums, the major ones being those of the Workmen's Circle in Liberty, New York, and the Denver Sanitarium, organized in 1904 by a committee of immigrant and native-born Jews. For many years one could find *pushkes* (collection boxes) for the Denver Sanitarium in stores, meeting halls, and homes in Jewish neighborhoods. The Denver Sanitarium was perhaps the best known of these tuberculosis hospitals,* but by 1922 there were places for over 1,100 patients in Jewish sanitariums throughout the country. Even so, the demand for beds was so great that most applicants had to wait several months before being admitted.

Despite the weight of these troubles, the immigrant Jews seem to have ended with a better health record than did other immigrant groups. In an 1890 New York census of vital statistics, death rates in predominantly gentile areas west of the Bowery are higher than death rates in predominantly Jewish areas east of the Bowery. The same pattern is repeated with regard to serious diseases, like pneumonia and diphtheria, and diseases attacking children under five.

Why this should have been so is mostly a matter of speculation. Perhaps because the Jews had behind them a long tradition of self-denial which had prepared them for still another ordeal; perhaps because their habits of abstinence spared them the ravages of alcohol; perhaps because *kashruth* protected them from certain diseases carried by pig's meat; perhaps because their training in self-help quickly prompted them to establish clinics, hospitals, and sanitariums; perhaps because their closely knit family structure brought them to a quicker concern for symptoms of illness (as well as to a certain shared hypochondria); and perhaps because Jews have had an overwhelming reverence for doctors, which made them regard medical aid as their first need.

The most visible threat to the health of the Jewish immigrant was the tenement, a mode of housing that in New York goes back to the earliest decades of the nineteenth century, when the raw and rapidly expanding metropolis of less than 200,000 people began to absorb waves of Irish and German immigrants. Many of these people settled in the Wall Street area and on Cherry Hill, a once attractive East Side neighborhood reduced to a slum by the end of the Jackson administration. With the further arrival of thousands of immigrants in the 1840's, row after row of single-family residences were transformed into multiple-dwelling units. No New York building proved too grand to be spared this fate. The house quartering President

---

* In the early twenties the Denver patients published a monthly magazine in Yiddish and English entitled *Hatikvah* ("hope" in Hebrew) which contained news items, gossip, health reports, jokes, and even bits of verse:

> He's a lunger
> Awfully pale,
> Thirty years old
> Thin as a rail.
> One eye black
> One eye glass,
> One leg wood
> The other brass.
> Teeth all out
> Ribs caved in,
> He's a darn good scout
> For the shape he's in.

Washington during his first years in office was reduced to a squalid tenement well before the Civil War. The Walton House on Pearl Street, with interior columns made of solid mahogany and regarded in colonial days as the most handsome in the city, was packed by the 1860's with Irish immigrants.

Throughout the nineteenth century, few building standards or regulations controlled tenement construction. A mushrooming of slums in Manhattan created filth and squalor equal to the worst in Europe or Asia. Even before the East Side became a Jewish quarter, tenements spread through its streets—as also in Cherry Hill, Five Points, and Mulberry Bend to the south; the "Bloody Sixth" west of the Bowery; and the Negro sections of Greenwich Village to the north. By the Civil War these areas had begun to take on a uniform cast, with gray brick boxes three stories or higher replacing colonial structures. Some faced the streets; others, often no more than a yard or two away, rested on rear lots.

The first Tenement House Act of 1867, riddled with loopholes, mattered mainly as a promise of things to come. All tenements were required to have fire escapes—or some other means of exit; cesspools were forbidden—except where unavoidable; water closets and privies had to connect with sewers—where such existed; a landlord was obligated to provide only one privy or water closet for every twenty inhabitants. Worst of all, insufficient funds were provided for enforcement, thereby establishing for the next half-century a pattern of failing to live up to regulations that were inadequate to begin with.*

The next important push for tenement reform occurred in an unlikely place: the pages of Henry C. Meyer's trade journal, *The Plumber and Sanitary Engineer*. In 1878 Meyer announced a prize competition for a tenement on a 25-by-100-foot lot, with the award going to the design that best combined maximum safety and convenience for the tenant with maximum profit for the investor (a formula always likely to lead to disaster). First prize was awarded to the dumbbell design of James E. Ware, which soon would become synonymous with the worst features of New York slum housing.

* Some sense of how difficult it was to enforce regulations is given in an 1896 letter from Jacob Riis to Lillian Wald:

My Dear Miss Wald,
    Over 10,000 orders to light dark hallways have been issued since spring by the Board of Health, and probably 50,000 more will have to be issued before the landlords trouble. I took a trip with Mr. Wilson (the President of the Board) early in the summer, through Eastside tenements to show him that the trouble was with the policeman who didn't know a dark hall when he saw it. Orders were then issued to the police to recognize the fact that they could *not* see whether the floor was dirty or not, or whether they were running a baby down, as evidence that the hall was *dark* in the meaning of the law. . . . I think we shall get the best of the evil in your section by degrees, for this is one of the things which may be reformed and unreformed again in five months.

It is [wrote Jacob Riis] the one hopeless form of tenement construction. It cannot be well ventilated, it cannot be well lighted; it is not safe in case of fire. It is built on a lot 25 feet wide by 100 or less in depth, with apartments for four families in each story. This necessitates the occupation of from 86 to 90 percent of the lot's depth. The stairway, made in the center of the house, and the necessary walls and partitions reduce the width of the middle rooms (which serve as bedrooms for at least two people each) to nine feet each at the most, and a narrow light and airshaft, now legally required in the center of each side wall, still further lessens the floor space of these middle rooms. Direct light is only possible for the rooms at the front or rear. The middle rooms must borrow what light they can from dark hallways, the shallow shafts, and the rear rooms. Their air must pass through other rooms or the tiny shafts, and cannot but be contaminated before it reaches them. A five-story house of this character contains apartments for eighteen or twenty families, a population frequently amounting to 100 people, and sometimes increased by boarders and lodgers to 150 or more.

The dumbbell tenement did offer a few advantages by comparison with older tenements—fireproof stairways, more privacy of halls, and better ventilation of water closets. The New York *Times* nevertheless concluded in 1879: "If one of our crowded wards were built up after these designs, the evils of our present tenement house system would be increased tenfold." This warning ignored, the dumbbell became the characteristic design for houses erected on the East Side between 1880 and 1901.

Jewish immigrants were ill-equipped for coping with the tenement problem. Many were too frightened, most too inexperienced in American ways to go and fight City Hall. The religious Jews were too withdrawn from the grime of pressure politics, the socialist Jews too superior to it. The growth of a new tradition of winning practical gains would have to wait upon younger American Jews throwing themselves into reform politics or learning to squeeze favors out of Tammany Hall. Meanwhile, it was fortunate for the immigrants that native reformers and muckrakers found in the East Side an outlet for their wish to ease the lives of the oppressed. Jacob Riis, a reporter for the New York *Sun*, published in 1890 his classic study of tenement life, *How the Other Half Lives*, and for the next two decades, through a stream of articles and books, he kept forcing upon middle-class readers an awareness of the horrors of the slums. Lawrence Veiller, a patrician radical, began as a naïve University Settlement House worker in the early 1890's and then became an agitator for tenement reform. Veiller and his friends hammered at this theme until finally, in 1901, a law was passed in Albany that put an end to further construction of the dumbbell tenement. The narrow dumbbell shaft was superseded by a court that could not measure less than four and a half feet in width. A separate water closet was required in each apartment, to replace the two-to-a-floor system dating back to 1879. The height of nonfireproof tenements was limited, with few exceptions, to five stories, and previous laws requiring that halls and stairs be fireproofed were strengthened.

On paper all this seemed impressive. In practice the new requirements were a good deal less so, especially on the East Side. Much of the damage had already been done. In the Tenth Ward the number of tenements had more than doubled in the preceding few decades, increasing from 534 in 1864 to 1,196 in 1893. By 1900 there was a building on almost every available East Side lot. And given the effective resistance to tearing down "old-law" structures, little opportunity remained for "new-law" tenements after 1901.

Still, improvements were introduced after 1901 by applying some of the "new-law" regulations to "old-law" buildings. To meet minimal standards, windows had to be installed in the walls of windowless rooms, and back-yard privies, of which 6,763 still served the poor of Manhattan in 1903, had to be replaced by water closets. Lighting in hallways had to be improved somewhat; cellar floors had to be waterproofed. And a large enough munici-pal staff was provided to insure more than token enforcement.

The New York Tenement House Act of 1901 was not replaced by another major act until after the First World War. Structural changes were made in older buildings, but no mere modifications of the dumbbells could begin to cope with the pouring in of immigrants. In the 1890's the popula-tion of Manhattan grew by approximately 400,000; in the 1900's, by ap-proximately 500,000. To have begun to handle the problem according to humane standards would have meant to rid the city of the Tammany ma-chine that, except for a few intervals, ruled it during all these decades; would have meant to stir up, somehow, a sense of collective responsibility in the hearts of the native population; would have meant to institute serious urban planning and public housing; would have meant to break with the American distaste for government intervention.

All through the decades of mass migration there were some Americans, men and women with a sense of social responsibility, who knew that housing in the cities was a scandal. As for the immigrant Jews themselves, their attitudes were complex and barely accessible to anyone beyond their cul-tural orbit. Over the centuries the Jews had learned to keep in mind two measures of response: the first, an austere balance sheet of the outrage to which they had been subjected and which, even without a final reckoning on earth, they did not propose to forget; and the second, a readiness to rejoice in the smallest gains that might nevertheless come to them. The immigrants suffering in East Side tenements knew that by American stand-ards they were victims of an outrage, and that good will and imagination might have gone far toward remedying it. But they also remembered that in the old country many of them had lived in hovels, fearful of stray peasants and drunken policemen who might wander by and break windows. So they responded to both the American immediacy and the European memory, submitting as best they could to their daily burdens, determined to escape as quickly as possible, and meanwhile finding solace—it was a genuine solace—in the fact that even in the short time since they had arrived in this country there had been improvements: a workable fire escape, a lighted hallway, a toilet for each family. Only people who have never known the absence of these rudimentary amenities would be inclined to minimize their value.

Working in the Shops

In 1890 the Baron de Hirsch Fund conducted a survey of more than 100,000 Jews on the East Side. Of the roughly 25,000 gainfully employed Jews among the respondents, more than 12,000 were listed as garment workers. During the decades to come, the number of Jewish workers in this industry would increase steadily. In 1900 over 40 percent of 35,000 female workers classified by the census as "Russian-born" and close to 20 percent of 191,000 male workers classified in the same way were listed as garment workers. Three decades later a much larger work force in the garment trades was still "predominantly Russian Jewish." The fate of the east European immigrants was to be crucially intertwined with the development of the garment trades.

It was a development almost entirely dependent on the rate at which hand sewing was replaced by machine manufacture, individually fitted by ready-made garments. As early as the 1850's machine-sewn vests, coats, and pants were being manufactured in the United States, but as late as 1890 the bulk of women's clothes, except for cloaks and mantillas, was still being sewn by hand, either at home or in small tailoring establishments. The women's clothing industry did not complete its transformation to machine manufacture until about the turn of the century. Meanwhile, garment centers were becoming part of America's rapid industrialization, particularly in New York, Boston, Chicago, and Philadelphia, all major places of Jewish settlement.

New York took and kept the lead. By 1870 it had a product value for men's clothing of over $34,000,000. Its large supply of cheap Irish and German labor, its rail connections, its tradition of hard work, all signified decisive advantages. In 1880, with a product value of $60,000,000 for men's clothing and $18,000,000 for women's (a sixfold increase over the 1870 figure), New York had outstripped the combined production of its four closest urban competitors.*

From 1889 to 1899 the growth of the garment industry in the United

---

* The rapid growth of the garment industry was stimulated by the ingenuity of clothing pioneers like Moritz Goldenson, credited with the "invention" of the alluring undergarment. In the 1870's he came out with a "bridal set" featuring a "bridal nightgown of the princesses and the brides of the Austro-Hungarian nobility and imperial court." His success in popularizing styles in women's underwear earned him an honored place in the history of American advertising.

States, measured by number of workers and value of product, was two or three times as rapid as the average for all industries. For the women's clothing industry, the years of sharpest growth were during this period, one that coincided with the upsurge of Jewish immigration. In 1900 the product value for women's clothing in the country as a whole came to $159,000,000, with New York's share a massive $107,000,000. By 1914 the American clothing industry consisted of nearly 15,000 establishments employing 510,595 wage earners and 61,919 salaried employees; its yearly payroll came to $326,605,102 and its product value to well over $1,000,000,000.

By the time east European Jews started to arrive in large numbers, a good part of the clothing industry was owned by German Jews, who had come here in the 1840's and 1850's and started their upward climb with clothing stores along Baxter and Chatham streets on the East Side. As early as 1851 Jewish "pullers-in" were sardonically called "Baxter Street merchants," and Chatham Street was called Jerusalem, "from the fact that the Jews do most of the business on this street [with] a Yankee stuck in now and then by way of variety." In an 1863 edition of the New York *Herald* Jewish names appear in twenty-three out of twenty-five advertisements for firms handling ready-made and secondhand clothing.

Finding it easier to deal with a German-Jewish employer than a gentile one, the east European immigrants moved into the garment trades. Other factors reinforced this trend: many of the immigrants had some experience in tailoring; jobs were not hard to come by in an industry that doubled its size with each decade of the Jewish migration from eastern Europe; and, perhaps most important, as the work became increasingly routinized, no very great skills were required for most of the available jobs.

This had not always been true, especially during the earlier years when the Germans and the Irish came over in large numbers. Under the family system of production that then prevailed, precut material was assembled at home into garments, with the head of the family, a skilled craftsman, doing the difficult work, while wife and children lent a hand with such easier tasks as basting, finishing, and buttonhole making. Gradually this inefficient method was replaced by one in which the job of putting together a single garment was divided among several semiskilled workers. The machine work would be given to an operator, the needle work to a baster and a finisher, and minor tasks, such as sewing on buttons, felling, and pressing, to still others. In one leading garment shop in New York at the turn of the century, no fewer than thirty-nine tasks were carried on by the same number of workers in order to manufacture a single garment.

Somewhat greater skill was required in the dress and women's cloak trades, at least until they caught up with advances in machine manufacture. But there were other women's garments, such as shirtwaists, which a newcomer could learn to work on in a short time. "As a rule, it takes 10 persons to produce the waists in the factories. . . . As a result of these divisions in labor, Jewish immigrants are able to master their jobs . . . usually in less than a month."

Such improved systems of production were at first conducted in large lofts, but with the arrival of masses of east European Jews the industry spilled over into sweatshops, unventilated tenement rooms packed with teams of eight to twenty who pored over worktables and sewing machines. With the growth and rationalization of the industry, conditions improved—but only a little. By 1911 foot power was still prevalent in women's garment shops, as were twenty-five-pound hand-operated pressing irons (a common cause of spinal curvature), leaky illuminating gas tubes, high temperatures, and bad light and ventilation. Shop walls and floors were grimy, separate washrooms an exception, lunch areas either nonexistent or in "a dark and dirty corner of the shop, or in the janitor's apartment on another floor." Water closets were often located in yards or halls; the legal minimum of one for every twenty-five workers was not met in many shops, some having only one for eighty-five workers; and many, lacking windows, passed odors directly into the work areas. "The adequate flushing of the closets," reported a shocked inspector, "suffers from their location and neglect, and their condition is, in many cases, scandalous."

In the shop itself the garment worker was plagued by a tyrannical "task system," a rudimentary kind of speed-up that increased his work load faster than his pay check. The evils of this system are explained by an Industrial Commission report:

> The contractor . . . would go to the manufacturer. Finding that there was but little work to be had, he would offer to take the coats cheaper than the price theretofore paid. When he came home, he would tell his men that there was not much work and he was obliged to take it cheaper, and since he did not want to reduce their wages and pay them less per day, all they would have to do would be to make another coat in the task. That is, if they were accustomed to make 9 coats in the task, they would be required to make 10, and then 11, and so on. The wages were always reduced on the theory that they were not reduced at all but the amount of labor increased. In this way intense speed was developed. The men who had been accustomed to making 9 coats in a task would make 10, and so on, up to 15, 18, and even 20, as is the customary task at the present time [1901]. The hours began to be increased, in order to make the task in a day.

Over the next decade the task system was to be one of the major targets of attack by the garment unions, but it was not until after the historic settlement of 1910 that it was significantly modified. The kind of life created by this work system is suggested by a few statistics in a 1911 Immigration Commission report on the clothing industry. A very small percentage of female garment workers, even those in the country more than ten years, were earning over $10 a week by 1911. Only 29.6 percent of the male garment workers of east European Jewish extraction who had been in the country less than five years were earning over $12.50 a week. Among east European Jewish immigrants in the garment industry who were over sixteen years of age at the time of their arrival, one out of two was earning more than $12.50 a week—compared with fewer than one out of three south Italian males, two out of three German males, and one out of twenty Russian-Jewish females. Jewish heads of families in the garment industry averaged $502 a year; most worked between nine and twelve months a year. Fully a third of Jewish heads of families earned less than $400 a year. What kept these people going was that most families had more than one worker, that they were well trained in the arts of self-denial, that they lived by a goal of expectation that gave some meaning to deprivations of the moment.

The pivotal figures in the garment industry were the contractors, a tough breed of underfinanced adventurers who sought out the owners of cloth (usually German Jews) in their Broadway showrooms and arranged to convert bundles of precut material into ready-to-wear clothing for a set price. Returning with these bundles to the shops, they would often work alongside their men, immigrants like themselves, into the far hours of the night.

Jacob Riis describes one such marginal "boss," visited in 1890:

> A sweater, this, in a small way. Five men and a woman, two young girls, not fifteen, and a boy who says unasked that he is fifteen, and lies in saying it, are at the machines sewing "knee-pants." . . . The floor is littered ankle-deep with half-sewn garments. . . . The faces, hands, and arms to the elbows of everyone in the room are black with the color of the cloth on which they are working. The boy and the woman alone look up at our entrance. The girls shoot sidelong glances, but at a warning look from the man with the bundle [the contractor] they tread their machines more energetically than ever. . . . They are "learners," all of them, says the woman, who proves to be the wife of the boss, and have "come over" only a few weeks ago. They turn out 120 dozen "knee-pants" a week. They work no longer than to nine o'clock at night, from daybreak.

Since the New York Tenement House Act of 1892, contractors had been forbidden to carry on manufacture in the home, but the law was slow to take effect and some years went by before garment production was actually confined to shops and lofts. (As late as 1911, thirteen thousand tenement houses in New York were licensed for home work by the Bureau of Factory Inspection, and that on a not very rigorous factory inspection.)

Wages in the garment industry remained low, even by contemporary standards, throughout the period of migration. In 1914 the average hourly wage of male clothing workers was about 35¢, a figure that exceeded only the rate for common building workers. By 1930 garment workers were receiving an average of $24.51 a week, $1.50 less than the pay of workers in stockyards and slaughterhouses.

A typical turn-of-the-century East Side sweatshop required the "inside"

Young sweatshop workers

services of thirteen Jewish workers in addition to six Italian women who did
felling (turning over the rough edges of a seam and sewing it down flat) in
their own homes. The "inside" group comprised three operators of foot-
powered sewing machines, three basters, three finishers, two pressers, one
trimmer and busheler (in this case, the contractor himself), and one button
sewer. In an average seventy-two-hour, six-day work week, three hundred
coats were assembled for a contracted price of $225 (75¢ a coat). Out of this
amount the contractor paid weekly salaries of $15 to each operator, $13.30
to each baster, $10 to each finisher, $12 to each presser, $18 to himself as
trimmer and busheler, $9 for button work, and $2 apiece to the Italian home
workers. After deducting his weekly rent of $6 and the $3 cost of oil and
repair, the contractor was left with a neat profit of $38.10, more than double

the wage paid to his most skilled workers. During prosperous times thousands of contractors made good returns on their tiny capital investments, often no more than $50 to $100—the cost of a few used sewing machines. But with the inevitable slack season, or, still worse, an economic depression, thousands of contractors, as many as one third of them in a typical year, went under: some because they agreed to prices lower than they could meet, others because their manufacturers went bankrupt, and still others as a result of exhaustion and ill health.

Rising in the World

A very few rose, quite literally, from rags to riches, from some obscure *shtetl* to a Fifth Avenue business address.

Even before reaching his *bar mitzvah*, Louis Borgenicht (1861–1942) had already earned a few pennies by selling fertilizing material (mostly old bones collected in abandoned fields) to peasants, delivering mail to the few landlords near his *shtetl* who could pay for the service, and peddling soda water at village fairs. "It boiled down," he would recall some sixty years later, "to a question of what storekeeper—what tobacco, notions, or drygoods man—I could persuade to take me as an apprentice." Born in Austria-Hungary, Borgenicht became an apprentice in a village tobacco shop at which peddlers would gather to discuss the ins and outs of their trade: where the best shawls could be bought at lowest prices, how to persuade a peasant woman to make a purchase. To these peddlers the boy once announced, "Piece goods will take me out into the world." The next week he was working in a drygoods store half a block away. He had by then mastered a valuable business technique: after clinching a bargain with a peasant woman for a shawl, he would snatch a slightly cheaper one from a shelf beneath the counter. "A little sleight-of-hand and it was the cheaper shawl which, wrapped and tied, was handed to the woman." Moving on to a better job at a drygoods store in the city of Jaslow, Borgenicht immersed himself in the clothing industry. "Days and nights," recalled this Jewish Kipps, "I pored over goods. I've always felt that it was impossible to sell something you don't believe in yourself."

Borgenicht soon recognized that he was caught in a backwater. "I saw those others . . . all the same men sitting behind counters and over desks . . . treading the same worn steps day by day, impervious to new ideas, unaware of the world moving around them, stifling in an ancient society where a man's life was determined by his birth." Impatient, nervous, Borgenicht opened a piece-goods store in a Hungarian town—but it was the same story, no manufacturing, everything made by hand, no demand for anything, a world frozen with boredom.

In 1888 Borgenicht and his wife sailed for America. Operating out of an eight-dollar-a month apartment on Eldridge Street, he tried his hand at peddling; frightened by stories of peddlers left dead on lonely country roads, he stuck close to home. He sold herrings out of a barrel on an East Side street corner. Business was good, the first week's profit eight dollars and the second, thirteen dollars. Taking a pushcart, he sold notebooks, bananas, socks, crockery—whatever he could buy for a nickel and sell for a dime.

A driven man, he understood that step-by-step improvements in income would never bring him to the place he dreamed of. He walked the streets, studying what people were wearing and what was being sold in stores, until one day he noticed a little Slavic girl with an apron utterly common in Central Europe but still unknown in America. This, thought Borgenicht, might be the item to make his fortune.

He bought 150 yards of material in a Hester Street store, and, with the help of his wife, he manufactured forty children's aprons in one day. Within three hours he had sold them all, realizing a profit of $2.60. He then invested all his remaining capital in gingham and white goods, and he and his wife labored six days a week from seven in the morning until late into the night, converting uncut material into enough aprons for him to peddle from house to house. Soon an eighteen-year-old apprentice was hired for six dollars a week. A bit later the Borgenichts rented a store on Sheriff Street and lived in its back rooms. Then a few girls were hired to work on machines in the store. In 1890, two years after his arrival, Borgenicht gave up peddling and concentrated on the manufacture of children's dresses. By 1892 twenty girls were employed in the back room of a large store, with dresses being sold to Bloomingdale's and Ridley Brothers.

Borgenicht still felt dissatisfied, restless, hemmed in. "I wanted to grow, to employ crowds of people. And here I was, cramped in a little retail-wholesale shop, dealing with customers who wanted one dress or two petticoats. At night I lay awake and thought of my frustration." Longing to break into "the real downtown merchants' district," Borgenicht gave up his East Side establishment and moved nearer to Broadway, where, by cutting expenses, he began to compete successfully with the German Jews. They paid an outside subcontractor to sew and finish precut materials, but Borgenicht followed the example already set by the Yiddish-speaking "Division Street moths" and acted as his own subcontractor. He did his own cutting, hired girls fresh off the boat at low wages, and made do with an inexpensive loft on Canal Street, off Broadway.

Though this operation prospered at first, a combination of unfortunate circumstances—overexpansion, an injudicious partner, uncollectable bills, an economic recession—drove Borgenicht into bankruptcy. Unbroken, he and his wife scraped together a few dollars, went back to Rivington Street, opened a small shop, moved on to a larger shop on Division Street, and then to a still larger one on East Broadway. In 1900 the East Broadway operation showed a ten-thousand-dollar profit.

Borgenicht expanded rapidly. By 1910 he was being called the "king of the children's dress trade." He now had a work force of 150, a yearly product value of $1,500,000, and a sales staff of 14 receiving orders from the country's largest stores. By 1913 Borgenicht employed 1,500 workers. A rich man, he divided his life between his office on Broadway, his uptown residence, and his summer estate in the Catskills, replete with stables, gardens, orchards, a tennis court, and a swimming pool. Later, looking back on his life, Borgenicht saw himself as a brilliant opportunist: "Starting from scratch in a strange land, I had established what was to all intents and purposes a new line. In twenty years I had watched it develop into a significant industry. . . . The concept was overwhelming to a man who had come to the U.S. with bare hands."

In the years of his wealth Borgenicht remained attached to the culture from which he had come; he served on the boards of synagogues, he contributed to HIAS, he gave food to poor Jews on holidays, he kept his factory closed on the Sabbath, he sent his sons to Hebrew school, he maintained a kosher home, he read the Yiddish papers until the day of his death. But gradually, with the drift of the years, there occurred subtle changes of stress and style. Borgenicht began to show concern for narrowing the social gap between himself and his more *hochwohlegeboren* coreligionists. At the plush family residence a *fraulein* was employed to teach the little Borgenichts German speech and manners. Upon joining an uptown Hungarian synagogue, he struggled to replace his coarse accent with more refined and mellifluous sounds. Even his appearance changed. Still driven, still restless, he nevertheless began to sport a carefully trimmed beard, and donned striped pants, cutaway jacket, and top hat for holidays and special occasions. The New York *Staats Zeitung* and the Metropolitan Opera were now taking almost as much of his time as the Yiddish press and theatre. Torn between the social possibilities created by his wealth and the pieties he still felt toward the East Side, Borgenicht ended as a man not quite comfortable in any world, visibly a success but uncertain where to register its impact, a stranger, perhaps, even to himself.

Like Borgenicht, the majority of east European Jews who succeeded in business did so in the garment industry. Oscar Berman, born in a wretched little Lithuanian village, worked his way up from traveling salesman in neckwear to head of the Crown Overall Manufacturing Company; Samuel Messing came out of an impoverished Warsaw childhood to reach the presidency of Messing-David Corporation, manufacturer of lingerie; Ben Pauker escaped an Orthodox family in Austria to become head of Pauker Brothers, manufacturer of sportswear; Louis Saffer left Vilna at the turn of the century and ended his life as a manufacturer of men's clothing. Of the two hundred or so prominent Jewish businessmen of east European extraction mentioned in the 1947 edition of *American Jews, Their Lives and Achievements,* most are clothing manufacturers of one kind or another. If they remained in the garment industry, it was unusual for such men to become extremely rich—multimillionaires, say. The really big money was elsewhere, in real estate and liquor, the movies and junk. This was the path of the Lefcourts, from rags to real estate, as also of the owners of one of the largest scrap-iron and steel companies in America, Luria Brothers and Company.

There were a number of other industries in which relatively large numbers of Jewish immigrants worked for a living. In the early 1900's 20 percent of the fifteen thousand cigar makers in New York City were Jewish. In 1909 a recently established union of butcher workers estimated that it needed to organize "at least a thousand men." Even before the turn of the century enough Jews were entering the building trades to cause resentment among better-paid carpenters, painters, and paper hangers:

> We are knocked out of the work of fitting up flats in the Harlem district [reports the secretary of a local building trade union] by lumpers who hire the cheapest labor in the market . . . from the other side . . . Swedes, Hungarians, and Polish Jews. They work for $1.50 to $2.50 a day. . . .
> We have lost all the work done east of Third Avenue, from the Battery to the Harlem River. The work there now is done entirely by Polish Jews . . . 1500 men . . . Polish Jews have injured our business. They are not good mechanics, and they will work for $1.15, $1.25, and $1.50 a day (compared with from $2 to $5 a day paid to union members).

Finding work in alteration and repair jobs, over 8,000 Jewish building workers formed a union in 1913. An Inside Iron and Bronze Workers Union, organized in 1913 under the United Hebrew Trades, reported a membership of 2,000 in 1918; a similarly sponsored Bakers Union numbered 2,500 in the same year. The United Hebrew Trades also sponsored a Bed Spring Makers Union of 150 members, a Chandelier and Brass Workers Union of 275, a Milk Wagon Drivers Union of 1,000, as well as small locals of shoe fitters, bag makers, metal workers, umbrella makers—even an East Side Newspaper Deliverers Union that met, appropriately enough, in the *Forward* building.

Wages and working conditions in most of these trades were often no better than those in the garment industry; sometimes they were considerably worse, as among Jewish butcher workers who, if we can believe a pioneer leader of their union, earned a mere $1.50 a week plus "board"—"a pallet or a narrow cot, in the back room of the foul-smelling, unheated butcher shop . . . and what the butcher's wife cared to send down to him." Nor were bakers better off. As late as 1912 the great majority of New York's 2,500 bakers were located in rat- and roach-infested cellars in which working conditions were appalling. Conditions in the cigar industry were hardly better, with the work unsteady, the pay equal to that of an ordinary semiskilled garment worker (in 1905 from four to seven dollars a week for women, twelve dollars a week for men), a sixty-hour week, and a serious child-labor problem.

In time, the East Side industries began to move upward and outward. After the First World War the clothing industry, now the fourth largest in value product in the United States, with close to 95,000 garment workers employed in Manhattan alone, graduated out of the ghetto into more sumptuous uptown surroundings. By 1930, with few exceptions, Manhattan's garment workers labored within a 150-acre area bounded on the east by Seventh Avenue, on the north by Times Square, on the south by Pennsylvania Station and on the west by Ninth Avenue. Surrounded by skyscrapers built on garment-earned money by Abe Lefcourt, Saul Singer, Mack Kenner, and other Jewish builders, the streets at noontime would be filled with hordes of Yiddish-speaking Jews shouting in an informal employment market, reading Yiddish newspapers, munching sandwiches and dill pickles. The Jewish workers, together with a growing number of Italians and blacks, benefited from improved physical conditions, labored five to ten hours less a week, and received real wages 20 to 30 percent higher than before the war.

Many immigrant workers could now experience the small pleasures of life—better food, clothing, housing. Of close to a thousand pensioned clothing workers interviewed in 1950, well over half reported having moved out of the East Side by 1930 to higher-rent areas. Many moved into three- to six-family apartment houses in Brooklyn and the Bronx, a notable distance from what they had left behind.

Ways to Make a Living

A good portion of the earnings of Jewish workers remained within the Jewish economy, paid out to landlords, storekeepers, and venders of services. Almost everything the immigrant needed, and some he did not, could be found within that economy. Listed in the 1890 Baron de Hirsch census of the Jewish East Side are 413 butchers, 370 grocers, 307 drygoods dealers, 120 restaurant keepers, 83 shoe dealers, 80 coal dealers, 31 hardware dealers, 58 booksellers.

The first decades of the century also showed a notable increase in the variety of East Side retail establishments and offices. During this period the *Forward* mentions an East Side photography business, a Jewish milk business, and a plethora of East Side drugstores and barbershops. Another source estimates that in 1907 200 physicians, 115 pharmacists, and 175 dentists served New York's downtown Jews—figures that appear somewhat high. By 1913, near the peak of its development, the East Side was bursting with sizable numbers of shops, offices, professional services. A survey in that year of only a fraction of the Jewish community, covering 57 blocks, lists 112 candy stores and ice-cream parlors, 70 saloons, 30 lunchrooms, 78 barbers, 40 dentists, 16 doctors, 38 drugstores, 2 optometrists, 3 piano teachers, 12 photographers, 23 lawyers, 43 bakeries, 93 butcher shops, 20 laundries, even a veterinarian.

One major route for social advancement was real estate. Though tenement properties on the East Side were expensive, ranging from $35,000 to $50,000 each, "thousands of humble immigrants" from eastern Europe, wrote one investigator, had become owners by 1907. This figure is probably exaggerated, but the description of how it happened remains valuable:

> First they become lessees. By constant saving the East Sider gets together $200 or $300, with which, as security, he gets a four or five years' lease of a house. He moves his own family into the least expensive apartment. He himself acts as janitor; his wife and daughters as scrub-women and housekeepers. He is his own agent, his own painter, carpenter, plumber, and general repair man. Thus he reduces expenses to the minimum. He lets out apartments by the week, always calling promptly himself for the rent. By thus giving constant attention to his work he has perhaps a few hundred dollars every year as profit. By the time his lease expires, this has swollen to a few thousand. With this he buys a tenement outright. He puts down from $3,000 to $5,000 on a $45,000 building, giving one, two, three, sometimes four mortgages in payment. . . . Then he repeats his old operation. . . . When the third or fourth mortgage comes due, he has invariably made enough out of the building to pay it off. He keeps on hard at work and likewise pays off the third and second. Then, as his rents still come in, he invests them in more tenements; until, as a monument to a life spent in the hardest sacrificial toil, he may own a string scattered all over the town.

Perhaps the most impressive, certainly the most colorful, of the immigrant businessmen were those who would later be known as the Hollywood Moguls, a dozen or so Yiddish-speaking Tamerlanes who built enormous movie studios and for nearly half a century satisfied the world's hunger for fantasy.

They began arriving in America during the 1880's, penniless boys who drifted restlessly from job to job. Carl Laemmele, who would head Universal Pictures for twenty years, went through a succession of youthful wanderings: furrier's apprentice in New York, errand boy in Chicago, supernumerary in an Edwin Booth production of *Julius Caesar*, farm hand in the Dakota plains, clerk in a jewelry store, bookkeeper in a stockyard. The others—Samuel Goldwyn, Louis B. Mayer, William Fox, the Warner brothers, the Schenks, the Selznicks, Harry Cohn, Jesse Lasky, Adolph Zukor—all followed pretty much in Laemmele's footsteps. Bored with sitting in classrooms, too lively for routine jobs, clever in the ways of the world, they were on the lookout, these *luftmenshn* in God's country, for a key to wealth and power.

They found it in the nickelodeon. Renting cheap stores in immigrant (mostly Jewish) neighborhoods, they charged a nickel a head for a showing of early movies to patrons who sat on rows of wooden chairs. The immigrants, like everyone else, loved these simple, flickering pictures, and soon the young entrepreneurs were making money—a little bit of money. It was a business that appealed to them: strictly cash, a minimum of goods and apparatus, and brand new. A bright young Jew could get in at the start without having to trip over established gentiles along the way.

By 1910 some of these young businessmen were already owners of small chains of moving-picture parlors that boasted whitewashed exteriors, uniformed ushers, and male vocalists. But the take from nickel-a-head shows was, after all, limited—the real money, it seemed, lay in distribution. They moved into the distribution of movies, and found that even there they had not yet reached the real money; so they moved into the production of movies, setting up pioneer studios in Hollywood and buying up whatever talent they could find. Banks lent them money; the capitalization, at first, was modest; and the economic boom of the First World War eased their way up. By the twenties, they had risen to become heads of empires employing thousands of actors, stagehands, writers, publicity men, and all-purpose flunkies. A decade later they were earning some of the largest salaries in the country—Louis B. Mayer's income was $1,296,503 in 1937.

The Moguls were mostly semiliterate men, ill at ease with English, but enormously powerful in their intuitive grasp of what American—indeed, international—audiences wanted. They were soon dining with heads of state, traveling among the international set, winning and losing fantastic sums at Monte Carlo, realizing their wildest personal fantasies, satisfying their every whim, amiable or sadistic. The marks of immigrant Jewishness remained on their every feature and every gesture, and the shrewder among them made no special effort to erase those marks. Some discarded worn Jewish wives for fresh gentile beauties, but except for Harry Cohn, who died a baptized Christian, that was as far as they cared or were able to go in shedding the past. They remained Jews, of a sort.

Often vulgar, crude, and overbearing, they were brilliantly attuned to the needs of their business; they commanded and used to the full a profound instinct for the common denominator of taste; and they left a deep imprint on American popular culture. Trusting their own minds and hearts, shrewd enough not to pay too much attention to the talented or cultivated men they hired, the Moguls knew which appeal to sentiment, which twirl of fantasy, which touch of violence, which innuendo of sexuality, would grasp native American audiences. It was something of a miracle and something of a joke. They had come from the Ukraine and Poland and Austria-Hungary; they still spoke with Yiddish accents; but it was they, more than anyone else, who reached the fantasies of America, indeed of the entire world—a universalism of taste which shaped the century and which they could shrewdly exploit because they innocently shared it.

An especially difficult path to economic advancement was to become clerks and salesmen in the "outside world." Accents, gesticulations, lack of familiarity with American manners, distrust of gentiles, religious habits—all combined with that world's well-rooted preconceptions about Jews to make it difficult at first for immigrants to obtain even the simplest clerical job in a municipal office or behind a department-store counter. It is hardly surprising that in 1900 only 2.3 percent of a sample of New York State's 73,000 Russian-born workers were employed as clerks, and only 3.2 percent as salesmen. Slowly the percentages rose in both fields. In the 1920 census, out of a sample of 400,000 foreign-born workers, 13,000 Yiddish speaking males held positions as store salesmen (though many, no doubt, in stores operated by Yiddish-speaking employers). While forming only 5.7 percent of the group studied, the Yiddish-speaking salesmen comprised 20 percent of those employed in the field. Yiddish-speaking women also ranked high in white-collar work, with close to 4,000 (over two fifths of the total) handling clerical jobs. By 1920 a major economic rise toward middle-class status had been begun—but no more than begun.

By 1912 enough second-generation Jews had entered the civil service to warrant notice:

> Twenty years ago the Irish occupied not far from ninety percent of all the positions in the city departments of New York. That was the period of the spoils system. . . .
> Now, however, nearly all of the 6,500 positions in the city government are awarded on the basis of competitive civil service examinations. As a result, the Jews are rapidly driving out the Irish, the Germans and the native Americans. The East Side branches of the public libraries find themselves unable to supply the demand for books that are supposed to prepare one for civil service examinations. The Jews study hard and long, and their examination papers are so immeasurably superior to the average offered by representatives of other races that they invariably secure preferred places. . . . They fill nearly all medical and laboratory positions. . . . They hold most of the minor legal positions. They are the city's searchers, process-servers, and law examiners. Most of the municipal office-boys are youngsters from the East Side; the stenographers and typewriters are nearly all Jewish girls.

The move toward the professions was, if anything, still more direct and massive. In 1891 only a few dozen east European Jews were doctors or lawyers in New York, and there were no more than a handful in dentistry and teaching. By the next decade, these few grew "into hundreds," though statistically they amounted to a mere 2.6 percent of the immigrant Jewish working population. By 1907 of 2,979 foreign-born male students in American colleges and universities, 37.1 percent were Jews. Moreover, of 6,652 native-born male students of foreign-born parents in such schools, 16.1 percent were of Jewish descent. In brief, the Jews constituted almost one fourth of these two groups of students, a percentage which was several times higher than the proportion of Jews to non-Jews in the general population.

This trend accelerated in the following decades, as larger numbers of second-generation Jews reached college age. In the early twenties Jews numbered 14,837 out of a total of 153,085 students in 106 institutions. Making up over 9 percent of the entire student body, Jewish representation in colleges had grown to three times their proportion of the general population. The New York figures were still steeper. During the scholastic year 1918–1919 the total number of Jewish students in a group of New York colleges and universities came to 7,148 out of a total of 18,552. About a quarter of the Jewish students attended courses in finance; in medicine and law the proportion of Jews was double that of non-Jews; in dentistry, almost triple. Only in teaching, among the professions to which Jews have customarily been attracted, was the gentile percentage larger. Studies in the mid-twenties placed between 9 and 10 percent of gainfully employed Jews in the professions, as many as 16 percent in clerical positions, and less than 50 percent in manufacturing and mechanical industries.

The trend that has since become the central socioeconomic fact of American Jewish life was well under way by the 1920's—toward the professions, toward small and medium entrepreneurship, and away from blue-collar occupations. A study of Jewish graduates of medical schools in ten American cities shows that from 1881 to 1885 there were 25; from 1891 to 1895, 153; from 1901 to 1905, 460; from 1906 to 1910, 716; and from 1916 to 1920, 1,273. In a thirty-five year period the number of medical graduates increased fifty times. A study dealing with the occupational distribution of first- and second-generation immigrants from Russia living in New York in 1900, most of whom can be assumed to have been Jews, shows that 61.2 percent of the first generation of male immigrants worked in manufacturing industries and 27.5 percent in trade (a category including peddlers). For the second generation the percentages are strikingly changed: 32.6 percent in manufacturing and 57.8 percent in trade.

Some cautions should be noted. Large segments of the American economy remained shut to the Jews, either immigrant or native-born. Corporations, banks, and other institutions kept Jews out of crucial managerial posts, not so much through formal decision as through informal understandings. Companies like the New York Telephone Company had a clear policy of discrimination. And at no point did the Jews really approach, let alone participate in, the central concentrations of wealth and economic power in the United States.

The Jews did make remarkable socioeconomic progress, a progress mirrored in the new neighborhoods to which some of them would move in the 1920's: Borough Park in Brooklyn, the Upper West Side of Manhattan, the west Bronx. Yet, it should be remembered, this was a move that left behind a majority of the Jewish immigrants, who remained workers and petty tradesmen to the end. Only in the second and third generations--native-born, well educated, and free of many of their parents' constraints—would the climb out of poverty and subjection be largely completed.

CHAPTER SIX

The Way
They Lived Then

F OR ABOUT thirty or forty years, a mere moment in history, the immigrant Jews were able to sustain a coherent and self-sufficient culture. It was different from the one they had left behind, despite major links of continuity, and it struggled fiercely to keep itself different from the one they found in America, despite the pressures for assimilation. Between what they had brought and half preserved from the old world and what they were taking from the new, the immigrant Jews established a tense balance, an interval of equilibrium.

Traditional faith still formed the foundation of this culture, if only by providing norms from which deviation had to be measured. The influence of Russian intellectual styles, in their moral gravity and self-conscious idealism, remained strong, especially among younger men and women aspiring to the life of the spirit. Secular Jewishness became a major source of ideas, blending with elements of religion to create a culture that served as surrogate for nationhood: a structure of values neither strictly religious nor rigidly skeptical. And then of course all things American kept pouring into the Jewish streets: ideas, styles, manners, language, more or less transformed by their absorption into the culture of *Yiddishkeit.*

Released from the constraints of Europe but not yet tamed by the demands of America, Jewish immigrant life took on a febrile hurry of motion and drive. After centuries of excessive discipline, life overflowed— its very shapelessness gave proof of vitality. Moral norms, while no longer beyond challenge, continued for a time to be those implanted by Orthodox Judaism, but manners changed radically, opening into a chaos of improvisation. The fixed rituals that had bound the east European Jews broke down under the weight of American freedom. The patterns of social existence had to be remade each day. The comedy of social dislocation gave edge and abundance to life.

Richer in morals than manners, stronger in ideals than amenities, the world of the immigrant Jews could not, in any ordinary sense, be called a "high" culture. It lacked an aristocracy to emulate or attack, it lacked a leisure class that could validate the pursuit of pleasure, it lacked an aesthetic celebrating the idea of pure art. It had no symphonies or operas, no ballets or museums; its approach to the treasures of the West was decidedly tentative. There were many persons of native courtesy and refined bearing in the immigrant world, but the aesthetics of behavior, a matter of deep moral consequence in traditional Judaism, could hardly be a prime concern on the East Side. The nuances flourishing in a society secure with its economic surplus and political strength had yet to appear; visions of life exalting the supremacy of play seemed distant; the European cult of the gentlemen was barely recognized. It was a society in which the energies of moral aspiration had not yet become settled, or dissipated, into a system of manners.

There had been rigorous, even rigid systems of manners governing every moment of life in the old world, but these had broken down with migration to America. Gradually, as they rebuilt the foundations of their life, the immigrant Jews re-formed its surface. David Blaustein lectured them on the need to "knock at the door" before going into someone else's room—a courtesy that would have more point once "someone else" had a room of his or her own. Abraham Cahan wrote in the *Forward* that table manners should not simply be dismissed as bourgeois adornments: "Not all rules are silly. You would not like my sleeve to dip into your soup as I reach over your plate to get the salt; it is more reasonable for me to ask you to 'pass the salt, please.' " And Marie Ganz remembered a striking incident when her landlord, Mr. Zalkin, barged into the apartment of Mr. Lipsky, demanding "de rent." "Never mind de rent," answered Mr. Lipsky, "What right you got to come in without being told 'come in'? . . . Take off your hat, go outside, knock on the door, and when I say, 'come in,' and not before, you can come in."

What the East Side lacked in sophistication, it made up in sincerity. It responded to primal experiences with candor and directness. It cut through to the essentials of life: the imperative to do right and the comfort of social bonds. Torn apart, as it soon would be, by insoluble conflicts of value, it lived out its inner struggles and confusions to the very brim of its energy.

At the Heart of the Family

An old man remembering his East Side childhood would say that on coming home from school he had a recurrent fear that his cot in the dining room would again be occupied by a relative just off the boat from Europe and given shelter by his parents. How many other Americans could share, even grasp, this order of experience? Space was the stuff of desire; a room to oneself, a luxury beyond reach. "Privacy in the home was practically unknown. The average apartment consisted of three rooms: a kitchen, a parlor, and a doorless and windowless bedroom between. The parlor became a sleeping-room at night. So did the kitchen when families were unusually large. . . . Made comparatively presentable after a long day of cooking, eating and washing of dishes and laundry, the kitchen was the scene of formal calls at our house and of the visits of friends and prospective suitors." Cramming everything into the kitchen during the evenings had a practical purpose: it saved money on gas and electricity. During the 1890's desperate families had put "three boarders in the front room and two *borderkes* [female boarders] in the kitchen, but today the rooms are too small," noted the *Forward* in 1904. Once boarders could be assigned separate rooms and neither kitchen nor dining room needed to be let, a major advance had been registered in domestic economy.

Only in the kitchen could the family come together in an approximation of community. On most days everyone ate helter-skelter, whenever he could, but on Friday nights, in the mild glow of the Sabbath, the whole family would eat together. Decorum reigned again, the pleasure of doing things as everyone knew they should be done. When a son failed to show up for Friday-night dinners, that was a signal of serious estrangement—not the least use of rules being that they lend clear meaning to violations.

Sitting around the wooden kitchen table that was covered with a white or checkered oilcloth, fathers read newspapers, mothers prepared food, children did homework, boarders gobbled meals. The father's eyes "often fell on the youth at the table who is studying 'Virgil' or on the girl seated in the rocking chair with the big geography on her lap serving as a desk. The atmosphere of the room was not altogether pleasant . . . due to the pail of refuse under the burning stove, which must remain in the house over night by an edict of the janitor."* When families took in work, perhaps "finishing" dresses, it was done in the kitchen. Night after night *landslayt* from the old country, recalls Sophie Ruskay, would come to sit in the kitchen, "waiting uncomplainingly until Mama was at leisure. . . . In Yiddish and with eloquent gestures they told the stories of their hardships." For the kitchen was the one place where immigrants might recall to themselves that they were not mere creatures of toil and circumstances, but also human beings defined by their sociability. The kitchen testified to the utterly plebeian character of immigrant Jewish life; the kitchen was warm, close, and bound all to the matrix of family; sometimes of course it could also be maddeningly noisy and crowded—"my own private Coney Island," Zero Mostel has remembered—and then the sole escape was behind the locked door of a toilet or down the steps and into the streets.

In the kitchen the Jewish mother was sovereign. "My mother," recalls Alfred Kazin in his lyrical memoir,

> worked [in the kitchen] all day long, we ate in it almost all meals except the Passover *seder*. . . . The kitchen gave a special character to our lives; my mother's character. All my memories of that kitchen are dominated by the nearness of my mother sitting all day long at her sewing machine, by the clacking of the treadle against the linoleum floor, by the patient twist of her right shoulder as she automatically pushed at the wheel with one hand or lifted her foot to free the needle. . . . The kitchen was her life. Year by year, as I began to take in her fantastic capacity for labor and her anxious zeal, I realized it was ourselves she kept stitching together.

Every recollection of Jewish immigrant life that is concerned with more than the trivia of "local color" notices that as soon as the Jews moved from eastern Europe to America there followed a serious dislocation of the family. Patterns of the family had been firmly set, indeed, had been allowed to become rigid in the old country: the moral authority of the father, the formal submission of the wife together with her frequent dominance in practical affairs, the obedience of children softened by parental indulgences.

An old-world mother—prototype of thousands who would come to America—is sketched by one immigrant:

> She was nervous, clever, restless, obstinate, quick-tempered and very active. She was capable of working from early morning until late at night for her husband and children. . . . Like most Jewish women of those days, she had not been educated. . . . She knew and observed, however, in every particular, all the rules and laws pertaining to the Jewish religion. . . .

* Is this perhaps unjust to janitors? One of them poured out his heart in the *Forward:* "Janitors aren't born with a broom in their hands. Janitors are the most unhappy people in the world. They work hard for a pittance. . . . The tenants want to 'rule.' They are oppressed in the shops, but when it comes to the janitor, every pauper is a boss himself. . . . And our heartache when we keep begging the women to separate the garbage from the ashes. . . . The janitor has a soul like everyone else."

The name of God was always on her lips. Always when she was about to start gossiping with other women, she would begin, "May God not punish me for what I am about to say. . . ."

To her children she was a loving despot. For the slightest offense she would curse, threaten, and quite often emphasize her indignation with slaps in the face . . . but soon after she would quietly ask God to forgive her. . . .

"Poor innocent lambs," she would whisper, "it is my fault, not theirs, that we are so poor and they do not get enough to eat. . . ." And so it would go on and on.

In a culture where men were supposed to be—and sometimes were—concerned mainly with the rigors of learning, the mother often became the emotional center of the family, the one figure to whom all turned for comfort and with whom constraints might safely be discarded. Whenever social arrangements demand a harsh discipline, there is likely to be a sanctioned outlet for the overflow of feeling. Among the east European Jews it was the mother. Her mixture of practical sense and emotional abundance was classically celebrated in Jacob Gordin's *Mirele Efros*, a Yiddish play enormously popular in both eastern Europe and America—half culture-myth and half tear-jerker in which errant, ambitious sons come finally to recognize the wisdom of the triumphant matriarch.

Not all or even most Jewish fathers in eastern Europe were learned, nor were all wives prepared to take on the burdens of breadwinning. Still, such families did exist and, more important, they set a standard honored even by those who could not live up to it. Some immigrants tried for a time to continue the old ways. "In our home," remembered Elizabeth Stern, the daughter of a rabbi, "the father was the head, revered and honored. One did not speak to him, nor of him, lightly. He represented an ancient civilization." So he did; yet in the new civilization of America it was to her mother, not her father, that the young Elizabeth turned for practical guidance.

In the turmoil of the American city, traditional family patterns could not long survive. The dispossession and shame of many immigrant fathers has been a major subject for fiction about immigrant Jews, both in English and Yiddish. For the Jewish wife the transition seems to have been a little easier. Having sold herrings in the market place of her *shtetl*, she could sell herrings on Orchard Street—and then, if a little more ambitious, open a grocery or drygoods store. Never having regarded herself as part of a spiritual elite, she did not suffer so wrenching a drop in status and self-regard as her husband. She was a practical person, she had mouths to feed, and, by and large, she saw to it that they were fed.

It was by no means typical of immigrant life that wives should continue to be or become the breadwinners. On the East Side only a tiny fraction of wives worked full time—though most girls did or tried to. If the husband was a responsible man and children began to arrive, the wife usually stayed home, sometimes earning an extra dollar with piecework taken from a garment subcontractor. Not only tradition but practical sense enforced this choice: it was so hard to maintain any sort of decent life in the tenements, it took so much energy just to cook and clean and shop and bring up children, that the immigrant wives, who in any case seldom possessed marketable skills, had to stay home. For both husband and wife, even if there were no children, to spend sixty hours a week in a shop would have made family life all but impossible. Nor did staying home mean leisure or indulgence for the wives. It meant carving out an area of protection for their families, it meant toil and anxiety, which all too often left them worn with fatigue, heavy and shapeless, prematurely aged, their sexuality drained out.

It was from her place in the kitchen that the Jewish housewife became the looming figure who would inspire, haunt, and devastate generations of sons. She realized intuitively that insofar as the outer world tyrannized and wore down her men, reducing them to postures of docility, she alone could create an oasis of order. It was she who would cling to received values and resist the pressures of dispersion; she who would sustain the morale of all around her, mediating quarrels, soothing hurts, drawing a circle of safety in which her children could breathe, and sometimes, as time went on, crushing her loved ones under the weight of her affection. The successful entry of the immigrant Jews into the American business world would require a re-assertion of the "male principle," a regathering of authority and aggression—at least outside the home. But in the early years of a family's life in America, it was often the mother who held things together and coped best with the strange new world:

> They were able [reads one account] to maintain the traditional, patriarchal structure. Pauline [the mother], a sensitive woman, declared that the children should not give their household contributions to her, even though she did the shopping and spent most of the cash. She understood the humiliation of Isaac [the unemployed father] and worked to preserve his old role and status, declaring that "Papa should be the manager, he being the head of the household." Thus the forms, if not the entire substance, of family relationships were maintained at the Jacobson home.

To preserve a portion of customary deference to her husband while acquiring the scrappiness demanded by the streets; to gratify her idea of what was morally right while yielding an inch or two to her children; to sustain her personal modesty while beginning to recognize that she was also a woman with desires of her own—it took strength, sometimes an excess of strength, to deal with these conflicting demands.

Quantities of time had to be consumed in finding out where a piece of fresh fish might be gotten for a penny less, or which butcher threw in a few extra bones with a pound of meat. The diet the immigrant mother provided her family was, at the outset, mostly an adaptation of what they had eaten in the old country; poor families were known to subsist for days on herring, bread, and tea, with potatoes and cheap meats like lung among the other staples. Except for horse-radish, carrots, cabbage, and beets, the early immigrants had little fondness for vegetables, though fruit was greatly liked. With time, lettuce and tomatoes came to be "good for the children"—the cult of the vegetable being transmitted to the immigrant kitchen by both the Yiddish newspaper and the American school. (The one provision that was usually delivered to immigrant homes was the plebeian bubbly known as seltzer, in white or blue bottles with a spray on top.)

For both the immigrant mother and her family, food remained at the center of existence. It would be a long time, certainly more than a generation, before one could take for granted having as much food as one might want. Fat meat, the bane of later Americans, seemed a privilege. "The sight of the roast sputtering with hot grease stirred me to ecstasy. In the old home [Europe] I had never had enough meat. . . . Now fat meat was mine for the asking, and what was more I learned that it was cheaper than lean meat, a strange subversion of good taste." To the immigrant mother these words of a young man from the East Side were a matter of course, barely requiring articulation.

If her allotted task was to be a *berye* (efficient housewife), worrying about food, rent, and runny noses, the immigrant mother also had some ideas of her own. In the earlier waves of immigration, many of the women were illiterate, but after 1904 or 1905 a good number could read and a few had even brushed against Russian literature, either directly or through Yiddish translations. It bears remembering that this Jewish housewife absorbed with the minutiae of domestic life had only a few years earlier been a girl working in a sweatshop where she had heard the exhortations of union organizers and sometimes responded to socialist appeals. If she now stayed at home, she learned a little, perhaps a little more than she let on, from Yiddish articles read aloud after dinner, from the religio-moral discussions held at the Passover *seder*, from the arguments of her menfolk, and from the scraps of knowledge her children brought home about George Washington's rectitude, the advantages of free enterprise, and the vital importance of clean fingernails.

She often had an eye for little amenities. Not always, of course—some Jewish mothers were *shlimazolnitses* (sloppy housekeepers). But, as a rule, once there was bread on the table, she grew eager for those social improvements that could brighten and refine life. She yielded happily to the craze for herding children to music lessons. She learned about American-style manners. She began to grasp the mysteries of balanced diet. And if she seldom shared the passion of her Italian counterpart for flowers, she soon came to enjoy keeping potted plants, especially, for some reason, the rubbery kinds. Rarely was there space, time, or inclination for domestic pets,*

---

* "Some time ago," wrote a *Forward* reporter in 1903, "I was walking on Henry Street. A wet snow was falling. I saw a crowd of boys chasing another boy, who was hiding something under his torn coat. Some of the boys ran into the hall of the

but many kitchens were graced with canaries, a bird for which Jews have had a special fondness.

Jewish folklore had elevated the mother to a figure of sanctioned tenderness, and now, together with a somewhat abrasive capacity for battling whatever might threaten her family, she became an object of sentimental veneration. By certain readings, the Oedipal romance was peculiarly Jewish, perhaps even a Jewish invention. Seldom has maternal adoration found so lyrical an expression as in *Call It Sleep*, Henry Roth's novel about the East Side. The mother, Genya, talks to her little boy, David:

> "It is summer," she pointed to the window, "the weather grows warm. Whom will you refresh with the icy lips the water lent you?"
>
> "Oh!" he lifted his smiling face.
>
> "You remember nothing," she reproached him, and with a throaty chuckle, lifted him in her arms. . . .
>
> "There!" she laughed, muzzling his cheek, "but you've waited too long; the sweet chill has dulled. Lips for me," she reminded him, "must always be as cool as the water that wet them."

Open sensuality of this kind was no doubt rare in the immigrant milieu, as in any other of the time, but what Roth rendered could be found elsewhere, muffled and shamefaced. More characteristic perhaps is a recollection of Samuel Chotzinoff in which his mother comes through as a shrewd manager whose

> resourcefulness in moments of economic crisis appeared unlimited. Some situations, like the purchase of clothes, seemed to demand the brashest of tactics. Others, like the ever-recurring crisis of the gas meter when there wasn't a quarter in the house, called for quiet diplomacy. Of an evening one of my sisters might be entertaining a gentleman who would, perhaps soon, we hoped, reveal himself as a suitor, when suddenly the gas would begin to flicker and go out. At such moments my mother would strike a match, reach for her purse, open it with her free hand, peer in it closely, and announce laughingly that she could find nothing but bills. The gentleman, hastily fumbling in his pocket, would produce a quarter, and the light would come on.

Time brought changes. Learning to relish the privileges of suffering, the Jewish mother could become absurdly, outrageously protective. From that condition, especially if linked, as it well might be, with contempt for

---

> building where I was visiting, others remained outside holding a sort of open-air meeting. It was about the small dog which the boy had been hiding and which now lay in his lap. The boys were discussing what to do with the puppy. No one dared take him home, because his mother would surely throw both of them out. The boys examined their new pet, touching his paws, ears, face, and tail. I left them in the middle of their discussion, suddenly recalling my own childhood in Europe, where we used to steal a dog from a rich gentile lady and play with him secretly for weeks, teaching him tricks and snatching food from our plates in order to feed him."

her husband, she could decline into a brassy scourge, with her grating bark or soul-destroying whine, silver-blue hair, and unfocused aggression. Nor was it unusual for her to employ ingenuity in order to keep her brood in a state of prolonged dependence, as she grew expert at groaning, cajoling, intimidating. Daughters paled, sons fled.

Yet even behind the most insufferable ways of the Jewish mother there was almost always a hard-earned perception of reality. Did she overfeed? Her mind was haunted by memories of a hungry childhood. Did she fuss about health? Infant mortality had been a plague in the old country and the horror of diphtheria overwhelming in this country. Did she dominate everyone within reach? A disarranged family structure endowed her with powers she had never known before, and burdens too; it was to be expected that she should abuse the powers and find advantage in the burdens. The weight of centuries bore down. In her bones, the Jewish mother knew that she and hers, simply by being Jewish, had always to live with a sense of precariousness. When she worried about her little boy going down to play, it was not merely the dangers of Rivington or Cherry Street that she saw— though there *were* dangers on such streets; it was the streets of Kishinev and Bialystok and other towns in which the blood of Jewish children had been spilled. Later, such memories would fade among those she had meant to shield and it would become customary to regard her as a grotesque figure of excess.

Venerated to absurdity, assaulted with a venom that testifies obliquely to her continuing moral and emotional power, the immigrant mother cut her path through the perils and entanglements of American life. Everyone spoke about her, against her, to her, but she herself has left no word to posterity, certainly none in her own voice, perhaps because all the talk about her "role" seemed to her finally trivial, the indulgence of those who had escaped life's primal tasks. Talk was a luxury that her labor would enable her sons to taste.

Boarders, Desertion, Generational Conflict

Composites, by their very nature, omit a wide range of eccentricity and variation. If the Jewish family was a major force making for stability in the immigrant world, it was also peculiarly open to the seepage of alien values. So many demands were made on it that sooner or later it had to show signs of strain and coming apart. No social arrangement as inherently delicate as the family could withstand the assaults that came from all sides—from the school, the street, the theatre, the gangs, the shops, the gentile world, all seemingly united in trying to rip apart the fabric of Jewish life.

If the memories of countless sons and daughters were of sustenance and warmth, the memories of others were of harshness, bickering, nastiness. Anyone reading through the "Bintel Brief" ("Bundle of Letters") column in the *Forward*, where readers declared their troubles with unnerving candor, might suppose that thwarted loves, broken homes, soured marriages, and heartless children were the norm of immigrant life. The Yiddish press of the early 1900's is filled with articles, some serious and others mere persiflage, concerning the damage wrought by boarders in immigrant homes. The sheer piling in of bodies into small spaces was itself enough to create psychic problems. Samuel Cohen has remembered how his brother Joseph rented a "large two-room flat" for ten dollars a month in order to be able to sublet the bedroom to four boarders, all of them drygoods peddlers, who kept their stock in the same room.

> Each boarder paid seventy-five cents a week, which was to include coffee in the morning and laundering. . . . Each would contribute six cents for a half pound of meat, thus making it two pounds in all, and two cents additional for vegetables in which the meat was cooked. . . . Every morning one of the boarders went down to the grocery store and bought four five-cent rye loaves. They would all breakfast on that with coffee. The remainder of each loaf was laid away for the evening meal. But my sister-in-law could not cut in on the loaves, for they all bore their owners' private marks!

What could happen in such a setting was described by one immigrant, Jacob Rosen, in a letter he sent to a Yiddish newspaper in 1903:

> My wife took in a boarder, a *landsman* who had a wife and three children in Europe. Soon he became chummy with my wife. She told me he wanted to buy her a hat and a skirt. At first I couldn't believe my ears, then I became jealous.
> One morning after I had left the house to go to my laundry, the boarder tried to attack my wife, but she escaped and locked him in the apartment. She came running to the laundry; I was furious but waited till I had calmed down. Then we went home. I took two sticks and we beat him so hard he couldn't go out for eight days. He gave us $80 and made us promise not to write to his wife.

Young wives might be stirred by visions of a more poetic or exalted mode of life—and how could husbands back from ten or twelve hours over a sewing machine satisfy such yearnings? No one will ever know how many Emma Bovarys lived and died on the East Side; but if we suppose Emma to represent an eternal possibility of human nature, there must have been a good many wives like her, restless and discontented, responding to the first tremors of Jewish romanticism. The majority of immigrant wives were, of course, committed to the sanctity of nurture and the ethic of self-sacrifice. Yet it is hard to suppose that without some deep-going disturbance in private life there would have been so many serialized novels in the Yiddish press about broken families, so endless an outcry of woe in the "Bintel Brief," so many nervously jocular references to the boarder's sexual exploits in Yiddish fiction, theatre, and folklore.

The most severe sign of disturbance was the persistent desertion of families by immigrant husbands. Records of the United Hebrew Charities in New York for the fiscal years 1903 and 1904 show that 1,052, or about 10 percent, of the applications for relief came from deserted women. In Chicago it was 15 percent. The Committee on Desertions of the Conference of Jewish Charities reported that in the period between October 15, 1905, and May 1, 1906, it handled 591 cases of desertion. Fifty-four of these were taken to court, with 33 agreeing to support their families, 18 serving a prison term, 2 released at the wife's request, and one simply destitute; 63 cases were settled out of court, with the husbands either returning to their families or agreeing to support them; 48 cases were pending; and the remainder, somewhat more than half, were "awaiting further information"—that is, the husbands could not be found. In 1911 this work was consolidated on a national scale through the establishment of the National Desertion Bureau. In 1912 it reported 561 cases among Jewish immigrants in New York alone. The reasons given for desertion were: 120, another woman; 47, bad habits; 134, insufficient dowry; 4, wife immoral; 3, another man, and so on. Because many deserted wives, out of shame or fear, failed to report their husbands, many of the men never were in fact discovered. The figures can therefore be taken as, at best, an approximation of how serious the problem was.

For years the *Forward* ran a feature, "Gallery of Missing Husbands," that contained photographs of men who had deserted and pleas that they get in touch with their families. The paper received letters from distant places, from abandoned wives in Russia and Galicia asking that their husbands be located in America, and, in one instance, from a black woman pleading for help because she had been left with a baby. Here are a few notices from a 1910 issue of the *Forward:*

> Sarah Solomon is searching for her husband who is now uptown, 38–40 years old, solid build, medium height, black eyes, black mustache, left me 2½ years ago. I offer $25 to anyone who will notify me of his whereabouts. He doesn't have to be afraid of divorcing me. Notify me at 132 Ludlow Street, in the restaurant.

> I am looking for my husband Nathan Cohen, known as Note Moshe Mendele Shenker's from Nashelsk, Russia-Poland, umbrella peddler, 22 years old, the little finger of his right hand is bent. He abandoned me and a 5-month-old baby in great need. Whoever knows of him should have mercy on a young woman and infant and get in touch with Bessie Cohen, 1415 Snagman Street, Chicago.

Jewish agencies pressed for legislation that would make desertion a felony rather than a misdemeanor (in 1905 such a law was passed in New

York State) and that would prevent deserters from evading their responsibilities by crossing state lines. The Yiddish world was full of discussions as to
the reasons for desertion, and an article in a 1910 *Forward* by M. Baranov
offered an explanation about as good as those that trained sociologists would
later provide. Baranov wrote that most of the desertions occur among "the
mass of uneducated young Jews." The old ones come to America "with
sacred traditions; the middle-aged Jews have rigid outlooks; the youthful
istn [political activists] have principles. But the young men without spiritual
roots are defenseless against American life." And then, quite in the spirit of
Durkheim, he continued:

> In Europe they were not responsible for their lives; they lived within the
> framework of police regulations, religious ritual, teachings of relatives and
> neighbors. Every step was decided beforehand. Their road of life was narrow,
> but they could not get lost. . . . In America young Jews are hurled into a
> world of freedom—no fences, no police, no communal judgment. It's every
> man for himself. Nothing sacred; you can buy or sell everything for money.
> The aim of life is amusement; conscience and honor fall by the wayside. . . .
> Such a young man gets married. In three or four years he has several chil-
> dren, who are a nuisance. His wife grows sickly. His wages are too low to
> allow him any fun. He fights with his wife, who doesn't let him out of the
> house. There are gay young girls out there, and carefree bachelors. The
> anarchists preach free love; the freethinkers guarantee there is no God and
> no punishment in the afterlife. The young man thinks, "I'm a free person,
> who cares what they say," and one fine day he leaves home and forgets to
> come back. He becomes a missing husband.

An extreme symptom, the desertion of husbands aroused abhorrence
among all segments of the immigrant world; but it did not really threaten
life at its center, certainly not as much as the friction between parents and
children. If conflicts between generations are central to the experience of all
immigrant groups, among the Jews these became especially severe because
of the persuasion that, at almost any cost, it was necessary to propel sons and
daughters into the outer world—or, more precisely, to propel them into the
outer world as social beings while trying to keep them spiritually within the
Jewish orbit. Morris Raphael Cohen, who grew up on the East Side, saw the
conflict between generations mostly as a struggle of ideas: "We called upon
the old religion to justify itself on the basis of modern science and culture.
But the old generation was not in a position to say how this could be
done. . . . What ensued was a struggle between old and new ideals. Homes
ceased to be places of peace and in the ensuing discord much of the prover-
bial strength of the Jewish family was lost." Cohen was surely right in the
long run, but it is arguable that during the years when the immigrant culture
was at its strongest the clash between generations lent it a kind of vitality, an
inner tension generating new energy.

Neither side could have known, nor gained much consolation if it had, that in the cramped precincts of the ghetto they were re-enacting tests of conscience that had shaken European intellectual life throughout the nineteenth century. Denounced as "a daughter of Babylon" when she first brought home earnings from her literary work, and excoriated by a father who cried out that "in America money takes the place of God," Anzia Yezierska was trapped in a heart struggle much like that of George Eliot with her father. The classic war to the death between father and son in Samuel Butler's *The Way of All Flesh* would find a small-scale replica in the fictional memories of Budd Schulberg's *What Makes Sammy Run?*:

> "I hadda chance to make a dollar," Sammy said.
> "Sammy!" his father bellowed. "Touching money on the Sabbath! God should strike you dead!"
> The old man snatched the money and flung it down the stairs. . . .
> "You big dope!" Sammy screamed at him, his voice shrill with rage. "You lazy son-of-a-bitch."
> The old man did not respond. His eyes were closed and his lips were moving. He looked as if he had had a stroke. He was praying.

This conflict between generations *had* to be unbearably fierce. Lincoln Steffens, for some years closely involved with the immigrant community, saw

> an abyss of many generations. . . . We would pass a synagogue where a score or more of boys were sitting hatless in their old clothes, smoking cigarettes on the steps outside, and their fathers, all dressed in black, with their high hats, uncut beards, and temple curls, were going into the synagogues, tearing their hair and rending their garments. The reporters stopped to laugh; and it was comic; the old men, in their thrift, tore the lapels of their coats very carefully, a very little, but they wept tears, real tears.

It was a struggle beyond conciliation, and the more it raked up old affections the more bitter it grew. Responses that few could allow themselves to recognize or name, responses of embarrassment, guilt, and shame, were brought into the open. One's parents were to be cherished yet kept in the background; to be loved yet brushed aside. Among one's friends, especially if they had some pretensions to culture, it was understood that parents were a cause for uneasiness—a reason, by the way, that so much of the younger generations' social life moved toward the streets. Arthur Goldhaft, son of an immigrant, has expressed with a rare honesty feelings of shame about parents he also loved:

> The [immigrant Jews] themselves seemed ready to accept the idea that they were nobodies. They were so scared that they even dropped the pride of a family name. Or maybe they had something deep in them that was a greater pride, that made all this name business a trifle . . . which we, their American children, didn't catch on to. This perhaps is the first key to what disturbed so many of us as we grew up—the feeling that our folks were just nobodies.

How could the younger people understand why their fathers felt that identity rested not in a name—Weisenberg or Weiss or Wiss or even White —but in unbreakable membership in a sanctified people? And even if sons and daughters could understand this, as Goldhaft struggled to, of what earthly use would it be when they began to push their way into American society?

The immigrant leaders and intellectuals tried to cope with the problem, but they were helpless. In 1903 Abraham Cahan printed a *Forward* editorial on baseball, a subject that until then had eluded his public scrutiny. A father had written in bemoaning his son's fondness for baseball: "What is the point of this crazy game? It makes sense to teach a child to play dominoes or chess." But baseball?* "The children can get crippled. . . . I want my boy to grow up to be a *mensh*, not a wild American runner." Poor Cahan, trying to cope with problems beyond the wisdom of a Solomon, replied cautiously that Jewish boys should be allowed to play baseball—as if anyone could stop them!—"as long as it does not interfere with their education." Chess was good, "but the body needs to develop also. Baseball is played in the fresh air. The really wild game is football, the aristocratic game in the colleges. Accidents and fights occur in football, but baseball is not dangerous." Even for Cahan there had to be a limit, his Jewish fright and socialist rectitude drawing the line at "aristocratic" football. He ended, however, with his usual good sense: "It is a mistake to keep children locked up in the house. . . . Bring them up to be educated, ethical, and decent, but also to be physically strong so they should not feel inferior."

Suspicion of the physical, fear of hurt, anxiety over the sheer "pointlessness" of play: all this went deep into the recesses of the Jewish psyche. It was a price, hardly the largest, that Jews had paid for the conviction of specialness. They could no more suppress their true feelings about the frivolities of street or gymnasium than they could deny the shudder that passed through them on walking past a church. A sensitive writer remembering his childhood in Brownsville would conclude that "intellectual and spiritual independence came easily to the Brownsville child . . . but the right to breathe freely, to use one's arms and legs and voice forcibly . . . these privileges had to be conquered inch by inch." Decades would have to go by before the sons and daughters of the immigrants could shake off—if they ever could!—this heritage of discomfort before the uses and pleasures of the body. What they were struggling for was nothing less than the persuasion that they had as much right as anyone else to feel at home on this earth, and what their parents were saying was no, Jews could not feel at home on this earth. Seemingly trivial or comic disputes over matters like

* " 'Stop! You—you—you baseball player you!' scolded grandma, hurrying after us into the hall. That was the worst name," recalls Eddie Cantor, "she could call me. To the pious people of the ghetto a baseball player was the king of loafers."

playing baseball released profound clashes of world view, perhaps nothing less than whether Jewish messianism still mattered in the new world.

Several years after Cahan's defense of baseball, the Yiddish poet Abraham Liessen published a lament, not the first and surely not the last, over the growing estrangement of Jewish youth. Writing in the summer of 1910, Liessen noted the growing number of Jewish graduates from schools and colleges but then went on to ask: "What has the Jewish quarter gained from all these intelligent young Jews?" Not much, apparently. The recent cloakmakers' strike, in which "priests and Fifth Avenue ladies are interested," was "ignored by intellectual Jewish youth. . . . These are the children of the workers who sacrificed themselves to give them an education. You see these workers every day, exhausted, pale, slaving over the machines. Why don't their intelligent children feel a debt?"

By 1910, according to Liessen, one could see an important social change in the East Side. A decade or more earlier, the usual kind of generational clash had occurred between Orthodox parents and radical children, while now it took place between radical parents and worldly, ambitious children. A cruel kind of justice—perhaps the sole answer to Liessen's question "Why don't their intelligent children feel a debt?"

While the generational struggle continued for decades, it would be some years before it seriously threatened the coherence of the immigrant community. Until the First World War large numbers of new immigrants kept arriving, with each new wave forced in part to re-enact the experience of the preceding ones. The institutional structure of the Jewish community kept growing in strength, a barrier against disintegration. And the struggle between old and young continued to be acted out mainly on immigrant territory, even the most rebellious sons still forced by circumstance and feeling to remain within the cultural orbit of their fathers. What would finally doom the immigrant Jewish culture was not any internal development at all, but the ending of immigration in the twenties—for that would signify a decisive tipping of strength in the struggle between old and new.

The Inner World of the Landsmanshaft

The old persisted, stubborn, rooted in the depths of common memory. As if to re-create in miniature the very world from which they had fled, the immigrant Jews established a remarkable network of societies called *landsmanshaftn*, probably the most spontaneous in character of all their institutions, and the closest in voice and spirit to the masses. While the Jews had seldom felt much loyalty to Russia or Poland as nations, they brought with them fierce affections for the little places they had lived in, the muddy streets, battered synagogues, remembered fields from which they had fled. The *landsmanshaft,* a lodge made up of persons coming from the same town or district in the old country, was their ambiguous testimony to a past they knew to be wretched yet often felt to be sweet.

The *landsmanshaft* began in the simplest ways. Immigrants, feeling themselves lost in American cities, would seek out old-country neighbors—the phrase *di alte heym,* the old home, keeps reverberating through Yiddish speech, writing, and plays. Coming together, they formed modest little organizations that kept alive memories and helped them fit into the new world.

Many of the *landsmanshaftn* formed during the last few decades of the nineteenth century were also *anshe,* congregations established according to place of origin or by occupation; but by about 1900 the majority of the *landsmanshaftn* were secular in character, some even adorning themselves with English names like the First Kalisher Benevolent Association, signs of a wish to hasten the process of *oysgrinen zikh,* ceasing to be greenhorns.

Why were the *landsmanshaftn* started? A 1938 survey by the Yiddish Writers Group of the Federal Writers Project yields replies by old-timers:

> The men here felt miserable, they left their wives or brides back home, so they used to get together in the house of a married *landsman* to drink tea or play cards.

> A *landsman* was about to be deported because he was sick, so the *landslayt* realized the importance of having their own organization for self-help.

> A *landsman* died in the factory. People think he is a Greek and bury him in Potter's Field. *Landslayt* hear about it, his body is dug up, and the decision taken to start our organization with a cemetery.

Before the First World War some of these secular *landsmanshaftn* had a semisocialist flavor, bringing together craftsmen from an old-country trade who had lived together in a town or neighborhood. But soon the kinds of immigrants who aspired to political action drifted away, either into the various parties or into the socialistic Workmen's Circle. The *landsmanshaftn* would experience two phases of looking outward, during the First World War, when they would send money to help their people back home, and during the thirties, when they would join the entire Jewish community in trying to help the victims of Nazism. But in the main, the *landsmanshaftn* were jealous of their self-contained character—that impulse to social inwardness which brought a member to the monthly meeting in an East Side hall, away from family quarrels, troubles of livelihood, and the noise of Jewish politics. When the political types dropped away, the remaining members seem to have been relieved, for they preferred not to be bothered by all those orators and intellectals. What they wanted was the closeness of familiars, the pleasures of smallness regained.

Societies from various east European regions would come together to set up a loose *farband*, or federation. A Galician federation of *landsmanshaftn* was formed in 1904, a Polish federation in 1908, a Romanian federation in 1909. By pooling resources, these federations were able to establish hospitals, convalescent centers, and old-age homes. But only seldom did these larger structures affect the inner life of a particular *landsmanshaft*.

In a good many of the *landsmanshaft* constitutions—and their founders were ferocious writers of constitutions—there is a proviso that as long as seven or ten members survive it is forbidden to change the name of the society, quite as if the name, token of an unrecoverable past, has taken on a sacred character. These constitutions reflect the pleasure the founders must have felt in setting up their own rules, perhaps the only place where they could set up their own rules. Most of the constitutions require that the books be kept in Yiddish, though one, that of Anshei Grodno, says that while business may be transacted in Yiddish, the constitution itself must be accorded the dignity of Hebrew. The Independent Mogilnitser provide that if anyone wishes to speak at a meeting in a language other than Yiddish he must first gain the permission of the chair.

Some constitutions offer homely statements of purpose, as the Ershte Turower: "This organization exists to help sick and needy brothers, also to pay expenses of death cases and endowments." More ambitious is the preamble of the Ershte Shendishower Galitzianer Khevra: "The goal of the society is to maintain the spirit of fraternity. . . . That ideal has to be kept alive among the younger generation born in this land and [as if to anticipate the outcry of every Jewish organization during the coming decades] an attempt must be made to plant in them an awareness of our origins."

The rules of the *landsmanshaftn* are like pocket mirrors to a culture. The Kolomeir constitution refuses admission to saloonkeepers. The Narevker declares that if a member marries, a committee of seven will be chosen to grace the wedding, with "hat check . . . on the account of the organization." The Pukhoveritser is strict as to decorum, insisting that "at the funeral of a member or his wife every member has the duty to dress neatly and arrive on time. . . . Every member must line up and is not allowed to smoke during the funeral, and when someone disobeys he will be fined fifty cents." With the Narevker Untershtitsung Fareyn, a member who marries is to receive a five-dollar gift, but only if he has belonged a full year; and the present must be given personally by the vice-president at the wedding. Virtually all the constitutions declare that if a member marries a gentile, he will be stricken from the rolls.

Marriage regulations are strict. Paragraph 13 of the First Kalisher Benevolent constitution specifies: "When a member gets married he must propose his wife to the society, the society will then appoint a committee, which will go to the doctor with her to obtain a statement about her health. In case the doctor declares her health to be unsatisfactory, the concerned member will remain single, or if he marries will not get any death benefit for his wife." The Anshei Kaminets di Lita offers meticulous instructions: "When a member marries off his child, he will get the *khupe* [bridal canopy] free and also the gas illumination in the *shul*. On the *shabes* after the wedding, he has the right to stand next to the president on the *bime* [stage]."

Constitutions provide for benefits, from those for sitting *shive* (mourning for the dead), usually five or seven dollars, to special sums for members stricken with tuberculosis. In the latter regard the Turower constitution is exemplary: "When a member gets ill from consumption he will receive one hundred dollars extra, besides the twenty-dollar-a-week benefit, which will be paid for five weeks. . . . When it will be found necessary to support him further, this will be discussed at a special meeting."

Some constitutions require that a member suffering from an "immoral disease" be denied sick benefits. Others specify the rights of the dead, "a hearse and two carriages" at the funeral. Anxieties sometimes break out concerning Americanization, as in the Krasilaver clause insisting that "a *ba'al tefilla* [prayer leader] who prays on High Holy Days in front of the lectern must not shave or cut his beard and must not be a desecrator of the Sabbath." How extraordinary a change in the nature of Jewish life is suggested by the mere thought that a *ba'al tefilla* might be a desecrator of the Sabbath!

In the constitution of the Sanover *landsmanshaft*, almost as if it had undergone a Masonic infusion, there are rules for elaborate rituals ("When you enter and the meeting has already started, you have to greet the president with the right hand on the left breast.") At least in this respect, the *landsmanshaftn* were not very different from lodges the world over, with their hocus-pocus and improvised designations of rank. "The raw elements among the immigrants who were working their way up," writes Borukh Rivkin in a thoughtful study of the *landsmanshaftn*, "accepted this theatricality with the lust for honor characteristic of those who had never had any. The lodge ceremonial supplanted the synagogue ceremonial. When could such Jews have imagined becoming head of a synagogue? But here they could even be a president!"

Moral refinements brighten up these constitutions, as in the Ponevesher rule that "a member who reproaches another with having accepted help [from the emergency fund] will be fined one dollar. The second time he will be turned in to the court." An equally delicate adjustment is proposed by the Ershter Turower Untershtitsung Fareyn: "If there are any misunderstandings between the Yiddish [of the constitution] and the English translation, the Yiddish must be given priority."

It would be foolish to suppose that all was kindness and light in the *landsmanshaftn*. How could it be? They shared in the narrowness of culture that marked the early years of the immigration, and frequently they helped to perpetuate it. In 1896, for example, the Khevre Khokhmes Adam Merplinsk stubbornly refused to pay a death benefit to a member's wife because of a rule that anyone whose husband died while residing above Houston Street was ineligible for such a benefit. The New York *Times*, not always amiably inclined toward the grubby folk below Houston Street, reported this news under the headline "Died Too Far Uptown." The *Times* also noticed that the same society was being sued by Mrs. Nathan Greenstein because it refused to pay a death benefit for her deceased husband, on the ground, as the *Times* slyly headlined, that "When He Fails to Pay an Assessment, Because He Is Dead Is No Excuse." In later years there would be a softening of spirit and a polishing of manner among the *landslayt*, yet those who could not pay their dues would still face expulsion.

The greatest difficulties of these societies usually arose from financial innocence. Most of them worked by the "assessment system," which meant that as members grew sick or died the others were taxed to pay the cost of benefits. Seemingly in accord with traditional Jewish ideas of equal sharing, it was a system that worked well enough when members were young and not likely to die in large numbers; but once the average age reached the fifties, the number of assessments increased so rapidly that they placed an alarming burden on the remaining members. Had the *landsmanshaft* founders known about actuarial tables . . . but if they had been the kind of people who knew about such things they would probably never have founded *landsmanshaftn*. After a few decades many societies faced financial disaster through a multiplication of assessments. Some turned for rescue to the national orders, like the Workmen's Circle, while in other instances, younger members split away to form their own societies, often with such prefixes as "The Young Men's" or "Progressive" in their names.

Rickety yet durable, the *landsmanshaftn* satisfied many needs. A member could assuage his nostalgia for the old country by listening to reports at the meetings from newly arrived immigrants or those who had gone back for a visit. He could share in the deeply rooted Jewish tradition of communal self-help, which in practice might mean sending money back home for Passover matzos or to repair the *shul*. The society would provide help for unemployed members, usually in confidential ways, and once the wives started their ladies' auxiliary, this task was often turned over to them, as appropriate to their superior sense of delicacy.

Landslayt tended to congregate in distinct parts of the East Side, the northeast corner of Clinton and Rivington streets, for example, being the hangout of those who had come from the Galician town of Lemberg. There were corners for those from Chortkov, Boiberik, Tarnopol, Prszemisl, and Kolomei, where "matchmakers come to make appointments, bosses look for hands, and people find relatives they haven't seen for ages." As things got a little better, the various societies would congregate in their own cafés:

> . . . you don't need a passport. . . . A Jew from Vilkomir can enjoy the chopped liver in the Minskers' café. . . . *Landslayt* in the cafés boast about their societies. . . . A young man from Minsk says his is the best, another jumps up to say his gives a hundred dollars to each member who marries, so

a third one yells out, "Sure, but you don't take in bachelors. . . ." On the whole, the *landslayt* cafés live in peace with one another. If there is a fire in a *shtetl*, everyone sympathizes; if a spinster finds a husband, everyone is happy; if a rabbi dies, even the heretics weep.

With its meager resources, the *landsmanshaft* ventured on a modest anticipation of social security: it provided sickness and death benefits, and it hired a doctor, himself often an immigrant just out of medical school, who for a small retainer, sometimes no more than a hundred dollars a year, would treat members at reduced rates. In fact, many a Jewish doctor began his practice as a "society doctor," a term that meant something very different from what it would come to suggest in later years. One of them recalls:

> With pull you'd get the job. If you were a doctor for a small *landsmanshaft*, one day you'd run to Brooklyn, the next day to the Bronx to treat a society patient. The society would pay me a certain amount for coverage for a certain number of patients—fifty cents for a single member every three months, seventy-five cents or a dollar for a family. Every member had a right to come to my office and ask me to call at his house. I took the job because in that way I was sure of being able to pay the rent for my office. On my own I took in very little.
>
> Some doctors were devoted, many not. Some patients took advantage of the system and it wasn't always very pleasant. Most society members treated their doctors with respect, but some said, "A society doctor? What can he know?" For more serious illnesses, they'd go to another doctor.
>
> I delivered babies in the house and would get a practical nurse to follow up for a week or so. The society member paid extra for the delivery of babies, something like ten or fifteen dollars, as I remember.
>
> The society member would recommend the doctor to his friends, and in that way you could build up a practice. But it was hard, lots of running up and down tenement stairs. When I moved my office to the Grand Concourse, I gave up the society.

For many members, the most important function of the *landsmanshaft* was that it ensured proper burial. As the Jewish historian Salo Baron has remarked, "The cemetery appeared as second only to the synagogue among communal institutions [in the life of European and Asian Jews]. In view of the possibility of private congregational worship, many communities sought burial plots even before erecting a house of worship." One of the first things every *landsmanshaft* did was to purchase a plot of land in a Jewish cemetery. The necessities of life might force a Jew to spend his days among strangers, but even if no longer Orthodox he wanted to spend eternity among Jews.

At meetings the members took care of practical needs. Insurance agents were notorious for belonging to many *landsmanshaftn;* so too young doctors and lawyers looking for a bit of income. Unemployed garment workers might soften the heart of an employer if he happened also to be a *landsman*.

Yiddish poets sometimes managed to persuade their societies to finance a thin volume: you didn't have to read the stuff to be proud of publishing "a famous writer."

There were other, less tangible, benefits. At the meetings or just after, you could relax over a game of pinochle, get caught up in an intrigue over who the next president would be, enjoy the solemnities of parliamentary ritual, and once in a while share the excitement following a treasurer's departure with the funds.

Best of all, there were seldom outsiders. Seldom union officials, seldom politicians, seldom "community spokesmen," seldom rabbis (except for a eulogy when a member died). In a community always in danger of becoming overideologized, the *landsmanshaft* served as a nonideological oasis. Is that not one secret behind its persistence—the need felt by ordinary people to be at home among themselves? Ideologues and intellectuals in the Yiddish world were always uneasy with these societies, sometimes mocking them as uncultured or deficient in the higher idealism. The founders of the early Jewish unions saw the *landsmanshaft* as a paternalistic barrier to class unity: it was hard to organize shops where workers came from the same town as the boss. The men who wished to create a self-conscious Jewish community saw the *landsmanshaft* as a provincial impediment. The men who dreamed of a rich Yiddish culture saw the *landsmanshaft* as a bulwark of parochial narrowness.

They were often right. Yet the masses of immigrants, though in time a good many would join the unions and the parties, remained faithful to their societies. In the *landsmanshaft*, through the very transparency of its ends, the immigrant Jews released their wish simultaneously to cling to the cultural tokens of the fading past and bend a little to the bruising present. The ranks narrowed; societies that had once proclaimed themselves "Young Men" from such-and-such a place had no members under sixty; minute books were lost or carelessly thrown away.

Estimates of the number of *landsmanshaftn* vary widely, from about three thousand to perhaps twice that number. Eighty percent of the societies sprang up between 1903 and 1909, and as late as 1938 there were still half a million members of *landsmanshaftn* in New York City alone, with another quarter of a million in the remainder of the country. Eighty-five percent of them were foreign-born; efforts to recruit sons never really succeeded.

Provincial as they were, and perhaps just because they were provincial, the *landsmanshaftn* would perform one last service for the immigrant Jews. After the Second World War, when the news of the Holocaust reached the United States, the *landsmanshaftn* began to issue *yizkor bikher* (memorial volumes) in memory of the *shtetlakh* from which they had come. Hundreds of such volumes have been published, some threadbare, merely listing names and printing photographs, but others, like the books issued by the Brainsker and Bialystoker societies, offering local histories of Jewish settlement. Some

of these *yizkor bikher* are heartbreaking: here is one from the town Volko-
visk, which in 1910 had 14,500 inhabitants, of whom 8,000 were Jews. It is a
990-page book rich with sociological and historical materials, with excellent
pictures of Jewish activities, not only those of rabbis and merchants but also
of boxers, cyclists, firemen, even skiers. Themselves harassed and driven out
decades ago, and their relatives taken from these little towns directly to the
ovens, the immigrant Jews nevertheless cherished memories of the mud and
sticks in the places where they had been born.

Long after the *landsmanshaftn* entered their decline, an interviewer
asked the president of the Ponevesher society about its ultimate purposes.
The answer came as unadorned as the *landsmanshaftn* themselves:

> To die but not to die off . . . everybody in his place tries not to die off but
> to prolong his memory. . . . Our *khevra kadisha* [burial group], besides
> taking care of the grave in accordance with the law of Israel, immortalize
> the name of each member by reciting it at *yizkor*. It is to be wished that our
> young members will join us so that this important institution will exist
> forever. Because we are all mortal.

Shul, *Rabbi, and Cantor*

In the communal life of the immigrants, the synagogue, or *shul*, remained the single institution everyone took for granted. Despite the rise of
secularist ideologies and the spread of a weary indifference among the
masses, few could envisage a time when the *shul* would cease to be at the
center of Jewish life. God could easily be neglected in New York, it was
probably not His favorite city, yet He was not at all forgotten. While only a
minority continued to follow the rituals with literal exactness, the aura of
faith, which is also to say, the particulars of old-world Jewish culture,
remained strong in the nostrils of the immigrants.

The *shul* formed an integral part of immigrant Jewish life, clearly so
for those who believed, but also, in part, for those who did not. For the
folksmasn, the great mass of ordinary people, the *shul* served as a visible
reminder of God: it did not command daily attendance as in the old country, it could no longer claim to be an exclusive arbiter of morals and manners, but it remained a large presence, registering Jewish continuity and
coherence. The connections between *shul* and immigrants were not necessarily formal—statistics relating to synagogue membership or attendance
never tell us very much about the religious sentiments of Jews. The bulk of
the immigrants simply assumed that it was desirable for the more fervent
among them to keep the *shul* alive, providing the daily *minyan*, or quorum

of worshipers, and maintaining the facilities that the majority could use on occasion.

Ordinary immigrants went to *shul* at least several times a year, especially on Rosh Hashonah and Yom Kippur—Yom Kippur, the Day of Atonement, having so sacred a resonance that they felt that to go then was to confirm one's identity as a Jew. In their homes they observed the rituals of *kashruth*, assuming as a matter of course that major ceremonials, *bar mitzvah* to marriage, would take place under the aegis of the *shul*.

Were they believers, these masses of immigrants? Perhaps not entirely, probably less so as the years went by, and certainly not with the rigor of their fathers.* Were they disbelievers? By no means, and surely not with the fanaticism of the more extreme radicals. "Many of the irreligious immigrants," remarked a keen American reporter in 1896, "relax their atheism on . . . Yom Kippur. . . . 'It is safe and does no harm,' said a non-believer who scorned the ignorance of the Orthodox and laughed as he told what his people do." To the immigrants God was a presence in Jewish life, just as the *shul* was the place where one reknit one's ties with Him, or at least renewed acquaintance. In the writings of Sholom Aleichem there is precisely the same inclination to dissolve formal issues of belief into an acceptance of custom and sentiment: God is someone to whom Jews must keep talking, and as for whether He "exists" or not, that is a problem for philosophers.

In principle, the *shul* claimed the whole of its members' attention, quite as it had in eastern Europe. It tried to provide a range of activities to rival that of the immigrant culture itself, for the believers feared, reasonably enough, that this culture was a threat to their hegemony. In the years shortly after 1900, the Forsyth Street synagogue, for example,

> has a *khevra kadisha* consisting of over twenty members who perform all the rites connected with the burial of the members: the *khevra* is social, for it gives banquets very often; on certain Sabbaths its members are accorded privileges at the reading of the law. The same synagogue has organized a *khevra schas* or *mishnayoth*. This society has forty or fifty members, and there are no dues; the members study the Talmud every evening in the vestry rooms of the synagogues. The Ladies Benevolent Society consists of over 150 members; the dues are paid monthly, and are devoted to charity.

Not many synagogues succeeded in maintaining these structures; competition from the secular institutions of the East Side was severe.

Some synagogues were fairly imposing; most were ramshackle and improvised. During the 1890's and 1900's the East Side had numerous tenement synagogues, often several of them occupying neighboring apartments and consisting of members who in the old country had lived in adjacent towns.

* "The Orthodox Jewish faith," reflected Abraham Cahan's protagonist in *The Rise of David Levinsky*, "is absolutely inflexible. If you are a Jew of the type to which I belonged when I came to New York and you attempt to bend your religion to the spirit of your new surroundings, it breaks. . . . The very clothes I wore and the very food I ate had a fatal effect on my religious habits."

In *shul*

Here, at 125 Rivington Street, is the Golden Rule Hall. [On Yom Kippur] five separate congregations worship on its five separate floors, and worship for twelve hours at a stretch. Crowds of young, middle-aged and old go in and out, up and down the creaky stairs, in intermittent unending streams. Grandsires gray, puling infants, tired women and struggling men, to whom Yom Kippur is more than Sabbath, are all there for this one day. . . . Within each steaming room some men chat and some women gossip at intervals, children are sleepily quiet, and devotees in grave habiliments occupy the corners. Wild is the recitative of the *hazan* [cantor]. . . . Conviction speaks from the depth of his being, and passionate devotion in his vibratory tones. His memory is marvelous. Not a syllable escapes that of one blind patriarch.

Somewhat less exalted is Samuel Chotzinoff's recollection of the crush at Yom Kippur worship:

> At least 100 men and boys were packed in a room that could not have accommodated 50. Like every Yom Kippur I had known before . . . this one was unbearably warm and humid. I had taken the precaution the day before of buying a tiny phial of "Yom Kippur drops" for a penny, and whenever I grew faint I would take a whiff and feel better for a while. But in the late afternoon there came a moment when the men removed their shoes and prayed in their stocking feet. Inured to individual odors only, I was unable to tolerate the massed onslaught. I fainted dead away.

The capacity of Jewish worshipers to combine disorder and fervor, odors and exaltation, was difficult for outsiders, even for children of the immigrants, to understand;* perhaps it had something to do with a feeling that matter and spirit, far from being split by a Protestant dualism, should dwell together. In any case, the High Holy Days soon became a major religio-social occasion for the immigrants, graced with such aesthetic adornments as virtuoso cantors and trained choirs. The adoration that worshipers gave a brilliant cantor was like the adoration opera enthusiasts shower on a brilliant tenor. When a famous European cantor arrived—Israel Cooper or Pinkhas Minkovsky in earlier days, Zavl Kwartin or Yossele Rosenblatt later on—the Yiddish press offered lengthy articles with expert scrutiny of their cantillation.

There was also a strong business aspect to the competition for cantors:

> The net proceeds from the sale of seats are in many instances the main source of the congregation's income. Hence, the hiring of a good cantor is generally viewed in the light of an investment. . . . Some celebrities are paid for the four principal services of the Days of Awe as much as $1,000 [in 1897], but such virtuosos apart, $200 would be a fair average of the cantor's fee, although the humbler congregations cannot afford to pay more than $50 for the season.

When Yossele Rosenblatt, whose voice was pure, high, and nimble, came to America in 1909 to sing at Ohab Zedek Congregation in Harlem, he was paid the astonishing salary of $2,400 a year. "There were occasions," his son recalled, "when an admission charge limiting the size of the crowd seeking entrance to the synagogue, was imperative. . . . As early as 2 AM the entire block of 116 Street would be black with men and women, some of whom had traveled great distances to hear Yossele Rosenblatt."

Observance among the immigrants was essentially Orthodox, few of them being tempted by the "flavorless" innovations the German Jews had

---

* "To look at this whispering, gesticulating, nodding, ecstatic crowd, it was almost hard to imagine them in any other role than holding communion with their Maker. . . . But *Minha* over, each at once assumed a work-a-day air, and as they kissed the *mezuza* parchment on the door-post in haste to get out into the noisy street, there was again a cluster of tailors, peddlers, store-keepers, each with the seal of worldly care on his face."

introduced as Reform Judaism during the nineteenth century. But if they clung to traditional modes of liturgy, they could not avoid changes in synagogue organization. Rabbis imported from Europe found it hard to adapt to the styles of American congregations and quickly had to confront a crisis in authority. Laymen in America, especially those who had grown wealthy and upon whom congregations depended, were likely to be more assertive—sometimes more vulgar—than in Russia or Poland. For the rabbis, this often meant grief and humiliation. So-called reverends, without rabbinic authority or competence, sprang up like parasites, quick to make a dollar by performing marriage ceremonies. In the early years "it was not the rabbi but the *hazan* who was considered the important functionary of the Orthodox congregations. . . . The rabbi, unless he was a popular preacher, was considered a somewhat superfluous burden; he received only a small salary, or none at all, having to rely for a living on the emoluments of the rabbinical office."

Gradually the governance of the synagogue shifted toward something like that of late Congregationalism, with decisive power in the hands of the "businessmen" and the rabbi regarded as an employee who might minister to the "spiritual needs" of his congregants but had best be cautious in making spiritual demands on them. "They let me be *frum* [pious] and I let them be free"—this sardonic epigram comes from a rabbi of a later decade, but if not entirely applicable to the years before the First World War it certainly points to a growing trend.

One major attempt had been made in New York to impose a quasi-theocratic framework on Orthodoxy. In 1888 a number of congregations, calling themselves the Association of the American Hebrew Orthodox Congregations, proposed to appoint a "chief rabbi," whose tasks would include ruling on matters of ritual and belief, raising the spiritual level of the faithful, and bringing order to the sale of kosher meat. A scholar of unimpeachable piety and sweet temper, Rabbi Jacob Joseph, was brought over from Vilna and installed with much enthusiasm. But once he actually tried to regulate the kosher-meat business, notorious for its strong-arm methods, he became entangled in a mesh of business interests he could not begin to cope with. The butchers and ritual slaughterers, as well as some rabbis, had repeatedly been locked in disputes over the income from *kashruth:* "fist fights were not uncommon and disregard for Jewish law and Board of Health ordinances was rampant." Rabbi Joseph and his Orthodox Association now proposed a penny tax upon poultry as the minimal cost of strict rabbinical control: "From this day forward," he proclaimed in the fall of 1888, "every bird slaughtered in the abbatoir under our supervision will be stamped with a *plumbe* [lead seal]."

This *plumbe* became a weight dragging Rabbi Joseph to depths of indignity. It reminded many Jews of the *karobka*, or Russian government tax on kosher meat—had they not fled the czar in order to avoid such impositions? The Jewish radicals started an agitation against the American *karobka*, as they called it; so did many butchers and slaughterers, who believed that inspection best which inspected least. Congregations drawn from Galician and Hungarian Jews, always discomfited by the intellectual superiority of the Litvaks (Lithuanian Jews), started looking for a "chief rabbi" of their own, and in 1892 appointed Rabbi Joshua Segal to the post. What followed was a squalid competition between the two "chief rabbis" and their partisans over the supervision of kosher meat and the issuance of decrees through their respective *bet din*, or rabbinical courts. In 1893 a third "chief rabbi" was added to the roster in New York, Rabbi Hayim Vidrowitz, who had come from Moscow, gathered a few Hasidic *shtiblakh* [prayer rooms], and hung out a sign reading "Chief Rabbi of America." Asked who had given him this title, Rabbi Vidrowitz replied "The sign painter."

Reduced to shame and parody, the whole project of declaring a chief rabbi collapsed, the Orthodox Association declined to a paper organization, and Rabbi Joseph, a child in the American wilderness, fell sick with paralysis, suffering neglect and poverty in his last few years. "It was unrealistic to expect to transplant the organizational form of religious life of the European community to American soil. There the rabbi was spiritual head of a community; in America a rabbi's authority extended only to the congregation he was elected to serve."

Versions of Belief

Orthodoxy survived this fiasco, just as it managed to overcome its incapacity to set up the kinds of centralized institutions that helped the Reform and Conservative wings of American Judaism adapt themselves to native circumstances. The Orthodox congregations in America tended to be jealous of their local rights and disinclined to build up elaborate national structures—though by the turn of the century Orthodox Jews in New York and Chicago had established seminaries that could train teachers and insure rabbinical continuity. What held the Orthodox Jews together was a conviction that they alone represented legitimate Jewish faith and that this faith should be maintained by holding fast to traditional patterns of ritual and worship. As long as the mass migration from eastern Europe continued, there were also new recruits to the synagogues in which Orthodoxy prevailed. In 1881 only 8 out of some 200 major synagogues in the United States were Orthodox, the majority then being committed to or verging upon Reform. By 1890 the number of synagogues had risen to 533, with the bulk of new ones set up by Orthodox Jews recently arrived from eastern Europe.

Of the major innovations in Jewish religious thought and practice that have occurred in the United States, only a few began among the east European immigrants. Neither believers nor agnostics saw much need for innovation. The minority of immigrants who had adopted the surrogate faith of radicalism was hostile to all religion, though in practice the skeptics often retained warmer sentiments toward Orthodoxy than to either Reform or Conservative Judaism. Before the First World War and often enough in later years too, the Orthodox congregation was likely to be both Yiddish-speaking and largely plebeian in tone and composition, thereby striking a Jewish skeptic as much more congenial than either Reform, disdained from a distance as the pallid voice of rich German Jews, or Conservative, regarded with some puzzlement as neither fish nor fowl. If our skeptic was moved on his deathbed to attend the word of the Lord, he would turn to an Orthodox rabbi, who represented "the real thing" and spoke in a tongue he understood. If, earlier in life, he had backslid so far as to want a religious wedding for his daughter, he would have sought out the same kind of rabbi, perhaps the only kind he had ever known. In a curious but significant way, the radicals and skeptics among the immigrant Jews contributed for a while to the stability, perhaps the stagnation, of Orthodoxy.

Among Orthodox communicants themselves, the incentive to innovation was equally small. The actively pious, a shrinking minority, rejected change in principle or wanted to confine it to a few external forms: that, as they saw it, was the major point of difference between themselves and the "deviant" branches of the faith. A larger fraction consisted of what Charles Liebman has called "the residual Orthodox": those who kept their membership, came to the services on the High Holy Days, and observed some rituals, though more out of cultural inertia than religious decision. Still less concerned with religious matters were "the nonobservant Orthodox," those for whom the faith had gone dead but who lacked the courage or clarity to acknowledge it.

The Orthodox rabbis from eastern Europe, loosely banded together in 1902 in a national organization (Agudath ha-Rabbanim), began to see quickly enough that they would have severe difficulties in trying to reach American-born Jewish youth, even the small segment of it that remained firm in Orthodox belief. "Very early, they began to labor for the creation of *yeshivot* in America of the old type, to produce not only learned laymen but also rabbis who would be as pious and as learned in the Talmud as their fathers, [and] who would also possess sufficient American education to be able to lead in the new land." Inevitably, the rupture between generations that was causing so much pain on the East Side also had to occur, though in less extreme ways, among the Orthodox Jews. In the early 1900's moods of discontent began to appear among younger Orthodox communicants, especially those who had been born in America; they grumbled over what they regarded as the rigidity of their parents' synagogues, sometimes over the gradual emptying out of faith among those who still went through its motions. In a good many synagogues run by older immigrants, the young people were kept from conducting services simply because they were clean-shaven and spoke English. Forming a self-conscious minority intent on creating an Orthodoxy suitable to American life, a handful of second-generation Jews on the East Side organized in 1912 the Young Israel movement, perhaps the one major religious innovation to be enacted primarily in the immigrant world.

At this point in the history of the immigrant Jews, the Orthodox synagogues regarded themselves as under mounting assault from what one chronicler calls the threat of "Reform, gangsterism, and anti-religious Socialism." In 1911 Rabbi Stephen S. Wise, a spellbinder from uptown who advocated a freewheeling ethical religiosity which he proposed to board with Reform, came to the East Side on a mission of conversion. Reform, or anything like it, had never been able to make a dent among the immigrants, but the charismatic Wise, holding meetings in Clinton Hall, "attracted many sons of Orthodox parents who had never before heard religion discussed in English." In the eyes of the Orthodox, both old and young, Wise "preached a foreign religion—and he passed a basket through the audience on Friday nights for contributions. Some Jews threw in buttons, others real money." The older generation of pious Jews was largely deaf to the fads of the faithless; it was the sons who feared Wise's invasion, perhaps because they were a trifle drawn to his eloquence and sophistication. Uncomfortable in the old-style *shul* yet determined to reject the watered-down beliefs of men like Wise, the Orthodox youth decided on a religious-intellectual assertion of their own. They formed Young Israel.

At first it consisted mainly of a program of public lectures held on Friday nights, at which an Orthodox "revivalism" was preached in English —itself a sufficient innovation in the eyes of the older people. Speakers of intellectual distinction, like Dr. Judah Magnes, who had abandoned Temple Emanu-El because he judged Reform Judaism to be "empty," Professor Israel Friedlander of the Jewish Theological Seminary, and Mordecai Kaplan, the distinguished theologian not yet in his heterodox phase, offered arguments in behalf of religion more sophisticated than the traditional Yiddish-speaking rabbis could summon. Gradually Young Israel became a religious tendency committed to Orthodoxy but, because its founders saw themselves as part of American society, rejecting "many of the folkways of their parents" and regarding old-style services as "without melody or emotion." They shaved their beards, dressed in modern style, listened to English sermons, and replaced the customary buzz of talk in the Orthodox *shul* with an atmosphere of decorum.

Less notable for theological boldness than for institutional coherence, Young Israel developed attractive social programs, learning to overlook the scandal of mixed dancing which the older rabbis excoriated. It set more rigorous standards for the education of its members and insisted that officers be Sabbath observers. It was a movement led mostly by educated lay figures, second-generation Jews who remained on the East Side at least for a time and "refused to defer to an Orthodox rabbinate who, they felt, lacked secular training, sophistication, and community status comparable to theirs." For its own reasons Young Israel continued within the synagogue that upheaval of power relations which wealthy immigrant laymen had begun somewhat earlier against rabbinical authority. The movement grew, becoming one of the strongest components of Orthodoxy. By the mid-sixties it was claiming 95 synagogues and 23,000 affiliated families. Over the years, like most groupings within American Jewry, it gradually lost some of the marks of its distinctiveness, but during the teens and twenties, within the East Side and then beyond it, Young Israel was the one successful effort to bridge the gap between the faith of the old world and the faith of the new.

By contrast, the relationship between the East Side and Conservative Judaism was a good deal more ambiguous. During the years of heaviest migration the Conservative movement never succeeded in establishing strong roots, certainly not a decisive organizational base, in the immigrant world; yet among the children and grandchildren of the immigrants, as they moved into comfortable neighborhoods in the cities and suburbs, Conservatism would become the dominant agency of worship, or at least affiliation, for those still wishing to maintain some identification with the faith.

In its origins Conservative Judaism goes back to nineteenth-century Jewish historicism, lodged mainly in Germany but with some intellectual branches in the United States. Like similar tendencies in the Christian world, the historical school proposed to examine Jewish religious experience as "an organic historical development based on 'the revealed Bible.'" And again like similar tendencies in the Christian world, the historical school, while earnest in religious devotions and serious in scholarly interests, may have helped unwittingly to further the very disintegration of faith it wished to halt.

In America this outlook acquired force and coherence when Solomon Schechter, a gifted religious scholar, became president in 1902 of the Jewish Theological Seminary. Gradually the Seminary established itself as the intellectual center of the Conservative movement, which in 1913 organized itself as a formal grouping. Both in its main line of development and its quasi-Tillichian offshoot, the Reconstructionism of Mordecai Kaplan, Conservative Judaism has been led by some of the most scholarly and intellectually serious figures in Jewish religious thought.

What such Conservative thinkers as Solomon Schechter, Louis Ginzberg, and Israel Friedlander hoped to find was a way of "defining a nonfundamentalist theology . . . that was convincingly traditionalist." All of these figures came out of the milieu of east European Orthodoxy, but all were also influenced by the German *Wissenschaft des Judentums*. Schechter summarized the leading themes of Conservatism:

The theological practices [of the historical school] may be thus defined: it is not the mere revealed Bible that is of first importance to the Jew, but the Bible as it repeats itself in history, in other words as it is interpreted by Tradition. . . . Since, then, the interpretation of Scriptures or the Secondary Meaning is mainly a product of changing historical influences, it follows that the center of authority is actually removed from the Bible and placed in some living body, which . . . is best able to determine the nature of the Secondary Meaning. This living body, however, is not represented by any section of the nation or any corporate priesthood or Rabbinhood, but by the collective conscience of Catholic Israel.

The very flexibility of this position, as it tried to yoke tradition and change, led to grave difficulties, not least of all "the practical difficulties of reconciling a corpus of law having no effective sanctions with the proclivities of modern man." Conservative Judaism has always been torn by internal divisions, with a "right wing" trying to hew closely to the injunctions of *halakha*, or Jewish law, and a "left wing" arguing that the need for change cannot be satisfied by strict adherence to Jewish law. The result has been a movement rich at its upper level in controversy and reflection while religiously eclectic, if not indifferent, in its ranks. Or, as one Seminary professor is supposed to have remarked, the rabbis deliberate and the laity decides.

What gave urgency to these problems of belief and made them seem relevant to some of the immigrant Jews was the difficulties that Orthodoxy had experienced in adapting itself to the American setting. During the earlier immigrant days, writes Marshall Sklare, Orthodoxy "functioned as a cultural constant in the life of the disoriented newcomer, as a place of haven in the stormy new environment." But as immigrants began to find a place for themselves, the claims of Orthodoxy to regulate Jewish life in all its essential moral aspects and social relations grew increasingly difficult to sustain. Orthodox synagogues did, of course, make some adaptations to American circumstances, but the clash, both in substance and in style, between the requirements of traditional Jewish observance and the requirements of American urban life was still severe. A pattern of Orthodoxy emerged, in Sklare's words, "which for all practical purposes overlooks certain requirements of the sacred system. While synagogue procedure has been kept intact, a strategic compromise has been effected by disregarding the degree to which the congregant adheres to the sacred system while *outside* the sanctuary."

Difficulties of this kind among the Orthodox helped prepare the way for the growth of Conservatism as the religious agency to which a good many descendants of the East Side chose to adhere. An indeterminate faith retaining essential portions of the remembered Orthodox ritual; a strong adherence to Hebraic worship with considerable English admixtures; a rabbinate able to bend with the winds of the twentieth century yet hoping not to break under their pressures—all this has suited the needs of second and third generations. Temperamentally and sociologically, Conservative Judaism came to represent the controlled thinning out of the religious fervor many immigrants brought from eastern Europe to the East Side. An intelligent rabbinical adherent has asked: was it "merely a stopover for Jews on the way from Orthodoxy to Reform and thence to whatever lies beyond? To borrow Emerson's wittily descriptive phrase about Unitarianism—'a featherbed for falling Christians'—is Conservatism a featherbed for falling Orthodox Jews? Will Conservatism be able to reproduce itself once the reservoir of human material reared in an Orthodox environment has vanished?" Such questions could be put to a great many other offshoots of the immigrant world as well.

From Heder *to Secular School*

The generational clash that kept erupting throughout the immigrant milieu was especially painful, and often rather squalid, in the dingy little *heder* (Hebrew school) that an unhappy *melamed* (elementary-school teacher) kept in a tenement flat or basement. Usually an elderly man who feared and despised everything he had found in the new world, the *melamed* turned to the teaching of children, whom he often also feared and despised, because he had a bit more learning than other immigrants and because he shared with them a need to eat regularly. Some were

> earnest, medieval men, zealously trying to impart unwished-for knowledge to unwilling youngsters. . . . [Others] are ignorant men who spend their mornings in peddling wares and evenings . . . selling the little Jewish knowledge they have to American children. . . . The usual procedure is for a group of boys to gather in the home of the self-appointed "Rabbi," and to wait their turn or "next." While one pupil drawls meaninglessly the Hebrew words of the prayer book, the rest play or fight.

Thousands of pupils would remember the *melamed* with a cordial hatred, though later, in the coolness of time, some Jewish historians would judge him to have been as much a victim of circumstances as were his victims. The sardonic Hebrew poet Menakhem Dolitsky recalled his stint as a *melamed:*

> A Jew rents a room, hangs up a gilt sign reading, "Expert Teacher, Alphabet, Bar Mitzvah"—and he's in business as a teacher. He doesn't make enough out of just teaching, so he takes on a few side lines, either because of their sacred or their beneficial character and he puts on his sign: "Expert *Mohel* [circumciser], Expert Marriage Performer, Expert Matchmaker, Expert Evil-Eye Exorciser, Expert Hemorrhoid Remover," etc.

Always on the alert for the mischief the young devils might invent, and with a stick in hand for admonitory persuasion, the *melamed* begins his class. First he drills his pupils, through mass repetitive chanting, in the *alef-bet*, or Hebrew alphabet, sometimes writing the letters on the blackboard or, if that luxury is lacking, on the wall. After the alphabet comes the recital of prayers from the Pentateuch, meant to prepare the child for the liturgy of the synagogue, though only a small number of pupils ever learn to read Hebrew passably well and fewer still to understand it. On occasion the *melamed* paces the youngsters through the *kaddish*, or prayer for the dead, though it is rare indeed for any effort to be made that might bring all this into a living relation with either the Jewish tradition or the American experience. Restless after a day in public school, where discipline has to be taken seriously, and bored by the rasping drone of the *melamed*, the pupils resent the *heder* as a theft of time that might better be used in playing stickball; soon they come to see it as a theatre of war in which their aim is to torment the *melamed* as ingeniously as possible.*

For the *melamed*, the whole experience is an indignity. Driven wild by the malice and indifference of his pupils, the *melamed* in Henry Roth's *Call It Sleep* cries out: "May your skull be dark! . . . and your eyes be dark and your fate be of such dearth and darkness that you will call a poppyseed the sun and a caraway the moon. . . . Away! Or I'll empty my bitter heart upon you!"

In a Yiddish novel by Joseph Opatashu, Friedkin, the head of a *heder* on the East Side, goes one afternoon to give a private lesson to the son of the school's president. The boy, Harry, comes into the apartment, sweaty from playing baseball:

> Running through Friedkin's mind was the thought that the piano teacher probably did not have to wait for his pupil. Friedkin categorized people and things strictly according to rank. He understood that piano playing occupied a higher rank than Hebrew; therefore the piano teacher was entitled to better treatment than the Hebrew teacher. In turn, he was treated better than the old man who had to instruct the girls in prayer-book reading in the kitchen. . . .
>
> "Come on, come on," barked Friedkin at his pupil. . . .
>
> "Suppose I haven't prepared my lesson?" Harry lifted his shoulders with a pitiful look and a silly smile on his face.
>
> Friedkin did not know what to do. Punish him? He was afraid to tangle with the boy. What could he do if Harry didn't want to study? Disregard

* Cf., in *Great Expectations*, Pip's education at the school run by Mr. Wopsle's great-aunt: "The pupils ate apples and put straws down one another's backs, until Mr. Wopsle's great-aunt collected her energies, and made an indiscriminate totter at them with a birch rod. After receiving the charge with every mark of derision, the pupils formed in line and buzzingly passed a ragged book from hand to hand. . . . When the fights were over, Biddy gave out the number of a page, and then we all read aloud what we could—or what we couldn't—in a frightful chorus . . . none of us having the least notion of, or reverence for, what we were reading about."

the boy's negligence? Again he was afraid—of the president. If the latter saw Harry was not making progress, he might change teachers.

Friedkin judged he'd better side-step the issue and opened the Bible to a passage Harry knew almost by heart. He calculated that if the father happened by, he'd hear how the boy swam through the text like a fish through water. . . .

Friedkin pretended not to see this. He felt nervous, as before an examination, and wanted to leave as soon as possible.

A veteran of the *heder* wars remembers his *melamed* as a man with "a straggly gray beard and reddish eyes and a fly-specked coat. I lasted only a few days in his class, because on the third or fourth day he caught me making some kind of trade, maybe with those cards with pictures of baseball players." Out comes the pointer to whip the miscreant's palm, but this one yells, "Don't hit me or I'll hit you." The infuriated *melamed* keeps coming, the boy climbs out of a window, jumping down to the roof of a shed, and so ends his time in *heder*. Others, of course, have greater capacities for endurance and submission.

The Yiddish press during the early years of the century constantly laments the condition of Jewish education. Under the headline "Jews Neglect Jewish Education and Blame America," the *Tageblatt* writes: "They are accustomed to sending their children to public school where they receive free books and education, and then expect the same from Jewish schools. But this is to forget that public schools also cost money." True enough; but for the immigrant wage earner it is a heavy burden even to pay his one dollar a month to the *melamed*, and sometimes, when he sees how little his child has learned or wants to learn, he throws up his hands and curses America as a *treyfene medine* (infidel land).

In 1909 a survey of Jewish education in New York by Mordecai Kaplan and Bernard Cronson found what most East Siders already knew: that equipment was lacking, discipline poor, attendance irregular, and qualified teaching rare. "The demand for Jewish education is comparatively small. Small as it is, the means and equipment which we possess at present are far too inadequate to meet the demand. Wherever that demand is met there is a lack either of system or content." Nine years later a comprehensive survey by Alexander Dushkin found that only 65,000 out of an estimated 275,000 Jewish children of school age were receiving Jewish instruction at any given time, and of these, 24,000 were being taught in a *heder* or by itinerant *melamdim* at home; that records were barely kept; that only about one eighth of the Jewish children given instruction were accommodated in school buildings, the remainder going to synagogue basements and rented rooms which the Health Department had condemned in 1915 for often being "filthy fire traps"; that most of the schools were losing more than half their pupils each year; and that average salaries of full-time teachers barely reached those paid to the lowest ranks in the New York public-school system.

The *heder* turned many Jewish children away from areas of knowledge they would later regret having missed. The immigrant Jewish community knew only too well that most of what passed for Jewish education was a disaster. Indeed, if there was one problem the Jewish cultural leaders tried seriously to cope with, it was that of finding better ways to educate children in Jewish subjects. They set themselves to learn about modern methods of pedagogy; they created special institutions for the training of teachers; they raised large sums of money to improve the synagogue schools, and in 1918 Dushkin could say that in contrast to the degeneration of the *heder* (which was privately run), the Talmud Torah (communally owned) had improved. In 1905 a National Hebrew School for Girls was started in Brooklyn, attempting to synthesize Hebraism, Jewish nationalism, and modern approaches to teaching. On the East Side a number of yeshivas were established as day schools to offer intensive traditional learning, usually with a thin smattering of secular subjects.

Inevitably there developed within these yeshivas conflicts parallel to the conflicts troubling every Jewish school—between those who wished to cleave unquestioningly to the methods of old-country instruction and those who saw a need for adapting at least minimally to American conditions. In May 1908, for example, an open struggle erupted in the Yeshiva Yitzkhok Elkhonen (later to become Yeshiva University) when fifteen students were "locked out" by the faculty. The *Tageblatt* reported that "the yeshiva students plan a mass meeting in order to demand elections of a new board of directors. They claim the entire subject matter must be changed so that the school can produce rabbis suited to American Jewry." These rebellious students did not prevail, but the complaints they expressed were to be heard repeatedly in the Jewish world.

Starting in 1910 the Yiddish secular movements organized their own schools. They were persuaded that neither traditional nor modernized Hebraic instruction could reach Jewish children in America and that, in any case, they should develop their own curriculums. The Labor Zionists, through their fraternal order, the Jewish National Workers Alliance, set up in Harlem the first of their Yiddish-Hebrew schools, de-emphasizing Hebraic traditionalism and stressing the contemporary values of the two Jewish languages. In 1912 a group of fervent Yiddishists, indifferent to religion and committed to a secular nationalism, founded the Sholom Aleichem Folk Schools, never to be large in number or student enrollment but steadily maintaining a high level. And in 1916 the Workmen's Circle began its own secular schools, quite the most ambitious of those devoted to Yiddish, with careful training of teachers, regular preparation of pedagogical aids, and the issuance of Yiddish books composed for American children.

Such schools could not, of course, be introduced without a buzz of ideological contention. In the eyes of religious Jews it seemed little short of apostasy to confine the education of children to secular Yiddish subjects; they claimed, with some justification, that even these subjects could not be understood apart from the context of classical Judaism. To such Hebraists as Nachman Syrkin, the theorist of Labor Zionism, setting up Yiddish secular schools seemed an act of cultural surgery that deprived children of their tradition. The intellectual leader of the campaign for secular Yiddish schools was Dr. Hayim Zhitlovsky, for whom Yiddishism had become a kind of national creed; what enabled him to gain converts was the wish of Yiddish-speaking radicals and Zionists to create for themselves a cultural haven, at once Yiddish, secular, and socialistic, that would survive between the Jewish past and the American future.

The work of these secular institutions was impressive. Their supervisors were serious men who frequently proved to be inventive at coping with American conditions and who showed an admirable readiness to learn from modern educational theorists. Their schools succeeded—but only in limited ways that they themselves would find dismaying. To a small remnant of young people the secular schools gave a portion of learning and often a strong attachment to Yiddish. But as first conceived, these schools were supposed not only to keep alive the ideas of secular radicalism but also to ward off the tide of Americanization threatening to wash away Yiddish culture. In these larger ends, the Yiddish schools did not and could not succeed. Twenty years after their inception, when they seemed still to be thriving, a Yiddish educator would write: "We thought we could raise our children according to our spirit, and through our schools insulate them from the community in which they grew up. Today we know that we cannot control the intellectual development of our children, and that both the home and community have a much greater impact on their education than we do." The Yiddishists had finally no choice but to scale down their expectations; yet they kept on with their work, determined to leave behind a few young people who would love their language and remember their ways.

Dreamers of a Nation

There were other dreamers on the East Side, those who dreamed, not of preserving Yiddish culture, but of re-establishing a Jewish nation. In the immigrant community Zionism was the slowest and the last to take root among all the major twentieth-century Jewish movements. During the most fervent years of East Side political-cultural life, between, say, 1900 and 1914, the Zionist organizations remained marginal and precarious, seldom rivaling Jewish socialism in active strength or intellectual influence. Zionism was still an ideological sect, quite unable to become the mass movement toward which it aspired.

Throughout the nineteenth century there had been pre-Zionist stirrings in America, some of them as a response to proclamations by European visionaries and occasionally in answer to Christian philo-Semitism which took a warm view, as in George Eliot's *Daniel Deronda*, of a Jewish return to Palestine. Lonely figures like Moredecai Noah and Warder Cresson issued appeals for Zion revived; the once-famous poet Emma Lazarus shared these visions; there was even, in 1884, a fragile American branch started of Hoveve Zion (Lovers of Zion), a Hebraist society that paved the way in eastern Europe for political Zionism. But these were isolated figures and groups, barely touching the masses of immigrant Jews. Hoveve Zion broke up into competing factions two years after its formation, along lines that would plague American Zionism for decades. One group, the activists, wanted immediate colonization and sought to prepare those few "who wish to settle in Palestine," while the other group, let us call it the sympathizers, saw its purpose "as the *mitzvah* (good deed) of aiding the colonization of the Holy Land by our poor persecuted Yehudim," that is, *other* Jews. Not until 1898, a year after Theodor Herzl convened the first International Zionist Congress, did some one hundred fraternal societies meet in New York to form a Federation of American Zionists, a very loose alliance of fraternal lodges, Hebrew-speaking clubs, and synagogue societies.

Until the First World War in 1914, writes a historian sympathetic to Zionism, the movement in America remained

> a small and feeble enterprise. It provided an outlet for some thousands . . . who met in their societies like votaries of some bizarre cult. They discussed the latest developments in the nerve centers of the World Movement, sold *shekolim* [shares], made collections for the Jewish National Fund and sang *Hatikvah*. The Movement remained an "East Side affair," which meant that it had no money or influence or social prestige. True, its leaders were not "East Siders," they were [German Jews] from the right side of the tracks, but they were like British officers in an army of "natives."

Nor were these leaders, in the formative years of American Zionism, very competent; few of them could hold their own in the rough tournaments of immigrant debate.

By 1905 the total Zionist membership (mostly on paper) came to 25,000, representing a tiny fraction of American Jews. Of these, only a few hundred were at all active. When Herzl sent requests from Switzerland for financial help, the Federation of American Zionists could rarely satisfy him. It could barely support a small staff and a monthly journal, the *Maccabean*. As a Labor Zionist memoir would later recall, perhaps with a touch of exaggeration: "The Zionist office had little contact with the Jewish masses. When General Zionism [the moderate wing of the movement] occasionally descended upon the Jewish ghetto, it appeared like a ghost wearing a silk topper."

It seems probable, though of course it cannot be proved, that among the immigrants there was a greater fund of latent sympathy for the idea of a regathered Jewish nation than the condition of early Zionism might suggest.

Anyone walking through the Jewish streets, then as later, would have encountered a great many little blue-tinted boxes into which people dropped a
penny to help the pious Jews of Eretz Yisrael. But the idea of a re-estab-
lished homeland, let alone a Jewish state, seemed so utterly utopian that it
could hardly form the basis for a viable politics within the immigrant milieu.
At best it struck even sympathizers as a dream beyond the reach of a broken
and scattered people.

Early American Zionism nevertheless served a number of positive functions within the immigrant community, less because of its ideological distinctiveness than those traits it shared with other immigrant movements.
Zionism played the role of a *maskilic* (enlightening) force among those it
reached, giving them a coherent view of the world and a sense of collective
purpose; it resisted "the vulgar acculturation typical of the *alrightnik* . . .
It laid the basis for Westernized Jewish culture in English." And it kept
insisting that nowhere in the gentile world, not even in America, could the
Jews find comfort or security. One of the more successful spokesmen for
early Zionism, Joseph Zeff, made a specialty of hammering at this theme:
"Don't fool yourselves that you are Americans. You are not counted as
Americans and never will be. . . . The Russians will be assimilated with the
Poles; the Germans with the French—all will become as one nation—but not
the Jews. . . . The Jew will always be alone. Against his own wishes, he
will remain loyal to his race and to his past."

In this formative period American Zionism was undergoing a process of
inner division that largely reflected developments within the world Zionist
movement. The religious Zionists, or Mizrachi, formed their own group in
1903 and the Labor Zionists, or Poale Zion, in 1905; there followed years of
fruitful co-operation-and-conflict. Neither group was anywhere near a mass
movement, but from the Zionist point of view each performed a useful role.
The Mizrachi broke down some of the hostility to Zionism among Orthodox
Jews, and the Poale Zion tried, mostly in vain, to breach the solidly anti-
Zionist front of the Jewish labor movement. New leaders began to appear,
talented speakers and writers like Judah Magnes, Stephen S. Wise, and Louis
Lipsky, though on the East Side the first two suffered from being regarded
as "outsiders."

Yet Zionism could not gain the mass response it would later command
among the immigrant (or native-born) Jews. Nor is it hard to understand
why. It struck most Jews as an exotic fantasy nurtured by littérateurs. The
first *Aliyah*, or settlement in Palestine, during the 1880's had been far from a
success, had indeed, been marked by extreme hardships; the Jewish community there, consisting mostly of pious town-dwellers, was supported
mainly by donations from abroad; and there was hardly much reason to
suppose that many Jews would want or be able to settle in a land notoriously
despoiled and ill-ruled.

Zionism ran head-on against the opinions and sensibililties of most
American Jews. A good number of Orthodox Jews regarded it as "Torah-

less," a heretical effort to transpose messianic expectation from the transcendent to the mundane sphere. The German Jews disliked it as a romantic-nationalist ideology that could threaten their increasingly secure position within the United States. Many Jews, admitted the *Maccabean* in 1908, "resent the idea of national interests apart from the general interests of the country." A few years earlier the Reform rabbis had passed a resolution declaring themselves "unalterably opposed to political Zionism" and, in a startling sentence, had added, "America is our Zion." The Jewish socialists regarded Zionism as a troublesome competitor, a bourgeois delusion that could only distract the masses from struggling for their liberation. The Yiddishists were enraged by the Zionist depreciation of the whole Diaspora experience. (Actually, the two groups shared certain judgments about that experience, such as the view that Jews ought to turn increasingly to "productive labor." The Zionists, however, were inclined to see *galut* mostly through images of deformation, whereas the Yiddishists saw it as a rich historical epoch.)

No Jewish movement encountering so many organized opponents among the immigrant (and nonimmigrant) Jews could have won easy victories. But there is another, perhaps deeper, reason for the early troubles of Zionism: by its very nature it was antipathetic to the whole Jewish migration to America. Hundreds of thousands of people had uprooted themselves at great cost from their accustomed life in eastern Europe; they had suffered in the new world; they were still—by, say, 1905 or 1910—finding it hard to establish themselves in the American cities. And then came a band of Zionists, *luftmenshn* of ideas, who told them in effect that they had journeyed in the wrong direction, America was not the answer to their problems, they must look elsewhere, to a land that seemed very distant and inhospitable. For most immigrants this was simply too much to accept: not even in imagination could they bear the thought of "another voyage." Few Zionist spokesmen were urging the immigrants to undertake "another voyage" immediately— but if they were not, what then did Zionism come to except fine sentiments, and how could it compete in the daily life of the immigrants with those socialists who kept urging concrete and immediate actions for improving their conditons? Even in later years, when Zionism became a powerful sentiment among American Jews, they would still be reluctant to accept *Aliyah* as an objective for themselves. Just as in their early poverty they could not bear to suppose they had come to the wrong place, so in their later comfort they could not take seriously the idea that their task was to leave it.

All of these difficulties found a temporary solution when Louis Brandeis, already a well-known lawyer and public figure, took over the leadership of American Zionism in 1914. Gathering around him a group of talented intellectuals and public men, so that the movement escaped the "stigma" of the East Side, Brandeis shrewdly emphasized the democratic and humanitarian aspects of the Zionist appeal. To counter the argument that

Zionism was incompatible with American loyalties, he wrote that it "is the Pilgrim's inspiration and impulse over again. . . . And what have been made the fundamentals of American law, namely, life, liberty and the pursuit of happiness are all essentially Judaistic and have been taught by them for thousands of years." This was a rhetoric with little precedent in the writings of American Zionists, and, more important, it came from a figure whose authority was unprecedented. The most qualified spokesmen for Zionism, men like Nachman Syrkin and Shmarya Levin, bore the stamp of Europe, having come out of Yiddishist and Hebraist traditions; but Brandeis, though deficient in personal Jewish culture, was the sort of public figure who commanded the respect of people whom Syrkin and Levin simply could not reach.

Brandeis kept quietly assuring American Jews that support for Zionism did not mean they would have to go to Palestine themselves—being a Zionist, to recall a phrase from a Hoveve Zion faction, was a *mitzvah*, a good deed, and few Jews could resist the claims of a good deed. "The place," wrote Brandeis, "is made ready; legal right of habitation is secured; and any who wish are free to go. But it is of the essence of Zionism that there shall be no compulsion." To older Zionists, especially those of Poale Zion, Brandeis's way of putting things seemed a dilution of principle. But in the short run it brought a new influence to the Zionist movement, not only in the Jewish community but in American politics as a whole.

In 1917 the movement reorganized itself as the Zionist Organization of America, now based on individual rather than group membership and thereby more effective than the earlier Federation. A women's affiliate, Hadassah, had been started in 1912; abstaining from inner polemics, it took on a broad humanitarian character and grew rapidly. Zionism now became a significant force, perhaps more so in American Jewish life as a whole than in the immigrant neighborhoods. Its great coup internationally was its success in persuading Great Britain in 1917 to issue the Balfour Declaration, which declared that His Majesty's Government "view with favor the establishment in Palestine of a national home for the Jewish people." Through the part they played as a pressure group helping to bring about this declaration, the American Zionists gained prestige both among their comrades abroad and the Jews at home. Their *mitzvah* was under way.

A Bit of Fun on the East Side

It will not do to be too serious: immigrant Jews also liked a bit of fun, even those high-minded ones who yearned for a religious or secular transvaluation. Their possibilities for amusement were limited, but with a long experience at "making do," the Jews improvised a scheme of pleasures ranging from those available within the East Side to those requiring forays beyond its limits.

From its earlier Irish and German days, the East Side had had its share of saloons; by 1899 there were still about 150 in the Eighth Assembly District alone, mostly between Allen Street and the Bowery, a distance of four blocks. Saloonkeepers regarded Jews as poor customers, but soon enough the immigrant community sifted out its share of what it called "the bums"— a layer of petty politicians, grifters, hangers-on, sporting enthusiasts, and gamblers. Others also found a home in the saloon, even some ordinary workers like the bakers whom Morris Hillquit, in the severity of his socialist youth, had noticed to be fond of their beer after quitting the cellars in which they worked. Still, drink was rarely a temptation for the Jews, most of whom turned to other kinds of amusement and relief.

Subsisting on a scatter of pennies, the candy store came to serve as an informal social center in the immigrant streets. It attracted adolescents who found their parents' apartment too stifling and dreamed of moving on to the glamour of Broadway or the big money of uptown business, prize fights, and rackets. It served a purpose somewhat like that of the barbershop in small-town America, harboring the gritty wisdom of street people, the undeluded "realism"—prey neither to social ideologies nor the mystiques of learning—that would flourish among Jewish cab drivers, fight managers, ward heelers, and the like. In the candy store these men could find coziness, gossip, tips about the big time; they could assert the commonplaces of human nature, talking about baseball instead of socialism, boasting about Jewish middleweights instead of philosophers, looking for tips at the races rather than paths to utopia. It was a relief, for young and not so young, occasionally to waste an hour or two near a soda fountain. The delicatessen also became an important place in every immigrant Jewish neighborhood, helping to maintain ethnic distinctiveness through tastes in food when other, more important signs of distinctiveness began to fade; but somehow, the delicatessen seldom served as the center for either adolescents or grownups that the candy store did. Perhaps—about such mysteries we can only speculate—the average candy-store keeper was so desperate for a penny or two of business that he was readier than anyone else to put up with the sorts of people who made his store their hangout.

Still, saloon and candy store were no more than marginal to the social life of the immigrants, serving mainly as recruitment centers for *di proste* (the common ones) as they prepared to slip off to the corners of American society where one might make a fast, or sleazy, dollar. A large part of immigrant social life centered, rather, on family and home, not merely on ceremonial occasions but also through the sharing of simple pleasures, like entertaining over a glass of tea and walking together to the park on warm evenings. Precisely this coherence of kin provoked young people to seek escape, and during the early years of the century a common way of escaping was to visit the dance hall.

There were, by 1907, thirty-one dance halls in a ninety-block district between Houston and Grand streets, east of Broadway. Eliminate park space and unused lots, and there remains a dance hall for every two and a half blocks! Here, in "the winter picnic-grounds of our district," fraternal societies staged their "balls," families celebrated weddings, and young people came in large numbers for an hour or two of dancing.

"Every once in a while there were scandals about the dancing schools. . . . The press and the reformers would pound the drums that these places were breeding grounds for white slavers. East Side girls, eager for recreation, would sneak out to the dance halls without telling their parents. Not having a hat, they would check an apron and pay ten cents." The *Forward*, forgetting its occasional recognition that even class-conscious workers needed some fun in life, would denounce evil "professors" who misled Jewish girls by teaching them "unbridled Coney Island and Haymarket dances." Some of these "professors" were guilty of routine commercial deceit, others were procurers. In either capacity they would rent a hall for thirty-five dollars a month, on the understanding that they could use it for midweek evenings only, since family celebrations took place on weekends. The usual cost of a three-month dancing course (two lessons a week) was six dollars. Long a favorite among Jews even in the old country, dancing became for the younger immigrants one of the few easily accessible pleasures: it enabled them to meet other young men and women, it brought a few moments of release.*

Accommodating between five hundred and twelve hundred people, the most popular East Side halls—the New Irving, the Progress, and the Liberty —were booked up in the winters for weeks in advance. "New Irving Hall can be rented for $30 a night for wedding or ball, and if the receipts from the box office are satisfactory on the night of a ball to the management, the same organization may have the hall free of charge for its next celebration." A young woman observing immigrant customs took a walk in 1904 along

---

* In 1912–1913 George Burns, later to become the well-known comedian, got a job as dance instructor at Bennie Bernstein's Dancing School at Second Street and Avenue B. Admission was ten cents for gentlemen and five cents for ladies.

"At the beginning of the evening, all the men would be seated on one side of the hall and the girls on the other. Bernstein would open the dancing by ringing a bell and announcing loudly, 'Ladies and gentlemen, when I give the signal, the gentlemen will cross over and ask the ladies to dance—no running, please. . . . Professor Heller's Double Brass Band will now play the mirror dance.'

"Professor Heller's Double Brass Band consisted of a piano player, drummer, and two trumpets. The mirror dance was an invention of Bernstein's. A girl sat in a chair in the middle of the hall with a mirror in her hand. A man crossed the room and looked over her shoulder into the mirror. If she liked his looks, she nodded yes, and got up and danced with him. If not, she nodded no, and the poor dope had to go back to his own side."

Grand and Clinton streets, where she "counted 19 different posters advertising 19 different balls in the near future." She transcribed a few of the posters:

Full Dress and Civic Ball
given by
YMHA
Grand Central Plaza
214–20 Broom St.
March 25
Music by Prof. L. Uberstein
Brass Band

And

Bob Adams will sing between dances
Reception and Ball
Turquoise Social Club
At Lenox Association
Saturday Night March 26
Music by Professor L. Fischer

Annual *Forward* balls, held in the Grand Central Palace and later in Madison Square Garden, were major East Side events. The Yiddish anarchist paper, the *Freie Arbeiter Shtime*, held *poyern balln* (peasant balls), which started with

a parade of the "priest" holding a crucifix and the "judge" with a lawbook, followed by "peasants." After the march the "peasants" supervised the arrest of the "bourgeois" guests and dragged them to the "judge." The "judge" had to act drunk, but since he was usually played by the anarchist leader S. Yanovsky, who loved his glass of whisky, this wasn't hard. Anarchist justice was then dispensed: fines for kissing a virgin, or for not kissing a virgin; for standing about too quietly, etc. All this was a way of raising money for the cause. "Marriage ceremonies" were performed by the "priest" in Latin and Yiddish, and paid for by a couple of nickels. The "marriages" lasted till midnight, and then you were free. If you didn't have your own girl you were out of luck, since the anarchist girls attached themselves to the leaders of the movement.

There were other sources of pleasure: efforts to fix up East River piers so that boys could dive off them in the summers; a few pathetic ventures in back-yard gardening, through the removal of layers of debris and the nurture of tomatoes and radishes in the shadow of the tenements; the construction of roof gardens for summer play on settlement houses.

More important were the East Side parks, few in number and always heavily crowded.

> On hot summer nights [we would] seek relief from the heat in Jackson Street
> Park. The park, innocent of grass and trees, was a large asphalted area close
> to the East River, with many lanes of benches . . . and a stone pavilion like
> a Greek temple, where a small brass band occasionally played and milk was
> dispensed at a penny a glass. The park was always crowded. The men were
> in their undershirts. The women, more fully dressed, carried newspapers for
> fans. Hordes of barefoot children played games, weaving in and out of the
> always thick mass of promenaders.

A *Forward* reporter made a tour of the few parks used by Jewish immigrants: Seward Park, where "older people come who have worked all day
and want some fresh air, though you wonder, looking at the skimpy little
trees, where they expect to find it"; Jackson Park, where "whole families lie
on the ground and couples sit on the benches in the dark and where Jewish
and gentile bums molest passers-by"; Hamilton Fish Park, where "I saw the
same tired faces and bent backs, though it is quieter than the other two";
and the Williamsburg Bridge, "mobbed with families, ten customers to
every seat, abounding in contrasts; elegant ladies and proletarian boys in
dirty nightshirts, bearded Jews and clean-shaven Jews." New and wonderful, the bridge "is international—you hear all languages. The air is clean and
sweet, and people run there."

By about 1908–1910 large numbers of Jews had moved out of the East
Side, and Prospect Park in Brooklyn and Central Park in Manhattan had
become favorite gathering places. Conflicts of the kind that would later
trouble other alien communities broke out between the Jews and the park
authorities, whose zeal for enforcing rules seems to have sharply increased
when the violators proved to be greenhorns. As the *Forward* remarked,
"The commissioner of parks wants to preserve the flowers; the Jewish
mothers want to preserve the health of their children." Many immigrants
could not read the signs saying "Don't Touch the Flowers," nor grasp the
norm of restraint that park authorities wanted to impose. Going to the park
and opening themselves to its beauty, some immigrants would want to take
home a branch or a flower; it was hard to understand that everything was to
be enjoyed but nothing kept. There were, of course, immigrants who
brought habits of sloppiness and destruction. In 1908 more than one hundred
Jews were arrested in Prospect Park after Inspector O'Reilly charged that
"they were turning the park into a garbage pail." Many were forced to
spend the night in jail and then, before a cruel magistrate, fined ten dollars
each. The *Forward* raged against police brutality and official harshness while
also lecturing its readers on the need for decorum: "It is very wrong to
litter the park with garbage, step all over the grass, tear the flowers, break
the branches, and make noise." To minority groups, who suspect it may be a
subtle device for their belittlement, the civic sense does not come very
easily; but with time the Jewish immigrants learned to live by the rules, or
how to change and bend them, so that tensions could relax.

Among the Jews themselves there could never be any doubt as to their most popular amusement: it was the Yiddish theatre, the central institution of their secular culture, speaking to their needs and gathering their fantasies. Whatever was noble, and much of what was coarse and decadent, in their culture found reflection on the stage. As a sort of grubby side show, the Yiddish music halls enjoyed a few years of prosperity. A contemporary account, reflecting the puritanism of the settlement-house worker who wrote it, yields a picture:

> [About 1900] the possibilities of the present Jewish vaudeville first dawned upon an East Side saloon keeper. He set aside the rear end of his establishment. . . . Here he constructed a small stage for the cheap talent he found. The rest of the place was utilized for chairs and tables where the patrons enjoyed their beer. . . .
>
> The performers are an ignorant lot. . . . Those actors who do a "turn" either sing and dance, or conduct a dialogue. There is a marked effort to imitate the poor English vaudeville actors; but the vulgarities are so exaggerated that they make the performance positively filthy. The songs are suggestive, the choruses are full of double meanings. . . . Children learn these ditties and often in all their glee sing them in the streets.
>
> There are a number of small music halls that seldom, if ever, have enough patronage to pay for running expenses. Still, these places keep open. . . . They are the rendezvous of well-known East Side Fagins, and of the moral leeches that fatten on the virtue of innocent womanhood.

When the Yiddish press wasn't campaigning against dance halls, it might turn to the obscenities of the music halls, but no outcry of reform could have stopped East Siders from frequenting them. What brought about their downfall was technology, not morality—the appearance of motion pictures in 1906 and thereafter. "Most music halls have shut down," reported the *Forward* in 1908,

> Yiddish theatres are badly hurt, and candy stores have lost customers. For only a nickel you can see a show, hear a song, and watch a dance. There are now about a hundred movie houses in New York, many of them in the Jewish quarter. Hundreds of people wait in line. A year ago there were ten Jewish music halls in New York and Brooklyn; today there are two. . . . The movies are not feeling the depression, for people must have entertainment, and five cents is little to pay. A movie show lasts half an hour. If it's not too busy, you can see it several times. They open at one in the afternoon, and customers, mostly women and children, gossip, eat fruit and nuts, and have a good time.

Six years later the *Forward* returned to the same theme: "Everybody loves the movies. Our Jews feel very much at home with the detectives, oceans, horses, dogs, and cars that run about on the screen." When it rained, Jewish customers tried to persuade the owners of the outdoor theatres that the rain would soon stop and the show should not be canceled.

People come in raincoats and with old newspapers to cover their heads. . . . Small boys sell old papers for two cents to be used as umbrellas. The people sit with the rain pouring down their necks; when the seats get too wet, they sit in the back; when it gets very bad, they gather under the operator's tent. The movies have candy nights, grocery nights, and chicken nights. At intermission the audience draws lots and the lucky ones win a present. You can pay a nickel or a dime and go home with a whole chicken.

These were all pleasures within the safety of the East Side itself, but for some, perhaps many, the thought of breaking out seemed still more exciting. What the old residents of New York might take for granted—Coney Island, the Bronx Zoo, the Metropolitan Museum of Art—the immigrants had first to discover, savoring the fact that Jews were not officially barred from public places of amusement, as they often had been in the old country. Museums were a novelty, few immigrants having ever seen one; but when Lillian Wald headed a campaign in 1891 to persuade the Metropolitan Museum of Art to stay open on Sundays, the one day workers might attend, fifty thousand of the eighty thousand signatures on the petition came from the East Side.

Jews are commonly supposed to be indifferent to the charms of nature, yet the truth seems to be that whenever they were able to, they stretched out their hands for a bit of grass. One old woman, no longer able to name the places of her remembering, tells us that "for entertainment we would walk over a bridge every Sunday where there were cows in the open air. This was in the Bronx. It was a place like an island. We used to go by an old train." A son of immigrants has written of the "excursions" Jews loved to take, in the early days up the East River and later on the lordly Hudson. Tammany Hall understood these longings and every fortnight in the summer would organize

> a dilapidated ferryboat filled with as many persons as it would hold. It left at the foot of Montgomery Street and plodded heavily, uneasily, and sagging on one side with its overload of people, up the East River, into Long Island Sound, and after three or four hours pulled up at some rural wharf. There the passengers were let loose in the adjoining fields for an hour, after which several long blasts of the ship's whistle brought them back.

Political groups were zealous in organizing such outings: it was a way of attracting converts while also indulging in a little pleasure. On hot Sundays the socialists

> would take the Grand Street ferry to Williamsburg, and then the horsecar to Prospect Park. It was a long ride, through sparsely populated sections with views of beautiful cottages and wide lawns with flowers. . . .
> There were other pleasures, the ride on the Staten Island ferry. . . . The ride lasted twenty minutes in each direction. We would remain on the boat, generally making two round trips.

Perhaps the most tender evocation of these pleasures is a memoir by Michael Gold of his family taking the long trip by elevated train one Sunday to Bronx Park. The train was "a super tenement on wheels," with "excited screaming mothers, fathers sagging under enormous lunch baskets, children yelling, puking and running under everyone's legs, a gang of tough Irish kids in baseball suits who persisted in swinging from the straps." Gold's mother, usually settled in kitchen and stoop, took her children into the woods, "smelling out the mushrooms" she had loved in her native Hungary, poking under trees and lifting her skirt to make a bag for the mushrooms, telling her children, as she never had before, that "birds talk to each other," and suddenly flinging her arms around Michael and his sister Esther to cry out, "Ach, Gott! I'm so happy in a forest. You American children don't know what it means. I am happy!"

Mrs. Gold, like other Jewish women, whose sons would not trouble to put their memories to paper, had gone to the woods with the hope of *khapn a bisl luft* (catching a bit of air), as they said in Yiddish. There was a whole philosophical persuasion in that phrase.

Up into the Catskills

As soon as the immigrants could break free of the crush of the tenements, they fled—people who have lived with poverty are rarely foolish enough to find it glamorous. In the years when they had no choice but to remain in the slums, they tried each summer to squeeze out a week or two away from the city, at least for wives and children. Most could not manage even that, but some did go to "the mountains"—which meant the Catskills. They went there because it was nearby and inexpensive, and because the German Jews had already cut a trail through gentile resistance in Ulster and Sullivan counties.

As early as 1890 a handful of east European Jews had begun to trickle into the Catskills. By 1893 the Rand McNally *Guide to the Hudson River and the Catskill Mountains* reported that Tannersville "is a great resort of our Israelite brethren, who love to gather where they can be together," the Israelite brethren no doubt being German Jews. By 1899 the Ontario and Western's annual *Summer Homes* listing carried its first report of Jewish boardinghouses, though the earlier presence of Jews is suggested by an 1892 announcement of the Carpenter Boarding House: "No Jews Allowed." In 1900 the High View Farm of Mountaindale restricted its clientele to "a good class of Hebrews only," presumably German Jews. That same year The Jewish Agricultural Society began to finance Jewish settlers in Sullivan County, with the hope that they would become truck or dairy farmers. (A hope not always realized, since some of the settlers, as a veteran hotelkeeper has recalled, would borrow money from the society's Ellenville office on the pretext that "it was for farming, but actually we used it to put up a resort.")

The local people were not enthusiastic. In the summer of 1899 the Ellenville *Journal* reported that residents of the Sandbergh valley were "seeking legal advice" because the increase of Jewish hotels had turned the Sandbergh River into a "mere sewage channel." Genuine as this concern over pollution may have been, "it was given added muscle by the hostility of many of the older valley people to the proliferation of Jewish boarding-houses which brought with them a way of life conspicuously different." By 1906 the *Journal* reported that in the previous six years twelve hundred farms had been sold to Jews, mostly in a ten-mile strip embracing parts of the valleys of the Sandbergh and the Neversink and also parts of Ulster County near Ellenville. "Nearly everyone of the purchased farm houses is used as a summer boarding house . . . the presence of these [Jews] does much to put money in circulation. . . . Their coming has enabled many a poor farmer to get rid of land from which he could not get a living." Such economic considerations were not, however, enough to put an end to prejudice: "There were cases of cruel harassment, there were fist fights, there was much concealed hostility." Still, Jews kept pouring in, a significant minority of them tuberculars seeking cures at the sanitariums in Liberty. Local railroads offered special fares to vacationers, the Hudson lines sold cheap river trips, but what finally opened "the mountains" to floods of New Yorkers were the automobile and the bus.

The Yiddish press started carrying advertisements for Catskills resorts as early as 1902, when three hotels, with special emphasis on "fresh-grown food," announced their custom in the *Forward*. Until then, apparently, guests had been recruited through relatives and by word of mouth. For the next ten or fifteen years most of the Jewish hotels were quite modest in what they could promise or provide, the High View optimistically advertising "no mosquitoes," and the Grand Mountain House boasting that "we have our own waterfall." These places were really no more than renovated, or unrenovated, farmhouses partitioned into small rooms for summer boarders. But even in the years before the First World War there began to emerge the kind of plush hotel for which the Catskills would become notorious. In 1904 the Evergreen Farm House offered facilities modest by later standards but decidedly more sumptuous than those of most competitors:

> Elevation, 2000 feet. Baths, toilets, cold and hot water on every floor. Fresh milk, butter and eggs from our own farm. Kosher. 500 fruit trees. Piano and other entertainment. Books and newspapers. Playground for children.

By 1906 the Park House informed Jewish readers that it had

> Electric lights in each room (something new), bells, hot and cold

water. Stables, carriages, telephone and telegraph, bowling, billiards,
a dancing pavilion, nightly concerts, a Ladies Orchestra. $10–15
weekly, children half price.

In 1920, flush with postwar prosperity, Schindler's Prairie House announced in the *Day* that it had hired "a special pastry chef" and now had six
thousand chickens on its farm, perhaps as good a sign as any of the mixture
of pretension and innocence characterizing such establishments.

For some immigrant Jews "the mountains" were an unqualified blessing.
In 1907 the gifted Yiddish poet Joseph Rolnick became ill and was advised
to go to Liberty. Since he was destitute, an "evening" was held for him at
Clinton Hall with admission charges of 25¢ and 35¢; it brought in $123.
Rolnick then spent ten weeks in Liberty

at a hotel that stood on a high hill. I slept in a tiny room on the third floor.
It was the first time in my life that I was so close to hills and clouds. . . .
Room and food cost eight dollars a week. . . .

We ate at two long tables. There was ample and delicious food. We had
meat twice a day. Big pitchers of milk stood on the table at all three meals.
The guests ate and drank more than they needed, because we all believed that
the more we ate, the sooner we would get well. In ten weeks I gained thirty-
eight pounds.

By contrast, a sardonic view of "the mountains," perhaps prompted by
anxieties that affluence might undermine socialist conviction, emerges in a
series the *Forward* ran in 1904:

It is a pleasure to breathe sweet air for a few weeks, see real grass and trees
and birds. But the pleasure is not an easy one. Nothing the worker enjoys
comes easily. One of the main drawbacks of the vacation is that a woman
needs a lot of pretty summer dresses; if not, her enjoyment is spoiled. In
many of the boardinghouses the women sit on the porch like a fashion show,
each one showing off her clothes and jewelry. Instead of enjoying the fresh
air, they try to make each other jealous.

These farms and hotels look more like hospitals than pleasure resorts.
Every room has as many beds as it can hold . . . four or five in a room is
not considered too much.

There are twice as many children as adults. A child is always crying;
another is getting slapped. When it rains four or five dozen women, girls,
children, and a handful of men are crowded into a small porch. The crying,
cursing, and slapping remind you of the Yiddish theatre. If one of the girls
volunteers to sing you have to stick it out because you can't insult her by
leaving, and she sings while the children are crying, the mothers are cursing,
husbands and wives fighting, and women are insulting one another.

The only good thing in the Catskills is the fresh air, but this is not the
fault of the farmers. No matter how hard they try, they can't spoil the air.
But the boarders don't take advantage of the fresh air. They sit either on the
porch or under a tree nearby.

When the husband of one of the women does come for a few days, she is very proud—and besides, it makes the other women jealous. They in turn can't stand it and send for their husbands. The visiting husbands set up pinochle games and play all day, forgetting their wives.

The girls are bored and try to find boys; when a young man wanders onto a farm they do their utmost to hold him there. Life in the Catskills is free; ceremonies are ignored, although the girls remain honorable. If a boy doesn't come along, the girls go to look for one, ostensibly paying a visit to another farm. There are twelve girls to every boy in the Catskills.

Some of the hotels have dances. They are free and people come from miles around. There are Chinese lanterns strung up half a mile from the hotel. The crowd in the dance hall is really happy, more than if it were a wedding.

On hayrides, which are very popular, the noise becomes deafening. They sing. "Let Us All Be Happy" from Libin's play *Broken Hearts* was popular this summer. . . . There are no seats on a hayride; the girls and women and few boys are all tangled up and every few minutes a girl "loses a leg."

In a few decades these plain boardinghouses would be replaced by the pretentious hotels—with their Miami architecture, Broadway entertainment, and piles of lox and bagels—which would make the "Borsht Belt" a convenient symbol of vulgarity, often mocked most bitterly by comedians whose careers had been launched in its casinos. As with so many other aspects of immigrant life, the *Forward* was there first, registering embarrassment before crudities it had to acknowledge as familiar.

But some fellow feeling ought to be possible for the people who flocked to the Catskills. They were tired; they had worked hard all year; they possessed no articulate tradition of nature romanticism; and a plenitude of food was still, in their eyes, a cause for wonder. Many of the men preferred to play pinochle, and many of the women to sit around gossiping, rather than commune with the famous beauties of nature; but it cannot be excluded that some Jewish vacationers did take walks in the woods. A few Yiddish-speaking boarders may even have stumbled upon words of praise for the countryside's "sweet air." The unadorned boardinghouse and the nameless *kokhaleyn* (where guests did their own cooking) were not the most refined of places, certainly not the most elegant; they were just farmhouses where ordinary people came for rest and diversion.

Matchmakers, Weddings, Funerals

As—or was it because?—the hold of Orthodox religion weakened, the immigrant Jews seemed to care more about traditional customs. Religion now began to require conscious assent, a sure sign of trouble; but custom, received and modified, could seem spontaneous, the "natural" way things were supposed to be done. Perhaps, too, religious energies, somewhat cut off from religious worship, were now being displaced onto all those modes of conduct and biases of value that made one a Jew no matter what one believed. Traditional styles, even as they were transformed in the new world, could thus be reaffirmed at the very moment when traditional beliefs were under assault. For the immigrants there were ceremonial occasions—the rituals marking turning points in life, such as weddings and funerals—that enabled an outpouring of emotions seldom permitted in daily existence.

" 'What,' said a shocked father" to the ever sympathetic Lillian Wald, " 'let a girl of seventeen, with no judgment whatsoever, decide on anything so important as a husband?' " Brushing aside the mockery of the young, many older immigrants still regarded the matchmaker, or *shadkhn*, as a useful figure; to rely on his arrangements seemed more sensible than to wait for the incomprehensible vagaries of their children. As late as 1916 a Yiddish reporter, S. P. Kramer, found that "hundreds or even thousands still use matchmakers, but the majority of people wait for love. . . . It is not so 'impersonal.' " The marriage broker customarily received 5 percent of the dowry in addition to a flat fee, neither one nor both enough to make him rich. Kramer found one

> *shadkhn* in a tenement house. After I gave him details about my job and background, he took a dollar registration fee and said, "I have Galician, Russian and American girls. Here's one who says she has five thousand dollars. Why waste time? I'll give you the address and you can go right over. . . ." When a young couple has a few dates they let the matchmaker know if they want to keep seeing each other or if he should find them new prospects. Many happy marriages are arranged, but there is a practical side to it all: bankbooks have to be shown, the boy and girl are very realistic.

Affecting an ecclesiastic bearing, the matchmaker wore a somber black suit with a half-frock effect, a silk *yarmulke* (skullcap), a full beard. A once legendary matchmaker, Louis Rubin, who claimed to have arranged over seven thousand marriages—"very few of them cut-rate"—was interviewed at the end of his career: he would never, he said, "take less than a hundred dollars a case." If clients had photographs Rubin would clip them to the folder, but he didn't insist on pictures unless the subject was unusually attractive. "In most cases it's just as well not to have pictures." Throughout his career Rubin advertised only through discreet handbills in Jewish neighborhoods and a modest notice in the *Day*. Less than 40 percent of his business, he said, came from young people wanting directly to get married; usually the parents started negotiations and, it need hardly be added, preferred college men as sons-in-law.

With the single exception of the birth of a son, the wedding was the most joyous moment in immigrant life. A Yiddish novelist, I. Raboy, has left a vivid picture of a wedding on Ludlow Street:

From the butcher they ordered two hundred chickens and fifty calves' livers; two hundred pounds of beef. From the baker on Essex Street white rolls and cakes; and they told him to bake sugar and honey cakes, fruitcakes and tortes topped with nuts. They went to the saloon on Suffolk Street and ordered twenty casks of beer, twenty gallons of wine and countless bottles of slivovitz.

A phaeton with two horses bedecked with ornamental trappings raced down the length of Ludlow Street bearing the groom to the house of the bride. . . . First the groom went into the bride's house. Both sides of the staircase were jammed with people. Soon the bride and groom emerged. A small boy and girl carried the long train of the bride's white dress. . . .

When the bride and groom entered the dimly lit hall, the electric lights came up with great brilliance. The bride and groom were seated at the head table and received the blessings of guests and relatives amid much kissing and happiness.

At the other end of the hall, on a balcony, sat the musicians with clarinets, trumpets, and two violins. There was a little Jew who played a tall bass, and there was a drum. When the bride's family entered the hall, the musicians played a *freylakhs* [a Jewish dance, very gay and lively].

The family in Raboy's story was more prosperous than most, but even the poorest Jews somehow found the money for a good wedding. Here are a few recollections of immigrant weddings, taken from conversations at a Jewish old-age home:

Everybody and his cousin were invited because my mother-in-law had a grocery store and it was good for business. We were married in the New Hennington Hall on Second Street and Avenue A. With the presents we practically furnished an apartment. Her mother gave us a thousand dollars, and in those days that was a real head start.

I had one dress and one pair of shoes to go out with until a cousin started making dresses for me, so you see I ended up dressed as nice as the next one. I had a good figure then. When I had a few dollars saved up I had a wedding on Essex Street. Fancy it wasn't, but still we had it in a hall. We had music. They danced Russian dances. But it wasn't a swell wedding.

I was married in 1904. I was still living on Houston Street. When people married and they invited guests to the wedding, they had to pay twenty-five cents for hat check, to go to the bride. These weddings were held in Liberty Hall on Houston Street. The people were usually very poor. But the food was good because Jewish people know how to outdo themselves.

I was married in Clinton Street. It was a big hall. The nicest wedding you could have. I was eighteen. I had about twenty carriages standing by the door and my husband kept paying but he didn't have enough so he had to ask my uncle to lend him fifty dollars. He had to pay the cook, pay this one and that one. To stop all this paying we had to leave the wedding early.

Nothing, it seems, can survive in a state of innocence: not even the Jewish wedding, with its rumbling sociability, its wail of clarinets, its

scurrying hordes of children, its amiable vulgarity. Refined immigrants began looking down their noses at weddings in halls, especially as these became
more expensive and ostentatious. The Victoria Hall at 80 Clinton Street
advertised an "electric *khupe*" (bridal canopy) in 1900, and the Grand
American Hall ("strictly union") featured "thousands of electric lights"
three years later. A Yiddish memoirist recalls that "the aristocrats and radicals preferred 'private weddings' without a big fuss," but ordinary people
were not "satisfied with this. They wouldn't forgo the opportunity of dancing at their own children's wedding. My parents and my wife's parents
insisted on a traditional wedding, and later I was not sorry."

A poor man's funeral was much like a poor man's wedding: rapid,
explosive, and with a large residue of bills. One estimate of funeral expenses
on the East Side that appeared in the *Evening World* in 1897 comes to a bit
more than $140, with the casket costing $70, five coaches $30, the hearse
$10.50—a staggering sum for most immigrant workers. Michael Gold once
coaxed a Jewish funeral driver to let him come along:

> at the tenement of the corpse . . . there was a crowd gathered. Weddings,
> sewer repairs, accidents, fires and murders, all are food for the crowd. Even
> funerals. . . . They made an awful hullabaloo. It pierced one's marrow. The
> East Side women have a strange keening wail, almost Gaelic. They chant the
> virtues of the dead sweatshop slave. . . . They fling themselves about in an
> orgy of grief. It unpacks their hearts but is hell on the bystanders.

Hell especially on younger bystanders. One of them, Marcus Ravage,
chanced to come back to the East Side after some years of absence and
heard

> a horrible wailing and lamenting on the street. A funeral procession was
> hurrying by, followed by several women in an open carriage. Their hair was
> flying, their faces were red with weeping. . . . The oldest continued me-
> chanically to address the body in the hearse: "Husband dear, upon whom
> have you left us? Upon whom, husband dear?" . . . The frightful scene,
> with its tragic display, its abysmal ludicrousness, its barbarous noise, revolted
> me. I had seen the like of it before, but that was in another life.

In his entangled feelings toward the funeral Ravage compounded two
ways of life, the way of outpouring and the way of restraint. Young people
like Ravage and thousands of others raised on the East Side had to live by
both responses, as heightened consciousness and nervous strain.

Old-world Jews were quite capable of experiencing embarrassment, but
rarely in regard to their own emotions. As immigrants, they could be embarrassed by their failures with English, their awkwardness with American
friends, and the incongruities they might sense between the kind of personal
relations they took for granted and the prevailing romantic ethos of the new
world, especially when it was declared by their children. But toward the
primary, root emotions of their life—toward the joy of bringing children

into the world, the gratification of seeing them securely married, the grief of persecution, the despair of death—they felt no embarrassment. Life was conceived in elemental categories, overpowering absolute moralities. Happiness came, misery followed. It was mostly a matter of fate, perhaps God's will, and in any case, beyond ready comprehension or control. The disciplines that sophisticated cultures impose on themselves, as mediating forces between man and the ultimate facts of his existence, had of course been present among the east European Jews, mainly as commandments and prohibitions. Their experience had been anything but carefree, their conduct too often bound by harsh constraints. But precisely because they felt themselves so helpless before the venom of the world, the Jews had established occasions that sanctioned the release of emotion in all its fullness or, if you prefer, excess. They were not controlled by the visions of the Gentleman, the Protestant, the Intellectual. Mostly their lives consisted of long stretches of denial and once in a while an outburst. If they laughed, it was with sardonic glee; if they cried, it was to the heavens. Letting loose their grief was, in Gold's wonderful phrase, a way to "unpack their hearts."

To the Brim

This emotionality, ranging from a rich abundance to wanton excess, permeated the whole of immigrant Jewish life. Coming to America, the immigrants brought with them a historically complex and deep culture. It was by now a culture mostly in fragments, brilliant particles in disarray. It was a culture that no longer had the inner principle of order—the assumption that God had stamped a unique destiny upon the Jews—which had once kept it in severe control. Freed from this discipline, the culture of the east European Jews gained in energy but lost in coherence. Nevertheless, the memory of what it had once meant still smoldered in the minds of the immigrants, more perhaps as sentiment of loss than formal idea.

To think of the culture brought over by the immigrant Jews as a "mere" folk culture is a patronizing error, though an error often indulged in by later generations of American Jews. There was, of course, an abundance of folk materials as these had arisen in eastern Europe—dances and jokes, proverbs and songs, legends and superstitions. There were also the lullabies like "Rozhinkes mit mandlen" ("Raisins and Almonds"), the holiday songs, the songs of courtship (*"Mirele, Mirele, zing mir a lidele, vos dos meydele vil"*—"Mirele, Mirele, sing me a song, what does the girl want?"), transported and sometimes transformed from *shtetl* to tenement. Some of these were, in the strict sense, folk songs, others were theatre songs or verses of Yiddish poets set to music which became so popular as to be all but indistin-

guishable from folk songs. There were the anecdotes about Hershel Ostropolier, the Yiddish scamp with a sharp tongue, "a man without respect,"
who mocked and scathed all Jewish institutions. There were the stories about
Chelm, the legendary town (based on a real place in Poland) populated by
fools and innocents, a kind of reverse mirror of the Yiddish world, in which
all the strains and excesses of intellectuality were mashed into amiable non-
sense. There were legends of the *dybbuks* and *golems*, through which Jews
could symbolize the powers of the uncanny, powers for which they might
lack a vocabulary in common discourse. There were dances, almost always,
like the *freylakhs* (a round dance), meant for a group, or for a social
enactment, like the *broyges tants* (dance of anger), performed at weddings
by father and daughter. There were the proverbs, crisp and scathing—"Send
a lazy man for the Angel of Death"; "When a poor man eats chicken, one of
them is sick." And there were the jokes criticizing, as Clement Greenberg
notes, "the Jew's habit of explaining away or forgetting the literal facts in
order to make life more endurable"—jokes that survived the transatlantic
journey but could not escape the mauling of Hollywood and the Catskills.

Attractive as these elements of folk culture may appear to strangers,
both gentile and Jewish, it would be a mistake to see them apart from the
encompassing discipline of the Jewish past. For every folk story there was a
Biblical legend, equally immediate but with far greater historical resonance.
For every folk song there was a cantorial melody tied to rituals of worship.
For every folk witticism there was a passage of rabbinical commentary,
speaking for the obligation to make moral distinctions.

All this—the heritage, the burden, the debris of centuries—the Jews
brought with them. In America images of piety remained in the imaginations of even the most ignorant and grubby, since the mere fact of being a
Jew imposed a distinctive consciousness. Stories of Jacob and Joseph, of
Esther and Ruth, may have become garbled, but they were still alive. Anecdotes of fearful massacre, centuries back, were repeated at night in kitchen
conversation. Judas Maccabeus, Maimonides, Khmelnitsky the butcher, the
Baal Shem Tov, such looming figures of the past were brought over too.

But the most urgent force in Jewish tradition, the force that could send
a quiescent people into moments of transport and even collective frenzy,
was the idea of messianism. The Messiah had not come, he might never
come, but he must come! This fervor, deriving at its purest from the tradition of prophecy and at its most debased from the tradition of apocalypticism, would flame in the immigrant world, a blazing secular passion
appearing first as socialism, then as Zionism, or the two together. The Messiah would be replaced by the messianic principle, the grandiose solitary
figure by a collective upheaval. The vocation for sacrifice, the pursuit of
martyrdom, even that strain of madness which has coursed through Jewish
life for centuries—none had yet reached exhaustion. Passed on from grandfathers to grandsons, sometimes through an apparently inert middle genera-

tion, the messianic impulse continued to burn in Jewish immigrant life; indeed, the first rush of free air from the new world caused it to flare still higher.

The emotionality of the Jews, often regarded with distaste by sophisticated gentiles and embarrassment by emancipated Jews, was a sign not merely that they had behind them a long history of tumult and woe; it was the psychic shadow of a great idea—the idea of messianism as sacred burden —which must surely be at the heart of any attempt to explain Jewish survival, if indeed it can be explained at all.

CHAPTER SEVEN

The Restlessness of Learning

No MATTER how cramped their lives might be, the immigrant Jews struggled against the assumption that they were locked into settled cultural molds. All the ideas and myths surrounding them—whether the traditionalism of their own past, the lure of American individualism, or their improvised culture of *Yiddishkeit*—helped arouse new energies of aspiration and discontent. It was inevitable that these energies should have no precise focus. In the early 1900's there was just not enough living space or time to make the kinds of distinctions between the life of the mind and a place in the world, between the ideal of universal justice and the thrust of ethnic striving, which later generations would find it easy, perhaps a little too easy, to make. Uneducated, ill-educated, narrowly educated, or educated according to premises that seemed not to bear on American life, the immigrant Jews now wanted to learn at least a fraction of what had long been denied them. The hunger for knowledge was widespread, and among a few it rose to a fierce and remarkable passion. Whatever time was left after a long day in the shop or store they often spent, sometimes misspent, in groping to discover what they did not know.

The immigrants had first of all to work out some relationship with the surrounding American culture. Learning the new language turned out to be difficult, partly because they had little experience in the methods of modern learning. "There are many intelligent people," bemoaned the *Forward*, who "spend their lives in a candy store on Ludlow Street, or a paper stand, wasting away" because they cannot master English. Still others did learn to read and write but found it a torment to speak: "Jewish young people know their English grammar, but they can't speak fluently. There is some hope for the youngsters, but the old people will never learn."

Between Yiddish and American English there rapidly developed an overlap that purists on both sides deplored but could do nothing to prevent. The Yiddish literary people, trying to discipline and chasten their language, feared that a mass invasion of English vocabulary would overwhelm them. Hayim Zhitlovsky spoke angrily of "the wild-growing Yiddish-English jargon, the potato-chicken-kitchen language"; but he was forgetting that the vividness of folk speech owed something to "the kitchen." Hundreds of English words—some because there were no Yiddish equivalents, some because they served so efficiently, some because they symbolized a rapid absorption into American life—invaded Yiddish speech in the early years of the century. *Hello, all right, good-bye, please, shut up* (the universal *sharrap*), *icebox, paint, landlord, tenant, sale, haircut, teacher, pants, graft, bum, crook, gangster, dinner, street, walk, floor* were quickly taken, with whatever twistings of pronunciation, into immigrant Yiddish and accepted by Yiddish editors with varying degrees of tolerance.

Perhaps a little more slowly, loanwords from Yiddish came pouring into English with equal force and color. Mencken listed many Yiddish words that were quickly accepted into American English: *makher, mamzer, shleper* (especially the verb *to shlep*). There are numerous others: *kibitz, ganev, pisher, shnorer, shpritz,* as well as idioms that are literal or twisted translations of Yiddish phrases, such as "I'm going on a marriage," "My liver is in the oven," "You should live so," and "He doesn't know from nothing." Yiddish vulgarisms, often used as a semiarcane mode of reference by Jews in the company of gentiles, also became popular in English, such as "futz around," "AK," "pisherke," and a rich variety of synonyms for the male sexual organ. There were still more complicated transpositions from Yiddish to English and English to Yiddish. The English term "pay day" was twisted in Yiddish into *payde*, meaning not the day one gets paid but the money one gets on that day.

> An interesting group of words consists of those that are partly analogical creations, partly the result of folk etymology, and partly the result of contaminations. Thus *afodern*, "to afford," in American Yiddish is apparently the Yiddish *fodern* contaminated by the English *afford*. The adverb *oysayd* is the English "outside" contaminated by the Yiddish *oys*, "out." The word *oysgen* in American Yiddish means "to take a walk," while in European Yiddish it means "to expire."

A whole sublanguage or patois grew up in the immigrant districts, neither quite English nor quite Yiddish, in which the vocabulary of the former was twisted to the syntax of the latter. Even those who tried systematically to learn English tripped over the cruelties of idiom: who, in truth, could explain or grasp the mysteries of English prepositions? In the Jewish quarter English took on a new inflection, with the voices of speakers allowed a wider melodic range than was customary among those who used "correct English." Yiddish phrases taken to be uniquely penetrating were imported into English, sometimes, it seemed, especially by those most determined to become English speakers. Words like *chutzpa* and *shlemiel* brought not only verbal richness but new slants of observation, curious intimations of irony. With enrichment came debasement, troubling lovers of English quite as it troubled lovers of Yiddish. But there was no stopping a process so deeply rooted in common experience, and in fact, English penetrated not only American but also European Yiddish. Writing in the *Forward* in 1930, Max Weinreich noted that such words as *business, bluff, peddler*, and *greenhorn* had become naturalized in European Yiddish, with *Der Bluffer* even used as the title of a humorous Yiddish paper in Warsaw.

The difficulties experienced by immigrants in learning English were not merely technical, like mastering the "th" and "w" sounds or coping with the chaos of English spelling; they were basically cultural. To plunge, however tentatively, into a gentile culture raised the fear of religio-ethnic abandonment: who could not remember his father's warning that a single step from the true path meant the risk of complete apostasy? Nor was it always easy for an immigrant six or nine months in this country to be persuaded that, out of genuinely benevolent motives, a government might really provide free schooling at night.

Nevertheless, thousands of immigrants took themselves off to the night classes that the Board of Education ran three and four times a week in the public schools. If one takes into account all those who passed in and out of these classes, often disoriented and discouraged, the number must have been enormous. (Yiddish journalists claimed that the majority of adult Jewish immigrants attended night schools at one point or another, but there is of course no way of verifying this claim.) In the popular histories, oral legends, and comic fiction (Leo Rosten's *The Education of Hyman Kaplan*), the night school has been endowed with an aura of tenderness and charm as an agency that helped ease immigrants into American speech and customs. For a lucky few it did. "The night school," wrote Boris Borgen, an immigrant who became an influential social worker, "brought me into another life. I discovered an evening school. . . . The teacher was Henrietta Szold, a quiet earnest young woman, absorbed in her work with an almost painful intensity." To have had as one's teacher so remarkable a woman as the American pioneer of Zionism, was of course a privilege; but for most immigrant students the experience of night school proved a good deal more abrasive. All too characteristic is Edward Steiner's complaint: "If our teacher had met us as men and not as children, if into that weary hour he had thrown a grain of humor to relax us, if someone would have sung a simple tune in English, more might have remained after a week than fourteen out of a class . . . ten times that number."

East Side spokesmen frequently charged that night-school teachers were patronizing, negligent, and overworked. The first two complaints were at least sometimes, and the last almost always, true. A sober student of the problem, not inclined to the exaggerations that kept flaring up in the Yiddish press, painted a depressing picture of what the night schools would be like once they opened in the fall:

> The immigrants will be pushed into school benches intended for eight year old children, their knees reaching to the very desks. They will be uncomfortable and sorely puzzled. And then a teacher, in all probability tired from a day's hard work, will undertake the task of teaching them English. For a few days perhaps he may have patience with pupils who are exhausted after their ten-hour day. He will treat them gently, sympathetically. But after a while his own fatigue will show its effect, and he will become capricious and unduly exacting. The students will lose heart. . . . One by one they will cease to come until barely a third of the original number is left. Then there will be talk in a different tone—censure, this time, of the laziness of the foreigner, of his unwillingness to make sacrifices to learn English.

The problem went beyond poor facilities and overworked teachers; as in later decades, there was a kind of cultural opacity, not always the result of ill will, in the efforts of educational authorities to "straighten out" the immigrants. An elementary reader often used in night classes—*The New American Citizens*, published in 1909 by Frances Sankstone Mintz—offers a muddle of baby-talk history, mindless civic lessons, anecdotes about American inventors, some insipid poems, a few patriotic songs, but nothing that touches on the experience or feelings of the immigrants themselves. With such texts the process of Americanization could only be a kind of cultural bleaching.

Still, many immigrants tried. At one point, for example, the Jewish bakers' union organized classes in the public schools for its members, mostly in the daytime so as to accommodate nightworkers. Hundreds came, dozens stayed. Perhaps no one was really at fault; perhaps the classes were organized on mistaken principles; perhaps the sheer circumstances of life were too hard (a grown-up man, worried about bread for his children, breaking his head over alien ABC's . . .).

The Orthodox religious groups did not care very much about learning English, and the Yiddishists were necessarily ambivalent, but those immigrant leaders who understood that their future lay in America kept pressing for English instruction. No one was more persistent in this demand than Abraham Cahan, who devoted many *Forward* editorials to the need for mastering English. Cahan, whose influence on this score was enormous, pressed his readers very hard: he was like a father thrusting a child into the water in the hope it will be forced to swim. In regard to the immigrant young there was perhaps something to be said for this approach, but with the older people it often meant prodding them into a shock of cold.

Might there not have been more humane arrangements that accepted the reality of bilingualism, a reality, after all, that encompassed the lives of most immigrants? Paul Abelson, a sensitive East Side educator who began as an immigrant boy and went on to earn a Ph.D., wrote in 1906: "It may be questioned whether to teach him the English language is the first and only requisite to assimilate the immigrant, and that, if he has not shown a readiness to acquire the language according to our methods, the task of assimilation is hopeless." Neither the well-meaning people at the Board of Education nor the immigrants themselves could quite grasp the point of such a remark: the one believed cold plunges were good for foreigners and the other accepted cold plunges as a fatality of existence.

"Americanizing" the Greenhorns

How to educate immigrants in both the English language and American customs became an issue that agitated the East Side for decades. A clean, ruthless sweep of everything they had brought with them? A last-ditch resistance to each and every new influence they now encountered? Not many people openly advocated either course, though there were a good many German Jews, well entrenched in American life, who wanted the first, and at least some Orthodox immigrants who favored the second. Step by empirical step, the immigrant community moved toward biculturalism, though its shrewdest spokesmen, like Abraham Cahan, understood that even if achieved, this equilibrium between past and present could not be maintained for very long.

Nor was it merely toward American culture that the immigrants had to work out some sort of relation. Between them and America stood the German Jews, for whom Judaism was more a faith than an encompassing way of life. With an ease the Russian and Polish Jews could not—indeed, seldom cared to—emulate, the German Jews had thoroughly Americanized themselves, many of them finding a road to the Republican party and bourgeois affluence. By the turn of the century, the tensions between the established German Jews and the insecure east European Jews had become severe, indeed, rather nasty—a glib condescension against a rasping sarcasm. The Germans found it hard to understand what could better serve their ill-mannered cousins than rapid lessons in civics, English, and the uses of soap. But even as they seemed maddeningly smug to the east Europeans, they were bound to them by ties they might have found hard to explain yet rarely wished to deny. A struggle ensued, sometimes fraternal, sometimes fractious, about the best ways to help the hordes of east Europeans find a place in the new world.

One focus of this struggle was the Educational Alliance, curious mixture of night school, settlement house, day-care center, gymnasium, and public forum. The Alliance represented a tangible embodiment of the German Jews' desire to help, to uplift, to clean up and quiet down their "coreligionists." Such conscientious leaders of the German-Jewish community as Isidor Straus and Jacob Schiff—men of wealth, men at ease in the new world, men who could pick up the telephone and get through to the mayor —brought about a merger in 1889 of three agencies, the Hebrew Free School Association, the Young Men's Hebrew Association, and the Aguilar Free Library Society, into one large center located in a five-story building on East Broadway and Jefferson Street. Named the Educational Alliance in 1893, it became for several decades a major source of help to the new immigrants, as well as a major cause of contention between uptown and downtown Jews.

In forming the Educational Alliance the German Jews were influenced by the settlement-house movement of the 1880's, through which such highminded men and women as Charles Stover, Felix Adler, Jane Addams, and Lillian Wald hoped to provide the poor with cultural and moral aids that would train them to help themselves. That the motives of the German Jews were often pure seems beyond doubt. They poured money, time, and energy into the Alliance, and often were rewarded by the downtown Jews with fury and scorn. Yet neither can it be doubted that the attitudes of the German Jews were calculated to enrage. An uptown weekly, the *Jewish Messenger*, announced that the new immigrants "must be Americanized in spite of themselves, in the mode prescribed by their friends and benefactors." The *Messenger* found these plebeian Jews "slovenly in dress, loud in manners, and vulgar in discourse," and would have liked to "pull down the ghetto . . . and scatter its members to the corners of the nation." Down on Rivington and Delancey streets there were people quite prepared with compliments in turn.

Throughout its life the Alliance was wracked by the question: to what extent should it try to "Americanize" the greenhorns? A historian friendly to the Alliance wrote that some of the "older Jewish settlers [a euphemism for German Jews] wished to effect a rapid change in the lives of these immigrants. Impatient with people with whom they were neither socially nor intellectually *en rapport* but whom they could not help acknowledging as their own, they advocated the immediate abandonment by the immigrants of their old world cultural patterns and the overnight transformation into full-fledged Americans." Especially in the early years of the Alliance, this often meant that it aped such public—day and night—school routines as flag saluting and patriotic singing, which annoyed the stiff-necked immigrants, both Orthodox religious and orthodox radical, who felt they had a fair portion of culture on their own.*

The sponsors of the Alliance soon realized that the immigrant's "spirit was not mute; that a great heritage lodged in him. . . . They therefore followed the wiser policy of . . . gradual adjustment." Slowly, very slowly, they came to understand that assimilation had to be seen as a process to be eased rather than a program to be legislated. Yet even this formula was hard to enforce. For there were always passionately held differences as to whether the Alliance should stress the old or the new, traditional Hebraic and Yiddish or American culture and customs.

In its best years, between the turn of the century and the First World War, the Alliance threw itself into communal aid and popular education with a kind of frenzy. In 1898 its directorship was taken over by David Blaustein, himself an east European immigrant who had made his way through Harvard, served briefly as a rabbi, and was now one of the first to reflect seriously upon the problems of Jewish social service. An intelligent man, Blaustein gradually softened the "Americanizing" pressures of the Alliance and came to feel that people like himself might even learn from their "clients." He was one of the first public figures on the East Side to move past the fixed rhetoric of Jewish ideology and, both in his practical work and in a series of sensitive essays, confront the particulars of immigrant experience.

Under Blaustein's leadership the Alliance bristled with activity. There were morning classes for children needing preparation to enter public school; night classes for adults struggling with English; daytime classes for waiters, watchmen, and bakers who worked at night; classes in Yiddish and Hebrew; classes in cooking and sewing; classes in Greek and Roman history taught by Edward King, a Scotch Comtean with leftist politics and a passion for enlightening the poor; classes for Hebrew teachers who might want to learn English—alas, admits the *Eleventh Annual Report*, "sparsely at-

---

* The Alliance's *First Annual Report* breathes an astonishing condescension: "The importance of physical training for our downtown brethren cannot be overestimated. Our coreligionists are often charged with lack of physical courage and repugnance to physical work. Nothing will more effectively remove this than athletic training."

The 1899 report of the Alliance's Committee on Moral Culture solemnly warned that "within the contracted limits of the New York ghetto . . . medieval Orthodoxy and anarchistic license are struggling for mastery. A people whose political surroundings have entirely changed, who are apt to become intoxicated with liberty of action which has suddenly been vouchsafed to them . . . is apt to depart from its mooring and to become a moral menace."

In later years the more sensitive leaders among the German Jews came to understand their errors in the Alliance and elsewhere. Louis Marshall wrote in a letter to a friend that the German Jews "held themselves aloof from the people. . . . They acted as Lords and Ladies Bountiful bringing gifts to people who did not seek for gifts. . . . The work was done in such a manner as not only to give offense, but to arouse suspicion of the motives."

tended," even though held "on the lines laid down in Spencer's *Essay on Education*"; enormously popular classes held in Yiddish by the spellbinding preacher Hirsh Masliansky, who combined Jewish uplift with a shrewd gloss on Americanism; classes in music and art (among the art students were Jacob Epstein, Ben Shahn, Chaim Gross, Moses and Isaac Soyer, William Zorach); classes at an offshoot called Breadwinners College, started by Thomas Davidson, a wonderfully zealous gentile teacher who created a sort of Ruskin College staffed by volunteers, to which, as the *Eleventh Annual Report* jubilantly noted, "belt-makers, button-hole makers, collectors, collar-makers, carpenters, cutters, cloak-makers, cigar-makers, embroiderers" came regularly, and where Morris Raphael Cohen taught the Book of Job on Monday and "Social Evolution" on Sunday.

The conductor of the children's orchestra at the Alliance, Sam Franko, would recall:

> My class was composed of about 35 members, ranging from 10 to 15 years of age, and distinguished more by ambition than by talent. Their parents, most of them immigrant Russian Jews, thought their offspring to be geniuses. . . .
> I have often reproached myself for the strictness and severity with which I treated these children, ill-clad and undernourished as many of them were.
> . . . When the rehearsals were over, everything was forgotten; the young students never missed an opportunity of accompanying me to the station. . . .
> It was a sight to see so many children marching in a body through the streets of New York, each armed with a violin case.

In turn, one of Franko's students remembered:

> The large room in which Sam Franko's orchestra rehearsed in the evenings was in the daytime a studio where art students drew, painted, and modeled with clay. The walls were hung with unframed paintings. . . . Before and after our rehearsals . . . I used to examine the paintings and the sculpture with interest. . . . The portraits were mostly of East Side types. . . . There were figures of children, fat, shrewd-looking women, and young and old men of the Hasidic type, with curled earlocks and beards, their faces a bright unhealthy hue, their eyes shining with a kind of rapture.

The Alliance tried almost everything. A People's Synagogue with sedate services in Hebrew and German was set up in 1900, never very successful. On the High Holy Days services were held for ten cents a ticket, "to combat . . . the opening of synagogues in dance halls and meeting rooms . . . presided over by officials imbued with mercenary motives only." At one or another time the Alliance had an orchestra, a Halevy Singing Society, an Anton Rubinstein Muscial Society, a Children's Choral Union. The passion for musical instruction, shared by even the least educated immigrants, was satisfied by low-cost lessons in violin, piano, and mandolin. In the 1890's Tuesday-evening concerts "of a very high order"—as if the German Jews would ever sponsor anything that wasn't!—were held for a five-cent admission charge. Art exhibitions; birthday celebrations of great figures ranging from Aristotle to Longfellow; a mass of literary clubs (the Carlyle, the Gladstone, the Tennyson), some of which, notes one *Annual Report* dolefully, collapsed into "mere social gatherings"; a roof garden opened in 1896 for the summertime use of children and mothers, where Nathan Straus established a depot for the sale of sterilized milk (average daily attendance in 1896 was 4,600); a boys' camp and a girls' camp in the summers; a school for physical culture; a Legal Aid Bureau to help deserted wives; endless theatrical performances—all this and more made the Educational Alliance into something like the "immigrant's university and club" that one of its *Annual Reports* boasted it was.

Yet for all its good works, the Alliance could never settle into harmony, either within its own institutional life or in relation to the immigrant masses. With the latter there was always distance and misunderstanding, an obtuseness of good faith. A report prepared in 1902 by Bernard Ernst, superintendent of the Alliance's camp for boys, catalogued the woes that East Side ragamuffins could inflict on social workers and camp directors:

> It is a discouraging fact that the East Side boy despises manual labor. . . . Apart from intellectual exertion, all labor appears menial to him. The few duties at the camp—none of them irksome or onerous—were shirked and evaded with perplexing regularity. Boys had to be literally driven to make their beds. . . . Larger boys bribe the juniors to do their work. . . . When asked to help to remove rocks from the baseball field, the reply was, "What has the camp got the farmer for?" When one senior was asked about the "philosophy" of dishwashing, his reply was, "What are the women for?"
>
> The East Side boy is accustomed to excessive over-feeding. He wants six thick slices of bread—over half a loaf at every meal. He loathes vegetables largely because he does not know them as food. Lettuce is called "grass" and not eaten; cauliflower is meant for cattle. . . . Table manners are woefully absent. Everybody puts his knife in his mouth.

It was probably no one's fault, this long tradition of misunderstanding. How could Mr. Ernst get through to boys needing six slices of bread with each meal? How could he understand the underflow of anxiety in Jewish life that the fixation on food released, caricatured, and assuaged? And how could he have supposed that in the eyes of his charges he was anything but a rather stuffy comic figure?

From the moment of its birth the Educational Alliance came under attack. Orthodox Jews were aghast at its innovations in prayer, socialist Jews at its devotion to petty reform. In 1900 a group of Yiddish intellectuals, with the playwright Jacob Gordin at their head, set up a rival institution, the Educational League, declaring it was time "the people down town cut away from the apron strings of the German Jews." A mass meeting brought together two thousand people in March 1903 at the Grand Central Palace, where Gordin presented a skit ridiculing uptowners and "social workers." Called "The Benefactors of the East Side," it has a pretentious German-Jewish philanthropist declare that he and his friends, "like Abraham Lincoln," are working to liberate the slaves. "To be sure, the East Side people aren't black, but they *are* Romanians. They aren't Ethiopians, but they *are* Russians." Gordin's sketch was as effective as it was nasty, and his audience loved it.

Gradually the Alliance bent under such attacks, learning to show a bit more warmth and respect for the people it proposed to uplift. But where the rival Educational League soon collapsed, the Alliance kept doing its work: Gordin could write rings around the Schiffs and the Strauses, but when it came to the day-by-day work any institution requires for survival, he was not much in evidence.

Nor was the Alliance without intellectual defense. In a once-influential book called *Jewish Philanthropy* (1917), Boris Bogen charged that the "leaders of the East Side were, practically speaking, indifferent to the matters pertaining to their immediate neighbors. They were busy with higher ideals; they were engaged in the strife of world-wide movements." This was a shrewd thrust, striking directly at a major weakness of the whole immigrant culture. Men dreaming of salvation, in this world or another, were seldom prepared for small, unglorious tasks such as the Alliance undertook.

The memories of those who read in its libraries and attended its lectures vary to an astonishing extent. Zero Mostel, who began to paint in its art classes, summoned his experience through an image of space: after the overcrowded apartment in which he grew up, "the Alliance gave me a new life—I had never seen such *big* rooms before!" Equally telling is the memory of a Yiddish poet, Joseph Rolnick, who in 1910 was living on Madison Street and each morning would walk to a garment shop on Chambers Street.

> While it was still dark I used to stop at a column of the el, scribble a few rough lines that came to me. . . . Sunday mornings I would go to the Alliance and there finish the poem. In the large reading room I often dozed off, together with others who grew sleepy from the warmth. The librarian used to walk up and down waking the sleepers . . . but I learned to hear her steps before she came near my chair. Not once did she catch me dozing.

The memories of Eugene Lyons were bitter:

> We were "Americanized" [at the Educational Alliance] about as gently as horses are broken in. In the whole crude process, we sensed a disrespect for the alien traditions in our homes and came unconsciously to resent and despise those traditions, good and bad alike, because they seemed insuperable barriers between ourselves and our adopted land.

The memories of Morris Raphael Cohen were warm:

> It was [at the Alliance] that my father and mother went regularly to hear the Rev. Masliansky preach . . . in Yiddish. It was there that I drew books

from the Aguilar Free Library and began to read English. . . . It was there that I first met Thomas Davidson who became the light of my life and of my intellectual development. . . . A window of my life opening on the soul-strengthening vista of humanity will always be dedicated to the Educational Alliance.

Who was right, Lyons or Cohen? Each in turn, both together, and neither alone. The German Jews, intent upon seeing that the noses of those East Side brats were wiped clean, surely proved themselves to be insufferable, and anyone raised in the clatter of Clinton Street or the denial of Cherry Street had good reason to rage against the uptown Jews. Yet, in a way, the latter were right: physical exercise and hygiene *were* essential to the well-being of their "coreligionists" and somehow, through prodding and patronizing, they had to be convinced of this. The east European Jews felt free to release their bile because they knew that finally the German Jews would not abandon them, and the German Jews kept on with their good works even while reflecting on the boorishness of their "coreligionists." Out of such friction came a modest portion of progress.

A Visit to the Cafés

Keidansky, an immigrant Jew stuck away in Boston, decided one year in the early 1900's to spend his vacation on the East Side. He wanted something exciting and new, not just to exchange the monotony of Boston for the monotony of the country. So he went to the cafés of the Lower East Side where, as he later told a friend, "people feel free, act independently, speak as they think, and are not ashamed of their feelings."

In those "universities of the ghetto," as he called the cafés, Keidansky found all social and cultural problems delightfully close to solution. The financial trusts? They are paving the way for socialism, explained a young man at his table, since industrial concentration is a prerequisite for the new society—otherwise, what would you do, run around the country organizing peanut stands? The future of war? Once the workers take over, no more war. Tolstoy? A great writer but a puerile philosopher, announced a red-haired fellow from behind a newspaper at the next table. Ibsen? There's a man who knows the tragedy of life—and what's more, our own Zangwill rates Ibsen higher than Shakespeare. But Shaw, isn't he still greater? Conversation shifts to Shaw's little book on Ibsenism, an astonishing number of the talkers claiming to have just finished it, and then to Georg Brandes, the Danish-Jewish critic. Brandes, says a pale-faced poet with a sweet smile, is the greatest critic of modern times. Thus far the talk has been mostly about the drama—but what about the novel, has it any future in these distraught times? Keidansky is somewhat alarmed at the news that the novel is in bad shape: it has proved unable to keep up with modern tempos. The short story of Maupassant, that's the form of the future, chimes in a journalist who specializes in twelve-hundred-word *feuilletons*. Yes, adds a Yiddish actor, you mean the Maupassant who's recently become a contributor to the *Forward*—a dig at the way Yiddish papers "borrow" European fiction. But what's wrong with making Maupassant a Yiddish writer? asks someone who has kept quiet until now. After all, didn't a nice Jewish man walk into the office of one of our magazines and ask to speak to Friedrich Nietzsche? Mention of Nietzsche brings the talk back to Wagner's music, Gorky's novels, Zola's realism, "all these things decided upon," observes Keidansky, "by people who understand them, more or less."

His sharp eye for bluffers notwithstanding, Keidansky is enchanted. "Everywhere you meet people who are ready to fight for what they believe in and who do not believe in fighting." It is getting late now, after eleven, and the intellectual stars begin drifting in—Alexander Harkavy, the Yiddish dictionary maker; Abraham Liessen, editor of the *Tsukunft* and a stirring, pure-spirited poet; Hillel Zolotaroff, the Kropotkin of the East Side; Jacob Gordin, the playwright, in all his dark stateliness; and others too: Hourwich the economist, Paley the editor, Louis Miller the acerb polemicist. Men aware of their place in the world, they make impressive entrances, some with thick Russian-style beards, others clean-shaven in the American fash-

In the café

ion. This is their territory, and here they are treated with a well-deserved respect such as the outer world has yet to accord them. A little later Hutchins Hapgood drops in, the charming young American who is getting his education by listening intently to Abe Cahan, walking the streets of the East Side, and going to the Yiddish theatre.

Back home in Boston, as he again settles into the staleness of provincial life, Keidansky tells a friend, "Why, I have gotten enough ideas on the East Side to last me for ten years."

By 1905 there were several score of these cafés, or, as they were sometimes called, coffee-and-cake parlors, on the East Side. Each café had its enthusiasts claiming it was the true center of Yiddish intellect. For the early playwrights and actors, it was Schreiber's café on Canal Street. For the serious young poets of 1907–1908 who called themselves *Di Yunge* (The Young Ones), it was Goodman and Levine's on East Broadway. For the radicals, as the veteran socialist Louis Waldman remembered, it was the Monopole at Second Avenue and Ninth Street, where Leon Trotsky once appeared in the flesh. But the most famous center for writers, actors, philosophers, and *kibitzers* who took pleasure in staring at the great, was the Café Royale on Second Avenue and Twelfth Street. For a dime (and a nickel tip) you could get a glass of tea and a piece of coffee cake while sorting out the celebrities of Yiddish culture and listening to the gypsy fiddler Ferenc Miklos, who played, said the critic Samuel Chotzinoff, "with a sumptuous tone that a great artist might envy."

Sooner or later, unless he were unusually skillful at sliding from table to table, a customer had to buy something. But once he had made his ten- or fifteen-cent purchase he could sit endlessly, in a not always clean but reasonably well-lighted place. "The cafés were kept going not by what the writers spent, but by those more numerous patrons who liked to pass an evening where writers congregated." And some glamour of the spirit apparently rubbed off on these onlookers, which made it a little easier for them to face the drabness of another day in the shops or streets.

A little easier too, it seems, for the Jewish women who frequented the cafés—not the sober housewives who would not have dreamed of wasting a minute on such frivolities, but the newly liberated young women dressed or draped in bohemian "Russian" styles and still either a little shy or inclined to be overassertive in their freedom.

> The hall bedroom is such a dingy, dreary place . . . [but the café] is light and cheerful. . . . If they are not the objects of fine courtesies and considerateness, [these bohemian women] do not miss them; perhaps they never knew them. . . . They sit there in an atmosphere of tea-steam and cigarette smoke . . . pallid, tired, thin-lipped, flat-chested and angular. . . . The time of night means nothing until way into the small hours. When one must sleep in a hall bedroom there is no hurry about bedtime.

The talk bubbles harmlessly, sometimes wittily, like new froth on an old culture, and for some who have no other place to go, it helps pass the time.

A Passion for Lectures

To most immigrants the café seemed an exotic or frivolous place, appropriate perhaps for *inteligentn* and associated idlers, but hardly for working people who had to earn their bread. What many of them did take seriously was the endless lectures that filled the nights of the East Side, especially on weekends. There were the lectures scheduled by the Educational Alliance and the People's Institute at Cooper Union. There were the Yiddish lectures arranged by Dr. Henry Leipziger for the Board of Education, which by 1915 were drawing 75,000 people a year. There were the lectures sponsored by the immigrant institutions themselves, the Workmen's Circle, the unions, the socialists, the Zionists, indeed any group with the faintest pretension to culture. At such evenings one could feel at home, perhaps even venture to ask a question or speak up without embarrassment.

November 1897: the William Morris Club sponsors a lecture on astronomy at the *Forward* building. January 1898: Dr. Ingerman offers a series on "The History of Ancient Greece" for the Workmen's Circle. September 1905: the anarchist Progressive Library features Dr. Hillel Zolataroff as its main speaker, flanked by Max Kornin reading from Sholom Aleichem, "Comrade Gorodetsky playing the violin," and Sara Edelstadt, sister of the late poet David Edelstadt, reading from his work—"admission 15¢, proceeds to help a sick comrade." In 1906 large crowds come to hear Dr. Isaac Daniely, delegate from the Russian Socialist Territorialist party, speak on the post revolutionary situation of his country; Dr. Shmarya Levin, a communal leader among the Russian Jews, draws "an immense audience at his first lecture in New York"; and the "Zionists find it profitable to send a Yiddish lecturer to New England towns." In 1915 the Ladies Waist Makers Union sponsors a series of lectures and concerts every Friday night, attended by fifteen hundred people, mostly girls. So it would go into the winter weeks, through the passing decades: the tribute immigrant Jews paid, sometimes beautifully earnest and sometimes mere blank-minded ritual, to the sanctity of thought.

When young Marcus Ravage went to work as a shirt operator a few years after the turn of the century, he found that almost all his fellow workers brought books to the shop, mostly in Yiddish but some in Russian, German, and English. During their lunch hour, unless they succumbed to the lure of a discussion, "the entire lot of them had their heads buried in their volumes or their papers, so that the littered, unswept loft had the air of having been miraculously turned into a library." One day a girl operator found Ravage glancing at her book and asked whether he went to lectures. A little ashamed, he said that he did not. "You know," she told him, "Maxim Gorky is going to speak tonight."

> I began to buy newspapers and watch for the notices. There were scores of lectures every week. . . . One night it was Darwin and the next it might be the principle of air-pressure. On a Saturday night there were sometimes two meetings so arranged that both could be attended by the same audience. I remember once going to a meeting at Cooper Union to protest against the use of the militia in breaking a strike somewhere in the West, and then retiring with a crowd of others to the anarchist reading-room on Eldridge Street to hear an informal discussion on "Hamlet versus Don Quixote."

For the East Side intelligentsia—a category hospitable enough to include immigrant workers, housewives, students, and storekeepers—these lectures were not merely a major outlet through which to release yearnings for mental growth, they were also one of the few kinds of recreation such people could afford or approve. "There would be 'balls' bearing no resemblance to any type of function usually designated by the name except that speeches would be followed by dancing and refreshments of tea and sand-

A Russian girl student

wiches—an obvious hang-over from the student 'balls' of Russia and
Switzerland, each of which was dedicated to a cause. One might meet Alexander Berkman and Emma Goldman unaccountably turning up at a social-
democratic ball despite their anarchism." Indeed, for the ideologically committed there was not much difference between learning and diversion—the
weekend lecture became an occasion at which all of one's deepest interests,
intellectual and personal, could be engaged.

To young people like Ravage, eager to swallow the world's culture at a
single gulp, it hardly mattered whether a lecturer spoke on popular science
or ancient history, German literature or Indian customs. "There was a
peculiar, intoxicating joy in just sitting there and drinking in the words of
the speakers, which to us were echoes from a higher world than ours." The
phrase is deeply revealing: "echoes from a higher world than ours," as if
somewhere in the distance there gleamed a true repository of learning,
beyond the reach of mere immigrants, or mere Jews, or, for that matter,
mere Jewish immigrant lecturers. Most of the lectures were on political and
social, sometimes cultural, topics; but one of "the echoes from a higher
world" the immigrants tried occasionally to reach for was that of elementary science, something their own tradition had been unable to cope with.

The lecturers were themselves often but a step or two ahead of their
listeners. Morris Hillquit, later to become a distinguished socialist, began his
career as lecturer by visiting a fraternal society of German-Jewish tailors in
behalf of the United Hebrew Trades. Unexpectedly, the chairman asked
Hillquit to address the meeting "on the Labor Problem," and the young
man, who had never before made a public speech, suddenly found himself
talking in German to several hundred attentive tailors about ideas he had
only a few days earlier picked up in Engels's *Socialism, Scientific and Utopian.* "As I spoke on, I warmed up to my subject. I soon forgot my audience
and overcame my stage fright. I was attempting to restate in simple language
and largely for my own benefit the lesson I had just learned. . . . I spoke
about half an hour, which seemed to be an eternity, and was warmly applauded. . . . Thus began my career as a public speaker. It has never
ended."

Among the scores of Yiddish lecturers there were some genuinely
learned men. Hillquit himself had dipped into the social sciences and tried
hard to avoid the pat formulas of his comrades. Shmarya Levin was a Judaist
of wide culture, as was the Labor Zionist theoretician Nachman Syrkin.
Moissaye Olgin, first a staff writer for the *Forward* and then the main
Yiddish spokesman for communism, had a firm grounding in Russian literature. Hayim Zhitlovsky, advocate of an eclectic Yiddishist nationalism, won
the admiration of the serious audiences.

How fearfully serious those audiences could be* is suggested by David

* Serious, but also wonderfully eager and warmhearted. One Yiddish lecturer tells
the story of an engagement he had in Chattanooga. It was in the dead of winter, a
tremendous snowstorm forced his train to stop for hours, and by the time he
reached the city it was midnight. He assumed his audience had long ago dispersed,

Shub, a Yiddish writer, who recalls a series of ten lectures Zhitlovsky gave shortly after arriving in New York in 1904. Bringing with him the credentials of a leader of the Russian Socialist Revolutionary party (a populist radical movement) and intent upon creating a major impression, Zhitlovsky chose as his topic "Marxism and Synthetic Monism." To stress the momentousness of his choice, he spoke in Russian, though he knew Yiddish quite well. Socialists, anarchists, the whole East Side intelligentsia, flocked to Clinton Hall.

Zhitlovsky spoke in "a fine literary Russian without a trace of an accent. He was a sparkling lecturer. . . . But I am certain," admits Shub, "that I was not the only one there who failed to understand even half of what he was saying." Zhitlovsky's philosophical assault on Marxism caused anxiety among the Yiddish-speaking socialists, and to seal off this wedge of heresy they sent Abraham Cahan to the platform—also speaking in Russian—with a lecture entitled "Is Marxism Scientific?" Pragmatist by nature, Cahan declared that Marx was not a philosopher at all, but rather an analyst of society, and that the claim for Marxism as science rested on its economic analysis of capitalism. Zhitlovsky sat through Cahan's presentation, and in the discussion period (where the two antagonists conveniently lapsed into Yiddish) he showed that Cahan had narrowed Marxism for his own polemical advantage and that, in fact, most of its European theorists did make philosophical claims. The bewildered young Shub, though a political ally of Cahan, had to admit that Zhitlovsky had gotten the better of the debate—as Cahan himself privately admitted several decades later.

Most of the Yiddish lecturers were neither as erudite as Zhitlovsky nor as sharp as Cahan. They lectured on the run, skimming fragments of knowledge from German or Russian books, scraping together tidbits from English magazines, and often relying on the rhetorical expansiveness of the Yiddish language. A good many of the lecturers were men who had been decently educated in traditional Judaism but who were ill at ease when it came to secular topics—and on the East Side it was secular topics that were mainly in demand.

It was not an easy life, being a Yiddish lecturer. When Benjamin Feigenbaum, the socialist propagandist, instituted a rule in the early 1900's of charging a flat fee (five dollars from organizations that could afford it), this constituted a major step forward in the profession. In one of Z. Libin's Yiddish sketches, a lecturer pours out his heart: After Rosh Hashonah, "the

---

but to his astonishment, there, at the station, was a committee cheerfully waiting for him. They told him that, the hall having shut down, the audience had gone to the house of an old Yiddishist. There the lecturer found a few dozen people prepared to hear him even though it was now past midnight. He gulped a cup of coffee aand began. No one stirred, no one left. By the time he had finished speaking and had answered numerous questions, it was deep into the night. Still, no one left. A breakfast was improvised, people talked, laughed, and sang, preparing to go straight to their morning's work. The committee then took the lecturer back to the station, and as he boarded his train, one of them said, "I bet you'll never forget the Jews of Chattanooga."

committees" are suddenly heard from, proposing engagements, but all summer long you might as well starve to death.

In her memoir of Nachman Syrkin, Marie Syrkin recalls being taken to endless public meetings by her father: "baby-sitters were an unheard of institution . . . the cost would have been prohibitive. Besides, I believe my parents felt that a bright ten-year-old should be able to appreciate political discourse at any hour." An important figure in the Jewish world and a man of intellectual attainments, Syrkin would spend his days at the Astor Library, which he made into his "office," writing essays and seeing associates. "Any crank or lunatic who wanted to find him—and the tribe was numerous—knew that he could discover Syrkin either at work in the Jewish Room or pacing up and down the corridor. To save the cost of lunch my mother would give him a sandwich cut into bite-size pieces which he would keep in his pocket and eat while reading."

The Syrkins lived for a time in the east Bronx and later in Flatbush. "Paying the rent was always postponed to the last possible day; the landlord turned out to be an admirer of my father's and was . . . elastic as possible in his construction of what date constituted the last day. The grocery storekeeper was apparently a less zealous reader of the Yiddish press." When things became desperate, Mrs. Syrkin went to work in a hat factory and the theoretician whose ideas would serve as the basis for the Israeli kibbutz felt overcome by shame. "To be a hungry student or a chronically indigent intellectual was proper . . . but for my mother to seek work in a factory was as great a loss of caste as if my father had become a petty shopkeeper." Nor was the condition of the Syrkins significantly better or worse than that of other Jewish intellectuals in New York during the years before the First World War. Writing for the Yiddish press, giving lectures, serving as leader of an organization—these were precarious ways to earn a living. And if the lecturer belonged to a political movement, he was frequently expected to speak without payment, sometimes without even recovering his carfare.

At home the rent might be overdue, but on the platform, summoning visions of universal justice or national liberation, the lecturer embodied a standard his audience respected. Marcus Ravage tells the story of a friend, one Wykoff, who planned to leave his job in the garment trades and become a dentist, so as to have "time to read and to think—to be a human being." What had crystallized this desire was a lecture by Benjamin Feigenbaum. "Did you hear him on 'Dominant Figures in World Literature?' It made my heart sick. Goethe, Calderon, Racine, Dante, what do I know about them?" For that matter, what did Feigenbaum himself know about them?

For forty years Benjamin Feigenbaum (1860–1932) kept bustling through the endless meetings of the East Side, a ubiquitous figure in its political and cultural life: half scholar, half agitator, wholly lecturer. If you went to a protest meeting after the Kishinev pogroms, Feigenbaum was likely to be one of the speakers; when two thousand girls in the shirtwaist industry met in 1909 to plan their great strike, Feigenbaum was on the platform exhorting them with his homely Yiddish eloquence; and in any given season, he could be heard speaking for the Socialist Labor party, then the Socialist party and the Workmen's Circle and the *landsmanshaftn* on topics ranging from the falsity of religion to the sanctity of culture. Earnest, winning, a little folksy, Feigenbaum was always at hand, more knowledgeable than most of his competitors but less so than his audiences may have supposed.

Feigenbaum was especially popular, wrote his old friend Abraham Cahan, "among those older socialists who in their youth had been educated in Holy Writ. With a passage from the Bible or the Talmud flavored by a preacher's metaphor, Feigenbaum would make a socialist concept graphically clear," for in his person and his thought he bridged the gap between the older *maskilim* (enlightened ones) and the younger socialists.

Born in Warsaw, Feigenbaum spent his youth in a strict Hasidic-rabbinical atmosphere, studying in yeshivas along traditionalist lines. At the age of twenty-two, like others of his generation, he saw the light of socialism and abandoned all he had been taught in order to become a relentless opponent of religion. Nimble in argument, he was soon the darling of the Yiddish-speaking radicals of Warsaw, who believed in him—the Yiddish novelist I. J. Singer would later recall—with the fervor that "Hasidim believed in their *tsadikim* [spiritual leaders]." Singer adds a story about Feigenbaum's abandonment of the faith: "As a young man after his marriage he studied in the hall of the Grand Rabbi of Ger. . . . One day he was inspected [since rumors of heresy had begun to be heard] and found not to be wearing the prescribed undergarments with ritual fringes. The enraged Hasidim laid him out on a table and beat him mercilessly." The memory of this humiliation remained an acute one for Feigenbaum, and, according to some of his friends, it kept spurring him to continued antireligious diatribes.

Fleeing Warsaw, Feigenbaum settled for a while in Antwerp, where he wrote for the Flemish socialist press, and then in London, where he became a correspondent for the New York *Arbeiter Tseitung*. In 1891 he arrived in New York, and gave his first public lecture in the New Everett Hall, where, as Cahan would remember, the crowd "was electrified with curiosity in the way a small town hears out a new cantor."

A natural popularizer, Feigenbaum wrote articles for the *Forward* on innumerable topics, many with a rather thin smattering of knowledge. He could speak on almost anything, and he did; but his specialty was religion. His assaults on the Almighty, to whom he paid more attention than many an ostensible believer, were fierce and sometimes a little coarse. "Our Jehovah," he wrote once, "showed a weak character in first creating man and then failing to hold him in check."

Feigenbaum touched the older Jewish workers not merely because he knew his way around the Talmud but also because he shared their deep moral conservatism even while preaching socialism. For all his tirades against "our Jehovah" he insisted on the rightness of those Jewish ethical precepts concerning marriage and sexuality to which his audiences still clung; he even saw them, with some shrewdness, as precepts sustaining socialist belief. Whether or not he knew it, Feigenbaum was preaching a Yiddish version of the "religion of humanity" that had been advanced by English intellectuals a few decades earlier, that sense of ethical obligation which they wished to remove from its religious context.

Feigenbaum was a man with a hunger for knowledge and a readiness to share it. Sometimes he shared a little too quickly, but in the circumstances of East Side life this was probably a venial fault, if a fault at all. The service that he, and others like him, rendered the Jewish immigrants was to throw up a footbridge, shaky and perilous, to the outer world of knowledge. In the winter of 1908, for example, he was giving a series of lectures, with a five-cent admission charge, for the Tombrezhberger Young Men's Educational Society, beginning with "Religion as Cultural History" and including such topics as "The Essence of Free Thought," "Secrets of the Torah," and "The God of Religion and the God of Understanding." The contents of these lectures have been lost, but if one may judge by Feigenbaum's articles and pamphlets, they were uneven mixtures of enlightenment and parochialism, firmly grounded in Jewish learning and somewhat less so in the popular agnostic tracts of his day. There is no reason to suppose they were any flimsier than a good portion of what would pass for higher education in America sixty years later.

The work of men like Benjamin Feigenbaum has been covered over by the dust of time; but every culture needs such men, those who sustain even if they also coarsen the tradition of learning.

The Self-Educated Worker

Like everything else on the East Side, the lectures came in for a share of caustic attack. "Knowledge among progressive workers," wrote A. Litwin in the *Forward*, "is superficial."

> As objective observers we must admit that the instruction provided is bad. . . . Our people are getting a chaotic education; our lecturers seize on topics that do not require exact knowledge or explanation. . . . After the lecture, when the chairman asks for questions, no one responds. If someone does, the question has nothing to do with the lecture. Sometimes the questioner is a fanatic and the lecturer, who had been discussing the differences between the drama and the novel, has to make it clear that he did not mean to insult the Socialist party.

The *Forward*'s pretension to the mantle of Matthew Arnold might bring smiles to the lips of Yiddish intellectuals, but there was no denying the accuracy of its diagnosis. The hodgepodge of topics, the dubious qualifications of many speakers, the weariness of the audiences, the lack of systematic instruction, the temptation to use the platform for proselytizing rather than teaching—these were severe weaknesses. It was probably inherent in the lecture system that it should lead people to take a first step but rarely the second. Yet, by any dispassionate standard, all of these complaints seem finally beside the point. The ill-educated or partly educated immigrants who kept coming faithfully on Friday and Saturday nights to the lectures would surely have profited from better programs, as they would have profited from a whole range of conceivable benefits. But it was in the nature of things on the East Side that such benefits be out of reach, while the lectures, good, bad, and indifferent, were always at hand. The lecture was the one pedagogical activity the immigrants could arrange for themselves, through their own agencies and with their own resources. The lecture was their ticket of entry into the world of knowledge—a world, as they recognized in their sober moments, they would never succeed in making their own. It was easy to scoff at the foibles of the lecture system, as a half-century later it would be easier still; but historical perspective, which may be no more than another name for decency of feeling, should instruct us that a certain grandeur of aspiration is to be found in this spectacle of overworked and poverty-stricken men and women submitting themselves to the routine of lectures.

The values embodied in these lectures could be found all through immigrant life. Morris Hillquit came to his first intellectual stirrings on the roofs of the Cherry Street tenements during the 1890's, inflamed by "the high themes which constituted [the] daily conversational fare." John Cournos, at about the same time, became a regular visitor at the home of a Philadelphia family named the Mayers—in Russia, the Mayorskys—where people talked about Swinburne, Wilde, and Whistler. Israel Davidson remembered Wolfe's drugstore as a "clubhouse" where East Side intellectuals, at least those he happened to know, gathered for discussions. "At Warschauer's Russian tea-house I often heard Bacon mentioned respectfully as a philosopher alongside Spencer," wrote Marcus Ravage. As a boy Samuel Chotzinoff stood enraptured in Katz's music store on East Broadway listening to conversations concerning the respective merits of Toscanini and Mahler as symphonic conductors. Abraham Walkowitz started the Art Culture League in 1900 to bring art to immigrants. Melekh Epstein remembered "enormous crowds" traveling up to Lewisohn Stadium to listen to Beethoven's Ninth Symphony. Recollections sweetened by the passage of time? Perhaps; but even with every discount of skepticism, these recollections turn us back to an impressive reality.

Out of this confusion of idealism and waste arose the most notable human type in the immigrant experience: the self-educated worker. What he or she learned from the Yiddish lectures, classes, rallies, and newspapers was incomplete, hazy, sometimes half-baked; but whatever remained was earned and felt. With a kind of passionate stoicism, these men and women struggled against the thickening of their capacities. They sensed that if they gave way to circumstances even once, they would be lost. They worked to open themselves to the world's beauties, stumbling into simple aesthetic experiences for which their tradition had made little allowance. They hoped to re-create themselves according to an ideal image—if not wholly, for they knew it was much too late for that, then at least in bits and patches. This image had come to them from a strange confusion of sources: from the old Jewish respect for learning, from the heightened morale brought by the renaissance of Yiddish culture, from the socialist vision of a humane existence.

The self-educated worker was a child of the nineteenth century, perhaps the most persuasive evidence for its creed of progress. Liberating energies from popular education, positivistic thought, scientific advance, socialist idealism—all came together to stir into consciousness the masses of the oppressed. The self-educated worker made his first appearance in Europe, attending labor colleges in the industrial towns of England, listening to August Bebel in Berlin paint a dream of proletarian emancipation, reading Tolstoy and Chernyshevsky in half-clandestine study groups in Petrograd. He appeared in America as a foot-loose Wobbly or a craftsman who had responded to the voice of Eugene Debs and begun to read Haldeman-Julius's Little Blue Books. Grappling to discover his sense of individuality, he wanted not merely to win some rights for his class but also to claim a modest share in the heritage of Western culture.

The self-educated worker was by no means unique to the Yiddish-speaking world, but as he came to the forefront in the Jewish quarters of Warsaw and Vilna, London and New York, he seemed a peculiarly intense figure—indeed, a peculiarly Jewish figure—who brought with him yearnings and capacities, aptitudes and inclinations that had been honed to sharpness by the pressures of ghetto life. It could not be said about the Yiddish-speaking worker, as it could about many of his European equivalents, that he had just emerged from centuries of illiteracy and muteness; his transformation was from a narrow but coherent religious culture to a quasi-secularized culture at once vibrant and amorphous. And not only was he a proletarian searching for articulation and dignity, he was also a Jew who had come to hope that by approaching Western thought he would both satisfy his own blossoming needs and help to remedy the disadvantages of the Jews as a people. All through the late nineteenth and early twentieth century, learning came to seem an almost magical solution for the Jews, a people that has always placed an enormous faith in the sheer power of words. Learning in its own right, learning for the sake of future generations, learning for the social revolution, learning in behalf of Jewish renewal—all melted into one upsurge of self-discovery.

On the East Side, no matter what the political or communal distractions of the moment, Abraham Cahan kept prodding the immigrants: "In America a worker can sometimes even go to college and get an education. But it takes a long time. *You must try to be an intellectual,* not just a doctor or a lawyer." One of Cahan's colleagues wrote: "We know workers have little time or strength to read after a day in the shop. But a half hour of serious reading every day for several years can provide an excellent education." A persuasion of restlessness moved these men—*you must try to be an intellectual!*—in behalf of a freedom they associated with the life of the mind. All gone now, almost forgotten, but the glory of the immigrant world.

They themselves would not have used such language, for in their quiet aspiration they kept more than a little of that sardonic spirit which seems inseparable from the Yiddish tradition. Here is a memoir of one such self-educated worker, characteristic in its blend of pride and resignation:

"Sometimes I think my life came to an end even before it began. I sit here talking to you this evening, a man of fifty-eight, with the feeling that there is little for me to look forward to. But that feeling doesn't make me sad. I have learned to accept it as I have learned to accept other things.

"While I was growing up in Russia, I developed a tremendous hunger for learning. It's a familiar story to you, and you've probably heard it many times—but all I can say is, it's true. I went for some years to the *heder* and got from it what I could, but all my religious education did was to teach me how little it could give me. I wanted to drink from strange wells.

"When I was about sixteen or seventeen, just a few years before I came to America, people of my generation became very restless. We heard of the Bund, which had recently been started, and to us it meant not only socialism but the whole idea of stepping into the outside world. When a speaker from the Bund came to our town, we saw him not just as an emissary of the organization but also as a new kind of Jew, someone with combativeness in his blood and a taste of culture on his tongue. How cultured was he? By now, who can say? He was our lifeline to the outside world, and that was enough.

"I began to take an interest in books. Some were by Yiddish authors, and some were Yiddish translations of Russian classics. Since I had also gone a little to the Russian school, I began to swallow—I mean, really swallow—Russian books. I read everything I could get my hands on. Turgenev was my favorite, perhaps because there is such a sweetness to his voice. And then Tolstoy and Dostoevsky. I read, of course, Sholom Aleichem, who made the ugliest things in life seem beautiful, and Peretz who, in his own way, taught me not to lose respect for myself.

"How can I describe to you, you who live with a mountain of books, the hunger that I and my friends felt? The excitement we shared when we would discuss Dostoevsky? The pleasure we took in going to a shabby little bookstore in our town? For us it was books and only books. We had nothing else. Here in America young people can choose from movies and music and art and dancing and God alone knows what. But we—all we had was books, and not so many of them, either.

"By the time I came to America, I had to pull my nose out of the books to get a job, but, thank God, things were not as bad for me as for others. I had a relative who broke me in as a garment worker, and after a while I became a cutter, which meant pretty good wages in those days. I was never a slave in the sweatshops. From the beginning I had a skill. What disturbed me most about my early years on the East Side—and this was after 1905—was not so much the physical suffering, but the feeling that I was lost, in a desert. My fellow workers weren't always friendly. Cutters, you know, aren't the most refined people in the world. So I learned to be quiet. I did my share of the work, no one had to prop me up, and what went on in my mind was my own business.

"I would go home in the evenings (I wasn't yet keeping company with my wife) and read translations of Gerhardt Hauptmann and Charles Dickens and your Edgar Allan Poe. I went to night school, and picked up a little English, so I could read the easier books. But it never seemed enough. I was like a hungry man who gets fed but either the food isn't right or it doesn't agree with him or maybe it's not what they call nowadays a balanced diet.

"And I went to lectures. God, those lectures of ours! The socialists by the dozens, the anarchists, the schools, everybody. I heard them all, and sometimes one of the poets would read, like Rosenfeld or Yehoash. They seemed educated men and they certainly knew more than I did. So when Zhitlovsky talked about Herbert Spencer—you can imagine how badly we needed Herbert Spencer on Delancey Street in those days!—I listened. And I thought to myself, maybe next time I can swallow it all.

"But I couldn't. I didn't know where one thing began and the other ended. What was the connection between Herbert Spencer and the Vilna Gaon? How did you bring together one piece of learning with another?

"I went to so many lectures that I began to wonder about them. Don't misunderstand me. I'm not saying that anybody got rich giving lectures. But I noticed they were always introductions, introductions to this and intro- ductions to that. If you want to be honest, that was really what we needed— but it made you feel as if you were in kindergarten all your life. And in unpleasant thought crept into my mind: how many listeners around me knew what the lecturer was talking about? Once I even began to wonder if *he* knew. Still, I kept going—what else was there to do?

"Sometimes I would see the Yiddish writers, on the street or in one of those cafés you Americans think were so wonderful. I would see Mani Leib and his friends, noisy and lively. I admired them. To be honest, I envied them. They seemed lucky in my eyes. I went to an occasional 'evening' where they read or talked, and I bought their books. The Yiddish word gave me pleasure, as it still does. Once or twice I looked into their magazines, but here I felt like an outsider. There were things they knew and talked about which shut me out. Even so, I kept reading and listening and squeezing myself.

"I got married, my wife was a sympathetic person with a mind of her own. Life became easier, I went into a business and while I never got rich—I wasn't a pusher—things were comfortable after a while. When the *Day* started coming out and it seemed to have finer writers than the *Forward*—men like Koralnik and Margoshes—I took it instead, or sometimes both.

"Still, if life became easier in some ways, it also became harder in other ways. I had to chase after the dollar and take care of my family. Each passing day I felt a little more tired. As a result I couldn't read as much as I had in my earlier years. It seemed more pleasant just to sit and talk with my wife. Even so, I kept on buying Yiddish books, because if people like me didn't, who would? In my house you can find almost every Yiddish poet.

"I had always been a disbeliever. It was part of being, among us, an emancipated person. But as I got older, I found that I enjoyed going back to old things, dropping in at the local *shul* to listen to the Kol Nidre or occasionally a religious discussion among the old-timers. I didn't change my ideas, you understand; but my mind seemed readier to take in things which in my youth it had shut out. After all, I was a Jew.

"What else can I tell you? My children went their own way. I am proud of them, but there are things we can't talk about. Still, I have no complaints. My circumstances were what they were. My family has been a whole world to me. I still take pleasure in a page of Sholom Aleichem, and to me Bazarov and Raskolnikov are like friends of my youth. But to think of them is to be reminded that there was a door which, for me, was never opened."

Fathers and Sons

Once the world of the *shtetl* began to crumble and the winds of the Enlightenment started to batter down its rickety frames, the Jews turned with a passion to the problems of secular history—to the *idea* of history—which they had scorned in the past. A culture that had never held great expectations in regard to tomorrow, since it knew that tomorrow could only bring the same injustice that had marked today, was now seized with orgiastic demands upon the dynamic of history. The Jews who in imagination had for so many centuries lived with the past now thrust their hopes and fantasies onto the future. Coming late, the Enlightenment struck the east European Jews with magnified force; gradually, a new secular utopianism infiltrated the old messianic desire; and the tradition of social passivity, a cost of Jewish survival over the centuries, now encountered the noisy impatience of the young.

The immigrant fleeing his *shtetl* and wearing out his eyes over piecework in the sweatshops would of course have spoken in less abstract terms. He would have used the vocabulary of his own needs and expectations. But it was characteristic of Jewish life that a sense of collective fate should become implanted in almost every Jew's personal experience, no matter how ignorant he might be and no matter how commonplace his experience. One could not grow up as a Jew without having some sense of occupying a distinctive place in the scheme of things, without having to accept a destiny that for better or worse would affect every moment of life. Abraham Cahan has written in his memoirs:

> Each new wanderer, ruined by a pogrom or seeking to improve his lot or caught up in the excitement of the exodus, thought he was trying to better his own condition only. . . . But soon every emigrating Jew moving westward realized he was involved in something more than a personal expedition. Every Jew, even the most ignorant, came to feel that he was part of an historical event in the life of the Jewish people. Ordinary Jews became as idealistic and enthusiastic as intellectuals. Even Jewish workers and small tradesmen who had managed fairly well sold their belongings and joined the . . . move westward to start a new Jewish life. They did so with religious fervor and often with inspiring self-sacrifice.

The social impatience that had seized the Jews of Russia and Poland toward the end of the nineteenth century was a major spur to the American migration. It drove them to hard work and sometimes blinded them with the vanities of success. Yet in their deepest feelings many people in this generation saw themselves as personally doomed*—indeed, one of the fascinating things about them was their underlying fatalism, the way even their social activism or personal ambition could sink back into a deep Jewish persuasion of the sheer recalcitrance of the world. They might prosper a little, but they could hardly feel at ease in the new world. "Home" remained a tiny speck of land in Europe, a place they would not see again. Journeying between worlds, they were not certain it would be a great blessing to reach port. In the language of a later time, they felt themselves to be a "transitional generation" for whom the pleasures of the new would come either too late or not at all.

Sholem Asch, in one of his novels, has a characteristically overstated yet pertinent passage:

> The deprivation in Lederer's youth had eaten into his blood and bones. He couldn't enjoy life, even though he had the means for it. To this day Lederer

---

* Lincoln Steffens caught this note in a sketch he published in 1896 about East Side life. A tenement worker says of a young girl given to unseemly lightheartedness: "Let her labor long and be silent, that her son's sons may sing songs."

weighed and measured his every step, to make sure it would not undo him. He begrudged himself a whole lump of sugar in his coffee, although sweet coffee was a great delicacy to him. He never spread butter heavily on his bread, although he madly loved lots of butter. He was miserly in small things; it was easier to get a thousand dollars out of him than a few cents.

The idea that they constituted a "transitional generation" was a major cause of that stoicism which colored the whole of immigrant life. And with gratifications postponed, the culture of the East Side became a culture utterly devoted to its sons. Onto their backs it lowered all its aspirations and delusions, expecting that the children of the new world would reach the goals their fathers could not reach themselves. In coming to America the immigrant Jews had brought with them visions of collective fulfillment and ambitions for personal ascent. Between vision and fulfillment there were complicated ties. By providing consolations of the ideal, their visions gave the immigrant Jews strength enough to survive the miseries of settlement. By releasing long-suppressed energies, their ambitions drove them to labor, sacrifice, obsession, and material conquest.

It would be a mistake to say that one group of immigrants held to visions, another to ambitions. Immigrant life was never so well defined. Almost everyone retained some strands of religious feeling, almost everyone regarded himself as something of a socialist, almost everyone hoped soon to improve the conditions of his existence. With time, visions of Jewish fulfillment grew more vague and ambitions of personal success more precise. As American society showed itself a good deal readier to accept the Jews than to indulge their programs, the immigrants learned to make their way into the alien precincts of business and professional life. Often enough it was the purity of their vision—the moral firmness induced by religion or set free by radicalism—that provided the energies for realizing their personal ambitions. Yet seldom did this transfer occur without guilt, and almost always it bore emotions of regret.

It was the unspoken hope of the immigrants that their visions and ambitions, the collective dream of Jewish fulfillment and the personal wish to improve the lot of sons and daughters, could be satisfied at the same time. They hoped, through earnestness and toil, to link spiritual fulfillment with material gratification, and at least some of them tried honestly to live according to both sets of values, the selflessness of a committed generation and the sober parsimony of a rising ethnic group. As life slowly became easier, the dream of liberation from the gentile yoke was to be realized through an immersion in the alien culture—but never a total immersion, always one that could be limited and controlled. The immigrant Jews would plunge into this alien world, they would gain its rewards, they would savor its pleasures and its wonders; but they would also make sure to keep their own standards and styles of life. It would take a long time and a good deal of pain before they could see that, in satisfying Jewish wants, America would show itself resistant to Jewish conceptions; that ambitions realized might mean visions abandoned.

Meanwhile, during the early years of the century, it was a common feeling among Jewish garment workers and bakers and storekeepers that, while they might succeed in working themselves up a little (*zikh aroy-farbetn*), they were still caught in the grip of the old world, the old ways. Many of them were fiercely proud of those old ways and ready to unleash attacks on anyone daring to question their value. Yet, personally, they felt trapped. They were trapped in the limitations of their skills, in the skimpiness of their education, in the awkwardness of their speech, in the alienness of their manners.

But the sons—*they* would achieve both collective Jewish fulfillment and individual Jewish success. Whether such a way of putting the matter would have occurred to many immigrants is hardly the point. They were seldom in a position to grasp the complex process by which ideas of collective fulfillment were transformed into goals of personal achievement. They simply lived it out in their own experience, only later coming to understand what had happened.

Gradually those messianic expectations that had colored the Jewish past —sometimes with feverish defiance and sometimes with subterranean faintness—were disciplined into personal values. Here is a passage from a manuscript autobiography* left by a Jewish immigrant who arrived in America in 1868 and became a banker in Boston, then a cattle dealer in Colorado:

> I was the victim of a severe conflict. If the American spirit would conquer, it would spur my efforts and energies and I could accomplish a lot. If the Russian spirit would conquer, I would become dependent and go around with a dream of forcefully bringing the Messiah . . . who would free the world from slavery and exploitation. Then my hands would not be lifted to do business and the ambition to work myself up in the world would be stilled.

When a generation of immigrants told itself, "My son shall not work in the shop," it was speaking from the bitterness of its parched days. In coming to America it had committed itself to what it saw as a materialistic society, and no matter what else might follow, it would first have to live by the code of that materialism. Yet these immigrants were still touched by ancestral emotions and prohibitions. That they had spent a few years in New York or Chicago did not mean that all they had inherited, the marks of their distinctiveness, had vanished.

The idea of shaking off the humiliation that had always been part of Jewish experience in the Diaspora was now to be realized *in the Diaspora itself*, the very land many Jews cursed with all their hearts, seeing it as a bastion of the Pharaohs. Orthodox Jews regarded the idea of fulfillment in

---

* It is one of scores of unpublished memoirs at YIVO, many of which keep returning to the theme of the retreat from political idealism to personal accumulation.

America with anxiety, because it signaled both a heresy and a danger that the faith might collapse. Socialist Jews looked upon the idea of fulfillment in America with repugnance, because it signaled opportunism and raised the heretical thought that utopia might become irrelevant. But the masses of Jews, those both a little Orthodox and a little agnostic, acted out of a deep, common impulse: America was different from all other countries, America —land of sweat and swinishness!—meant that the sons could find a path such as Jews had never before been able to discover. The fathers would work, grub, and scramble as petty agents of primitive accumulation. The sons would acquire education, that new-world magic the Jews were so adept at invoking through formulas they had brought from the old world. And even those Jews who looked upon this idea with repugnance found they had to acquiesce in it when they thought of *their* sons.

Let us turn to homelier language. Max Gordon, a Broadway producer, has left a vignette of his East Side family:

> Of culture in my house there was none. No one in my home had any im-
> pelling drive toward serious music, or art, or reading. Aside from the daily
> Yiddish newspaper that my father read after dinner, aside from the prayer
> books read by my father and mother, there was no other reading in the home.
> *That seemed to have been left to me.* As the baby in the family, with none of
> the responsibility for helping to support the household, I was the one whose
> schooling was important. . . . By my tenth year I had become an omniverous
> if indiscriminate reader, a regular visitor to the library on Grand Street and
> the happy discoverer of the Educational Alliance. [Emphasis added]

Gordon's failure to enter imaginatively the life of his father, a man who read "only" the Yiddish paper (after how many hours of work in which sweatshop?), is no more obtuse than other failures of more distinguished sons. What is striking in this passage, however, is the sentence "*That* [get- ting an education] *seemed to have been left to me.*" This Benjamin of the slums was testifying to the decision of immigrant fathers that everything was now to be staked on their sons, a decision any Jewish father could share without even being aware of it, so deeply had it come out of the reserves of common desire. In behalf of its sons the East Side was prepared to commit suicide; perhaps it did.

When Hutchins Hapgood came to the East Side at the turn of the century, he saw how the Jewish family was being twisted into new shapes:

> In Russia the father gives the son an education and supports him until his
> marriage, and often afterward. . . . The father is, therefore, the head of the
> house in reality. But in the New World the boy contributes very early to the
> family's support. The father is in this country less able to make an economic
> place for himself than is the son. The little fellow sells papers, blacks boots,
> and becomes a street merchant on a small scale. As he speaks English, and his
> parents do not, he is commonly the interpreter in business transactions, and

tends generally to take things into his own hands. There is a tendency, therefore, for the father to respect the son.

Writing in 1902, Hapgood focused on the East Side during its more difficult years, and even then he clearly exaggerated the extent to which the father had been dispossessed. Yet he did notice that one crucial result of the migration was that changes in Jewish family life often led to a flow of power toward the mother. If she often used this power with legendary selflessness, it could also seize her like a *dybbuk*, transforming her into the brassy-voiced, smothering, and shrewish mama upon whom generations of unsettled sons would blame everything from intellectual sterility to sexual incompetence. There followed also the gradual emergence of the daughters, some already among those fiery girls, the *farbrente*, who made Jewish socialism so brilliant an occasion, but more of them gliding into education, work, assertiveness, and independence.

Hapgood saw how the crisis set off in the Jewish family by its adaptation to American life produced unexpected troubles for the sons—a whole new load of Jewish woe lowered on their backs at the very moment they seemed on the edge of liberation.

> While yet a child [the Jewish boy] acquires a self-sufficiency, an independence, and sometimes an arrogance which not unnaturally, at least in form, is extended even toward his parents.
>
> If this boy were able entirely to forget his origin, to cast off the ethical and religious influences which are his birthright, there would be no serious struggle in his soul. . . . He would be like any other practical, ambitious, rather worldly American boy. The struggle is strong because the boy's nature, at once religious and susceptible, is strongly appealed to by both the old and the new. At the same time that he is keenly sensitive to the charm of his American environment, with its practical and national opportunities, he has still a deep love for his race and the old things. He is aware, and rather ashamed, of the limitations of his parents. He feels that the trend and weight of things are against them, that they are in a minority; but yet in a real way the old people remain his conscience, the visible representatives of a moral and religious tradition by which the boy may regulate his inner life.

The sense of shame that Hapgood observed has been poignantly confirmed by a son of Jewish immigrants:

> One morning my father took his box and started out. I followed. Maybe that was the first time in years that I had taken a good look at my father. As I had never grown very tall, but was in fact a shrimp, he still towered over me, but he seemed an old man now, bent, and I hated the discolored yellowish beard, and the general shabby air of him. With terrible anger I felt myself seeing him as an old sheeny peddler, too.

The complicated feelings with which sons could look back upon the hopes of their fathers has been well expressed by Alfred Kazin: "It was not for myself that I was expected to shine, but for them—to redeem the constant anxiety of their existence. I was the first American child, their offering to the strange new God; I was to be the monument of their liberation from the shame of being—what they were."

The fathers had borne intolerable burdens and now the sons did too. The sons knew how great, how oppressive, was their debt and how little they could show by way of gratitude; they knew how enormous was the distance between the circumstances that had confined their fathers and the circumstances now opening to them. The distance between generations came to be like a chasm of silence which neither affection nor good will could bridge. Inner shame, outer irritation, a rare coming together in grief— life ripped people apart, and when fathers and sons could manage a little objectivity they might acknowledge that finally no one was to blame.

There is a haunting story by Jerome Weidman called "My Father Sits in the Dark." A son speaks, troubled that each night his immigrant father "sits in the dark, alone, smoking, staring straight ahead of him." The father sits in the kitchen, on an uncomfortable chair. "What are you thinking about, Pa?" "Nothing." "Is something wrong, Pop?" "Nothing, son, nothing at all." Coming home late one night, the son "can see the deeper darkness of his [father's] hunched shape. He is sitting in the same chair, his elbows on his knees, his cold pipe in his teeth, his unblinking eyes staring straight ahead." There is nothing to be said, neither quarrel nor reconciliation. "What do you think about, Pop?" "Nothing," answers the father, "nothing special."

CHAPTER EIGHT

Growing Up in the Ghetto

THE STREETS were ours. Everyplace else—home, school, shop—belonged to the grownups. But the streets belonged to us. We would roam through the city tasting the delights of freedom, discovering possibilities far beyond the reach of our parents. The streets taught us the deceits of commerce, introduced us to the excitement of sex, schooled us in strategies of survival, and gave us our first clear idea of what life in America was really going to be like.

We might continue to love our parents and grind away at school and college, but it was the streets that prepared the future. In the streets we were roughened by actuality, and even those of us who later became intellectuals or professionals kept something of our bruising gutter-worldliness, our hard and abrasive skepticism. You could see it in cab drivers and garment manufacturers, but also in writers and professors who had grown up as children of immigrant Jews.

The streets opened a fresh prospect of sociability. It was a prospect not always amiable or even free from terror, but it drew Jewish boys and girls like a magnet, offering them qualities in short supply at home: the charms of the spontaneous and unpredictable. In the streets a boy could encircle himself with the breath of immigrant life, declare his companionship with peddlers, storekeepers, soapboxers. No child raised in the immigrant quarter would lack for moral realism: just to walk through Hester Street was an education in the hardness of life. To go beyond Cherry Street on the south, where the Irish lived, or west of the Bowery, where the Italians were settling, was to explore the world of the gentiles—dangerous, since one risked a punch in the face, but tempting, since for an East Side boy the idea of *the others*, so steadily drilled into his mind by every agency of his culture, was bound to incite curiosity. Venturing into gentile streets became a strategy for testing the reality of the external world and for discovering that it was attractive in ways no Jewish voice had told him. An East Side boy needed to slip into those gentile streets on his own. He needed to make a foray and then pull back, so that his perception of the outer world would be his own, and not merely that of the old folks, not merely the received bias and visions of the Jews.

When he kept to the Jewish streets, the East Side boy felt at home, free and easy on his own turf. Even if not especially friendly or well mannered, people talked to one another. No one had much reason to suppose that the noisiest quarrel between peddler and purchaser, or parents and children, was anything but a peaceful ritual. Within the tight circle of the East Side, children found multiple routes for wandering, along one or another way:

•   Toward Canal Street, "suit-hunting avenue," as they called it, the stores bright with ties, *mezuzas*, hats, Hebrew books, *taleysim*, where you could jest with the hawkers, stare at the bowls shaped like hourglasses and filled with colored liquids which were kept in the drugstores, feast on windows, savor the territory.

•   Toward Hester or, a bit later, Orchard Street, pushcart territory: shawls, bananas, oilcoth, garlic, trousers, ill-favored fish, ready-to-wear spectacles. You could relax in the noise of familiars, enjoy a tournament of bargains, with every ritual of haggling, maneuver of voice, expertly known and shrewdly appraised. "After a light diet of kippered herring I would wander among the pushcarts for my dessert. I developed a knack for slipping bananas up my sleeve and dropping apples into my blouse while the peddler was busy filling some housewife's market bag. I used to pack a peach into my mouth with one snap of the jaws and look deeply offended when the peddler turned suspiciously upon me."

•   Toward Rutgers Square, with a stop in the summer to cool off at the Schiff Fountain, and then a prowl into the crammed adjacent streets: boys playing stickball or stoopball, and "on one corner the water hydrant turned on to clear the muck of the gutter. Half-naked children danced and shouted under the shower. . . . They pushed out the walls of their homes to the street." At night Rutgers Square changed colors, and it was fun to sidle along, watching the intellectuals as they strolled on East Broadway, and street speakers variously entertaining, some with little more than lung power, others artists in low-keyed enticement.

•   Toward the East River, in warm months, with a dive off the docks, where a blue film of oil from passing tugs coated the water "and a boy who didn't come out looking brown hadn't bathed." Once, after "washing away our sins in the water, we had to pass by gentile lumber yards, and the men there used to throw bricks at us. Then some of us got together and beat them up with sticks, and they never bothered us again."

•   Toward Allen Street, center of darkness and sin, "with its elevated structure whose trains avalanched between rows of houses and the sunlight never penetrated. I see the small shops, which somehow never achieved the dignity of selling anything new . . . a street which dealt in castoff merchandise. Even the pale children seemed old, second hand."

These "ways," while hardly as elegant as more celebrated ones in modern literature, tracked discoveries into the familiar and the forbidden, into that which stamped one as a true son of the immigrants and that which made one a future apostate. Learning the lessons of cement, one lost whatever fragments of innocence remained. The apartments were crowded, the streets were crowded, yet for boys and girls growing up in the ghetto, the apartments signified a life too well worn, while the streets, despite their squalor, spoke of freedom. Freedom to break loose from those burdens that Jewish parents had come to cherish; freedom, if only for an hour or two, to be the "street bum" against whom fathers warned; freedom to live by the senses, a gift that had to be learned and fought for; freedom to sin. Cramped or denied, shushed or repressed, sexual yearnings broke out on the streets and were expressed through their grubby poetry, in hidden corners, black basements, glowering roofs: wherever the family was not.

To be poor is something that happens to one; to experience poverty is to gain an idea of what is happening. All the evidence we have suggests that the children of the East Side rarely felt deprived. They certainly knew that life was hard, but they assumed that, until they grew up and got a grip on things, it had to be hard. Only later, long after the proper occasion had passed, did self-pity enter their psyche. In the actual years of childhood, the streets spoke of risk, pleasure, novelty: the future—that great Jewish mania, the future.

Legends of retrospect, woven from a wish to make the past seem less rough and abrasive than it actually was, have transformed every Jewish boy into a miniature scholar haunting the Seward Park library and, before he was even out of knee pants, reading Marx and Tolstoy. The reality was different. Scholarly boys there certainly were; but more numerous by far were the street boys, tough and shrewd if not quite "bums," ready to muscle their way past competitors to earn half a dollar, quick to grasp the crude wisdom of the streets. Sammy Aaronson, who would rise to distinction as a fight manager, spent his boyhood as a street waif, sometimes sleeping in the Christopher Street public baths, sometimes at Label Katz's poolroom in Brownsville, sometimes riding the subways all night for a nickel. His family was the poorest of the poor, his mother worked as a junk peddler, their furniture often landed on the street after an eviction, but "there was nothing particularly tragic about that. . . . We didn't feel sorry for ourselves and nobody felt for us." Harry Golden, whose youth was softer, assures us that he too was no Goody Two-shoes. "I played hooky and went to the movies. . . . I was unconscionably capable of forging a note the next day to explain my absence. 'My son Herschele was sick yesterday. (Mrs.) Anna Goldhurst.' Instinctively I knew 'Herschele' and the parentheses would lend absolute verisimilitude to my forgery." Eddie Cantor, before he began to appear in vaudeville skits in Chinatown, did come close to being a "bum." By the age of thirteen, he had "socked a teacher," lost a job through talking too much, perfected his game of pool, learned to hustle a few pennies by jigging and singing on a street corner, and taken up with an immigrant Russian girl, not Jewish, but with melancholy black eyes.

The streets were the home of play. Jewish boys became fanatics of baseball, their badge as Americans. In the narrow streets baseball was narrowed to stickball: a broomstick used as a bat, a rubber ball pitched on a bounce or sped into the catcher's glove, the ball hit high to fielders pinched into the other end of the street, with quarrels as to whether passers-by or wagons (later, cars) had hindered ("hindoo'd") the play. Or stoopball, with a rubber ball thrown smartly against the outer steps of a tenement—a game mostly for eleven-to-fourteen-year-olds.

> We'd go to play ball in Tompkins Park. If we couldn't afford a bat we'd bat a can around. The girls played jacks. We'd make a big circle and play marbles. The highly colored ones we called "immies." I couldn't tell my father I played ball, so my mother would sneak out my baseball gear and put it in the candy store downstairs. . . . Later, when I played semipro baseball I'd bring home five dollars and give it to my mother.

Jewish boys were said to be terribly competitive at games, as if already playing by adult norms: "You see it in the street where they delight in 'spiking' tops, playing marbles 'for keeps,' and 'pussy cat,' in all of which the sole idea is to win as an individual boy." The East Side allowed no lingering in childhood; it thrust the ways of the world onto its young. In their middle teens the boys turned clannish, forming "social and athletic clubs," partly to imitate American models.

Girls had their own games, since "the separation of boys and girls so rigidly carried out in the public schools also held for the street; boys played with boys, girls with girls." Sophie Ruskay, who lived on Henry Street, continues:

Occasionally we girls might stand on the sidelines and watch the boys play their games, but usually our presence was ignored. . . . We knew it to be a boy's world, but we didn't seem to mind it too much. . . . Tagging after us sometimes were our little brothers and sisters whom we were supposed to mind, but that was no great hardship. We would toss them our bean-bags [to play with], little cloth containers filled with cherry pits. . . . Then we could proceed to our game of potsy. Mama didn't like me to play potsy. She thought it "disgraceful" to mark up our sidewalk with chalk for our lines and boxes; besides, hopping on one foot and pushing the thick piece of tin, I managed to wear out a pair of shoes in a few weeks.

Neither my friends nor I played much with dolls. Since families generally had at least one baby on hand, we girls had plenty of opportunity to shower upon the baby brothers or sisters the tenderness that would otherwise have been diverted to dolls. Besides, dolls were expensive.

Regardless of season, the favorite game of both boys and girls was "prisoner's base." We lined up on opposite sides of the curb, our numbers evenly divided, representing two enemy camps. One side turned its back to invite a surprise attack. Stealthily a contestant advanced and either safely reached the "enemy" and captured a "prisoner," or, if caught, "became a prisoner." When a sufficient number of prisoners had been taken, a tug of war followed to rescue them. Trucks and brewery wagons lumbered by. We looked upon them merely as an unnecessary interference.

The streets meant work. Children, like nine-year-old Marie Ganz, went out to pick up bundles of sewing for her mother and was told they could bring in "maybe five dollars a week if she's a good sewer." But the full-time employment of children in shops and factories was rare on the East Side, partly because there was not much use for them in the "Jewish industries," partly because the Jewish sense of family prompted fathers to resist with every ounce of their being the idea of children as full-time workers.

By about 1905 most immigrant Jewish families were trying to keep their children in school until at least the age of fourteen; but almost all of them worked in the afternoons, evenings, weekends. Henry Klein, whose story is quite ordinary, peddled matches at the age of six and a bit later, with his ten-year-old brother Isadore, shined shoes at the Houston Street ferry. When he became experienced, he peddled with a professional named "Sammy" Cohen, working after school and earning twenty-five cents an hour extra when he taught English to his boss. He sold vegetables, fruit, fish; he hauled coal and wood from the Rheinfrank coalyard at the foot of East Third Street and ice from the Fifth Street dock. While attending high school and, later, City College, he spent weekends selling lozenges in Central Park, fearful of the police because he had no license and making his sister Estelle sit on the benches with boxes of lozenges hidden under her skirt. He would average about two dollars a day, on good days as much as three.

Parents and Children

Between Jewish immigrant parents and the world of the streets there was a state of battle, not quite a declared war but far from a settled peace. To the older generations the streets enclosed dangers and lusts, shapeless enemies threatening all their plans for the young. The parents could not, nor did they really wish to, distinguish between their received sense of the gentile world and the streets to which their children fled. The older immigrants were too suspicious, too thoroughly under the sway of past humiliations, to believe there might really be some neutral ground, neither moral nor immoral, neither wholly purposive nor merely corrupting, for the years of adolescence. Immigrant parents feared the streets would lure their children from the Jewish path, would soften their will to succeed, would yield attractions of pleasure, idleness, and sexuality against which, they suspected, they were finally helpless.

"We push our children too much," wrote a Dr. Michael Cohen, who lived on the East Side. "After school they study music, go to Talmud Torah. Why sacrifice them on the altar of our ambition? Must we get *all* the medals and scholarships? Doctors will tell you about students with shattered nerves, brain fever. Most of them wear glasses. Three to five hours of studying a day, six months a year, are better than five to twelve hours a day for ten months a year." The *Forward* labored to explain to its readers:

> There is no question but that a piano in the front room is preferable to a boarder. It gives spiritual pleasure to exhausted workers. But in most cases the piano is not for pleasure but to make martyrs of little children, and make them mentally ill. A little girl comes home, does her homework, and then is forced to practice under the supervision of her well-meaning father. He is never pleased with her progress, and feels he is paying fifty cents a lesson for nothing. The session ends with his yelling and her crying. These children have not a single free minute for themselves. They have no time to play.

The testimony we have on these matters comes from the sons and daughters, hardly a word from the older people. What might *they* have said? That they brought with them a bone knowledge of the centuries and that being born a Jew meant to accept a life frugal in pleasures? Or that, seeing opportunities for their children such as Jews had never dreamed of, they felt it was necessary to drive them to the utmost?

The costs were high. "Alter, Alter," cried a mother, "what will become of you? You'll end up a street bum!" What had this poor Alter done? He had been playing ball on the street. Later, when he broke a leg, his mother came weeping to the hospital: "Alter, Alter, do you want to kill me?" Trying to joke, he answered, "Wait, Mama, whose leg is broken?" But as he realized later, "to the folks from the old country sports always remained something utterly pagan." A good many Jewish children would always suffer from a life excessively cerebral and insufficiently physical; they would always be somewhat unnerved by the challenge of the body and fearful before the demands of sports.

By their mid-teens, if not earlier, the children of the immigrants began to shift the focus of their private lives from home to street. The family remained a powerful presence, and the young could hardly have envisaged its displacement had they not kept an unspoken sense of its strength. But in their most intimate feelings they had completed a break which in outer relations it would take several years to carry through. This was, in part, no more than the usual rupture that marks the storms of adolescence, but among the immigrant Jews it took a peculiarly sharp form, a signal for a Kulturkampf between the generations.

The immediate occasions for battle were often matters of private experience. That sex could be coped with only through stealth and secrecy, and in accordance with norms appropriated from the outer world—most East Side boys and girls simply took this for granted. Sex was not merely a pleasure to be snatched from the meagerness of days, it was the imaginative frontier of their lives, a sign of their intention to leave behind the ways of their parents. Sex might begin as an embarrassed fumbling toward the life of the senses, but it soon acquired a cultural, even an ideological aspect, becoming an essential part of the struggle to Americanize themselves. Day by day, the wish to be with one's girlfriend or boyfriend, modest enough as a human desire, brought the most exasperating problems. "On the East Side there was no privacy. Couples seized their chance to be together when they found it; they embraced in hallways, lay together on roofs. I passed them all with eyes averted."

In this tangle of relationships, the young could rarely avoid feelings of embarrassment. One's mother spoke English, if she spoke it at all, with a grating accent; one's father shuffled about in slippers and suspenders when company came, hardly as gallant in manner or as nicely groomed as he ought to be; and both mother and father knew little about those wonders of the classroom—Shakespeare, the Monroe Doctrine, quadratic equations—toward which, God knows, they were nevertheless sufficiently respectful. The sense of embarrassment derived from a half-acknowledged shame before the perceived failings of one's parents, and both embarrassment and shame mounted insofar as one began to acquire the tastes of the world. And then, still more painful, there followed a still greater shame at having felt ashamed about people whom one knew to be good.

> There never seemed any place to go. The thought of bringing my friends home was inconceivable, for I would have been as ashamed to show them to my parents as to show my parents to them. Besides, where would people sit in those cramped apartments? The worldly manner affected by some of my

friends would have stirred flames of suspicion in the eyes of my father; the sullen immigrant kindliness of my parents would have struck my friends as all too familiar; and my own self-consciousness, which in regard to my parents led me into a maze of superfluous lies and trivial deceptions, made it difficult for me to believe in a life grounded in simple good faith. . . .

So we walked the streets, never needing to tell one another why we chose this neutral setting for our escape at evening.

Delinquents and Gangs

When Alter's mother grew fearful that her son would end as a "street bum," she was not merely indulging a fantasy. All through the decades of immigration, the East Side and its replicas elsewhere in the country were harassed by outbreaks of juvenile crime and hooliganism, ranging in character from organized bands of pickpockets to young gangs half-social and half-delinquent. Crime had flourished in the Jewish immigrant quarters since the early 1880's (see pp. 96–101) but the rise of a distinctive youth delinquency seems to have become especially troubling shortly after the turn of the century. The mounting congestion of the East Side drove more and more children into the streets, while the gradual improvement in economic conditions enabled them to acknowledge the extent of their desires.

By 1902, reported Louis Marshall, there were "upwards of 300 boys and girls of Jewish parentage" in the House of Refuge on Randall's Island, the New York Juvenile Asylum, and other municipal and non-Jewish institutions. By 1904 the children's courts, "which handle children under fifteen, are packed. Police courts are filled with boys over fifteen, second and third offenders who started at age thirteen–fourteen." The *Forward* printed discussions as to whether erring children should be driven out, as they sometimes were by enraged Orthodox fathers, or kept at home; its editors favored the latter course, "since if you let them out they will go to the dogs completely. They have aggressive natures; if they can't get to their sister's pocketbook for a few cents, they'll try to get the money by stealing. It is preferable that parents should suffer from a bad child."

In 1906 the head of the New York YMHA, Falk Younker, reported that "between 28 and 30 percent of all children brought to the children's court in New York are Jewish. There are three and a half times as many children among this number who are the children of recently arrived immigrants as there are of native born parents. Fifteen years ago Jewish prisoners were an unknown quantity." The main reason cited by Younker was blunt enough: "home life is unbearable."

So acute had the problem become by 1902–1903 that communal figures like Louis Marshall and Jacob Schiff—once relations with government were involved, German Jews still took the lead—started to apply pressure on municipal authorities. They proposed that Jewish children under sixteen committed for misdemeanors be sent, with a subvention from the city, to a reformatory organized by the Jewish community itself. A similar arrangement was already in effect within the Protestant and Catholic communities. Mayor Seth Low vetoed the necessary bill in 1902, but Marshall was a very stubborn man and he kept badgering city officials until the bill was passed a few years later. With a $110 annual contribution per child from the city, and a building fund of several hundred thousand dollars from wealthy donors, the Jewish Protectory Movement built the Hawthorne School, a reformatory in Hawthorne, New York, and supervised probationary work in the city. It tells us something about the magnitude of this problem that the Protectory Movement had to continue its work through and beyond the First World War.

In the gap between Jewish family and gentile world, the children of the immigrants improvised a variety of social forms on the streets. At one extreme were the good and earnest boys, future reformers and professionals, who organized the Social, Educational and Improvement Club of the late 1890's, built up a treasury averaging $11.50 in any given month, and listened to talks by "Mr. Ordway on his experience in the Arctic" (it seems, the secretary archly noted, that "he received a warm reception in a cold climate") and by Mr. Mosenthal on "the theory of our government." At the other extreme were the "tough" gangs, made up of boys from six to twenty years of age, popularly known as "grifters," or pickpockets. These gangs, devoted more to thievery than violence, were sometimes so successful that they could hire furnished rooms to shelter those bolder members living away from home. Their customary hangouts were street corners, alleyways, poolrooms. Crowded streetcars and parks were favorite arenas for "grifting." A frequent strategy would be to start a fake street fight between two of the older members and then, as a crowd collected, the younger ones would go through to pick pockets.

Members of these gangs would later graduate into the ranks of Jewish criminality, such figures as Arnold Rothstein and Legs Diamond becoming masters of their craft; but in any sober light, these formed only a small, marginal group. Far more characteristic were the gangs combining an urge toward social ritual and a staking of turf with occasional forays into petty lawbreaking. Rough schools of experience, these gangs were seldom as violent as those that would later spring up in American urban life. On the East Side they gave a certain structure to the interval between childhood and independence—half-illicit, half-fraternal agencies for a passage into adult life.

Girls in the Ghetto

For girls in the immigrant Jewish neighborhoods there were special problems, additional burdens. Both American and Jewish expectations pointed in a single direction—marriage and motherhood. But the position of the Jewish woman was rendered anomalous by the fact that, somehow, the Jewish tradition enforced a combination of social inferiority and business activity. Transported to America, this could not long survive.

In the earlier years of the migration, few Jewish women rebelled against the traditional patterns—life was too hard for such luxuries. Early union organizers repeatedly found, Lillian Wald reported, that a great obstacle to organization was "a fear of young women that it would be considered 'unladylike' and might even militate against their marriage." In the 1890's, after the Council of Jewish Women was started, with a membership drawing only slightly on immigrant women from eastern Europe, Rebecca Kohut "was sent on a series of speaking tours, and I frequently had to face hostile crowds" in Jewish neighborhoods. For "Jewish women were expected to stay at home. . . . To have opinions and to voice them was not regarded as good form even in the home."

A glimpse into the conditions under which immigrant shopgirls had to work is provided by Rose Schneiderman's sober account of her teen-age years:

> So I got a place in the factory of Hein & Fox. The hours were from 8 AM to 6 PM, and we made all sorts of linings—or, rather, we stitched in the linings —golf caps, yachting caps, etc. It was piece work, and we received from 3½ cents to 10 cents a dozen, according to the different grades. By working hard we could make an average of about $5 a week. We would have made more but we had to provide our own machines, which cost us $45. . . . We paid $5 down [for them] and $1 a month after that.
>
> I learned the business in about two months, and then made as much as the others, and was consequently doing quite well when the factory burned down, destroying all our machines—150 of them. This was very hard on the girls who had paid for their machines. It was not so bad for me, as I had only paid a little of what I owed.
>
> The bosses got $500,000 insurance, so I heard, but they never gave the girls a cent to help them bear their losses. I think they might have given them $10, anyway. . . .
>
> After I had been working as a cap maker for three years it began to dawn on me that we girls needed an organization.

It made all the difference, growing up in the ghetto, whether a girl had come with her parents from Europe or had been born here. The *Forward*, with its roving sociological eye, noted that

When a grown girl emigrates to America, she becomes either a finisher or an operator. Girls who have grown up here do not work at these "greenhorn" trades. They become salesladies or typists. A typist represents a compromise between a teacher and a finisher.

Salaries for typists are very low—some work for as little as three dollars a week. . . . But typists have more *yikhes* [status] than shopgirls; it helps them get a husband; they come in contact with a more refined class of people.

Typists therefore live in two different worlds: they work in a sunny, spacious office, they speak and hear only English, their superiors call them "Miss." And then they come home to dirty rooms and to parents who aren't always so courteous.

Other kinds of "refined" work were even less lucrative, department stores paying salesgirls in 1903–1904 only ten dollars a month to start with, and rarely more than five dollars a week when experienced. Librarians in those years started at three dollars a week, even though special training was required. The most desirable job for a Jewish girl, then as later, was felt to be in teaching, but this meant that she had to be supported in her schooling until she was at least eighteen or nineteen. Many families could not do that. Or, if they had to choose between keeping a son in college and sending a girl to high school, they would usually prefer the former, both for traditional and economic reasons.

Even Jewish girls who had come from Europe as children and were therefore likely to remain fixed in the progression from shopgirl to housewife, found themselves inspired—or made restless—by American ideas. They came to value pleasure in the immediate moment; some were even drawn to the revolutionary thought that they had a right to an autonomous selfhood. Carving out a niche of privacy within the cluttered family apartment, they responded to the allure of style, the delicacies of manners, the promise of culture.

Hannah Chotzinoff, going out one evening to a ball at Pythagoras Hall,

looked radiant in a pink silk shirtwaist and a long black satin skirt. . . . [How had] Hannah obtained her beautiful outfit? There never seemed to be an extra quarter around the house. . . . If the pink silk shirtwaist was an extravagance, Hannah took measures to preserve its freshness. She had tied a large white handkerchief around her waist, so arranged that it would protect the back of her shirtwaist from the perspiring right palms of her dance partners. . . . To [those who placed their hands above the handkerchief] Hannah said politely: "Lower, please."

Girls like Hannah were close to the small group of young immigrants who tried to model themselves on the styles of the late-nineteenth-century Russian intelligentsia. Tame enough by later standards but inspired by a genuine spiritual loftiness, the style of these young immigrants might be described as a subdued romanticism, a high-minded bohemianism. One of the topics in the air during these years was

the double standard of morality. The Russian author Chernyshevsky had
written a novel on the subject, and the book, though not new, was enjoying
a vogue on the East Side. . . . It posed for its heroine and, by extension, to
all women, the question of the acceptance or rejection of the hitherto unchallenged promiscuity of males. . . . It was earnestly debated in my own
house, on the sidewalks, and on the benches by the Rutgers Square fountains.
. . . The male arguments against a single standard appeared to lack force,
and almost always capitulated to the sterner moral and spiritual convictions
of the opposition.

Though snatches and echoes of such debates occasionally reached them,
the double standard could hardly have been a major preoccupation of most
immigrant shopgirls. Their lives were too hard for anything but the immediacy of need—especially those who, because they had come to America by
themselves or had lost their parents through death, were now forced to live
alone in hall bedrooms and support themselves over sewing machines.
Lonely, vulnerable, exhausted, these girls were the lost souls of the immigrant Jewish world, rescued, if they were "lucky," by marriage or solaced
by political involvement. In the years slightly before and after 1900, the
Yiddish press carried reports of such girls taking their lives—"*genumen di
gez*" ("took the gas") ran the headlines.

For the Jewish girl who had been born in America, or had come here at
an age young enough so that she could learn to speak English reasonably
well, there were other difficulties. Jewish boys faced the problem of how to
define their lives with relation to Jewish origins and American environment,
but Jewish girls faced the problem of whether they were to be allowed to
define their lives at all. Feminism as a movement or ideology seems to have
touched no more than a small number of Jewish girls, mostly those who had
already been moved to rebellion by socialism. (The fiery socialist Rose
Pastor became famous only after, or because, she married the millionaire
Graham Stokes; the idea of a red Yiddish Cinderella made its claims on the
popular imagination as the idea of a brilliant rebel girl could not.)

What stirred a number of young Jewish women to independence and
self-assertion was not so much an explicit social ideology as their fervent
relation to European culture, their eager reading of nineteenth-century Russian and English novels. One such young woman, Elizabeth Stern, recalls
how her father

had come to look with growing distrust on my longing to know things; upon
my books especially. . . . He discovered me with *Oliver Twist* bulging from
the covers of my prayer book where, with trembling hands, I was trying to
hide it. He flung the novel on top of the book case. He told me in his intense
restrained angry voice that my English books, my desire for higher education,
were making me an alien to my family, and that I must give up all dreams of
continuing beyond the grammar school.

A subdued romanticism

An intelligent woman who wished to be just toward her own memories, Elizabeth Stern remembered that her father later spoke in "a voice of rare tenderness" when he told her that "he wished me to grow up a pride to our people, quiet, modest. . . . I was to marry; I too could be another Rachel, another Rebecca." Her father "would joyfully sacrifice himself for any of his children, that they might follow the path he believes the ideal one. He could not see that I might have ideals different from those held by him."

When the moment came to decide whether Elizabeth would continue with her studies, her father kept repeating "impossible"—though all the poor girl wanted was to be allowed to enter high school! Finally her mother intervened with a memorable remark: "Let her go for a year. We don't want her to grow up and remember that we denied her life's happiness."

So it was with many other Jewish girls. Golda Meir, growing up in an immigrant home in Milwaukee, had to run away in order to assert her independence. Anzia Yezierska (1885–1970), for a time a well-known novelist, was locked in a struggle with her father that lasted for years. Her story, quite typical in its beginnings, turned at its end into an American legend:

She arrived in New York in 1901, sixteen years old. Her first job was as a servant in an Americanized Jewish family "so successful they were ashamed to remember their mother tongue." She scrubbed floors, scoured pots, washed clothes. At the end of a month she asked for her wages, and was turned out of doors: "Not a dollar for all my work." Her second job was in a Delancey Street sweatshop kept by "an old wrinkled woman that looked like a black witch." Anzia sewed buttons from sunup to sundown. One night she rebelled against working late and was thrown out: "I want no clock-watchers in my shop," said the old witch.

Her third job was in a factory where she learned a skill and, luxury of luxuries, "the whole evening was mine." She started to study English. "I could almost think with English words in my head. I burned to do something, be something. The dead work with my hands was killing me."

She began to write stories with heroines—Hannahs and Sophies—who were clearly projections of her own yearnings. They were not really good stories, but some streak of sincerity and desperation caught the fancy of a few editors and they were published in magazines. By now, she was no longer young—a woman in her mid-thirties, trying to make up for years of wasted youth.

A first novel, *Hungry Hearts*, won some critical praise. Like all her books, it was overwrought, ungainly, yet touching in its defenselessness. No woman from the immigrant Jewish world had ever before spoken with such helpless candor about her fantasies and desires. In one of her novels, *Salome of the Tenements*, a young immigrant girl named Sonia says of herself: "I am a Russian Jewess, a flame, a longing. A soul consumed with hunger for heights beyond reach. I am the ache of unvoiced dreams, the clamor of suppressed desires." Sonia meets and marries a Yankee millionaire, the elegant Manning, and for a moment she thinks that she has won the world; but it all turns to dust, as in such novels it has to, and in the end what remains is the yearning of a Jewish girl, far more real than anything else in the book.

All the while, in the forefront of her imagination, loomed the figure of her father, a stern pietist who regarded her literary efforts with contempt. "While I was struggling, trying to write, I feared to go near him. I couldn't stand his condemnation of my lawless, godless, selfish existence." There were bitter quarrels. "He had gone on living his old life, demanding that his children follow his archaic rituals. And so I had rebelled . . . I was young. They were old."

Her first book published, Anzia confronted her father. "What is it I hear? You wrote a book about me? How could you write about someone you don't know?" Words of wrath flew back and forth, but Anzia, staring at her father in his prayer shawl and phylacteries, "was struck by the radiance that the evils of the world could not mar." He again threw up the fact that she had not married: "A woman alone, not a wife and not a mother, has no existence." They had no meeting ground but anger.

One morning a telegram was delivered to her room: ten thousand dollars for the movie rights to *Hungry Hearts*! She went to Hollywood, Yiddish accent and all; she wore expensive clothes, enjoyed the services of a

secretary, met the "greats" of the movie world. But alas, not a word came
out of her. The English she had worked so painfully to master ran dry.

Back home, defeated, she drifted through years of loneliness and poverty again. A few books published but little noticed: all with her fervent
signature, pitiful in their transparency. At sixty-five, quite forgotten, she
wrote an autobiography, *Red Ribbon on a White Horse*, summoning memories of the time when she had been a young immigrant woman locked in
struggle with her father. By now she shared his view that the fame and
money of her middle years had been mere delusion, and for the title of her
book she chose a phrase from an old Jewish proverb: "Poverty becomes a
wise man like a red ribbon on a white horse." In some groping, half-
acknowledged way she had returned to the world of her fathers—a final
reconciliation, of sorts.

The case of Anzia Yezierska was an extreme one, in that she had to
confront, at their stiffest, the imperatives of both Jewish and American
culture. Most Jewish girls of her day were neither wholly submissive nor
wholly rebellious; within the bounds of the feminine role they found strata-
gems for cultivating their private interests and developing their private
sensibilities. By 1914 a growing number of girls from East Side homes were
going to high school and a small number to college; by the mid-twenties,
about a generation later than the daughters of the German Jews, a good
many girls from east European Jewish families had begun attending Hunter
College and, in smaller numbers, Barnard.

A check of the graduating classes at Hunter—admittedly imprecise,
since it is difficult to know whether certain names are Jewish, let alone
German-Jewish or east European–Jewish—confirms this trend.

Year of Graduation	Number of Graduates	Estimated Jewish Graduates	Estimated East European Jewish Graduates
1906	156	43	13
1910	186	40	25
1912	155	36	25
1913	295	85	56
1914	273	102	66
1916	245	71	58

If these figures are at all indicative, it would seem that by the years
immediately before the First World War, the girls from east European
Jewish families had become the majority within the graduating Jewish
population at Hunter. Since there is no reason to suppose that the number of
German-Jewish girls going to college declined, it would follow that at about

the same time numbers of German-Jewish girls started going to private colleges like Barnard.

With eager if shy determination, the Jewish girls were redefining their lives. Elizabeth Stern, having won the battle for high school, found that she "wanted a room in which one simply sat. I had no clear idea of what I would do in it. But I had no room of my own yet. . . . Neighbors and relatives laughed in amusement at my wish." Like thousands of others, this young immigrant woman struck intuitively upon the demand that Virginia Woolf would voice in another setting: a room of one's own, a room with a view.

Going to School

As a young woman Myra Kelly worked for a few years teaching first-graders at P.S. 147 on the East Side; apparently she was a good teacher and a warmhearted person who felt affection for the immigrant "scholars" she kept drilling in English reading, writing, and spelling. Irish girls and young men, often themselves the children of immigrants, were pouring into the school system, and over the next several decades would become its dominant group. Myra Kelly differed from the others in one respect—she wrote quasi-fictional stories about her experiences as a teacher. *Little Citizens*, published in 1904, has as its heroine Constance Bailey, also Irish, also a first-grade teacher, also sparkling with lace-curtain wit and trim shirtwaists. The "long-suffering" but loving Miss Bailey melted before the eagerness of her Jewish boys and girls to please and to shine, though as a realistic teacher she could also regard them as "a howling mob of little savages." She "delivered daily lectures on nail-brushes, hair-ribbons, shoe polish, pins, buttons, elastic, and other means to grace. Her talks on soap and water became almost personal in tone."

Myra Kelly's ear for Jewish accents was atrocious, but it would be hard to expect someone raised with the beauties of Irish speech to be sympathetic to the way East Side children mangled the English language. What won her heart was their brightness of mind and softness of emotion. In one of her stories, set just before Christmas, all the children are planning ingenious gifts for Teacher, while her special darling, Morris Mogilewsky, lacks even a nickel for a ribbon; but then, with a smile of triumph, he brings Miss Bailey a present his father had gleefully given his mother: "the receipt for a month's rent for a room on the top floor of a Monroe Street tenement."

Remembering her days of the three R's "and deportment," Sophie Ruskay evoked a scene in which an equivalent of Miss Bailey ruled with firm kindliness:

When teacher called out in her sharp, penetrating voice, "Class!" everyone sat up straight as a ramrod, eyes front, hands clasped rigidly behind one's back. We strived painfully to please her. . . .

Beautiful script letters across the huge blackboard and a chart of the alphabet were the sole adornments of the classroom. Every day the current lesson from our speller was meticulously written out on the blackboard by the teacher who, whatever else she lacked, wrote a lovely, regular hand. . . .

We had to learn our lessons by heart, and we repeated them out loud until we memorized them. . . .

The window was opened a fraction of an inch and the teacher, standing on her little platform, snapped, "Breathe in! Breathe out!" The hissing sounds as we "exhaled" must have reminded the teacher of a school of porpoises at play.

The bulk of memoirs dealing with East Side childhood contain warm, sometimes remarkably tender descriptions of the years in school. That many of the Irish and Yankee teachers, as well as the growing number of Jewish teachers, were kind to immigrant children and that some of these teachers were excited by the potentialities of the children's intellect and the pathos of their striving, seems entirely credible.* Old-line Americans teaching in the schools often brought with them a fine sense of rectitude; Irish teachers with memories of how their own people had suffered upon coming to America were likely to be affectionate, though sometimes a bit condescending toward Jewish speech and manners. Still, one wonders, were there no petty tyrants, no mean-spirited bigots teaching school in the immigrant Jewish neighborhoods? Very few, if one goes by the pupils' remembrances.

Perhaps, in gratification at having escaped from the hardships of their youth, the writers of such memoirs indulged in a certain romanticizing of their days at school—though with regard to other youthful experiences they could be caustic enough. And perhaps they were still captive to the view their parents had often taken toward the American school. For on this matter there was a firm if unspoken consensus among immigrant Jews. It appeared first as the familiar Jewish respect for institutions of learning,

* Arriving in America at the age of eighteen, Israel Davidson entered the first grade, sat patiently with small children, climbed from grade to grade as he began to understand a little English, and in a year had completed the whole elementary curriculum. Here is a letter he wrote to one of his teachers:

Dear Sir and instructor.

As I found out that you take much interest in helping those who languish for help, I encouraged my heart with a few days before, to impart to you some of my inner thoughts about study, but on account of your words spoken to me; "don't speak about things but do them" I changed my mind and now I thank you for telling me of my misdoings, because they are my faults and I have to be gratitude to their corrector who is in the same time my benefactor. I have courage enough to look straight in the face of truth even if she blames me. I know that men surely gain by being blamed and perhaps lose by being caressed.

Your obeydient
Israel Davidson

with the sheer architectural impressiveness of the newer school buildings helping occasionally to induce a sense of awe; and it emerged a bit later as a kind of idealistic calculation, with the school commonly taken to be a sure path to advancement. If one's children had to put up with some taunting, even a little abuse, from gentile teachers or classmates, well, that was a price worth paying. Hadn't Jews put up with far worse in behalf of far less?

At least in the earlier years of the migration, Jewish parents were decidedly reluctant to visit the schools. They felt uneasy before intellectual authority, abashed at having to use their broken English—but most of all, they assumed it was probably necessary for the children to accept an irksome discipline. Those Jewish children who did progress in school often decided, at some level beneath explicit speech, that it was best to hide or suppress resentment at whatever slights or slurs might come their way. And in the classroom itself many were so earnest and obedient that they won over teachers whose preconceptions about Jews had not been of the kindliest. Myra Kelly might make fun of her pupils' speech and feel embarrassed at their surging emotionality, but after visiting their homes she gained a strong respect for immigrant parents. Better still, she found herself "densely puzzled and pondering as to whether she could ever hope to understand these people."

Not all teachers could be expected to show this breadth of response, nor did they. A gentile teacher is quoted as saying about her Jewish pupils: "They are mentally alert, colorful, intelligent, the backbone of my class, but they can be an insufferable nuisance because of their constant desire to distinguish themselves." This eagerness to excel—to excel publicly and conspicuously—softened the hearts of some teachers, hardened the hearts of others. A school principal is quoted as saying of his Jewish pupils: "Their progress in studies is simply another manifestation of the acquisitiveness of the race"—a remark by no means unusual, as witness reformer Jacob Riis declaring that the aptitude of Jewish children for "mental arithmetic" showed "how strong the instinct of dollars and cents is in them." And a study of Jewish teachers in the years of the First World War speaks bitterly of bias in hiring and promotion, the deprecation of Jewish students by gentile instructors, a growth in racial antagonisms, all the result, perhaps, of an increase in the number of Jewish students and teachers to the point where they were seen as threatening gentile dominance.

The experience of immigrant children in the public schools was surely a little less rosy and more abrasive than most memoirists acknowledge. (Writing in their adult years, they may have felt an impulse to join in that nostalgia about childhood which has been so powerful an element in American culture, as if wanting to show that "we too" could have idyllic memories.) There was the pleasant side recorded by Mary Antin: "What a struggle we had over the word 'water,' Miss Dillingham and I . . . and when at last I could say 'village' and 'water' in rapid alternation, without misplacing the two initials, that memorable word was sweet on my lips. For we had conquered, and Teacher was pleased."

But there was also the aspect recorded by another child of immigrant parents, who grew up in the east Bronx in the twenties:

> At the age of five I really knew Yiddish better than English. I attended my first day of kindergarten as if it were a visit to a new country. The teacher asked the children to identify various common objects. When my turn came she held up a fork and without hesitation I called out its Yiddish name, a *goopel*. The whole class burst out laughing at me with that special cruelty children can have. That afternoon I told my parents I had made up my mind never to speak Yiddish to them again, though I would not give any reasons.

The pained embarrassment that seeps through this recollection was due less to anyone's malice or ill-will than to inherent difficulties in making the transition from immigrant home to American school. And about that there was little parents, teachers, or children could do.

Jewish Children, American Schools

For the New York school system, the pouring in of these immigrant Jews—as well as Italians, Germans, Poles, Slavs—seemed like an endless migraine. Language, curriculum, habits, manners, every department of the child's life and study had to be reconsidered. While the educational system was mostly in the hands of the Irish, there were a good number of German Jews among both administrators and teachers, and it was they, "progressive" in educational thought and eager to speed the assimilation of their east European cousins, who developed new educational strategies for the immigrants. Given the poor conditions—overcrowding in the schools, fear and suspicion among the immigrants, impatience and hostility among some teachers, and an invariably skimped budget (often worse during reform administrations than when Tammany dealt out the spoils)—a summary conclusion would be that the New York school system did rather well in helping immigrant children who wanted help, fairly well in helping those who needed help, and quite badly in helping those who resisted help.

In 1905, a peak year of immigration, the Jewish pupils on the East Side were concentrated in thirty-eight elementary schools. These contained 65,000 students, of whom some 61,000, or almost 95 percent, were Jewish. Certain schools, like P.S. 75 on Norfolk Street, were totally Jewish. That condition which a half-century later would be called *de facto* segregation did not deeply trouble the Jewish immigrants—on the contrary, they found a certain comfort in sending their children to public schools overwhelmingly Jewish. Children who knew a little English served as translators for those who a week or two earlier had stepped off the boats. In the years between, say, 1900 and 1914 there were sporadic efforts by Jewish groups to pressure the Board of Education with regard to overcrowding of schools, released time for religious training, and the teaching of foreign languages; but we have no record of major objection to the racial homogeneity of a given school or district.

"The school personnel," writes a historian of New York education,

> considered it easier to teach English to a class in which all the youngsters spoke the same foreign language. . . . Only the social workers raised questions about the ethnic homogeneity of the schools. The assimilation of the immigrant would be retarded, they feared, and the learning of English impeded when the children used their native tongue everywhere but in the classroom. . . . But even the settlement house workers concentrated their fire on the methods of Americanization they saw [in the schools]. . . . They commented angrily on the gulf the teachers were creating between the foreign born parents and their native born children. Grace Abbott, Jane Addams, and Sophinisbe Breckenridge exhorted the schools to recognize the importance of foreign cultures.

From the immigrant spokesmen there were similar complaints, often furious in the Yiddish press and stiff even in the writings of so reasonable a man as David Blaustein. "Respect for age," he noted, "is certainly not an American characteristic, and this is an upsetting of all the immigrant's preconceived idea of society. . . . The children are imbued with the idea that all that is not American is something to be ashamed of. It is an unfortunate but indisputable fact that cheap and superficial qualities are the more likely to be assimilated."

But segregation of Jewish pupils failed to arouse any concerted protest among immigrant parents. It was a condition to which they had long been accustomed; it helped make the first years of settlement somewhat less frightening; and it also seemed, in its distinctive American form, a social springboard for plunging into the new world. The immigrants were prepared, indeed, eager, to have their children Americanized, even if with some psychic bullying, but they did not want to see themselves discarded in the process. As time went by, however, they came close to accepting even this fate as a price that had to be met.

Not without some dragging of feet—a mode of locomotion endemic to educational bodies—the Board of Education began to restructure the New York schools in order to "connect" with immigrant children. Good and even imaginative work was undertaken. Bilingualism in the schools was rejected out of hand: the authorities never saw it as a serious option, the immigrants would have been deeply suspicious of it. But an effort was made by such East Side superintendents as Gustave Straubenmuller, a specialist in teaching English to foreigners, and Julia Richman, an enthusiast for "progressive" education, to make their teachers sensitive to the special problems of Jewish pupils. One study of these problems, after listing the familiar virtues of Jewish students ("idealistic, thirst for knowledge," etc.), is candid enough to mention "other characteristics" that teachers might find disturbing: "occasional overdevelopment of mind at expense of body; keen intellectualism often leads toward impatience at slow progress; extremely radical; many years of isolation and segregation give rise to irritability and supersensitivity; little interest in physical sports; frank and openminded approach in intellectual matters, especially debatable questions."

Public school curriculums were revised to place a smaller stress on the memorizing of fixed materials (e.g., dates and names in American history) and a greater stress on what Julia Richman called "practical civics," study of the actual workings of American government and society. Schools and playgrounds were opened for afternoons, evenings, and weekends, to provide social centers for children and to lure them away from the streets. (Nothing could finally do that . . .) Emphasis was placed on manners, grooming, little courtesies, often annoying to immigrant pupils but which in later years they would be wryly grateful for. Miss Richman, ruling her school district with a stern hand, instituted a range of practical reforms, from regular eye examinations for children to the organization of parent groups.

The main problem, of course, was to teach children to read, write, and speak a new, a *second*, language. Good sense, even imaginative sympathy, is shown in a 1907 syllabus designed for special English classes for immigrant children:

> Spoken language is an imitative art—first teaching should be oral, have children speak.
> Teach children words by having them work with and describe objects.
> Words should be illustrated by means of pictures, toys, etc.
> Presentation of material should keep pace with the pupil's growth in power.
> A bright pupil should be seated next to one less bright, one should teach the other.
> In copying, the purpose is language, not penmanship.

Until 1903 immigrant children had been placed in classes together with much younger American-born children, and as the English of the immigrant pupils improved they were promoted into classes with children nearer their own age. But by 1903–1904 the Board decided, in accord with a plan developed by Straubenmuller, that this method no longer worked, since it tended to humiliate the immigrant children and slow down the American ones. Special classes were therefore set up to teach pupils of foreign parentage whose intellectual condition was in advance of their ability to express themselves in English. Pupils would remain in these special classes for a period of four or five months and then, having gained the rudiments of English, be assigned to regular classes.

Of the 250 special classes organized in 1905, 100 were held on the East Side. Most were smaller in size than normal classes, containing 30 to 35 pupils rather than the usual 45 to 50. The peak year for these special classes was 1912, when 31,000 pupils attended them; after that, the number steadily declined.*

Once immigration came to a stop with the outbreak of the First World War, these problems, though still unsolved, seemed less acute. Yet as late as 1914 a law was enacted in New York stipulating that children under sixteen who left school would have to complete at least the sixth grade—indicating, it would seem, that a good number were still failing to get through grammar school. It is chastening to note that in 1910 only some 6,000 out of 191,000 Jewish pupils in New York were attending high school. One out of three pupils in New York was Jewish, but only one out of four high-school pupils was Jewish. Allowing for the probability that the proportion of Jewish children under high-school age was greater than among the rest of the population, these figures still suggest that the dropout rate among Jewish children at or before the end of grammar school was not significantly better than for the remaining two thirds of the school population taken as a whole. It was better, however, than for other immigrant segments such as the Irish and Italians. A 1908 study of laggard students in the New York schools showed that no simple correlations could be established between command of English and classroom performance: children of German-born parents did better than children of American-born parents, the latter better than children of Russian-born parents, and the latter better than children of Irish- and Italian-born parents. The bulk of Jewish immigrant children, studies indicate, were not very different in their capacities or performances from the bulk of pupils from most other ethnic groups.

During the years between 1900 and 1914 the Board of Education published quantities of material on these matters, some of it notable for flashes of insight and sympathy in regard to immigrant children, but still more for

---

* To deal with varying abilities of the immigrant children, a complex system of special classes was elaborated in 1905–1906. "C" classes were held for immigrant pupils between eight and fourteen years old who could speak no English. After a few months of intensive work they were either sent to regular classes or shifted to a special "E" class. The "E" classes were for pupils over the normal age who were enabled to advance rapidly through a modified course of instruction that relaxed the usual demands with regard to English. Most children in "E" classes were between eleven and fifteen. Finally, "D" classes were organized for children approaching fourteen who had no prospects of finishing the eighth grade; they were given the bare elements of literacy so they could get working papers. Over the years, the "E" classes became the most numerous and important, while "D" classes were gradually eliminated.

This system worked with a certain rough effectiveness—best, as usual, for the best students. In a little while, however, it began to decline into an informal track system, especially in schools with the least sympathetic principals: slow pupils and those for whom English formed a hopeless barrier were allowed to linger, or waste, in the "E" classes. One East Side principal, Edwin Goldwasser of P.S. 20, complained about this trend in 1912 and proposed that "E" classes be abolished; he wanted immigrant children to be either transferred quickly from special to regular classes or directed toward entering the labor force in their mid-teens.

honesty in grappling with problems of handicapped, ungifted, and recalcitrant children. Conscientious efforts were made to provide the rudiments of
learning to immigrant children, within the financial constraints imposed by
the city and the intellectual limits of a culture persuaded that a rigorous,
even sandpapery Americanization was "good" for the newcomers. To read
the reports of the school superintendents is to grow impatient with later
sentimentalists who would have us suppose that all or most Jewish children
burned with zeal for the life of the mind. Some did, seemingly more so than
among other immigrant communities, and these comprised a layer of brilliant students who would be crucial for the future of the American Jews.
What made the immigrant Jewish culture distinctive was the fierce attention
and hopes it lavished upon this talented minority.

Immigrants and the Gary Plan

Despite their tacit policy of maintaining a respectful distance from the
school system, the immigrant Jews tried occasionally to exert pressure upon
it. Rabbis were outspoken in asking that distinctly religious (in practice,
Christian) ceremonies be removed from the schools, and in 1907 the Board
of Education did prohibit further singing of sectarian hymns and the reading of religious books other than the Bible. Around Christmastime disputes
would flare up over the singing of carols, but not very violently, since most
Jewish parents seem to have taken an attitude of pragmatic neglect toward
such matters. The Yiddish press raged intermittently against abuses, denouncing in 1906, for example, proposals to bus Jewish children from East
Side schools to less crowded ones on the West Side. In 1911 the *Forward*
launched a campaign against the high-handedness of Superintendent Julia
Richman, regarded as fair game since she was herself a German Jew.
("When she visits a school, it is like Yom Kippur.") And throughout these
years the immigrant Jews were bothered by the fastidiousness, and often
rather worse than fastidiousness, of the school system with regard to the
English pronunciation of candidates for teaching jobs—many a Jewish boy
and girl had hopes destroyed because of an inability to pronounce the "ng"
sound in "Long Island" quite the way the examiners insisted. Once in a rare
while, the Yiddish papers would take an uneasy glance at the school curriculum, wondering, cogently enough, why teachers gave their pupils no reason
"for multiplying a fraction in just this way. . . . The children get rules,
they do examples, and that's it. They have to finish in the allotted time, and
then it's 'pencils down.' Like soldiers, they are made to stop at exactly the
same moment, even though some children are naturally faster and others
slower." In the main, however, the immigrant Jews looked up to the school

system as an agency meriting respect and a little fear—since it was a power that, through incomprehensible edicts, could satisfy or destroy all one's hopes for one's children. The Yiddish press often had to urge immigrant parents to draw a little closer to the schools, advising them, for instance, to pay attention when children brought home notes from school doctors recommending dental care, eyeglasses, and operations for tonsillitis.

Not until the appointment of Joseph Barondess to the Board of Education in 1910 did the east European Jews gain formal recognition as a constituency that had to be heeded by the educational bureaucracy. From about that time onward, the immigrant Jews felt free, or at least somewhat freer than in the past, to intervene in the politics of education. Their first major intervention, in the struggle that took place over the Gary Plan between 1913 and 1917, was of an urgency which in this area they had never been able to release before.

It was a struggle that aligned a group of high-minded but obtuse patrician "reformers" against a range of immigrant and plebeian communities fearful of cultural dispossession. In 1914 Mayor John Purroy Mitchel, a wealthy lawyer elected as an anti-Tammany reformer, became intrigued with a new educational approach pioneered in Gary, Indiana. The Gary Plan, writes a historian of education, "discarded the old progressive tenet of 'a seat for every child' as an inefficient use of classroom space and the teacher's time." It also relied on departmental teaching; instead of one teacher instructing the same group of children all day, each class moved to a different classroom for major subjects. To put the plan into effect, a school had to be equipped with extensive shops, laboratories, and recreational facilities. The plan had special appeal to New Yorkers because it made possible the accommodation of nearly twice as many students in one school building as there were classroom seats.

Intellectuals like Randolph Bourne wrote admiringly about the Gary Plan as a partial fulfillment of John Dewey's educational ideas; the Mitchel administration also admired the plan, but mostly as a way of saving money. From the outset, the plan met with resistance among teachers, students, and parents, in part because of ingrained fears of anything that seemed novel, in part because of cultural distaste for the kinds of people now in City Hall, and in part because of suspicion that the plan would mean that the children of the poor would linger on a vocational track rendering them unable to compete with the children of the rich. Benevolent in intent but elitist and parsimonious in approach, the people who began putting the plan into effect in several New York schools quite ignored these signs of popular uneasiness. But Tammany Hall did not ignore them. On the lookout for an issue that would help it regain power, it saw here the possibility for playing on the prejudices and fears of large segments of the population.

In the 1917 election, when Tammany ran a dismal hack named John Hylan against Mayor Mitchel, it pledged to "banish the imported Gary system, which aims to make our public schools an annex to the mill and factory." Hylan stumped the city crying that "our boys and girls shall have an opportunity to become doctors, lawyers, clergymen, musicians, artists, orators, poets or men of letters, notwithstanding the views of the Rockefeller Board of Education."

The Gary Plan became a central issue in the campaign, and the Jewish community responded strongly, with a new self-confidence though not with complete lucidity. During the previous year or two Jewish groups ranging from the B'nai B'rith to Orthodox rabbinical associations had been applying organized pressure on the Board of Education to drop the plan. Now, a few weeks before the elections, riots broke out in a number of schools, most of them in such Jewish neighborhoods as the East Side, Harlem, and Brownsville. The majority of students arrested were Jewish, for by this point, under the incitement of both Tammany and the Socialists, many immigrant Jews believed the plan was a scheme to cut their children off from routes to professional advancement. And it was much too late for the mayor and his supporters to say anything that might dissolve these fears. Hylan won the election overwhelmingly and the plan was scrapped.

Was the Gary Plan, in intent or likely consequence, a device for choking off the ambitions of immigrant and lower-class communities? Certainly not in its original formulation by William Wirt, the Gary school superintendent hired to advise the New York schools, nor even in the minds of the New York officials who proposed to adopt it. But the actual introduction of the plan into the New York schools was a fairly shoddy business, since the idea of a richer curriculum soon faded, while the scheme for doubling up on class space kept the interest of city officials. Even this vulgarization of the Gary Plan need not have brought quite so fierce a reaction in the poor neighborhoods, both Jewish and non-Jewish, nor need it have allowed Tammany so brilliant a political advantage. What was finally at stake was the relationship between rulers and ruled, patricians and plebeians, those who "knew better" and those nominated to be the beneficiaries of that superior knowledge. When the immigrant Jews lined up, most of them, with the forces attacking the Gary Plan, they fell prey to political demagogy; yet they were also expressing an oblique insistence that their voices be heard by the city's educational authorities, their opinions consulted and prejudices taken into account.

City College: Toward a Higher Life

By the 1890's a small trickle of boys from east European–Jewish families had joined the several dozen German-Jewish boys entering City College each year. The great Jewish inpouring to the college would not really begin until after the First World War, but the deep attachment felt toward the college among the immigrants was firmly established by the first years of the century. Of all the institutions they or their children might encounter in the new world, City College came closest to fulfilling Emerson's promise that "this country, the last found, is the great charity of God to the human race."

It is far from clear, however, that in the eighties and nineties City College wholly deserved the affection of the Jewish immigrants. Located at Lexington Avenue and Twenty-third Street, it was by no means a distinguished college. Staffed by a mediocre faculty and headed successively by two presidents, Horace Webster and Alexander Webb, who had both come from West Point, City College maintained a semimilitary discipline in its treatment of students. In the 1880's and 1890's the average graduating class was about fifty, though several times that number passed through each class in a given year. Many boys entered at fourteen or fifteen and graduated at nineteen or twenty; in both curriculum and atmosphere, City College was actually a combination of high school and college. Upon graduating from grammar school, boys could take an entrance examination and those scoring at least seventy would be admitted to "the sub-freshman class" in which they were expected to cram somewhat less than an equivalent of high school into one year's work. High-school students who had done well in their first year were also allowed to transfer to "the sub-freshman" or freshman classes. This meant a fairly liberal policy of admissions and a high rate of casualties—by 1906 the graduating class contained 140 boys, though it had begun five years earlier with close to a thousand. Many dropped out for financial reasons, others because of academic failure. But for the gifted and hard-working the college meant opportunity, and to the Jewish boys that seemed quite enough. By 1903, when Dr. John Finley took over the presidency and began to raise the academic level of the college, more than 75 percent of the students were Jewish; in the graduating class of 1910 at least 90 of the 112 students were Jewish, and of these the great bulk came from east European families.

In the earlier years, especially the eighties, life at the college was not always pleasant for the handful of Jewish students. The professors maintained a tone of Protestant moralism, with slight allowance for the distinctive backgrounds and interests of their students; and anti-Semitic incidents, while not condoned, were not rare. In 1878 the Greek-letter societies barred Jewish students—a slight that for years would rankle such Jewish alumni as Bernard Baruch. In 1881, when a student paper called the *Free Press* started to campaign for internal college reforms, it was denounced by the *College Mercury* on the ground that its editors, Rosenberg and Rothschild, "of the Semitic race," had gotten their material about college affairs "from a certain Jewish library." Rosenberg and Rothschild answered: "Why this particularization? It smacks strongly of the student persecution of the Jews in Germany." (Besides, added the *Free Press* editors, they stood close to the top of their class while the gentile lunkhead editing the *Mercury* was at the very bottom!) Two years later there occurred a more serious incident. Professor Charles Anthon made anti-Semitic remarks in his classroom, Jewish students instituted a boycott of his classes, a formal investigation followed, and the professor was granted "a leave of absence for two months, on account of ill health."

As the number of Jewish students increased and "the Semitic influence" settled in, the college took on an atmosphere of greater tolerance. Even in its early days, the distinctive character of City College was more the work of its students than its faculty. Bernard Baruch, the park-bench financial wizard, who graduated from City College in 1889, set down impressions that could easily have been written by a graduate fifty years later: "Each year the College Athletic Association sponsored a track and field meet. . . . My class would talk a blue streak in the debating forums but we couldn't run very fast." Morris Raphael Cohen, remembering his student days in the late 1890's, was caustic about the faculty: "Rigid discipline and pursuit of marks were more important to most of the teaching staff than love of learning. But what the professors lacked in love of learning, the student body made up." That, too, could have been said, though with greater qualifications, by a graduate of the thirties.

Yet the Jewish students loved the place, loved it utterly, hopelessly, blindly. What Bernard Hershkopf, '06, wrote could and would be repeated by innumerable others:

> The classrooms were bare, the chairs and desks of the plainest. The blackboards were grayed over with the chalk dust pressed into them over many years. The library was crowded and old; it had not really been well kept up for a number of years. . . .
>
> The physical properties and appearance of the old City College were not in any sense beautiful or inspiring.
>
> But, as against that, there were the students. Scores of them thirsted for learning as men long lost in the desert must thirst for water. None could halt or defeat such deep-rooted determination to learn. We knew it as gospel truth that this plain College was for each of us a passport to a higher and ennobled life.

Jewish boys excelled in mathematics, history, and literature, but other subjects, like shop and "mechanical drawing," they often regarded as meaningless burdens that alien powers had lowered upon them:

> The drawing lesson was the bane of his existence. He just could not draw, and besides was still not very familiar with the language. The instructor one day demanded, "go to the blackboard and draw a carrot." He was nonplussed. He did not know what a carrot was. . . . The class, realizing his embarrassment, tried to help him by whispering, "Draw something round." So he drew what he thought was a circle. It turned out to be elliptical enough to look like a carrot and the day was saved. By dint of much torture, he managed to receive 40 percent in the course, hardly a passing mark.

Such were the ways in which Jewish boys stumbled through the non-academic portions of the curriculum, turning out clumsy breadboards in shop, struggling with parallel bars in gym, and often even learning to swim. In the years between world wars, City College took on a legendary character, a school at once grubby and exalted: the passionate alcoves where revolutionary position-takers argued "the correct line"; the triumphs in basketball "based on the principle of a weave around a flexible pivot"; the somber classrooms where overburdened teachers and bristling students found "the world of knowledge and meaning and commitment . . . there for us to explore." City College became the haven of Jewish minds, and none shone more brightly, triumphing over pretension and murk, than the mind of Morris Raphael Cohen (1880–1947).

At the beginning his story is quite like those of other East Side boys. He was born in Russia, speaking Yiddish as his first language and tasting in child-hood the bitter fruits of poverty. In 1892 he came to New York with his parents, and as he grew up he almost left school in order to help support the family, worked for a while in his father's soda-water stand in a pool room, and savored dreams of intellectual distinction and self-sacrificing public life. He wrote in his diary at the age of seventeen: "My principal characteristic is a love for books. Every cent I can lay my hands on goes to buy some book. . . . The next principal characteristic is my great desire to do good, in the full sense of the word, and my impotency to comply with this desire. . . . I am not only a reformer but a revolutionist. I detest customs that are shams."

Delicate, bookish, quick-witted, the boy made his way through City College in the late nineties, learning more on his own than he could from the not very glittering faculty, and reading with that concentrated rapacity that would remain with him throughout his life (Mommsen, Gibbon, and Green as a freshman; the classical French playwrights as a sophomore; the pre-Socratics, Plato, and Aristotle in his last two years). That he was remarkably gifted soon became obvious, but he retained enough critical realism to measure his faults: "Am too conceited in argument . . . My natural tendency to conquer my opponent is stronger than reason." In his own aggressive way, Cohen was driven by a Jewish eagerness to break into the knowledge of the world, "to possess the fruits of the Age of Reason." His youthful socialism, he later wrote, "was a protest against economic conditions," but it was "also directed primarily to the conquest and democratization of the things of the spirit."

What first inspired Cohen to think of himself as an intellectual, a philosopher living for the disinterested pursuit of truth, was a chance encounter with Thomas Davidson, a free-lance educator devoting himself to the irregular teaching of poor boys and girls on the East Side. From Davidson, Cohen learned the beauties of skepticism, the pleasures of reflection. At a summer school Davidson ran in the Adirondacks in 1899, where Cohen earned his keep by doing odd jobs, the pupils studied the *Divine Comedy*, struggling through the *Inferno* in the original Italian. The nineteen-year-old Cohen read Plato systematically, discussed Parmenides with Davidson, and studied Latin. Mary Rypshin, soon to become his wife, studied beside him and wrote letters home date-lined "Paradise."

The Cohens scraped together their pennies and sent Morris to do graduate work in philosophy at Harvard, where from 1904 to 1906 he worked with William James, Josiah Royce, Hugo Münsterberg, and Ralph Barton Perry. From all of these remarkable men he learned, but of none did he become a disciple. As a mature man Cohen would call himself "a stray dog" in philosophy, alien to systems, indifferent to converts, forever a man of questions.

With some difficulties, Cohen began his career in 1912 as teacher of philosophy at City College, where he would remain until close to the end of his life. Lacking, he said, verbal facility, Cohen started to teach according to the Socratic method, with one question chained to another, and all of them devoted to testing, or assaulting, the coherence of the philosopher under discussion. In a typical session, the assigned text might be a Santayana essay on aesthetics, in which that philosopher had offered a wonderfully inclusive definition of "the aesthetic." A student, picked at random, would have to answer: what does Mr. Santayana mean by "the aesthetic?" The student knew his lesson. Did he agree with Mr. Santayana? The student, also knowing his part in the unfolding ritual, answered hesitantly, y-e-s. Cohen would then begin to shred Santayana's statement, question after question driving toward a demonstration of how difficult it would be to see anything as other than "aesthetic" if one accepted Santayana's definition of it (a method similar to the one Cohen notably employed in attacking John Dewey's use of the term "experience"). A few minutes before the end of the class, the exhausted but still pugnacious student had been led into a definition of "the aesthetic" completely at variance with the one by Santayana which he had endorsed forty-five minutes earlier. "So who is right?" Cohen would ask. The bell rings, students rush up to find out Cohen's opinion, and with a wicked grin he says, in the Yiddish accent he kept throughout his life, "What does it matter what *I* think?"

Cohen became the culture hero of the City College boys, at least the brighter and tougher ones, who learned not to fear (too much) his probing, combative style, "a kind of smiling struggle to the death. The room was electrified, we jumped to the defense of our fellow-student, but our teacher took us all on, in a razzle-dazzle of knowledge, of analytic power, of fighting intellect. Truth was the quarry, and we were really fellow-participants in the hunt."

It was a terrifying, sometimes even a sadistic method of teaching, and only the kinds of students that came to Cohen could have withstood it— Jewish boys with minds honed to dialectic, bearing half-conscious memories of *pilpul*, indifferent to the prescriptions of gentility, intent on a vision of lucidity. "He never let us down, we always left a bit more confused, a bit wiser, always more hopeful, even giddy with hope, for he was a living example of the power of reason."

Cohen's ferocity in the classroom was quite impersonal. "For most of us," recalled the historian Richard Morris, "to be corrected by Socrates seemed neither a surprise nor a disgrace." To some it even seemed a reason for pride, signifying acceptance into a superior realm where all that mattered was the clash of minds and the hunger for truth. Formidable as he seemed on the lecture platform, everything about Cohen testified that he shared with his students common origins, common experiences, common values. He might pummel them in the classroom, but they knew that in conflicts with the college authorities, a rather common occurrence at City College, they could count on his sense of fairness, even compassion. "I could not feel that the defects of our boys in point of manners," he wrote in a characteristic sentence, "were as important as their extraordinary attachment to the values of spirit."

After his death, in 1947, little remained of Cohen's influence—a fate he was to share, in the age of analytic philosophy, with other, more productive, American philosophers, like Santayana and Dewey. Cohen founded no school, left no central or easily popularized idea, failed to publish a great book. Even *Reason and Nature*, his most distinguished volume, was little read. He was not among the "one-eyed men," those thinkers who pursue a single idea with ruthless exclusion and thereby end with at least a familiar tag dangling from their names; he was a "two-eyed man," stressing the principle of polarity, by which he meant the need for examining claim and counterclaim, subjecting both to the razored test of logical analysis, and not allowing the philosophical passion for truth to decline into an ideological passion for system.

Cohen himself had foreseen his decline of influence and even noted his own limits of creativity. His mind, he wrote late in life, had "none of the vitality and flare of genius of James or Santayana, the fruitfulness of Peirce or Royce, or even the solid substantiality of Dewey. Yet withal [it showed] a tenacious clinging to truth." This characteristic suspicion that, for all his erudition and critical powers, he was a philosopher characterized by a certain dryness—his opponents would say aridity—of mind, clearly troubled Cohen, yet in the end, with his mixture of Jewish stoicism and philosophical resignation, he came to accept these limitations as intrinsic to himself. Was there perhaps a sense in which these were also limitations of his culture, or at least of its secular-rationalist segment? Pride in argument, vanity of dialectic, a gleaming readiness for polemic—if these traits sometimes characterized Morris Cohen, so too might they be found in the culture from which he emerged and in the younger philosphers he helped to shape. Yet his poignant codicil, "a tenacious clinging to truth," spoke for the antiseptic virtues of criticism, the bracing disdain of pretension. And these virtues, too, were not Cohen's alone, even if he gave them a dramatic rendering that none of his contemporaries could equal.

To Jewish boys who had come from the East Side, Brownsville, or the Bronx to study at City College, there were no doubts or qualifications: Cohen was a great figure. What did he leave them? A vision of mind, a style of quest. And a storehouse of anecdotes, hundreds of them, either true or apocryphal, about his scathing rigors of mind. Nor does this seem, upon reflection, a scant legacy. The anecdote has always been a favorite among sages, and those students who, in Sidney Hook's phrase, bore "the mark of Cohen" often responded to their teacher as if he were a *tsadik* and they Hasidim hanging on his words. But with one crucial difference: they had been taught by Cohen not to expect anything so commonplace as answers.

At one of his classes, a student insisted to Cohen that "a thing isn't real unless it can be touched, tasted, and worked with." Cohen responded by telling a story about three businessmen confronted by the Devil. "You three have had too good a time," he told them, "and you're coming below with me." When they pleaded for mercy, the Devil agreed to give them a chance —if he could not do what they asked, he would let them go. The Frenchman challenged the Devil to turn a nearby lake into Burgundy wine—flash, the Frenchman disappears. The Irishman challenged the Devil to turn a nearby mountain into gold—flash, the Irishman disappears. The Jew thought and thought, and suddenly he began to whistle "Dixie." "Sew a button on that," he told the Devil.

Another story has a student bursting into Cohen's office and crying out that he is very upset. "What is the matter?" "It's just been proved to me that I don't exist." "Why are you coming to me?" "I want you to prove that I *do* exist." "Well," said Cohen, "it is not impossible, but tell me, young man, to whom should I address the proof?"

A third story has Cohen replying to someone who had said that he, Cohen, was merely a critic in philosophy: "Hercules cleaned out the Augean stables—should I fill them up again?"

The ideal audience for such anecdotes, what Paul Goodman once called "wisdom stories," extends through time from Rabbi Nachman of Bratslav, the Hasidic teller of tales, to Hershel Ostropolier, the legendary Jewish scamp, to Sholom Aleichem and Peretz, the major Yiddish writers, and then to those students at City College who felt that, for reasons they could not always express, these anecdotes brought grace to their lives.

CHAPTER NINE

Jewish Labor, Jewish Socialism

B Y THE opening years of the century Jewish socialism had become a vigorous strand of thought within immigrant life, but as an organized movement it was very weak. After twenty years of meetings, groupings, splits, regroupings—all the busywork of left-wing politics interrupted by desperate strikes in "the Jewish trades"—there was still no mass socialist movement on the East Side or its replicas in other cities. Nor did it matter much whether the Yiddish-speaking socialists belonged to the increasingly sclerotic Socialist Labor party or the livelier Socialist party, which Eugene Victor Debs and Morris Hillquit formed in 1901: they were boxed into "discussion circles," handfuls of people distant from the center of either the Jewish community or American socialism.

There was, by now, an immigrant Jewish proletariat of considerable size in the American cities, a proletariat intensively exploited and inclined every few years to outbursts of extreme discontent. There was an immigrant community numbering at least a million and a half Jews, gathering its strength, finding points of sociopolitical power in the municipalities, and developing its own fairly complex class structure. The "objective conditions" for a mass socialist movement, about which left-wing theorists kept writing, seemed surely to have become ripe. Yet, despite their intellectual aggressiveness and their strength in the garment unions, the Jewish socialists could not find a path that would lead them out of the miseries of sectarian life.

When the Yiddish socialist monthly, the *Tsukunft*, resumed publication in 1902 after a lapse of four years, its editor, Abraham Liessen, had to admit that "many of our best people have disappeared. Once, even our older comrades were youthful in spirit, but now our young people seem spiritually aged. And this is true not only for individuals but for the movement as a whole." A Chicago comrade described the situation of these years: "In the Jewish quarter there was such benightedness, you had to feel your way like a blind man. Socialist movement? What movement? The word 'socialism' became a term of contempt. Our Jewish workers were dead souls."

So it remained until about 1908. "The Jewish socialist branches, few in number, neither discussed major issues nor undertook large activities. . . . The more active branches distributed socialist literature in English, since we had hardly any Yiddish material. Once in a while there'd be a street meeting." In 1904 the Socialist party hired the ubiquitous Benjamin Feigenbaum as its Yiddish-language secretary; he made a national tour, lecturing in his familiar manner, but nothing changed. Among the Yiddish-speaking socialists there spread a mood of profound discouragement, leading some to propose that they abandon the Jewish arena entirely and try to join the ranks of native American socialism—if only they could find a way of slipping past the linguistic and cultural barriers that rose between themselves and the English-speaking comrades.

To unburden "the bitterness of their hearts," the Jewish socialists in the New England region organized a conference in 1903 in Providence, Rhode Island. This modest gathering decided to set up an "Agitation Bureau," which would prepare Yiddish leaflets; but at the same time, and characteristically, it rejected a proposal from a minority of delegates that "the Jewish question" be put on the agenda. It seemed pointless to discuss this question, since most of the delegates were convinced that the only solution to the Jewish problem was socialism and anything else was either diversionary or a retreat to "Jewish nationalism." In opposition to this view, Morris Winchevsky, the Yiddish labor poet, remarked at the conference that "we'd be more successful in our propaganda if we took some real interest in the problems of our fellow Jews, and did so as socialists." But then, as later, such sentiments were looked upon with suspicion by many of the Jewish socialists—which may explain why the "Agitation Bureau," and a nationwide equivalent started four years later, turned out to be so feeble.

Early Weaknesses

Why were the Jewish socialists unable to form an organization of strength? If they could lead enormous strikes, why could they not also bind their followers into a compact movement?

Organization, especially that which looked outward toward the native American milieu, was always difficult for the immigrants. (The *landsman-shaft*, perhaps their most stable grouping, largely drew minds away from America and back toward the security of nostalgia.) Life in the American cities was hard, work exhausting, the imperative of daily need overwhelming. Suppose you thought of yourself as a socialist—which, in one or another sense, a considerable minority of Jewish immigrants did. That meant going to an occasional lecture, being prepared to join a strike when it erupted, reading the *Forward*, joining the Workmen's Circle (the socialist fraternal order) and, much less often, joining "the party." But to be active in a Socialist branch, to pay dues, attend meetings, hand out literature, speak at street meetings, all this signified a disciplined commitment that in the nature of immigrant life, and perhaps the nature of humanity, was hard to come by. Most people, especially if they have labored throughout the day, find regular "party work" tiresome; add the disputations of ideologues who may not have to get up early the next morning, and it is not hard to understand why even left-leaning immigrant workers failed to participate in the Jewish socialist groups as intensely as their leaders desired.

There is another reason for the organizational weakness of Jewish socialism, one that touches rather deeply on the immigrant psyche. Modern Jewish life has been characterized by a mixture of idealism and skepticism and, at its extremes, yearnings for apocalypse and drops into nihilism. The fervor for socialist revolution could be very high among some of the immigrants, yet this fervor was often undercut by a nagging pessimism as to the possibilities of *any* Jewish politics. Even if the entire Jewish working class were converted to socialism tomorrow, how would that change anything fundamentally in the country? Such doubts had already led young Jewish revolutionaries in eastern Europe to abandon their own people and try to lose themselves in the Russian movement. For all their readiness and volubility, Jewish radicals did not matter enough *insofar as they remained Jews;* they could fulfill themselves as revolutionists only through the self-denial of assimilation. So had argued Jewish leftists in Warsaw and Moscow, those who opposed the Yiddishist orientation of the Bund; and so argued (or felt) many immigrants who sympathized, yes, with Jewish socialism but wondered what it could lead to beyond noise and self-agitation on "the Jewish street."

Even the Jewish unions, on which the socialists rightly staked so much, found it terribly difficult to survive as stable institutions. By 1904, when there were about 200,000 workers in the New York garment industries, the vast majority was unorganized and few of the unions were more than skeletal groups. Heroic effort in strikes, followed by a partial victory won at great cost, and then a leakage of these gains through carelessness and lassitude—this pattern among immigrant workers led to a disillusionment with the whole idea of unionism. It was surely a fine idea in general, but the personal cost was so high and the long-run benefits so far off. . . . Within the unions some people began to say that, by injecting their ideological concerns, the socialists stood in the way of small but solid gains; and while this view, represented by such early union leaders as John Dyche and Abraham Bisno, was not yet prevalent, it would win adherents over the years.

Perhaps, thought some observers, the very enterprise of unions ran counter to the "Jewish spirit." Among American unionists, by no means eager to get caught up with contentious immigrants, and also among scholars like John Commons, a notion became popular that the Jewish workers, lacking discipline and susceptible to petty-bourgeois moods, did not provide good material for unionization.* That such questions could even be raised in the early 1900's was deeply discouraging to the Yiddish-speaking socialists.

A large share of the trouble came from the Jewish socialists themselves. Their politics was often marked by a dogmatic absolutism ill-adapted to the needs of the masses. Too much of it derived from a ferocity of denial, the trauma that only a decade or so earlier had accompanied their rebellion against religion. They had seized upon the categories of Marxism, but often what excited them most was the polemic against theology.

The socialism of the immigrants in New York and Chicago, probably still more so in the smaller cities, was in good part an émigré movement, emotionally focused on the old country and finding its intellectual sustenance in European traditions. When the Bund, the Jewish socialist group in Poland, withdrew in 1903 from the Russian Social Democratic party to declare itself an autonomous party, this event shook the Yiddish-speaking

---

* What Commons wrote in the 1901 Industrial Commission report became, for a time, fairly standard opinion: "The Jew's conception of a labor organization is that of a tradesman rather than that of a workman." Selig Pearlman, a historian of American labor, reports that Beatrice Webb, the English Fabian writer, had similar notions "about the extreme individualism of the Jewish immigrants from East Europe and their eagerness to 'get out of their class,' traits for which she had a scornful reaction." Mrs. Webb, in her study "The Jews of East London," wrote in 1902 that "it is by competition, and by competition alone, that the Jew seeks success. But in the case of the foreign Jews, it is a competition unrestricted by the personal dignity of a definite standard of life, and unchecked by the social feelings of class loyalty and trade integrity."

Mrs. Webb wrote this just three or four years before the revolutionary activities of the Polish Bund and seven or eight years before the enormous strikes of Jewish workers in the United States.

left of the East Side far more than anything happening in this country. And insofar as Jewish socialism in America resembled an émigré movement, it bore many of the scars of such movements: cramped isolation, ugly internal quarrels, soured romanticism.

Rebelling against the parochialism of traditional Jewish life, the Jewish radicals improvised a parochialism of their own—but with this difference: they called it "universalism." In one leap they hoped to move from yeshiva to modern culture, from *shtetl* to urban sophistication, from blessing the Sabbath wine to declaring the strategy of international revolution. They yearned to bleach away their past and become men without, or above, a country. To show any sensitivity, let alone fellow feeling, for the religious or cultural sentiments that immigrant workers had brought from Europe, was to open oneself to ridicule for still being under the sway of Jehovah. To recognize that Jewish socialists had to write and speak in Yiddish not merely because it was the only language the immigrants understood but also because there were urgent Jewish problems touching all Jews, including the "emancipated" radical ones—this led to insinuations of "nationalism." And before the charge of "nationalism," courageous men quailed, as their grandfathers might have quailed before charges of heresy.

A Chicago witness offers an anecdote about the "cosmopolitanism" of the Jewish socialists:

> Once I came to a lecture at our La Salle Club. The lecture was on a deeply Jewish subject and was held in Yiddish. Afterward, the chairman spoke in English, appealing to the audience to join the party. So I got up to ask a question: My God, all of us here are Jews, you make your appeal to Yiddish-speaking workers, so why don't you speak Yiddish? They answered me that they had been speaking Yiddish for a long time and it hadn't done any good, so now they were going to try English.

The need to shake off the common Jewish past which, unbidden, still hovered over them obsessed the older Jewish socialists—those like Feigenbaum, who wrote that "all true socialists without exception are opponents of nationalism"; or those like Michael Zametkin, a veteran of the eighties, who bemoaned the fact that immigrant workers, not knowing English, had to use "the mishmash of the Russian-Hebrew-German jargon" that went under the name of Yiddish; or those like the *Forward* editorialist who wrote, "We will consider our task done when we have so awakened our readers' interest in socialism, literature, and science that they will turn to other languages, and most of all to English."

In the pages of the *Tsukunft* there kept winding a heated but inconclusive debate between the "cosmopolitan" socialists and those sympathetic to Jewish sentiments. When Feigenbaum, an uncompromising assimilationist, sardonically inquired, "What kind of Jewish 'cultural' independence is it that 'enlightened' socialists wish to maintain?" he was answered by a comrade: "To be national means to possess national self-consciousness—that is, the recognition that certain individuals belong to my nation, and that my nation is no better and no worse . . . than all other nations, and has the same right to exist as all other nations. 'National' and 'international' are not opposites, but concepts that complement each other."

In turn, the "cosmopolitans" argued that once religion was discarded, Jewishness had no real substance, becoming a mere indulgence of nostalgia: "What special demands can [Jewry] present as a nation? What do Jews have in common besides a synagogue, a *mikve* [ritual bath], a *hazan* [cantor], a *shokhet* [ritual slaughterer], and a solemnizer of weddings? Give Jews civil rights and what remains of the national demands?"

There was no inherent reason why this debate could not continue indefinitely—and, insofar as it raised issues of lasting concern to Jewish radicals, it has. By about 1910, however, the issues were resolved decisively in favor of the "more Jewish" Jewish radicals, primarily because a large number of Bundists reached New York in the years after the collapse of the 1905 Russian Revolution. Experienced, self-confident, and with an aura of revolutionary sacrifice,* the Bundists brought with them a worked-out ideology, and a sophistication in expressing it, that old-timers like Feigenbaum and Zametkin could not cope with. The Bund had maintained a structure of sympathizing branches in America, some sixty of them by 1906; their three thousand members considerably outnumbered the enrollment in the Jewish branches of the Socialist party. Bundist leaders like Mark Liber and Raphael Abramovitch made extended lecture tours in America, raising funds for their movement. During the 1905 revolution, the Bundists in America mobilized in behalf of their comrades in Europe, sending them for several months the considerable sum of five thousand dollars a week. After the collapse of the 1905 revolution, a widening stream of Bundist immigrants began to arrive, some of them, like David Dubinsky and Sidney Hillman, to become crucial figures in the trade unions, and others, like B. Charney Vladeck and Nokhem Chanin, to lend strength to Jewish socialism in America. The New York "ambassador" of the Bund, Dr. Moshe Gurevitch, decided to remain here and in 1907 opened a Russian-Jewish bookstore, which served as port of call for arriving comrades.

The Bundists had the advantage not only of political experience but also of sustained discussions regarding the relationship of Jews to the socialist

---

* An aura often gained through imprisonment in czarist jails. B. Charney Vladeck, who began his political career as a Bundist and later played a major role in the affairs of Jewish socialism in America, wrote in an unpublished autobiography that "the whole experience" of his imprisonment "was in a way a repetition of the Talmudic Academy. . . . The days passed in endless discussions of party programs and platforms. The role of the peasantry in the revolutionary movement, the historic mission of the working class, the kind of government to be set up after the revolution, the role of the individual in society, the question of national minorities—all these were discussed in their relation to Karl Marx and Bakunin, Plekhanov and Lenin. . . . For the first time in my experience I had an opportunity to become familiar with the theories of the international labor movement. Also, there for the first time, I came across Emerson in a German translation."

movement. They inclined politically to the left wing of international social- ism; they were strongly oriented toward practical work in the trade unions; they believed in fostering a coherent Jewish culture, secularist and modern in outlook and based on Yiddish as the language of the Jewish masses. Committed to Jewish national survival (or, as they put it in Europe, "auton- omy"), they were nevertheless strongly opposed to Zionism, which they dismissed as a utopian fantasy. They wanted the Jews to form a distinct national-cultural grouping within the countries where they lived, and the Jewish workers to be part of, though organizationally separate from, the socialist and labor movements in those countries. In Poland this had led to organizing a Jewish socialist party, the Bund; in America, where a separate party was clearly unrealistic, it led to the organization in 1912 of the Jewish Socialist Federation as an autonomous subdivision of the Socialist party.

Despite their relative sophistication, the Bundists who came to America after 1905 had difficulties in adjusting to the new world. Emotionally, many of them still lived in the old country, their imaginations excited by mem- ories of revolt and their consciences troubled by reports of comrades suffer- ing from czarist reaction. They often looked down upon the older Yiddish- speaking socialists as deficient in theoretical subtlety and victimized by the flatness of American society. "Everything in America seemed to them pro- saic. Another lecture, another hundred votes gained at election time—who could be excited by that?" Still, as people of energy and conviction, they threw themselves into the movement in this country and succeeded in giving it a new forcefulness.

In Europe the Bundist position had been attacked as a disguised version of Jewish nationalism; Georgi Plekhanov, the Russian Marxist theoretician, had made a famous joke dismissing the Bundists as Zionists with seasickness. More cogent perhaps than the ideological attacks of orthodox Marxists like Plekhanov was the argument that the Bundists proposed to stop history at precisely the point where they had first encountered it. They accepted the breakup of the traditional Jewish world view; they favored the fracturing of opinion and pluralism of tendencies within Jewish life that followed upon the end of religious hegemony; yet they strongly resisted all proposals or inclinations toward a further assimilation into the gentile world. They wanted to remain Jews—nonbelieving, radical, modern, but Jews.

Both religious and secularist Jews criticized the Bund on the ground that the Yiddishist phase of Jewish history which it hoped to preserve would, of necessity, be short-lived. Either—said these critics of both right and left—the Jews will return to their traditional faith or they will proceed to total assimilation; it is unrealistic to expect a prolonged historical period in which the Jews would maintain themselves as a distinct people yet be without religion or territory.

There was, it now seems, a certain validity to these criticisms, but in 1910 or 1912, before modern Jewish history had reached its denouement, the Bundists played a vital role in the immigrant community. They grasped, better than anyone else, that the problems of the immigrant Jewish working class were not merely problems of organization but, still more, of morale. They grasped that it was necessary to forge a Jewish working class that would have a sense of its own worth. Too many Jewish workers still lived under the sign of fear, too many still bore the stigma of *shtetl* passivity, too many still thought of self-exploitation as a strategy for escaping exploitation. The Bundists understood that they had to confront a major problem in collective self-regard. Victories in trade-union struggles were, of course, essential to that end, but greater internal coherence and solidarity were a prerequisite for giving those victories a lasting institutional base. What the Bundists brought to the socialist and union movements in this country was not merely their élan, combativeness, and sophisticated conviction; it was a Jewish dimension, the persuasion that when garment workers won strikes, as they began to do in 1909, this was a victory not merely for workers who happened to be Jews but for *Jewish* workers. The class struggle pursued within the Jewish community would be a means of enriching the life of the Jewish workers, while enriching their life was a precondition for a success-ful pursuit of the class struggle.

Recognizing that they were now in America to stay, the Bundists joined the Socialist party, became active in the Workmen's Circle, and provided new leadership in the Jewish unions. There were bitter fights between the *"grine" sotsialistn*—greenhorn socialists, mostly Bundists—and the *"gele" sotsialistn*—"yellowed," or less greenhorn, socialists, mostly old-timers from the 1880's and 1890's. In Chicago, for example, where the *"grine"* proposed to create a Jewish Socialist Federation, the *"gele"* howled them down: "You want to make a Bund in America, do you? You want to celebrate your own private Sabbath? No, sir; here in America we have only a unified Socialist party."

The Bundists and their allies won out, with the Jewish Socialist Federa-tion representing, in good part, their adaptation to American circumstances. A number of Yiddish-speaking socialists of the "cosmopolitan" wing, espe-cially in their Brooklyn stronghold, refused to have anything to do with the "nationalistic" Federation (which, in reality, devoted much energy to at-tacking the Zionists). Under the leadership of J. B. Salutsky, later known in the labor movement as J. B. S. Hardman, the Federation nevertheless thrived. A year after its formation in 1912, it had sixty-five branches with a membership of 2,500. On the face of it, this was a small number, but because these people were active and articulate, they were able to exert considerable influence in the immigrant world.

Several factors helped the new Federation. Ever since the Kishinev pogroms of 1903 there had been a greater readiness on the Jewish left to acknowledge the depth and validity of national sentiments; such prominent East Side anarchists as Hillel Zolatoroff and Moshe Katz returned "to the people" and became Labor Zionists. Though not yet a mass movement, the

Zionists lent intellectual respectability to national sentiments among secular Jews, thereby forcing the Socialists to adopt less doctrinaire positions.

Within the American socialist movement as a whole, there had been going on a sharp debate about the problem of immigration. The Socialist party leadership, seeking to win over major segments of the trade-union movement and itself not quite free of prejudice, was torn between the traditional socialist principle that immigration should everywhere be unrestricted and the AFL stand favoring severe limits on Oriental immigration. The Jewish community, of course, favored unrestricted immigration, as did almost all the Jewish socialists, both out of principle and a recognition that anything less would leave them utterly vulnerable to attack by political rivals. At the 1908 Socialist party convention a fight broke out over the immigration issue, with one or two party leaders (Victor Berger and Ernest Untermann) indulging in openly racist remarks. Morris Hillquit, appalled at some of the things he heard yet seeking a formula that would prevent a rupture between the Socialists and the AFL, introduced a resolution that accepted some restrictions on immigration, not on the grounds of race, religion, or nationality, but whenever it threatened to "weaken American labor." This waffling formula gained a narrow majority of the convention; it was opposed by the Jewish delegates from the East Side, led by Meyer London, who fought for unrestricted immigration. That the issue could arise in so bedeviling a way, even within the radical movement, greatly strengthened the hand of those who argued that a distinctive Jewish Socialist Federation was needed.

Finally, it was the pressure of events that settled this dispute. The years 1907 and 1908 had brought a severe depression, and partly in reaction, a series of major strikes broke out in the Jewish industries. There could be no question that these strikes represented a fulfillment of hopes shared by all Jewish socialists nor that they represented an outburst of rage and yearning within the Jewish community as a whole. Polemics were put aside for a while, and the work of the moment began.

The Girls and the Men

Bad as things were for the Jewish socialists in the first years of the century, they were worse still for the Jewish unions.* Socialist groups can

---

* An imprecise but unavoidable designation. "Jewish unions" refers to those in the needle trades, and sometimes elsewhere, which have had either a majority or a crucial plurality of Jewish members and in which the leadership has been heavily Jewish. At a minimum, this would include the unions in the women's clothing, men's clothing, fur, and hat industries. Over the years, a number of other unions, such as locals of the bakers' and painters' unions, could also be called Jewish.

survive on ideology, factionalism, and visions, but unions either perform concrete tasks or go under. The largest and most important Jewish union, the International Ladies Garment Workers Union, was organized in 1900 at a New York conference opened by Joseph Barondess, the all-purpose plenipotentiary of the East Side, and Herman Robinson, representing the American Federation of Labor. Eleven delegates were present, claiming to speak for two thousand workers. With a treasury of $30, the ILGWU began to make what its officers regarded as "modest progress": its total income for 1900–1901 was $506, a sum deemed sufficient to appoint Bernard Braff as part-time secretary-treasurer at $5 a week. The next year his salary was tripled, on condition he give full time to union duties.

The early account books of the ILGWU tell a story of their own. From June 1902 to May 1903 the cost of clerical help came to nineteen dollars. Since Braff wrote poorly, his son, a high-school student, "smoothed out the English of his immigrant father and embellished the official reports with literary allusions to Mark Twain," for which service the 1903 convention voted the boy a ten-dollar present. At the initiative of Benjamin Schlessinger, a young activist who would later become president of the ILGWU, the convention passed a resolution of friendship for the Socialist party, though the union itself was tactically conservative in these early days, avoiding rash strikes and trying to move step by step toward solid organization. This strategy was strengthened by the new secretary-treasurer chosen in 1903, John Dyche, whose views on unionism were fairly close to those of Samuel Gompers but whom the Jewish socialists respected as a devoted and serious man.

About 1904 the ILGWU started going downhill: internal wrangling, raids from the syndicalist Industrial Workers of the World, disastrous strikes, decline in membership. A 1908 conference led certain active figures to consider abandoning the union: "Some of us," recalls the early leader Abraham Rosenberg, "cried bitterly at these words." When a decision was made not only to keep the union afloat but also to open a new office for its New York Joint Board, the first month's rent could be paid only because Meyer London, the Socialist leader, advanced twenty-five dollars from his own pocket. Rosenberg writes that when the New York tailors' Local 9 had to induct new members, it often could not collect a quorum of old ones. "Well, we found a way out. Just before the meeting we borrowed a dozen operators who were meeting in the same building and a few skirtmakers, and we elevated them to the rank of tailors for that evening." As for the International, Dyche spent a good part of his time evading landlords and other bill collectors: he "would come into his office early in the morning, snatch up his mail, and be gone for the rest of the day."

And then, with a momentum and rapidity that may resist full explanation, everything changed. In 1909 the United Hebrew Trades, a federation of the Jewish unions, had forty-one affiliates in New York, with perhaps five thousand members; many of these locals were paper organizations wistfully held together by five or six people. Yet within a few months there erupted a series of strikes unprecedented in Jewish life for their size, duration, and fury. First came the bakers, two thousand of them, striking in the spring of 1909 against conditions that were regarded as shocking even on the East Side. Soon the offices of the United Hebrew Trades were besieged by groups of workers demanding they be organized, and the UHT leaders—Bernard Weinstein and Max Pine, aided by socialist irregulars like Hillquit, Cahan, and London—were racing about from meeting to meeting.*

Why the change? Because the 1907–1908 depression had come to an end, there was more work in the Jewish industries, and a slight rise in income fortified the workers to demand more. Because the IWW, mostly an irritant in the needle trades, had been beaten off. Because the post-1905 wave of immigrants began to assume leadership in the unions. And because the realization kept growing among immigrant Jews that for good or bad they were in America to stay: "Their hopes in the Russian Revolution began to wane. . . . The idea of going back home to Russia gave way to the realization that America was 'home.' As a result, many of these immigrants turned their attention to their immediate environment."

Helpful as such explanations may be, they all seem finally not to satisfy. Perhaps the most cogent thing to be added is that the massing of tribulation and anger which in the past had recurrently erupted as strikes now reached another climax of explosion—this time among the Jewish girls.

On November 22, 1909, twenty thousand shirtwaist makers, most of them girls in their teens or early twenties, and about two thirds of them Jewish, went on strike.

The manufacture of shirtwaists, or blouses, was a relatively new segment of the garment industry. Since 1900 it had been growing rapidly, its

---

* As a central agency of the Jewish socialists in the unions, the United Hebrew Trades came in for severe attack from leaders of the American Federation of Labor. In general, the tension during these early days between Jewish unionists of socialist inclination and the more conservative AFL has been minimized by historians who respond to the leadership of the Jewish unions as it is now and forget what it once was. A major point of contention was the immigration issue, with the UHT favoring unrestricted immigration and most AFL unions restrictions of varying severity. In 1901 the AFL organizer Herman Robinson urged local unions not to affiliate with the UHT since it knew "little or nothing about the trade union movement; its entire knowledge of unionism extends from East Broadway to Houston Street, and from the Bowery to Sheriff Street."

  This kind of sparring continued for a good many years. In February 1918 the AFL Executive Council ordered all affiliates in New York to leave the UHT on the ground that it maintained close relations with the Amalgamated Clothing Workers and the Cloth, Hat and Cap Makers Union, both of which were independent unions led by immigrant Jews, many of them socialists, and both of which were in conflict with older, moribund AFL affiliates.

  It would take several decades before this clash between the Jewish socialist union leaders and the official AFL leadership came, not to an end, but at least to a point where it could be quietly contained.

1909 output in New York alone reaching fifty million dollars. Physical conditions in the shirtwaist shops tended to be better than in other parts of the industry, mostly because these shops were newer, cleaner, and more likely to use electrical power; but the girls were subject to many small tyrannies, sexual discrimination on top of class exploitation. "Inside subcontracting" was common in the shirtwaist shops, which meant that male employees would themselves employ several "girl helpers," who earned no more than three or four dollars a week. These doubly ill-used "learners," who sometimes kept "learning" long after there was nothing left to learn, formed 20 to 25 percent of the work force. Female workers were charged for needles, power, and supplies at a profit of 20 percent; taxed for the chairs on which they sat; made to pay for clothes lockers; fined if they came to work five minutes late. Sporadic efforts to organize them had failed, and the common view of the time was that, because they were girls who hoped soon to marry, they could not be unionized.*

When the strike began, the shirtwaist makers' union, Local 25 of the ILGWU, had slightly more than one hundred members and some four dollars in its treasury. Limited strikes had already been called against several firms, the Triangle Waist Company and the Leiserson Company, but these seemed on the edge of collapse because the employers, mostly east European Jews, had used strikebreakers and thugs to frighten the girls. In desperation, the leadership of Local 25 began to consider the total gamble of a "general strike" in the shirtwaist industry.

On November 22 it called a meeting of workers at Cooper Union. Thousands came, with crowds spilling over into other halls. Gompers spoke; so did Mary Dreier, head of the Women's Trade Union League; and, as usual at such meetings, Jacob Panken and Meyer London, the big guns of Jewish socialism. But no clear strategy had been worked out by the Local leadership, and the speakers, hesitating before the prospect of an ill-prepared general strike, could not quite decide between exhortation and caution. As the evening dragged along and speaker followed speaker, there suddenly raced up to the platform, from the depths of the hall, a frail teen-age girl named Clara Lemlich, who had been picketing at the Leiserson plant day after day. She burst into a flow of passionate Yiddish which would remain engraved in thousands of memories: "I am a working girl, one of those striking against intolerable conditions. I am tired of listening to speakers who talk in generalities. What we are here for is to decide whether or not to strike. I offer a resolution that a general strike be declared—now."

A contagion of excitement swept the meeting, people screaming, stamp-

---

* "Our organizing," recalls the secretary of the shirtwaist local, "was generally carried on in a stereotyped way. We would issue a circular reading somewhat as follows: 'Murder! The exploiters, the blood-suckers, the manufacturers. . . . Pay your dues. . . . Down with the capitalists! Hurrah!' The employers would be somewhat frightened and concede to the demands of the union. [Then] the workers would drop out."

ing feet, waving handkerchiefs. The chairman, Benjamin Feigenbaum, stood on the platform trying to restore order, and when finally heard, asked for a second. Again pandemonium, the whole crowd shouting its second. Shaken by this outburst, Feigenbaum cried out: "Do you mean it in good faith? Will you take the old Jewish oath?" Thousands of hands went up: "If I turn traitor to the cause I now pledge, may this hand wither from the arm I raise!"

Week after week the strike went on. Most shops were closed, a few tried to use scabs. The Jewish socialists threw themselves into the day-to-day work. The Women's Trade Union League sent help to the picket lines, sharing blows and abuse with the Jewish and Italian girls.* Lillian Wald and Mary Simkhovitch did publicity. Wealthy New York women such as Mrs. Oliver Belmont and Anne Morgan, sister of the banker, provided bail money. Wellesley students donated $1,000 to the strike fund. In the first month alone, 723 girls were arrested and 19 sent to the workhouse; the average daily bill for bail came to $2,500. Sentencing a striker, Magistrate Olmstead declared: "You are on strike against God and Nature, whose firm law is that man shall earn his bread in the sweat of his brow." About which Bernard Shaw, in reply to the Women's Trade Union League, wired: "Delightful. Medieval America always in the intimate personal confidence of the Almighty."

Nothing in the strike was as remarkable as the girls themselves. Some turned out to be natural leaders, fighting with great boldness, even ferocity. "Into the foreground," wrote an observer, "comes the figure of one girl after another as her services are needed. With extraordinary simplicity and eloquence, she will tell before any kind of audience, without any false shame and without self-glorification, the conditions of her work, her wages, and the pinching poverty of her home."

A young reporter for the New York *Sun*, McAlister Coleman, went down one morning to the garment center. It changed his sense of things forever,

to watch a picket line form in front of a struck shirtwaist-factory.

The girls, headed by teen-age Clara Lemlich, described by union organizers as a "pint of trouble for the bosses," began singing Italian and Russian working-class songs as they paced in twos before the factory door. Of a sudden, around the corner came a dozen tough-looking customers, for whom the union label "gorillas" seemed well-chosen.

"Stand fast, girls," called Clara, and then the thugs rushed the line, knocking Clara to her knees, striking at the pickets, opening the way for a

* At a strike rally for the shirtwaist makers, Morris Hillquit commented on the relationship between immigrant working girls and native middle-class women who were helping them: "It is no mere accident that in this fight the striking Jewish and Italian girls, the poorest of the poor, have the sympathy and active support of the suffrage workers of all classes. There is a certain common bond between women fighting for civil rights and women fighting for industrial justice."

group of frightened scabs to slip through the broken line. Fancy ladies from the Allen Street red-light district climbed out of cabs to cheer on the gorillas. There was a confused melee of scratching, screaming girls and fist-swinging men and then a patrol wagon arrived. The thugs ran off as the cops pushed Clara and two other badly beaten girls into the wagon.

I followed the rest of the retreating pickets to the union hall, a few blocks away. There a relief station had been set up where one bottle of milk and a loaf of bread were given to strikers with small children in their families. There, for the first time in my comfortably sheltered, upper West Side life, I saw real hunger on the faces of my fellow Americans in the richest city in the world.

The strike dragged on until mid-February 1910, and was finally settled with improvements in working conditions but without the formal union recognition for which the ILGWU had held out. A victory or defeat? In the eyes of some intransigent leaders, probably a defeat; in retrospect, a liberating event for the Jewish workers. By the strike's end, Local 25 had grown to ten thousand members. In the immigrant world, the shirtwaist makers had created indescribable excitement: these were our daughters. The strike came to be called "the uprising of the twenty thousand," and the phrase should be taken as more than socialist or Jewish rhetoric, for it was indeed an uprising of people who discovered on the picket lines their sense of dignity and self. New emotions swept the East Side, new perceptions of what immigrants could do, even girls until yesterday mute. *"Unzere vunderbare farbrente meydlekh,"* "our wonderful fervent girls," an old-timer called them.

What the girls began, the men completed. Five months after the shirtwaist makers strike was over, the cloakmakers declared their general strike. "In the women's strike, the social consciousness of the community was a potent factor. In the men's struggle, labor faced capital directly. One was a sudden emotional outburst; the other was carefully planned. In the former, about 20,000 workers were involved. In the latter, the number of strikers was three times as large. . . . The shirtwaist makers' strike was an 'uprising.' The cloakmakers' strike was 'the great revolt.' "

No Jewish union in the United States had ever before gone about its preparations with such care and method. Members were systematically enrolled. The Cloak Operators Union, Local 1 of the ILGWU, which in 1908 had only two hundred members, increased its ranks to two thousand by June 1910. In April the union began issuing an irregular paper, the *New Post*, in English, Yiddish, and Italian.* "Wherever cloakmakers gathered, one would find groups of workers discussing [the proposal for a general strike] in the most heated manner." The AFL hierarchy was enlisted and Samuel Gompers came to New York to speak at a prestrike rally in Madison

* During the early 1900's there had been a steady influx of Italian immigrants, mostly women, into the garment trades. In later years the Italians would form a powerful minority within the ILGWU, concentrated in Local 89 under the leadership of Luigi Antonini.

Brown Brothers

Delivering bundles of clothes, 1910

The Granger Collection, New York

Orchard Street, 1910

East Side newsboys starting off to work

International Museum of Photography at George Eastman House, Rochester, N.Y.

The air shaft of a dumbbell tenement, *c*. 1900

Brown Brothers

Girls at their machines in a garment shop

A sweatshop on Ludlow Street

Museum of the City of New York

International Museum of Photography at George Eastman House, Rochester, N.Y.

Communal faucet in a tenement hall, 1910

Museum of the City of New York

Clotheslines in a New York slum

Skipping rope on the roof playground of the Hebrew Institute

Making things clear, 1912

The Granger Collection, New York

Batter up, with small fry watching from a wagon, in a tenement alley, *c.* 1910

Brown Brothers

Old and young resting in an East Side park, *c.* 1910

Friendly argument on an East Side street

The New York Public Library, Local History & Genealogy Division

Courtesy of YIVO Institute for Jewish Research

Saluting the flag on Americanization Day
at the Educational Alliance, 1910

Brown Brothers

Abraham Cahan, editor of the *Jewish Daily Forward*

UPI

Culver Pictures

Meyer London, Socialist congressman
from the East Side

Morris Hillquit: from Cherry Street
to American Socialism

Rose Schneiderman at a street rally

wn Brothers

Brown

"In Union There Is Strength": placards in many languages

After the Triangle fire: bodies on the sidewalk

Policemen bending over Triangle fire victims

Courtesy of the International Ladies Garment Workers Union

Clara Lemlich, teen-age firebrand

Samuel Gompers speaking to the shirtwaist makers at Cooper Union, 1909

Brown Brothers

Square Garden—the first time a Jewish union had ventured to hire so large a place. Thousands could not get into the hall, so enormous was the outpouring of workers. Many stood on the streets listening to speeches from rented trucks. Elaborate arrangements were made for raising funds from friendly organizations, with Morris Winchevsky, the Yiddish poet, in charge of this campaign. (Where but in the Yiddish world could a poet have been the chief fund-raiser for a general strike?) Close to $250,000 was collected, with about two thirds of that sum to be distributed as weekly strike benefits.

On July 2 and 3 a secret vote of all the locals in the cloak industry favored the strike by 18,771 to 615. On July 7 the strike began. Abraham Rosenberg, then president of the ILGWU, summons the moment:

> About two o'clock some members of the strike committee went to the cloak district to see how the order of the strike committee would be received. . . . Among those who were eager to see whether the workers would respond were Abraham Cahan and Benjamin Schlessinger, editor and manager of the *Forward.* Our people naturally were excited, their hearts beat fast, and every minute seemed an age to them. When at ten minutes past two there was no worker to be seen, Cahan ironically asked, "Well, where are your strikers . . . ?" Hardly had he spoken, when we saw a sea of people surging out of the side streets toward Fifth Avenue. . . . By half past two, all the streets were jammed with thousands of workers. . . . Many of our most devoted members cried for joy at the idea that their lifelong labors had been crowned with success. In my mind I could only picture to myself such a scene taking place when the Jews were led out of Egypt.

All was precise, orderly, well managed: something new among the immigrant workers. "Every hall where the strikers met was in charge of a hall chairman. . . . Each shop elected its own shop chairman who was responsible to the hall chairman. The shop chairman kept a list of all the workers in their respective shops. Twice a day they took roll call. If any strikers were absent more than once or twice, committees were sent to look them up." Strike benefits were distributed as regularly as finances allowed, one to two dollars for unmarried workers and two to four dollars for married ones.

The union was asking for a forty-nine-hour week, the employers offered a fifty-three-hour week. Wage demands also began to seem negotiable once representatives of both sides started to meet. But the one point that seemed beyond compromise was a union demand that the employers bind themselves to hire only union members. When the strike dragged through the summer, the suffering of the workers grew severe, as did the losses sustained by the smaller employers. A number of Jewish public figures proposed that the Boston attorney Louis D. Brandeis, by then well known in American life, be invited to serve as negotiator. He accepted, and with the aid of Louis Marshall and Jacob Schiff, both of whom feared that the strike might tear apart the Jewish community, he gradually worked out an agreement.

In principle an opponent of the closed shop, Brandeis improvised a formula that would later be used for settling many industrial disputes. He proposed a "preferential union shop," that is, "a shop in which union stand-ards prevail and the union is entitled to preference." At first the Jewish socialists denounced this formula, the *Forward* calling it, not very accu-rately, a scheme for "the scab shop with honey." But pressures for settle-ment were mounted against both sides, and finally, on September 2, a "Protocol of Peace" was signed that gave the cloakmakers substantial im-provements (a fifty-hour week, wage increases, abolition of inside subcon-tracting, and a version of the "preferential union shop" that in practice would not be very far from the "closed shop.") As soon as word of the agreement reached the East Side, people started streaming toward the square in front of the *Forward* building on East Broadway. "Everywhere men and women, old and young, embraced and congratulated one another on the victory. It was early morning, Saturday, September 3, before the streets were emptied of the masses of humanity. . . . Saturday afternoon, trucks decorated with flags, with bands of music, and carrying crowds of cloak-makers drove through the streets, announcing the strike had been settled."

The East Side had earned its joy. Until now there had been no more than a large scattering of Jewish immigrant workers who would sometimes cohere for a fierce outbreak and then crumble into isolated persons; by 1910 one could speak of a Jewish working class, structured, disciplined, self-conscious, and with a much stronger tie to socialist politics than character-ized the American workers. Through a bitter struggle against Jewish em-ployers, the immigrant workers helped to create a new Jewish élan, a greater sense of strength and possibility, which extended beyond their own ranks and into the immigrant community as a whole. Through an internal class struggle they helped form a communal, even "national" consciousness. The words of Abraham Rosenberg—"I could only picture to myself such a scene taking place when the Jews were led out of Egypt"—were acute in their linkage of class and communal motifs.

Historians of American Jewish life have often seen the Protocol of Peace as a sign that, even when struggles broke out between Jewish workers and Jewish employers, the traditional values of Judaism still contributed to modulating the conflict. A sense of belonging to a community in which norms of justice, no matter how frequently violated, continued to operate; a sense that Jews could find ways of settling disputes among themselves short of open battle; a sense that Jews had moral obligations to one another that would at least soften the ravages of class conflict—all these, it has been suggested, helped make possible the Protocol of 1910.*

* Will Herberg, in his important study of Jewish labor, writes that Jewish em-ployers and employees shared "a common social and cultural background," which included "an age-old tradition of arbitration, of settling their often bitter disputes within the Jewish community. . . . They shared too, as a heritage of centuries of self-enclosed minority existence, a marked concern for the reputation of the Jewish community with the outside world. New World conditions undermined and con-fused these traditional standards, but did not entirely destroy them."

There is obvious truth in such claims. The Protocol did advance norms of collective bargaining far ahead of those prevailing in most American industries, and it would take some decades and a good many violent strikes before the major American corporations would agree to similar terms. No doubt, some of the Jewish manufacturers wanted, as their lawyer, Julius Henry Cohen, wrote, "to put the industry upon a higher plane and to make of the business something which would not make them shamefaced when admitting to their neighbors or children that they were cloak manufacturers." No doubt, such employers encountered moral pressures from friends, neighbors, fellow members of societies and synagogues: pressures likely to be all the more stringent because the immigrant Jews were still packed into a tight physical and social space.

Yet the point can easily be exaggerated into a Jewish sentimentalism. For, as one historian asks, "How do we reconcile [the supposed effects of] the Jewish heritage with the brutality accorded strikers in 1909, 1910, 1912, and 1913 by Jewish employers?" Or with the efforts of the manufacturers to discard the Protocol entirely in 1916? Or with the brutal history of industrial relations within the garment industry all through the 1920's and 1930's? If the moral imperatives of the Jewish tradition acted as a restraining force upon the garment manufacturers, their own economic interests usually proved to be stronger. They had to. The employers were caught up in an industry where competition was murderous, profit uncertain, bankruptcy frequent. To survive, they had to take these realities into account, which meant that their Jewish consciences, keen or dull, had to be kept in the background. Had the immigrant workers not forced recognition of their unions and improvements in conditions, most Jewish employers would not, and probably could not, have allowed traditional sentiments of justice to overcome economic urgencies. Still, it seems fair to add that in some ways—their susceptibility to pressure from leaders of the immigrant community, their grudging readiness to accept arbitration during the 1910 strike—the employers did show themselves to be still responsive, if only residually, to the moral claims of the Jewish tradition.

This tangle of mixed feelings and confused values showed itself in the third major strike of the period, the 1910 general strike of men's clothing workers in Chicago. Dragging on for more than four months, it was an especially bitter strike, in part because the workers were caught between their employers, mostly Jewish, and the United Garment Workers, a sluggish organization that looked with suspicion on the "radical Jewish tailors." The hub of the strike was the huge factory of Hart, Schaffner and Marx, employing six thousand people. Here a young man named Sidney Hillman, later to be a major figure in the Jewish labor movement, sprang forward as the local leader, shrewdly fighting off both the New York–based bureaucracy of the United Garment Workers, which at one point tried to make a deal with the employers over the heads of the Chicago strike committee, and a group of intransigent leftist workers influenced by the IWW and unwilling to end the strike unless the closed shop were won. Except at Hart, Schaffner and Marx, the terms of settlement were close to being a defeat for the strikers, yet in the long run constituted an entering wedge for the unionization of the industry. What broke the unity of employer resistance was, to some extent, the moral qualms of Joseph Schaffner, who so took to heart the criticism of rabbis, ministers, and social workers that he began to wonder whether he was "a moral failure." "This strike," he told a friend, "is killing me." Schaffner then negotiated with Hillman an agreement superior to those in other segments of the industry—here conscience, Jewish or not, does seem to have played a role.

Four years later, after much quarreling with the leaders of the United Garment Workers, the Jewish unionists in the men's clothing industry set up a new organization, the Amalgamated Clothing Workers, with the twenty-eight-year-old Hillman as president and a veteran socialist, Joseph Schlossberg, as secretary-treasurer. Though it soon became the dominant union in the men's clothing industry, organizing shops that the slow-footed UGW never even approached, the Amalgamated had to live outside the ranks of the American Federation of Labor, the leaders of which kept insisting that the UGW was the only legitimate union. This isolation did the Amalgamated little harm. Blending Hillman's pragmatic reformism with Schlossberg's radical sentiments, the Amalgamated became a major presence within the Jewish labor movement, less socialist in tone than the ILGWU and less involved with Jewish communal affairs, but in many ways a pioneer in developing the "progressive unionism" of later decades, that is, a unionism extending its range of concern to the social and political reforms that would be characteristic of the welfare state. Its independence from the AFL hierarchy allowed the Amalgamated a freedom to experiment with liberal programs that was by no means common among American unions.

The Triangle Shirt Fire

After 1910, strike followed strike, one after the other, in all the Jewish industries. Long-contained emotions poured into these strikes, outcries of men and women calling for a recognition of their worth. And then, in the spring of 1911, the nerves of the East Side broke. One of the largest garment shops in the city, the Triangle Shirtwaist Company, at the edge of Washington Square, burst into flame, and in the eighteen minutes it took to bring the fire under control, 146 workers, most of them young Jewish and Italian girls, were burned to death.

A reporter passing through the square would remember how

a young man helped a girl to the window sill on the ninth floor. Then he held her out deliberately, away from the building, and let her drop. He held out a second girl the same way and let her drop. He held out a third girl who did not resist. They were all as unresisting as if he were helping them into a street car instead of into eternity. He saw that a terrible death awaited them in the flames and his was only a terrible chivalry. He brought around another girl to the window. I saw her put her arms around him and kiss him. Then he held her into space—and dropped her. Quick as a flash, he was on the window sill himself. His coat fluttered upwards—the air filled his trouser legs as he came down. I could see he wore tan shoes.

Investigations, recriminations, exonerations: none could quench the grief of the East Side. What did it matter whether the Triangle building had violated the fire code or the fire code had been inadequate to start with? The charred bodies spoke of endless pain, remembered burnings. The East Side broke into scenes of hysteria, demonstrations, mass meetings, as if, finally, its burdens were just too much to bear. Morris Rosenfeld, the Yiddish poet, printed a threnody that occupied the whole front page of the *Forward*. A few lines:

> Over whom shall we weep first?
> Over the burned ones?
> Over those beyond recognition?
> Over those who have been crippled?
> Or driven senseless?
> Or smashed?
> I weep for them all.
>
> Now let us light the holy candles
> And mark the sorrow
> Of Jewish masses in darkness and poverty.
> This is our funeral,
> These our graves,
> Our children. . . .

A more severe eloquence was that of Rose Schneiderman, the tiny firebrand of the Women's Trade Union League, who spoke in a whisper at one of the memorial meetings:

The old Inquisition had its rack and its thumbscrews and its instruments of torture with iron teeth. We know what these things are today: the iron teeth are our necessities, the thumbscrews are the high-powered and swift machinery close to which we must work, and the rack is here in the firetrap structures that will destroy us the minute they catch fire. . . .

This is not the first time girls have been burned alive in this city. Every week I must learn of the untimely death of one of my sister workers. Every year thousands of us are maimed. The life of men and women is so cheap and property is so sacred! . . .

I can't talk fellowship to you who are gathered here. Too much blood has been spilled. . . . It is up to the working people to save themselves.

It was from such experiences that the immigrant Jewish working class emerged in America.

The Jewish Working Class

Has there ever been another working class quite like it? Still pocked with the scars of Jewish fear*—a legacy of the past that could not be erased through mere will—the immigrant working class showed deep resources for sacrifice, powerful sentiments of solidarity, and a capacity for organization that made the hasty impressions of labor historians like John Commons seem a little absurd. There was a visible communal pleasure, a grim sort of pleasure, in testing out this new sense of combativeness. Abraham Liessen wrote a sentence about the striking cloakmakers of 1910 that would be widely quoted on the East Side: "The 70,000 zeros became 70,000 fighters." Radical or not, the immigrant Jews took pleasure in this observation: it spoke to their morale.

To be a fighter, to act in concert with other workers, to bring to one's tongue such inspiriting words as "respect" and "dignity"—all this testified to the forging of collective selfhood. Almost every ideological segment of the immigrant community stressed the goal of achieving "a normal life," and part of that "normal life" would consist in a readiness to demand from the world what other people never hesitated to demand.

As a class in its merest beginnings, the Jewish workers had no traditions, no depths of experience to draw upon. They had to improvise their own myths, transmuting emotions of millennial expectation, or perhaps merely the frustrations of immigrant life, into visions of proletarian solidarity. The belief of the radicals that fulfilling this vision would also, somehow, sustain Jewish identity, may now seem to have been too facile; but in 1912 the formation of an immigrant Jewish working class helped to cohere and define the entire immigrant Jewish community. An old-time Jewish leftist has remarked, "It's my idea that the Jewish community in the United States was not really a Jewish community, it was just something in fermentation until the labor movement came along. That gave the Jewish community its character, its face." An exaggeration, but a useful one.

Meanwhile, yielding inspiration, there were stories brought across from Europe about the new fighting spirit of Jewish Warsaw and Lodz, though in truth this went no further back than a quarter of a century. There were

---

* "We were a frightened people," recalls a veteran of Jewish unionism.

also, as both inspiration and admonitory examples, the efforts of the earlier immigrant generations to fall back upon, though gaps of remembrance had already begun to crack open here. So the Jewish activists in the unions, most of them socialists, had to create their own symbols, their own legends, their own rhetoric, drawing upon whatever sources they could. That was why their imaginations were stirred by the spontaneous boldness of Clara Lemlich, the unknown girl racing up to propose a general strike of the shirtwaist makers. That was why their pride was gratified by Liessen's epigram about the zeros becoming fighters. That was why they responded warmly when European socialist and Zionist leaders came over with reports that other Jews were starting to raise their heads.

The Jewish immigrants were a community triply uprooted: from their old homes, from their religious traditions, and from their customary work and culture. Uprooted, yet able to enjoy the sensations of unfettered speech, they found in their very deracination ground for a new assertiveness of strength. They could speculate freely, *luftmenshn* of programs. They could excite themselves with illusions of possibility. They could dream of bringing together their homely Yiddish with red visions of a beneficent future. The moral and psychic restlessness that seized the Yiddish-speaking Jews both in Europe and America hardened into a social restlessness. It was an overwrought community, dizzied from the freedom it had won in crossing the ocean and angered by the wretchedness it had encountered after the crossing. Tuned to a pitch of intensity, the immigrants seemed sometimes to behave as if intensity were a good in itself, a pleasure to be savored and indulged.

All this, we may ask, about immigrant workers, overstrained, illlettered, provincial, and with the marks of the *shtetl* still upon them?

Like most people, the mass of immigrant workers lived or tried to live by the values of private life; yet a significant number, a vital minority, thought in terms of political goals and collective fulfillment. Perhaps more important, the sentiments of this minority had a way of penetrating and sometimes inspiring those workers who were not active in the unions and did not consider themselves to be radicals. The outlook of a community is almost always expressed by its articulate minority, and the test of that minority's right to speak for the others is whether, at crucial moments, it anticipates their sentiments, putting into language what they could not articulate themselves.* True as it may be that for the bulk of the immigrant workers the unions counted mainly as agencies for securing immediate benefits, it is also true that—for a sizable minority, always, and for the majority,

---

* A personal recollection: in a strike of garment workers in 1933, my parents were suddenly swept into strike activity. Neither had ever shown any interest in unionism or politics; yet in the immigrant milieu the moral authority of the unions, or the *idea* of unions, was so great that once the strike began, they simply took it for granted that it was their duty to join, work, and make sacrifices in its behalf. And this attitude was widespread among Jewish workers.

now and again—unions figured in larger, more "ideal" ways. The rise of Jewish unionism cannot be understood without acknowledging "the decisive role that can be played by purely moral factors in the life of a people."

How deeply these moral factors could penetrate the life of simple people is evoked by a letter sent in 1902 to the pantsmakers' local of Boston by a member expelled for scabbing in a strike. The original is in Yiddish:

> I appeal to you, President, and the members of the Union. I would call you brothers, but I know you will not take it in good faith. I know that you will say, "What think you of the boldness of this scab; he even calls us brothers?" . . .
>
> Dear Brothers, I beg you to have mercy on my children. If you would come into my house you would see how frozen my stove is, and how my children shiver with cold—on empty little stomachs—just as I do. But I can only answer my children with a sigh: "I was a scab, therefore we must starve from hunger and cold. I cannot justify myself against the union. . . ."
>
> Dear Brothers, I will ask you something, but answer me feelingly. Are my children responsible for my being a scab? Are they to be blamed because their father is a fool? Answer me, are they to be blamed? I beg you in the name of my little ones to let me back into the Union; we are cold, we are hungry, you are men, have mercy, Brothers.
>
> Sam Schaeffer

The Boston pantsmakers took back the contrite brother and gave him a union card.

By their very nature, the Jewish unions were different from those prevailing in the United States during the early years of the century. In tone and quality, they resembled the unions established by European Social Democrats and anticipated the "social" unionism later to be introduced by the CIO. Where most American unions focused on immediate bread-and-butter issues and were likely to be hostile to heterodox ideas, the Jewish unions reached out toward a wide range of interests, from social insurance plans to co-operative housing, educational programs to Yiddishist cultural activity. Especially in the earlier years of their insurgency, the Jewish unions were not merely bargaining agencies, they were centers of social-cultural life, serving some of the same functions as the *landsmanshaftn*, though with a much more enlightened outlook.

A politics looking to the future blended with a tradition of *tsedaka*, or communal responsibility, drawn from the past. The unions established a custom of contributing generously to other unions, Jewish or not, as well as to innumerable social and communal agencies. When the furriers went on strike in 1912, the cloakmakers, themselves barely established, gave $20,000. During the great steel strike of 1919, the Jewish garment unions contributed $175,000, an enormous sum for the time and half of what all the unions in the country gave. Later, in the thirties, the Jewish unions were equally helpful to the new CIO unions.

There were other signs of distinctiveness. In the early days, meetings of locals were often conducted in Yiddish, or mainly in Yiddish, though the garment unions were careful to recognize the claims of multilingualism in locals with other ethnic pockets. The fervent atmosphere of these years is recalled by Charles Zimmerman, who would become a leader of the Communist bloc in the needle-trade unions during the twenties and a major figure in the ILGWU afterward: "[In 1914] our whole young crowd, we hadn't much to eat, so we used to gather at my house. My mother would cook a big pot of potatoes, we used to buy a couple of herrings, and we would sing Edelstat's [Yiddish] poems. Also those of Bovshover, but mainly Edelstat, his proletarian songs. Such was the spirit of the East Side at that time."

This blend of social radicalism and cultural romanticism not only shaped the awareness of many early leaders of the Jewish unions;* it also helped bring those unions a little closer to the Jewish community than some socialist leaders really desired, since it encouraged a recognition of how deeply the unions were becoming involved in the daily course of immigrant affairs.**

There remains the most fascinating characteristic of the immigrant Jewish workers: that many of them should be simultaneously inflamed with revolutionary ideas and driven by hopes for personal success and middle-class status. Writing about these aspirations for social ascent, Nathan Glazer has remarked that

> the explanation of Jewish success in America is that the Jews, far more than any other immigrant group, [had been] engaged for generations in the middle-class occupations. . . . Now the special occupations of the middle class—trade and the professions—are associated with a whole complex of habits. Primarily, these are the habits of care and foresight. . . . The dominating characteristic of [the middle-class person's] life is that he is able to see that the present postponement of pleasure (saving money is one such postponement) will lead to an increase of satisfaction later. . . . [Jewish workers] were not, like the other workers who immigrated with them, the sons of workers and peasants, with the traditionally limited horizons of those classes. . . . [Their] background meant that the Jewish workers could also immedi-

---

* A more sardonic version of this idea is expressed by a Yiddish journalist reminiscing about his immigrant years: "The East Side waited for the paradise promised by the socialists, and while waiting, it sang the Yiddish songs of Edelstadt, Rosenfeld, and Winchevsky."

** "The position of Jewish labor in the American Jewish community was strange and hard to define. In New York particularly, it was a very important part of the community and yet was, in a way, alien to it; in the 'provinces' (outside of New York) this alienation was even more marked. Jewish labor was an important part of the community because, in the larger centers, it constituted a major section of the Jewish population and set its mark on the emerging American Yiddish culture. But the radicalism of the Jewish labor movement, especially its secularist, anti-religious bias, actually made it a schismatic element in American Jewish life, very much as it had been in earlier days in eastern Europe."

ately turn their minds to ways and means of improving themselves that were quite beyond the imagination of their fellow-workers.

How then was it that these immigrant workers, or at least a good number of them, also became solid unionists and dedicated socialists? In part through the very traits Glazer assigns to the middle class—traits also needed by proletarian unionists and radicals, for whom the postponement of gratifications would come to be a familiar experience. In part because the Jewish immigrants brought with them not merely habits derived from petty trading but also such traditional elements of Jewish experience as messianism, which could be adapted to secular persuasions. And in part because the first shock of encountering America brought a shattering disappointment, especially to the earlier immigrants. Frustration paved the way for new political faiths, as it already had in the old country.

Many immigrants paid no attention, of course, to any programs for radical liberation: they saw their chance in America and they took it. Only a few would remain in accord with the aging Jewish unionist who explains that he was never inclined to set up his own business because "I didn't want to be an exploiter, that's all." But many others yielded themselves to dreams of fulfillment ranging from international socialism to a little business of one's own, from the regathering of the Jews dispersed in *galut* to a professional career for one's son. The fulfillment could be collective, it could be personal—or, as the immigrants felt, why not both? As either descriptive or judgment, the term "middle class" does not even begin to do justice to the shadings and complexities of Jewish desire.

Like no other group in modern history, the immigrant Jewish workers meant to realize the Marxian idea that the task of the working class is its self-abolition. They can hardly be blamed that this did not occur quite according to plan.

The Socialist Upsurge

By 1910 the Jewish socialists had begun to deepen their roots in the East Side, breaking out of their earlier sectarianism and approaching the condition—as well as the problems—of a mass movement. In America itself socialism was on the upsurge, reaching its peak of influence in the years between 1912 and 1916. The Jewish socialists felt themselves to be part of a movement that, in the foreseeable future, could sweep to victory, and in 1908, when Eugene Victor Debs ran as Socialist candidate for president, they organized enormous campaign meetings for him throughout the East Side. His voice trembling with apostolic passion, Debs stirred audiences of tens of thousands at Hamilton Fish Park and then at Rutgers Square, just across from the

Forward building, as he held out the vision of "a new and shining era of human brotherhood."

In their own neighborhoods—the East Side, Harlem, Brownsville—the Jewish Socialists were steadily growing in number (more followers than members), starting to learn the arts of electoral politics, and consolidating their intellectual position, partly through the arrival of writers from Europe and partly through the maturing of spokesmen like Morris Hillquit. Intense and excitable, with a loftiness of spirit that even its opponents envied, the Jewish Socialist milieu gave people a sense of home and of mission. Spurred by the example of their parents or by the eloquence of orators like Panken and London, young sons and daughters of the immigrants would turn "naturally" to the idea of socialism; it became their initiation into the world, for a few the belief to which they would pledge their lives and for most a first inoculating touch of idealism before passing on to other, worldlier affairs.

The Jewish Socialists worked in several arenas. There was the union movement, now starting to provide a major institutional base. There was the network of inner activity: meetings, conferences, committees, lectures, social events, parades, soapboxing, selling literature, all of which brought people together into comradeship yet differed from other Jewish institutional life in that it directed attention beyond itself, outward, toward national affairs and international politics. "One need only go," remarked a gentile visitor, "to a Sunday morning Jewish Socialist Sunday school to get a glimpse of the leaven of socialism that is among all ages of Jewry. There over 100 children spend an hour in singing, and a second hour in classes, eagerly discussing questions as to the relation between the wages John Wanamaker pays his employees and moral goodness." Especially important in this thickening infrastructure of Jewish socialism was the Workmen's Circle, the fraternal society founded earlier in the century, which doubled its New York membership from five to ten thousand in the years between 1905 and 1908 and provided the political activists with financial aid and a "mass base."

Apart from strikes, the most exciting activity open to the Jewish Socialists was the recurrent election campaigns. At first, in orthodox Marxist fashion, they saw such campaigns merely as occasions for propaganda and recruitment, but by about 1910 they began to be lured by the thought of victory. In the electoral campaigns, confined mostly to the Jewish districts but sometimes with darts into adjacent German and Irish neighborhoods, such masters of the soapbox as the booming and indefatigable Jacob Panken reached thousands of listeners. On the East Side a lively street meeting meant an evening's free entertainment and casual enlightenment: it was an important part of neighborhood life. Election by election, the Jewish Socialists became more professional in their methods, providing lists of registered voters in the *Forward*, organizing impromptu leagues of supporters in the unions, arranging torchlight parades, printing literature, and sending their sharpest debaters, like Hillquit, to outwit opponents. Yet, for a good many years, the results of the elections—impressive enough by comparison with later radical efforts—were deeply disappointing to the Jewish Socialists. As one of them wryly observed: "During the campaign weeks the East Side districts rocked with socialist agitation. The Socialist candidates were hailed as Messiahs. The open air meetings were monster demonstrations of public confidence and affection. . . . The marvels of the Socialist strength would grow until the day of the election. Then during the twelve hours between the opening of the polls and their closing, the strength would melt away."

One reason, probably overstated by the Socialists, was the skill and persistence with which Tammany Hall used "repeaters" at the polls, stole votes, and so on. Another reason was the continual movement of Socialists out of the East Side to Brownsville and the Bronx ("as the ships bring the greenhorns, the moving vans take out the radicals"). Still another reason was the feeling among Jewish voters that while it was ennobling to listen to London and Hillquit, they preferred not to "waste" their votes on the Socialists. (A feeling especially strong when there were "reform" candidates or when William Randolph Hearst, the demagogic publisher then in his populist phase, ran for mayor or governor.) And still another reason for Socialist electoral disappointments was that large numbers of immigrants never troubled to become citizens. In 1912 the proportion of registered voters on the East Side was the lowest in the city. A few years earlier the *Forward* was bemoaning the fact that in Jewish electoral districts containing 250,000 people, only 12,000 had voted. "Our Exile has created neglect of bureaucratic formalities. . . . For the same reason American Jews do not take out citizenship papers—who wants to bother with the formalities and the paper work? Peddlers and storekeepers have to be citizens in order to obtain licenses, and they don't want to start up with Tammany." But the immigrant workers, especially those whom Hillquit called "ready-made Socialists" from Poland and Russia, were less inclined to observe such bourgeois legalities as citizenship. An old-timer remarks in his memoirs: "I know of one great Socialist propagandist who was in America thirty years before he became a citizen." There were others.

The major reason for electoral disappointment, however, was one that Jewish Socialists were reluctant to confront: the movement in New York was predominantly Jewish in composition and leadership, with only a few pockets of Irish, German, and native American members. The very successes of the Jewish Socialists in their own districts underscored their difficulty in reaching apathetic or hostile gentiles and brought home a realization that victories won within a minority subculture had only a limited value for advancing the Socialist cause. Had the Socialists been able to register support in other parts of New York to the extent that they could in the East Side or Brownsville, that might well have triggered a multiplying effect among the Jewish voters. As it was, potential supporters in the Jewish neighborhoods must have turned away from Hillquit and London out of a persuasion that socialism was still mostly a Jewish tempest in a Jewish teacup, both tempest and teacup rather small. And for the Socialists themselves, it raised the deeply troubling question of why they could not penetrate other ethnic groups with the degree of success they were beginning to show among the Jews.

In the Ninth Congressional District, which covered the heart of the East Side, the Socialists kept increasing their strength, almost from election to election. In 1904 their vote came to 21 percent. In 1906, when Morris Hillquit ran for Congress in the Ninth, he polled 26 percent. In 1908 the party put on a major effort, again nominating Hillquit. Distinguished outsiders, like William Dean Howells and Charles Edward Russell, endorsed the Socialist ticket; during the peak of the campaign there were an average of 25 street meetings a night on the East Side; Big Tim Sullivan's Tammany machine seemed genuinely alarmed. Yet, when the results were in, Hillquit ran a poor second behind Tammany's Henry Goldfogle, the Socialist vote having declined from 26 to 21 percent.

All the previously cited reasons for electoral disappointment were discussed by the Jewish Socialists, but there is one additional factor that needs examining, though at the time it was not often faced with candor. Once it began to seem possible that in a three- or four-sided race the Socialist candidate in the Ninth might win by polling about 40 percent of the vote, the temptation naturally arose to pick up some extra votes through campaign appeals that the more intransigent comrades would regard as not "strictly Socialist." For some, such appeals seemed the rankest opportunism. But those Socialists who responded to the problems and feelings of their district not just as Socialists but also as immigrant Jews, honestly believed that to campaign in the Ninth with the mere abstract slogans of socialism was utterly insufficient. It showed an insensitivity to the life of the Jews, it signified a doctrinaire narrowness in one's conception of politics.

The old problem of the relation between socialist principles and Jewish sensibilities, which had troubled the East Side a decade or two earlier, was now reappearing in a new and heightened way. To what extent was it intellectually honest and politically appropriate to appeal to Jewish interests that "went beyond" or "left behind" class divisions? There was, for example, the endlessly troubling matter of immigration. There was the extremely sensitive issue of Jewish pride, which had been wounded by Police Commissioner Bingham's attack (see p. 134) and which could be rubbed the wrong way when radicals kept harping on the social evils of the East Side.

Hillquit tended to emphasize a purist approach. He had no strong feelings, or none he showed in public, for Yiddish as culture or language; he was a cosmopolitan, not in the narrow-spirited way of those earlier radicals who had exhausted themselves attacking religion, but in the sense that he cared mainly about establishing a nationwide American movement. At a 1908 rally, he spoke with candor: "The interests of the workingmen of the Ninth

District are entirely identical with those of the workingmen of the rest of the country, and if elected to Congress, I will not consider myself the special representative of the alleged special interests of this district, but the representative of the Socialist Party and the interests of the working class."

But was it really self-evident that the interests of workers in the Ninth were "entirely identical" with those of workers in the rest of the country? On some issues, like the crucial one of immigration, a strong case could be made for the opposite view. Hillquit was clearly distinguishing himself from those comrades who wished to give electoral acknowledgment to "the alleged special interests" of the East Side, and his opponents, both on the right and the left, quickly grasped his point. For as one historian has remarked, the Jewish Socialist movement was unique on the East Side in "preaching . . . concern for issues transcending the ethnic group."

Hillquit's opponents handled him roughly. The *Varheit,* a Yiddish daily edited by ex-Socialist Louis Miller, kept asking where Hillquit had been during the 1903–1904 protests against the Kishinev pogrom. (Miller had in mind a statement of the New York Socialist party, shortly after the pogrom, warning its members not to be swept away by "Jewish nationalism.") The conservative *Tageblatt* wrote that "Hillquit belongs to those who hide their Jewish identity . . . who crawl after the *goyim.* . . . He supported closing the door of the land of freedom to those who like himself wished to find a home in America." Such thrusts were wounding, with the *Varheit* further damaging Hillquit by reprinting attacks from the left, some by Bundists and some by Daniel De Leon, the polemicist of the Socialist Labor party.

That Hillquit was seriously concerned with trying to maintain good relations betweeen American Socialists and the trade unions (without which, he believed, it would be impossible to build a significant Socialist movement in America); that he had Asiatic immigration in mind when he wrote that he opposed immigration of workers from backward countries "who are incapable of assimilation with the workingmen of the country of their adoption"—such facts, whether mitigating or not, helped him little. For "the Jewish quarter insisted on an unqualified stand for unrestricted immigration. As a spokesman for American Socialism, Hillquit could not meet this sectional demand. He spoke with the circumspection of a presidential nominee and not with the regional partiality expected of a Congressional candidate." Neither Goldfogle, the Tammany man, nor De Leon, high priest of the sectarian left, needed to worry about such problems.

Whether by plan, intuition, or a little of both, the Jewish Socialists began to bend to the sentiments of the East Side. In 1910 they nominated for Congress Meyer London, like Hillquit a veteran comrade and lawyer for the garment unions but also more deeply placed in the immigrant milieu. If Hillquit had no choice but to become entangled with complications of national politics, London, a supporter of unrestricted immigration, spoke to the immediate sentiments of his community.

Running far ahead of the other Socialist candidates, London brought the congressional vote up to 33 percent. The left wing of the party charged that campaigners had urged the East Side to "split for London," thereby abandoning the other Socialist candidates, and Louis Boudin, a theoretician of the left, wrote bitterly that "racial and subracial prejudices of voters were appealed to. The Russian Jews were appealed to because Comrade London was also a Russian Jew." For Boudin this was prima facie a betrayal of principles; in the eyes of the London supporters, an overdue acknowledgment of the legitimacy of ethnic demands. ·

Running again in 1912, London did almost as well, with 31 percent of the vote. The portents were clearly good, since this was the year of Theodore Roosevelt's Progressive party, and its candidate for Congress in the Ninth, the respected social worker Henry Moskowitz, won 22 percent of the vote, at least a portion of which could be expected to go Socialist the next time.

Apparently it did. In 1914, with the now-strengthened garment unions plunging into the campaign, London brought his vote up to 47 percent (just under six thousand votes) and won the election. That election night there occurred one of those emotional outpourings which seems to have been a profound need of East Side, perhaps of all Jewish, life. Crowds started gathering at dusk on Rutgers Square, facing the *Forward* building; at two in the morning, recalls an old Socialist,

> Tammany leaders conceded London's election. Joy broke out among the assembled mass. Men sang and danced. . . . London was brought to the square at four in the morning to head an impromptu demonstration. The writer still remembers the march over the streets at early dawn; M. Zametkin [a venerable comrade] speaking from the balcony of the *Forward*, lifting his hands to the rising sun, exclaiming, "Perhaps the sun will shine on the East Side from now on."

The following Sunday the Socialists held an overflow celebration at Madison Square Garden, and London spoke simply and modestly: "I do not expect to work wonders in Congress. I shall, however, say a new word and I shall accomplish one thing that is not in the platform of the Socialist Party. I hope that my presence will represent an entirely different type of Jew from the kind that Congress is accustomed to see." It was, in good part, for this last remark that the East Side had chosen Meyer London.

Meyer London (1871–1927) and Morris Hillquit (1869–1933) were the best, morally and intellectually, that Jewish Socialism had to offer. Both were born in eastern Europe, and both came to America in their late teens, gifted youngsters who turned spontaneously to the radicalism of the East Side. London, whose father ran an unprofitable anarchist print shop, tutored pupils in order to get himself through high school and then, in 1896, NYU law school. Hillquit, whose family was squeezed into a two-room apartment on Clinton Street, worked for a few months as a shirtmaker but proved too frail for factory life; he then spent some time as a four-dollar-a-week clerk in the Socialist Labor party office and as a contributor to the Yiddish radical press before also entering law school. London trained himself through English-language amateur debates at the Educational Alliance, Hillquit through nighttime political discussions in Yiddish, Russian, and English on the roofs of Cherry Street. Both were enthralled by an idea, but in temperament and style they expressed, almost too neatly, variant possibilities open to young radicals at the turn of the century.

London never left home. He lived his entire life on the East Side, a man neither quite of the people nor apart from the people; he belonged to that small group of immigrant professionals still closely tied to the working-class milieu, men and women with strong cultural inclinations but not, in a narrow sense, intellectuals. London's strongest feelings were stirred by the ordinary—he might have said extraordinary—workers who pioneered in forming the Jewish unions. For them he served as advocate, adviser, and, sometimes, informal loan agency; labor people loved to tell stories about his generosity in donating services and refusing fees. A modest man, quite without the flamboyance or falsities of an earlier figure like Barondess, he lived austerely, sometimes simply closing his law office in order to work for the cause. He was the respected tribune of the East Side plebs, sharing their values and never, apparently, tempted to leave them for more attractive quarters. His daughter has remembered a family atmosphere that could have been found in other immigrant homes as well:

> The lack of money never affected me, largely, I believe now, because nobody we lived among had any more than we did. . . . Our traditions did not include money as a problem to be discussed. . . . I don't recollect [London] buying me toys, but we did talk about books a good deal. There wasn't much buying of anything; there was a good deal of improvisation, but my childhood was a very happy one.

And what a leader of the fur workers' union has recalled about London during a grim twelve-week strike in 1912 could have been said over and over again by everyone else in the Jewish labor movement:

> London battled and suffered with us. I shall never forget one little incident that occurred during the fourth week of the strike. We came to London with our usual tale of woe, told him of the desperate plight of the strikers' families. On the table near him were lying an unpaid gas bill for about $18 and a pass book from a bank. London picked up the book . . . consulted his check stubs. Then he remarked that his bank balance was $35, made out a check for the sum and gave it to us.

London had little to offer as a socialist thinker, but as an example of socialist man, a great deal. Though not a Yiddishist—he did his public speaking in English, with a strong accent and without the bearish melodrama affected by some of his comrades—London lived in essential moral harmony with his milieu. He was rewarded three times, in 1914, 1916, and 1920, with election to Congress, not (as some historians would later suggest) despite his socialism, but because, in the eyes of the immigrant masses, he was uniquely *their* socialist and consequently something other or more than a socialist.

Hillquit, in approach more reflective, in temperament more withdrawn, in style more cosmopolitan, chose a role difficult, perhaps impossible, to fulfill in the circumstances of American life. While maintaining as his political base the Jewish districts of New York and working as closely with the garment unions as London did, he also became the main intellectual guide of American socialism. Regarding himself as a Marxist in the tradition of Karl Kautsky and the German Social Democrats, he soberly tried to steer his party into the American mainstream, between the extremes of antipolitical syndicalism and incoherent reform which have always threatened American socialism. Whenever it was necessary to put forward a spokesman in public debate, whether against Samuel Gompers of the AFL or Bill Haywood of the IWW or any number of intellectuals who volunteered to defend capitalism, Hillquit was usually his party's choice. He spoke with lucidity, argued cogently, and kept to a stance of civilized discourse; he also learned to write English well, though with a certain Victorian stiffness. If not an original thinker, he became a figure of intellectual force.

More complex than London, Hillquit was given to sardonic moments and uneasy reflections, troubled by the embarrassments of reconciling his career as highly paid lawyer with his vocation as Socialist spokesman, and inclined to retreat from his comrades into a shell of personal cultivation. London was a natural leader, though in a confined constituency; Hillquit, a highly developed political man who would have made a first-rate European parliamentary spokesman but in America had no proper outlet. London fulfilled himself by staying within his culture, but thereby shrinking the terms of his fulfillment; Hillquit suffered frustration by confronting the problems of connecting Jewish socialism with American politics, but thereby gained in breadth of perspective.

The First World War put both men to a harsh test. Many, probably most, American socialists were shocked by the collapse of the European movement before the power of nationalism: the European Socialists, who had kept saying that an imperialist war would be met with a general strike, now rushed to vote war credits for their warring governments. The Hillquit leadership in America, however, proposed to remain loyal to the traditional Socialist view on the war. In April 1917 Hillquit wrote his party's famous Saint Louis Declaration, pledging continued opposition: "We call upon the workers of all countries to refuse support to their governments in their wars. . . . As against the false doctrine of national patriotism we uphold the ideal of international working class solidarity. . . ."

Courageous and principled, Hillquit's stand nonetheless brought down upon his party mounting governmental wrath and occasional mob attacks.

The solitary Socialist in Congress—and from a Jewish district, at that—

London faced a lonely task. He bore himself with dignity and judiciousness, he worked hard at preparing his speeches, he won the respect of the more serious Congressmen. This was, indeed, "an entirely different type of Jew from the kind that Congress is accustomed to see." He introduced bills against child labor and for minimum wages and unemployment insurance—"wild socialist schemes" sidetracked in committee. "I remember," said London, "when I made my first speech, one of the most extreme of the Republicans made his way across the House and peered into my face as if to discover what kind of a weird creature from some other world had found its way to this planet."

Though convinced that Hillquit's Saint Louis Declaration was too extreme, London did his best to oppose the gradual American drift into the war, arguing against "preparedness" and urging the United States to mediate between the warring sides in Europe. No one in Washington listened. Once the United States entered the war, he felt it wrong to impede its military measures, even by the symbolism of a vote. He therefore voted "present" (a way of abstaining) on a measure for issuing war bonds and on a war-appropriations bill—for which the left wing of the Socialist party would never forgive him. In 1916 the Brooklyn branch had already decided not to circulate London's congressional speeches on the ground that he was fudging the party's antiwar stand; now, in 1917, Ludwig Lore, a left-wing spokesman, charged that London was deliberately neglecting "every opportunity of manifesting serious opposition to war, in direct violation of our Saint Louis program."

Under the multiplying pressures of the war years, London's political base began to crack. Feelings on the East Side grew inflamed: some found him too antiwar, others not enough so; some thought him a fanatic, others a temporizer. In 1918 the Labor Zionists, who until then had supported London, turned against him because he evaded their request to introduce a congressional resolution supporting the Balfour Declaration recognizing the right to a Jewish national home in Palestine. Answering the Labor Zionists, London rehearsed the standard socialist arguments, including a warning against "forcible annexation" of Arab properties. In his own quiet way, London was a stubborn man who proposed to act in accord with his convictions even if that meant displeasing political allies.

Attacked on all sides, from right and left, in the press, in Congress, in his own party, London was no longer the adored tribune of a coherent community. In 1918 he failed to be re-elected, losing by a few hundred votes. Two years later he ran and won, for the last time; but by then, with the devastating split in the Socialist party, which prepared the way for a Communist movement in the United States, his victory was at least as much personal as political. In 1922 a gerrymandering of the Ninth District and the banding together of Republicans and Democrats behind a single candidate insured London's defeat. He never ran again.

In June 1927, while crossing Second Avenue, London was struck by a taxi and fatally injured. His coat pocket, as he lay dying, held a copy of Chekhov's short stories.

After London's congressional victories in 1914 and 1916 there occurred one last and overwhelming upsurge of immigrant Jewish socialism. In the mayoralty campaign of 1917 Hillquit pulled together the hopes of East Side radicalism, bringing it to a high pitch of ecstasy, perhaps delusion; he drew as well, though not nearly as much, upon the unpolitical antiwar sentiments of the Irish and Germans. The campaign meetings were enormous; thousands of East Siders, belonging to no party, worked as volunteers for Hillquit; and even he, usually so restrained, was shaken by the enthusiasm.

> One evening [he wrote] I was to speak at three meetings in the East Side. A gigantic parade was formed spontaneously. The whole East Side seemed to be on its feet, and for three hours countless thousands of men and women surged and swarmed through miles of streets before and after the car in which I made my laborious progress from one hall to another. They sang and shouted and cheered, and their numbers swelled incessantly. It was a touching scene never to be forgotten.

The magnitude of Hillquit's campaign set into motion a backlash among New York's Jews, some of whom, newly prosperous and respectable, were afraid that Jews would be smeared as radicals and war "shirkers." As seldom before, the East Side was polarized into hostile camps. A great deal was now at stake in politics; one's ideology signified more than the luxury of "taking a position." Obliquely but sharply the whole question of immigrant relations with American society was being fought out in the campaign.

Joseph Barondess, now supporting the Republican candidate, led an attack on his old comrade: "Every cheer we give to those [like Hillquit] who are betraying the government is a betrayal of our sons in the camps." Louis Marshall, usually a sober man, wrote that he was "alarmed at the thought that the Jews of New York, by supporting Hillquit's policies [which Marshall described as favoring 'a premature peace'] shall be charged by the American people . . . with virtual treason and sedition." Samuel Untermeyer, a lawyer associated with Tammany Hall, struck the same note: "The Jews are generally regarded as the backbone of the Socialist party in this city. With your aid, this sedition appeal will die the death it deserves. If, with your aid, it should succeed, the responsibility and shame will be yours." And the New York *Times*, in a touch of nastiness, wrote: "It is a singular genius of Mr. Hillquit that he seeks at once to betray the land of his birth and the land of his adoption."

What all such appeals shared was not an effort to prove the Socialists mistaken but the threat that a Socialist victory would be used against the Jews; or, more bluntly, that Jews should not permit themselves to hold unpopular opinions because that would unleash anti-Semitism. Replies came from several directions. A conservative English-language journal, the *American Hebrew*, attacked "the shortsighted policy of making the Jew the scapegoat for all radical movements." The *American Jewish Chronicle*, another English-language paper, charged that the Jewish leaders promoting the fight against Hillquit were themselves "the authors of the talk about a Jewish vote," and asked, "Why must we Jews always be under the spell of what gentiles will say?" Most biting of all was the *Forward* in an article entitled "Be Afraid and Be Hypocrites!":

> A Jewish multimillionaire in today's free, proud, democratic America comes and tells us to be afraid, to conceal our feelings, not to do what we consider decent and honest. . . . We should not vote, he says, for the man we love and respect and trust but for the others who don't give a damn for the people. . . . If you Jews [he tells us] are true to yourselves, America will hate you.
>
> From what medieval cellar come these words? From what terrified, broken Jew, with wobbly knees and bent back? Is this the voice of an old-time innkeeper who kissed the whip with which the Polish nobleman slashed him across the face? No, it is the voice of an American Jewish millionaire. . . .
>
> The most loathsome aspect of the whole business is that they are not trying to persuade us, they are playing upon our fear. They do not really believe in America or its democracy.

Once the vote was in, it became clear that both Socialist expectations and anti-Socialist anxieties had been excessive. Hillquit polled a very impressive total of 145,332, an increase of nearly 500 percent over the last Socialist candidate for mayor; 22 percent of the city's voters (31 percent in the Bronx) supported him. But this was still far from the electoral victory that people had been talking about. In the three assembly districts containing the bulk of East Side voters, Hillquit gained 11,911 out of 22,299 votes, a clear majority (but also indicative of how small the immigrant Jewish vote still was). A breakdown of city-wide returns by later scholars has indicated that Hillquit's vote was not simply "a Jewish vote"; clearly, however, his strongest electoral support and the bulk of his active workers came from the immigrant Jewish community as it now spread out from the East Side into a number of satellite neighborhoods in Manhattan, the Bronx, and Brooklyn.

The Jewish Socialists had reason for celebration: they elected, in "their" districts, ten state assemblymen and seven city aldermen, as well as a municipal court justice. It seemed, not only to them, that they were on the way to becoming the second party in New York City (there had also been large Socialist gains elsewhere in the country). But that, of course, was not to be. Harsh internal splits, a repressive national atmosphere in the early twenties (reflected in the expulsion of several Socialists from the New York State Legislature in 1920), and a distinct improvement in economic conditions, especially for the Jewish immigrants—these were among the reasons for a reversal of political fortunes.

The Meaning of Jewish Socialism

From the distance of half a century—and at a moment when our controlling assumptions seem radically at variance with those of Meyer London and Morris Hillquit—what are we to make of immigrant Jewish socialism?

To a few elderly survivors it may still seem like a golden time of hope and fervor. For their sons and daughters it can often evoke a glow of warmth, sometimes framed in condescension: the struggles and dreams of the past are done with forever, yet those were really wonderful days. . . . Such feelings have found a sophisticated analogue in the theories of a number of historians who have written about the radicalism of the immigrant Jews.

The objective function of the Jewish Socialist movement, argue these writers, was to acclimatize the immigrants to American life. This was neither the intent of the Jewish radicals nor a judgment they could be expected to welcome; nevertheless, during the first two decades of the century Jewish socialism in America was primarily a vehicle of "transition and acculturation." It built up the morale of the Jewish workers, enabling them to move into American society; it helped integrate them "into American political life" by providing, through the unions, "a laboratory and training-ground of collective self-government." These ends achieved, it was then all but inevitable that the radicalism of the immigrant Jews should fade away.*

Clearly, there is a portion of truth to this view of Jewish unionism and socialism. The garment unions were, in fact, becoming deradicalized even as they kept using socialist rhetoric; a good many Jewish Socialists were, in fact, being absorbed into communal and labor organizations as their fervor cooled and their ideas changed. For many immigrant and even American-born Jews, their stay in the Socialist movement served as a kind of prep school for later careers. At a Socialist branch meeting you learned how to make a motion conforming with *Robert's Rules of Order*—which gave you an advantage over most workers in your union. At a YPSL (Young People's Socialist League) meeting you learned how to make a speech, even if sometimes a bombastic one—which gave you an indispensable skill for becoming

---

* This approach to Jewish socialism is most thoroughly developed in Will Herberg's essay on the American Jewish labor movement; it appears obliquely in Daniel Bell's history of American socialism; and a cruder version can be found in Benjamin Stolberg's book on the ILGWU ("the garment workers were Americanized in the melting pot of their own union, which burned out the many isms and in the end produced an essentially progressive trade unionism").

an official of some communal agency or a business agent of a union. At a meeting of a Socialist faction you learned how to "theorize," or at least mimic the posture of theory—which gave you a certain facility when you went on to college and became a sociologist or an English professor.

Stressing articulateness, rapidity, coherence, generalization, the Socialist milieu provided skills that in later, more "realistic" years could be put to worldly advantage. That was true, of course, for every Socialist movement throughout the world, but all the more so for the Jewish movement in America, where political training enabled careers venturing not only upward, in status, but also outward, beyond the ghetto.

It was not an inexorable process. Individuals could cling to old convictions even while escaping the social milieu that had helped form them. Some "of the most fervent Socialist agitators soon became doctors, lawyers, and teachers, but as a rule, they did not sever their connections with the radical or labor movements out of which they had come." But the organizations of Jewish labor had less leeway: they found that, if they were to survive, certain adaptations to American circumstances were essential. Unions had to accept the rules of collective bargaining within capitalist society; they sometimes had to help small employers stay in business so as to insure jobs for their members; and they had to deal with unsavory politicians if they wished to protect themselves.

Nor was the process of adaptation entirely one-sided. "In the course of winning a better place in our society, those who became the nation's tailors developed a fresh view of the functions of a trade union," so that in time they exerted a transforming influence upon the American labor movement. For decades a minority, sometimes a scorned minority, within the American labor movement, the Jewish unions contributed heavily to the transformation of American unionism which began in the 1930's. The Jewish Socialists, though failing to build a durable mass movement, brought to public attention a cluster of social proposals that would be debated and fought over for decades, some later to be enacted as domestic policy.

Still, the fact remains: it was the Jewish unions and the Jewish Socialists that had to do most of the adapting, it was they that had to modulate their earlier political ideas as they found themselves gradually being absorbed into American society.

Yet, for all its pertinence and shrewdness, this approach to immigrant Jewish socialism betrays the bias of a later moment, the tendency of ex-radical historians to dissolve the Jewish radical experience in the acids of retrospection. They assume what remains, or ought to remain, an open question: that the course of adaptation from the "excesses" of Jewish socialism to liberal moderation or even conservative comfort was entirely desirable, a token of what is called "maturing." They treat immigrant Jewish radicalism in a manner oddly similar to that in which the immigrant Jewish radicals used to treat religion. Jewish socialism becomes a colorful trauma in the process of adjustment, to be stored in the attic of memory, just as religion had been dismissed as a mere sublimated version of unfulfilled historical yearnings or a mere social agency holding in check oppressed masses. In both cases, the explanation explains away too much too easily. The historians refuse to confront Jewish radicalism in its own right, even as they make shrewd remarks about its unanticipated role; the Jewish radicals, in similar fashion, refused to confront religion in its own right, even as they made shrewd remarks about its unacknowledged uses.

But while there is no reason whatever to take Jewish socialism at its own valuation, there is good reason for confronting it on its own terms. Whatever undesired or alien functions it came to serve, Jewish socialism was primarily a political movement dedicated to building a new society. It was part of a great international upsurge that began in the nineteenth and has continued into the twentieth century; and while there were, of course, distinctive traits in Jewish socialism testifying to a unique historical background, there were also many ideas and values shared with the other socialist movements of the world. Had the Jews, upon entering modern history, not participated in this movement, that would have perhaps required more of a special explanation than the fact that some of them did. Sharing the program of international socialism, the Jewish socialists largely shared its fate. There is a simple, perhaps decisive sense in which Jewish socialism can be said to have failed, quite as American or French socialism failed: it did not lead to the creation of a new society in which all men would live without want, in freedom and fulfillment. But just as international socialism helped to transform the consciousness of humanity, so did Jewish socialism transform the consciousness of the Jews. International socialism placed upon the historical agenda the idea of human liberation; it brought to unprecedented intensity the vision of a secular utopia; it enabled masses of previously mute workers to enter the arena of history. Jewish socialism (and Zionism also) transformed the posture of Jewish life, creating a new type of person: combative, worldly, spirited, and intent upon sharing the future of industrial society with the rest of the world.

To see Jewish socialism, then, as mostly an episode in the adjustment of immigrants to American society is to deny it the dignity of its historical range and ambition—even the dignity of its failure. It is to assume that the yearnings that gave rise to Jewish socialism have been more or less satisfied; it is to assume that not only were some adaptations of the Jewish Socialists to American society unavoidable but that most of them were desirable. There is, however, another possibility. In bending when it had to, Jewish socialism may have bent more than it had to. In yielding to American ways, it may have lost some essential strength of vision.

We have no reason to suppose that there will occur a revival of Jewish socialism in quite the forms it took during the first few decades of the century, any more than we have reason to suppose there will occur a similar revival of American socialism. But abiding needs and desires can take new expression. Has American society shown itself to be so splendid and so solicitous of its members that the views of the Jewish Socialists no longer retain an edge of truth? Are the adjustments and adaptations of their later years, made at some expense of earlier vision, to be seen as an unqualified good? Were all the hopes and ideas of the immigrant radicals mere soft-hearted delusions?

Perhaps so. Yet if Jewish socialism had to yield some of its intransigence before American society, American society still has something to learn from Jewish socialism.

CHAPTER TEN

Breakup of the Left

F OR MOST American Socialists, and particularly the Jewish ones, the two Russian revolutions of 1917—February, overthrowing the czar, and October, establishing Bolshevik rule—seemed proof that the moment had come when the proletariat would take power throughout Europe.

The whole of immigrant Jewry welcomed the February Revolution: an end to the hated czars and government-arranged pogroms! With the October Revolution all the talk of the radicals, everything that must sometimes have seemed elusive to even the most sanguine among them, took on the strength of reality. That a working-class state could be proclaimed in the most backward country of Europe, that the Lenin who had yesterday been a mere émigré in Switzerland should today command the palace of the czars: this seemed radiant evidence that the victory of socialism was at hand.

Until the formation of the Communist International in 1919, and for a while afterward, there was hardly a radical in America who did not support the Bolshevik revolution, though some had begun to dissociate themselves from Bolshevik theories. One reason was that for a time hardly anyone in America really knew what was happening in Russia, most reports in the press being so drenched with malice as to discredit the possibility of serious criticism. Once, however, John Reed started filling the pages of the *Liberator* with his brilliant narrative about "ten days that shook the world"—an account of the Bolshevik revolution with the imperial simplicities of myth—then the American radicals could find a source of guidance and inspiration: *this is how it happened, this is how it's done.*

In the Yiddish press, by contrast, there was at first a strain of skepticism toward the Bolsheviks. The *Tageblatt* hewed to its conservative line: "A strong government based on law and order will not be established in Russia until the Bolsheviks have failed." The socialist *Forward,* uncertain in its view of the Bolsheviks, printed an editorial on November 17, 1917, favoring a coalition of all the Russian Socialist parties, a proposal Lenin had already dismissed. The next day the *Forward* ran a pugnacious article by Moissaye Olgin, then an anti-Leninist but later to become the main Yiddish spokesman for Stalinism. Lenin, wrote Olgin, "is a master at devising slogans for uninformed masses. . . . But when it comes to governing a powerful state or being responsible for improving the life of millions, he may not be so keen." It was only after the Bolsheviks had consolidated their power and begun to cast their voices across the whole of Europe that the Jewish left in America largely abandoned, at least for a few years, its impulse to criticism.

Among the more radical immigrants there now arose a movement to return to Russia: it brought together motifs of nostalgia, political romanticism, and disillusionment with America. Between 1917 and 1920, some 21,000 people left the United States who declared themselves to be "Hebrews" and "Russians": 3,760 of the former and 17,355 of the latter, though we can safely assume that a good many of the "Russians" were also Jewish.

> A Chicago Yiddish daily published a poem in which the author thus expressed his feelings about new Russia: "Forgive me, I did not know you,/I was afraid of you, because of the Czar's crown on your head. . . . I have escaped from you/ to a strange land over the sea." The Socialist *Forward*'s manager, Baruch C. Vladeck, wrote: "Life is strange: my body is in America. My heart and soul and life are in that great wonderful land, which was so cursed and is now so blessed, the land of my youth and revived dreams—Russia."

Especially in the months between the fall of the czar and the rise of the Bolsheviks to power, the East Side was caught up in heady sensations of political fervor. On July 9, 1917, thousands came to a demonstration in front of the Henry Street Settlement, at which the new Russian ambassador, M. Bachmatiev, spoke: "I salute you in the name of my sisters who were tortured in Russia; of brothers who were tortured in Siberia; and of my dead father, whose eyes were burned out in a pogrom." With unusual lyricism, Abraham Cahan wrote that Yiddish culture in America would now enter a higher phase through interchange with the newly liberated Russian. In May 1917 a group of about a hundred, calling themselves the "Former Prisoners," left New York to return to revolutionary Russian via Japan and Siberia. It was a moment of great expectations and only a few sober voices:

When New York Jews found out about the Russian Revolution [wrote A. Litwin in the *Forward* on May 4, 1917] they were exuberant. . . . We would all leave America and fly to Russia, and Jewish New York would be emptied out; East Broadway and Harlem and the Bronx would be covered with grass, as they were fifty years ago when the first Litvaks [Lithuanian Jews] set foot in America. But we are sobering up and realizing that Jews in America are here to stay. I talked with lots of people; only a few thousand can and will leave immediately. Most of these are greenhorns who can't assimilate, *luftmenshn* drifting between the United States and Russia and always ready to move. The majority of the two million Russian Jews in America have struck roots and will remain. They have hundreds of cemeteries here, where their relatives are buried. Those with children born here will remain. And economic ties are strong.

Those few who dared express doubts about Bolshevism had a rough time of it, especially at Jewish meetings. Emotions of revolutionary fraternity seized the left-wing public, so much so that even the usually prudent Hillquit was swept along. "The Socialist picture from 1917 to 1921," notes Daniel Bell, "is not a simple one of 'left' vs. 'right,' but a *complete* shift of the entire socialist movement to a frame of reference completely outside the structure of American life." In a book Hillquit published in 1921, *From Marx to Lenin*, there is some criticism of the Communist International as "essentially Russian in structure, concept and program," but far more noteworthy was his endorsement of "the dictatorship of the proletariat" as a form of power compatible with democracy. If this reflected a desire by Socialist spokesmen to keep the favor of their leftward-swinging constituency, it is also true that the leaders were themselves caught up in the same enthusiasms.

Inevitably there sprang up a left wing in American Socialism hoping to transform itself into a Communist party, and inevitably this left wing found adherents in the Jewish quarter. With their major source of inspiration the political turmoil of Europe, the left wingers succumbed to a sectarian outlook utterly out of rhythm with American events. Through a series of splits and splits within splits, often ugly, sometimes bizarre, there gradually emerged the feeble beginnings of American Communism.*

At first it seemed that the Jewish Socialist Federation (see p. 294) would escape the worst excesses of factionalism, since it was already to the left of the American Socialist party and thereby somewhat less vulnerable to the pull of those urging an immediate split. Some of the Federation leaders also felt that the inner cohesion of the Jewish radical world would make the prospect of a split seem especially disturbing. But there was finally no way of insulating the Jewish left in America from the convulsions of world

---

* A story that need not be repeated here. Narratives detailing it, of varying outlook and reliability, can be found in Melech Epstein, *The Jew and Communism;* Theodore Draper, *The Roots of American Communism;* Daniel Bell, *Marxian Socialism in the United States;* Irving Howe and Lewis Coser, *The American Communist Party.*

socialism. In 1917 a meeting of Manhattan Socialists saw the loose beginnings of a left wing influenced by Leon Trotsky, then a refugee living in New York.* By 1919 the *Forward* was describing the inner situation of the Federation as hopeless: "The majority of the branches are divided into warring camps which refuse to listen to or understand one another. It is impossible to carry on constructive activity. . . . Might not a divided existence be more practical than a forced coexistence?"

Earlier that year a left wing had been formally established in the Federation by five young members of its East Side branch; like all radical factions, they started publishing a paper of their own, the *Kamf*. In May 1919 this small group, led now by Alexander Bittleman, withdrew from the Federation and started its trip into the semiunderground of American Communism. "The young men of this group," scoffed Moissaye Olgin, "live in a little world created in their own imagination where everything is as they like it to be. The workers are united, class conscious, organized and armed. Only one thing remains to be done: begin the final conflict." J. B. Salutsky, the leader of the Federation, wrote with still greater vehemence: "According to the Moscow prescription, the new [Communist] International is to be a religious, fanatical, intolerant sect of *hasidim* adhering to one rabbi only."

So powerful, nonetheless, were the leftward propulsions within Jewish Socialism that precisely leaders like Olgin and Salutsky would be the ones to break the Federation away from the Socialist party. Trying to walk a thin political line—pro-Soviet but critical of Communist parties—the Federation leaders in 1921 declared their organization autonomous, apart from both the Socialist and Communist parties. A minority, consisting mostly of *Forward* people, left to form their own group, the Jewish Socialist Farband, which maintained ties with the Socialist party. It tells us a good deal about the temper of the Jewish left at this time that the Farband's weekly could say as late as 1921: "We are not an organ for attacks on the Russian Bolsheviks. We have the greatest respect for the leaders of the Soviet government." Not until another two years or so did this "respect" come to an end—by 1923 the Farband was sharply anti-Communist and would remain so to the end.

Only a few voices within the Jewish left offered a critique of the now-homeless Federation majority. Philip Krantz, veteran radical of the nineties, denounced it as "a *gilgul* [transmutation] of De Leonism"—not quite accurate, but a sharp thrust. More serious were the warnings of Vladimir Medem, the Bundist leader recently come to the United States, who argued at the Federation's 1921 convention that "the dictatorship of the proletariat"

---

* At this meeting, where "fist fights kept breaking out in the hall as partisans of opposing factions split into little sub-meetings, without benefit of parliamentary procedure to abate their passions," Trotsky was the leader of the extreme left while Hillquit led those who, while against the war, proposed to confine their opposition to "the tradition of American parliamentarism."

 Trotsky would later speak with contempt of immigrant Jewish Socialism, calling Hillquit "a Babbitt of Babbitts . . . the ideal Socialist leader for successful dentists."

must necessarily degenerate into a dictatorship of the ruling party over the proletariat. Only through democracy, Medem insisted, could socialism be fulfilled.*

The Jewish Socialist Federation soon became entangled in negotiations with some of the underground Communists, hoping thereby to establish a revolutionary movement more combative than the Socialists but less doctrinaire than the Communists. These negotiations completed, the most prominent Federation leaders, like Salutsky and Olgin, joined with the Communists in establishing an aboveground organization, the Workers party, in December 1921. For the Communists, the Workers party was a "legal front"; for the Federation people, a venture in good faith. Stricken at the moment of birth, the Workers party did not last long. Salutsky and some of his friends became disillusioned and quit; others returned to the *Forward*, sadder and perhaps a trifle wiser; hundreds drifted out of left-wing politics entirely; and a small group, led by Olgin, became hard-line Communists. In a play on Chekhov's phrase, Olgin explained his political choice: "But I want to go to Moscow!" So in the coming decades would a good many others, Jewish and non-Jewish.

If the number of card-carrying Jewish Communists in the early twenties was small (perhaps fifteen hundred in all the garment unions, for example), their influence in the Jewish labor movement was large. A militant segment of needle-trade workers responded with enthusiasm to the call of Lenin; the majority of left-wing Jewish writers, intellectuals, and speakers faced left; while those who remained with the *Forward* and the Socialist party were mostly the "practical workers," trade-union functionaries, and the like. Among the Jewish radicals who had the perception and courage to criticize the Bolshevik regime were some who, a few years earlier, had gone back to Russia in a flush of enthusiasm. The anarchist leaders Emma Goldman and Alexander Berkman had at first praised the Bolsheviks for "their glorious work," but by June 1921 Emma Goldman was writing from Russia, "I am trying desperately to get out now that I have come to the conclusion that the situation here is utterly hopeless as far as Anarchist activities are concerned." From the red scare in America to the red terror in Russia, they were hounded for their beliefs, and when they came back their accounts of what they had seen in Russia were denounced not only by the Communists but also by many liberals.

Never before, remarked Vladimir Medem sarcastically in 1921,

* In a long-forgotten article published in a 1918 issue of the Warsaw Bundist paper, *Lebns-Fragen*, Medem wrote: "The guns of the conscripted Bolshevik soldiers are directed not only against the bourgeoisie. They are turned against the socialist working class. The day is not far when revolutionary tribunals of the more 'kosher' Bolsheviks will be set up to shoot the more 'suspect' of their own comrades. . . . And if today Lenin yearns to shoot Abramovitch [a Menshevik leader], may he not wish to shoot Trotsky tomorrow?

"A socialist government that turns to the methods of terror signs its own death warrant."

have I seen so many people inclined toward Bolshevism as here in America. And precisely among the affluent, the "alrightniks." If you see a Jew who drives a car, you can be almost certain that he will be chanting Sabbath hymns for Bolshevism. And the better the car, the warmer his "sympathies." . . .

What is lacking [in the American Jewish milieu] is firm socialist will and clear socialist thought. . . . Zionism, communism, anarchism, all are mixed into one pot, and no one knows where one ends and the other begins. Chaos reigns.

In this atmosphere of unsorted enthusiasms there began to emerge the community of Yiddish-speaking Communism.

Civil War in the Garment Center

From the very start it was characteristic of the Jewish Communists that they should be marked by a deep ambivalence toward everything Jewish. They were hostile to religion, Zionism, any "deviation" into Jewish nationalism; they used Yiddish simply because it was the language of the immigrant workers and not out of any principled attachment—or so they said. But they were themselves also immigrants, whose language was Yiddish and whose culture consisted mainly of the very elements of the Jewish tradition they were rejecting. For Jewish radicals this was not a new dilemma, but among the Communists it was driven to an extreme. They declared themselves internationalist, even cosmopolitan, in outlook and concerned mostly with rousing the class consciousness of all workers, yet they could not escape the impulse common to many immigrant Jews of building a hermetic community of their own, one in which the overtones and associations of Yiddish played a far greater part than their ideology allowed. This problem was to plague the Yiddish-speaking Communists for many years, with party functionaries issuing "directives" that Jewish comrades must abandon their provincial ways and plunge into mass work within the American proletariat. All very well; except that it was entirely beyond the reach of most immigrant Jews, Communist or not.* In the early twenties, however, another kind of

---

* "In Norfolk, Virginia, the [Communist] party unit [in the early thirties] is 'a Jewish-speaking one.' A non Jewish member stops coming to meetings because he can't understand what is being said. The Norfolk branch, reports a party functionary, 'has adopted a white chauvinist attitude. . . . The unit members cannot go about the task of organizing the Negro, conscientiously, because . . . they are now in the businesses, exploiting the Negro workers.' No doubt; but might not a little humaneness prompt one to add that these Yiddish-speaking members in Norfolk are old-time Jewish radicals who drifted South in order to earn their livings as tailors and grocerymen?"

"mass work" did come within their reach, and that was the fierce Communist effort to capture the garment unions.

William Z. Foster, a left-wing trade unionist who had led an unsuccessful steel strike the previous year, organized in 1920 the Trade Union Educational League, which was to serve as a focal point for militant unionists in the established labor movement. The early Communists were at first contemptuous of Foster's plan for working within the AFL; but as he drew closer to them politically and became their outstanding public leader, they realized the TUEL could have its uses. Campaigning for industrial unionism, the TUEL picked up considerable support at first, but by 1923 it had narrowed into a Communist agency. An AFL convention of that year denounced it as a dual-union tendency.

One of the few places where the TUEL had real strength was in the garment center of New York. There was a long tradition of "opposition groups" fighting inside the garment unions against the traditional leadership. There were acute economic grievances as a result of the decline of the cloak trade, the spread of the contracting system, and the flight of employers to open-shop towns away from New York. There were internal fissures within the ILGWU leadership which could be exploited. And there were militants, perhaps two thousand of them, belonging to the four main garment unions, who were not members of any Communist group yet followed the Communist line with devotion. During the recent splits a good many of the more energetic younger radicals had turned toward the left; the Communists could now assemble such gifted leaders as Charles Zimmerman and Louis Hyman in the ILGWU and Aaron Gross and Ben Gold in the Fur Workers Union. By the end of 1924 the TUEL had won majorities in the executive boards of three large ILGWU locals in New York and had also made sizable inroads in Boston, Chicago, and Philadelphia. The struggle between left and right grew more brutal and demoralizing each day.*

At the head of the ILGWU stood Morris Sigman, a veteran Jewish unionist who had been an IWW organizer in his youth and still remained a bit of a syndicalist at heart. Ill at ease with the *Forward* crowd, suspicious of all political interference in trade-union affairs, and convinced almost religiously of the virtues of the rank and file, Sigman was an honest man who lived by the pioneer psychology of early Jewish unionism and felt increasingly out of place in these more complex times. At first he was prepared to tolerate the Jewish Communists, hoping they would work as gadflies to sting complacent leaders, but he soon came to see that there was something new about the Communists, very different from all earlier radical "oppositions,"

---

* "Left" and "right" signify Communist and Socialist. But with complications. Some adherents of the "left" regarded themselves not as Communists but merely as militant unionists. On the "right" were not only the Social Democrats of the *Forward* type but nonpolitical business unionists as well as a group of Jewish anarchists, led by Louis Levy, who tried to maintain a position somewhat critical of the Socialists while forming with them a joint front against the Communists.

a rule-or-ruin outlook that would not rest short of total domination. Blunt in his methods, Sigman started to attack the Communist bloc in early 1925. He charged the TUEL leaders with violating the union constitution—specifically, with having arranged a May Day meeting at which the loose-tongued Moissaye Olgin had cried out from the platform, "Long live a Soviet America!" The three locals under TUEL control were suspended and the headquarters of two were seized in the night by Sigman cohorts; but the third, Local 22, repulsed the raid and became a center for the Communist-led opposition.

Contesting the legality of Sigman's action, the suspended locals set up a Joint Action Committee (JAC), which became the directing body for all left-wing work in the garment unions. Its nominal leader, Louis Hyman, was not a CP member but behaved pretty much as if he were; a radical *magid* (preacher), he had a way of endearing himself to union members whenever he got up to speak. The brains of the JAC and probably the most able Communist in the garment unions was Charles Zimmerman.* Led by these gifted men, the JAC kept intensifying the struggle. Scores of young Communists from the colleges, Bronx housewives, and party members from the entire city joined the left-wing garment workers in guarding their headquarters. There was civil war in the garment center, with that peculiar venom which only fratricide can induce.

In the past almost all radicals had shared the premise that factional disputes must not be allowed to go beyond certain limits, but this restraint was now abandoned. Importing "the methods of the class struggle," the Communists fought the old-line union leaders as if Jewish socialism were

---

* Zimmerman, who would break from the CP with the Lovestone group in 1929 and later become a major leader of the ILGWU, is one of the best examples of the self-educated intellectual, a shopworker in his early years, that the Jewish union movement developed. His youthful ambition after arriving in the United States in 1913 was "to study. . . . I didn't have any particular profession in mind, I just wanted to study. I went to night school and then to Manhattan Preparatory School" to gather enough credits for college. "But with the coming of the Russian Revolution things changed. I joined the Socialist party in 1917," and since the revolution seemed at hand, "what was the use of going to school? I became more active in the union and the radical movement."

In 1920 Zimmerman joined the Communist party and attended Sunday-afternoon lectures that a now-forgotten party ideologue named Harry Waton gave on Marxism and, oddly, Spinoza's First Principles. Imbibing these linked fundamentals, Zimmerman also developed larger curiosities. In 1922 he and some friends, all Jewish radicals, "bought a jalopy and started traveling across the country." They worked for a time in the hayfields of Montana and as lumberjacks at Yellowstone Park, meeting with veteran Wobblies (IWW members, for whom Zimmerman felt a sentimental attachment). Having smashed their car, the young East Side radicals hitchhiked up and down the Pacific coast. This trip, which Zimmerman would remember a half century later as "carefree but not aimless," was followed by several years as leader of the Communist group in the ILGWU. Later Zimmerman felt that poking around in the Northwest and along the California coast might have given him a certain insight into American life enabling his break from the Communist movement.

their main enemy. And, as they saw things, perhaps it was. If anything, the Jewish Communists were more ferocious than their gentile comrades, for when Joseph Boruchowitz, the Communsit leader in the cloak union started debating with a *Forvetsnik* (a *Forward* supporter), what erupted was not just a difference of opinion but a seething hatred between men who only yesterday had known one another intimately.

At first the violence was mainly symbolic. Left-wing women would form what their opponents called "fainting brigades"—when a right-wing leader opened a local meeting, these women would pretend to faint, perhaps out of sheer incredulity at what they were hearing, and the result would be a brilliantly contrived chaos. Then there were the "spit brigades," groups of women ostentatiously spitting into the gutter whenever a right-wing union official passed them in the garment center. Childish as all this may seem, it often managed to unnerve its victims, especially those still inclined to think of themselves as socialists who had given their lives to building unions. And in their disdain for civility, the Communists moved from the symbolism of disruption to the actuality of violence. Both sides began using *shtarke* (strong-arm men), first amateurs and then professionals. In the headquarters of the furriers' union, Room C became known as a place where opponents could be roughed up a little. Rarely, if ever, had such methods been seen in the earlier years of Jewish radicalism, and the fact that they were now on the way to becoming commonplace signified a shared moral decline.

Functioning as a union in all but name, the Joint Action Committee collected dues, serviced grievances, negotiated with employers. But since the Communists were still reluctant to embark on a dual-union policy, Zimmerman and Hyman avoided the trap of proclaiming the JAC a separate union. Its main slogan, they took care to stress, was the "full reinstatement" of the left-wing locals.

That the left wing commanded enormous influence among the garment workers in the mid-twenties was admitted even by its enemies; it succeeded, for example, in calling a mass demonstration at Yankee Stadium in July 1925 to which forty thousand cloakmakers and dressmakers came, and it then organized a work stoppage in which thirty thousand workers left the shops and filled seventeen halls to listen to its speakers. A majority of the New York garment workers, certainly a majority of the active ILGWU members, supported the left wing, not necessarily because of its Communist leadership but because they felt—with some reason—that the suspension of the left-wing locals had been undemocratic.

The Sigman leadership was forced to retreat. Resuming negotiations with the left wing, it agreed to reinstate the suspended locals and call a special convention of the ILGWU. When this convention opened in Philadelphia on November 30, 1925, the two sides were about evenly matched, and for a moment it seemed that the largest of the Jewish unions might fall into the lap of the Communists. After fifteen days of wrangling, in which the Communists demanded proportional representation (it would have assured them control, since they represented the larger locals), a convention committee proposed more representation for the big locals but not proportional representation. Zimmerman leaped up to remind the right wing of an earlier informal agreement for a referendum on this issue, but the chairman, David Dubinsky, ruled that no previous arrangement could be binding on a sovereign convention.

A remarkable incident now occurred. Louis Hyman shouted, "Let's walk out," and the entire TUEL group left the hall. This was not, however, a calculated bit of Communist strategy, it was an impulsive act initiated by Hyman. The top Communist steering committee, Ben Gitlow and William Dunne, immediately ordered Hyman to reverse his course—dual unionism was not yet the order of the day. When Hyman refused to lead his delegation back to the convention hall, Dunne told him bluntly, "Then you'll crawl back on your belly!" Bowing to Communist discipline, the TUEL forces returned to the convention that evening.

A compromise was patched up and the right wing kept control of the ILGWU, though by a frail margin. The TUEL continued to gain strength; it soon took over the New York Joint Board, the single most important segment of the union, with Hyman becoming general manager and Zimmerman head of the dressmakers' department. In a short time, it seemed almost certain, the Communists would control the whole ILGWU.

Yet within a year there followed so radical a shift of fortunes that the power of the TUEL was all but shattered. In 1926 the Communist leadership of the New York cloakmakers called a long, violent, and disastrous strike. It grew out of a debate within the ILGWU over the report of a commission appointed by Governor Alfred E. Smith to consider ways of rationalizing the garment industry. So close did this report come in its particulars to earlier ILGWU demands that President Sigman advised accepting it as a basis for negotiations.

The Communist group running the New York locals now faced a crucial choice. Hyman and Zimmerman were not at all enthusiastic about calling a strike, for they realized that the odds against success were high; but behind them pressed the Communist party, actively demanding an immediate strike. This pressure, in turn, was almost entirely the result of a violent faction fight that was then being waged within the party. Neither of the two factions, one led by William Z. Foster and the other by Jay Lovestone, was willing to risk the "onus" of opposing a strike and the accompanying charge of being insufficiently "Bolshevik"; both knew that in actuality a strike would have little chance of victory; but each was more concerned with factional advantage than the future of the union. Out of such unsavory motives, the Communist leadership finally drove its supporters in the ILGWU to call a general strike in the cloak trade on July 1, 1926. The response of the workers was immediate and predictable: the shops were closed.

During the first months of this bitter strike, almost the entire Jewish community supported the cloakmakers, despite the leftist character of their leadership. Had a settlement been negotiated within a reasonable time, the workers would have profited and the Communist leadership in the ILGWU emerged with heightened prestige. But the strike was not settled in time. Hyman and Zimmerman negotiated informally with the employers and by the eighth week of the strike reached what seemed to them favorable terms. Only one barrier remained: approval by the Communist apparatus. And again factional interests proved decisive. Neither the Lovestone nor the Foster group within the party was willing to endorse a settlement that, in the eyes of Moscow, might make it seem pusillanimous. The party there-upon ordered its people in the union to reject the proposed terms of settle-ment—a decision for which the cloakmakers paid heavily. Yet their ranks held firm: no group of Jewish workers had a longer experience in strike discipline than the cloakmakers.

Finally, on December 13, the International suspended the left-wing New York leadership and settled the strike as best it could. Prolonged for six months and costing $3,500,000, it had brought misery to thousands of workers, mostly because their leaders were subject to an external political decision. It would take the ILGWU years to recover from this shattering defeat.

The Yiddish-speaking Communists continued to offer battle within the union, issuing "bonds" in a campaign to reinstate their leaders and raising $150,000 from sympathizers. But their moment had passed. They had held the fate of thousands of workers in their hands and had treated them with gross irresponsibility. The cloakmakers gradually drifted back to the old-line leadership; the "bonds" were never redeemed. Though they could still launch punitive guerrilla raids, the Communists would never again be in a position to take control of the union. In the shops and on the streets fist fights, sometimes with knives and blackjacks too, continued to break out regularly.

Not only was the struggle within the Jewish unions organizationally damaging, it was an experience that brutalized everyone involved. All par-ticipants were stained, right and left. The ethos of Jewish socialism would never again have the moral glow of its earlier years. In the whole immigrant Jewish experience there was probably nothing to match the civil war in the garment center for sheer ugliness.

One major reason for the success of the Communists in gaining support among garment workers was that a good part of the traditional leadership—socialist, nominally socialist, ex-socialist, or nonpolitical—had been losing its spiritual élan. "There was much in the union—ancient abuses, narrow-visioned, overcautious policies, undemocratic structures and practices—against which 'idealistic' members might revolt." That unions, like all other organizations, should become bureaucratized may be inevitable, and not even the most idealistic leadership can prevent this merely through an exercise of will. A vigorous opposition, acting in good faith and loyal first of all to the members, would have done the ILGWU a world of good. The possibility of such an opposition, however, was foreclosed by the Communists, with the result a hardening of bureaucratic arteries in the right-wing leadership.

A veteran of Jewish Communism, later supporter of the right wing, has left a picture of how a bureaucratic "machine" could grow up in a union local:

> A machine was built primarily by placing supporters in the best shops or by satisfying their craving for prestige. As voluntary [union] work was now paid for, an unscrupulous officer could oil his machine by padding committee expenses to give his men a few extra dollars.
>
> A machine manages to remain in power through deals when it lacks popular consent. It also tends to develop contempt for the people. Some of the [ILGWU] officials had no trouble convincing themselves that the good of the union demanded their remaining in office. And if the ballot proved disappointing, they did not shrink from improving the results.

Feeling that their very survival as public men was at stake, and privately somewhat doubtful that they could cope with the sharp-tongued leftists in debate, the right-wing leaders sometimes found themselves using methods and making alliances within the unions that they would have felt ashamed of a few years earlier. The struggle hurt both sides but, in a sense, the right more than the left. Having surrendered to the "higher" requirements of ideology, the Communists were all but indifferent to ordinary moral constraints: they were open to large brutalities, rarely to petty corruption. The Socialists, more humane and commonplace, could slip, by contrast, into small weaknesses, the routine failures of union bureaucrats. Recognizing as much, some of the better Socialist leaders tried to warn their followers. At the 1924 ILGWU convention Morris Hillquit said: "People have become cynical. . . . You must maintain the highest sort of idealism, for that is one of our greatest assets. The union should not be purely a business organization which discards all questions of theory, philosophy, or idealism."

Four years later, at a convention that was trying to pull the union together after the 1926 disaster, Hillquit came back to the same theme: "In the years of spiritual indifference that had taken hold of the whole country and all movements [during the early twenties], your union . . . began to conduct itself too much as a business enterprise. There was not enough soul in it."

Such appeals, Hillquit must have known, could hardly undo the damage of the mid-twenties. For not only had the opposing sides themselves resorted to brutal methods, the struggle had also enabled gangsters to enlarge their foothold in both the industry and the union. During the 1926 strike, the employers hired the notorious Legs Diamond mob to terrorize pickets, and the left-wing locals responded by hiring a rival mobster, "Little Augie"

(Jacob Orgen). When violence splattered across the streets, the International appealed to A. E. Rothstein, a respected manufacturer, to intervene with his son, Arnold Rothstein, then absolute boss of the New York underworld. Arnold had once met a few ILGWU people—Charles Zimmerman had appealed to him to remove gangsters who were terrorizing union pickets. He had taken a liking to Zimmerman and obliged. Now, eager to please his father, he again obliged, this time by telephoning Legs Diamond and Little Augie, both of whose gangs he controlled, and suggesting that they calm things down. They did.

Yet the mere fact that some locals could become mixed up with gangsters, even if only to arrange "protection" for their members, signified a sad decline for the Jewish union movement. For some years after the strike, the gangsters kept sliding into both the industry and several ILGWU locals. Murder Inc., run by the notorious Lepke and Gurrah, seized control of trucking within the garment center, edged its way into the top rung of a few locals, and made deals with a number of union officials (several, like Harry Cohen and Abraham Beckerman, old-time Socialists, were removed from union office because they collaborated with gangsters). It was not until the mid-thirties that the Jewish unions would be able to shake off these unsavory connections.*

It was a deadly combination: Communist ruthlessness, the decline of integrity in the union leadership, and the mushrooming of gorilla methods. Even after their hold on the ILGWU was consolidated in the late twenties, the right-wing leaders were, in crucial respects, damaged men. Many had been badly shaken by the years of poisonous factionalism, shaken out of complacence but also out of idealism. They felt wearied, ill-used, drained, little appreciated. Some grew bitter, others cynical. A rigid anti-Communism became a reigning passion. Without quite acknowledging it, some of the Jewish union leaders were now inclined to do precisely what Hillquit had warned them against: to treat the union not as a "cause" but as a businesslike institution requiring efficiency and meriting honesty, while leaving the rhetoric of socialism to nostalgic banquets and the Sunday pages of the *Forward* (where it had also lost its original glow). Hillquit was still

---

* A writer very close to the garment unions, J. B. S. Hardman (once J. B. Salutsky, leader of the Jewish Socialist Federation), offers testimony as to "these disastrous invasions" of the racketeers: "The strategic New York cutters' local of the Amalgamated Clothing Workers fell under underworld dominance in the early 1920s, and not until ten years later did the national union leadership mobilize enough power to end it—in cooperation with fair-minded employers and, of all politicians, Mayor Jimmy Walker. In the meantime the entire membership . . . suffered from the abuses the racketeers inflicted on the trades via the cutters' corrupt leaders. Did the non-cutters' local unions tolerate it? Some were hoping for the best, some were 'taken care of,' some fought back futilely, one absorbed a gun bullet for non-compliance. Did the members of the cutters' union approve their leaders' course? Some profited by the crooked development and kept silent. The mass of them were badly scared."

respected, but for only a few union leaders did he remain an unquestioned moral guide. Something had burned itself out in the civil war of the garment center, some fires of youth and hope.

There are many reasons for the gradual decline of Jewish socialism in America—its very success in creating labor unions that improved the lot of immigrant workers, its inability to stake out a *modus vivendi* with native American radicalism, its failure to break past the boundaries of ghetto life, its hesitation to acknowledge the distinctiveness or "exceptionalism" of the American experience, its later excessive submission to the welfare liberalism of Franklin Roosevelt, and more. But in the actual experience of the leaders of the garment unions, nothing was more damaging to their earlier visions than the struggle with the Communists in the twenties.

Dual Unions—and the Furriers

With one major exception, the Communist penetration of the garment unions is, from here on, a story of decline, even fiasco. By the late twenties, when the Communist International decided upon the policy of dual union-ism (the building of Communist-led "revolutionary" unions in opposition to the established "reformist" unions), Communist strength in the garment trades had badly shrunk. On New Year's Day, 1929, they nonetheless orga-nized the Needle Trades Industrial Union, which set itself up as a competitor to the four major garment unions. Only a few thousand workers joined this dual union, mostly furriers, long to constitute a bulwark of Yiddish-speaking Communism, and dressmakers, who had not participated in the 1926 strike and were therefore less likely to be hostile to the Communist leadership. In a little while a number of left-wing leaders, including Hyman and Zimmer-man, broke with the Communists and returned to leading posts in the ILGWU. Some embittered right wingers were reluctant to welcome them back, but David Dubinsky, now becoming the dominant leader, understood that these men would be especially useful in rebuilding a shattered union.

The other major garment unions differed sharply in their relation to the Communists. In the Amalgamated Clothing Workers, Sidney Hillman's guile prevented the Communists from making permanent inroads, though they did command some influence during the mid-twenties. A master Machiavel-lian, Hillman pursued during the twenties a generally pro-Soviet line in public, thereby pleasing the left, while at the same time keeping it firmly under control in his locals. In the Fur Workers Union, however, the Com-munists established a strong and enduring base. Here the fight between factions began to look like a gang war, and for years the New York fur market would be the scene of mass violence. Inflamed young Jewish workers, joined by a few hundred militant Greek furriers, battled on picket lines and in the shops: sometimes against the Industrial Squad of the Police Department, sometimes against right-wing opponents, sometimes against hoodlums. The Communist furriers developed a psychology rare in modern Jewish history and previously unknown in the immigrant milieu: the psychology of shock troops, a sort of paramilitary vanguard handy with knives, belts, pipes. No one in the garment center was tougher than they, no one claimed to be.

Within the fur union the Communists had two first-rate leaders, Aaron Gross, a quiet tactician, and Ben Gold, a flaming rabble-rouser. In 1926 the furriers called a strike of their own, fought out with gorillas and *shtarke;* it ended with the first forty-hour week in the garment trades as well as a 10 percent wage increase. The fur industry was small and compact, and the majority of its workers skilled craftsmen; it could be organized much more easily than either the dress or cloak trades. Except when yielding to ideological agendas—and since they had a mass following within the union, they could often establish some independence from the party representatives— the Communist leaders of the fur workers were resourceful unionists.

In the whole immigrant world there was no one quite like Ben Gold (1898–   ). Gold's natural setting was a meeting hall at Manhattan Center or a platform at Seventh Avenue and Twenty-eight Street during lunch hour. With or without amplifier, he would rise to speak before thousands of garment workers milling about in the streets and ready for a few minutes of excitement: the followers whom he sent into transports of adoration, the opponents whom he scandalized, and those who savored his gifts with the neutral objectivity they might turn upon the technique of a great cantor.

Physically, Gold was not an overwhelming figure at all. He was slight and, in his younger years, good-looking in a raffish sort of way. Quivering with nervousness, he experienced a kind of transfiguration when he opened his mouth, as if seized by some spirit of fury and negation. A stream of fire came pouring out of him, not always as grammatical speech, either in Yiddish or English (which he used interchangeably), and not always elegant, either; but as a rush, a flood of rage, summoning the anger of his listeners and teaching them they had funds of anger of which they had not even known.

A virtuoso of invective, he poured endless scorn on the heads of the "Socialist fakers" and "AFL misleaders." Union rivals would remember with a tremor of astonishment his resources for *sheltn,* a Yiddish verb connoting curse, denounce, excoriate. When Gold reached *"dem tsentn shtok,"* the tenth floor of the *Forward* building, where Abraham Cahan had his office, there tumbled out of him arias of abuse as his voice, always high and thin, rose to a piercing shriek. His hysteria ate into his audiences, and they reveled in it, they found it bracing and cathartic, they gained some vicarious strength from it.

Part of his power derived from the ideological energies of Bolshevism, but part, too, had indigenous sources in the turbid streams of Jewish apocalypticism. Anyone familiar with east European Jewish history would not have found it difficult to imagine Gold as a disciple of the would-be Messiah Jacob Frank, predicting an end to days and an escape from mundane torments, in a voice that leapt through the higher octaves of yearning and release.

Gold had been born in Bessarabia, the son of a radical Jewish craftsman. In 1908 his father, Israel, came to the United States, and two years later brought his wife and children. The boy quickly began working at all sorts of trades, pocketbooks, dresses, paper boxes. At thirteen he took his first job in a fur shop, earning nine dollars a week as an operator. "In May 1912 Israel Gold gave Ben $1.25 to pay for a union book, and the young boy joined the furriers union. When the 1912 strike started, Gold [all of fourteen] was assistant chairman of the shop of Pike and Rabinowitz. . . . During the strike Gold became acquainted with men and women active in the Socialist party. Though much older, they took the young boy into their confidence and taught him many things."

In 1916 Gold joined the Socialist party; his temperament made it almost certain that he would later follow the left wing into the Communist movement. Within the Fur Workers Union, he became the acknowledged Communist spokesman, profiting greatly from the guidance of Aaron Gross. Beaten up by thugs after the 1926 strike, Gross left for California, physically broken and politically disillusioned—one of the very few Communist furriers to join the dissident Lovestone group. Whereupon the Communist party sent in another "representative," Irving Potash, who took over Gross's role of helping, steering, and restraining Gold.

The Communist line of starting dual unions in the late twenties upset Gold severely, his every instinct as a mass leader telling him it was a dreadful mistake. For three days and nights he walked the streets of New York with his friend Charles Zimmerman, trying to decide what to do. Zimmerman proposed quitting the CP, Gold resisted. "Gold's real motive," Zimmerman later felt, "was a fear for his future. He knew well that in a break with the party he would be unable to carry the entire fraction [of the Communist furriers] with him. . . . Besides, Gold's vanity could not face the prospect of being castigated by those who now worshipped him as a hero."

And a hero Gold would remain all through the thirties and deep into the forties for the left-wing Jewish workers: a combative, shrewd, imperious, and somewhat impulsive leader, a tribune of the streets, a *shtime* (voice) that even anti-Communist Jewish workers held in awe. More flamboyant than most other Jewish union leaders, Gold had a dash of personal style and an easy way with women; his vanity expanded; the Communist machine tended the expansion.

After the Second World War, the furriers' union had to face new problems. The McCarthyite atmosphere made it vulnerable; an anti-

Communist drive in the CIO threatened to destroy it; other unions began raiding its shops, especially in the leather division. In 1954 Gold publicly resigned from the Communist party, stating that he had no serious political differences but was taking this step to comply with the Taft-Hartley Act, which required that union presidents sign affidavits that they were not members of the Communist party. He was nonetheless prosecuted by the government and found guilty of swearing falsely; later, the case was thrown out by the courts. But the meaning of all these events was clear: the fur union had been put on the defensive.

Grappling for shelter, party strategists proposed that the fur union become a subdivision of the Amalgamated Meat Cutters Union—and for this, pay the price of yielding some of its independence. Gold rebelled. Though he did not formally attack this proposal, he suggested conditions so unlikely to be accepted by the meat cutters that in effect his line meant that the fur union should fight independently to the end. Very probably, the end would have been the destruction of the union. The party fraction within the union, together with non-Communist leaders concerned primarily with organizational survival, gave Gold a sound thrashing in the internal dispute which now took place. Without the Communists, Gold was no longer a hero, or, if still one in the eyes of the fur workers, he was a hero without strength. For a few months he returned to work in a shop, hoping to build his own group within the union and thereby take back the leadership of what was now the fur and leather division of Amalgamated Meat Cutters. Twice, an opposition group inspired by Gold ran candidates for office in the New York fur union, and twice it was badly beaten. Gold had misunderstood his relationship to the party; he had failed to see that by now the mood of the fur workers was defensive and resigned.

By about 1960 Ben Gold left the union, retired to Florida, and there wrote a nostalgic Yiddish novel called *Yene teg* ("In Those Days"). To a casual eye down there on the beach, he might have seemed just another aging Jew, quiet and bent, among many.

A Network of Culture

Beginning in the early twenties, the Yiddish-speaking Communists built up a network of social and cultural institutions, masquerading as nonparty, which are still astonishing in their range and variety. It was as if the traditional fondness of immigrant Jews for a thick structure of organizations was now being taken over by the very movement that refused all principled Jewish ties.

First came the *Freiheit*, the Yiddish Communist daily started in 1922, which for six or seven years enjoyed a good share of literary talent. Its editor, Moissaye Olgin, wielded the most vitriolic pen in the immigrant quarter, delighting in polemics against his old friends on the *Forward*. And a number of serious Yiddish writers, men naturally inclined toward the left and seeking acceptance for fiction and verse more experimental than Abraham Cahan tolerated in the *Forward*, began to contribute to the Communist paper.

Had the *Freiheit* been able to confine itself to the inner affairs of the immigrant Jews, it might have gained steadily in circulation and influence. The Communist upsurge in the needle trades during the mid-twenties was an obvious source of strength, as was the widespread sympathy for "the Russian experiment." But what reduced the *Freiheit* to grief was its lock-step loyalty to the international Communist movement. Let a conflict arise between Jewish interests and the Communist line, and the *Freiheit* almost always stood fast by Moscow, even though its editors knew that it would cost them heavily in the Jewish world. One such conflict occurred in 1929, after an Arab guerrilla raid brought death to a number of Jewish settlers in Palestine. The first response of the *Freiheit*, presenting the news as a tragic event in Jewish life, was in accord with the natural feelings of its writers and readers. But a few days later, prodded by the Jewish Bureau of the Communist party, the paper turned about to hail the Arabs as "fighters for national liberation." Adding to the injuries caused by the party line was the insult of William Gropper's *Freiheit* cartoons, gross caricatures of Jewish leaders in a style more fitting for a Nazi sheet than a Yiddish paper. By the late twenties the *Freiheit* lost most of the Yiddish writers who had agreed to appear in its pages, such figures as H. Leivick, Lamed Shapiro, and Menakhem Boraisha turning away in dismay.

Among the immigrant workers, however, the Communists maintained a following of some strength. The loyalties of workers, once formed, are slow to change—or so twentieth-century experience seems to indicate. All through the twenties the Communists had built up dissident fractions within the Workmen's Circle, tearing away from it both a number of children's schools and the New York summer camp, Kinderland. In 1930 they started their own fraternal society, the International Workers Order, which would prove to be a rich source of recruitment and finances. Meanwhile, they were building a maze of local groups devoted to Yiddish folk singing, co-operative housing projects (in the northeast Bronx), mandolin ensembles, summer camps (Nitgedeyget—"No Worries"—in Beacon, New York), amateur theatre, sickness and death benefits, radical Jewish schooling, not-quite-modern dance, and literary discussion. For newly arrived immigrants who leaned politically to the left, such groups provided a welcoming and reassuring environment. For some talented people in Yiddish culture, such as Jacob Schaeffer, a choral leader who worked mostly in Chicago, the left-wing societies meant a new opportunity—sometimes the only opportunity—to do their work.

What hindered the growth of these groups was the very politics that had often been a reason for starting them. The initial impetus behind the *Freiheit* Mandolin Ensemble or the Jewish Workers Musical Alliance may have been vaguely leftist, but that does not mean all of its members were concerned with each turn of the party line. On the contrary; to be a non-party leftist engaged in "cultural activity" probably made it a little easier to tolerate political doctrines that a strict scrutiny might have found intolerable. And it would be a mistake to suppose that for even the intransigent Yiddish-speaking Communists the cultural aims of these groups were merely a ruse or maneuver; many of them, quite like the Jewish Social Democrats, felt strong attachments to their past and had yearnings toward cultural expression which might not be quite in accord with their ideology.

Absorbed in the internal life of these institutions, the nonparty Jewish leftists were able—some for their whole lives, others for decades—to put up with a great deal from their Communist mentors. Consider the matter of religion. When the *Freiheit* started publishing in 1922 it tried to avoid the sort of antireligious polemics that had characterized immigrant radicalism in the late nineteenth century. During the 1922 Passover holiday the *Freiheit* devoted a whole page to depicting Moses as an agitator, perhaps even a "terrorist," who was guilty of not being close enough to the rank and file. Pharaoh, by contrast, was unwilling to make compromises until threatened with the "slaying of the firstborn." In the succeeding centuries, Pharaoh would always reappear with renewed vigor, until finally the Bolshevik revolution "brought him to old age." Whatever its value as history, this sort of "clarification" signified an effort not to run head-on against the sentiments of ordinary Yiddish readers.

But by the time the Communist International embarked on its ultra-leftist Third Period, in 1929, the Communists not only reverted to, they sometimes surpassed, the crudities of the pioneering immigrant radicals. The Jewish organizations in the Communist orbit held mock *seders* on Passover, social affairs on Rosh Hashonah, lectures on Yom Kippur. It was customary for all Yiddish papers not to publish on the High Holy Days—even the newsstands closed down on the Jewish streets; but, as if from spite, the *Freiheit* would appear on Yom Kippur, often with antireligious material. "The yearly antireligious demonstration organized by the Jewish Bureau of the Communist party on Kol Nidre night," wrote the *Freiheit*, "has become a recognized institution among revolutionary Jewish workers who fight darkness and religious poison." In the children's schools run by the International Workers Order, all Jewish subjects, even secular history, were banned, and the curriculum slanted entirely along Marxist (or Stalinist) lines. Kalmon Marmor, a Yiddish intellectual who served as educational director of the IWO, wrote that the aim of these schools "is not to teach 'Jewishness' but to educate the children of Jewish workers" in politics. At the Kinderland camp the children in the thirty-six bungalows were dutifully herded into "thirty-six little Soviet republics."

The coming of the Popular Front period in 1934–1935, when the Communist International decided upon alliances with socialist and liberal groups, brought a sense of relief to many Jewish Communists. It would now be possible to speak more easily to the immigrant masses. The Communists could say a kind word for Palestine. They could acknowledge they were coming a little closer to the political outlook of those right-wing Socialists or ex-Socialists who controlled the Jewish labor movement. And they could even find virtues in Jewish cultural traditions for which they had previously shown contempt. The Communists, Moissaye Olgin announced, would now be "the best sons and daughters of the Jewish people." In former years, "we managed to alienate the Jewish masses. More than that, we conveyed the idea that the Communists are hostile to Jewish national aspirations. We fought Zionism, which was correct, but in fighting Zionism, we forgot that many progressive elements of the Jewish people were Zionistically inclined. We forgot also that the craving, the desire, for nationhood is not in itself reactionary."

The earlier Communist attitude toward Zionism, Olgin repudiated as "national nihilism." To his somewhat bewildered Jewish comrades he declared, "we must learn not to scoff at religion." And he proposed as a road to the Jewish masses that the Communists establish themselves as "inheritors of the best in Jewish culture."*

Particularly successful in tapping the latent idealism and personal anxieties of immigrant workers were the numerous Workers Clubs established by the Jewish Communists. Needs ranging from culture to flirtation could here be satisfied, all under a benevolent antifascist aura yet without the risks of party affiliation. Melekh Epstein has left a description of such a club:

> The inner walls were taken out, and a stage built on one side. The walls were painted and decorated with posters and placards, and the ceiling was festooned

---

* Some fellow-traveling groups lingered on from the past, small in membership but useful, sneered the *Forward*, as a *Komunistishe pushke* (Communist collection box) —such as ICOR, the Organization for Jewish Colonization in Russia, which in the early thirties had seized upon an ill-fated plan for settling Jews in the Siberian province of Biro-Bidjan. The International Workers Order, by contrast, grew steadily, becoming a mass organization claiming over 100,000 members in the early forties, with 35,000 of them in the Yiddish speaking branches. The activities of this society were extremely wide-ranging, from social insurance to party-line children's schools, from Yiddish publishing to summer camps. The IKUF, or World Alliance for Jewish Culture, founded at an international conference in Paris in 1937, brought together the usual "figures" from the Jewish left with an array of Yiddish writers whose anxiety over the rise of fascism led them to overlook the politics of their new allies. Local groups were formed throughout the country, and a letter from Detroit in the organization's monthly, *Yidishe Kultur*, gives a characteristic picture: "At these functions a few women comrades gave public readings of poems and stories. These were then discussed. Nor is material support for the progressive movement forgotten." The adult schools run by the Jewish Communists adopted new names but served the same function, in earlier years as the Jewish Peoples University and later as the School for Jewish Studies. At various festivals the left-wing dance now permitted itself a touch of Jewish content, Lillian Shapero producing a "Purim Dance" and Anna Sokolow a "Kaddish."

with colorful crepe paper. Facing the stage was a buffet . . . served by the girls. . . .

Friday night was lecture night, Saturday was given over to dancing, Sunday, to the literary evening. . . .

The clubs were more spacious and comfortable than the cramped bedrooms, where the young people lived in twos. The clubs were an outlet for native talent . . . and boys met girls there.

In these clubs there broke out, during the late twenties, a conflict between the "proletarians" and the "culturists" that reflected far-reaching differences within the entire Yiddish-speaking world. The "culturists," influenced by such Yiddish writers as S. Niger and H. Leivick, took seriously the idea of creating an autonomous and "progressive" Yiddish cultural life, while the "proletarians," inspired by the Jewish Bureau of the Communist party, saw "cultural work" as strictly subordinate to political ends. At a November 1929 conference of the New York clubs, the "culturists" were "wiped out," according to an article in *Funken,* the journal published by the Workers Clubs.

The greatest contribution of the left-wing immigrant Jews to the Communist movement was, finally, neither their time, nor money, nor minds; it was their children. Through the Young Pioneers, a children's group, and then the Young Communist League, which during the thirties built up powerful student branches, largely Jewish in composition, at such schools as City and Hunter colleges, a whole new generation of fervent comrades came into being. Working as party organizers in the industrial cities of the Midwest, writing for the *Daily Worker* and the *New Masses,* and some of them dying in the Spanish Civil War, these sons of the immigrants were well educated, articulate in English, and free of their parents' inhibitions. From the ranks of these young people came not only such party leaders as Joseph Starobin, Joseph Clark, and John Gates, but a considerable number of middle-class members and fellow travelers—teachers, social workers, dentists, accountants, lawyers, and doctors. Those who threw themselves full time into party work would customarily drop every sign of Jewish identity. Taking "party names," they made certain to choose non-Jewish ones, with the rationale that this was necessary in order to approach American workers, but with motives surely more complicated. The veteran Yiddish-speaking leftists did not always know how to feel about this "Americanizing" of their sons, whether to regret the cultural tearing apart that it signified or to see it as still another sacrifice for the cause.

All might have continued well for Yiddish Communism had there not burst upon the world in 1939 the Hitler-Stalin pact. Most Communists of Jewish descent no doubt suffered some shock when they saw the picture of Ribbentrop and Molotov shaking hands, but those who represented themselves as *Jewish* Communists, speaking to a distinctive Jewish consciousness, suffered the greatest emotional turmoil. Heated meetings were held by the Yiddish-speaking Communists and sympathetic groups, at which some members announced their withdrawal and harassed leaders tried to justify the unjustifiable. A *Forward* correspondent described a Yiddish meeting in the Midwest at which a prominent fellow traveler rose to say he was not really concerned with Russia's betrayal of England and France but felt that "all of us who put our trust in Stalin were exposed naked in front of the world as a pack of idiots."

At first the *Freiheit* claimed there was nothing necessarily wrong with nonaggression pacts and that, in any case, they did not conflict with the antifascist Popular Front. This justification crumbling, the Jewish Communists tried to console themselves with the notion that the pact contained a secret clause voiding all relations between Germany and Russia in case Germany attacked a third nation. Once Germany did attack Poland, the Jewish Communists used a "special" argument among their followers. The partition of Poland, said the *Freiheit*, was "good for the Jews." For while two million Polish Jews had thereby fallen under Hitler's power, another million had been "saved" by Russia.

The Labor Zionist weekly, *Yidisher Kemfer*, attacked this argument, noting that it had been the pact which first precipitated the war by freeing Hitler from the threat of an eastern front. In any case, "we reject with loathing the saving of a million Jews when it is bought at such a price." As the *Kemfer* wrote: "Explanations [for the pact among Jewish Communists] changed daily. . . . It was difficult not to form the impression that the faithful did not themselves believe in their own arguments."

A stream of desertions began from the Yiddish-speaking front groups. Yiddish writers like Opatashu, Leivick, Nadir, and Hirshbein, some of whom had contributed to the *Freiheit*, drifted away. Leading members of the *Freiheit* staff—Melekh Epstein, Louis Hyman—resigned.

In the Jewish unions, the pact brought the Communists frequent embarrassment and measurable losses. By far the most important of these, and certainly typical of others, occurred in Local 22 of the ILGWU, which contained twenty thousand Jewish dressmakers and had long been a radical stronghold. In the fall of 1939 a group of dressmakers presented a petition signed by five hundred members of the local calling upon its executive committee to pass a resolution denouncing the Hitler-Stalin pact. To prevent a split in the local's leadership, which still contained a minority of Communists, the executive committee turned down this request, but in statements to the Yiddish press, the manager of the local, Charles Zimmerman, expressed his personal agreement with the petitioners.

Again, ideological war in the garment center. Communist leaflets were distributed in the dress market saying that "Lovestoneites [Zimmerman had been one years back] betray the workers and are attempting to force them into support of the present imperialist war." At the next meeting of Local 22, held in October 1939, the issue came to a head in a way that was characteristic of many other Jewish unions. Sensing the angry mood of the meeting, the Stalinist leaders confined themselves to speaking about such things as bad conditions in the trade—but the ranks would not be placated. Hissing spread through the hall. Fist fights broke out, and Zimmerman barely managed to control the meeting. The outcome of it all was that six leading Communists, all on the executive committee of Local 22, resigned from the party. Once they left, the CP lost whatever prestige it still had in the local, as it would in other segments of the Jewish labor movement.

In the last months of 1939, the Yiddish press was filled with jibes and taunts, all focused on the question: are the Communists still in favor of the boycott of Nazi goods that had been carried out, almost as a matter of course, by all American Jews? William Z. Foster's answer for the CP was no, and for weeks the *Freiheit* avoided printing his statement. Finally, it had to admit shamefacedly that the Jewish Communists now favored dropping the boycott of Nazi Germany. A kind of pall fell upon the Yiddish-speaking community; it all seemed beyond credence.

During the war years, because the party again changed its line to a version of the Popular Front, the Jewish Communists recouped some of their losses; but the memory of the pact was too strong among the immigrant Jews, and for many there could no longer be any trust in the Soviet Union. Still, a hard core of Yiddish-speaking Communists remained faithful: they had pledged their lives and they lived out their pledge. The will to believe, whatever it was that drove them, ran very deep; the emotional investments of a lifetime could not be abandoned; and always there remained the hope that the Soviet Union would yet prove to be the land of freedom and socialism about which they had dreamed. When dream turned to nightmare, some left with admissions of shame. Those who remained may have felt that nightmare was better than nothing.

Recovery, Growth, Adaptation

Coming directly after the murderous feud between right and left wings, the depression of 1929 brought chaos to both the garment industry and its unions. What little remained of union control was wiped out; the old sweating came back; strikes failed; gangsters flourished. One unhappy result of the factional wars was an ILGWU decree banning organized factions except during brief preconvention periods, a sign that "the traditional habits and concepts of trade union democracy were considerably weakened." The inner life of many locals grew flaccid, enabling careerist officials to tighten their hold.

The ILGWU claimed some forty thousand members: it would have been cruel to check the claim. In 1929 the union was two million dollars in debt, partly because the International had taken responsibility for the "employer security" funds* which the left-wing Cloakmakers Joint Board had improperly spent in the 1926 New York strike. There were times when the telephone at the International office was disconnected and the staff unpaid. The other garment unions may have been a little better off, but not much.

Slowly, through the will of a devoted handful, the Jewish unions began to pull themselves together. They enacted harsh economies, and found new, pragmatic leaders. By 1932 there were a few strikes that brought in some members. In April 1933 the ILGWU scored a success in a Philadelphia strike which led to a quick recognition of the union. "Much of the renewed vigor of the needle trade unions in this period can undoubtedly be traced to the return [to posts of leadership] of a considerable number of former Communists"—most of them drawn from the Lovestone group, expelled in 1929 from the Communist party.

By the time President Roosevelt's National Industrial Recovery Act (NIRA), with its Section 7A guaranteeing the rights of unions to organize, came along in 1933, the Jewish unions had on their 'own partly—but only partly—regained their strength. The struggle with the Communists turned out to have one useful result: the Jewish union leaders were psychologically prepared for a new course that would take them to the mainstream of American life. When signals started coming from Washington they leaped to respond. For better or worse, they had unburdened themselves of the old ideological baggage; they judged the New Deal, not as socialist theoreticians reckoning its ultimate implications, but as hardheaded unionists who saw a chance for growth.

Leaders of the ILGWU and the Amalgamated were soon traveling to Washington to help prepare the NRA "Codes," which set minimal work standards in varous industries and gave a cue for extended union organization. In the dress trade, where fewer than 15 percent of the New York workers belonged to the union, the ILGWU felt that a strike would have to be called before any "Code" could be written, since only through a militant action could the union regain the loyalties of the workers. The strike began in August 1933, when seventy thousand workers shut down the entire industry. It turned out to be a great triumph for a union that only yesterday had not even been certain it could survive, and it revealed again how deep was that sense of solidarity which underlay all the moods of the Jewish workers. For many of these people the 1933 strike was probably a turning point in their lives, since their work conditions, if never to be exactly wonderful, would never again be so bad as in the past.

Taking advantage of the new atmosphere created by the Roosevelt

* These funds were deposited by employers with the union in order to make certain that if a shop suddenly went out of business or disappeared, workers could be paid their concluding week's wages. It was, of course, morally impermissible for the union to use this money for any other purpose.

administration, the Jewish unions grew at a phenomenal rate. By the spring of 1934 the ILGWU had risen to 200,000 members. The growth of the Amalgamated, while also rapid, especially in scattered small-town shops, was not so spectacular only because it had never sunk so low as the other unions. Serving in Washington as labor adviser to the NRA, Sidney Hillman also worked closely with the garment unions back in New York, often cuing in their organizational drives. David Dubinsky, who became president of the ILGWU in 1932, brought a feverish energy to its campaigns, as if he were undamaged by the events of the twenties. Under the new agreements, more than 90 percent of the dress workers now had a thirty-five-hour week and wage increases from 20 to 50 percent. By the time the Supreme Court declared the NRA unconstitutional in 1935, the garment unions were so strongly entrenched among the "NRA babies," as the new members were called, that no significant relapse in wages or work standards was possible. The ILGWU and the Amalgamated now became powerful institutions, with large staffs, swelling treasuries, and substantial influence in the politics of both Washington and New York.

Within the Socialist ranks there now broke out a fierce factional fight regarding the attitude the American left should take to Roosevelt's New Deal. On one side was the "old guard," veterans of the movement who had kept it alive through the lean twenties and were based mostly in the Jewish trade unions; on the other side, younger and more militant members centered around Norman Thomas. At a Socialist rally in Madison Square Garden, Abraham Cahan had delighted some comrades and shocked others by saying that Roosevelt ought to take out a card in the Socialist party, so strongly was he carrying through proposals that Socialists had always favored; while the Thomas wing, though also prepared to support specific welfare measures introduced by Roosevelt, saw the New Deal as a patchwork meant to save a sick and unjust social system. Behind this clash lay all-but-irreconcilable political views, and in 1933 the party split, with the old guard taking the Jewish unions and prepared to end the policy of socialist isolation and enter the New Deal coalition, while the Thomas wing hoped to build a fresh and intransigent party.

The more leftist leaders of the Socialist movement, winning Thomas to their views, criticized the New Deal with some cogency. They pointed out that it had not really ended unemployment or changed the basic life situation of the worker in capitalist society. But the Jewish unionists knew that with the accession of Franklin Roosevelt to office something crucial *had* changed for them. Thousands of workers were being swept into union ranks; new contracts were being signed, gains won, future victories made possible. Roosevelt became an adored figure in the Jewish unions, with the social reforms of his administration signifying the kind of concrete goals that, for most Jewish workers, would gradually replace the ideal of socialism.

Whether or not the split among the Socialists was inevitable, it might now, decades later, be worth asking whether there could have been a more flexible socialist stand, one that would acknowledge the New Deal as a significant step toward the welfare state, bringing desirable reforms yet by no means removing the need for a basic socialist critique. Might not even electoral support of Roosevelt have been combined with socialist pressures to extend, and then perhaps transcend, the limits of the welfare state? Perhaps so; but at the time such a nuanced course was almost impossible for both sides. The leaders of the garment unions were so entranced with their immediate possibilities, they had no interest in a politics requiring qualifications. The left wing in the Socialist party was so persuaded that a worldwide social transformation was an immediate urgency, it had no patience with the "opportunism" of the unionists. In these single-minded perspectives Jewish socialism in America, and perhaps American socialism as well, exhausted itself.

But not the Jewish unions. They were now full of vigor, energy, expectation.* They were enjoying their plunge into American politics and starting to wield a new influence in the American labor movement. In the mid-thirties, still functioning as the more "progressive" wing of the AFL, the Jewish unions lent strong support to the new industrial unionism that was organizing steel, auto, and rubber, and would become a major transforming power in American society. At first the garment unions joined in setting up the Committee for Industrial Organization which, under John L. Lewis's leadership, worked as a caucus within the AFL. Once, however, Lewis made it clear he was going to set up his own labor federation, the ILGWU pulled out and in 1940 rejoined the AFL. The Amalgamated remained with the new Congress of Industrial Organizations, though Hillman and his colleagues would soon be distressed by Lewis's sudden turn against Roosevelt. But whether in the AFL or the CIO, the garment unions found themselves for the first time close to the center of American labor, breaking down traditional hostilities of antisocialist (and anti-Jewish) leaders and gaining the confidence of such new industrial-union leaders as Walter Reuther.

In politics, too, the Jewish unionists discovered that they had considerable power, if only they chose to use it. They joined or improvised a series of political agencies, from Labor's Non-Partisan League, sponsored by the CIO, to the American Labor party in New York, controlled by Dubinsky and Hillman. Socialist-inclined garment workers could thereby ease their

* One of the happiest signs was the enormously entertaining revue *Pins and Needles*, which was put on by an ILGWU-supported group in 1937 and survived through three and a half years of revised productions and tours. Professional but not too professional, *Pins and Needles* ranged from satirical songs and sketches about intra-union quarrels ("Papa Lewis–Mama Green") to exhortatory pieces like "Take Me Back to the Sewing Machines." The show opened with a cry by the ensemble, "We're from the shops . . . Dressmakers, cloakmakers," etc., all of whom want to "put our foes on pins and needles."

transition into old-party politics, voting for Democratic candidates under transparent new labels. When the ALP was infiltrated by Communists, the ILGWU and a number of other Jewish unions left, to form the Liberal party in 1944.

Such political activity was something very new for the garment workers. They had been taught all their lives that between the two capitalist parties there was little difference and that a socialist vote was an elementary moral obligation. Now, the persuasions of a generation were being brushed aside—perhaps because these had already lost their inner urgency. Most garment workers followed the political signals of their leaders, voting for New Deal candidates on minor party lines and, after a while, the Democratic ticket. Abandoning formal socialism, they seemed to feel they were preserving something of its original moral intent.

It was a political shift that reflected a deeper and more gradual change among the immigrant Jewish workers. Consider the garment unionists who, by 1935, had reached their fifties: They had lived through an exhausting series of strikes and conflicts, they had witnessed the shattering of early hopes associated with London and Hillquit, they had suffered through the demoralizing feuds of the twenties, they had been shaken by the depression. They were tired, and had every right to be tired. Even the younger ones, those who had come to America in the early twenties, were not very different. Idealism many of them still had, but idealism is not a plant which thrives in isolation, it must be combined with other needs, other nurturance. Some true believers remained faithful to the Communist movement, but for most of the garment workers, their idealism had been bruised by a surplus of experience and complicated by that weary skepticism which seems all but inseparable from modern urban life. (Who, going to and from work on the New York subways for over a quarter of a century, could retain an untarnished faith in the nobility of mankind?) The new political turn of the Jewish unions was by no means a mere shrewd adaptation to American politics, it also reflected deep, unspoken needs of the garment workers themselves.

The dominating figure—perhaps the representative man—in this new phase of the Jewish labor movement was David Dubinsky (1892–   ). At Washington dinners, Sidney Hillman took the spotlight, but Hillman was already somewhat distant from the garment workers. He fitted in too easily with the bureaucrats, politicians, and social workers; he no longer seemed to feel uneasy at having backed out of the Jewish milieu. But Dubinsky not only held control of the largest Jewish union, he remained "one of us" in manner, speech, and outlook. A pudgy little fellow, unpretentious and brash, he was at ease with his own people, the highly paid cutters and lowly paid finishers, the business agents, the comrades—and the bosses too. He had never gone far in that smoothing of rough edges which Hillman had completed years earlier. Dubinsky still seemed a *folksmensh*, plain and plebeian. And just because he shared so many traits of the garment workers, he had a gift for getting at their moods and feelings. Out of the ferment of Jewish socialism, the cruel factionalism of the twenties, and the new openings of the thirties, he stirred up a mixture of shrewd calculation and carefully measured idealism which spoke to the immigrant Jews.

Born David Dobnievski, he grew up in Lodz, an ugly industrial city where the new Jewish working class labored twelve to fifteen hours a day. He went to school until he was thirteen, became a master baker in his father's shop at fourteen, and was elected secretary of the bakers' union at fifteen. In a strike that followed, he helped shut down his father's little shop. The police came for him, and the father calmly gave him a bit of money and a ritual garment to wear. Ten days and one bribe later, he was released from jail on condition he leave the city.

A year later Dubinsky was again arrested, at a meeting where the Bundists were trying to organize bakery workers. This time the arrest was much more serious, with the police banishing him to Siberia, where he had to live under surveillance. In Warsaw and Moscow prisons he met a spectrum of political prisoners: it fired his mind, completed his education. In Siberia, "after ten days I made up my mind to escape. I managed to place myself at the very end of the convoy and . . . lagged further and further behind." This simple plan succeeded: it was a time when simple plans still could. Back in Lodz under a false name, young Dubinsky returned to the bake shops, hiding out each night in a different place. Finally, his brother sent him money for a ticket to America, and on July 1, 1911, he arrived in New York.

So far his story is not very different from that of hundreds, thousands of other young Jewish revolutionists. But Dubinsky was not really cut out to be a revolutionist. His mind was not speculative, not "theoretical" enough. His temperament drew him to the concrete. For a few months the Dubinsky family hoped that David would study to become a doctor, but that seemed too distant, almost as distant as making the revolution. Instead, he slipped into Local 10 of the ILGWU, the powerful cutters' local. As a cutter you might make almost as much money as a doctor, and without having to learn English.

Local 10 was one of the few locals which had begun to use English at its meetings, and for young Dubinsky that presented a problem, as, less openly, it would throughout his life. Local 10 was stiff-necked and "conservative," comprising a needle-trade aristocracy, and restricting membership through high initiation fees and a six-month probationary period. A "progressive" opposition formed by the socialists, calling itself the Good and Welfare League, arose within the local; this group of some eighty members upset the old-line leadership in 1917, and soon Dubinsky was on the executive board. In 1920 he became assistant manager, in 1921 manager of the local. A stronghold for the right wing in its battle against the Communists, Local 10 would be Dubinsky's impregnable base for years to come. People liked him. He was blunt, peppery, shrewd. He had endless energy. He could wheedle and bluster, maneuver and compromise. He was still a socialist, but not what would later be called an "ideologue." He liked to get things done.

In the twenties Dubinsky led the right wing in the ILGWU. For the Communists he became a kind of devil-figure, hated with a venom they reserved only for a few others, like Hillquit and Cahan, and hated perhaps even more than anyone else, since he was not a "sensitive" intellectual, but roughhoused with them in a style they understood. A friendly reporter wrote that

> He was not over-fastidious about his use of weapons. Communists and those suspected of leftist sympathies were hurtled incontinently out of the locals. . . . When the Communists would fire off a barrage of broadsides, picturing him as the leader of "sluggers and gangsters," the head of a "fat-bellied clique of job-holders," and announcing "on behalf of the rank and file," that "we are through with Dubinsky," the little man would promptly hand in his resignation. As a result, vehement protests would pour in from hitherto neutral rank and filers, Dubinsky would withdraw his resignation—and be reelected by a large majority.

The methods used by Dubinsky and his friends—they would have said, the methods they *had* to use—in these internecine fights left their mark on later years. Relatively peaceable as the ILGWU became after Dubinsky assumed its presidency in 1932, he would always have a dread of resumed factionalism. His leadership was characterized by a blend, not at all unknown in American unions, of democracy and "Bonapartism," a reasonably firm adherence to rules and a stringent domination from on top. And very much in the style of many immigrant Jews, Dubinsky managed to reconcile a ripe sentimentalism with a harsh toughness. He found it hard to fire old pals who had been useful to the union in the past; he could be ruthless with officials who crossed him. At a Jewish Museum exhibit held in the sixties, Dubinsky stood in front of a blowup of the *Forward* front page carrying Morris Rosenfeld's poem about the victims of the Triangle fire and wept unashamedly; at about the same time he was pursuing ILGWU organizers who dared propose a union for themselves.

Within the union he became a rampaging "papa," quick to lose his temper and indulge his generosity. He ran the union as a good, an intelligent, often a brilliant "papa," but the sons, that phalanx of leaders draped about him, some of whom were men of talent, suffered for years from his high-handedness, as sons of powerful papas do. Dubinsky had a way of personalizing things, naïvely identifying himself with the union, which most of his predecessors would have thought it a scandal to do. "Our enemies," he said about his decision to support John Lindsay for mayor of New York, "they were dancing already on my grave. Not only dancing but they already had me buried. But then they forgot that little fellow, Dubinsky. They left a little hole; they didn't cover me up. That little fellow, Dubinsky, he'll slip through the eye of a needle." That little fellow certainly didn't have a little opinion of himself.

Not a first-rate orator, Dubinsky was masterful, however, at intra-union politics; at negotiating with the employers (many of them also immigrant Jews who spoke with the same Yiddish accent and could be gotten to with the same sentimental toughness); and at dealing with gentile liberals (with whom he would shrewdly take advantage of his own deficiencies—as he felt them to be—of speech and manner, so as to make them feel superior.) Busy, always busy, Dubinsky liked, as the Yiddish proverb has it, "to dance at all the weddings." A close observer would recall: "He used to take tickets at union functions, adjust the microphones, peel off his dinner jacket to help the waiters set up extra banquet tables, quarrel over the price of floor tiles and switch off the light in empty union offices, leaving behind a note with some such reproof as, 'What's the matter, Edison gives it to you free?' "

Master in his own house, Dubinsky often felt uneasy in the outer world. Some of his associates, trying to understand the vivid contraries of his nature, even came to say that basically he was a shy man: which, if true, could be demonstrated only by pointing to the opposite in his behavior. Within the AFL, of which he became a vice-president in 1934, he had to sit with gentiles who were, he knew, suspicious of everything about him: his speech, his background, his opinions, his "race," his wit. During the forties and fifties he fought a good fight against racketeering in the unions; at the 1940 AFL convention he was assaulted by Joe Fay, an official of the Operating Engineers who would soon be jailed as a convicted extortionist. Dubinsky's sport was bicycling, not fisticuffs, but he survived with a bruise or two and a glow of reputation. Meeting "really big people," patricians like Eleanor and Franklin Roosevelt, he did feel a little shy, though he charmed them, perhaps more than he knew, with his cleverness.

To the end Dubinsky remained himself, at home in the world that had made him, still an immigrant among other immigrants, adept at Yiddish, never inclined to deny his past. He stemmed less from the intellectual side of the Yiddish tradition than from those ordinary but vigorous folk who brought flesh, blood, noise, and strength to Jewish life. That sometimes he may still have been the immigrant boy staring into the sweetshop of gentile America, hardly distinguished him from—or endeared him any the less to— his own people.

In the Dubinsky era, the ILGWU experienced a transformation not only in political and social outlook but also in ethnic character. Like the other garment unions, it became "more Jewish" in outlook and "less Jewish" in composition.

Abandoning the "cosmopolitanism" of the older Jewish socialists, the garment-union people now felt free to share in Jewish concerns transcending class or labor lines. They reacted to the growth of European anti-Semitism with a new feeling of "Jewish identification." The anti-Zionism of the Jewish labor movement, by now more habit than conviction, all but disappeared. In 1934 the garment union leaders set up the Jewish Labor Committee as a defense agency for Jewish interests in the American unions; somewhat later they would strike up a friendship with Histadrut, the Israeli labor federation. "The truth is that, although the development was continuous, the term 'Jewish labor movement' meant something very different in the 1930's from what it once had. Once it had meant a compact bloc of labor organizations . . . making use of Yiddish as their vehicle of communication. Now . . . the term referred to a kind of semi-organized grouping of Jewish labor leaders, combined for the purpose of promoting relevant Jewish interests."

Internally, the Jewish unions were experiencing a major change. In 1913 over 80 percent of the men's clothing workers were Jewish; by 1950 less than 30 percent of the ILGWU and about 25 percent of the Amalgamated were Jewish. By the late forties there were few, if any, Yiddish-speaking locals. And these trends held at least as well for the other clothing workers' unions. One estimate of membership in the Jewish or once-Jewish labor organizations runs as follows:

Membership in Jewish Unions, 1951

Union	Total Membership	Jewish Membership
ILGWU	400,000	120,000
Amalgamated	375,000	95,000
Cap and millinery	45,000	25,000
Furriers	40,000	25,000
Other Jewish unions	60,000	40,000

In a 1953 study, "Old-Timers and Newcomers," Will Herberg offered valuable material about the ethnic changes in Local 22, the dressmakers union:

> Jews constituted 70.5 percent of Local 22 in 1934, but only 63.4 percent in 1946, and barely 51 percent in 1953. The fact of the matter was that Jewish dressmakers were not taking their daughters, much less their sons, into the shops to succeed them. . . . The Jewish membership of Local 22 was becoming older; many were dropping out or retiring, and their place in the shops was being taken partly by Italians of Local 89 but primarily by Negroes, Puerto Ricans, and 'others' who were joining Local 22.

One consequence of these ethnic changes was the growth of serious conflicts within the union, conflicts understandably minimized by the leadership, which had always looked upon racial or ethnic discrimination as scandalous but which could not always cope with the emotional reactions of either its members or itself.

> Most revealing perhaps is the feeling of embitterment of some [Jewish] old-timers at the prospect of the union which they had built eventually passing into other and "alien" hands, for they see, clearly enough, that in another generation Local 22 will be only insignificantly Jewish in comparison with the growing non-Jewish majority. A few say so in just so many words, but there are many others who, though they would be shocked at its overt expression, feel the same embitterment and share the same sense of frustration.

For the aging leaders of the Jewish unions, this transformation was painful. That the "newcomers" were people needing help and meriting fair treatment everyone agreed, but there was a feeling of disappointment with their seeming lack of interest in union affairs and their lack of "leadership qualities." Surrounded by hordes of alien members with whom they could not even converse, the veteran Jewish leaders tended to erect a defensive psychology, bristling with impatience at even well-intentioned criticism.

The Jewish unions could no longer be called socialist, but they were still, and more effectively than ever, *social* unions. Broad-gauged in their involvements, they functioned efficiently within the framework of the welfare state, a phase of capitalism that requires the kinds of pressures social unionism can provide in order to advance a step or two toward the humanization of society. Some of the Jewish unionists liked to feel they were still socialists at heart, but success, they knew, was tricky, far more so than failure. With mounting responsibilities, they cared less and less about the ultimate goals of socialism, indeed, about any ultimate goals. Not that many turned to bourgeois fleshpots. Few Jewish union leaders were tempted by high living, and in comparison with most of their American equivalents, they were downright ascetics. It was simply that, as the years slid by, they could no longer pretend that the small material gains won by the union were anything but a proper—and perhaps sufficient—end in themselves. Like other people trapped between remembered sentiments and pressing circumstances, the Jewish unionists improvised formulas of reconciliation, splitting themselves between daily practice and Sunday speeches. With time, they made fewer Sunday speeches.

What then remained, halfway through the century, of immigrant Jewish socialism? Warm memories remained, large and unforeseen practical achievements, an intellectual tradition still savored by some younger people and—the Workmen's Circle, that tenacious fraternity which kept the past alive if only through nostalgia and a declining number of witnesses. It was this organization in which shards and reminiscences of Jewish socialism could still be found. To turn back to its beginnings is to round out the end.

From Politics to Sentiment

When the Workmen's Circle (Arbeiter Ring) was created, in 1892, the handful of Jewish immigrants who started it had not the slightest thought of modulating their convictions. They wanted to set up a society that would bring together workers of socialistic persuasion, while also providing them with those scanty but essential benefits—sick care, burial service—which the traditional *landsmanshaftn* offered. Once the Workmen's Circle became a national body, in 1900, the general intent was quite the same. A circular put out a few years earlier had said, "the member of the Workmen's Circle spends his time in scientific discussions, listens to a scientific lecture, which develops his morals and clears his mind of the dust of the factory; it encourages him to think and to open his eyes to the fact that he is a human being with energy, courage and spirit." High-minded words, in accord with the spirit of early Jewish socialism. All through its early years the Workmen's Circle stressed its radicalism, its strict opposition to Jewish nationalism, its hostility to religion. Yet even at the outset there were some socialists who sensed that the mere fact of starting such a society might signify a watering of their belief.

The organization grew and prospered. By 1910 it had close to 39,000 members; it carried $11,680,000 worth of insurance for them; in the previous year it had paid out $62,000 in sick benefits and $20,000 in death benefits. But it was typical of the inner strain in the minds of the socialists leading the Workmen's Circle that precisely these signs of success made them uneasy—as failure might not have. B. Charney Vladeck noted that during a given year "no less than one thousand lectures are held at the branches . . . but they are carried out . . . so as to provide minimal accomplishments," for the lectures tend to be superficial and include an odd mixture of topics such as "Yiddish Literature, Free Love, Socialism, Electricity, Religion, and Canine Teeth."

That, apparently, was what the members wanted. The heart of the problem, continued Vladeck, was that "as long as the WC was not very strong, people joined not only for the benefits but for the higher purposes as well. Now, however, the Workmen's Circle is a secure place for insurance and other practical services, with the result that there gravitates to it a mass of people remote from radical and social purposes." Was this good, or was it bad? Vladeck spoke about the Workmen's Circle as one might speak about a radical party, which has a right to demand discipline and coherence of belief; he could not decide whether such criteria should also be applied to a fraternal order. And he hesitated to acknowledge what it might reveal about the larger drift of the Jewish working class.

It is at about this point that we come upon the distinctive character of the Workmen's Circle in immigrant Jewish life. It keeps growing, to the point where in the thirties it has almost eighty thousand members; it steadily widens the scope of its cultural work; it sets up a sanitarium for tubercular members in Liberty, New York; it becomes a major agency for the diffusion of secular Jewish culture. And its success depends precisely on keeping intact its inner contradictions as these mirror, with a faithfulness no other institution could match, the changing experiences of the radical Jewish workers. Were it ever to resolve its problems, either by becoming a strictly socialist group or by totally abandoning the socialist tradition, it would, to that very extent, cease being close to the center of the immigrant Jewish experience.

As it was, the Workmen's Circle satisfied the needs, because it yielded to the mixed desires, of those Jewish workers who retained some secularist and radical opinions. It provided a setting in which they could meet under pleasant conditions, where they could sit down to a glass of tea and exchange small talk and large ideas. It arranged a minimal version of social security. It gave its members some possibility for quenching their thirst for learning, through classes and lectures admittedly uneven in quality but still precious to those who had no chance to acquire formal education. It gave them a way, through its afternoon schools and high schools (*mitelshule*), to provide their children with "a secular Jewish education," thereby finding, perhaps, some middle path between a complete break from Jewishness and a lapse into faith. And it gave them an honorable basis for feeling that, if no longer the zealots of their youth, they still *cared* about socialism—or at least social reform. With an intuitive shrewdness beyond the reach of the more ideological socialists, the Workmen's Circle knew exactly what masses of immigrant workers wanted.

Over the years the Jewish aspect of its work grew dominant and the socialist aspect weaker. In 1919 it started an extensive chain of Yiddish-language schools for children. Perhaps its single greatest achievement, these schools were often conducted on a high level. What their curriculum should be was a constant subject for debate: a strict radical-secular education conducted in Yiddish? A somewhat more inclusive "Jewish content" through acquainting children with Jewish history? (But how could that be done without bringing in Jewish religion?) A schedule of holidays established by the Workmen's Circle schools in 1919 amusingly reflects these problems: it includes Passover (but not Rosh Hashonah and Yom Kippur), May 1, Paris Commune Day, July 4, and the anniversary of the Russian Revolution (whichever Russian Revolution the local school preferred, February or October). Such debates, reflecting the internal contradictions of the organization, could not be resolved; such debates, preserving those internal contradictions, were fruitful.

In time the Workmen's Circle experienced the troubles characteristic of all Yiddish-speaking organizations. Attempts were made to set up English-speaking branches, but only with middling success. Many members began to prosper in the years after the Second World War, and it became something of an embarrassment as to whether businessmen could remain in a society calling itself the Workmen's Circle. Embarrassment or not, they remained. The holidays kept shifting further, away from May 1 and Paris Commune Day and back to traditional Jewish ones.

In a sense, then, those Jewish Socialists who in the early 1900's had been dubious about starting such a fraternal order were now being proven right. The Workmen's Circle did reflect a drift away from early Jewish radicalism, it did accept the later Jewish easement into American society, it did embody the gradual reconciliation of the Jewish working class with Zionism. But what the early socialist skeptics could not have understood was that in their uneasiness they were anticipating the central course of immigrant Jewish life. As it now appears, their real objections were not to the comrades who started the Workmen's Circle but to the whole Jewish experience in America, which the Workmen's Circle faithfully reflected. Still less could they have foreseen that this organization would come to seem emblematic of the way Jewish socialism gradually transformed itself from a politics into a sentiment—a sentiment tended with affection and respect but no longer from the premise that the will or even heroism of an immigrant generation could change the world.

CHAPTER ELEVEN

Getting into American Politics

O<small>F ALL</small> the sectors of American life that were open to them, old-party
politics was the one that immigrant Jews were the slowest to enter. Work
was a necessity for survival, education seemed an entry to the future, but
politics—it would take several decades before east European Jews could feel
at home with the big-city machines, their strange skills, codes, corruptions,
and vulgarities.

The east European Jews brought with them a skimpy political experience. To the Orthodox the idea of a secular politics was inherently suspect,
to the radicals an untried if tempting possibility. In the political life of
czarist Russia Jews had been allowed at most a token representation, more
humiliating than enabling. Many were still in the grip of the traditional
Jewish persuasion that it was best to keep as far away from politics as
possible, since any involvement with the affairs of the gentiles would probably be dangerous and certainly degrading. Within east European Jewish
life, secular politics was a novel experience; mostly, it was an "internal"
politics, necessarily abstract and visionary, without much grounding in the
realities of power or administration. Sharing this limited background in
public life, both the Orthodox and the radical immigrants tended to look

upon the politics of American cities as still another antic of the gentiles, an antic that a needy Jewish lawyer might have to join in, but which was not thereby any the more estimable. And last but hardly least among the reasons for the slowness with which the east European Jews entered American political life was the fact that by the 1880's urban politics had come increasingly under the sway of the Irish. Themselves only several decades in this country, the Irish had shown a rare genius for improvising the styles and perquisites of the big-city machine, and they were hardly inclined to allow any latecomers, least of all Jews from Poland and Russia, to threaten their control.

In the last third of the nineteenth century, some immigrant Jews, mostly German, became prominent in the Republican party. Arriving in mid-century as sympathizers with the democratic spirit of '48, the German Jews usually sided with the northern cause; it seemed only natural that they should rally to the banner of antislavery and the party of "Father Abraham." In the decades after the Civil War their allegiance remained largely with the Republicans, and this no doubt played a certain role in prompting Republican administrations to make diplomatic representations in behalf of persecuted Jews in Europe. (When the Republican leader William Howard Taft spoke out against anti-Semitic excesses in Russia, the Orthodox Yiddish paper, the *Tageblatt*, wrote that "his goodness lies all over his face.") With time, as the Republicans showed themselves to be the party of respectable conservatism, the German Jews, increasingly affluent and at ease in America, tended to drift in the same direction. They gained places of honor in the party's ranks, some, like Edward Einstein and Israel Fisher, being sent to Congress by Republican majorities in New York. Oscar Straus and Simon Wolfe, both prominent German Jews, were awarded second-rank diplomatic posts abroad. And by the turn of the century, a number of high-minded German Jews in New York, led by Jacob Schiff and Louis Marshall, came to see the Republican party as the necessary antagonist to Tammany corruption.* A minority of German Jews, like Henry Morgenthau, Sr., and the millionaire Straus brothers, chose to become Democrats, identifying with the national party (the "Cleveland Democrats") and refusing to work with the corrupt bosses of Tammany Hall. But on a national scale and for some years into the twentieth century, the majority of American Jewish voters preferred the Republicans. In every presidential election between

* In the course of establishing themselves in this country, the German Jews built up a number of national organizations devoted to fraternal and quasi-political ends, ranging from B'nai B'rith to the American Jewish Committee. Later, the east European Jews would begin to enter and slowly transform these organizations. In accord with the experience of the European Jews that even while trying to influence gentile political parties it was best to keep a certain distance from them, these national Jewish organizations proved to be effective at quietly lobbying in behalf of Jewish interests. The strength of their own communal organizations may thus have been one reason for the caution with which both German and east European Jews made their way into American politics.

1900 and 1928, with the possible exceptions of 1900 and 1916, more Jews voted for Republicans than Democrats.

It was a preference that seldom extended to local politics. In the cities Jewish voters were inclined, though by no means invariably, to support the Democrats. The Republicans were feeble in most New York neighborhoods with large Jewish populations; they seemed out of touch with immigrant groups; and while sometimes virtuous, they were rarely men of the people. Spokesmen for Republican or Fusion reform movements would travel down to the East Side a few weeks before Election Day, hold rallies, announce a crusade to rid the city of Tammany corruption, and appeal for Jewish support. Rarely did such efforts fail completely—or persist for more than a few years. As an East Side gangster remarked: "These reform movements are like queen hornets. They sting you once, and then they die."

In 1894 the reform candidate for mayor of New York was William Strong, an upright conservative banker who won a clear victory with the help of a considerable Jewish vote. Though Strong proved to be an honest and efficient mayor, he soon managed to antagonize a large part of the East Side by insisting on a strict enforcement of all city ordinances—which meant that the police had to crack down on violators of the antipushcart and Sunday blue laws. Thousands of Jews who were Sabbath observers and chose to work on Sundays, as well as those who scraped out a living from pushcarts, decided it might, after all, be better to go back to the manageable corruption of Tammany. In the 1897 election Strong was beaten by a Tammany hack named Van Wyck, in part because Jews abandoned the reform ticket. This pattern would be repeated through several surges of reform, most dramatically in John Purroy Mitchel's years as mayor, 1914 to 1918, when his patrician insensitivity to immigrant fears of the Gary Plan for the New York schools (see p. 278) enabled Tammany to pile back into office.

In the early years of the twentieth century the Republicans still kept a strong hold on Jewish voters, at least during presidential elections. Theodore Roosevelt's progressive rhetoric and philo-Semitism won their hearts: it was pleasing that so *echt* an American should seem so well disposed to them. "In the presidential campaign of 1904 Yiddish community leaders enrolled 4,000 voters in the Independent Roosevelt Committee. For the first time in thirty years the Austro-Hungarian [Jewish] Sixteenth Assembly District, a banner Tammany district, elected a Republican assemblyman. What is more, the Roosevelt landslide nearly carried a Republican into Congress." In New York City the Republicans were usually more generous than the Democrats in nominating Jewish—mostly German-Jewish—candidates for local office, if only because a Republican nomination seldom brought much chance for election and could therefore be dispensed to marginal groups with a ready show of benevolence.

For the east European Jews, apart from those who gave themselves to the cause of socialism, the major arena in American politics would always be the Democratic party. These were the decades, all through the late nine-teenth and early twentieth centuries, when Tammany Hall ran New York City with a hard fist and an eager palm, in tacit accord with John Ran-dolph's famous judgment that politics rested on seven principles: "two loaves and five small fishes." George Washington Plunkitt, the turn-of-the-century Tammany leader who doubled as its streetside Machiavelli, re-marked that Tammany's "like the everlastin' rocks, the eternal hills, and the blockades on the 'L' road—it goes on forever." The founding father of modern Tammany, Boss Tweed, had been a Protestant rascal, but his reign, ending with an 1873 jail sentence due to certain financial irregularities, be-came more and more dependent on Irish rascals. With time the Irish gained support from German, Jewish, and even Italian rascals, though these new-comers were never allowed to share equally in rewards or decisions. Once Tweed was locked up, "Honest John" Kelly took over the leadership, and from then until at least the Second World War Tammany meant Irish power.

It was a power resting on a generous endowment of will, talent, and energy, but still more on a shrewd adaptation to big city life. The Irish, notes Daniel Moynihan, brought with them attitudes and aptitudes that no other ethnic group could match: "There was an indifference to Yankee proprieties," deriving no doubt from an earlier contempt for English preten-sions; there was "a settled tradition of regarding the formal government as illegitimate, and the informal one as bearing the true impress of popular sovereignty,"* which led to a kind of standoff between machine and govern-ment; and there was the fact that "most of the Irish arrived . . . fresh from the momentous experience of the Catholic Emancipation movement," pro-viding them with a tradition in mass politics that could be put to good use in American cities. Irish nationalist activity continued in America itself, and this, remarks William Shannon, "provided experience in building voluntary organizations, in working for large, impersonal goals, and in writing and reading lively polemical articles." One advantage of the Irish in American politics was the gift many of them had not only for speaking English but for speaking it beautifully. Not, however, all of them; before 1870 a number of the west of Ireland immigrants could speak only Irish.

The strategy they developed for dominating American cities rested on an amiable pluralism of graft in which social groups were rewarded with patronage in rough accordance to their political strength and reliability. It was a system resting on intense loyalties within the machine, so that a combination of local bosses dividing the spoils could also become a fellow-

* The point is reinforced by a personal communication from Andrew Greeley: "A major factor [in preparing the Irish for their political activities in the U.S.] was the west of Ireland Irish-speaking personal-fealty approach to politics. Irish-speaking Ireland was historically without governmental or legal enforcement structure. . . . The society was run to a very considerable extent on personal loyalty to one's colleagues, friends, and relatives—even to a greater extent than would have been the case in feudal Europe, where there was at least the symbol of central government."

ship of allies ("All there is in life," said Boss Croker, "is loyalty to one's family and friends"); on a deep collaboration with the police, so that even when elections were lost Tammany could maintain some of its strength and income; on tending to social needs and soothing of minor troubles among poor constituents (free coal and food to the needy, fixing traffic tickets, interceding with officials for jobs, entry of children into college, etc.); on an acute sensitivity to the feelings of ethnic groups just starting to settle into American life; and on a style of conduct and speech authentically popular in its outrageousness, its crudeness, its humor ("I seen my opportunities," said Boss Plunkitt, "and I took 'em").

About politics in any larger sense, about the craft and purpose of government, the Irish politicians were notoriously weak, and the more clever among them took pains to avoid holding office so as not to expose this poverty of mind. They were usually content to keep hands off the operations of government, if only they continued to get their "normal" share of loot; and in later years, when Al Smith became the leading Democratic politician in New York, they showed themselves ready to support progressive social legislation as long as it did not undermine their power within the party. Their attitude toward politics as a calling was a humorous combination of cynicism and benevolence; what they hated most was moral or ideological zeal, postures of rectitude. Plunkitt and Croker, Sullivan and Murphy, all would have agreed with the character in a Trollope novel who bursts out, "I hate Purity. . . . I hate the very smell of it. When I see the chaps [reformers] come here and talk of purity, I know they mean that nothin ain't to be as it used to be. Nobody is to trust no one. There ain't to be nothing warm, nor friendly, nor comfortable any more."

When extra votes might be needed, Tammany could use brass knuckles and its crew of "repeaters" from the Irish and Jewish gangs; the day before an election was customarily "dough day," when district captains would receive money for judicious distribution, usually at the rate of two dollars a vote, by no means a small sum for a poor man with a large family. But essentially the power of Tammany depended on the insight that in a society composed of ethnic groups not yet at ease with native mores, the politics of corruption might best be lubricated by a moderate infusion of social services. Plunkitt, who worked hard between apothegms, gave his biographer an account of an active day that began with racing to a fire at 6:00 AM, fires being "considered great vote-getters" because victims helped by the machine remained loyal when marking their ballots; then continued with visits to the police court in order to bail out some drunks and to the municipal court in order to help a widow dispossessed from her lodgings; proceeded to funerals for Italian and Jewish constituents, as well as conspicuous appearance at "the Hebrew confirmation ceremony in a synagogue"; continued with a meeting at which district captains were lectured on strategies for the next election, then a meeting with pushcart peddlers complaining of police harassment, "a

Hebrew wedding reception" and finally, at midnight, "in bed." Performing these errands, Plunkitt understood the dynamics by which large taking and small givings could be combined. "The politician who steals," he said, "is worse than a thief. He is a fool. With the grand opportunities all around for the man with political pull, there's no excuse for stealin' a cent."

How effective the Irish ward boss could be, and how complex his obligations could become, was acknowledged in a remarkable tribute by one of his fiercest opponents, the social worker Jane Addams:

> The Alderman bails out his constituents when they are arrested, or says a good word to the police justice when they appear before him for trial; uses his "pull" with the magistrate when they are likely to be fined for a civil misdemeanor, or sees what he can do to "fix up matters" with the State's attorney when the charge is really a serious one.
>
> The Alderman gives presents at weddings and christenings. He seizes these days of family festivities for making friends. . . . On their side it seems natural and kindly that he should do it.
>
> Such a man understands what the people want, and ministers just as truly to a great human need as the musician or the artist does. . . . [His constituents value] the consciousness that they have a big, warm-hearted friend at court who will stand by them in an emergency. *The sense of just dealing comes apparently much later than the desire for protection and kindness.*

Miss Addams did not conclude that the ward boss should be admired or kept in office; she merely insisted that if reformers or radicals, or even ordinary citizens, wished to undermine his power, they would first have to understand its sources.

Getting on with Tammany

Throughout the eighties and into the nineties, relations between Tammany and the immigrant Jews were neither close nor sustained. The tough-minded Tammany leaders had no intention of dealing any new ethnic group into the division of the spoils unless they were forced to; clearly, more profit could be had when the number of claimants was limited. There were other, perhaps deeper reasons for Irish reluctance to bring new immigrant groups to the center of Tammany power. Not only did Tammany serve material ends, it also yielded rewards of mutual esteem and personal coziness to the leaders and hangers-on, making Irishmen feel better about being Irishmen. But how was the sense of clan to be maintained if places had now to be found for east European Jews, so odd in their excitability, their abstractness, their discomfort before the pleasures of life? What could an "Honest John" Kelly make of an astringent Abraham Cahan?

By the late eighties, it is true, a small number of Jewish figures routinely won nominations in New York from both major parties, usually for such modest posts as coroner and alderman-at-large. But since the Jewish voters, estimated at 11,000 in 1880, were scattered throughout the city and not yet able to command decisive strength in a single district, Tammany had little reason to be generous. And for their part, the east European Jews had at first little taste for the rough-and-tumble of low-level municipal politics. They were often contemptuous of American politics for ideological reasons and sometimes fearful for religious reasons; they did not always bother to become citizens; they seemed still too absorbed with their own inner life to respond to the politics of the city.

The settlement-house worker Mary Simkhovitch would remember that at election time Martin Engel, boss of the Eighth Ward at about the turn of the century, "used to drive through in an open barouche, his fingers laden with diamonds, and more diamonds shone from his cravat. The intellectual Jewish East Side for the most part did not comprehend the game played by the political leaders. But they dimly realized what benefits accrued from keeping in with the forceful ones." And what they did understand of local politics, many East Siders hated: "Traffic in votes was quite an open business in those days. . . . I saw the bargaining, the haggling between buyer and seller; I saw money passing from the one to the other. . . . Favors, favors, favors! I heard that word so often, in connection with politics, that the two words became inseparable in my mind. A politician was a 'master of favors,' as my native tongue would have it."

It is a nice irony of immigrant life that the one event which seems to have persuaded Tammany to start paying close attention to the East Side was a plunge by Jewish immigrants into left-wing American politics. In 1886 the United Labor party, a rickety alliance of radicals, trade unionists, and liberals, ran the single-tax theorist Henry George as its candidate for mayor. Earnest in speech and radical in views, Henry George won the hearts of many immigrant Jews, and for the first time a sizable number of them became active in local politics. Henry George clubs were set up on the East Side, street meetings were held in Yiddish, and, a few days before the election, a large rally was organized at which George made an impassioned speech comparing the liberation of the Jews from the Pharaohs 3,500 years ago with his campaign to ease the lot of New York wage earners. George polled 68,000 votes; his Democratic opponent, Abraham Hewitt, 90,000, and the Republican candidate, Theodore Roosevelt, 60,000. Even in nonradical circles it was commonly believed that an honest count (no easy matter in New York) would have given the election to George. In the Jewish wards he ran especially well, and in the city as a whole his total Jewish vote was estimated as anywhere between five thousand and fifteen thousand.

Whatever its exact size or meaning, this vote was taken by Tammany as a clear signal that politics in New York was changing, and with the accession of Richard Croker as boss in 1886, the Hall began to adapt itself. The coalition behind George soon disintegrated, as such coalitions usually do, but for the Jewish immigrants this first taste of politics had by no means been bitter. At least some of them showed a flair for politics; they were slowly beginning to discover, as the *Tageblatt* would say in a brilliant phrase, that "a Jew in Exile has no power other than his mouth"; they were ready to work hard for candidates whom they trusted; and if someone would only manage to enroll more of them as citizens, they could become a significant political force within a decade or two.*

Jewish candidates who had previously felt it wise to identify themselves as civic-minded gentlemen of German descent now felt it wiser not only to announce they were Jews but also to appeal directly to Jewish interests. The famous problem of whether there is a "Jewish vote" and whether it can be "delivered" by one or another communal leader began to be discussed, seemingly without end. Slowly, not yet on a major scale, the Jews were granted larger slices of patronage, and with time, more of it to east Europeans than Germans: four or five places in the State Legislature, a seat in 1910 on the Board of Education, and once in a while nomination to higher office (Simon Rosendale as Democratic candidate for state attorney general in 1891). Political advertisements, an indirect sort of ethnic patronage, began to appear in the Yiddish papers; handbills were printed in Yiddish; district leaders learned the date of Jewish holidays. A few efforts, never very successful, were made to encourage ethnic clubs tied to Tammany: "The Russian American League of the 8th A.D.," reported the *Tammany Times* in 1897, "is pledging its support to the Democratic Party. Alexander Grossman is president. . . ." And Tammany grew more careful of Jewish sensibilities: its house organ, the *Tammany Times*, which still permitted itself dialect jokes in the early nineties ("Repecca, you shall nod shpeak mit dot Silverstone boy vonce more") began to print respectful notices about Jewish dignitaries.

The custom of small favors was systematized, as was the network of relations between Tammany and the Jewish saloonkeepers—the latter insignificant within the Jewish world itself but of growing importance for the Jewish penetration of Tammany. And with their usual responsiveness to the feelings of ethnic constituents, the Tammany leaders regularly took stands opposing immigrant restrictions—they, at least, were not inclined to share Protestant fears that the country was being overrun by alien hordes.

But while Tammany established itself as the dominant force in East Side politics, it never quite won the unquestioning adherence among immigrant Jews that it enjoyed in other parts of the city. An eloquent Socialist, a

* But the 1910 census showed that only 18.6 percent of foreign-born males of voting age in the Second, Fourth, and Eighth assembly districts, all heavily Jewish, were naturalized. In part, this low percentage was due to the enormous influx of immigrants after 1905, but it also indicated what was common knowledge on the East Side, that many Jews did not trouble to become citizens.

righteous voice of Fusion, a deeply American figure like Theodore Roosevelt, could lure away Jewish votes. There were always some unreliable pockets, like the Sixth Assembly District in the upper portion of the East Side (extending slightly north of Fourteenth Street), where the shrewd Hungarian Jew, Samuel Koenig, had organized the Federal Club in 1891, wrested local control from the native boss George Hilliard, and made the district, rapidly filling up with Jews, into a Republican stronghold. The heavily Jewish Eighth Assembly District voted for the Democrat, William Jennings Bryan, in 1900 and the Republican, Theodore Roosevelt, in 1904; its "representative in Albany is alternately a Republican and a Democrat." Immigrant Jews were too restless and too indifferent, too skeptical and too utopian—all together, in an improbable mixture—simply to yield their souls to a political machine. They recognized its power and acknowledged its uses, but unwavering surrender to any gentile institution was not a course to which they could readily accommodate themselves.

There was a major sociological reason for this. Tammany could provide valuable services for the minority of immigrants who were coming into regular contact with agencies of government: it could bring relief to peddlers facing court fines, smooth the way for storekeepers needing the benevolence of local police, and, later on, help real-estate men and contractors gain favors from City Hall. But those Tammany services which might be described as a miniature anticipation of the welfare state—charity, social work, medical help, burial arrangements—seem to have counted somewhat less among Jews than other immigrant groups. For the Jews, persuaded by their entire history that they had to take care of their own, brought with them a tradition of keeping an elaborate network of social and charitable agencies, and once these were re-created on the American scene, the district captain's largesse came to seem, if not unwelcome, then certainly less important. The very coherence of Jewish life enabled a good many immigrants to maintain a satisfying distance from the political machine. Only when immigrant Jews started moving outward in large numbers, toward the business and professional centers of the city, could Tammany be of crucial help as a link to agencies of power.

By the nineties, ambitious young Jews were beginning to be accepted as Tammany hangers-on, messengers, and flunkies. About the turn of the century Leon Stand, father of the Tammany luminaries Bert and Murray Stand, became the first Jewish lieutenant of John F. Ahearn, the powerful Tammany leader of the Fourth Assembly District in the heart of the East Side. An old-timer recalls the workings of the Jewish officialdom in Tammany, still very small-fry, during the nineties:

> On a hot night of June 1894, Tammany's Jewish politicians were holding a special session in the rooms of the Fourth Ward Club. Max Hochstim . . . was to give them a pep talk. They had to deliver more than the usual vote in the coming election or "your names will be mud."

Hochstim spoke the language of the district, not the high-falutin' English of the Fusion agitators who came downtown to address outdoor meetings. "Boys," he said, "we're in trouble. If we lose this election we lose our jobs. And jobs, you know, are hard to get right now." This was the language the assembled could understand. "Them reformers have given us a bad name. . . ."

The [local process server] "counselor" Julius Melkin arose in all his diminutive dignity . . . and addressing the visiting statesmen as "your honors," he cleared his voice and said: "I have a slogan. Jews have not been getting political jobs. Everything goes to the Irish. Where do you see a Jewish copper, a Jewish fireman, a Jewish street-cleaner, a horse-car driver or conductor? To get out the vote we must demand our rights. . . . I have the slogan which will get out the vote for Tammany: 'Jobs for Jews.'"

Prolonged applause. Mr. Hochstim shook hands with Julius and congratulated him. Said Max: "Counselor, you are an asset to the party. We won't forget you." And then Max delivered the famous line which won the municipal elections . . . "Boys," said Max, "we will beat them uptown bums yet. Get busy, go out and scratch. *To hell with reform!*"

After the turn of the century political conduct became a little more circumspect, and unsavory characters like Max Hochstim were replaced by young men who had gone to high school or even become lawyers. Still, a Jewish aspirant casting his fortune with Tammany had to take on or simulate a certain rough plebeian gloss. He learned to chew, smoke, and gamble. He made himself visible in the clubrooms, he peddled chowder tickets, he put placards in store windows. He rooted himself in the neighborhood as the agent of the Irish leader—though in so doing he sometimes harmed his own prospects, for by cutting himself off from Jewish communal life and devoting himself entirely to the machine, he might become excessively dependent on the leader. Once he had proven his loyalty and worth, he would be taken into the leader's confidence and receive assignments of some importance. Henry Schimmel, later a state assemblyman and local magistrate, was recruited to the John F. Ahearn Association in 1908 by Aaron Jefferson Levy. Mr. Ahearn saw in Schimmel a willing worker and assigned him to go to court with peddlers who had received summonses.

Usually they'd be fined a dollar [recalls Schimmel]. But they didn't like the idea of waiting in court. So I asked Ike Rice, the court clerk, if I could plead their cases in their absence. He had no objections, so that's what I did. I developed quite a reputation as a result. Whenever someone got into trouble, they'd say, "Give it to Schimmel, he'll take care of it!" In fact, "Give it to Schimmel" became a slogan in our neighborhood. Later I'd check to see whether a fellow for whom I had done a favor voted for the ticket, and if he didn't I'd let him know about it.

That Tammany leaders allowed a few Jewish handymen to scoop up minor spoils does not mean they were ready to share power with the Jews or anyone else. For decades, even in those districts with overwhelming

Jewish majorities, most of the crucial posts remained in Irish hands. The kind of business conducted by Tammany leaders depended on confidential relations within a clan, a stained brotherhood in which benefits and burdens were quietly shared and the links between henchmen cut far deeper than mere common interest. Tammany signified shared background, experience, sentiment. Internecine warfare could, and often did, break out within the Hall, but most of the time that signified a fissure, not an abandonment, of loyalties.

The Jews were "different." Leaders like Plunkitt might learn to attend Jewish weddings and keep their hats on when visiting a *shul*, and a bit later Big Tim Sullivan might give out two thousand free pairs of shoes to the East Side needy in sacred memory of his mother's birthday. Yet such men felt uncomfortable with most immigrant Jews, as, for that matter, most immigrant Jews with them. In the eighties and nineties, only a few Jews, like "Silver Dollar" Smith, a saloonkeeper who had shown himself free of traditional Jewish scruples against the use of fists, were allowed to become district leaders. (As late as 1907 there was still only one Jewish district leader in the whole of Tammany.) Most Jewish politicians did not really command much power within Tammany, the mere ability to make a speech or even win elections never unduly impressing its leaders. An exception was Aaron Jefferson Levy, "as likable a rascal," remembered a henchman, "as ever donned a legislator's toga." When Tammany jammed through impeachment proceedings in 1913 against Governor William Sulzer, who had been treacherous enough to show some independence after being elected, it was Aaron Jefferson Levy, now majority leader in the State Assembly, who served as "prosecutor." "Aaron did not personally dislike the Governor. But once his unpleasant assignment was outlined, he went diligently about the task"—for which he was later rewarded with a municipal judgeship.

Equally loyal was Henry Schimmel. When Mr. Ahearn chose him to be a candidate for assemblyman in 1913—Schimmel, "an unknown, a nobody," ahead of such true-blue members as Max Lipman, Izzy Scherer, Hymie Turchin, and Sam Dickstein—no one at the county convention dared ask, "Who's Schimmel?" For even if some wondered what the Boss had in mind, "they all knew their place." Schimmel ran home crying all the way like a baby. Later he figured it out. "It was my honesty that Mr. Ahearn liked. And the fact that I was supporting a mother." To Schimmel and others like him, Mr. Ahearn would always be a great Christian gentleman who dispensed justice to his Jewish retainers.

During the four years he served in the Assembly, Schimmel voted regularly with the party, but when it came to after-duty hours, a night's drinking or more intimate diversions, he preferred to go his own way, apart from his party colleagues. He just didn't go out much with the boys up there, nor did they expect him to. The Jewish assemblymen from both parties were quieter, inclined to keep to themselves and sometimes have dinner together. For them, as Schimmel would remember it, life in Albany was somewhat "lonely." On the few occasions when a measure came up in the Assembly involving distinctly Jewish interests, there was hardly any need for Jewish members from the two parties to caucus. "We just worked together automatically. There was a bond of loyalty cutting across party lines."

What sort of young men gravitated toward the East Side Tammany clubs? "As a rule," wrote an observer, they were

> of a lower order, having nothing but regularity and party fealty as their redeeming features. Usually, their education has ended with a course in public schools. From that time they are close readers of the *Daily News*, the *World* and the *Journal*, and keep "posted" on all political questions. Add to this the mellowing influence of the Tammany leaders' discourse and society, and the young men are fit for any office within the gift of the "people."

If this seems snobbish, it was a snobbism probably shared by a good many immigrant Jews. Becoming a Tammany *meshores* (messenger boy) didn't strike fathers and mothers as a worthy career for their sons; they hoped for something a little more ennobling, or at least more secure and independent. Yet once their sons became lawyers, it was often an economic necessity that they tie in with the local clubs. In 1908 Henry Schimmel graduated from NYU law school and, in exchange for office space, did free legal work for Aaron Jefferson Levy; when Levy took him to the Ahearn clubhouse, Schimmel started picking up scraps of business that brought in a few pennies.*

There were other Jewish recruits to the party clubs who found a home of sorts under the wings of Irish leaders.

It was a turning point in his life, Louis Eisenstein would always feel, when he joined the John F. Ahearn Association in 1917, recruited by the veteran member and former assemblyman, Henry Schimmel. At first Louis drew the usual drab errands, but once he established his worth he was chosen to be a precinct captain. Holding this post meant being "friend, confidant, political and social worker" for about a thousand voters. One day

---

* This pattern would be repeated almost twenty years later when another young Jewish lawyer, Louis Lefkowitz, found himself without clients or income. He turned to the local Republican boss, Herman Marblestone, who lived in the same Houston Street apartment house as the poverty-striken Lefkowitz, and Marblestone told Louis to come over to the Republican clubhouse. Because this happened to be within a Republican enclave that extended on the East Side from Houston Street to Sixteenth Street, Lefkowitz found it prudent to become a Republican: after a while, it brought him a few ill paying clients. Forty-five years later he was frank enough to admit that, while the Republicans had seemed a little more "elevated" than Tammany, his main motive for becoming a Republican had been simple: it was necessary to eat. And in the Republican party, far more porous in structure than Tammany, a bright young fellow like Lefkowitz might rise faster than in Tammany.

a year, Election Day, Louis received his reward. "It was for me, not my party's candidates, that my constituents cast their ballots."

Louis knew that in entering the Ahearn Association he had joined a fine company of men. Mr. Ahearn kept his promises, spread out the rewards of victory, helped care for the electorate, and, unlike Tim Sullivan, leader of the nearby Eighth Assembly District, refrained from excessive greed. When an old Yiddish-speaking man came up to the clubhouse on 290 East Broadway, Mr. Ahearn would say, "Louis, talk to this man in his own language, he didn't come here to see a show." Louis enjoyed being useful to both his leader and a fellow Jew.

Decades later, after the Ahearn dynasty had fallen, Louis would think back on its fifty-six years, feeling somewhat like a Roman stoic who in times of decadence recalls times of honor. He would remember the days when "Mr. Ahearn's authority was never challenged . . . and he ruled like a benevolent country squire." On Monday and Thursday evenings "the District's Congressman, State Senator, State Assemblyman and Alderman were present and accounted for at the club." Once, when a young lawyer failed to fulfill his promise that he would defend a poor peddler in court, Mr. Ahearn sternly banished him from the clubhouse. Mr. Ahearn would assign tasks, or, as they were called, "contracts," and the precinct captains took them seriously: "no promise that could not be kept was made, no promise was made that could not be kept." In the summers the association held its annual outing, "a pleasant boat ride up the Hudson [toward a spot where East Side folks could enjoy] the aroma of fresh, green grass. . . . At night a torchlight parade slowly wound its way from the boat landing up South Street to the Ahearn clubhouse." Shopkeepers along the way spread sawdust on their sidewalks in the shape of letters spelling out Mr. Ahearn's name. "Wetted with gasoline, and ignited by match, the emblem burst forth into flames just as the marchers passed by."

Those were good days. "No religious rebellion took place. . . . The name 'Ahearn' was good enough for everyone." It didn't matter, in the Tammany clan, whether you were Irish or Jew; after a while, it didn't even matter whether you were Italian, just as long as you played by the rules—though, truth to tell, the Irish tended to be rather contemptuous of the Italians and to trust them less than the Jews, who if suspect as a group were loyal and brainy as individuals.

Louis met important men in the political world. There was Aaron Jefferson Levy, perhaps not quite as strict as he should have been in his career as a judge, but still "a warm and humane friend." There was Sam Koenig, the wily Republican boss who extracted profit from defeat by "working closely with Tammany leaders on patronage." (Once, at a banquet, Sam whispered, "We Republicans and Democrats fight only one day a year," and Louis nodded in happy agreement.) There was Sam Dickstein, who succeeded Henry Goldfogle in Congress, and there was the astute Sam

Mandelbaum, the Fourth's assemblyman, and most of all, there were the Ahearns, John F. and his son Eddie.

Thanks to such friends, Louis was awarded a post-office job in 1920, though, to his surprise, he had to work hard. Accused of being a "Jew shirker" by the foreman, Louis dumped a mail bag on the man's head and was fired. Next morning Louis arrived with a stern note from Congressman Goldfogle and in a few minutes was back on the job. Justice in those days was direct, personal, immediate, and you knew where to turn for it.

Later came other jobs, not exactly plums, more like leavings, but Louis wasn't the one to complain. When Eddie Ahearn got into a fight during the twenties with the Tammany leadership and patronage dried up for the association, Louis remained a liege faithful to his lord. When Eddie died, in 1934, things really began to go bad, and Louis ran into hard days. A Jewish triumvirate, Murray and Bert Stand and Henry Schimmel, tried to hold things together by steering the new leader, brain-damaged Willy Ahearn, but it didn't work. Bert Stand knifed Louis politically, but then how could anyone compare a man like Bert Stand to a Mr. Ahearn?

It wasn't as if Louis failed to see that some stripes on the Tammany tiger shone less brightly than others. He recognized that "in the dim back rooms of many Tammany clubhouses" there was gambling, though most of the games were "clean. That is, they were run as legitimately as you could run an illegitimate activity." He knew some of the district leaders were plain thieves. And he even had to admit that upon becoming Manhattan borough president in 1904 Mr. Ahearn had made a grave error in closing his eyes to the corruption that flourished under him—and for which he was removed from office during one of the city's flare-ups of reform. But to the end Louis was convinced that Mr. Ahearn himself had never dipped a hand into the till, it was just that "as Borough President [he found himself] unable to avoid the pitfalls" of corrupt underlings.

In later years Louis watched the Ogilvies, the Currys, and the De Sapios take their turns as Tammany leader. One evening at the Commodore he listened with quiet scorn as the hacks sang a song for Boss Curry:

> So here's to John Curry,
>   The Chief of the Clan;
> We won't have to worry
>   While he's our head man.

By the thirties, things were falling apart. The Hall suffered poor leadership; La Guardia would soon be ripping it to pieces; Irish and Italian blocs were at war, "with Jewish district chiefs gravitating from one clique to another." Such ethnic battles seemed unworthy to Louis, a desecration of the spirit of the old days when Mr. Ahearn ruled without challenge and his Jewish boys obeyed without hesitation, all of them together honoring the association's motto, "Without Favor or Price." For Louis the clubhouse had been "a welcome oasis in a sea of uncertainty," and later, in the time of his aging, he knew those days would never come again.

The Jews and the Irish

During the years when young men like Henry Schimmel and Louis Eisenstein were making their way into the party, relations between Irish and Jews within Tammany were generally amiable, seldom close, and far more complicated than either side recognized. Very few of the Jews who turned to old-party politics were fervent men; some were decent, many shrewd, most practical; but they were hardly the sort of burning moralists or fanatic idealists who would disturb the peace within Tammany. They took positions subordinate to the Irish leaders, and within the scale of their perspective, it made good sense that they do so. They lacked the confidence, experience, and toughness that would have been required to challenge Irish power, and even if they had tried and succeeded in one or two districts, they would have been crushed within Tammany as a whole. Besides, their interests were different in character from those of the entrenched Irish leaders, so that for some decades the two groups could live together in a makeshift division of labor and rewards. The main Irish interest lay in controlling the machine as a clan preserve; the main Jewish interest in the advancement of individual careers, through appointive jobs or elected office. (Among Jewish political advisers who worked with but not in Tammany, there would also be an element of social concern and idealism.)

Thinking in personal rather than ethnic terms, the Jews in Tammany showed no desire to unseat the Irish leaders, even in districts where the Jews had become the overwhelming majority—though on occasion they might join with one Irish leader against another, as in the fight between Eddie Ahearn and John Curry in the twenties. Only by the late twenties and thirties does one hear grumblings among Irish machine workers that the Jews, especially those serving as advisers to Al Smith and Franklin Roosevelt, are getting too powerful. But in the earlier decades men like the Levys, Goldfogles, and Dicksteins were content to sup off Irish plates; and they seem to have shared the view that Henry Schimmel would express many years later, that if a Jew became district leader in the Fourth Assembly District it would lead to bitter warfare because other Jews would then feel the post was within their reach, while if a feared and admired Irishman like Ahearn held the power, he would keep both the peace and a rough sort of justice among his Jewish retainers.

As for the Irish leaders in heavily Jewish neighborhoods, self-preservation required a bending of manner and tactics. But as men naturally inclined toward friendliness and, often enough, a feeling for impoverished minority groups, some Irish leaders could genuinely warm toward the immigrant Jews. That "John Ahearn loved the Jews," as Henry Schimmel would later recall, may have been an overstatement; that he got along well with them is not. After the famous riot at the funeral for Chief Rabbi Jacob Joseph (see p. 123), where gentile workers in the R. H. Hoe factory threw objects at mourning Jews in the streets, Mr. Ahearn ordered his men to break all the windows in the factory as a sign of his displeasure. "The Jews loved him for that," as well they might, and when word got around the East Side it made him more political friends than could any number of food baskets. Eddie Ahearn continued in the steps of his father, once beating up a fireman who ranted against Jews and many times announcing, with good reason, that he "owed everything" to them. When he died, in 1934, some twenty thousand people on the East Side attended his funeral, clear enough evidence that, for good or bad, the Irish dynasty had won the hearts of Jewish immigrants.

Yet the Ahearns were not above an occasional crudity toward their Jewish followers, in part to remind them who was boss, in part to have a little fun along familiar gentile lines.

> Sometimes [recalled Henry Schimmel] Mr. Ahearn would play tricks on us. I remember when I was an assemblyman, there was a Jew named Wennig who kept a fish store open on Sundays. The priest next door, a Father McIntyre, did everything to impede Wennig. So Wennig tells his troubles to Mr. Ahearn. The Boss asks Mike Looney to talk to the priest, but Mike says no. He asks Scully and Devlin, but they also turn him down. Next he asks me, so I go to see Father McIntyre in his parish house. Before I can do more than introduce myself, he calls me a liar and throws me out. When I return to the clubhouse and tell the Boss what happened, he laughs and laughs. Only then do I find out that Father McIntyre has a notorious reputation for temper, a regular fire-eater. Next day the Boss pays a call on him and the problem is resolved, but meanwhile I've been made to look a little foolish.

Louis Eisenstein tells a similar story about Eddie Ahearn and Congressman Samuel Dickstein:

> On one particularly frigid Monday night [Dickstein] knocked on the door of Eddie's office. . . .
> "Sorry, I can't see you right now, Sam. But hang around," said Eddie, mysteriously. "There's something I want to talk over with you. Not in here though. Wait in front of the building. I'll be out in a few minutes."
> Sam waited on the sidewalk in snow several inches deep. . . . Must be pretty important, he figured, if the chief wanted to see him alone out here. A half hour passed. Then almost an hour. Sam still waited. He shook the snow from his shoulders. . . . At last the door creaked open and Eddie appeared—with several of us.
> "Sam," he said, "what on earth are you doing out here shivering in the snow? I thought you left."
> "But you told me to wait . . ." replied the chattering Congressman.
> "Wait?" Eddie responded with a look of mock amazement. "Why

should I have you wait in the middle of the blizzard? Do you think I'm crazy? Go home and warm up!"

In Washington a lawmaker, at the clubhouse Sam Dickstein was still one of Eddie's boys, subject to the whim or, on occasion, the sadism of his boss.

The first crop of politicians to emerge from the east European Jewish milieu was not very impressive. Henry Goldfogle, a shrewd fellow, proved adept at adjusting Tammany interests to Jewish sentiments, and gained a sort of fame for regularly introducing resolutions in the House denouncing Russian mistreatment of Jews. When a successor had to be chosen in 1922, Henry Schimmel wanted the nomination, but Eddie Ahearn decided to give it to Dickstein. And for a good reason: Schimmel had submerged himself in Tammany chores while Dickstein was building his own, independent support in the Jewish community and therefore seemed a stronger candidate. As a boy Dickstein had organized the Knickerbocker Club, meeting at Pitt and Rivington streets, with the purpose of teaching "immigrants to distinguish between the chaff of radicalism and the wheat of patriotism." On the lookout for a Yiddish-speaking antagonist to Jewish socialism, John Ahearn had noticed young Dickstein and adopted him as a political protégé. Once in Congress, Dickstein would usually cast a liberal vote on social and immigration bills—his political survival depended on that—but neither in politics at large nor in Jewish affairs in particular did he play a role of much distinction.

The same was true for other Jewish congressmen from New York—Sol Bloom, who wrote honestly enough that he had been chosen by Tammany because "I was an amiable and solvent Jew," and William Sirovich, self-proclaimed "Father Confessor of the East Side," who titillated Congress with his baroque rhetoric ("I regard Congress as the uterus and myself as the fertilizer preparing it for pioneer measures"). Emanuel Celler of Brownsville was a notch or two higher, coming to exert a considerable power in Washington.

These men represented the compromise the East Side, and its offshoots in other boroughs, had to make with America, perhaps the compromise immigrant Jews had first to make with themselves in order to confront America. Rather little of what gave immigrant Jewish life its moral and intellectual glow remained with the men it sent to the nation's legislatures. The most distinguished minds of the East Side, the most pungent and authentic Jewish personalities, neither turned to old-line politics nor could have succeeded had they tried. The early Jewish politicians in Tammany were not bad men, they were just commonplace men, signaling the price—perhaps not excessive, but a price nonetheless—the Jews would have to pay for their entrenchment in the new world.*

* This is not merely a retrospective judgment. There is a story told about Hymie Shorenstein, for decades a Democratic district leader in Brooklyn, whose "Yiddish accent was as thick as good sour cream. He ran his district with the traditional iron

For most of the Jewish politicians, their Jewishness had become the largest of the political fences to be mended back home; it was seldom the substance of strong conviction. When Emanuel Celler reported that he had found it an "agony" to listen to the anti-Semitic diatribes of Congressman John Rankin of Mississippi, he was entirely sincere. Yet apart from political necessities and defensive reactions, most Jewish politicians tended to be somewhat denatured Jews, the markings of their youth rubbed down by the pressures of wheeling and dealing. Perhaps the career of politics required that the immigrant tone, the Jewish fervor, be gradually discarded in favor of a hardheaded "pragmatism." And as for ideas about American society as a whole, this was hardly something to be expected from the Jewish men of Tammany. What American politics got from the Goldfogles, Dicksteins, and their like was shrewdness, oratory, philistinism, and a voting record at least as liberal as that from other sections of the country.

Maneuvering Within the City

In the political life of the big cities, the east European Jews slowly became a recognized force, not merely on Election Day but also with regard to such daily unglamorous matters as attention and patronage. Attention, an

---

hand." One year he nominated a young man for the assembly. The candidate, taking himself seriously, began to prepare speeches and opinions; but as weeks went by he received no call from the party. He tried to meet Shorenstein, but without any luck. Finally on the club night, he joined a long line of constituents waiting to see the leader. When his turn came, the following conversation took place:

"Mr. Shorenstein," he began, "do you remember me?"

"Sure," came the reply.

"I'm running for the Assembly."

"I know," grunted Shorenstein. "I picked you."

"But I've been running for six weeks and nobody knows it. No speeches, no rallies, no literature. What shoud I do?"

"Go home," said Shorenstein.

"But—"

"Go home."

As the young man, dismissed, started out the door, Shorenstein relented.

"Young man," he said. "Come back." "Young man," he said. "You ever been to the East River?"

"Yes."

"You see the ferryboats come in?" asked Shorenstein.

"Yes."

"You see them pull into the slip?"

"Yes."

"You see the water suck in behind?"

"Yes."

"And when the water sucks in behind the ferryboat, all kinds of garbage comes smack into the slip with the ferryboat?"

"Yes."

"So go home and relax. Al Smith is the ferryboat. This year you're the garbage."

element of local politics that has not been sufficiently studied, refers to the capacity of a group—ethnic, racial, class, neighborhood, ideological—to regularize the expectation that its demands, complaints, and sentiments will be heeded promptly, if not always satisfied entirely, by the authorities. To gain such attention, a group must be able to prove its capacity not only for controlling a segment of votes but also for establishing its presence in the day-to-day bargaining by means of which power is exerted and decisions are made.

It took some years for the immigrant Jews to learn to play this game: they had first to shake off some of their best and worst traits, a good part of what made their culture at once exalted and provincial. To suggest a precise date would be pointless, but our impression is that only with William Gaynor's maverick administration as mayor (1910–1914) did the East Side really begin to exert an influence at City Hall commensurate with its numbers and social weight in the city. Until about then, the immigrant Jews had available a number of institutions and power brokers for the exercise of pressure, but lacked the necessary experience, self-assurance, and, most of all, outgoingness.

As early as the 1890's, candidates for major office had begun regularly to speak at East Side rallies—a few years later, also in Brownsville and the Bronx. In the 1897 mayoralty campaign, for example, the reform candidate, Seth Low, addressed large audiences on East Broadway, Orchard Street, and Columbia Street. But such meetings were still somewhat erratic, as may be gathered from a report in the New York *Sun:*

> *Low Invades the Orient.* All the audience wanted was someone to give them the cue in Hebrew or Yiddish, for none of them understood a word of English. Chairman Rothschild introduced Mr. Low. The crowd had been coaxed into the hall by a band of musicians. The audience soon fell into a conversational acquaintance with each other and the men on each bench held little arguments with each other. Mr. Low waited for peace and then seeing it was a "hopeless hope," as they say on the East Side, he started off again to tell them who he was and what he was there for. . . . A cry shut Mr. Low off. When he inquired what it meant he was told that the crowd said, "What does he mean?" Becoming satisfied that the East Side did not understand him, he bowed and hurried from the hall.

That the major parties nevertheless came increasingly to the East Side meant that the East Side could go increasingly to City Hall. Throughout the administration of Tammany's Robert Van Wyck, mayor from 1898 to 1901, there was a constant, sometimes rather strained, relationship between semi-informal (often self-appointed) agents of the immigrant community and representatives of the mayor. In 1900, for example, when protests were made by David Blaustein, head of the Educational Alliance, against police tie-ins with East Side vice, they were answered with an alacrity that had not always existed in the past. A small enough courtesy; but in fact it signified a consolidation of Jewish political strength to the point where some attention had to be paid—even if, at times, with grumblings about those contentious Jews.

Relations between the immigrant Jews and the various agencies of city government were repeatedly aggravated by disputes over such "courtesy" issues as Sunday blue laws, Sabbath observance by Jewish workers, the demands of teachers that they be paid when they stayed home on Jewish holidays, Christmas observance in the public schools, and in later years the bitterly contested issue of "released time" in the public schools for religious instruction. Some of these issues touched sore spots in the feelings of both Jews and gentiles; others raised difficult problems regarding the relation between church and state, since the general principle of separation could not provide guidance for particular ambiguities.

Sunday blue laws were enforced sporadically, sometimes by reform administrations preferring legalism to tolerance. For Jewish storekeepers these bursts of strictness meant irritation and harassment. The wish of religious Jewish workers to stay home on Saturday and work on Sunday, especially important before the five-day week, was a constant subject of dispute, often without easy resolution. As late as the Equal Employment Opportunity Act of 1972 efforts were still being made to work out reasonable terms: the act recognized the right of Sabbath observance provided it did not cause undue hardship to the employer. Christmas ceremonies in the schools were always likely to rouse strong feelings on both sides, with Jews persuaded that such ceremonies threatened the religious integrity of their children and Christians feeling that the Jews were unreasonable in trying to prevent children from enjoying what had in effect become a universal holiday.

In 1906 this dispute came to a head when New York rabbis and some Yiddish papers urged parents to keep their children out of school during Christmas as a protest against "sectarian ceremonies." Between 20,000 and 25,000 children, about a third of the East Side school population, joined the boycott. Jewish sensibilities had been exacerbated by a recent trial of a Brownsville school principal, Frank Harding, charged with trying to convert Jewish pupils. The local school board had exonerated Harding, the Board of Education had reprimanded him. Shortly before Christmas, a Jewish delegation appeared at the Board of Education to argue that "all of these things [pictures of Madonnas, compositions about Jesus, Christmas trees, etc.] should be done away with as completely as should corresponding symbols of Judaism, Mohammedanism, or infidelism." Seeing itself trapped between aroused constituencies, the Board voted to let individual principals use their judgment as to which ceremonies were appropriate, which not.

Politically, these conflicts bore explosive possibilities. Glancing through the dry minutes of the Board of Education yields an impression that among some of its gentile members the Jewish demands evoked strong irritation, as if they felt the Jews were "pressing too hard" or forgetting that, while, yes, church and state were separate, still this was a *Christian* country. Such matters seldom came to the forefront of urban politics, but they simmered in the background. Precisely because they could not be settled by legal decisions and involved delicacies of relationship between adjacent communities, they were usually treated informally, through private discussions between "communal representatives" or power brokers and city officials.

One of the most indefatigable power brokers linking the immigrant Jews to American politics was Joseph Barondess (see pp. 113–15), who by 1905 or a bit sooner had graduated from the socialist and trade-union milieu to become a sort of all-purpose *shames* (sexton) or *makher* (operator) on the East Side. Reading through the enormous Barondess correspondence, one can easily misperceive him as a mere comic figure, the quintessential busybody poking his nose into everyone's affairs. In actuality, Barondess was beginning to master the American art of political pressure: he begged, he cajoled, he whined, he threatened, often for good causes (unrestricted immigration), sometimes for a crumb of patronage for East Side cronies, occasionally for a personal favor. Quite poor himself, and only recently having learned to write a passable English letter, he nevertheless won the ears of the mighty and the influential, more, it would seem, through persistence than power. "I want to impress upon you," he writes to Congresman William Sulzer, "that it is very important that you accept the invitation [from the Liberal Immigration League]. You have been our staunchest friend, and your presence will add a great deal of weight and importance to the banquet." To the Honorable William S. Bennett he writes asking for help in getting a Russian passport for the Yiddish actor, Boris Thomashefsky. To Mayor William Gaynor he writes complaining of how "brutal some of our police officers are." Barondess's letters to Gaynor are especially frequent: he sends a synopsis of Jacob Gordin's play *God, Man, and the Devil* asking the mayor to attend the opening of David Kessler's production; he writes in behalf of "the Jewish Fourth of July Celebration," thanking the mayor for allowing the East Side "to participate in a purely American festival"; he sends information on the mugging of Israel Goldstein, charging that the police know it to be "a common occurrence for loafers to attack Jewish pedestrians . . . but they don't do anything to stop it"; he whimpers that "it is impossible for me, without absolutely . . . and utterly disgracing myself to inform the Board of Directors of the Beth Israel Hospital of your intention [i.e., the mayor's] not to be present at their annual meeting." Just as it had been the custom in the old country for unlettered people to employ a scribe for communications of business, faith, and love, so on the East Side those who needed a favor or pushed a cause but felt uneasy about writing directly to "*di Amerikaner*" would turn to the ever available Barondess.

Gaining political attention meant not only that municipal government grew responsive to Jewish feelings and pressures, it meant also that a share of each party's nominations went regularly to Jews and that special efforts, compounding the sincere and demagogic, were made to win Jewish support at election time. That this often led to vulgar ethnic claims by candidates; that politicians speculated on whether or how a distinct Jewish vote could be won; that many a local candidate gained votes simply because he had the "right name" for a given district; that such practices signified a complex mixture of legitimate group interest and a debasement of the democratic process—all this may be taken as axiomatic.

Common clay, the Jews were open to appeals that they support Jewish candidates simply because they were Jewish. But most investigators have come to the conclusion that ethnic appeals to Jews, especially if unveiled by some "higher" element of idealism, were a little less likely to succeed than among other groups. There was a streak of skepticism and independence in the immigrant Jewish world which, if seldom strong enough to deprive the Democratic party of predictable majorities, sometimes led to flares of electoral irregularity, even to tacit revulsion against coarse ethnic appeals.

In 1920 the progressive Republican Fiorello La Guardia ran for Congress in East Harlem against Henry Frank, a pedestrian Jewish lawyer put up by Tammany Hall. The district, which had for some years given the socialist Morris Hillquit a high vote, was part Italian and part Jewish, like La Guardia himself. Frank, knowing he could not reach the Italians, concentrated on the Jews by issuing a series of attacks on La Guardia, through an anonymous "Jewish Committee," which charged that he was "a pronounced anti-Semite and Jew-hater." In an ordinary election this sort of thing might have worked, but La Guardia, a spectacular campaigner, made sure it would not be ordinary. Having learned Yiddish in his youth and aware that Frank, though Jewish, could not speak it, La Guardia challenged him to a public debate "conducted entirely in the Yiddish language." Frank panicked, reached for excuses, pulled back. La Guardia then made several Yiddish speeches in the district attacking his opponent for having set loose a vulgar racial campaign which Jews especially should repudiate. And then La Guardia topped it off with a neat wisecrack: "After all, is he looking for a job as a *shames*, or does he want to be elected Congressman?"

Jewish audiences appreciated La Guardia's politics almost as much as his wit, and his wit almost as much as his Yiddish. While Frank won a majority of the Jewish vote, it was not large enough to deprive La Guardia of victory. For once, a slanderous racial campaign backfired, and La Guardia emerged as a man of principle.

Did he remain one? In the 1933 mayoral campaign he was opposed by a good-natured Tammany hack, John O'Brien, who wished no one ill, and an independent candidate, "Holy Joe" McKee, a righteous Catholic who said La Guardia was "a Communist at heart." McKee fought a rather dirty campaign, insinuating that the reformer Samuel Seabury, a La Guardia supporter, was attacking Governor Lehman out of anti-Semitic motives. Whereupon La Guardia made public an article that McKee, as a young high-school teacher, had written in 1915 for the *Catholic World,* a piece of high-minded bigotry deploring the rise of atheistic Jews in the New York school system. "Surely," McKee had concluded, "we cannot look for ideal results from such material." McKee was not exactly a lovable man, and to uncover something that an opponent had put in print could easily be construed as acceptable politics. But as La Guardia's biographer, Arthur Mann, has written: "Even if he had disliked Jews as Jews in 1915, which is by no means clear, McKee, according to reliable testimony, was no anti-Semite in 1933. To insinuate that he was, as La Guardia did, was to be unfair because it was untrue." The La Guardia of 1933 was not quite the La Guardia of 1920.

As for the Jews, it became clear to some, though never enough, of them that they were receiving kinds of attention in American politics that should make them profoundly uneasy. How much of a role La Guardia's attack on McKee's alleged anti-Semitism played in the 1933 election no one can say with certainty, but what seems clear is that, like other benefits in this life, the winning of political attention could yield morally distasteful, even dangerous, consequences.

Together with increased attention there came, over the years, a decidedly less punctual increase of patronage. The first jobs made available to immigrant Jews were petty assignments in city departments; later they were given more attractive posts as clerks and, in a few instances, made magistrates in the minor courts. In time, it became a tradition that the Tammany Law Committee serve as a Jewish preserve, and, later, that important but little-noticed technical posts be filled by Jewish specialists, such as Jake Lutzki's management of the Board of Estimate. High-level appointments came a good deal more slowly in New York, at first mostly to board memberships rather than to commissionerships of major departments. These were —one gathers from looking through a file of municipal appointments for the first half of the century—mainly in the areas of health, education, and social service, where Jews had strong interests and skills. On the Board of Education, consisting between 1918 and 1948 of seven unpaid members, the Jews were customarily allotted one place, though at some points they had two. In 1948, the Board of Education was enlarged to nine members, in order to take care of emerging new ethic groups, and for some years thereafter the city had a fixed pattern of three Catholics (including at least one Italian), three Protestants (including one black), and three Jews (by now with distinctions between German and east European Jews). Jews were also frequently appointed to the unsalaried Board of Health, because of the large number of Jewish doctors in the city and the fact that this was not a political plum. By the twenties Jews were also often being made commissioner of health. But the jobs in city government bringing political power and patronage largely eluded Jews until the forties.

It is interesting to note that, while the majority of New York Jews were supporters of the Democratic party, their entry into "cabinet" posts in city administrations was largely facilitated by the minority party—Republican-Fusion Mayors Low, Mitchel, and La Guardia, each of whom appointed larger numbers of Jews than had their Democratic predecessors.

> As early as 1902–04, Jews were receiving 5 to 8 percent of the Mayor's top appointments [with the limitations noted above]—closer to 10 percent under Mayor Mitchel [1914–1918]. Mayor La Guardia was the watershed for Jewish and Italian patronage, almost doubling the representation for both groups between 1933 and 1945. Largely due to La Guardia's appointment pattern, ethnic and religious representation entered a new, perhaps stable phase: the balancing of appointments in a manner resembling the balancing of electoral tickets, in rough proportion to group electoral strength.

By contrast, a "fair share" of national patronage was slow in coming to the Jews, largely because the Republican party, usually in control of the White House during the first three decades of the century, neither owed nor paid many debts to the East Side.

Low Roads, High Roads

Once begun, the influx of east European Jews into politics took on a momentum of its own, operating at every level of social life, from street hoodlums to public-spirited men of rectitude. By the 1900's the methods of the Jewish gangsters had become more efficient than those of Monk Eastman and other pioneers in the field. Working in close partnership with Big Tim Sullivan, a major Tammany leader, such Jewish gangsters as Herman Rosenthal set up shabby storefronts on Second Avenue which featured a game called stuss, while other East Side mobsters, like Bridgey Webber and Sam Schepps, preferred to co-operate with a rival Tammany group led by Charles Murphy.

Most of them rather little fellows, the Jewish gangsters abandoned such crudities as fists and lead pipes and mastered instead the revolver and the use of speedy cars for getaways. Herman Rosenthal, at fourteen a poolroom runner, discovered that "the way to get ahead in the New World was to hang around Big Tim Sullivan's headquarters. . . . Sullivan made a special pet of young Rosenthal. For the rest of his life Rosenthal's fortunes would flourish and decline in tandem with those of the big Tammany Irishman."

In 1911 Rosenthal ventured beyond the Jewish streets, opening a gambling place in the Tenderloin district, north of Times Square. But here he ran afoul of his rival, Bridgey Webber, who regarded the Tenderloin as Murphy country. Some months later, in 1912, Rosenthal was murdered; a police lieutenant named Charles Becker, notorious for involvements with corruption, was charged with the murder and convicted—erroneously, it would seem from Andy Logan's entertaining account of this once-famous trial. In any case, the close relationship between the higher rungs of Tammany and the lower depths of the East Side was emblazoned in the city's newspapers, and thereafter "the political bosses and outlaw elements [concluded] that the financial arrangements between their two groups would have to be put on a more businesslike basis, a resolution that caused them to install Arnold Rothstein [another East Side gangster] as the czar of the New York underworld." Also a protégé of Big Tim Sullivan (who had a soft spot for smart Jewish lads unburdened by scruples), Rothstein helped establish a more mature, indeed professional relationship between the Tammany machine and the East Side thugs. In his own way, he was still another Jewish boy who had made good.

More reputable links were gradually forged between the immigrant Jews and the old-line parties. A garment manufacturer on the West Side needing to have trucks parked at illegal hours found it profitable to contribute a few hundred dollars to the district leader's campaign. A supplier of office machines looking for municipal contracts quickly saw that it was essential to be a regular supporter of the party, even if his checks were made out in his uncle's name. A lawyer on the lookout for a piece of business would find the Tammany machine, with its tentacles reaching into various city departments, of distinct service, especially if he in turn were moved to generosity.

It was precisely facts of this order that caused the East Side intelligentsia and the German-Jewish establishment to disdain the New York Democratic party. Not until about 1912, when Woodrow Wilson, an earnest intellectual who had been head of Princeton University, ran for president, did significant numbers of Jews start turning toward the national Democratic slate. Leaders of the German-Jewish establishment like Henry Morgenthau, who had earlier become disgusted with politics, and Jacob Schiff, who had always voted Republican, now made their influence and pocketbooks available to Wilson. Morgenthau "saw in Wilson a man of lofty idealism, and a knightly spirit"—a judgment shared by many liberals, intellectuals and, apparently, Jewish voters. When Wilson ran for president a second time, in 1916, he received a majority of the Jewish vote, thereby breaking the hold that Republicans had maintained in national elections. German-Jewish money, from men like Morgenthau and Bernard Baruch, by then established as a millionaire-sage, became a significant factor in Democratic politics; wealthy Jews with civic consciences would prove to be especially generous toward liberal and moderate candidates. Perhaps most important in this gradual shift of the more affluent and better-educated Jews from Republican to Democratic affiliation was the role Louis Brandeis played as Wilson's close adviser. A major critic of the trend toward monopoly and the concentration of wealth in American society, Brandeis helped shape Wilson's social thought so that the growing discrepancy between urban, industrial reality and *laissez-faire* ideology could at least be confronted.

When Wilson first took office in 1912, he hoped to select Brandeis for a cabinet post, but the opposition was so severe that he had to back down—

opposition from those who disliked Brandeis because he was a Jew, those who distrusted him as "a radical," and those in the German-Jewish leadership who felt uneasy because he did not seem to them, as Jacob Schiff put it, "a representative Jew." By this last they seem to have meant that Brandeis kept clear of the Jewish organizational milieu. Four years later, when nominated to the Supreme Court, Brandeis no longer had to suffer the coldness of the German-Jewish leaders, perhaps because they had come to see that this "radical" hardly threatened the survival of either the nation or their class, and perhaps because he had become head of the American Zionist movement in 1914, thereby taking his place, if not in an organization Jacob Schiff and Louis Marshall could quite approve of, then at least as "a responsible Jewish leader."*

For the East Side Jews such high-level maneuverings, if they knew of them at all, mattered less than the steady rise to power of Al Smith—a significant new development in New York politics. Smith represented something fresh in American life. He spoke in the accents of the urban masses; he cleared a path for recently arrived immigrant groups as they stumbled into mainstream politics; and at times he raised their inchoate needs and complaints to the level of serious issues. During his years in the State Assembly, beginning in 1903, and then as governor, beginning in 1918, Smith came to lead a "Jacksonian upheaval" that combined social reform with party regularity, new ideas with old styles. "Millions of half-enfranchised Americans," remarked Walter Lippmann, were "making their first bid for power" through Smith's candidacies for governor in the early twenties and for the presidency in 1928.

Raised in a poor Irish-Catholic family on Olivers Street, at the southern tip of the East Side, Smith went to work as a boy in the Fulton Fish Market. Throughout his career he remained an unreconstructed plebeian, with the traits of his people, both crude and delicate, expressed in his every gesture. He was a man at home with himself, free of pretense or self-consciousness, unlike the hordes of politicians masquerading in costumes of "the common man." He was wonderfully agile and playful in the years of his political prime, a "natural" leader of large intuitive gifts. He made the people of the slums—Irish, Jewish, Italian—feel that they too had begun to count for something in this world: "When tough, heavy-set men of the alleys . . .

* A supposition derived from Professor Yonathan Shapiro's study of Brandeis's political career. Still, it is by no means clear why the German-Jewish leaders, stiff-necked in their anti-Zionism, should have felt more at ease with Brandeis once he became a Zionist leader—unless we suppose that for men immersed in organizational life, even the act of joining the "wrong" organization seems better than belonging to none. Another scholar, Ben Halpern, rejecting Shapiro's view that Brandeis's turn to Zionism was opportunistic, argues that it was a deeply felt commitment: "Brandeis had come home. He was not, to be sure, after all those years . . . much of a home body; and his home life as a Jewish leader and a Zionist had its quarrels and partings. But this new belonging was a bond he never relinquished." Halpern's view is persuasively supported by another scholar, Stuart Geller, who sees Brandeis's turn to Zionism as "an extension of his own social philosophy that held dear the value of democracy."

would throw a rock at an old peddler merely because he had a beard," recalled Eddie Cantor, "Al Smith would come to the old man's aid and put his arm around him like a brother. It was the downright, simple heroics of the thing that struck the slum boys with wonder."

Poorly educated, too impatient to read much, Smith had only a small gift for abstract thought. Yet he guided through the legislature complex bills—the first steps limiting the exploitation of labor and giving legal recognition to the rights of workers—that in sum would comprise an entry into the welfare state. All the while he remained a loyal ally of Tammany, supporting bills to fatten its patronage, helping to push through a disreputable gerrymander of New York election districts, and voting, acknowledges a biographer, "as he was told"—with Boss Murphy doing the telling. When Smith did get into a harsh fight with some Tammany leaders in 1922, it was to thwart the ambitions of William Randolph Hearst, the journalist whom he rightly despised as a demagogue, and to limit the power of a new and ineffectual Tammany boss, George Olvany. But the system of bosses Smith never challenged: it seems, for him, to have been in the very nature of things.

Even immigrant Jews ordinarily contemptuous of old-party politics were delighted by Smith's career. If they could not quite see him as one of their own, they felt him to be a sort of kinsman, an *Irisher mensh* who lived only a few blocks away, on a street no more imposing than their own. And they felt this kinship not just because Smith had enough Yiddish to charm audiences with a good story, but because he too was an outsider who had smarted under native American snobbism yet made it seem good to have grown up on the East Side. Socialist candidates always had a hard time against Smith, whom they attacked less for his record than for his associations. To the more doctrinaire Jewish radicals, he was something of a puzzle, for they could not understand how a man so clearly decent in his social impulses could get along so smoothly with the Tammany hacks. Among the intellectuals of the East Side Smith's career was regarded as a paradox, and only later did it become clear that this order of paradox was rooted in the nature of American politics. For what Smith brought to focus between 1911 and 1928 was an upheaval of lower-class ethnic and urban groups *within* the shabby precincts of Tammany Hall.* That no one had quite foreseen an upheaval of this sort did not make it any the less real.

* An upheaval, apparently, that did not leave some of the Tammany leaders totally unmoved. The reformer Henry Moskowitz noted in 1918 that "Settlement workers, designated by an East Side mother as 'paid neighbors,' have helped to modify the point of view of Tammany's elementary neighborliness. Big Tim Sullivan reformed a little before he died. Who would have thought that this charming 'Robin Hood' . . . would sponsor the Fifty-four Hour Law for women workers in the State of New York and the bill advocated by Benjamin C. Marsh doubling the tax on land values? Tim told a settlement house worker that he appreciated the evils of congestion, for in his newsboy days he saw the toll of the slums in death, disease, and degradation. Whether Tim was 'kidding' the settlement worker or not, he acted as a reformer in spots."

Smith eased the way for second-generation Jewish intellectuals, the kind who a decade or two earlier might have been socialists, to enter old-line politics. Social workers, lawyers, writers, free-lance reformers, began to cluster around him during his years in the Assembly, providing him with solid research on social issues and, in turn, being initiated by him into the mysteries of American politics. Abram Elkus, a lawyer of progressive inclinations who had done a solid job as counsel for the New York Factory Commission in 1911, managed Smith's first campaign for governor in 1918, and brought with him a junior partner, Joseph Proskauer, who would become a speech writer and policy adviser in Smith's later campaigns. Henry and Belle Moskowitz, Robert Moses, and Clarence Lewis were among the Jewish political technicians who helped Smith reach a larger vision of American society. There were others, not directly at his side, who opened his imagination, fiery leaders like Rose Schneiderman of the Women's Trade Union League, selfless figures like Lillian Wald. In his private life Smith had known only the traditional kind of wife or mother; but once he encountered such vivid and articulate people as Rose Schneiderman and Belle Moskowitz, women who could be *interesting*, he came to respect and admire them.* They brought a whole new world of thought, and he was keen enough to want it.

Many of these people had first reached political consciousness in the East Side settlement houses, where the social fervor of immigrant Jews rubbed against the moral earnestness of young Americans responsive to the idea of service. Here, socialism and puritanism came together in a compound of practical selflessness; here, men who later might compromise, hedge and retreat were fired by sentiments of social compassion. Henry Moskowitz came out of the Madison Street Settlement, Belle Moskowitz out of the Educational Alliance. Herbert Lehman said that his sense of social responsibility had first been stirred up by Lillian Wald. Adolph A. Berle, Jr., Henry Morgenthau, Jr., and Sidney Hillman all worked as young men at the Henry Street Settlement; Eleanor Roosevelt at the Rivington Street Settlement; Harry Hopkins at Christadora House. All of these people contributed to the social changes of the twenties and thirties, some remembrance of East Side settlement-house idealism shaping, perhaps stiffening, their late conduct.

In 1906 or 1907, remarks a biographer, Al Smith would still have "laughed at [the East Side reformers, the women activists] as 'highbrows and crackpots' . . . . Over many an Albany bar, in those days, he made smart cracks about such folks, to the enthusiastic applause of his fellow legislators." But as he gained authority in office and began looking for ways to help the kinds of people among whom he had been raised, Smith needed

---

* Also to work with them for humane legislation. In 1923, after the State Assembly had voted down a bill to limit the working day of women to eight hours, Rose Schneiderman and a number of other women rushed downstairs to the governor's office. Overstrained by the fight she and her friends had put up for the bill, Miss Schneiderman burst into tears. In his pseudogruff manner Smith turned to her and said, "What's the matter with you girls? Are you getting tired?"

more than his friendly habits and humane inclinations. From men like Tom Foley and Charlie Murphy, the Tammany leaders who had launched his career, he could get no intellectual guidance—indeed, he was lucky that, out of respect for their protégé, they did not stand in the way of his larger purposes. For social ideas, hard knowledge, specific bills, he had to turn to people like the Moskowitzes, either experts themselves or quick to know where to find them. Smith's old cronies at the Hall were deeply suspicious of his new friends and new ideas, sneering that having "moved uptown and deserted the Fourth Ward, Al had surrounded himself with Jews." They even composed a little song, with a nice touch of self-mockery: "And now the brains of Tammany Hall/ Are Moskie and Proskie and Mo-o-o-ses."

The "Moskie" who darkened Tammany hearts was Belle Moskowitz (1877–1933), the single most powerful figure among Smith's Jewish advisers. She was neither an agitator like Rose Schneiderman nor a patient healer like Lillian Wald; she lived neither by the ideologies of feminism and socialism nor by the traditions of feminine service. She was a woman who had made up her mind that she would simply go about her own business, without complaint or uproar, as if being a woman were no particular handicap. She evaded the whole elaborate network of male condescension by pretending she could not see it or by persuading men she was so competent they dared not treat her as anything but an equal. To politics she brought the style of Fabianism, the rationality of the social planner whose memories still flicker with social outrage. The utopianism and intellectuality of the Jewish socialists seem never to have attracted her, though she would probably have gotten along with people like Sidney and Beatrice Webb, the English Fabian leaders whose theories led them to appreciate people devoted to the pragmatic.

She remained behind the scenes, caring nothing for publicity or advancement. Becoming Smith's confidential adviser, she prepared factual material for his speeches, tried now and then to untangle his grammar, handled relations with the press, managed his campaigns, worked up schemes for legislation, and made her quiet self into a bridge between the world of thought and the world of action. For about a decade, from 1918 to 1928, though decreasingly so after 1926, when Smith began to drift toward conservatism, Mrs. Moskowitz commanded a good deal of power in New York, and most politicians and reporters wanting to reach Smith knew it was advisable to reach Belle first. If all her "ambition and sublimated love were . . . centered in Alfred Smith," it was nevertheless with the calculation that she had found the one leader—an intuitive and sympathetic genius sprung from the people—who could charm the country onto a course of social betterment.

She was born Belle Lindner in 1877, daughter of an east European Jew who ran a watchmaking shop in Harlem. Bright and self-assured—also, apparently, beautiful in her youth—she acquired more education than most Jewish girls of her time. Graduated from Teachers College, she plunged into social work, serving at the Educational Alliance as director of entertainments for five hundred dollars a year. The Alliance left its mark, some touch of East Side passions that would never quite fade away. In 1903 she married a Sephardic architect, Charles Israels, who donated time to the Alliance; she bore him three children; and when he died in 1911 she went to work again, to support her family—and because work, she knew, was the portion of men and women with a purpose in life. In 1914 she married Henry Moskowitz, an East Side reformer with a Ph.D. in philosophy, who served as head of the Madison Street Settlement. Partners in a common enterprise, theirs was a busy and amiable relationship.

Settlement work, for such people, led to politics. Mrs. Moskowitz battled with city officials over their coarse treatment of "wayward girls," and came to see that the patience of settlement people could not by itself significantly affect conditions in the city. In 1912 she became active in Theodore Roosevelt's third party, campaigning for Oscar Straus, the Progressive candidate for governor of New York. Two years later she joined the fusion movement that sent John Mitchel to City Hall as mayor. By now Mrs. Moskowitz was becoming known as a woman, indisputably Jewish, of good ideas and first-rate political talents.

In 1918 she became active in Smith's first campaign for governor. There was, at the outset, a sternness of sorts in her treatment of Smith, as if she were a teacher trying to resist an especially charming student. Women had just won the vote, and when she asked Smith to speak for the Women's University League, he took the assignment as a lark, proposing to tell "a funny story perhaps, and some hot air about how glad he was that women had received the vote." Mrs. Moskowitz caught him short: no, he was making a mistake, these were educated women who wanted to hear something of substance. Taking her advice, Smith gave a serious hour-length talk which impressed his listeners; and from then on, the story goes, he listened to Belle Moskowitz on just about everything. She "had the greatest brain of anyone I ever knew," he later said.

It was an extraordinary relationship, this political alliance between stout Jewish matron and debonair Irish governor. Mrs. Moskowitz was more than a mere assistant, and Smith seems to have treated her with consistent delicacy, sensing that she was easily vulnerable to his hurt. She, in turn, understood that the slightest hint of intellectual condescension would be fatal. The passage of influence from one person to another, one milieu to another, is finally a process complex beyond description. Smith's political instincts were conservative in quite conventional ways, he rarely saw himself as an insurgent, and if nevertheless he proved to be a central figure in the introduction of welfare measures in American society, that was partly because there were people like Mrs. Moskowitz gradually persuading him that both elementary humaneness and the preservation of the social order required such measures. Yet Mrs. Moskowitz was by no means imposing her ideas on him—he was far too intelligent and strong-willed a man to allow that. She was, rather, bringing to explicit form some of his own intuitions.

Unavoidably, there sprung up malicious gossip about the nature of their friendship, and this convinced Mrs. Moskowitz all the more that she had to keep in the background. She refused to take any job in Albany, choosing instead to work out of a tiny office in Manhattan. "Powerful Tammany leaders . . . would have guaranteed her election to any post that would have removed her from close contact with the Governor," but Mrs. Moskowitz preferred to offer her opinions through telephone calls to Albany and, once a week, on Friday nights, to take the milk train for weekend conferences with the governor.

Vincent Sheean has left a vivid portrait:

> From the moment she came into the room, deep-voiced and thoughtful and sure, I was one of her devoted admirers. . . . Her serene face was still un-lined, with a sensitive mouth and dark, thoughtful eyes. She dressed always in black, moved slowly, and spoke—when she spoke at all—in a dark thought-ful voice. . . .
>
> I used to see "Mrs. M."—as the people in the political offices called her—at her desk in the headquarters of the Democratic National Committee [in 1928], as busy as a general directing an advance, and far calmer. . . . She did not allow people to shriek or get excited in her room, and her own slow movements acted as an anti-hysteria medicine on everybody who came near her. . . .
>
> Whatever she did was done by personal power alone. Tammany Hall loathed her; the Roosevelts disliked her; she had no kind of "organization" or clique to support her view of things, although it could be said that the most intelligent and socially conscious among Smith's advisors were her friends.

When Smith was badly beaten in the 1928 presidential campaign, Mrs. Moskowitz's political career came to an end. Smith tried to persuade his successor in Albany, Franklin Roosevelt, to take Mrs. Moskowitz as private secretary, but Roosevelt was too shrewd to want as his close assistant a woman whose loyalties had long been yielded to his predecessor. Mrs. Moskowitz neither whined nor grumbled; she returned to private life as a public-relations counselor. Far more important, and painful, to her was the slow decline of her relationship with Smith as he drifted rightward politi-cally. "It was Belle Moskowitz," said a close friend, "who had kept Smith on the liberal side until 1928, after which . . . she lost her influence with him."

Though still active in women's and Jewish organizations, "Mrs. M." now kept strictly apart from politics. She never indulged the vulgarity, so common in later years, of printing "revelations" about her political career; if she felt any bitterness about Smith's changing opinions, she kept it to her-self. She had done her work, she had enjoyed her moment, and now she would be still.

On the day in 1933 that Smith went up to Albany to attend Herbert Lehman's inauguration as governor, she died of a heart attack. Hearing the news, Smith immediately turned around and headed back to New York.

The political patterns introduced during Smith's years in office—rudimentary welfare measures, explicit appeals to plebeian interests, Jewish intellectual advisers—served as informal precedents for the emergence of the New Deal coalition in the thirties. Partly because he later turned into a hard-bitten reactionary denouncing Roosevelt's policies, Smith has not been accorded his due as a major innovative figure in American politics. What he began, hesitantly and on a small scale, was given a more conscious application by Franklin Roosevelt and Herbert Lehman. A key figure in this gradual transformation of the Democratic party in New York, Lehman was a German-Jewish banker of great wealth and keen conscience, who in 1926 lent the ILGWU fifty thousand dollars with which to recover from the disaster of a strike that Communist-led locals had prolonged for political reasons. To the Jewish garment workers this seemed a gesture of remarkable friendliness, and it became a foundation for the steady support they gave Lehman when he ran for governor and senator. About him no one could feel, as many had felt about Schiff and Marshall, that he condescended to east Europeans from a haughty Germanic perch; he was a simple man, modest in speech, and, if anything, earnest to a fault. Lehman became the first German-Jewish figure whom the east European Jews could accept without reservation, adopting him as quite one of their own. This was a fact of some importance, since it helped heal the split between the two main strands of American Judaism. And in politics at large, Lehman served to bridge the distance between Smith and Roosevelt by securing the loyalty of large numbers of working-class Jewish voters.

The way was now being prepared for the last, and perhaps major, step that would carry the radical or once-radical Jewish workers into the traditional milieu of American politics. But again, not without hesitations and halfway stops.

In 1936, on their way back from a CIO meeting, several Jewish trade-union leaders—David Dubinsky, Max Zaritsky and Sidney Hillman—began discussing the idea of a new party in New York, one that might run its own local candidates while on a national scale supporting Roosevelt and his New Deal. Such a party would give the Jewish union leaders a new leverage in local affairs and would allow the Jewish workers to vote for Roosevelt, which most of them clearly wanted to do, without having to struggle against the ingrained distaste many felt toward pulling the lever of an old-line party. Thereby was formed the American Labor party. In 1936 Norman Thomas's Socialist vote fell to a mere 187,342, of which 86,897 were in New York, while the ALP contributed nearly a quarter of a million votes to Roosevelt's total, not, as it turned out, crucial to the outcome but decidedly significant for the future of the Jewish unionists in the politics of New York.

With the formation of the ALP and then, in 1944, its successor, the Liberal party, there occurred an all but complete separation of the radical segment of the immigrant Jewish workers from the socialist movement—not perhaps from their old radical persuasions, or whatever remained of them, but certainly from any effort to build an independent party of socialism. As a result, the ALP—which, until the Communist infiltration of the early forties, meant mainly the Jewish garment-union leaders—was now in a position to bargain for political influence and patronage within the New Deal coalition and, to a lesser extent, the politics of New York City. Remaining outside the Democratic party, the ALP functioned in some ways as if it were a tendency within it—which, in time, it became. And except for a handful of stalwarts, the Socialist party could no longer attract the kinds of idealistic young Jews who had been a major sustenance in the past. Such people, following the path that reformers like Henry and Belle Moskowitz had begun to cut fifteen or twenty years earlier, found it entirely logical in the mid-thirties and later to enter the Democratic party, or at least to put one foot in its door through the ALP.

All this was merely the organizational reflex of a massive enthusiasm for Roosevelt within the Jewish community: the whole of it, from working class to bourgeois, from east European to German, from right to left. To the garment workers, Roosevelt's proposals for social security, unemployment insurance, and legislation enabling union organization seemed like a partial realization of their old socialist program—even if capitalism remained. To the Jewish community at large, Roosevelt's militancy in attacking Nazism and his evident preparations to back the European countries that would soon have to fight against Hitler seemed an essential course for survival—even though the record of his administration in helping to save or admit Jewish refugees was not at all a good one.* After 1936, Roosevelt's pluralities in

* The understatement of this book. For the truth is that, with regard to the Jewish refugees in Europe, the record of the Roosevelt administration was shameful.

Historical evidence concerning this matter has been accumulated in two careful and heavily documented works of scholarship, David S. Wyman's *Paper Walls* and Henry L. Feingold's *The Politics of Rescue*. About the best that can be said for the United States is that it did admit more refugees than the other Western nations: about 250,000 of them between 1933 and 1945. But, as Wyman remarks, "American ability to absorb immigration was vastly greater than that of the small European countries. . . . Viewed in relation to capacity, the English, Dutch, French and others in western Europe were more generous than the United States."

Blocking the path of Hitler's victims were the national origins quota system, which restricted the number of people allowed to enter from a given country, and, still more, a mean-spirited administration of this system by the State Department. During the thirties there was little possibility that Congress could be persuaded to liberalize the immigration laws; in fact, liberals both in and out of Congress hesitated to raise the issue out of fear that restrictionists would proceed to curtail immigration even further.

A bill introduced in 1939 by Senator Robert Wagner of New York and Representative Edith Rogers of Massachusetts provided for the admission of ten thousand refugee children for each of the years 1939 and 1940. Favorably reported out of a

Jewish districts kept rising until, by 1944, they often topped 90 percent. Indeed, the Jews constituted the only ethnic group in America that kept increasing its support for Roosevelt from term to term. "In several Brooklyn precincts in 1944 even the persons serving as Republican watchers voted for Roosevelt." As the veteran Tammany politician Jonah Goldstein quipped, "The Jews have *drei veltn—di velt, yene velt, un Roosevelt*"—three worlds—this world, the other world, and Roosevelt (the rhyme, unfortunately, is not as complete in English as in Yiddish). And thereby, the process was all but complete which over half a century brought the immigrant Jews from eastern Europe into the old-party politics of America.

---

joint subcommittee of the two houses, the bill was then killed through asphyxiating amendments in the full committees. It never even reached the floor of either house; such Jewish members of Congress as Emanuel Celler, Sol Bloom, and Samuel Dickstein, though chairmen of important committees, were helpless against the massed weight of opposition from the State Department and widespread indifference and hostility among southern and western members of Congress. Nor was this indifference and hostility confined to Washington. A Gallup poll in early 1939 found that only 26 percent of the population approved of the proposal to rescue twenty thousand children.

People feared that refugees would compete for scarce jobs. Anti-Semitism, fanned by demagogues like Father Coughlin, played its part. A security-obssessed country was afraid that Nazi spies would creep in with the refugees, and Assistant Secretary of State Breckenridge Long, an anti-Semite and professed admirer of Mussolini's fascism who was in charge of refugee policy, systematically exploited these feelings.

The climax of disgrace came in June 1940, when the State Department cut the refugee flow in half by shutting off most immigration directly from Germany and the rest of central and eastern Europe. "The half-filled quotas," calculates Wyman, "of mid-1940 to mid-1941, when refugee rescue remained entirely feasible, symbolize 20,000 to 25,000 lives lost because of the changed American policy." At least as damaging as this policy was the actual administration of refugee affairs by consuls steadily instructed by Long and other State Department officials to slow the entry of refugees into the United States.

The final responsibility rests on Franklin Roosevelt. As both Wyman and Feingold show in overwhelming detail—it takes strong nerves to read their dispassionate accounts—President Roosevelt never tried to exert moral leadership on the refugee issue, rallying the people in behalf of humane rescue and appealing to the deep if latent sentiments of decency in the American character. During the prolonged public debate over the Wagner-Rogers bill, he maintained an unbroken public silence. While on a Caribbean cruise in February 1939, he received a wire from his wife, Eleanor Roosevelt, asking if she could inform Undersecretary of State Sumner Welles that they approved passage of the bill. Roosevelt cabled, "It is all right for you to support child refugee bill but it is best for me to say nothing till I get back." In June the president was asked by Representative Caroline O'Day of New York for his views on the bill, and he wrote in pencil on her message: "File No action FDR."

By the time of the Holocaust itself, writes Feingold, "the Administration's reluctance to publicly acknowledge that a mass murder operation was taking place [in Germany and eastern Europe] went far in keeping American public opinion ignorant and therefore unaroused, while it helped convince men like Goebbels [the Nazi propaganda chief] that the Allies approved or were at least indifferent to the fate of the Jews."

Roosevelt's evasions and failures on this issue were compounded by pressures from the reactionary State Department. The security psychosis was widespread.

Right-wing groups, ranging from the American Legion to the Daughters of the American Revolution, raged against the idea of admitting helpless Jews. A commitment to a policy of rescue, adds Feingold, "entailed a political risk which Roosevelt was not willing to take, and the Administration's response was to go through the motions of rescue without . . . implementing them. . . . By concealing the anti-Jewish character of the Nazi depredations [in official American statements] behind a neutral or interdenominational cover, Roosevelt may have sought to lessen the predictable outcry about favoritism toward Jews at home."

As for the American Jewish organizations, they proved to be ineffectual. Some, like the American Jewish Committee, still confined themselves to the tradition of Louis Marshall, quietly lobbying in corridors—which, in this case, proved to be utterly inadequate. Others were frightened by the rise of domestic anti-Semitism: might not raising the refugee issue in too forceful a way play into the hands of the Jew-haters? All the Jewish groups were hindered by bickerings and uncertainties of policy: it was hard to imagine that the sufferings of the European Jews represented something different in kind from traditional and endurable sufferings of the past, it was hard to believe that anyone could be so insane as to wish to exterminate a whole people. And the Jewish organizations lacked political leverage with the Roosevelt administration precisely because the American Jewish vote was so completely at the disposal of the president. Had they been able to threaten that, unless the government took more courageous steps to save the refugees, crucial swing votes in crucial states might be withdrawn, it is at least possible that they could have had some effect.

And then again, perhaps not. They may simply have lacked the strength, and perhaps at this point no one cared very much about Jews. But what seems beyond comprehension is that the American Jewish organizations made so few efforts to challenge the Roosevelt administration publicly—as, incidentally, the liberal weeklies, the *New Republic* and the *Nation*, to their everlasting credit, did. Still less understandable or forgivable is that even in later decades, when the story of the American record toward the refugees had become well known and exhaustively documented, it did not seem to have appreciably tarnished Roosevelt's reputation among American Jews.

CHAPTER TWELVE

American Responses

A s EARLY AS the 1880's the descent of thousands upon thousands of east European Jews—their speech a brittle jabber, their clothes fiercely bizarre, their manners seemingly crude and frenetic—had become an occasion for journalistic response. A quick trip to Rivington Street was always good for colorful copy. Stereotypes of the Jew as an Oriental figure hoarding secrets of recondite wisdom and trained in the arts of commercial deception fill out even the most casual reportage of these early years. Almost as prominent are images of Shylock and Fagin: the Jew as a figure of surreptitious accumulation, gothic or medieval in style, performing mysterious rites in the dives of the modern city. When journalists of the eighties or nineties wanted to show sympathy, as some of them did, they informed their readers that most Jewish immigrants were quite free of the jewels with which legend had adorned them, in fact were pathetic in their poverty and bewilderment. Some newspapers were openly hostile, not precisely in the language of anti-Semitism, but with that resentment which native Americans were coming to feel toward whatever seemed exotic and perhaps depraved among the aliens. While free, as a rule, of explicit Jew-baiting, the journalism of these years betrays a nervous anticipation that the immigrant Jews, despite their momentary wretchedness, will yet come to exercise powers of the uncanny. The Jew is treated as a stranger not merely to the American experience or the Protestant imagination, but to the whole of the Western tradition; and thereby he comes to seem a source of possible infection, a carrier of unwanted complications—as if the Europe that had been left behind decades or centuries ago were approaching too closely.

On the simplest level there was a quantity of nastiness. The New York *Tribune* wrote in 1882 that "Hebrew immigrants" were "obstructing the walks and sitting on chairs" (!) at the Battery Park. "Their filthy condition has caused many of the people who are accustomed to go to the park to seek a little recreation and fresh air to give up this practice." The *Tribune* saw the Jewish quarter as a place of embarrassing fecundity: "Clambering upon every wheel, sprawling in every vehicle that comes to a momentary stop, and dodging among the heels of the horses is a crowd of children that puts numbers to shame. Children on the paving stones, children in the gutter, children in the ash-barrel, children on the stoop, children overhead, children underfoot, children fighting." A Dr. James, assistant sanitary superintendent of New York, found the residents of the East Side responsible for their own unhappy conditions, and the *Tribune* made much of his findings: "They are filthy in their habits and most obstinate in their mode of living. They persist in keeping live fowls in their rooms. . . . They keep chickens in the cellars and even in their bedrooms. . . . It is not an unusual thing for an inspector to cause the removal of garbage from sinks and upon returning to the place half an hour later to find the sinks full again."

The *Herald*, no doubt after a comprehensive survey, gravely reported that Jews "were accustomed to taking only one bath a year." That "they are utter strangers to soap and water," wrote the same paper, "and are on social terms with parasitic vermin, was apparent to the most casual observer." The *Times*, more august but hardly more charitable, wrote that "much thievishness and still more dirt have given the Jew from Poland an unenviable reputation, and he has grown to be looked down upon as a despised one among those of his own race." Even a serious magazine like the *Nation*, while refraining from a close inspection of immigrant fingernails, wondered in 1891 whether the moral composition of the masses pouring in from eastern Europe was satisfactory: "Some of this immigration is of excellent character, and some of it quite the reverse."

In a few years the response to the Jewish migration, especially in the better magazines, became more sophisticated—or at least more guarded. During the nineties there was a good amount of intelligent reporting, with men like Jacob Riis, Lincoln Steffens, and Richard Wheatley studying immigrant conditions closely. For a time Steffens became a sort of Jewish convert, so strongly was he drawn to the intensities of the East Side. Riis wrote *How the Other Half Lives*, the most influential of the early muckraking books, out of a reformer's zeal but with only a limited capacity for seeing the people he proposed to help. What he described of "Jewtown" was accurate and—in behalf of tenement reforms yet to come—very useful. But Riis was a cold writer, deficient in that play of humane sympathies which lights up the work of Steffens and Hutchins Hapgood. "Money," Riis could say about the immigrants, "is their God. Life itself is of little value compared with even the leanest bank account." This not only restated an ancient stereotype but was also painfully obtuse, for never in his book did Riis ask himself why the immigrants were so eager to save a few dollars or to what uses they might put their savings. His eye was sharp, but it was the eye of an outsider content to remain one, and eager as he was to remedy the conditions of the immigrant poor, he was equally clear in his mind as to the distance he meant to keep from them.

Still, the work of the muckraking journalists did help make people aware that terrifying social problems were blighting the cities. Energetic reformers, especially social workers like Lillian Wald and Kate Claghorn, made the cause of the immigrants their own. Philo-Semitic sentiment among portions of the educated classes visibly increased after the pogroms in Russia, the ritual murder charges in Hungary, the Dreyfus case in France. Some of the journalists who spent time among immigrant Jews, like Richard Wheatley, author of a fine series in the *Century Magazine* of 1892, were touched by the keenness of family life, the visible hunger for learning, the tradition of caring for one's own sick and poor. Such journalism seldom went very deep, and sometimes it was overcome by its own large-mindedness (it seems that if you pricked a Delancey Street peddler he bled). But it was a beginning.

In a valuable study of popular American responses to the Jews at the turn of the century, Oscar Handlin has found several recurrent figures. There was, for example, the Jewish peddler or old-clothes dealer or pawnbroker, Isaacs or Cohen, Ikey, Jake or Abie, whose

> garments were either old and shiny with an inevitable black derby hat, or else . . . ludicrously new and flashy.* His hooked nose stood prominently forth from his bearded face and his accent was thick. He was invariably concerned with money. . . . Some Jews were [shown as] just on the edge of dishonesty like the Bowery shysters, Katch & Pinch. But even a likeable chap like Old Isaacs . . . in the popular play [Charles Blaney's *Old Isaacs from the Bowery*] tells his daughter, "why, I vould trust you mit my life, Rachel. But vid mein money, ach, dot vas different."

Handlin notes that such caricatures, though certainly lending themselves in later years to anti-Semitic exploitation, were neither so intended nor so taken; they reveal an edge of cultural contempt but that is rather different from social and political enmity.

---

* This figure may well have been somewhere in Edith Wharton's mind when she drew the newly rich Jew, Sim Rosedale, in *The House of Mirth* (1905).

In the nineties a second stereotype became prominent, mostly in popular novels: the fabulously rich Jew entwined with international finance, a figure who must have had some connection with nativist and populist notions concerning foreign conspiracies and international bankers. There was also a vogue in these same years of cheap fiction in which beautiful Jewesses, literary descendents of Scott's Rebecca, served as nobly suffering but flawed heroines: Noel Dunbar's *Jule the Jewess*, Harriet Newell Baker's *Rebecca the Jewess*, and so on. About most of these writings the immigrant Jews knew little or nothing; they had more urgent matters to attend. But about the atmospheres that enabled such stereotypes to flourish they knew perfectly well. If America would finally turn out to be a land of opportunity for the immigrant Jews, they also realized that the welcome they were receiving was far from unqualified.

The Native Reformers

It was a welcome not even unqualified within the community of reformers who from the late eighties until the First World War kept attacking the evils of American society. These admirable men and women were among the small number of Americans emotionally prepared to find the immigrants a natural object for their sympathies. The immigrants, like the blacks of a later moment, seemed to provide the most dramatic instance of the costs that an acquisitive society could exact from its victims. But it was far easier to rally support for the immigrants than it would be for the blacks, since none of the immigrant groups, not even the scorned "hunkies" or "wops" or "sheenies," roused such primitive guilts and revulsions as would the blacks.

As high-minded men and women stamped with the moralism of native Protestant thought, the reformers found the Jews especially interesting. The Jews, it is true, have figured in the Christian imagination as mercenary, grasping, vulgar, and worse. But the Jews, as Edmund Wilson has remarked in writing about the New England Puritans, have also figured as the people of the Old Testament, the chosen, or at least the chosen who had strayed. Even in the strange and grubby figures of the ghetto, an eager Christian imagination could find traces of ancient glory. By the last few decades of the nineteenth century a gingerly philo-Semitism, exemplified in George Eliot's *Daniel Deronda*, became fashionable among men of good will who tried to link the stoic virtues of the early American patriots with the generous sentiments of the new American progressivism. That the immigrant Jews conformed to such native values as industriousness, sobriety, and thrift made it easier for the reformers to speak in their behalf and easier, also, to check that fastidious distaste which a visit to Jewish neighborhoods could induce.

It took some years before the native reformers could feel at home with—or in—the East Side. When Henry Codman Potter, Episcopal bishop of New York, decided in 1895 to spend a month working in the Cathedral Mission on Stanton Street, it created a stir both in the New York press and among the Jewish residents. "Don't imagine," wrote the bishop to a colleague, "that there is anything heroic in my going there or any especial risk. There are certain questions concerning the problem there to which I cannot get an answer *secondhand.*" And to a *Times* reporter the bishop remarked, with evident self-consciousness: "I don't believe in slumming . . . I will not go into the houses of the people looking around me as though I were in an old curiosity shop."

A good and honest man, and notably courageous as one of the first American ministers to help the labor movement, Bishop Potter was nevertheless troubled about Jews in a way characteristic of many early reformers. In an 1898 letter to Jacob Schiff—written, as he himself said, with "great unreserve"—Bishop Potter could say, "I am told that ['the Hebrew race'] is the only race in Wall Street whose word is not as good as its bond . . . the contention is made among the people whom I have again and again approached that the hostility to the Hebrew is because, in ordinary business and personal transactions, he is tricky and untrustworthy." Bishop Potter hastened to append his understanding that "such characteristics . . . have largely been begotten by the persecutions of Christian people"; but what mattered was that even so decent a man should still find it possible to indulge this weariest of stereotypes. Schiff's reply was appropriately stiff, as if he felt unable to cope with the accumulated sludge of history.

The vision sustaining the reformers

> never quite shed its cast of gentility, philanthropy, and detachment from the plight of the unfortunate. Not that condescension was intended. But the reformers' call at times seemed as remote as a Washington Square drawing room. Felix Adler and Bishop Potter . . . Jacob Riis and Charles Sprague Smith, Frank Damrosch and Thomas Davidson reflected that tone of an era in which the educated, socially advantaged and finally privileged, confronted the realities of New York and attempted in conscience to efface the evils with good works. . . . [But] an easy comradeship with tenement dwellers eluded the reformers.

Groups like the City Reform Club and the People's Municipal League kept attacking the iniquities of Tammany Hall throughout the eighties and nineties, but these earnest professionals and upright businessmen, mostly native Protestants though including a few Catholics and German Jews, were simply unable to respond to the emotional texture of urban life. Tammany was shamelessly corrupt, but its people were warm, available, and unpretentious; the reformers were men of rectitude, but often chilly, distant, and genteel. Throughout the 1890 municipal campaign, in which the People's Municipal League ran an unsuccessful candidate against Tammany, it

> consistently expended most of its energies upon simply condemning Tammany abuses. . . . The reformers paid scant attention to the difficulties of laborers and the new immigrants. . . . Richard Welling [a reform leader] interviewed a number of workingmen after the election and ascertained that workers considered the League to be composed of wealthy men who cared little about the plight of the lower classes. . . . Having abandoned hope of gaining a significant number of Irish votes, the League did nothing to gain the votes of Jewish or Italian immigrants.

This was a pattern ingrained in reform politics, to be repeated again in the effort of the newly formed Citizens Union to influence the 1897 municipal campaign. Men like Welling might gain the respect of a few East Side intellectuals, but the Tammany captain was quickly learning that it paid to attend weddings and *bar mitzvahs* of ordinary people. And ordinary people could feel that the fraternity of the corrupt might benefit them more than the honesty of the elite.

Only with the greatest difficulty was the distance narrowed between the reformers and the objects of their solicitude. At times it could simply be gotten round by good works, such as the construction in 1887 of several model tenements on Cherry Hill, undertaken by a special company formed in response to Felix Adler's agitation against slum housing. The buildings were *there*, and they served a purpose regardless of whether Adler felt at ease with the people who lived in them.

In the eighties the Episcopal church, spiritual guide of the city's upper classes, began to notice the evils of the slums. Bishop Potter organized in 1887 the Church Association for the Advancement of the Interests of Labor, which gave help to striking workers. Neither radical nor very successful, this group set a precedent for other, more aggressive churchmen who would preach the social gospel for and in the slums. A wavering line of descent can be traced from the ministers of awakening conscience in the eighties to the more assertive Christian Socialists who took to the picket lines two decades later. Inevitably, many of those picket lines were in behalf of immigrant Jewish workers.

If the reformers were to be trusted, they first had to become part of the neighborhood they proposed to help. Starting with the Neighborhood Guild in 1886, the settlement-house leaders, especially such devoted men as Stanton Coit and Charles B. Stover, sank roots into the East Side, learning to share its opinions, hardships, and emotions. When Coit hired a mover to take his furniture from Park Avenue to Forsyth Street, the Irish truckman said, "You really don't mean to move to Forsyth Street. I just moved out of there meself. It ain't a fit place to live in for the likes of you and me." To the immigrants themselves, the quixotic gestures of these Christian idealists were not entirely unfamiliar: many could remember, and a few participated in, that movement of the Russian intelligentsia known as "going to the people."

Coit left the East Side after a while, but Stover stayed on for many years, serving as head of the University Settlement, working actively in the East Side Civic Club, and becoming an admired figure in the immigrant community. Shy in manner but stubborn in pursuit of his ends, Stover made this work into the whole of his younger life; like Lillian Wald and a number of others on the East Side, he lived by the ethic of self-abnegation. His tiny apartment, Miss Wald later said, "became a Mecca to people with problems. I remember tall and high-booted callers, lusty husky men from Rumania or some unhappy corner of the earth, filling his room to ask for help or inter-pretation." John Jay Chapman, the critic, spoke of Stover as "a sacred man, a sort of priest, almost inarticulate, yet affecting everyone who met him." The example of Stover's work inspired others—Lillian Wald, for one, start-ing a settlement at 95 Rivington Street. As a girl, Eleanor Roosevelt spent two years doing volunteer work at the University Settlement, acquiring a sense of the life of the poor that would play its part during the years of the New Deal.

By about 1890 the settlement houses began to move beyond social work and into public agitation in behalf of reforms ranging from tenement legisla-tion to Stover's special interest, the creation of small parks on unused lots. Later he would become New York City parks commissioner, and he was a very good one, but in his younger years he wholly shared the life of the immigrant Jews, professing for them "a special affinity, and going so far as on one occasion to suggest that his middle name Binstein was of Semitic origin." In 1903 he published a touching little article, "Loyalty to the East Side," in which he urged young residents not to leave its streets even if they could afford to. By remaining on the East Side—and here he sounds like a confirmed Yiddishist—they would make it into "a giant, capable of winning its own battles, without the help of uptown reserves." At least for a handful of pure-souled men like Stover, the gap between the generalities of the reforming mind and the immediacies of urban experience came to be bridged.

Stage, Song, and Comic Strip

By the 1880's the popular arts had begun to acknowledge the presence of immigrant Jews: German or east European, it hardly mattered which. In a successful play like George Jessop's *Sam'l of Posen* (1881) the vulgar but kindhearted Jewish commerical traveler entered the ranks of American stereotype; in the vaudeville routines of Frank Bush the "Jew comic" took his bow, wearing a rusty plug hat, a gabardine, and a long pointed beard, and singing, "Oh my name is Solomon Moses/ I'm a bully sheeny man." Not until the 1900's, however, did the "stage Jew" and the "Jew comic" become fixtures of the American theatre, straight, vaudeville, and burlesque. The popular arts came to serve as a sort of abrasive welcoming committee for the immigrants. Shrewd at mocking incongruities of manners, seldom inclined to venom though quite at home with disdain, they exploited the few, fixed traits that history or legend had assigned each culture. They arranged an initiation of hazing and caricature that assured the Swedes, the Germans, the Irish, and then the Jews that to be noticed, even if through the cruel lens of parody, meant to be accepted—up to a point.

One of the first dialect comedians was David Warfield, born David Wohlfelt, who began as a member of the famous Weber and Fields vaudeville team and then rose to straight drama. A natural mimic, Warfield alternated Irish, German, and Jewish skits, but his reputation depended mainly on the Jewish ones. A popular skit featured him as a storekeeper watering some items of clothing and sticking "damaged by fire" signs over them—what a contemporary reviewer called "all these tricks that are not always funny or necessary, but cling to the Hebrew as frogs hang around the Frenchman and frankfurters around the German." Wearing the makeup of "the guileless, guileful Jew"—ears bulging, nose swollen, jaunty derby on the head, and "a few lines around the eyes to lend them an air of crafty cunning"—Warfield would proceed to mangle the English language with thick lumps of Germanic or what audiences took to be Judaic phrasing. The "Dutch" (German) routine had by then become standard in vaudeville and to slide from "Dutch" to Jew required little effort and not much of an ear. It was not subtlety audiences were looking for, it was not subtlety they got. In a skit called "Whirl-i-Gig" that Warfield did for Weber and Fields, he played Sigmund Cohenski, a Jewish millionaire vacationing in Paris. His daughter was in love with the dashing Captain Kingsbridge, U.S.N.

> "The Captain is my idea of a hero," Uneeda told her father.
> "A hero! Is dot a business? A tailor is a business, a shoemaker is a business, but a hero? Better you should marry a bookkeeper."
> "A bookkeeper? I suppose you think the pen is mightier than the sword," the girl sneered.
> "You bet my life," said Papa Cohenski. "Could you sign checks with a sword?"

Rough but not merely ill-natured, such humor was in the tradition of American demotic contempt for refinement. It struck at all ethnic groups but seldom struck them down. When Warfield, as Cohenski, bought dinner for Lillian Russell, playing Fifi, there followed an exchange:

> FIFI: You might bring me a demi-tasse.
> COHENSKI: Bring me the same, and a cup of coffee.

In such gags traditional American humor was adapted to new situations: the uncouth American stumbling over European sophistication becomes the uncouth Jew stumbling over European sophistication. Audiences enjoyed this. They seemed to need a few simple and unvarying traits by which to keep each group of "foreigners" securely in mind, traits that would induce an uncomplicated recognition. And as for the comedians themselves, they had at most ten minutes in which to develop a routine: which meant rough, broad, crude strokes. Their humor gained some of its thrust from contempt, and when Jewish comedians acted in these skits, as they often did, they took over the attitudes of the gentiles even while sometimes trying to soften and humanize the material.

Ambitious for the higher reaches of art, Warfield turned to straight theatre in 1902, playing in *The Auctioneer*, a successful melodrama produced by David Belasco. Warfield appeared as Simon Levi, using his traditional Jew costume but aiming at more elevated effects ("I've tried to keep the noses down to normal dimensions," said Belasco to the newspapers). Starting from poverty, Simon Levi rises to riches, falls back into poverty and then, a minute before the curtain drops, regains his money. Enabling Warfield to blend old tricks with new pathos, the play seems to have pleased the many Jews in his audiences. Impressed with his new status, Warfield wrote solemn articles about his "studies of the Hebrew race." "The expression of the eyes . . . is pleading, fearful, intelligent and gentle. The voice corresponds with the face . . . the favorite tone is a piano and often a pianissimo." Weber and Fields, brought up on the raucous streets of the East Side, no doubt had some pungent reflections about their former partner.

"Hebrew" roles became popular. The veteran Frank Bush sang, "I keep a clothing store 'way down on Baxter Street,/ Where you can get your clothing now I sell so awful cheap." Julian Rose worked up a skit called "Levinsky at the Wedding": "I got my invitation. It was printed on the back of her father's business cards. Old ones. On the invitation it says 'your presence' is requested. Right away the presents they ask for." Joe Welch did a *shlemiel* number, dragging himself onto the stage to funereal music and opening with a line that became famous: "Mebbe you tink I'm a heppy man." Andy Rice had a monologue about Sadie's debut in society. Ben Welch worked "Hebe" parts in the burlesque skit "The Parisian Widow's Show," and Abe Reynolds played a Jewish sultan in "Runaway Girls." Younger comedians were a trifle more subtle: Eugene and Willie Howard parodied earlier Jewish comics, Smith and Dale presented "Dr. Kronkeit," Lou Holtz started polishing his Sam Lapidus sketch.

On the legitimate stage Lew Welch, a veteran comic, appeared in 1907 as the touching old Jew in Hal Reid's *The Shoemaker*, and a year later scored a major success with a similar role in *The Peddler*. Road companies used *The Peddler* for some twenty years, and for all we know, this asthmatic melodrama may have done more to shape native feelings than works by our more distinguished playwrights. Reversing the formulas of the "stage Jew," *The Peddler* did justice to the Jews, "rich, creamy, lime-lighted justice," as one reviewer wrote, "that made you lick your chops."

Jewish themes spread to other media. By the First World War Eddie Cantor had become known for such ditties as "Cohen Owes Me Ninety-Seven Dollars," "Sadie Salome Go Home," and "Yiddle on Your Fiddle." Other "Yid" songs followed: "At the Yiddishe Cabaret," "Becky, Stay in Your Own Back Yard," "Who Married My Sister, Thomashefsky?" For decades Henry Wehman published butcher-paper compilations of ethnic humor, the one entitled *Hebrew Jokes* displaying on its cover a banana nose worthy of Julius Streicher's Nazi sheets. But in the main, the treatment of immigrant Jews became softer, or at least more cautious. Fanny Brice did her dialect numbers with at least an echo of the Yiddish stage in the background. Harry Hershfield's *Abie the Agent*, dealing sympathetically with a Jewish businessman, ran for years as a syndicated comic strip. Milt Gross ("Nize Beby, itt opp all de rize witt milk so Momma'll gonna tell you a Ferry Tail from de Pite Piper of Hemilton") mangled all languages, English, Yiddish, whatever.

Popular for a time and a little more pretentious were Montague Glass's "Potash and Perlmutter" sketches, in which two cloak-and-suiters, hearty *alrightniks*, keep a sharp eye on the dollar while displaying generosities that make them "lovable." Glass collected these pieces into several books, starting with *Potash and Perlmutter* (1910) and *Abe and Mawruss* (1911); a stage adaptation in 1913, featuring Alexander Carr opposite Barney Bernard, was the longest-running play of the year. Alternating his own stodgy prose with poorly recorded dialect (he had no ear for the differences between German-Jewish and east European–Jewish speech), Glass hit upon a shrewd formula. There was enough stress on the commercial tightness of Jews,

> "That's all right, Mawruss," Abe declared. "Business is business and charity is charity, y'understand; but even in charity, Mawruss, it don't do no harm to keep the expenses down."

and enough mockery of failures in etiquette,

> "R.S.V.P.," Morris replied, emphasizing each letter with a motion of his hand, "means, 'Remember to send vedding present.' "

so that the usual denouement, stressing Potash and Perlmutter's kindliness, became a little easier to swallow.

How did the immigrant Jews react to the caricature of stage, song, and comic strip? So far as one can tell, without much excitement or anger—even though comedians like the Howard Brothers and Lou Holtz appealed in their dialect sketches to immigrants and immigrants' children becoming Americanized. Many of these skits were funny, some perceptive; Jews had long experience in laughing at, often mocking, themselves. Absorbed with the trials of daily life, they were seldom inclined to blanch before mistreatment in the serious or popular arts; ethnic sensitivities were not yet institutionalized. By 1912, to be sure, Joe Welch ran into trouble when the

Chicago Anti-Stage Jew Ridicule Committee objected to his material, and at about the same time there were also protests against Potash and Perlmutter. By 1914 Willie and Eugene Howard were telling a reporter, "You should put it down that we take the greatest care in our impersonations of Jewish character. . . . Every gag we have ever used we have submitted to a rabbi who is a friend of ours and who must approve it before we use it." Actually, neither the Howards nor the other comedians were quite as stuffy as they thought it convenient to appear.

As the Jews settled into American life and became better able to acknowledge their own emotions, the problem of caricature came to seem more irksome. Some heard malevolence in every snatch of dialect, others thought of it as good, clean, or not so clean fun; but one historical fact warranted the Jewish feeling that ethnic parody constituted a difficulty for them as it hardly did for any other immigrant group. An attack on German or Irish immigrants might be unpleasant, even wounding, but as a rule it had no deeper potential of meaning—rarely did it signify a hatred cutting through all historical periods and social classes. But an attack on Jewish immigrants always raised the fear of consequences far beyond what the performers might intend. This fear could be exploited, as it was exploited, by prigs and busybodies, but that did not warrant its dismissal.

Except when indulging in pieties of camouflage, the comics themselves did not worry about such matters. They found approval and prosperity in the American theatre; they were admired by almost everyone in the Jewish quarter; and many of them were extremely talented entertainers. Without intending or knowing it, they were doing the work of the host culture: they were helping to integrate the Jewish immigrants into American life.

From Henry Adams to Henry James

The figure of the immigrant Jew entered serious literature much more cautiously than he did the popular arts. Despite the cultural vitality of the East Side, it did not often strike our better novelists as a tempting locale for works of fiction. Perhaps it seemed a place too bizarre, too ill-fitted when set against the bulk of American society. Perhaps they were quick to sense the difficulties of trying imaginatively to penetrate an alien culture. The most we have by way of literary response during the years before the First World War is a small quantity of impressionistic writing and one or two books of a high imaginative order.

No American writer, certainly none before Ezra Pound, has ever been more obsessed with "the Jew" than Henry Adams. So obsessed, indeed, that he never troubled to spend a few days inspecting actual immigrants. When he snarled at the thought of "four-hundred-and-fifty thousand Jews now doing Kosher in New York,"* it was as if he were taking at face value the worst caricatures of the "Jew comics," a mistake ordinary people were unlikely to make. Adams's hatred for the Jews flourished in his later years, after the mass migration from eastern Europe had reached its climax and he himself had entered an intellectual phase Paul Elmer More would call "sentimental nihilism." Neither evidence nor observation could shake Adams: he *knew* all he needed to know about "the Jew." Seeing the Jews as agents of international finance who polluted the American landscape, Adams wanted to "put every money-lender to death." In his *Education*, writing about himself in the third person, he connected the Jews with a melancholy decline in native virtue: "Not a Polish Jew fresh from Warsaw or Cracow—not a furtive Yacoob or Ysaac still reeking of the Ghetto, snarling a weird Yiddish to the officers of the customs—but had a keener instinct, an intenser energy, and a freer hand than he—American of Americans, with Heaven only knows how many Puritans and Patriots behind him." It is hard to know which motif is stronger here: the self-pity of the displaced patrician or the contempt of the haughty Anglo-Saxon.

Adams's response to the Jews was the morbid symptom of a man no longer able to bear the strains of his own thought and thereby inclined to lay "the burden of guilt for the growth of capitalism upon the Jew who was supposed to have misled such gentiles as sneaked away from the Table Round to follow the stock-market quotations." Yet a curious admiration wove its way into Adams's feelings about the Jews. When he complained that no one would read as many as fifty pages of his book on Chartres, he made an exception for "a few Jews." When he visited Poland and wrote that the Jews of Warsaw made him "creep," he also noticed that both he and they were cut off from the materialist vulgarity of the modern world. The Jews were full of energy and therefore to be despised; the Jews survived against incalculable odds and were therefore to be suspect; the Jews could adapt themselves to industrial civilization (though at what cost Adams never knew) and were therefore to be scorned. And as if in tribute from the enfeebled to the vulgar, the Jews were also to be envied.

William Dean Howells did take the trouble of visiting the East Side and allowing his friend Abraham Cahan to guide him through streets and tenements. What he wrote about the Jewish quarter in 1896 was characteristically decent: "always the one room, where the inmates [of the tenements] lived by day, and the one den, where they slept by night, apparently all in the same bed, though probably the children were strewn about the floor." He compared the tenements "for darkness and discomfort to the dugouts or sod huts of the settlers on the great plains." He admired "the splendid types

---

* The entire passage, in a 1906 letter to Brooks Adams, is worth quoting: "God tried drowning out the world once, but it did no kind of good, and there are said to be four-hundred-and-fifty thousand Jews now doing Kosher in New York alone. God himself owned failure."

of that old Hebrew world which had the sense if not the knowledge of God when all the rest of us lay sunk in heathen darkness." And for all its distracting vividness, he struggled to look beneath the surface of the immigrant scene. "There may have been worse conditions of life" than those on Rivington Street, but "if I stopped short of savage life I found it hard to imagine them." Yet the immigrants persisted, they "had not the look of a degraded people, they were quiet and orderly."

Keen as such observations were, they seem less notable than Howells's own scruples and self-doubts: "There is something in a very little experience of such places that blunts the perceptions, so that they do not seem so dreadful as they are. . . . I soon came to look upon the conditions as normal, not for me, indeed, or for the kind of people I mostly consort with, but for the inmates of the dens and lairs about me."

Howells knew how strong was the temptation of smugness at the very moment of his admiration; he sensed how large was the gulf between the life to which he had grown accustomed and the life he was glimpsing. He had the imagination of the victim, a rare capacity for crediting the humanity of the stranger, and not least of all, he was a genuinely friendly man. These were all qualities that made him respond with a hesitant warmth to the East Side.

To a visitor like H. G. Wells, who had no reason to share the fears of native Americans, the Jewish quarter in 1906 figured mainly as a spectacle of energy. He was struck by the common will among the Jews to make order out of squalor, he was moved by the sight of little immigrant boys saluting the American flag. The immigrants, he wrote, "come ready to love and worship. . . . They give themselves—they want to give." What Wells saw here was the power of the idea of America even among those who had barely brushed against it, an idea certain to triumph over Henry Adams's fears, if only because it was so much more openhearted and generous.

Henry James, also an "early American," shared Adams's alarm that the native strain in American life might be overwhelmed or adulterated, but as a novelist James felt it a test of his powers that he encounter these hordes of strangers, immigrants of a hundred grating tongues and assertive manners. When he came to the East Side in 1904, James experienced some of the emotions of dispossession that were troubling other Americans. The immigrant Jews struck him as strange, they represented everything that might mean an end to the America he had grown up in; yet these Jews were also a supreme testimony to the rightness of that America. James wrote a fine passage on Ellis Island—"before this door, which opens to them there only with a hundred forms and ceremonies, grindings and grumblings of the key." Thinking about the immigrant Jews, he noted "that loud primary stage of alienism which New York most offers to sight—[it] operates, for the native, as their note of settled possession . . . so that *un*settled possession is what we, on our side, seem reduced to." Such remarks have been taken as hostile, but it might be wiser to see them as an effort to be candid about ambivalent feelings. For James's heart, if visibly sinking, could also remain open: "Truly the Yiddish world was a vast world, with its own deeps and complexities, and what struck one above all was that it sat there . . . with a sublimity of good conscience that took away the breath, a protrusion of elbow never aggressive, but absolutely proof against jostling."

In the final reckoning James found himself overwhelmed by this "Yiddish world," unable to move beyond a quizzical uncertainty and a sensory fastidiousness. (He left a Yiddish play after the first act, because the smell of the place was offensive; he did not ask, at least in print, why it should have been so.) Tantalizing as his pages are about the immigrant Jews, they do not and could not have the wholeness of feeling he commanded upon returning to the places of his youth, the Hudson and the Saco he had known as a boy.

The one American writer who yielded himself imaginatively to the world of the immigrants—freely, happily, with fraternal ease—was not a novelist at all. Hutchins Hapgood, with the quiet help of Abraham Cahan, began to write his newspaper pieces about the East Side for the *Commercial Advertiser* and the *Atlantic Monthly* in the years between 1898 and 1902. When he put the sketches together in 1902 as a book called *The Spirit of the Ghetto,* he was fortunate enough to have the charming illustrations of an unknown young artist from Hester Street named Jacob Epstein. "In my lingerings in the cafés of Canal and Grand Streets," wrote Hapgood, "I had met this young Jew and he had invited me to his garret and had shown me some of his sketches: of old Jewish applewomen below his window, of poverty-stricken old Jewish rabbis, of anaemic feverish writers on the Yiddish newspapers."

Talking, listening, taking pleasure in the impressions he received, Hapgood roamed through the East Side. He brushed past the trivialities of "local color" and came to see that in the clamor of these streets was being created a culture that could challenge the premises of American life. The East Side "helps you to see the limitations of respectability. . . . It wears away the unnecessary, calls aloud for essential humanity, points with eloquence for justice, for truth and for beauty, of the human being who has reached the 'limit' and is therefore reduced to fundamental ideas." Hapgood confronted, less through polemic than oblique suggestion, the fear of native Americans that the immigrants would dispossess them, the prejudice that the immigrants brought a repugnant "commercial instinct"—it was almost as if he were writing with Henry Adams in mind. As far back as 1878, when the stage comics Burt and Leon did one of the pioneer Jewish skits, they had "Ikey" reply to the question "Are you a foreigner?" by anwering, "No, I'm an American from de oder side." What the comics had intuitively grasped, perhaps better than the intellectuals, Hapgood also understood. All of his pages, whether reporting the confusions of a young immigrant boy torn apart by opposing systems of value or picturing the rough simplicities of the Yiddish theatre, breathe the same spirit of American friendliness. The immigrants could ask for nothing more.

Legal Rights, Social Rebuffs

Can we locate, finally, a dominant American response to the migration of the east European Jews? Officially, there was an all but universal agreement that Jews, like other immigrants, should be accorded those benefits of legal equality that are contingent upon citizenship. In practice, these rights might sometimes be violated, but the mere idea of them was precious to the immigrants. Together with the official response, however, there was a complex of attitudes more difficult to isolate—attitudes ranging from the Judeophobia of the nativists to the fastidious sympathy of patrician reformers. In the last two decades of the nineteenth century social anti-Semitism became a serious problem, and later, in the chauvinist atmosphere induced by the First World War, it flourished once more. Social anti-Semitism refers to that informal system of exclusion which made it possible for native Americans to keep at a minimum their social relations with Jews, as well as to prevent all but a tiny number of Jews from entering the corporate bureaucracies and fashionable clubs. This structure of prejudice was confined mostly to personal and business relations; it was not a strategy for depriving Jews of their rights as citizens. The Jews were to be given opportunities, and it was expected that they would take advantage of them through exertions beyond those which might be forthcoming from gentiles; but the Jews were not to be cordially received into that network of clubs, universities, schools, and places of recreation in which the American elite flourished. The Jews were to be allowed, even required, to become Americans—but at arm's length. And in this policy there was a paradox that gentile America has never been quite able to resolve: Jews were steadily criticized for being too clannish, yet if once they moved onto the avenues leading toward assimilation they found many barriers on their path.

Piquant though it might seem in its color and vitality, the Jewish subculture was radically different from the dominant Protestant culture and was therefore an object of suspicion, sometimes contempt. True, this was a difficulty not unique to the Jews; Italian immigrants also suffered from the condescension of old-line Americans, and so did the Irish. Yet between the Italians, say, and the Jews there was a crucial difference: the Italians, even if benighted Papists, were Christians, and the Jews were not. Traditional stereotypes that had accumulated in Western culture regarding the Jews had been brought across the ocean along with more enlightened precepts. Jews were still seen as creatures of greed, exoticism, vulgarity. They were a pariah nation, suffering the curse of Judas. And perhaps most decisive was the recognition that the Jews formed a minority that could not be fully assimilated into the dominant American culture.

The Jews were to be kept at a distance not because of anything they might do in America, but simply because they were Jews. For a time most of them accepted this social exclusion, if only because they had more pressing worries as well as tempting opportunities; they complained only when the line between legal rights and social discrimination became blurred—that is, when informal systems of bias threatened formal assurances of rights, or when the benefits enabled by legal equality were in fact blocked by social prejudice.

Discrimination against Jews began to be practiced in a serious way some years after the Civil War, perhaps the most notorious instance being the refusal in 1877 by a leading Saratoga Springs hotel to receive the German-Jewish banker Joseph Seligman. In the years that followed there were a good many similar exclusions, but while arousing strong protests, these did not closely affect the lives of most immigrant Jews. Not many were able or cared to attend plush American hotels, and most of them were busy creating a complex of social and cultural institutions that shielded their personal lives from rebuff. Once, however, discrimination spilled over into areas that might hurt their careers in business or the professions, they spoke out forcefully. In 1898, for example, Jacob Schiff wrote a bitter letter to Bishop Potter of New York attacking "the spirit which, as by a tacit understanding, excludes the Hebrews from the Trustee-room of Columbia College, of the public museums, the public library, and many similar institutions." Schiff placed the blame on the Protestant leadership: "The river cannot rise higher than its source, and for the prejudice and intolerance which exist, the large mass of people are far less to be blamed than those who have the influence and the power to counteract it."

Once the Jews started to rise economically, "native Americans threw new obstacles across their path. Already shut out of clubs, most summer resorts, and many private schools, Jews found it increasingly difficult in the early 20th century to enter college fraternities and faculties. Restrictive covenants became common in urban residential areas. More important, job opportunities were beginning to contract."

Odious as such practices were, they must still be distinguished from anti-Semitism sanctioned or enforced by the state. Indeed, the commitment of American society to legal equality came to be a powerful weapon in the hands of those fighting informal discrimination. There were painful and humiliating incidents—the worst was the 1914 lynching in Georgia of Leo Frank, son of a wealthy New York merchant, and the subsequent justification of this lynching by Tom Watson, the southern populist leader. Yet these were acts of mob violence and demagogic viciousness, repudiated by the established spokesmen of American society, who felt it was one thing to keep a Jew out of one's country club, quite another to bend to gutter racism.

The response of American society, then, was mixed and sometimes confused. In popular discussions of the Jews, the image of the "melting pot" became a favorite—with clear presuppositions as to who would melt whom. An educator writing in 1909 could say as a matter of course that "everywhere these people [southern and eastern Europeans] tend to settle in groups or settlements, and to set up here their national manners, customs and observances. Our task is to break up these groups or settlements, to assimilate and amalgamate these people as part of our American race." Writers of a more reflective bent might not deny the possibility that America could be enriched by alien cultures, but the mass spirit of nationalism spoke otherwise. Even Woodrow Wilson could say in 1915 that "America does not consist of groups. A man who thinks of himself as belonging to a particular national group in America has not yet become an American." The blacks, to be sure, were an anomaly—native Americans yet denied legal rights and subject to brutal exclusions; the Jews were another kind of anomaly, accepted by the formal value system yet subject to milder if sufficiently irritating discrimination.

As for the immigrant Jews themselves, their deepest persuasion was that if only they were allowed to compete on equal terms in the worlds of business, education, and culture, they would thrive well enough. The view that individual merit should determine a man's place in the world was the position for which they fought the hardest. They did not ask for special accommodations; they were confident in their ability to survive and even distinguish themselves, if only they were granted equality of opportunity or something close to it. During the years immediately after the First World War this meant especially removal of the quotas which some of the most distinguished American universities set up against Jews. Social discrimination had already been experienced by young Jews in the colleges: they were generally kept out of the honor societies and eating clubs at Yale and Princeton; in 1913 a fraternity suspended its CCNY affiliate because "the Hebraic element is greatly in excess"; and it was commonly charged against them that by studying too hard ("They memorize their books!") Jews made non-Jewish students uncomfortable and thereby threatened the social poise of college life. All such affronts Jews bore more or less with patience, but quotas threatened them in a way they could not accept.

Between 1920 and 1922 Columbia University instituted regional quotas, and since most Jewish applicants came from the East, this cut the proportion of Jewish students from 40 to 22 percent. Enrollment of Jewish students at Harvard, the most liberal of the Ivy League schools, having risen from 6 percent in 1908 to 20 percent in 1922, the university issued a formal statement in 1922 saying in part: "It is natural that with a widespread discussion of [whether to limit the number of students] there should be talk about the proportion of Jews at the college." Behind this remarkable candor—no refuge in vague phrases about "social balance" or "regional distribution"— lay the decision of President Abbott Lowell that Harvard should face the "problem" of Jewish students without resorting to "the indirect methods" employed at other schools. It was his desire, read a release issued by his office in reply to criticism, that both "anti-Semitic prejudice and Semitic segregation [be] abolished in this country"—the effort to keep down the percentage of Jewish students at Harvard, it was thus suggested, had its origin in a wish to maintain harmony between gentile and Jew. In any case, by the mid-twenties it was common knowledge that quotas regarding Jews had been established at the prestige universities in the East.

For a generation of younger Jews, born in America of immigrant parents or themselves recently arrived, these genteel barriers were deeply offensive. Few thought of storming the executive chambers of General Motors, but many hoped to become doctors, lawyers, and teachers. Some paths to professional advancement were especially treacherous for Jews—engineering, for instance, and the teaching of English literature. Jews, it was often suggested, could not register the finer shadings of the Anglo-Saxon spirit as it shone through the poetry of Chaucer, Shakespeare, and Milton. (Christians did not seem to be similarly incapacitated with regard to the Old Testament.) It is instructive to read the grief-stricken record left by Ludwig Lewisohn, a man of literary distinction. Having finished his graduate work at Columbia in 1922, he encountered repeated rejections from heads of English departments throughout the country, some of whom did not even trouble to veil their true reasons. From his own professor at Columbia Lewisohn received a chilly note remarking on "how terribly hard it is for a man of Jewish birth to get a good position." Ablaze with the hope of achievement, young Lewisohn sat in his boardinghouse "playing with this letter. . . . I ate nothing till evening when I went into a bakery, and, catching sight of myself in a mirror, noted with dull objectivity my dark hair, my melancholy eyes, my ummistakably Semitic nose. . . . An outcast."

Nor was Lewisohn's experience unique. Writing about a period approximately a decade after Lewisohn caught sight of his nose in the mirror, Lionel Trilling has recalled how rare it was for a Jewish student to gain an appointment in a college English department. His friend Elliot Cohen

> had given up the graduate study of English because he believed that as a Jew he had no hope of a university appointment. When I decided to go into academic life, my friends thought me naïve to the point of absurdity, nor were they wholly wrong—my appointment to an instructorship in Columbia College was pretty openly regarded as an experiment, and for some time my career in the College was complicated by my being Jewish.

Precisely the kinds of treatment men like Lewisohn and Trilling suffered made any thought of a total assimilation into American life not only unrealistic but lacking in simple dignity. For the masses of Yiddish-speaking immigrants there was, in any case, neither choice nor problem: they wished to live out their lives within the subculture of *Yiddishkeit,* a thoroughly "natural" setting. In time there were intellectual efforts to validate a process that actually left little room for choice. Sensitive gentile intellectuals like Norman Hapgood and Randolph Bourne, who found much to admire in the culture of immigrant Jews, wrote articles urging the Jews to maintain their distinctiveness. "Democracy," said Hapgood in 1916, "will be more productive if it has a tendency to encourage differences." The infusion of alien cultures, added Bourne, signified an opportunity to create "a novel international nation, the first the world has ever seen." Horace Kallen, writing from a secular Jewish point of view, had already developed by 1915 his classic statement of "cultural pluralism." The idea of democracy, he argued, should apply not merely to individuals but also to groups, and the notion of the "melting pot" was antipathetic to democracy insofar as it denied ethnic groups the right to a continued existence. Envisaging "a cooperative of cultural diversities, as a federation or commonwealth of national cultures," Kallen provided the essential argument by which American Jews could reasonably declare their position within American society. They would be in it, at least as much as they were allowed to, but not entirely of it. They would accept its rules, its norms, and its obligations, but would retain their distinctive styles of culture. If they were to remain Jews at all, they really had no other choice. Their own desires led to this course, and so too did the response of the native culture.

THE CULTURE

3

OF YIDDISH

CHAPTER THIRTEEN

The Yiddish Word

THE BEGINNINGS of Yiddish literature in America are prosaic in circumstance, utilitarian in purpose, often crude in tone. The poetry and prose that Yiddish writers started publishing in the 1880's appeared mostly in newspapers devoted to ideological persuasion; it was written mostly by semi-intellectuals who regarded themselves as apostles of political liberation or by shopworkers struggling for the dignity of speech; it had to compete with a mushrooming of cheap popular romances, *shundromanen*, bought for a few pennies by the immigrant masses; and it was cut off from both world literature and the blossoming of Yiddish prose fiction that had begun in eastern Europe. At a time when Yiddish poets in America were still entangled with the rudiments of craft, Mendele, Sholom Aleichem, and Peretz, the classical trio of Yiddish literature, were producing major works in Poland and Russia. Yiddish writing in America, at this point, had a relation to Yiddish writing in eastern Europe somewhat like that which a century earlier American writing had had to English.

How deep the rupture went during the 1880's and 1890's between the life of the immigrant Jews and the life of the old-country Jews is rather hard to say. Connections were kept up, opinions exchanged, books sent. Yet it seems clear that during the migration from eastern Europe there occurred a kind of cultural roughening, the loss of a good part of the tradition, once the immigrants settled into America. A pioneer Yiddish novelist, Leon Kobrin, would testify that when he began writing in New York he knew almost nothing about the Yiddish masters writing in Europe; he read Mendele and Peretz mostly in Russian translations! Jews had always prided themselves on being a people of the book, but when they arrived here in the late nineteenth century they left behind them a good part of both their old and their new books. Only after the migration took on a mass character could the settlers reconquer some portions of their culture, and in the course of reconquering, transform it radically.

Their circumstances made the immigrants ripe for a new kind of literary expression, a poetry and fiction blunt in speech, fiery in politics,* breaking away from the passivity of traditional folk material. It would be unsophisticated in technique but stormy in voice, and directed toward the surging emotions of the Jewish masses as they tried to cope with poverty and deracination. Those emotions were available before anyone could articulate them: there were Yiddish readers in America before there were Yiddish writers. When the labor, or "sweatshop," poets came to the fore in the 1880's and 1890's, they arose organically out of a Jewish immigrant life already formed and spoke intimately to the sentiments of the Jewish workers. A Yiddish critic, B. Rivkin, remarks:

> A huge mass of potential Yiddish readers was gathering in the cities. Even if they had not wished to, they really had no choice but to learn Yiddish. It was the only language that could gradually lead them into the life of the new country. . . . They felt themselves lost in a "desert" where men seemed like grains of sand and the new language, English, was difficult to learn. So they naturally turned back to Yiddish. . . . Even complete illiterates—and there were quite a few among the early immigrants—as well as the many half-illiterates, who could spell out a few words in the Hebrew prayer books, now troubled to learn the alphabet in order at least to be able to read a daily Yiddish paper.
>
> The first immigrant generation and most of the writers were Jews without Jewish memories. . . . Even the few who did maintain traditions forgot them in their flight. . . . They shook them off in the boat when they came across the seas. They emptied out their memories. If you would speak with disrespect, they were no more than a mob. If you would speak with respect, they were a vigorous people.

* "We always try to provide," wrote the *Arbeiter Tseitung* in 1897, "novels that ignite the minds of ordinary readers but are also good and realistic literature. . . . We print such novels not to preen ourselves, but so that the reader who likes them may also read the things in behalf of which we publish. The main point for us is propaganda for socialism."

Is there anything comparable in the whole modern period? An up-rooted people, a broken culture, a literature releasing the crude immediacies of plebeian life, at once provincial in accent and universalist in its claims. As their lives fell into routine, the Jewish immigrants displayed strong if primitive cultural appetites.

> Poems and stories helped them to understand their new environment . . . and most of all themselves. They sought in literature the same thing they wanted in a newspaper: a way of becoming somewhat less of a "greenhorn," a way of escaping a little from their loneliness. And when poem and story gave them a certain enlightenment about mankind in general, the greenhorns began to feel they were becoming a little Americanized.

Between untrained writers and plain-minded readers there grew up the closest emotional ties, indeed, so close as to make difficult the emergence of a sophisticated literature.

> It was hardly an accident that so many people in the 1880's and 1890's wrote poems. Every speaker, agitator, journalist, and a great many folk intellectuals turned to poetry. It is enough to mention such names as Abe Cahan and Morris Hillquit [socialist leaders who composed occasional verse]. . . . Some, however, were not sure that it was proper for solid publicists and working class leaders to beguile themselves with poetry. That is why so many pseudonyms were used.

The writers had barely any tradition by which to temper their work; the very language they used was unsettled, a Yiddish coarsened with Germanisms and syntactically insecure; few critics could apply literary standards; most of the editors were uncultivated journeymen; and only gradually did there begin to appear a layer of readers responsive to more than calls for revolt and vignettes of proletarian deprivation. Often naturally talented, these early Yiddish writers in America were hemmed in by the tyranny of their moment. But of one thing there was no lack: blazing passions of romantic-revolutionary idealism, passions that ran like a red flame between readers and writers and for a time made critical judgment seem all but irrelevant.

The first volume of Yiddish poetry published in this country appeared in 1877, the work of an unorthodox rabbi named Jacob Sobel. Written in stilted Yiddish, Sobel's verses are typical Haskala preachments, though with some reflections of the confusion suffered by a generation uprooted from the old world. A more interesting early figure is Eliakum Zunser, who had achieved a reputation in eastern Europe as a *badkhn*, or wedding bard, improvising verses and tunes. Unpretentious, composed with a keen sense of what could move the hearts of mothers, brides, and relatives, and sometimes sprinkled with a dash of satire, Zunser's verses represent that stage of nineteenth-century Yiddish culture which brings together folk and artist.

Sweatshop Writers

The central figure, though not the best writer, in the sweatshop school of poetry was Morris Winchevsky, the only one among these writers to bring a rich Jewish culture to America. Speaking in the accents of a *maskil*, or enlightener, Winchevsky bridged the gap between the Haskala and Jewish socialism—indeed, one reason he was so brilliant a propagandist in verse was that he had worked in the German socialist movement and then, as an emigrant to London, became a friend of William Morris and wrote declamatory odes in behalf of justice and socialism. Among his more vivid poems are a group of "London Silhouettes" sketching urban wretchedness:

> The youngest is out selling flowers;
> the second cries "Laces!" all day;
> the oldest comes by in dark hours,
> and bargains her body away.

Upon his arrival in America, in 1894, Winchevsky was already a folk hero; his bristling verses spoke to the ideological fevers of the moment, and his cleverness satisfied readers who retained a smattering of Talmudic discipline. But of distinctively Jewish content there is rather little in Winchevsky's verse, since, like almost all the early Jewish socialists, he regarded Yiddish simply as a vehicle to the masses.

A more poignant figure of early Yiddish poetry in America was David Edelstadt, who, unlike Winchevsky, actually sweated in the garment shops. As a youth in Russia Edelstadt had no Yiddish at all, but upon coming to the United States and deciding to throw himself into the proletarian movement he learned Yiddish, though not with complete mastery. In his photograph he seems a composite of all those pure-souled romantics one associates with late-nineteenth-century Russia: bearded intense face, burning eyes, an air of abstracted spirituality. To his poems Edelstadt brought a heroic elevation of tone.* In his calls to rebellion and martyrdom—

> . . . the sufferer's every sigh
> resounded in my breast
> and turned into a battle-cry:
> "Revenge for the oppressed!"

—language, form, rhythm are all inferior, yet to the Yiddish reader they still yield a distinctive pathos, for they seem to come out of the collective

* Editor for a brief time of the anarchist *Freie Arbeiter Shtime,* Edelstadt also had his caustic side: "Already I can see our golden future/ When the state will be crowned;/ Socialist policemen/ Will crowd every corner/ From the president on his throne/ To the sheriff tightening his rope/ —All will be socialists./ What do you say to such a happy prospect?"

experience itself, fevered with dream and trouble. Dead at twenty-five from tuberculosis, this high-minded rebel was that rarity of rarities: a genuine working-class poet.

By far the most gifted of the sweatshop poets was Morris Rosenfeld, a man of flamboyant personality and troubled character who was the first Yiddish writer to dramatize the immigrant worker's life. One of his best-loved poems, "Mayn Yingele" ("My Little Boy"), describes his grief—his own grief, Morris Rosenfeld's, not that of some abstract proletarian—at having to work such long hours that he never sees his child except when it is asleep.

> The time-clock drags me off at dawn;
> at night it lets me go.
> I hardly know my flesh and blood . . .

No Yiddish writer before Rosenfeld had touched so closely the intimate experience of his audience, all the buried anger of the immigrant's days, and for that he was celebrated in the shops and the halls, wherever Jewish workers reflected on their condition.

Rosenfeld's radicalism was not as ideological as Winchevsky's nor as selfless as Edelstadt's; it was the radicalism of the Jewish masses brought to a high pitch of pathos, the cry of a generation that cared more about its plight than its programs. Later in his career, he would try to blend his socialism with Jewish nationalism. "I sing about what moves me," said Rosenfeld, and

Morris Rosenfeld

often he would recite with florid gesture or sing aloud his poems to working-class audiences. The *badkhn* tradition of a Zunser could still be detected in his recitals, though now given a new urgency by the pressures of immigrant life. The Yiddish critic A. Tabachnik remarks that where a poet like Winchevsky "went to the Jewish masses, Rosenfeld came from the Jewish masses," and where Winchevsky wrote socialist hymns, Rosenfeld composed "Jewish-social" outcries. In Rosenfeld, adds Tabachnik, there was already present an incipient personal lyricism, but "until the twentieth century, the lyrical 'I-poem' was a second- and indeed third-class genre in Yiddish poetry." That a poet might speak out of his private experience, that he might care to "represent" no one but himself, was an idea with which Yiddish literature could not yet be at ease. The first-person singular, except as a convention for voicing common aspirations, seemed a frivolity Yiddish writers could not afford.

For a decade Rosenfeld labored in the sweatshops, and the poems drawn from that experience, set to stirring music and once familiar to Yiddish readers throughout the world, can still communicate a somewhat sentimental force.

> I work, and I work, without rhyme, without reason—
> produce, and produce, and produce without end.
> For what? and for whom? I don't know, I don't wonder
> —since when can a whirling machine comprehend?
> Away rush the seconds, the minutes and hours;
> each day and each night like a wind-driven sail;
> I drive the machine, as though eager to catch them,
> I drive without reason—no hope, no avail. . . .
>
> the clock wakes our senses, and sets us aglow,
> and wakes something else—I've forgotten—don't ask me!
> I'm just a machine; I don't know, I don't know.

Rosenfeld was the first Yiddish poet in America to achieve some fame in the gentile world, and, as with a number of later Yiddish writers, it turned his head. In 1898 his poems were translated into English by Leo Weiner, a professor of Slavic literature at Harvard, and for a time Rosenfeld enjoyed a certain vogue among American literati and German Jews. But soon, his moment of novelty over, he had to return to the Yiddish world and scrape together a living from journalism and readings. The Yiddish writer Leon Kobrin has left a painful memoir of Rosenfeld at a reading in Philadelphia:

> He wore a long black Prince Albert coat with silk lapels, wrinkled trousers of a nondescript color, and shoes with run-down heels. . . .
>   There were about fifty people in the hall. Rosenfeld stood on the platform singing his songs in a pleasant tenor voice—like an actor. Then he recited a few.

At the end he said to the audience, "These poems, to sing and recite, are all in my book. Twenty-five cents—to sing and recite. Not expensive!" Since the audience didn't make a move, the poet got down from the platform with the books under his arm and walked among them, "For singing and reciting, twenty-five cents."

His smile no longer caressed, but begged and begged, perhaps cursed. . . . He sold about ten books, and my heart ached for him.

Later that evening . . . he made an angry gesture. "I didn't even make enough for a ticket back to New York."

The humiliation of such public performances was shared by almost every Yiddish writer of his day and later. But having supped a little at the sweetness of fame, Rosenfeld found his decline particularly hard. First the darling of the ghetto and then forced to confront his unpopularity with later Yiddish poets who dismissed his work as coarse and tendentious, Rosenfeld knew the tragedy of a writer who has outlived his moment. Only later, when it became possible to see what had been authentic in his poems— the intimate portraiture of the sweatshop, the fire of the immigrant cursing his fate—was he again honored in the Yiddish literary world. One of the poets who at first had attacked him, Moshe Leib Halpern, would say, "Rosenfeld is in the blood of every one of us."

The last of the important sweatshop poets, Joseph Bovshover, arrived in America at eighteen, became a furrier, and soon was composing revolutionary verses in the manner of Edelstadt, but with a psychic distance from his themes that would set him apart from the others. Learning English, Bovshover came under the spell of Shelley, and began to translate his own verses. Not a natural fighter like Winchevsky or Edelstadt, he experienced severe emotional difficulties in his chosen role. One critic has called him "the first Bohemian in Yiddish poetry," and indeed his work is marked by a romantic estrangement from all collective enterprises. In his late twenties he was removed to a hospital because of severe depression and remained there till his death.

For twentieth-century readers the work of these sweatshop poets may not prove satisfying; it never found a secure place between folk expression and sophisticated writing, nor could it break past the nagging dilemmas of propagandist art. But if naïve writers, the sweatshop poets were naïve in ways that yielded strength. Nothing could be more mistaken than to confuse their verse with the kind of "proletarian literature" that appeared, both in Yiddish and English, during the thirties. Edelstadt, Rosenfeld, and Bovshover wrote directly out of their own turmoil, their own travail, and even at their most propagandistic they were never middle-class literati engaged in poetic slumming. Winchevsky and Edelstadt would never have claimed they were sacrificing a poetic gift to a political cause, for to them such a distinction would have seemed unreal. For Rosenfeld and Bovshover the idea of a poetic career apart from the social muse may have begun to seem tempting, but they had little choice, they were locked in the grip of their moment.

Shortly after the sweatshop poets had established themselves on the East Side there began to appear in the Yiddish papers fictional sketches by writers like Leon Kobrin, Z. Libin, and S. Levin that also dealt with the life of the immigrant workers. Among historians of Yiddish literature it is a standard view that these early prose writers were inferior to the poets, but this view will not withstand fresh scrutiny. For while the fiction of this period does seem threadbare by comparison with the work of later Yiddish novelists and story writers, it has one lasting value: it yields a picture of the early immigrant milieu which precisely in its naïve transparency seems fresher than the rhetoric of the poets.

Kobrin, who began with newspaper sketches and turned to popular novels and plays, was an instinctive melodramatist who satisfied appetites for strong stuff: torn hearts, torn passions, torn lives. His fiction stands uneasily between the *shundroman* and the naturalism of writers like Asch and Opatashu. More available to later readers is Z. Libin, whom Hutchins Hapgood described as "a dark, thin, little man, as ragged as a tramp, with plaintive eyes and a deprecatory smile. . . . He . . . writes an occasional sketch, for which he is paid at the rate of $1.50 or $2.00 a column by the Yiddish newspapers." "My muse," said Libin, "was born in the sweatshop, beside the Singer machine where I first heard her outcry"—and that dissonance remains in all his stories. One story depicts a timid little man who, after a brutal encounter with workers in a shop, wins them over through a sweet

S. Libin

rendition of Yom Kippur chants; another, the misery of a worker upon learning that "a law" now restricts labor to ten hours a day, so that he cannot earn enough through piecework; a third, the fear of a worker that because a wall blocking his window has been torn down he will have to pay more rent. Dominating these ashen sketches is the spiritual impoverishment of early immigrant life, that heavy fear which had been brought across the ocean and continued to cloud the psyche of the Jews. In one Libin sketch, "A Picnic," which shows the result of an immigrant family's sudden desire for a bit of fresh air, a man cries out, "I don't know what possessed me. A picnic! . . . A poor worker like me has no business to think of anything but the shop."

Poets of Yiddishkeit

By the turn of the century, what the raw Yiddish literature developing in America needed most was to reestablish ties with the traditional culture of the east European Jews. With time, there were growing connections between Yiddish writers on both continents, for as life in the new world eased a little, it came to seem desirable that one turn one's eye back to what was being written in Warsaw and Vilna. Books published on one continent were bought and read on the other, though most Yiddish publishing still took place in the old country. In 1894 there appeared in the New York *Arbeiter Tseitung* a poem by Peretz indicating that he had followed the sweatshop school with interest: "A poem one can write/ That will move stones and mountains/ That will ring through all of Poland/ That will make the whole world tremble./ Rhymes and ideas I have in plenty/ But regretfully I have no hero." Seeing an ideological opportunity, Winchevsky replied: "In our midst/ Your wise and beautiful muse/ Would find a true hero/ In a proletarian blouse."

The interweaving of socialist and nationalist themes—both responses to the desperation of Jewish life—found its strongest expression in a group of writers who first became known in eastern Europe but reached the peak of their careers after migrating to America at the turn of the century. Abraham Liessen, Yehoash (Solomon Bloomgarden), and Abraham Reisen were writers of greater self-consciousness than the sweatshop poets. The slogans of internationalism, even if still gaining their consent, evoked in them a measure of Jewish irony. Grounded in Jewish tradition, their work signified a healing of the rupture between old and new worlds.

Liessen was primarily a poet of ethical declamation, admired for his loftiness of tone—no longer, like Winchevsky, a journalist in verse, but rather an essayist in verse, forever returning to the glories of the Jewish past. Trapped for a time between the ideologues of socialism and the partisans of nationalism, he lived in a sort of cultural limbo, though his yearning

Abraham Liessen

for a union of these two outlooks would be widely shared by the masses. Yehoash was more interesting as a poet, a lyricist caught between the clashing impulses of traditional folklike song and modern idiosyncratic speech. He was perhaps the first to write pure nature poems in Yiddish, apprehending the external world as an object of beauty in its own right. Sometimes Yehoash composed lyrical exotica, willfully distant from any Jewish experience, as in a group of poems devoted to Chinese figures ("The Empress Yang-Ze-Fu/ Has palaces fourscore/ A hundred rooms each palace has/ Each room, a golden door"). His finest achievement, however, was the first complete translation of the Old Testament into Yiddish, a work in which he could bow to the controls of a great text and thereby escape the conflict of inclinations that beset his own writing.

With Abraham Reisen we come to the first major Yiddish writer to spend the bulk of his life in America, a wonderfully gentle and lovable figure—one would say "Franciscan" were not Reisen the quintessence of ethical *Yiddishkeit*. In his hundreds of little stories, written without dramatic accent or visible plot line and sometimes reading like muted prose lyrics, Reisen has provided one of the truest portraits of Jewish life in eastern Europe,* and to a lesser extent of immigrant life in America. His

* "If every record of Yiddish life were lost, Jacob Glatstein once told me, a future archaeologist could reconstruct it all from the stories of Reisen. But could he learn

sketches depend so heavily on the tacit co-operation of his audience, they assume so deep a sharing of knowledge and value, they draw so heavily on shared silences, that to the unfamiliar reader they sometimes seem more like clues than embodiments. Focusing upon familiar situations—a cantor has lost his voice, a poor householder cannot pay rabbinical tuition for his son— Reisen wrote in a manner that reminds one of those designers who by manipulating a few sticks create the illusion that a bare stage is Lear's palace.

Reisen's lyrics, most of them employing simple rhyme schemes and a regular four-beat meter, drew heavily on Yiddish folk songs and poetry. Though an educated man who knew and loved Heine, Pushkin, and Nekrasov, and who would remain forever under the spell of nineteenth-century European romanticism, Reisen was at his best as a poet crystallizing the feelings of *Yiddishkeit*.

> In the quiet field I wandered where
> All my troubles had driven me,
> Till I stood waiting, silently,
> And heard the whole world's sorrow there. . . .
>
> The sum of the world's suffering,
> The sorrows of her years, past me
> Rode along there, silently,
> Fluttering by, and echoing.

The antiheroism, the anti-Prometheanism of *Yiddishkeit*, as it arose in eastern Europe and persisted in the immigrant world of America, found in Reisen's poems its classical expression. The sanctity of the poor, the celebration of *dos kleyne menshele* (the little man), the urgency and pathos of revolt, the transience of beauty, the shy flowering of a puritan romanticism, the ingathering of familiars—these are Reisen's themes. He could say with honesty:

> If all the world were on the rocks
> And I alone in clover,
> I'd open wide my door and bid
> The sorry world come over.

He could wonder ironically:

> A new world being made—one hears
> In childhood that it has begun;
> Then comes the passage of the years—
> Is it not yet fully done?

So thoroughly was Reisen at home in his culture, so free of any wish to move back to a Hebraic milieu or forward to a cosmopolitan one, he could write as if to be explicit were an indelicacy. Many of his lyrics were put to music and accepted by Yiddish audiences as folk songs. This popularity did

---

from Reisen so elementary a fact as how the Jews had perpetuated themselves? For that, shot back Glatstein, he would do better to go to the Bible."

not, however, keep Reisen from the usual impoverishment of the Yiddish writers. Moshe Nadir, a witty younger writer, recalls "an evening" in honor of Reisen:

> I collect some money and buy him a gold watch . . . I only wanted to make sure that, just in case . . . he would be able to pawn it. Reisen, dressed in a black tuxedo with the gold watch chain gleaming from his pocket, has no patience with the "honor" and no money for his rent. His Swedish landlady is after him for money. . . . The speeches are let loose—steam, smoke, words false and sincere. . . . A few intimates remain. . . . Sholem Asch has gotten a terrible toothache from all the praise given to Reisen, and he too must leave. . . . What's left? The groom himself, a huge bouquet of flowers in his hands, and I. We look at each other and at the flowers. What shall we do? I fling the bouquet over my shoulders. . . . We wander around for half an hour and don't know what to do. We pass Columbus's monument on Fifty-ninth Street and Reisen says, "You know what, Nadir? Put the wreath on *him*. It's *his* America." I climb to the top and put Reisen's wreath on Columbus's head. But Columbus ignores me, he says nothing.

The miracle of a Reisen was not that he derived from the people, but that he could remain at harmony with them, coming and leaving, always distinct from yet always able to return to their inner life. Precisely because he regarded being a Yiddish-speaking Jew as utterly "natural," his poems and stories need never explain or justify, they rest securely within the frame of a shared ethic. The poems emanate from a quiet flash, an ironic turn—what in Yiddish is called a *kneytsh*, literally a crease but suggestive of a slight surprise, a sudden access of sadness or bitterness.

> I wrote my songs through many a dark night,
> Choosing my rhymes like jewels, rare and bright.
> In all those nights they flamed upon the dark,
> But on my life they never shed one spark.

Yiddishkeit as the world outlook of a small world finds its consummate expression in Reisen's work, a modest idealization which the reader can take as a norm of existence. Further than this Yiddish literature cannot go with its native materials, so that the poets who follow him, as B. Rivkin writes, "could take Reisen as their model only for a short while. They had to create for themselves a lyric through their personal struggle, and for this he could not be their guide."

The Rise of Di Yunge

The beginnings of a distinctively modern Yiddish literature can be dated with precision. In 1907 a group of immigrants, new to America and oppressed by their isolation, started to publish a little magazine called *Yugend* ("Youth"). Some of them had begun to write while still in Europe, but derivatively, without a personal style. What soon made them a revolutionary force within Yiddish literature was that they refused political commitment and denied any obligation to speak for national ideals. Never at home with either America or the English language, these young men turned to world literature and, most of all, ideas of aesthetic autonomy and symbolist refinement.

Most were shopworkers, few had an extended secular education, almost all were cut off from writers in other languages. As they hurried to and from the shops, they read with eagerness the modern European poets, and in the evenings, nursing a glass of tea in Goodman and Levine's café, they would discuss impressionism, expressionism, symbolism. Sharing the lot of millions of Jewish immigrants and never able, in their writings, to detach themselves from the preoccupations of the immigrant world, these young men really lived, when they were most free imaginatively, in the lofty spaces of European poetry. One of them, Reuben Iceland, has recalled:

> Most deeply satisfying to us were the alien poets we were then encountering for the first time; we learned the most from the Russian, German, Polish, and French moderns. Baudelaire, Verlaine, and Rimbaud, whom we could read only in translation, became our daily poetic fare, and so too did Sologub, Bryusov, and Blok, and Liliencron, Dehmel, Rilke, and Hofmannsthal. With Stefan George and Theodor Storm we became acquainted somewhat later.

In poetry the leading figures were Mani Leib, Zisha Landau, Reuben Iceland, Joseph Rolnick, and Moshe Leib Halpern; in prose Joseph Opatashu, David Ignatow, and I. Raboy. At first *Di Yunge* was a term of contempt bestowed by older writers on the young heretics with their fancy aesthetic notions, but after a while Mani Leib and Landau, the leaders of the group, accepted the label with pride. Some important Yiddish writers, like Halpern and H. Leivick, merely brushed against *Di Yunge*, sharing with them not so much a creed as a common rejection of earlier tendentious writing. *Di Yunge* directed their main fire against the journalistic spirit; they wished to free Yiddish writing from the crushing weight of ethicism; and they felt, as Landau joked, that until their appearance, Yiddish poetry had been little more than "the rhyme department of the Jewish labor movement."

Like most intelligent Jewish youth in eastern Europe, these poets had been touched by the revolutionary ferment of Russia, but they came to America after the failure of the 1905 revolution, when moods of defeat swept through the Jewish intelligentsia. Their rejection of grandiose rhetoric was not merely an aesthetic response, it also reflected a sense of weariness and resignation in a bad time. One of Mani Leib's most beautiful lyrics, "Shtiller, Shtiller"—

Hush and hush—no sound be heard.
Bow in grief but say no word.
Black as pain and white as death,
Hush and hush and hold your breath.

—is simultaneously a credo for a poetry of nuance and understatement, a kind of allegorical reflection on the state of modern Jewish life, and a play upon the messianic expectation that runs through the whole Jewish experience.

Most of *Di Yunge* kept themselves fiercely apart from the journalistic excitements of the immigrant Jewish world.* Scraping together a few dollars, they would publish over the years a series of little magazines and anthologies—*Literatur, Shriftn,* the *Inzel.* If they did occasionally serve as a voice of collective aspirations, it was not by intent but simply because they were loyal to their own experience. (Iceland has written that in Mani Leib's lyric "Shtiller, Shtiller" "resignation is raised to heroism," a remark that applies both to the literary sensibilities of *Di Yunge* and to those traditional Jewish themes they supposed themselves to be putting aside.) Their Jewishness showed in the dependence of their work on traditional materials: Mani Leib on folk songs and legends (especially the Elijah motif), Landau on Hasidic tales. But with *Di Yunge* the voice of the poet—his voice in its own right, quite apart from Jewish problems—comes through in fullness: the voice of the poet as it might reflect moodiness or sensual pleasure, sanctioned or illicit responses. Inevitably, *Di Yunge* could never be as close to the Yiddish audiences as a Rosenfeld or a Reisen had been; they accepted as a fact of creative life that they had to remain cut off from the mass of Yiddish readers, quite as the European poets they most admired were cut off from *their* readers.

Setting out to purify the Yiddish language, *Di Yunge* expelled from their poems both newspaper locutions and the Germanisms beloved of earlier writers. They were also chary in using Hebraisms, because they knew that for a Yiddish writer to employ a Biblical phrase or rabbinical reference can often be a lazy substitute for discovering his own image. "Sentimentality," wrote the novelist Opatashu, "had to be smoked out. Among our Yiddish writers, the trees swayed too often in afternoon prayer, the sky was too often enveloped in a prayer shawl."

* As also from the American literary world, such as it was in the years just before the First World War. One American poet, Walt Whitman, did have an impact on *Di Yunge*, not particularly for his meters or diction, but for his expansiveness of spirit and egalitarian values. Whitman's "Salut au Monde" was translated by I. J. Schwartz into Yiddish and published in 1912 in *Shriftn,* a magazine of *Di Yunge:* some years earlier Morris Rosenfeld had written an ode in honor of the American poet. In 1919 L. Miller translated several Whitman poems for *Shriftn.* And in the twenties, David Ignatow and Meyer Shtiker put into Yiddish—very effectively, too —some chants of the American Indians. These were years in which *Di Yunge* were trying consciously to widen their poetic horizons, and their magazines published translations (not always directly) from Japanese, Chinese, Egyptian, and Arabic poetry.

Di Yunge were devoted to metrical proprieties and regularities; they experimented not so much with forms as with language, playing upon the flexible Yiddish vocabulary in a way no earlier poets had dreamed of doing. They were much concerned with the musicality of verse, revising their poems to make them smoother and more melodious. While most of them expressed a thoroughly romantic sensibility, drawing upon nineteenth-century European models, they lacked strong classical models in Yiddish poetry against whom to react or rebel. Even while proclaiming their modern distinctiveness *Di Yunge* had to establish their own poetic terms and boundaries; they had, so to speak, to do the work of both classicism and romanticism.

Di Yunge claimed to be indifferent to the very idea of subject matter, but what they really meant was that they were in rebellion against the subject matter of past Yiddish poetry, that romantic-heroic bombast which could be recited "with stirring effect" at public gatherings. They wished to write a personal and muted poetry, chamber music instead of brass bands. As late as 1925, when the original cadre of *Di Yunge* was publishing a journal called the *Inzel* (the "Island"), Landau would still feel obliged to remark, "We suffer from an epidemic of profound subject matter. It is considered a scandal to wife and child if we so much as treat an ordinary event." And in a passage that might have been duplicated in every language of the world, Landau continued: "The prophet, the preacher, the politician, have distant goals; distant and often obscure. And frequently calculation takes the place of goals. Only we, the aesthetes, have no goals and no purposes. Certainly no calculations. The tree blooms—the tree is beautiful. . . . Everything that is here is beautiful; and because it is here. This is the truth known to all who live with their senses."

"Live with their senses": that phrase, by now so commonplace in Western culture, could still arouse strong discomfort in the Yiddish world, seeming to suggest something frivolous and gentile, perhaps even "decadent." Indeed, the term "decadent" was often used against *Di Yunge* by hostile critics,* though from the vantage point of time we are far more likely to be struck by the purity and even innocence of their romanticism.

They dreamed of being pure poets and saw themselves as unrecognized distant cousins to the great Europeans from Pushkin to Rilke. But they were also poverty-stricken immigrant workers: Mani Leib a shoemaker and for a time a laundryman, Landau at first a house painter, Leivick for many years a

---

* Here is a critical attack on *Di Yunge* that combines this sort of crudeness with keen observation: "The home-brewed aesthetic of *Di Yunge* was an expression of our immaturity. . . . When all literary traditions were crumbling, when art for art's sake had expired in Europe and even its heirs, expressionism and dadaism, had vanished, here in America we imported it right to Sholem's café and enthroned it before a cup of coffee and cream. *Di Yunge* did not write about the growing metropolis of New York. . . . They did not write about Jewish life exploding in front of their eyes. . . . They did not address themselves to operators, candy-store keepers and peddlers."

paper hanger, Halpern a jack of all trades. Nothing else underscores so sharply the reason they never could become "pure poets" in Yiddish. Imagine in any other literature the turn to impressionism or symbolism being undertaken by a shoemaker and a house painter, the dismissal of the social muse by men laboring in factories! Proletarian aesthetes, Parnassians of the sweatshop—this was the paradox and the glory of *Di Yunge*. As late as 1934, when Leivick's poems and plays had been translated into many European languages, he could still be seen in the streets of New York carrying his paint bucket and wallpaper. And the bohemianism of these poets, tame enough by later standards, had still to be enacted within the tight confines of the immigrant world. As Iceland would recall:

> The majority of *Di Yunge* were shopworkers. To miss a day's pay often meant not to have a pair of shoes for one's child or be short three dollars toward the rent. Yet when we came into the café we found the gang, though we knew each of us should be in the shop. . . . Many a day I had my lunch in the shop out of fear that if I went out to eat I would not have the strength of will to complete the day's work.

Di Yunge yielded too much to their desire for chiming melodiousness and painterly harmonies, and their verse may sometimes seem to be lacking in dramatic marrow. But as they continued to write, it became clear they could never fully turn away from the realities of Jewish experience. They could not shake off the images, figures, and references that were rooted in their minds, nor the consuming homesickness they shared with so many other immigrant Jews. Homesickness colors the work of all *Di Yunge*, indeed of almost every immigrant poet, revealing less about the charms of the old country than estrangement from the new; it can be found both in a quiet lyricist like Joseph Rolnick, prompting him to compose pastorals of remembered scenes, and in a turbulent city ironist like Moshe Leib Halpern, who writes about New York, "If a wolf stumbled in here/ He'd lose his wits,/ He'd tear his own flesh apart!" *Di Yunge* were modern poets, but, more important, modern Yiddish poets. More than they knew or could suppose, they shared in the experience against which they rebelled.

Three Yiddish Poets

Cracking apart the earlier molds of Yiddish literary personality, *Di Yunge* liberated writers for new styles and postures. Three major Yiddish poets were thereby enabled to create for themselves more complex and various personae than Yiddish literature, either in America or abroad, had yet seen.

Into the unsettled world of American Yiddish literature Mani Leib brought a sensibility of high refinement and an intense love of language. Where did he acquire these persuasions, this half-taught immigrant who had no·formal training, who adored Pushkin, Blok, and the Yiddish folk song, and who, of modern languages, knew only Yiddish well? From the intense love the east European Jewish intelligentsia had developed for nineteenth-century Russian poetry; from the inner Jewish tradition of *edelkeit,* a term signifying both delicacy and nobility.

Mani Leib, wrote the poet Itzik Manger, "was the Joseph among the brothers of Yiddish poetry." He purified its voice, demanding that it shake off bombast and journalism, and insisted that Yiddish poets adhere to "the principle of strict word choice." The poem as self-contained pattern of musical harmonies, as taut structure linking theme and connotation, found its first major Yiddish fulfillment in Mani Leib's lyrics. He represents a new type in American Jewish life, and perhaps in the whole of modern Jewish life: the literary man who lives for the word.

> But blessed be, Muse, for your bounties still,
> Though your granaries will yield no bread—
> At my bench, with a pure and lasting will,
> I'll serve you solely until I am dead.
>
> In Brownsville, Yehupetz, beyond them, even,
> My name shall ever be known, O Muse.
> And I'm not a cobbler who writes, thank Heaven,
> But a poet, who makes shoes.

Mani Leib was not an experimental poet. Through most of his life he continued to use a conventional quatrain of rhymed iambics or a number of other set lyrical forms with traditional rhyme and metrical schemes. He believed—in the East Side, in the east Bronx!—that "beauty" is a self-contained quality, separable from the mere matter of the poem and to be evoked through diction and sound. His themes are sometimes disturbing, but his poems rarely disturbed; they are marked by that clarity and serenity he praised in one of his loveliest lyrics, "Come, Serene Plainness":

> Come, serene Plainness, with your bare blade cut
> Through my soul's black entanglements until
> My world, from heavy, sullen fetters freed,
> Shines like a burst of sun upon my sill.

He was a writer for whom the idea of becoming a poet seemed a sacred obligation: "Poetry was for us [*Di Yunge*] the meaning of life. Poetry lit up our gray days of hard physical labor at the sewing machines." If, as a result of his self-conscious aestheticism, his earlier poems are sometimes marked by a lack of substance and force, that is in part because for writers like him the struggle for literary autonomy could never be fully won.

In his final years, worn down by the vicissitudes of immigrant life, Mani Leib composed a series of sonnets in which aestheticism has been put aside somewhat and the language is firmer and richer. He responds now with greater openness to the stones and streets of his days:

> Of all rich streets, most dear to me
> Is my shabby Jewish East Broadway.
> Graying houses—two uneven rows;
> Frail, restless and exhausted bodies.

He opens himself to the pleasures of the physical world:

> My Indian summer, like an offering,
> Burns into gold and spirals of smoke.
> With brown hand, I push my last
> Starry ember through the ash.

About Mani Leib's position in Yiddish literature one might say what Dryden said about Edmund Waller: "The excellence and dignity of rhyme were never fully known until Mr. Waller taught it; he first made writing easily an art. . . . Unless he had written, none of us could write."

Completely different is H. Leivick, a visionary figure at the center of modern Yiddish poetry. Born in Russia, sentenced in his youth to six years' imprisonment for activity in the socialist Bund, and later driven to a wretched Siberian exile ("Even now/ on the roads of Siberia/ you can find/ a button, a shred of one of my shoelaces"), Leivick came to the United States in 1913. After years of hard work, he contracted tuberculosis and in the early thirties spent three years in a Denver sanatorium. All his life Leivick aspired toward pain, both as a way of sharing in the ordeal of his people and in an effort to gain a kind of anonymous sanctity. Throughout his voluminous writings—realistic plays, poetic dramas, psychological verse narratives, sonnets, lyrics, prose autobiography—the theme of suffering runs like a channel of blood.

While drawing upon a major element of Jewish experience, the martyrdom inherent in *galut*, this mystique also brushes against heretical possibilities. Of all Yiddish writers Leivick most closely approaches the religious passion of Dostoevsky as it declares the value of receiving pain in order to open to grace. Though not so complex a writer as Dostoevsky—he lacks Dostoevsky's gift for comic mockery—Leivick shares with him a belief in the redemptiveness of the passive. Like Dostoevsky, he sees the crucifixion as the common lot: all religious exaltations of pain, if pushed far enough, come to seem alike. Some of Leivick's Yiddish critics attacked his obsession with suffering as "masochistic" and a little beyond the edge of Jewish values—for, they argued, if the Jewish experience is indeed one of recurrent martyrdom, there is nothing in the Jewish tradition that warrants a celebration of pain. But while certain of Leivick's inferior works do seem to revel in self-torment, his obsession with suffering does not really derive from any mere literary or alien source, nor is it the kind of cultural posture that can be found among Western writers; it stems from a complete submission to the Jewish experience, a willed defenselessness before the mystery of its torment, which for Leivick is what it means to be "chosen."

Leivick wrote mainly out of the ethos of the east European Jews. The iron grip of their ethicism can, for him, never be loosened:

> A voice calls out: "You must!"
> Must what? O voice, explain!
> Instead of an answer I hear
> That call again. . . .
>
> It cries, "You must! you must!"
> And only God can tell
> Whether *must* is my redemption,
> Or *must* will be my hell.

If at times Leivick veers beyond the perimeter of strict Jewish belief, it is for reasons that a writer like Isaac Bashevis Singer also veers beyond it: the sheer intolerableness of Jewish life in the last century. In his identification with all those cut by the lash, Leivick is the poet of *galut* as it yields an ecstatic mystique of martyrdom.

Speaking in 1957 at a conference of Israeli writers, Leivick recalled an incident of his childhood.

> The teacher began the lesson for the day, the verses about the sacrifice of Isaac. Isaac accompanies his father Abraham to Mount Moriah, and now Isaac lies bound upon the altar waiting to be slaughtered. Within me my heart weeps even harder. It weeps out of great pity for Isaac. And now Abraham raises the knife. My heart is frozen with fear. Suddenly—the angel's voice: Abraham, do not raise your hand against your son, do not slay him. You have only been tested by God. I burst into tears. "Why are you crying now?" asked the teacher. "As you see, Isaac was not slaughtered." In my tears I replied, "But what would have happened had the angel come one moment too late?" The teacher tried to console me by saying that an angel cannot be late.

This image of the angel delayed would receive a large-scale embodiment in Leivick's ambitious verse drama *In the Days of Job*. The sheep that replace Isaac at the altar cry out against the common feeling that, Isaac having been spared, all will now be well. Leivick remains forever haunted by the thought that the terms of existence always require still another victim. It is an idea barely manageable this side of the morbid, but Leivick develops it with the groping intensity that is the mark of the visionary who cares not a damn that he may seem ridiculous to ordered, or ordinary, minds. In the spectrum of Jewish values Leivick stands at the opposite pole from the *sabra;* his vision of life is neither "healthy" nor "balanced"; as he speaks in the accents of Jeremiah, he does at times slide into the posture of an ascetic in the desert. Yet in some terrible sense Leivick has been vindicated by history: what had been regarded as neurotic excesses have come to seem anticipations of reality.

Leivick wrote in almost every poetic genre available to the modern Yiddish writer, and his work, because it is put to the service of so distraught a sensibility, is often marred by obscurities. There are points at which one senses in his poems a gap between the visionary strained beyond endurance and the craftsman who cannot reach a disciplined realization of his themes. At his best, however, he has left a body of lyrics, concentrated, gnarled, quivering—

> In the aftermath of storm
> the Milky Way is spun.
> God's sweet scent
> still rides around the sun.

—which speak to the union of transcendence and martyrdom possible only to those who continue to live by messianic expectation. Auschwitz and Treblinka haunted Leivick in his final years, but somehow, perhaps through sheer will, he remained open to "God's sweet scent."

No such hope could light up the days and nights of Moshe Leib Halpern, perhaps the most original Yiddish poet to have appeared in America: not the central figure, not the most fulfilled writer, but the fiercest and most forceful. In his abrasive poems, half song and half curse, Halpern brought together the traditional resources of *Yiddishkeit*, the satiric thrust of Mendele, and the parodic-violent sensibility of modernism. A rebel against his poverty-stricken life, he grew into a rebel against his own rebelliousness: "Help me, O God, to spit on the world and on you and on myself." Halpern introduced into Yiddish the disgust, the raging imprecation, the livid self-assault we associate with modern poetry.

A demon races through Halpern's lines, the demon of self. In his weaker pieces this causes a drop into self-pity, but in the strong ones it becomes objectified through a brilliant persona, *Moshe Leib der takhshit*, Moshe Leib the rascal. At best there is a cruel interplay between the speaker of the poem and the *takhshit* he addresses: Moshe Leib the wolf tearing at his own flesh; Moshe Leib the buffoon dancing in Coney Island or warning his young son that, whatever else, he is never to become a poet—

> My son and heir, I swear that, just
> As none disturb the dead in their rest,
> So, when you have finally grown,
> I'll leave you thoroughly alone.
>
> Want to be a loan shark, a bagel-lifter?
> Be one, my child.
> Want to murder, set fires, or be a grifter?
> Be one, my child.
>
> But one thing, child, I have to say:
> If once ambition leads you to try
> To make some kind of big display

To write about moonlight and the moon,
Or some poem of the Bible, poisoning the world,
Then, my dear,

I'll chop up, like a miser shredding
Cake for beggars at a wedding,
All the ties that bind us now.

—Moshe Leib becomes the name of his discontent.

Halpern steadily approached, but in his best poems went beyond, the mode of romantic irony; but in the spiraling of his mind there was no fixed point at which his irony could settle. He said of himself that he was "everywhere a stranger struggling anxiously like my brother Don Quixote with windmills." He had no patience with the cult of beauty to which *Di Yunge* had pledged themselves: "Much as I struggle only to see what is beautiful, I see only what is repulsive, a piece of rotten carcass." Overcome by yearning for the old country, he turned back in imagination to his *shtetl*, Zlochev, but then, remembering its muddy streets and pinched minds, he exploded: "This is the only solace to me/ That I won't be buried in thee—/ My home, Zlochev." For the new world, where "everything is turned into gold, made of iron and blood," he had no more affection. In a brilliant, soured fantasia called "The Bird," a voice is forever warning against those who want "to get at the hidden bit of cheese/ under my ass, behind my knees"—the poem is an ultimate assault on the moral and psychic impoverishment of the immigrant world.

Halpern was one of the first Yiddish poets to turn to the Communists, contributing poems to their paper, the *Freiheit*, when it began appearing in 1921. He was one of the first, four years later, to break from them, outraged at their efforts to make writers toe the line. He worked as a waiter, a sign painter, a pants presser,* a hack writer for a comic Yiddish weekly, and at none could he persist. He turned to private craftsmanship, making furniture for his home, sewing garments for his wife. He became a serious amateur painter. He went through a brief phase of nature romanticism, evidently a contrivance of desperation. His earlier bohemianism had long come to an end, and in his last few years—he died at forty-six—he entered a terminal serenity, no longer possessed by rage.

Nihilism ate into Halpern like a parasite, but what kept him from mere misanthropy was a tenderness he could never quite suppress, as if Moshe Leib the wolf had become Moshe Leib the lamb, as if the city poet summoning the powers of darkness could still find within himself one of Reisen's refined souls. And what saved him from chaos was a hopelessly

* In 1910–1911 a friend of the Yiddish poets, Isaac Bloom, had a dry-cleaning store in the Bronx that became an occasional hangout. One day Halpern asked for work as a presser. "It was worth something to see how Moshe Leib stands there with a heavy iron in his large, powerful hands and presses a pair of pants, mumbling to himself some lines for a new poem. . . . Suddenly—a burning smell. 'Moshe Leib, the pants are burning!' . . . He looked at me like a guilty child."

unbreakable tie with the Jewish immigrant masses he could neither abide nor abandon, with "the insulted, the deluded, the overburdened, the plain *folks-masn*." In another culture he might have become a desperado like Rimbaud or an aristocrat of letters like Stefan George; but here he has no choice, he dies in the east Bronx, in the shabbiness of the litter of Wicks Avenue.

Yiddish critics have compared Halpern to Baudelaire, and their reasons for doing so are clear: the turmoil of urban malaise, the exhaustion of spirit that the two poets share. But the comparison is valuable mostly for the differences it brings out. Halpern lacks Baudelaire's obsession with the idea of sin, lacks Baudelaire's intellectual equipment, but he has a playfulness, a gift for fooling, that Baudelaire lacked. In his poems he loves to clown, dance, croon, murmur. He introduces into Yiddish poetry not merely the grotesque, but the whole idea of self as drama, chaos, fire. Yet he cannot find solace in beautiful words, or ugly ones either; for him art is a sacred plague, and he is envious of all those who can gain relief in daily life. He writes in a 1922 letter—and this Baudelaire would have understood:

> The most ordinary ignoramus, the tough on the street, does not make a *tsimes* of his woes. He neither transfers them to parchment nor decks them out with a Torah cover. When his anger reaches the boiling point, he isn't ashamed to show that stones can fly like birds. But when the artist gets angry, he runs home and fusses with words until he grows sick of himself. I would like to believe that those artists who still retain some humanity must carry their art as if it were a boil under their arm. And their whole longing is to be redeemed from it.

In the end Halpern is lost, his struggle with self apparently beyond solution. He assaults himself with a barrage of self-contempt, succumbs at moments to impatience with culture and mind. It is as if he feels the absolute urgency that the Messiah come; but that if He were to come He would not be welcome; and in any case, depend on it, He will not come. And just this conclusion is unbearable.

Halpern's mastery of Yiddish is radically different from that of his predecessors; he breaks from refinement, mellifluousness, smoothness. His images wound, like glass crushed in one's hand. His language is a stylized imprecation, a thrust of mockery against the family sweetness of Yiddish culture. Like Mayakovsky, he stamps "on the throat of his poems."

Not only did *Di Yunge* enable such major Yiddish writers as Leivick and Halpern to go their own ways; the group also stimulated other writers in both verse and prose. J. I. Segal, who had brushed against *Di Yunge*, would make the details of ordinary Jewish life in the new world the substance of living poems; Joseph Rolnick composed muted portraits of country life that bear a curious resemblance to some of Robert Frost's poems; and I. J. Schwartz wrote long verse narrative about the immigrant experience in the provinces, notably in an uneven work called *Kentucky*. Schwartz had settled for a time in Lexington, Kentucky, and his quasi-

Whitmanesque descriptions of southern life, especially the life of the blacks, have a slightly puzzled, slightly exotic tone, as if they were studies of a foreign country. *Kentucky* opens:

> Broad, open and free lies the land,
> Drawing toward distant horizons.
> The sandy red tract stretches out
> Far and alien and lonesome . . .
>
> From a great distance comes a Jew
> With pack on shoulders, stick in hand,
> Into the new and free and spreading land. . . .

The Modernist Poets

Rebellion prompts rebellion, often against itself; after the First World War there appeared a new group of Yiddish writers calling themselves *In Zikh* (Introspectivists) led by Jacob Glatstein, Aaron Glanz-Leyeles, and N. B. Minkoff. The *In Zikh* poets, who brought Yiddish writing to the edge of modernist experimentation, directed their rebellion against *Di Yunge*, by 1920 a dominant tendency in American Yiddish literature. In retrospect it seems plausible to see *In Zikh* as heir to *Di Yunge*, at least insofar as it continued the movement away from didacticism and toward individuality. But when Glatstein and his friends first appeared, there were hot debates in Yiddish literary circles about the step or two they proposed to take beyond *Di Yunge*. In a sparkling piece of impudence called "A shnel-loyf iber der Yidisher Poezie" ("A Quick Tour of Yiddish Poetry"), published in 1920, Glatstein slashed away at his poetic elders with the recklessness of a young man determined to incite the anger of those he admires. The Yiddish poet, asked Glatstein, "who is he? What is the color of his soul? . . . of his despair and exaltation? . . . A pity that our writers regard themselves as missionaries, mere blind instruments, servants of the folk, its consoler and awakener." Glatstein attacked the leading spirits of *Di Yunge*, Mani Leib and Landau, as too "poetic," too cut off from the blunt realities of Jewish experience, too devoted to the poem as a smoothed-out and nicely rounded form. Many years would pass before a reconciliation between the two groups was possible; it occurred only after it had become clear that in maturity neither could cling to the programs of youth.

There were differences other than aesthetic. Most of *Di Yunge* had been workers, at least in their youth chained to the ships; the *In Zikh* writers had received a certain amount of education in America, some going to college for a time. Few of *Di Yunge* ever mastered English, and in their imaginations most of them lived with European literature; writers like Glatstein, Glanz-Leyeles, and Minkoff had read, or soon would be reading, Pound, H. D., Eliot, and Stevens. Indeed it was in the work of the *In Zikh* poets that one can see, for the first time, a major impress of American upon Yiddish poetry.

Where *Di Yunge* still conformed to metrical regularity and verbal decorum, the *In Zikh* poets turned to free verse, intensely personal themes, incongruities of diction and sound. The poetry of Whitman seems to have had some effect on them, but Glatstein would insist that the cadenced verse of the Bible was the greater influence. In their opening manifesto the *In Zikh* group developed aesthetic principles notably similar to those put forward by the imagists in America and other modernist groups in Europe:

> We introspectivists want, first of all, to present life as it actually is, with precision. . . . In what form? The complexity of verse . . . comes in the form of association and suggestion, the two elements most important in poetic expression. . . . These are best suited to express the complicated feelings of present-day man.
>
> Form and content are one. A poem that can be paraphrased is not a poem. Its major characteristic is rhythm. . . . For us free verse is not a "must." One may write an introspective poem in a regular meter. We believe, however, that free verse is best suited for our individuality.

All of this may seem familiar, but it is familiar because fifty years ago it was new. In the world of Yiddish such views struck home with a special force. What was most disturbing to the Yiddish public was the way in which the *In Zikh* writers drove to an extreme the views of *Di Yunge* which relieved Yiddish writers of national-social obligations: "For us there does not exist the sterile question as to whether the poet should write about national and social or personal problems. We make no distinction between poetry of the heart and poetry of the mind. . . . Whatever a Yiddish poet may write about is *ipso facto* Yiddish. One does not need specifically Jewish themes."

In the history of Yiddish literature the *In Zikh* group marks a major turning point, one at which Yiddish poetry almost—*almost*—joins the mainstream of Western poetry in the twentieth century.

Literary Life on the East Side

For most Yiddish writers, the conditions of their literary life were at once profoundly sustaining and intensely constricting. At least until self-conscious literary groups began to develop—which signified, of course, an estrangement from popular audiences—Yiddish writers enjoyed a spiritual intimacy with their readers that writers of other Western cultures might well have envied. The sweatshop poets had been popular tribunes; a poet like Reisen was a kind of a folk hero; and when Sholom Aleichem died in New York in 1916, some 100,000 people came to his apartment house in the east Bronx to share in the mourning, a tribute no other Western writer of comparable stature could expect in the twentieth century.

The advantages of this closeness between reader and writer hardly need elaboration: the reader was quick to respond to thematic allusions, the writer felt a strong responsibility to the needs of his reader, and both shared a sense of common experience, plebeian fraternity.* They lived in the same tenements, worked in the same shops. At least in its early decades, immigrant Yiddish culture was an organic culture, without avant-garde estrangement or aristocratic pretense.

There were related disadvantages. Even those Yiddish writers who saw themselves as self-conscious rebels rarely felt free enough to tinker and play, to write with an eye toward the horizons of their imagination rather than the limitations of their readers. Much can be said, no doubt, for the idea of literature as communication, but the Yiddish writers might have profited from indulging the idea of literature as expression. At first too close to their audience, they later found themselves, once they began to improvise modernist styles, too far from it. The transition from organic culture to coterie alienation, which in other literatures has taken centuries, Yiddish literature packed into a few decades.

Yet a coherent Yiddish avant-garde could never really settle into place; there were several beginnings, but each time one started to flourish it would come up against the severe limits of immigrant life. The readers who might have been the natural audience of a Yiddish avant-garde—sons and daughters of immigrants, now going to college and becoming sophisticated, more or less, about world literature—would soon turn their backs on Yiddish entirely. The potential readers of Glatstein became the actual readers of Eliot.

In their day-to-day existence Yiddish writers frequently had to face a difficult choice: either work by the sweat of their brows, which did not leave enough time or strength for their own writing, or become dependent on the newspapers.** Now, it is true that the better Yiddish papers gave more

---

* When Sholom Aleichem wrote for the New York Yiddish press in 1914-1915, his daughter recalls, he "ran his home address in the newspaper so that anyone who wished could contact him—and many did, all sorts of people. Some were just bores, and our problem was how to hasten their departure. Others had information to offer, what America was like, how people lived here, and the stories of their own experience in the land of Columbus. . . . My father absorbed it all in amazement. . . . With some of these people he visited such places as a modern laundry, a grocery, a tailor shop. At each place he would want to know how it operated, the working process as well as the working conditions."

** When Sholom Aleichem settled in New York in 1914, by then a world-famous writer and the one absolute Yiddish genius, he immediately had to start writing for the newspapers in order to support his family. The Yiddish papers competed for his name, and the *Day* signed him to a contract providing a hundred dollars a week for two pieces each week. After a year the paper could no longer afford to pay this

space to literary work than did the American papers; many of the best Yiddish novelists first printed their work in the *Forward* and the *Day*. But there was always tension between editors and writers; there had to be. The editors were scrambling for circulation, and that meant keeping a sharp eye on readers whose education and tastes, even when conventionally good, did not encourage modernist innovations. As a result, by the time *Di Yunge* came onto the scene, many Yiddish writers felt it necessary to keep a distance from the papers, sometimes printing a poem or story in one of them but eager to avoid complete dependence.

During the years that Yiddish literature thrived in America, say, between 1905 and 1940, a large number of little magazines were published: the *Naye Lebn*, the *Freie Shtunde*, the *Naye Land*, *Yugend*, *Shriftn*, *Literatur*, the *Inzel*, as well as some in Boston, Chicago, and California. Few of these magazines could last very long, though their contents were often on a high level. The little magazine depends on the presence of an avant-garde audience, and that the Yiddish writers could not find—nor were many of them sure they wanted to. Only journals with the backing of political groups, like the socialist *Tsukunft* and the Labor Zionist *Yidisher Kemfer*, lasted through the years. The Yiddish reader had been taught to take his literature with his politics, usually a little of the former and a lot of the latter. He was intensely faithful to his newspaper, expecting as a matter of course that it would offer stories, poems, serialized novels. He might occasionally be lured into buying a Yiddish book. But the little magazines seldom reached his eye, and if they did, he was likely to feel they were not really meant for him. They were not.

That gifted novelists and poets appeared regularly in the Yiddish papers was surely a boon for their readers, both those who might occasionally glance at a poem and those who really cared about literature. The regular publication in the Yiddish papers of writers like Asch, Reisen, Opatashu, I. J. Singer, and others must surely have helped to raise the cultural level of the Yiddish public. But for the writers themselves the blessing was a mixed one, since it made them too dependent on the commercial needs of the papers and too caught up with the topicalities of journalism.

Where else could they go? In the Yiddish world there was no equivalent of the American university in its recent phase of hospitality to writers. There were no foundations, no publishers ready to offer large (or small) advances, and only rarely private patrons. Nor could the Yiddish writer

---

salary, and Sholom Aleichem found himself in financial trouble. Abe Cahan, the truculent editor of the *Forward*, refused to consider Sholom Aleichem as a contributor because a year earlier he had failed to accept the *Forward*'s offer. Desperate by now, Sholom Aleichem agreed to do his stint of two pieces a week for the *Varheit*, the least prosperous of the Yiddish dailies; for these he was paid forty dollars a week. All this occurred at a time when the Yiddish press was at the peak of its strength—and the terms offered Sholom Aleichem were decidedly better than those enjoyed by other writers.

retreat to the comforts of bohemia: the café to which he went on a Saturday night was not something apart from, it was completely interwoven with, the life of the immigrant world.

While Yiddish still flourished, a few writers could work for one of the comic weeklies, like the *Kibitzer* or the *Kundes*. Moshe Leib Halpern and his friend Moshe Nadir, a clever writer of *feuilletons*, would sit in Tompkins Square on summer nights

> and collaborate on a crazy poem and bring it to the *Kundes*. We laugh a lot, and we take along some friends to help us laugh, and we fall into the editorial offices laughing loudly. The editor starts to laugh . . . and we swindle a few dollars out of him, in cash, and spend it wildly in a couple of days and remain the same poor but aesthetic poets we were, concerned only with beauty and art.

A bit later Nadir went to work for the *Kundes:*

> I was hired as an editorial assistant. I knew a lick of German and a teardrop of English, so I stole jokes from *Punch* and *Simplicissimus*. As you know, *Punch* is dry as an old maid, and *Simplicissimus* stout and silly as a bourgeois *mädchen*. From the English plum pudding and German meat loafs it was my job to make Jewish *kneydlakh*.
>
> Marinov, the editor, had once been a blacksmith. . . . He valued literature by the pound. His motto was "If you sweat it's good; if you don't it's bad." A good writer was one who weighed fifteen pounds less after finishing a piece.
>
> . . . When Marinov needed you he'd promise to make you into a second Mark Twain. When you worked by the piece and managed to earn as much as fifteen dollars a week, he decided it was better that you work by the week. When you worked by the week, he screamed that you were ruining him—too much time reading and not enough writing. "You eat like a horse and give out like a bird."

At least as precarious were the occasional efforts of Yiddish writers to earn their livings through translating from English, German, and Russian. As the Yiddish reading public grew acquainted with the more accessible modern works, the demand for translation kept increasing; but the pay for translating into Yiddish was at least as bad as it has always been in other languages, and the standards were often execrable. Unstable Yiddish publishing houses offered "sets" that were sold by traveling salesmen who'd go to meetings of Jewish organizations and spread the word about the wonders of alien authors. During the early decades of this century, such sets—sometimes "reworked," which meant cut and vulgarized—were issued of writings by Andreyev, Goethe, Zola, Jack London, Tolstoy, Dostoevsky, and Shakespeare. The Russian novelists were especially popular, since their names had first been heard in the old country. As for the level of these translations, they ranged from the mediocre to the shabby; given the financial risks, no one connected with such an enterprise could afford to be overly careful.

The East Side also had its hacks, as tireless as if they had stepped out of Smollett's London. Abner Tannenbaum, who turned out a stream of books "based on Jules Verne," as well as on Goethe's *Faust* and *Secrets of the Imperial Russian Court*, claimed more readers than Mani Leib, Halpern, and Leivick put together.

There were also serious translations, usually labors of love issued at the translator's expense. Some Yiddish writers felt a need to learn from older or more sophisticated literatures, and there was no better way to do this than through translation. As far back as 1899 the poet Bovshover put *The Merchant of Venice* into Yiddish; twenty years later I. J. Schwartz translated *Hamlet* and *Julius Caesar* tastefully. The writers around *Di Yunge* translated a good deal: Mani Leib from Slavic songs, Landau from Scottish ballads and Russian symbolist poetry. In later years B. Lapin issued a careful Yiddish version of Shakespeare's sonnets, and another poet, Meyer Shtiker, performed the virtuoso feat of rendering the first part of *The Waste Land* in Yiddish. But these were solitary efforts by serious writers, without hope of reward.

Nor was there much profit when Yiddish writers saw their own work issued by the few publishers, erratic when not unscrupulous, that sprang up on the East Side. During the earlier years Yiddish publishing houses put out unauthorized editions of Mendele, Peretz, and Sholom Aleichem for which the authors never received a penny. "All the authors got," writes a chronicler of Yiddish literary affairs, "was aggravation, because of the tasteless ways in which their work was issued." The pirated volumes were then sent to Poland and Lithuania, where they undersold Yiddish books put out by respectable European publishers. New York houses "also published collections of American Yiddish writers, reprinted from the daily press and never decently edited. The authors might receive a pittance, and helplessly watch their most immature work being reprinted for the sole purpose of filling as many pages as possible, so that the publishers could attract naive readers with bulky 'goods.' "

Some efforts were made during the years before the First World War to set up serious publishing houses devoted to Yiddish. The war itself was a temporary boon, since competition from Europe was cut off and American readers became somewhat more prosperous. Among these reputable houses were the Max Maisel Company, the Literarisher Ferlag, and Naye Tsayt, which showed some responsibility to both author and text. With the end of the war, however, a number of these firms collapsed, and Yiddish publishing would never again have any commercial success.

To avoid the plague of publishers entirely, Yiddish writers tried issuing their books co-operatively or through communal institutions. *Di Yunge* formed Inzel Ferlag during the 1920's and brought out volumes of poetry by Leivick, Rolnick, Mani Leib, and others; the novelist Ignatow founded a firm called Amerika "to protest the exploitation of Yiddish writers by Yiddish publishers." Such ventures invariably failed. Soon Yiddish publishing fell mainly to cultural institutions or the writers themselves. Branches of the Workmen's Circle would occasionally subsidize a Yiddish book. In 1925 the Yiddish secular education movement, known as the Sholom Aleichem Folk Institute, founded a publishing house, Ferlag Matones, which for a time engaged in some distinguished publishing. But all too often the Yiddish writers, including the most famous ones, had to pay for the cost of printing their books, then stack them in homes or cellars and slowly try to dispose of them. The story had come full circle, with many writers, just like Morris Rosenfeld half a century earlier, offering their wares to lecture audiences that seldom bought.

Yiddish Fiction in America

Only rarely was the course of Yiddish literature in America seriously affected by these material factors. Sooner or later books got into print, and those who cared, read. The fact that Yiddish book publishing came to be commercially hopeless gave the literature a certain freedom, enabling it to fulfill itself without having to worry too much about the dollar. It was a fulfillment that occurred with sharply different rhythms in poetry and prose. In the United States before, say, 1920, Yiddish fiction lagged in quality behind Yiddish poetry, a situation quite the reverse of that in eastern Europe. The work of the prose writers close to *Di Yunge* was not nearly so distinguished as that of the poets. A certain charm still resides in a novel like Isaac Raboy's *Mr. Goldenbarg,* an idyllic account of a young Jewish farmer in North Dakota who decides to move to Palestine. The very locale of this novel (where, after all, *is* North Dakota?) must have struck readers on East Broadway as exotic, but what impresses one about such fiction a half-century later is that it really has no roots anywhere, neither in the new nor in the old world, since it reflects mainly the deracination of the immigrant intelligentsia.

Yiddish fiction in America came into its own after the First World War, a period in which there occurred what S. Niger has called "the modernization of the Yiddish novel" and what might be called, more generally, the internationalization of Yiddish culture. With two strong and populous centers in eastern Europe and the United States, as well as smaller settlements in western Europe and Latin America, Yiddish culture displayed a peculiar mixture of provincial strength (its special concerns and references) and universalist uncertainty (its strivings toward world recognition, employment of "modern" themes, and dispersion across the continents). By 1925 it was not unusual for a Yiddish poet to live in New York and publish a book in Vilna, nor for a Yiddish novelist to live in Warsaw and publish his work in the New York *Forward.* Writers shuttled back and forth between continents, with some of the important Yiddish novelists of eastern Europe —Sholem Asch, I. J. Singer, Zalman Schneour—settling permanently in New York. All of these men had won solid reputations during the early years of the century and then, after coming to the United States, continued their literary work here.

Coming after the classical trio of Mendele, Sholom Aleichem, and Peretz, this generation of novelists was remarkable for its sheer energy, and for its readiness to expend that energy in a passionate struggle with the tradition that had formed it. Though many of these writers had been personally encouraged by Peretz, almost all had to break away from his influence. They wished to discard the thin elegiac style, the bare linear story, the winding rhythm, the ethos of *edelkeit*, the antiheroic protagonists—in short, the kind of *khokhme* (wisdom) story Peretz had perfected. Such novelists as Asch, I. J. Singer, Schneour, and Joseph Opatashu all tried to bring into Yiddish fiction a number of new elements:

•   A wider range of subject matter, including themes borrowed from Western literature and not significantly present in the work of Mendele, Sholom Aleichem, and Peretz.

•   The discovery of social layers in the *shtetl* which earlier writers had neglected, and of the whole new world of Jewish urban life.

•   A readiness, sometimes an eagerness, to expose themselves to the influence of modern European writing as a counterforce to their still-powerful native tradition.

•   A willingness to deal not merely with Jewish experience in eastern Europe but also with universal themes—class struggle, personal relations, sexual impulse, urban anomie—transcending or undercutting the Jewish experience.

•   A celebration of energy as a principle of human life, and especially of Jewish life, in opposition to the attachment of earlier writers to the values of reflectiveness, patience, and endurance.

•   An eager, often naïve interest in physical existence, whether of the natural world or the human body, such as can rarely be found among the Yiddish masters.

Other innovations in subject matter came quickly, and with them a new Yiddish prose: coarse, thick, vivid, erotic. Sholem Asch and Joseph Opatashu turned to the life of the Jewish underworld, both in Europe and America, and suddenly, as if out of nowhere, a parade of thieves, swindlers, bullies, confidence men, and toughs pushed their way through Yiddish fiction. In Asch's *Mottke the Thief* and Opatashu's stories there is a curious oscillation between realistic and romantic motifs: a desire to portray the Jewish underworld in its blunt misery coupled with a sense of how exciting it seemed that there should be a Jewish underworld at all.

Zalman Schneour was one of the first programmatically to introduce themes of eroticism in Yiddish literature. Sholem Asch discovered new human resources among the east European Jews, his story "Kola Road" becoming famous as a celebration of the *proste,* the common folk, and the *grobe yungn,* the vulgar ignoramuses.* Opatashu, wishing to supplant the pale little heroes of Peretz and Reisen, wrote stirring historical novels about Jewish heroes who, it turned out, could curse, revel, whore, drink, and fight. Above all, fight.

> Where are you now [wrote Zalman Schneour in his novel *Noah Pandre*], you Jews like oaks, with your broad-capped jack boots and squashed, burned noses like those of lions? You coachmen, butchers, water carriers, plasterers, hewers of wood. . . .
>
> You were always redolent of forests, cart grease, corn flour, fresh hides. Even on the Sabbath eve, after you had come from the baths and crept into your fine cloth gaberdines and surtouts—grown tight since your wedding day —you gave off a smell of birch and bark and the plenty of a full week. You held your prayer books gingerly as if they were fluffy yellow chicks, held them with the tenderness and compassion of strong men, and piously swayed over them. And with the same calloused and scarred fists you tossed five-hundredweight loads out of the barns, onto your carts and from your carts into the barns as if they were balls of wool.

But even as such writers drew away from the Yiddish masters, they remained far more subject to the "classical" tradition than they supposed. Like Peretz and Sholom Aleichem, they simply could not conceive of literature as a mere exercise in objective portrayal, let alone a mode of imaginative play. But now they chose new objects for celebration, since they felt the time had come to put some blood and muscle into Jewish life. Turning

---

* In an Opatashu novel set on the East Side, a Hebrew school teacher named Friedkin visits the home of the school's secretary, to meet his daughter. Friedkin is sullen because he believes the girl beneath him, and his behavior is described by Opatashu in terms deliberately coarse and vulgar:

> The secretary took tiny steps like a cat about to embark upon theft. While walking he opened and closed the fingers of his right hand and grimaced. . . .
>
> The secretary's wife, fat and still spreading, met Friedkin with a greasy smile. She kept wiping her hands.
>
> "Welcome."
>
> The gnome of a husband stared at his wife as though about to devour her and indicated she should not keep Friedkin in the kitchen. . . .
>
> Friedkin took off his hat and wiped his brow. Sensing himself in a place where he was respected, he spread out on the chair, peered at the girl and let out a tired yawn. . . .
>
> Friedkin hardly paid any attention [to the secretary's wife praising the charms of her daughter]. He just kept eating preserves, licking his lips, and was sure it must hurt them to see how he was devouring everything in sight. . . .
>
> Suddenly he started to laugh. The girl grew flustered, thinking he was laughing at her: "What's the matter, Mr. Friedkin, are you laughing at me?"
>
> He stopped, curled his lips, pulled at his shaven chin with animal delight and held himself back from guffawing. He peeled an orange, took a slice in his mouth, sucked at it, and spit the skin into a saucer.

their eyes downward, to the depths of Warsaw or New York, they wrote with a sense of consecration that had marked the work of Peretz when he looked upward. In the literature of an oppressed people, the romantic impulse can never be entirely absent.

Arriving in America during their mature years, these novelists would often make an effort to engage themselves, if not with America as such, then with the narrow arc of Jewish experience in America; but as a rule, the contours of their imagination had already been shaped, they were far more at ease in rendering places they remembered than those to which they had come. Sholem Asch wrote several novels about Jewish life in New York (*The Mother, East River*) but not nearly with the authority he had shown in earlier fictions set in Europe, such as *The Town* and *Sanctification of the Name*. Opatashu has a good many stories reflecting the moral chaos of life on the East Side, and once Sholom Aleichem even encouraged him to "write about Jews in America—that is your genre"; but Sholom Aleichem was wrong, for Opatashu did his best work in a novel like *In Polish Woods*, an earthy rendering of Jewish life in eastern Europe at the moment when Hasidism and the Haskala clashed. Whenever such writers tried to deal with the new world there was a lack of that assured intimacy which is essential to fiction.* Descriptions of place seem a trifle askew, evocations of atmosphere done from slightly too great a distance, the dialogue assigned to characters not heard with sufficient exactness. Whatever a writer of fiction has not completely assimilated in his youth is always likely to be recalcitrant to his imagination.

These writers constituted the sacrificial generation of Yiddish literature. They rebelled; they turned from the moldiness of the *shtetl* toward metropolitan excitements; they opened themselves to new, forbidden sensations; they welcomed history. And most of them paid a price. Yiddish writers trying to do what Western writers had long been doing, seldom did it as well. Precisely their "universality," that eager striving to emulate modern European literature, has come to seem most "provincial."

If any exceptions can be found to these judgments, they are two enormous novels, Sholem Asch's *Three Cities* and I. J. Singer's *The Brothers Ashkenazi*, both written in New York and once popular with English-reading audiences. Asch and Singer, the latter with more distinction, were among the first Yiddish writers in America to write the kind of thick, leisurely social novel that had dominated European literature earlier in the century. Intent upon portraying the social changes in Jewish life between

---

* This holds even for Lamed Shapiro, the most meticulous craftsman among Yiddish writers of fiction in the United States. Shapiro began with pogrom stories, but, coming to feel they were too crudely done, he set himself the task of widening the range of his subject matter and refining his style. From Chekhov he learned the possibility of employing tonal effects as the unifying principle of a story; from Flaubert, the virtues of economy and detachment. Shapiro's stories are notable for their tightness of structure, their terseness of style. Yet even as his technique is quite modern, his best stories are still set in the old country.

shtetl and city, I. J. Singer built his work upon spacious architectural principles, composing in the manner of the early Mann. More than most Yiddish writers, he mastered the problems of construction peculiar to the "family novel," such as maintaining an even, impersonal style and managing multiple layers of plot. He learned—it was something Yiddish writers had to learn—that modern society is a complex organism with a life of its own, a destiny superseding or canceling out the will of its individual members. And he absorbed the dictum of Turgenev and Flaubert that the novelist should keep himself out of the events he describes, as if in literature he were an invisible hand somewhat like that of Adam Smith's in economics. The idea of aesthetic distance signified that the writer had torn himself away, in partial estrangement, from his own culture. With Singer the distance from his work, like the estrangement from his culture, was a sign of the gradual secularization of the Yiddish intelligentsia—though in his own case also a sign of a temperament somewhat rare in the Yiddish milieu. Singer was a writer of deep skepticism, which he released not merely toward the ideologies agitating "the Jewish street" but also toward the whole human enterprise. Even in his short novel *Yoshe Kalb* (in English *The Sinner*), a caustic picture of the disintegration of Hasidism, Singer wrote from a tight-lipped, enigmatic distance. He was one of the few Yiddish writers able to establish a critical disengagement from the norms of his culture while remaining at home with its materials.

No such poise marked the fiction of Sholem Asch, in the decades between wars the most popular Yiddish writer in America. Asch brought together two strands of the Yiddish tradition: the tendency to idyllicize the past, bathing it in a Sabbath light, and the tendency to enlarge upon the pathos of martyrdom. He was an instinctive romanticist of the kind in whom the romantic soon melts into the sentimental. His true gift was for painterly verbal effects, remembered scenes drawn with slapdash primary colors—someone has said he wrote Yiddish as if the language were a personal enemy. But his ambition drove him toward massive literary structures he could not justify. Lacking the natural intelligence of Sholom Aleichem or the intellectual control of Peretz, Asch turned out middlebrow narratives with the kind of "power" certain to endear him to popular audiences in Yiddish and other languages. Under the shrewd hand of his translator, Maurice Samuel, he often read better in English than in Yiddish.

Only once did Asch's popularity suffer a major drop within the Jewish world, and that was when he published his best-selling Christological trilogy (*The Nazarene, The Apostle, Mary*). Appearing at a time when the Jews were suffering the most terrible ordeal in their history, these novels were bound to provoke a Kulturkampf among Yiddish critics and readers. The *Forward*, which had printed Asch's fiction for many years, refused in 1939 to accept *The Nazarene*. Some of the attacks launched in Yiddish publications against Asch were very nasty: the chauvinism of Jews is no more attractive than that of anyone else. To charge Asch with proselytizing for apostasy, as some Yiddish journalists did, was outrageous, and he was surely right in saying, "It is entirely untrue that I am preaching Christianity to the Jews. Christianity is simply the stuff from which I create."

Still, the mere fact that Asch had chosen to write about Jesus in a sympathetic vein struck many of his Yiddish readers as a provocation. They could hardly have been expected to make cool distinctions between the intrinsic merit of his books and the problems raised by the moment in which they appeared. Nor did Asch display much moral tact. Asked by the *Christian Herald* which Christian saint might best become the heavenly patron of the Jews, Asch replied that his candidate was Peter. This brought from the Yiddish writer Hayim Greenberg an appropriate rebuke. Noting that Peter was commonly recognized as the founder of the Catholic church, Greenberg wrote, "Is it necessary, in 1944, to remind a Jew what memories are evoked in Jewish consciousness by the papacy? Yet you [Asch] decided that our patron saint should be the man who stands at the fountainhead of the papal dynasty . . . what a lack of elementary decency toward your own people!" And even S. Niger, the Yiddish critic who had always spoken up for Asch, had to acknowledge that "Jewish readers and writers cannot remain neutral to the Nazarene. . . . It is natural, in view of Jewish suffering at the hands of those who turned Jesus into a God, that his name should be taboo."

In these circumstances the trilogy itself could hardly receive a dispassionate criticism, and perhaps that was just as well. For it comes to little more than an exercise in historical sentimentality, full of that damp ecumenical piety which signifies an earlier collapse of religious belief. Except for a few critics, the Yiddish literary public had steadily overrated Asch's work, and now it was paying the price for slackness of standards.

One aspect of the Asch controversy, at the time not much noticed, raised some delicate problems concerning Yiddish literature as a whole. Niger was entirely right to say that "the theme itself [Jesus as a figure in ancient Jewish life] has long been accepted in Yiddish and Hebrew literature. . . . In many poems and stories by American Yiddish writers the figure of Jesus is shown as a Jewish one and the legends woven around him are illuminated by Jewish concepts." And Niger went on to add that throughout his career Asch had shown inclinations toward sentimental Christianizing, even in so early a story as "In a Carnival Night" (1907). In *The Town*, Asch's first major work, there is a passage that anticipates his later turn to Christian sympathies, and some of his early stories contain warm responses to the Virgin Mary. Nor was Asch the only Yiddish writer who drove traditional Jewish sentiments to a point so extreme they might link up with primitive Christianity. Leivick has an early poem called "He" in which Jesus speaks comfortingly to Jews beaten in a pogrom, and some of Itzik Manger's early poems also reveal signs of attraction to the Christ figure.

How can we explain this? A Yiddish writer, compulsively focused on certain elements within his tradition—passivity, martyrdom, suffering—could move toward a *Weltanschauung* akin to that of early Christianity. Committed to the ordealist strand of the Yiddish tradition, a poet like Leivick would naturally find himself stirred by the story of Jesus, the archetypal martyr of Western culture. "I saw him as a prisoner," said Leivick, anticipating word for word what the Italian novelist Ignazio Silone would say years later.

Many Yiddish writers had been formed intellectually in the Russia of the late nineteenth century, when the idea of a "purified" or "inner" Christianity was popular among the gentile intelligentsia. It was an idea bound to leave an imprint on young Yiddish writers just beginning to approach the possibilities of alien culture. While exiled in Siberia for radical agitation, Leivick read Vladimir Soloviev, a major Russian spokesman for this effort at Christian renaissance, and there remain clear touches of similarity between the martyrological poems Leivick wrote in his later years and Soloviev's belief in "the quality of *sophia* in Christ himself."

If one reason for the warmth some Yiddish writers showed to Jesus was their obsession with martyrdom, another was the desire some felt to break out of Jewish parochialism. Young writers, usually ill-educated in anything but traditional Jewish learning, could easily confuse the universalism they sought with the Christianity they found. In east European Jewish life the very mention of Jesus had evoked images of persecution. But when a young writer began, say, in 1900 to peek into gentile culture he might discover that it contained more humane versions of Christianity than he had ever heard of in his *shtetl*, as he might also discover the extent to which Christianity seemed inseparable from Western culture. For such a young writer the problem was by no means an easy one—it has never been easy for any sensitive Jew upon first coming to hear the great voices, at once forbidding and enticing, of Christian culture. Not only the desire for universalism but also hesitant inclinations toward aestheticism could bring a Yiddish writer to an unexpected interest in Christian symbolism. Christological temptation had coursed through Yiddish literature as a narrow underground stream; what made a recurrence of it so painful for Yiddish readers was that it should surface precisely at the most dreadful moment in the history of the Jews.

After the Holocaust

About the ultimate preoccupation of Yiddish writing after the Second World War there can be no doubt. All schools, groups, and tendencies melted away: every Yiddish writer felt himself under the most sacred of obligations: the thought of the Holocaust was crushing.

It did not help, for the thinning ranks of Yiddish poets and novelists, that the world catastrophe of the Jews coincided with a visible disintegration of their own culture in America. Speeches might be made about the miraculous persistence of Yiddish, but the writers, whose eyes were as keen as those of anyone else, knew they were coming to the end. That in poetry, at least, the end was also a moment of creative upsurge—some wonderful Yiddish poems were written in America during the decades after the war— only made their fate more bitter. A number of the Yiddish writers sought consolation, perhaps even dreamed innocently of a literary resurrection, in the prospect of having their work translated into English. If it had happened to Asch in the thirties, and was happening to Isaac Bashevis Singer in the fifties and sixties, why not to them? Alas, they failed to understand that some edict of fate, or whim of taste, allows only one Yiddish writer at a time to be popular with American readers. There was a growing amount of translation in the fifties and sixties, some of it accomplished; yet no one could suppose that this brought about a genuine revival of Yiddish literature. In a bitter poem called "Yiddish Poets," Leivick wrote about his rage and frustration, how "the words go dumb," when reflecting on the condition to which they had come. A striking stanza portrays the Yiddish poets "dragging their poems by the neck through the streets of New York" like bewildered cats dragging their kittens. Another major poet, Jacob Glatstein, chose to emphasize his pride of self-sufficiency, his readiness to live within the narrowing circles of Yiddish. Yet he too knew the realities well enough, once saying with a sardonic smile to the author of this book, "What does it mean to be a poet of an abandoned culture? It means that I have to be aware of Auden but Auden need never have heard of me."

Lyrics on the usual range of topics and stories on the usual range of situations continued to be written, but Yiddish literature now returned, as it had to return, to its original concern with Jewish destiny. The future of Yiddish became an obsessive theme, with the writers oscillating between fierce gestures of persistence and sorrowful questions about the future. What S. Niger wrote in 1947 remains true for the years to follow:

> The tendencies characteristic of Yiddish poetry in the last few years have more to do with motives, ideas and thematic material than with artistic form or style. This is not because Yiddish writers no longer strive to create works of art. On the contrary. It is fair to say that no representative of Yiddish literature today has attempted to make it solely into an instrument of ideological expression. Ideas and a variety of psychological and ethical matters are for Yiddish literature, as for any other, the raw material which requires expression in pictorial, lyrical or rhythmic structure. But this is something Yiddish writers have recently ceased to emphasize. . . . Insofar as Yiddish writers are conscientious—and they are—they no longer want to be reckoned with as artists or "mere" artists. It is as if they feel guilty that their people's and their own tragedy has become no more than a "theme" for their poems and stories.

In the desolation of memory Yiddish poets found themselves turning back to the old Jewish God. He was not so much the God of Orthodoxy or even the God their fathers had worshiped, but a God inseparable from Jewish fate. He was a God with whom one pleads and quarrels: a figure or force, even if projected through images of denial and accents of reproach, in whom the sheer possibility of meaning continues to reside.

There was a recurrent doubt, even guilt, about the very act of continuing to write stories and poems, continuing to care about mere characters and meters. Aaron Zeitlin, a Yiddish poet with strong religious convictions, wrote: "Were Jeremiah to sit by the ashes of Israel today, he would not cry out a lamentation, nor would he drown the desolate places with his tears. The Almighty Himself would be powerless to open up his well of tears. He would maintain a deep silence. For even an outcry is now a lie, even tears are mere literature, even prayers are false." And in the moving lines of Zeitlin's long poem, "I Believe":

> Can I then choose not to believe
> in that living God whose purposes
> when He destroys, seeming to forsake me,
> I cannot conceive;
> choose not to believe in Him
> who having turned my body to fine ash
> begins once more to wake me?

The Yiddish writers kept returning over and over again to the *khurbn* (Holocaust) theme: they could stay neither with it nor away from it. And since it was impossible or perhaps useless to talk to men, they steadily turned back to the God who had been silent. Leivick implored Him:

> O, who on the steps of the path to Treblinka
> Will forgive me the sins of my song?

Kadia Molodowsky bitterly demanded:

> O God of Mercy
> For the time being
> Choose another people.
> We are tired of death, tired of corpses,
> We have no more prayers.
> For the time being
> Choose another people.

For the Yiddish novelists and story writers, the destruction of European Jewry brought difficulties beyond overcoming. The life of the old country was little more than a memory, no longer able to yield fresh experience, while the life in this country they had rarely been able to treat with authority. For the poets, precisely this constriction of subject matter became a major theme. All but destroyed in Europe, Yiddish poetry in the United

States now enjoyed a flare of late glory. Some gifted poets, increasingly masters of their language, kept writing in Yiddish: Aaron Zeitlin, holding fast to traditional feelings, denying all deniers, still adoring the Jewish God—

> Being a Jew means running forever to God
> Even if you are His betrayer,
> Means expecting to hear any day,
> Even if you are a nay sayer,
> The blare of Messiah's horn;

Itzik Manger, satirist and balladist deriving from the Yiddish folk singers and tavern entertainers, a witty voice in a time of gloom; Chaim Grade, survivor of the Holocaust, whose work is haunted by scenes of recollection and marked by an unnerving intensity; and Kadia Molodowsky, an exquisite lyricist who in her journeyings decides to

> Pack in all my blackened pots,
> their split lids, the chipped crockeries,
> pack in my chaos with its gold-encrusted buttons
> since chaos will always be in fashion

and asks,

> Take me somewhere to a place of rest,
> of goats in belled hats playing on trombones—
> to the Almighty's fresh white sheets
> where the hunter's shadow cannot fall.

Alone, wearied, proud, unheeded, tending their skills in defiance of fate and probability, aware that only a fragment of their audience remained, the Yiddish poets and novelists persisted in writing and publishing.

Two figures stood out in the post-Holocaust years, each a man of talent and fierce will—the poet Jacob Glatstein, hardly known outside the Yiddish perimeter, and the fiction writer Isaac Bashevis Singer, who gained an international reputation.

Glatstein had begun, in the early twenties, as a dissident voice in Yiddish literature. Together with his friends of the *In Zikh* group, he had called for the revolution in sensibility that we now recognize as modernism—the assault on rationalistic decorum, the claim that self-consciousness has an inherent value, the premise that urban turmoil is the proper locale for poetry, the impatience with fixed forms, received modes, binding traditions. Through Glatstein and his friends there entered into Yiddish poetry free verse, Whitmanesque rumination, personal outcry, nervousness of rhythm.

Glatstein introduced a subjective first-person voice into his work that Yiddish had hardly known before; he wrote about his own experiences, his own emotions. Like other Yiddish poets of his generation, he insisted upon his right to shake off the burdens of folk and the curse of history. In a poetry overcrowded with arias, he brought the freshness of recitative. And for a time it seemed that he had achieved his goal. He wrote objectified vignettes and reflections that remind one a little of Wallace Stevens; he brought to Yiddish poetry a sharper intellectual thrust than it had usually had; he did not hesitate to roughen the melodic line of his verse in behalf of his thought.

Yet precisely the need felt by almost every generation of Yiddish poets to struggle for individual sensibility testifies to the power of collective fate. In the end, the luxury of choice would be denied to them, quite as much to Glatstein as to the more traditional poets. No sooner would the idea of an autonomous literature, sought by group after group of Yiddish writers, seemingly be found than it would prove to be a chimera. There was no choice but to come back, with blessing or curse, to the themes of the fathers.

In his earlier years Glatstein had written almost every kind of short poem that is possible to the modern imagination; yet even in these poems, with their supple free verse and sardonic tone, it is perfectly clear that one is reading a poet in the central line of the Yiddish tradition. Just as Mani Leib kept listening for the footsteps of Elijah, and Moshe Leib Halpern kept echoing Purim theatricality, so Glatstein achieved some of his most brilliant successes in dramatic monologues spoken by Hasidic sages. The critic A. Tabachnik has made the point well: "The more modern our poetry became in form, the more Jewish it grew in spirit."

After the Holocaust Glatstein became, in effect, the major Yiddish literary figure in America. He was least impressive in his journalism, where he saw himself as a defender, one of the very last, of the Yiddish word. Speaking for the honor of a shattered people, he gave no quarter, accepted no compromise, refused to see the kinds of qualification that in his poetry he could see as a matter of course. Often his polemics were excessive, as in his blinding attacks on Boris Pasternak for passages slighting Jewishness in *Doctor Zhivago*. Yet to say this is perhaps to speak from a stance of detachment which cannot fully apprehend the character of Yiddish writing in the post-Holocaust years.

In his poems Glatstein made of Jewishness a cry of assault against the moral ugliness of the world:

> Good night, wide world
> Big stinking world!
> Not you but I slam the door.
> With my long gaberdine,
> My fiery, yellow patch,
> With head erect,
> And at my sole command,
> I go back into the ghetto.

Sometimes a note of exasperation crept into his poems, as in a rasp called "Brokers," in which he addressed himself to the "dear Jewish children," and begged them not to serve as brokers between the world and the Jews. Better that "you leave us alone/ and go to all the devils/ in the arms of your own/ black fear." But in the main this was not the tone of Glatstein's Holocaust poems, which are among the very few bodies of literary work that begin to cope with this impossible subject.

Social-national poet he might now have become, and at the very center of the Yiddish tradition too, yet it is notable that in his Holocaust poems Glatstein retained the personal voice with which he had begun as a young modernist, at once stern and sardonic, quiet and beyond grief. The platform rhetoric that has been so disastrous an element in Yiddish literature is rarely present in Glatstein's poetry, and even when it is, it appears with some ironic or mocking intent. In the Holocaust poems Glatstein continued the Yiddish tradition of direct speech with God, an affectionate quarrel in which the demand for justice, or at least explanation, is never allowed to lapse:

> Who will dream you?
> Who will remember you?
> Who deny you?
> Who yearn for you?
> Who, on a lonely bridge,
> Will leave you—in order to return?

The God that figures in these poems is hardly the omnipotent one of traditional belief, yet neither is he a mere construct of modern religiosity; he is an indestructible presence in Jewish life, beyond acceptance or denial. "The God of my disbelief is magnificent"—this was as far as Glatstein could go in reconciliation. What remained was anger and incomprehension:

> The Torah we received at Sinai,
> And in Lublin we gave it back.
> Corpses do not praise God.

An Unyielding Voice

Isaac Bashevis Singer was the one living Yiddish writer whose work caught the imagination of the American literary public during the years after the Holocaust. At first this might seem surprising, for Singer's subjects are remote and exotic: in *Satan in Goray*, the orgiastic consequences of false messianism among seventeenth-century Polish Jews; in *The Magician of Lublin*, a Jewish magician–Don Juan of the late nineteenth century who exhausts himself in sensuality and ends as a penitent; and in his stories a range of demonic, apocalyptic, and perversely sacred moments of *shtetl* life. Yet his readers seem to have felt that he spoke in a voice they could immediately respond to, a voice of modern sensibility.

They were partly right, for Singer had long ago cut himself off from the traditional assumptions of Yiddish literature. But they were partly wrong, for any effort to assimilate Singer entirely to literary modernism is bound to distort his meanings. Those meanings are often enigmatic. Singer's stories prey upon the nerves. They leave one unsettled and anxious, and, unlike most Yiddish fiction, neither round out the cycle of their intentions nor posit a coherent universe. They can be seen as paradigms of the arbitrary injustice at the center of existence, offering instances of pointless suffering, dead-end exhaustion, inexplicable grace. And sometimes, as in Singer's great story "Gimpel the Fool," they turn about, refusing to stay with the familiar discomforts of the problematic, and drive toward a prospect of salvation on the other side of despair. One thinks of the exalted final paragraph of this story:

> No doubt the world is entirely an imaginary world, but it is only once removed from the true world. At the door of the hovel where I lie, there stands the plank on which the dead are taken away. The gravedigger Jew has his spade ready. The grave waits and the worms are hungry; the shrouds are prepared—I carry them in my beggar's sack. Another *shnorer* is waiting to inherit my bed of straw. When the times comes I will go joyfully. Whatever may be there, it will be real, without complication, without ridicule, without deception. God be praised: there even Gimpel cannot be deceived.

The prospect of salvation in Singer's work does not depend on any belief in the comeliness or lawfulness of the universe. Whether or not God is there, he can hardly be supposed a protector. ("He had worked out his own religion," writes Singer about one of his characters. "There was a Creator, but He revealed himself to no one, gave no indications of what was permitted or forbidden.") In Singer's calculus of destiny, the world is merely a resting place and what happens within it, even within the enclave of the Jews, is not of lasting significance. Thick, substantial, and attractive as it comes to seem in his fiction, the world is finally but lure and appearance, a shadow of larger possibilities.

The norm of collective Jewish life is still active in Singer's fiction, but mostly as a tacit assumption in the background. His central actions consist of ecstatic lawbreaking within the iron bounds of law, moving either backward to the abandon of messianism or forward to the doubts of modern sensibility.

That Singer has always been regarded with some uneasiness in the Yiddish literary world is hardly a secret. His powers of evocation, his resources as a stylist are acknowledged by almost every Yiddish critic: anyone with half an ear for the cadence of Yiddish must respond to his prose. Yet many

Yiddish literary people have been troubled by what they see as his exploitation of sexuality, his surrender to the irrational, his indifference to the humane ethic of *Yiddishkeit*, his seeming readiness to move with equal ease to the sensational or the ascetic. "Old-fashioned" these responses may be, and sometimes ungenerous too; but they register something of importance. For in all of Singer's work there is a deeply ambivalent connection to the antinomian strand in Sabbatianism, that strand of ecstatic apostasy which declared the Messiah would have to descend to the nethermost depths of the world in order to climb to the heights of salvation. This is a kind of experience that has been important in the Jewish past but has rarely figured in Yiddish literature. Bringing such material to contemporary readers, Singer wrote in Yiddish but often quite apart from the tradition of *Yiddishkeit*. For Singer was a writer of both the pre- and post-Enlightenment who would have been equally at home with a congregation of medieval Jews and a gathering of twentieth-century intellectuals. He evaded both the religious pieties and humane rationalism of east European Jewishness. He shared only a little in the collective sensibility of the Yiddish masters; he was impatient with the sensual deprivations implicit in the values of *edelkeit*, refinement or nobility; and he moved away from a central assumption of Yiddish literature —that an immanent end can be located in human existence (*takhles* in Yiddish).

Once these qualifications have been registered, what astonishes one in reading his stories is the sheer energy and joy with which Singer held on to the Jewish past. In his best stories and novels he wrote about a world destroyed beyond hope of reconstruction, yet he seemed to take entirely for granted his role as traditional storyteller speaking to an audience responsive to his every hint and nuance. And he did this without a sigh or apology, without so much as a Jewish groan. It could strike one as a kind of inspired madness. A clever and sophisticated man, living in New York City, composes stories about Frampol, Bilgoray, Kreshev, as if they were still there, as if the world of the past were still radiantly alive: the Hasidim still dancing, the rabbis still pondering, the children still studying, the poor still starving, and nothing yet in ashes.

A few Yiddish writers remained, a dwindling handful, who remembered those that had come before them, the labor poets and the aesthetes, the celebrants of the *shtetl* and the portraitists of immigrant America. Somewhere between lapsed faith and mere skepticism the Yiddish writers found an uncomfortable resting place, making a home for the ethical style of *Yiddishkeit*. That the culture of *Yiddishkeit* was transient they all knew, no matter what they said; but they wrote as if there were a specific Jewish time untroubled by the tyranny of the clock.

Collapsing the distinctions of history, Yiddish literature bridged the gap between eternity and time. The prophet Elijah stepped into its pages with the assurance he must have felt in crossing the plains of Palestine; he jostled greenhorns on the Lower East Side, Yemenites in Israel, rabbinical students in Vilna. The central premise of Jewish survival is a defiance of history; the cost, beyond measure. What could not be carved out in the actuality of space and time was carved out in the rhythms of fiction and images of verse. As against the crumbling of history, the Yiddish word remained an unsleeping witness.

CHAPTER FOURTEEN

The Yiddish Theatre

The public is always and everywhere the same: intelligent and foolish, cordial and pitiless. . . . You are outraged because it laughs uproariously at flat jokes and applauds resounding phrases, but then it is none other than that same foolish public that fills the house when *Othello* is put on and, when it listens to the opera *Eugene Onegin*, weeps as Tatyana writes that letter of hers.

—CHEKHOV

In the Yiddish theatre as it began to appear during the early 1880's the East Side found its first major outlet for communal emotion. This was a theatre of vivid trash and raw talent, innocent of art, skipping rapidly past the problems of immigrant life, and appealing to rich new appetites for spectacle, declamation, and high gesture. To the gray fatigue of Jewish life it brought the gaudy colors of Yiddish melodrama. It was a theatre superbly alive and full of claptrap, close to the nerve of folk sentiment and outrageous in its pretensions to serious culture.

The writers and actors of this early Yiddish theatre understood instinctively that their audiences, seemingly lost forever in the darkness of the sweatshop, wanted most of all the consolations of glamour. They wanted spectacles of Jewish heroism, tableaux of ancient and eloquent kings, prophets, and warriors; music, song, dance, foolery (*a bisl freylakhs*, a bit of fun) evoking memories of old-country ways; actors of a majesty and actresses of a fieriness beyond their own reach. In exploiting these desires, the writers and actors betrayed a mixture of shrewdness and innocence that would often characterize Yiddish theatre in its later, more imposing days.

Contempt for "Moshe," the ill-lettered immigrant, soon began to be heard around the Yiddish theatres, and actors who were themselves greenhorns with little theatrical or any other culture started to assume aristocratic poses. Yet in spirit and mind they were still very close to "Moshe"—that was a good part of their strength as performers.

In the opening years of the Yiddish theatre, hardly a glimmer of serious realism could break through. Realism seldom attracts uncultivated audiences: it is a sophisticated genre resting on the idea that a controlled exposure to a drab reality will yield pleasure. To the masses of early Jewish immigrants, most of whom had never before seen a professional stage production, realism seemed dry, redundant, without savor. What stirred their hearts was a glimpse of something that might transcend the wretchedness of the week: a theatre bringing a touch of the Sabbath, even if a debased or vulgarized Sabbath.

In the experience of the east European Jews, Yiddish theatre had deep roots but only a brief history. Among the Jews in the Diaspora theatricality had long been suspect as a threat to social discipline, yet it had all sorts of oblique ways of creeping into their culture: through "the high-church impressiveness of the reading of the Torah," the virtuoso performances of cantors and preachers, "the protocol of the Passover feasts, with the theatricality of suspense in the opening of the door for the invisible prophet Elijah." During the Purim festival, when moral constraints were relaxed and drinking and practical jokes tolerated, it became customary for comic-heroic performances to be improvised. By the early nineteenth century the *purim-shpil*, composed in homely Yiddish, was a regular feature of that holiday. But there were really no professional Yiddish actors until the middle of the nineteenth century, when groups of minstrels, acrobats, and singers began to wander from *shtetl* to *shtetl*, half-welcomed and half-scorned as ragamuffins of the culture. One such group, the popular Broder Zinger (folk singers from Brody, a Galician town), introduced a few strands of dialogue as continuity between songs. They were then persuaded by Abraham Goldfaden, a writer of Yiddish songs, to do a simple performance of a play he had composed; this performance, which took place in 1876 at Jassy, Romania, in a wine cellar, marks a formative point in the history of Yiddish theatre. Goldfaden wrote a good many other plays rich in folk motifs and enlivened with charming songs, some of which like "Rozhinkes mit mandlen" ("Raisins and Almonds"), became in effect folk songs. A few theatrical troupes, harassed by czarist officials and disdained by the rabbinate, were formed, soon forced to break up, and sometimes formed again; but in truth, the birth of Yiddish theatre occurred almost simultaneously in eastern Europe and the United States, with many of the more ambitious actors opting for the freedom and supposed riches of the new world.

The first Yiddish stage production in New York was held on August 12, 1882, at Turn Hall on East Fourth Street between Second and Third avenues. A troupe of six men and two women, supported by local musicians and a choir from a nearby synagogue, put on Goldfaden's *The Sorceress*, "an operetta in 5 acts and 9 tableaux." Since no one in New York had a text of the play, it was patched together, like the choreography of a ballet, from the performers' memories of a European production. One of the actors, a plump sixteen-year-old named Boris Thomashefsky, would soon become a matinee idol, and in the memoirs he wrote many years later he tells a vivid story about hordes of Orthodox Jews angrily protesting the very idea of a stage production; the prima donna, Madame Sarah Krantzfeld, being pressured to drop out entirely; and he, Thomashefsky, racing to her apartment a few minutes before the show was to start and begging her to appear: "We will starve, they'll lynch us." The prima donna's husband, according to Thomashefsky, then explained: "They promised me a candy store and even a few hundred dollars if my wife leaves the play." Who "they" were is not clear: apparently German Jews or Orthodox east European Jews grouped around the newspaper the *Yidishe Gazetn.* An even greater bribe, continues Thomashefsky, persuaded Madame to come to Turn Hall. But by then it was quite late, the musicians had left, Madame refused to sing without them, and the audience hissed. A few weeks later Thomashefsky had to lead his fellow artists to employment in a cigarette factory.

The historian of Yiddish theatre, B. Gorin, concluded some time later that Thomashefsky's account had been exaggerated: there were neither crowds nor riots nor intimidations, and as for Madame Krantzfeld, she had simply been inconvenienced by a cold. Yet Thomashefsky's version, if weak on facts, touched a certain truth. For there was opposition from Orthodox Jews, who looked upon theatre as a shameful trifling, and from German Jews, who feared that the coarse downtown brethren might embarrass them. One of the early Yiddish companies, reports Gorin, "behaved badly behind the scenes," becoming known as a "hangout for loose women," so that "respectable people kept away from the theatre as if it were a plague."

They could not keep away for long. From start to finish, the theatre would be their great cultural passion. In a few months a regular Yiddish company began to perform on weekends at the Bowery Garden, with the puffy young Thomashefsky delighting audiences through renditions of women's parts. (Actresses were still scarce: respectable fathers forbade their daughters to go on stage.) The repertory of this little company consisted mainly of comedies by Goldfaden, the most popular Yiddish playwright in eastern Europe but never, once in America, able to adapt himself to the rough conditions of New York theatre. Battening on the whole of European drama and opera, taking his tunes impartially from Offenbach and synagogue chants,* Goldfaden wrote genre pieces that shrewdly sketched the

* "Almost all the music in the early Yiddish theatre," writes Joseph Rumshinsky, the veteran Jewish composer, "was based on cantorial compositions. . . . Abraham Goldfaden was not a professional musician; he played his melodies with one finger,

major east European Jewish character types. Among his plays of these early years were *The Capricious Bride*, *The Fanatic*, *The Sorceress*, and, a particular success, *Shmendrik*, an amusing folk comedy featuring a hapless ninny who would become a stock presence in Yiddish farce. Soon there were two, sometimes three, competing companies at the Bowery Garden and the National and Thalia theatres. Most of the actors shuttled between shop and stage, according to where they could earn their bread.

In May 1884 there arrived in New York the Russian-Jewish Opera Company, led by Max Karp and Morris Silberman, the first more or less professional group to perform in Yiddish; its nine members had had some training with Goldfaden in Russia and among them was a "company dramatist," Joseph Lateiner, who had an acquaintance with European languages and a facility for twisting European plots to Jewish ends. The actors took themselves with a certain seriousness, announcing that Madame Sonya Heine would play feminine leads, Madame Esther Silberman supporting "soubrettes," Lateiner "serious youths to old men," and that Morris Heine would be "chief comic." The East Side was captivated, and even the stodgy *Yidishe Gazetn* acknowledged some delight.

The Vital Hacks

For the next decade or so, the Yiddish theater was dominated by two rival companies led by their dramatists, Joseph Lateiner at the Oriental Theatre and "Professor" Morris Horowitz* at the Romanian Opera House. Indefatigable hacks, Lateiner and Horowitz turned out more than two hundred plays, usually naïve mixtures of historical pageantry, topical reference,** family melodrama, and musical comedy. Because the audience for

---

but he had a natural sense of rhythm. He surrounded himself with cantors and singers, but his chief collaborators were two musicians, Michael Finkelstein and Arnold Perlmutter, who had been choirboys and later violin players in orchestras. Thus they knew both liturgical and secular music, mainly German and French operettas. They introduced German and French marches and waltzes into the historical plays of Goldfaden, Horowitz, and Lateiner. This created a conglomeration of cantorial prayers, secular marches and waltzes, with occasional original numbers by Goldfaden."

* A self-bestowed title that would work wonders in gaining the respect of Jewish audiences. Other "Professors" soon appeared. As late as 1937, when Zalme Zilberzweig published his bilingual *Album of the Yiddish Theatre*, he still referred to Horowitz as "Professor."

** In the forgotten novel *Joseph Zalmoneh* (1893), Edward King describes a Yiddish play called *Judith and Holofernus*. The complicated plot has a noble Jewess slipping into the camp of the evil king in order to destroy him; at one point Holofernus's eunuch Mufti—"bulbous beard, parchment face sown with comical wrinkles, puffy lips"—"came forward to the footlights, and, stepping out of the historical

Yiddish theatre was still small, lengthy runs were impossible and each company needed a large repertoire—though what it billed as different plays would often be no more than a new title, a few twists of action, and a fresh song or two tacked onto the same old plot. Lateiner and Horowitz could produce a play in a few days, Horowitz boasting he could write one in a single night—he would sketch the central situation and speeches, and his actors could easily fill in the rest. Lateiner leaned toward the "romantic" play, usually an adaptation from Russian or German nineteenth-century drama sprinkled with homely Jewish touches, while Horowitz specialized in bombastic and wildly inaccurate renderings of Jewish history. Writing about figures like the Biblical Joseph, King Solomon, Judas Maccabeus, and Bar Kokhba, Horowitz perfected a Yiddish subgenre he called the "historical opera." When business was bad, competition between the two companies grew murderous. Placards smeared rival managers, actors were stolen away, and titles were pilfered. In 1887 Lateiner's company produced *King Solomon's Judgment*, an immediate success that ran for two weeks; a month later Horowitz countered with *King Solomon, or the Love of the Song of Songs*, which ran for four weeks. When Horowitz's company produced *Don Isaac Abravanel*, "an Oriental opera in four acts" that had nothing to do with the historical figure after whom it was named, Lateiner's company countered with *Don Joseph Abravanel*, reputedly authentic.

Performances tended to be long, usually lasting until midnight. Jewish audiences relished the details, often demanded that songs be repeated, took special amusement from couplets denouncing rival companies, shouted denunciations of villains, and showed no displeasure with the mixture of tragedy and vaudeville, pageant and farce—nor even with the intrusion of personal affairs in the midst of performances ("occasionally an actor would invite the public to his wedding, or inform his audience about his relations with his wife"). Remembering how hard it had been to earn their few pennies, the audiences liked to feel they were getting a "full" evening. For lovers of Yiddish, the language of these plays was excruciating: Lateiner and Horowitz gave their "high" characters speeches in *daytshmerish*, a heavily Germanized and pompous version of Yiddish, while reserving what Horowitz called *kuglshprakh* ("pudding language," demotic Yiddish) for the "low" characters. When Jacob Gordin introduced realistic motifs into the Yiddish theatre during the 1890's, Horowitz complained that he used the same language on the stage as in daily life: "If Gordin were to produce *Hamlet* he would let him talk Hester Street language! Did you ever hear a prince talking Yiddish? A prince must talk German."

When one of his scripts was not quite ready, Horowitz would dress up

---

play, sang, now in guttural tones, now in highly pitched key, a 'topical song' which discussed everyday occurrences in East Broadway . . . the roar of applause was loud and prolonged." King's description suggests he may have had in mind the gifted comic Zelig Mogulesco.

as King Solomon or Maimonides, step out at the end of the third act, deliver a speech for three quarters of an hour on the plight of the Jews, somehow tie it all in with his play, and top the evening with the massed company singing a Hebrew hymn or Yiddish tune.

It was the actors who ruled this theatre, enthroning themselves as aristocrats of the immigrant world. "Once, in the summer of 1888," recalled Abraham Cahan, he saw the actor Jacob Adler "strolling along East Broadway—tall, wearing a high hat and long coat and carrying a fancy cane in his hand. I had to stop and watch—not Adler but the people who followed him, their faces shining with adoration and enchantment and awe." Most of the plays were little more than occasions for display by the actors. Leon Kobrin, whose realistic plays would be produced somewhat later, found the early Yiddish stage a place in which "clowns and comedians with glued-on beards and earlocks, sometimes in long coats but mainly in 'royal' robes with tin swords and crowns of gold paper" declaimed at the top of their lungs. The historian Gorin complains that "an actor did not make his entrance like an ordinary person, he came on with a wild leap or dance." Yet sometimes "the wooden people in Horowitz's plays might suddenly begin to talk like human beings and really touch the heart. These were in borrowed scenes from great foreign plays, though without any connection to the events being shown. A simple tailor jealous of his wife would make a speech taken from *Othello*."

One eyewitness remembers a Thomashefsky performance:

> He had a vibrating, crackling voice, somewhere between baritone and tenor, going into falsetto in the upper ranges. When he sang "A Brivele der Mamen" ["A Letter to Mother," enormously popular on the East Side], the whole audience found it impossible to hold back their tears. No matter if the scene was laid in the hot sandy desert or the Halls of the Inquisition, Thomashefsky always managed to get in a song about Mama.
>
> Thomashefsky played Hasidic rabbis and Cardinal Richelieu, Elisha ben Abuya and Judas Maccabeus. In the early days he often appeared on horseback, naked to the waist, with his legs in golden tights. . . . The theatre was drafty and Thomashefsky suffered from continual colds.

A shrewd contemporary judgment of Yiddish acting appears in an anonymous letter in an 1885 issue of *Yidishe Gazetn*. The writer is discussing a new Horowitz play in which Bar Kokhba, leader of the doomed resistance to the Romans, escapes his tormentors by jumping into the sea and riding away on a fish: "The closing scene is too natural. The supernumeraries have poured their hearts into the scene with such force that they beat each other as in a real war. It is a miracle that none of them has been crippled. . . . They should remember that their enemies on stage are not real Romans, and there is no need for vengeance."

In 1891 Lateiner's company, touring in Philadelphia, presented *Exile from Russia*, which an astonished reviewer for the *Record* described as "a

tragical-musical melodrama or an operatic realistic drama . . . with a terrific climax in which three of the leading characters die violent deaths [followed directly by] a comic, topical duet." The play starts with a scene in a
Moscow tavern, where the Jewish owner is forced to dance by tipsy Russian
patrons, who then oblige with dancing of their own. The hero, Ossip, "with
a wealth of bushy black curls . . . and a face pallid from ardent study"—
Boris Thomashefsky, of course—debates with himself whether to convert to
Christianity or abandon hope for university study. Scenes follow of Russian
life, with a gentile heroine, daughter of a general, declaring her love for
Ossip if only he will convert, and Ossip deciding to leave the faith. When a
pogrom threatens, Ossip hurries home to lead his family to safety; he is
spurned—no help wanted from apostates; the drunken soldiers beat the Jews
"most realistically," and Ossip a little too. After more shooting and stabbing,
the play ends with an historical coda set in New York: "The end comes
with a parade of New York's foreign citizens, all in red, white and blue
regalia and red flannel yachting caps, who are headed by a brass band playing 'The Star Spangled Banner.' . . . Then a tableau is formed: the Stars
and Stripes wave side by side with the scarlet socialistic banners."

Harassed by a growing number of competitors, Lateiner and Horowitz
also began working up the *tsaytbild*, a sketch of the day, or in the later
phrase, a living newspaper. Lateiner produced *Under the Protection of
Moses Montefiore;* a new playwright, John Paley, did *The Johnstown
Flood;* whereupon Horowitz unleashed his own *Johnstown Flood.*

It is characteristic of the Yiddish theatre during these years that together with *shund* (trash) it should turn to productions of Shakespeare,
Schiller, and Goethe, done in hopeless translations but also reflecting an
innocent respect for the idea of culture. Some Shakespearean productions,
undertaken by serious younger actors like Jacob Adler, used more or less
straight translations and were commercial failures, though Gorin reports
that "after the first performance of *Hamlet* the audience was so pleased that
it called for the author." (Adler is supposed to have replied that the author
was an Englishman and hence not immediately available.)

Classics sufficiently "adapted" to Jewish life quickly won over the audiences. *Romeo and Juliet,* starring Thomashefsky, was given an old-country
setting, with the Capulets and Montagues turned into feuding religious
parties, the rationalist Mithnagdim and the pietist Hasidim. Romeo, now
Raphael, and Juliet, now Shaindele, played the balcony scene in a synagogue, with Raphael telling his beloved, "Look yonder! See the Eternal
Light! It is a sign that the Jewish love of God is everlasting." A witty touch
was the transformation of Friar Laurence into a Reform rabbi.

Within the Yiddish world the standard judgment of the early Horowitz-
Lateiner theatre was advanced by the writer David Pinski: "tomfoolery,
clownishness, and degeneracy, a caricature of Jewish life." There is obvious
truth in these words, but finally they settle into a judgment a bit too simplis-

tic. For the serious theatre that began to flourish in the 1890's not only arose
in reaction to, it also drew much of its vitality from, the earlier theatre:
fondness for spectacle, love of extreme chiaroscuro in emotional effects,
stylization of intensity. In any case, it is a common experience in the history
of cultures that changes which to their participants seem radical breaks later
come to look like continuities in a tradition. And had there been Yiddish
critics in, say, 1910 familiar with *commedia dell'arte* or able to take pleasure
in what later generations would call "happenings," the primitive vigor of the
early Yiddish theatre might have won a more tender judgment.*

Time of the Players

A beser teyater!—better theatre! This cry began to be heard in intellectual and theatrical circles during the 1890's, as if the Yiddish theatre, until
now snug in its local charms and vulgarities, were bent on connecting itself
with the great European traditions. A wave of reforming enthusiasm swept
across the East Side; talk was heard of a Yiddish drama sharing the seriousness of Ibsen and Hauptmann; names of great writers unfamiliar to ordinary
theatregoers were invoked in discussion and printed criticism. The main
figures at the head of this impulse toward self-improvement were Jacob
Gordin, a playwright strongly influenced by nineteenth-century Russian
literature, and a group of remarkable actors, led by Jacob Adler and David
Kessler.

A handsome stump of a man, with a thick black beard and soulful eyes,
Gordin looked and acted the very model of the enlightened Jewish intellectual, the sort who was imbued with a misty Tolstoyan idealism and was
intent upon lifting the masses out of superstition and into culture. Like
many half-deracinated Jews of his and later generations, Gordin was mad
for culture, which often meant a smattering of references and notions about
nineteenth-century European literature together with a neglect of native
traditions and values.

In Russia Gordin had never so much as seen a Yiddish play, and when
he came to America in 1891 he was by no means in secure command of

---

* A colleague who is an expert in Elizabethan literature suggests a comparison
between early Elizabethan and early Yiddish theatre: "Many of the early Elizabethan
and early Yiddish plays were shortlived and hastily written combinations of genres
and styles. The rivalry between acting companies, the boisterousness of the audience,
the postludes of jigs and songs and prayers, even the high productivity and generally
low literary merits of men like Peele, Greene, and Dekker, with their heroes full
of bombast and rodomontade, remind one of the early Yiddish theatre on the
East Side. The Elizabethan and the Yiddish theatre clearly had both actors and
audiences delighting in what Bottom was hoping for, a part to tear a cat in."

Yiddish as a literary medium. To feed his family he wrote sketches for a Russian-language paper in New York, one of which attracted the notice of Zelig Mogulesco, a gifted comedian in Jacob Adler's company. A meeting was arranged between Gordin and Adler and Mogulesco at a New York café—Gordin, apparently unaware that he was betraying the condescension of the *maskil* toward the *masn*, described what happened:

> I was curious to meet a Yiddish actor. . . . I thought that as soon as I told him I wanted to write a play, he would start emoting: wipe his nose on his sleeve, jump on a chair, and recite one of the popular tunes of the day ("Tsigele migele"). Imagine my surprise on meeting gentlemen with silk hats and handkerchiefs who talked intelligently. In their eyes I even detected a spark of talent. But if Yiddish actors are like other actors, why shouldn't Yiddish theatre be like all other theatres? At my first visit to the Yiddish theatre [a short while earlier], everything I saw was far removed from Jewish life: vulgar, false, immoral.

Always in awe of intellectuals who spoke Russian fluently, Adler commissioned Gordin to write a play, and the result, a fresh note in Yiddish theatre, was *Siberia*, produced in November 1891. Gordin evoked the ordeal of a Russian Jew who in his youth had been sentenced to Siberia, had then escaped, assumed another identity, become wealthy, and now, in the time present of the play, is betrayed to the police by a business rival. The actors were at first reluctant to do *Siberia*, which they judged to be weak in theatricality, but Adler, who took the leading part, stood firm by his new author. Though concessions were made to popular taste, such as inserting bits of song-and-dance routine, it looked on opening night as if the play would fail, since the restless audience was obviously unprepared for Gordin's sort of "realism." Stepping onto the stage before the third-act curtain, Adler made an urgent appeal: " 'I am ashamed because you do not appreciate this masterpiece by the famous Russian *pyesatl* [writer] Yakov Mikhailovich Gordin. If you understood how great this play is, you wouldn't laugh.' Adler then burst into tears, and the audience, deeply impressed, began to applaud." So at least does Leon Kobrin, a literary disciple of Gordin, tell the story.

Siberia was far from a masterpiece and Gordin was by no means a famous *pyesatl*, but Adler knew what he was doing. He knew that if he wept and thundered, threw in a Russian phrase, and appealed to the audience's respect for "culture," he might change its mood. He did. In the final act, where the hero is dragged away by the czarist police, the actors and audience began sobbing together, as if in common recall of a still painful past. Though greeted by Abraham Cahan in the *Arbeiter Tseitung* as "a complete revolution on the Yiddish stage," the play was only a moderate success. Years later Cahan would write more circumspectly: "Today *Siberia* would be regarded as a weak melodrama. . . . Then, it established Gordin's reputation."

Jacob Gordin

For some two decades Gordin would be a central presence in the Yiddish theatre. A man of strong will and uneven talents, he did his best to make "the Yiddish theatre like all other theatres," untroubled by the thought that this might entail losses as well as gains. He planted Yiddish drama in the soil of common life, bringing, as his rival "Professor" Horowitz sneered, "Hester Street onto the stage." He banished the highfalutin Germanisms of early plays, though his own Yiddish was no more than serviceable. He enforced a percussive moralism, what the critic Jacob Mestel called "folksy didacticism," or "lecturing on stage."* He translated or borrowed from Hugo, Ibsen, Gogol, Shakespeare, Ostrovsky, whomever he could find in German or Russian. He "fell into line with the Russian spirit of realism now so marked in intellectual circles in the ghetto" and was largely responsible for the tendency of Yiddish writers and audiences to use "realism" as a term of automatic approval, even though fairly little of what happened on the Yiddish stage could properly be called realistic. Above all, he brought discipline to a stage marked by highjinks and chaos, insisting upon strict adherence to scripts, battling actors accustomed to the *laissez-faire* of ad-lib, and attempting to create a decent system of rehearsals.

* Replying to an inquiry from an encyclopedia editor, Gordin offered his aesthetic principles: "The drama is not for amusement, merely, but for instruction as well. The greatest educational institution of the world is the theatre. The theatre socializes great ideas, and brings men of widely different social ranks to one intellectual level. The *realism* of a literary work is analytic in portrayal of characters and types of society. In *ideas* is vested the synthetic power of a work of art."

Once, during a rehearsal of *Siberia,* Mogulesco broke into a song-and-dance routine; Gordin violently protested; Mogulesco, screaming that Gordin was an anti-Semite, stormed out of the theatre; the actors sided with Mogulesco. Adler worked out a compromise that brought Mogulesco back to the stage and banned Gordin from rehearsals. On the opening night of a later Gordin play, *The Pogrom,* Bina Abramowich acted a Jewish matron who receives a visit from a Russian police inspector, played by Gordin himself. Miss Abramowich offered him fish and tea, wished him a good appetite, and suddenly whipped out an aside to the audience: "He should choke on it!" Gordin, infuriated and forgetting he was on stage, slammed his fist on the table and cried out, "Stop it, that's not in the script." Theatrical history does not record Miss Abramowich's reaction, but one may suppose she felt Gordin was out of his mind for trying to deprive her of this juicy bit of stage business.

Several of Gordin's plays became standard in the Yiddish repertoire, and even now, a good many decades later, they still have their moments of tension, their fragments of nice perception.* One of his early successes, *The Jewish King Lear,* bends Shakespeare's plot to a Jewish milieu: David Masheles, old and wealthy, makes the same mistake with his three daughters that Shakespeare's character had made centuries earlier, and with similar results. The play is set in Russia, but its themes—torments of parents, ingratitude of children—are perennial to Jewish culture and especially acute with regard to the immigrant milieu. In writing this play, which gave Jacob Adler one of his most spectacular roles, Gordin was criticized for borrowing liberally from Shakespeare, but he replied cogently enough that since Shakespeare had himself borrowed plots, why should not he, Gordin, do the same? Indeed, he shrewdly made this dependence on old plots into an element of his plays: "There is a point at which David Masheles is told the story of Shakespeare's play [by Jaffe, a character functioning as *raisonneur*] and warned that he might be heading for a similar fate. . . . Gordin is making sure his unevenly educated audience knows exactly what he is up to. He is giving them a lesson in literature."

Somewhat less parasitic on classical texts are two of Gordin's later plays. *God, Man, and Devil* reworks the Faust story, setting its action in a little Russian town where weaving is a main occupation. Hershele, a poor

---

* One fragment deserves preservation. In Gordin's play *The Russian Jew in America* there is an opportunistic Jewish labor leader called Huzdak who keeps repeating a tag line: "What do I need brains for when I've got a constitution?" At an early performance Abraham Cahan, incensed at this "slur" against the labor leadership, jumped from his seat and cried out, in Russian, "That's a lie." This led to a fierce quarrel between Cahan and Gordin, with Cahan attacking Gordin endlessly in the *Forward* and Gordin making speeches of reply from the stage. Cahan's general criticism of Gordin's plays—that they tended to exhort more than to dramatize—seems well grounded, but he was hardly the one to notice that in Huzdak's tag line Gordin had vividly captured a type that would become more and more prevalent in the immigrant world.

weaver, buys a lottery ticket from a salesman who is actually the Devil in disguise. Hershele wins, of course, becomes a manufacturer and a cruel sweater of labor, so that "the holy prayer shawls are wet with tears of the crushed poor," and at the end, murmuring that "man is like a vapor that rises to the clouds and vanishes," hangs himself in remorse. *Mirele Efros*, first called the *Jewish Queen Lear*, is a warhorse of a play in which the Lear theme turns into a celebration of Jewish matriarchy, providing an endlessly usable vehicle for actresses in the grand style, from Kenni Liptzen to Ida Kaminska.

By the early 1900's Gordin had become an East Side culture hero. His concern with "deep" problems, his anticlericalism, his Russian soulfulness, his obtrusive ethicism, his acquaintance with European drama, his dismissal of Yiddish folk motifs in favor of "universal" themes, all spoke to the needs of the East Side, especially those radicalized workers beginning to find a new self-assurance. "The Jewish immigrant sought a transfiguration; Gordin tried to present him as a new man, closing out his past." Yet precisely those aspects of Gordin's plays that struck his audiences as most enlightened now make him seem most dated, while the more innocent pieces of Goldfaden, untroubled by echoes of European culture and rooted in Jewish folkways, have preserved a bloom of freshness. "Closing out [the Jewish immigrant's] past," Gordin discarded his religion, folkways, idiom—quite as the travail of immigration had begun to do in reality.

Gordin's plays, said David Pinski, are a kind of "semiart. . . . He doesn't really write plays, he writes roles." Though meant as a critical thrust, Pinski's remark illuminates Gordin's strength in the theatre, since to provide strong "roles" for actors like Adler and Kessler was perhaps quite enough. "Roles" meant loose, expansive outlines of characteristic behavior which the actor could fill in with voice, body, gesture, mime. On the printed page, the main figure in Gordin's *Jewish King Lear* or Kobrin's *Yankel Boyle* might come to no more than a rough sketch, but when Adler, or Kessler, took the part in hand, there followed a wonderful realization of cultural detail, toward high romantic drama with Adler and strong genre drawing with Kessler. Cues from the culture, these roles were just sufficiently outlined to enable actors to begin the job of creation.

The generation of Yiddish actors flourishing at the turn of the century—Adler, Mogulesco, Kessler, Bertha Kalish, Kenni Liptzen, Sarah Adler—represented a large release of Jewish creativity. Unschooled and with the merest slapdash sort of training, these performers burst into an expressiveness so brilliant, it is only natural to ask: where did they come from, what were the sources of their talent? From the *hazan's* dramatism, the *magid's* eloquence, the *badkhn's* clowning—no doubt. But, still more, from the very depths of the Jewish past. These actors vibrated with energies for which official Jewish culture had made only the sparsest provision, but which had nevertheless always been present in the life of the Jews. The roughnecks played by Kessler, the *shlemiels* elevated by Mogulesco to a purity of humor, the shielding mothers Bina Abramowich made her specialty, the flaring tragic heroines of Liptzen and Kalish—such figures came out of the Jewish experience itself, where passionate outbursts had been only "natural," so precarious did life always seem and so close to the edge of blood. These figures were cultural types filled through the plenitude of memory and then, on stage, heightened and enlarged. Jewish life itself had been heroic and deformed, rich in extremes, drenched with abundance of feeling. The "excesses" of the Yiddish stage served as a kind of magnifying glass to the "excesses" of Jewish life. Very little in that experience could have persuaded anyone toward a style of understatement, or that cramped signaling through eyebrow and shoulder that would later flourish on the American stage.

Joseph Buloff, a brilliant Yiddish actor, came to America in the late twenties after having played with the Vilna Troupe, an east European company favoring a modernist style of shadowy quiet. Trying out for Maurice Schwartz's Yiddish Art Theatre, which still preserved some of the Adler-Kessler expansiveness, Buloff encountered astonishment: he did not gesture elaborately, nor storm about, nor declaim in the top register. As if speaking for the whole tradition, Schwartz asked him: "But how will the fellow in the last row of the balcony hear you?"

Buloff tells another story illuminating the dominant style of American Yiddish theatre. Playing Willy Loman in a Yiddish version of *Death of a Salesman*, Buloff, a rather slight man, made his entrance between two large suitcases which rendered him almost invisible to the audience. He thought this a rather keen stroke for evoking the theme of the play, but his dresser, a veteran of the Yiddish stage, was troubled by the "feebleness" of Buloff's entrance. "A Yiddish star," said the dresser, "comes in proud and upright, like Jacob P. Adler"—and the dresser drew himself up in majestic posture to stride across the room.

Yiddish actors, in the age of Gordin and Adler, were committed to a style of baroque expressiveness. Hutchins Hapgood felt they performed "with remarkable sincerity," and no doubt they did; but that tricky word meant something different then from what it has since come to suggest. For us, more than seventy years later, "sincerity" implies an emotional dynamic confined to the plain and the muted, but that can hardly have been what Hapgood saw when he went to the theatre of Adler, Kessler, and Thomashefsky. For the actors dominating the stage in, say, 1900, an effort to be "sincere" would mean a performance that opened up new possibilities of experience, evoking life through the larger-than-life and moving from the modest matter of the script to the enlarging gestures of the stage. Harold Clurman remembers Yiddish theatrical style as "realism with a little extra"—and what was distinctive was just that "little extra," lavish and exuberant.

Almost all the early Yiddish actors shared the view that man had been given a voice to shout, curse, whisper, weep, and woman to solace, scold, suggest, sing. Life on stage should be grander than on the street, for the Yiddish imagination was best released through images of potentiality. The leading Yiddish actors tended to be men of virility and heft, accustomed to filling the spaces of the stage. Actresses were ample, encompassing, womanly, who took in the whole of a rendered experience and formed worthy partners in stories of endurance. *Shund* plays might indulge in vulgar innuendo, but the Yiddish theatre as a whole kept shy of sexuality. Love, in Clurman's words, remained "behind the curtain," though he also remembers the actresses as "very sensual," bearing an aura of pride in their fullness.

A Theatre of Festival

The Yiddish theatre was a theatre of primary, unevaded emotions, Jewish emotions that had only yesterday escaped from the prisonhouse of Europe. Brushing past the drab recognitions of the week, this theatre created an atmosphere of holiday, a secular Sabbath still in touch with received associations of religion. It was a theatre that staked almost everything on a high romanticism of gesture, a theatre of festival.

Nesher hagodel, a Biblical Hebrew phrase meaning "the great eagle" (in Yiddish Adler means "eagle")—so his admirers called Jacob P. Adler (1855–1926) and so he often called himself. Where Jewish life had been mean and drab, he would make it princely and grand. It was all part of that trying on of roles, that delight in assuming new identities, which Jews began to experience after the emigration from eastern Europe. Benny Leonard was proving that a Jew could be the champion lightweight boxer, Arnold Rothstein that a Jew could be the most powerful of New York gamblers, Morris R. Cohen that a Jew could be the intellectual peer of George Santayana; and Jacob P. Adler, by the sheer force of will and blessing of physique, intended to prove that a Jew could make himself into an aristocrat, glittering in Prince Albert coat, dress shirt, spats, and diamond pin.

His early years were undistinguished. Born in Odessa, he drifted through nondescript jobs, a bit of dandyism along Odessa boulevards, a share of sexual adventure, some acting in a Goldfaden troupe, and then emigration in 1882, when the Russian government banned the Yiddish theatre. There followed a few years in London, unsuccessful and close to hunger, a journey to America in 1887, some desultory acting in Chicago, a return to London and Warsaw, and back to New York in 1890. Clearly a man uncertain of his vocation.

Teaming up with Thomashefsky, Adler toured the Yiddish theatres in

Chicago and Philadelphia, hardly an experience calculated to reinforce theatrical idealism, and then, in New York, became a partner with Kessler and
Thomashefsky in Poole's Theatre on the Bowery. The three actors produced melodramas and operettas, floundering aesthetically and sometimes
commercially, torn between the rewards of *shund* and the goals of art. For
Adler and Kessler this would always be a genuine problem, both of them
aspiring to serious theatre and goading themselves with self-contempt when
they had to do trash; for Thomashefsky, despite intervals of high-mindedness, *shund* was a natural milieu. As Mrs. Thomashefsky later said:
"While the others were creating their fame, we were creating our fortune.
Well . . ."

Adler was by no means a quick success. He did not sing or dance well, a
serious handicap in the early Yiddish theatre. Even when he began to be
accepted by immigrant audiences, he remained restless, though unable to put
his discontent into clear words. Like many other Jews of his time, Adler had
caught "the Russian flu," that yearning for high artistic and moral ideals; but
on the Yiddish stage there was as yet no way to realize them. The growth of
his powers as an actor depended, first, on his ability to create for himself
that public personality which soon took over the whole of his being, in or
out of theatre, and, second, on a meeting with Jacob Gordin, who gave him
the idea, the *word* by means of which to satisfy his longings. (This search
for a *word*, some clue to the significance of their art, was recurrent among
Yiddish actors: David Kessler would stammer to playwrights and colleagues,
"*gib mir a varum* [tell me a why].")

Adler's first important role was in Gordin's *Jewish King Lear* in 1892;
two years later he produced three Gordin plays; through the nineties, also,
translations from Shakespeare and continental writers, not always marked
by scrupulous fidelity. In 1901 he did a powerful Shylock on the Yiddish
stage, and two years later the same role in a Broadway production, with the
other actors speaking their lines in English and Adler in Yiddish. By now it
was a commonplace to describe him as the greatest Yiddish actor in
America.

For Adler "realism" would always be a sacred word. What Gordin and
he meant by it was that their plays should deal with the lives and problems
of "ordinary Jews," heads of households, matriarchs running businesses,
immigrants disoriented, families torn apart by generational clashes. But
Adler's style as an actor was not, by any serious standard, "realistic" at all; it
tended toward the grand, the picturesque, the flamboyant. He may have
begun, in many of the Gordin plays, with ordinary Jewish life, but his urge
as an actor was to magnify that life to the heroic, as if he were speaking less
to the immigrants' experience than to their desires. The usual formulas—that
an actor submerges his personality in the role he is playing, or that he allows
his personality to violate the role—did not really apply to an Adler performance. For him the whole point of a production was to imbue the role with

the colors of his personality, transforming a Gordin protagonist into a figure of Adlerian temperament. Brilliant and satisfying this often evidently was, but hardly realism.

A good bit over six feet in height, with a nobly expressive face, Adler could not have avoided a romantic approach to the drama even if he had wished to. Leon Kobrin remembered him as "remarkably handsome and dignified. . . . The Jewish sigh is in his voice, the Jewish tear in his sigh. He has the anger of a great temperament, the tenderness of great love. Frequently he declaims or is too dramatic, a poseur. But all this is illuminated by a feeling of festivity. . . . He has a plastic beauty which imbues every gesture and glance." Sholem Asch recalled that Adler "looked like a lord, dressed like two, and carried himself like a king." Another Yiddish writer said that "Adler prepared himself for a new role as a saintly scribe might prepare a new Torah scroll."

Adler's inclination toward a style of high bravura was somewhat muted in his rendering of Shylock. An Elizabethan Shylock was, of course, out of the question for a Yiddish performer; he *had* to bend the text toward his own purposes. A critic writing for the *Theatre Magazine* in 1902 quoted Adler, in words obviously put into his mouth yet faithful to his meaning:

> The opportunity is [Shylock's] for one moment of ineffable triumph and scorn, holding in his hands the very life of his former insolent persecutor. . . . Having purchased so dearly the right to his contemptuous opinion of his Christian fellow-townsmen, is it not certain that he will consummate his brief triumph by walking out of that court with his head erect, the very apotheosis of defiant hatred and scorn? That is the way I see Shylock.

Writing about the 1901 production, the Yiddish critic B. Gorin praised Adler for his "naturalness, absence of affectation." Two years later a New York *Times* reviewer praised Adler for his "simple, unaffected and naturalistic rendering" while remarking that Adler's difficulties with the role were due to "the fact that to make Shylock fully sympathetic to a Jewish audience is virtually impossible." What Adler could not achieve—given his reading of the part, necessarily so—was "the grim authority of an Irving or the malignancy of a Mansfield."

It did not take long for the Adler myth to spread beyond the boundaries of the East Side. Isadora Duncan, seeing in Adler, somewhat improbably, "a reincarnation of ancient Greek beauty," attended his performances worshipfully. When Adler was doing Tolstoy's *Living Corpse*, John Barrymore came frequently to admire and study his performance.

Theatricality, which may also signify a certain ruthlessness, was in Adler's bones. He tampered with scripts, pasted on touches of blowsy rhetoric, and once, when doing Kobrin's *Nature, Man, and Animal* (Yiddish playwrights like comprehensive titles), added an entire fourth act on opening night. "When I confronted him," recalls Kobrin, "Adler replied that the fourth act of the original script had gotten lost; either someone stole it or the mice had eaten it. So he wrote a new act himself. Still, how marvelously he performed in that play!"

In 1902, when Adler was seriously ill, he had an announcement placed in the Yiddish press saying that he was dying and wanted his admirers to come to the hospital on Saturday afternoon to bid him good-by. Thousands came, with Adler standing at the window to wave farewell. That afternoon all the Yiddish theatres were empty—Adler later said he had meant to show the theatre managers that he had the power to spoil even such a sure thing as the Saturday matinee.

Playing once in Baltimore, Adler and the composer Rumshinsky went off to a *landsman's* restaurant for a glass of tea.

> I was sure [wrote Rumshinsky] that Adler had lost his mind. He rose slowly from his chair, put on his hat at a rakish angle, and we finally arrived at the theatre. It was 10:00 PM, and the play had started with Anshel Shor doing Adler's role. I wanted to take Adler to the stage door, but he ran into the lobby. By this time I was convinced he was insane.
>
> Adler ran down the aisle, stopped in the middle, and shouted in Russian, "*Gospoda, ya s'vami!*" and in Yiddish, "I am here, I am with you! We'll play for you, we'll give you good theatre!" The curtain came down, and in his dressing room Adler began to apply make-up. He said to me, "Rumshinsky, my friend, I love theatre! But I'm on stage only two or three hours a day, so I have to turn the rest of my life into theatre!"
>
> When he was ready, the curtain rose and the play started again, from the beginning.

Life itself became theatre. By about 1910 Adler was earning large amounts of money and living in high style, the boy from Odessa resplendent and regal, staying in expensive hotels, dining expensively, and moving from woman to woman, regardless of expense. (Adler is said to have left behind a trail of illegitimate children, but this is beyond the historian's capacity to check.) Yet, with all his pretensions, he retained a touch of plebeian Yiddish humor. When Sholem Asch once took him to a posh London restaurant, Adler, in full regalia, asked the waiter for *bebelakh un kliskelakh* (beans and eggdrop), explaining that this was an "American aristocratic dish."

To his admirers in the Yiddish world, Adler was all but exempt from criticism. Puritanical as the immigrant ethos may have been, reticent as the East Side was about sex, theatrical royalty was granted special dispensation. Celia Adler, a daughter of Jacob by his first marriage, asked her mother, the veteran actress Dinah Feinman, whether she had felt any anger toward Adler after divorcing him because of his incorrigible skirt-chasing. Said the first Mrs. Adler to her daughter:

> Anger toward him? Never, my daughter. He was not to blame: women just would not leave him alone. He was too beautiful, the child of one of God's

rare moments of grace. . . . I remember when as bride and groom we walked through London's West End, everyone would stop to look at him. He wore bright blue clothes with a cape and top hat. "He's an ambassador or a prince," they would say. . . . I consider it my great good fortune that he crossed my path. . . . What would have become of me without him?

When Adler died, in 1926, his funeral was entirely worthy of him: he had taken pains to make sure it would be. His coffin was carried reverentially from Yiddish theatre to theatre; he lay in a black mourning coat with Windsor tie and *talit*, dual symbols of his life; thousands of people swarmed through the streets. As the first shovelful of earth was cast upon his coffin, a wail rose from the crowd of mourners: "the king is dead!"

There were others, equally or almost as talented. David Kessler excelled at depicting *proste yidn*, the sort of lusty common fellows whose experience carried an inherent dramatic tension. The American producer Jed Harris praised Kessler as the best actor he had ever seen, and Harold Clurman would write that Kessler "possessed animal force, a peasantlike strength." A tormented man, Kessler found it hard to articulate his theatrical intuitions. Lacking the culture that might bring his talent to the level of consciousness, he would break into wild rages if he could not explain to his cast how he wanted it to act. At the end of his life, when need drove him to a wretched operetta, Kessler was asked by a friend what he was doing: "He broke a toothpick and put down a piece of it on the table; he added a little bread, a bit of dirty paper from the floor, sprinkled some salt, pepper, and ashes from his cigar, mixed it all up with his finger, spat on it, and said, 'That's what I'm playing.' "

No such conflict between art and trash troubled Zelig Mogulesco, the first great Yiddish comic in America. He would simply turn on his high piping voice and delicious smile, begin to sing and dance, and for a few moments everyone would be transported into another world, innocent and sweet.

Once, at a performance of Horowitz's *Mishka and Mashka* there was an old woman on the stage, with a wrinkled face, who looked as though she had mistakenly wandered in from the street. The action took place on a ship en route to America. She had to be vaccinated and put out her skinny trembling arm; her whole body quivered; every wrinkle in her bewildered face fluttered. . . . The curtain fell and the audience cheered, "Mogulesco!" The old woman appeared, smiled charmingly, and bowed. . . . Afterward I went backstage and met Mogulesco, slim and elegant, a sensitive cheerful face, not a sign of the exhausted old woman.

The same memoirist summoned a picture of Mogulesco's last role, when illness had destroyed his voice and he had to "sing" with his eyes, his face, his limbs:

David Kessler

By now very weak, Mogulesco played a Jew afraid of his wife. His son-in-law convinces him that he should show her who is boss by vigorously stamping his leg. But when he sees his wife, the leg gives such a diffident and fearful shake that one can see the whole timid soul of the little Jew crouching in that leg. All season long audiences came to the Thalia Theater just to see Mogulesco's leg.

The actresses were at least as gifted. Kenni Liptzen, "with a kind of Toulouse-Lautrec head crowned (offstage) by burning red hair," became in Gordin's *Mirele Efros* (which she is said to have done fifteen hundred times) or the Yiddish version of Grillparzer's *Medea* a fierce tragic actress. Bertha Kalish, "the female counterpart of Adler," with a "regal carriage and a marvelous voice," specialized in elegant romanticism; she began as a Yiddish prima donna, starred on the English stage, and at the end, almost blind, returned to do Goldfaden's *Shulamith* in Yiddish. Sarah Adler, Jacob's second wife, was a veteran of the nineties, "the very emblem of womanliness, sensuous and discreet, with deep stores of elemental feeling."

The central impression of this period is of a bizarre unevenness: flaring brilliance and brutal waste all but indistinguishable. It took a long time for the conventional disciplines to be routinized in the Yiddish theatre—by the time they were, the theatre was already in decline. Lengthy rehearsals were unknown and, indeed, impossible, since each company had to keep a large number of plays on the boards. During a five-day period in November 1914, for example, Kessler's theatre advertised seven different plays!—two by Gordin, one by Asch, one by Pinski, and three more or less miscellaneous *shund*. Even the most conscientious actors could not possibly learn all their parts in advance; they had to pick up their lines as they went along, depending heavily on the prompter (who sometimes doubled as half director)* and on their intuitive grasp of the likely plot lines of Jewish drama. Despite the reforms begun by Gordin, playwrights were seldom accorded much respect (not that many deserved it!) and the stars could be ruthless in "fixing" scripts.

Among Yiddish intellectuals and journalists, who by now had to give sustained attention to the theatre, there were frequent complaints about the star system and appeals for ensemble acting. "The star," wrote the critic Jacob Mestel, "controlled the staging and 'direction,' ignoring the technical and ideological matter of the play, and was concerned mainly with dominating and outshining his colleagues. The star's role had to be 'sympathetic,' and scenes were frequently 'worked in' to prepare for his appearance."** There were plenty of grounds for these complaints, though, at times, especially hard times, when the stars had to combine companies, with Kessler going to work for Adler or Adler for Thomashefsky, they would share major and minor roles, sometimes even making an effort at artistic discipline. Yet in a theatre that rested on virtuosity of performance far more than on the depth of its plays or the coherence of its direction, the star system was not only unavoidable, it was a precondition for its erratic brilliance.

Yiddish theatre, then as later, depended heavily on "benefit nights," with Jewish organizations buying blocks of tickets at sharply reduced prices, usually for midweek performances.*** In 1914, Kenni Liptzen's theatre an-

---

* When Celia Adler was once brought into a Kessler play as a replacement, the only rehearsal she received was a kindly prompter's demonstration of where she was to stand and move at various points.

** Gorin wrote in 1902 that in a Yiddish version of *A Doll's House* a fourth act had been tacked on, with Nora returning happily to her husband. The sanctity of the family was one of the few absolutes of Yiddish stage convention.

*** It also depended, less heavily, on tours to outlying cities where the Yiddish-speaking communities, feeling themselves cut off from the centers of their culture, welcomed theatrical groups with an enthusiasm they did not always merit. "So big a crowd," reported the Pittsburgh *Dispatch* of May 13, 1915, "took possession of

nounced that $105 worth of tickets (individual tickets were then selling for 15 to 50 cents) could be had by *landsmanshaftn* for $30; later, especially during the depression years, the discount rate for "benefits" rose as high as 80 percent. Still, the benefit system had certain advantages: it brought in a steady if much reduced income, it forced unlettered immigrants to attend (having been pressured to buy a ticket you might as well go . . .), and it enabled theatres to do their "better plays" on midweek nights, when they had a semicaptive audience, while saving the trash for the weekends, when they had to take in money. Things didn't, of course, always work out so simply, for the society "buying the theatre" for a benefit night might insist that it be offered one of the more popular plays. *Landslayt* were not always thrilled at the prospect of seeing Shakespeare or Strindberg.

Except for a handful of stars who grew wealthy at about the time of the First World War, the theatre brought little material reward to Yiddish actors. They were a hardy lot: delicate souls didn't gravitate toward the theatre, in fact, "you had to be something of a rascal to become a Yiddish actor in those days." Managers were notorious for their brutal ways. In 1900, when one manager beat up a member of his company, forty-five Jewish actors came together to form a union, declaring a strike at the People's Theatre until the victimized colleague was rehired. Soon, all but the handful of top stars joined the union, the formation of which was helped by the omnipresent Joseph Barondess. "We are persecuted by the managers," read the union's opening declaration. "We play kings on the stage but our families are starving. We are part of the exploited proletariat and want to join with the labor movement." Within about a decade, the actor's union became very powerful, so much so that European actors as well as American beginners trying to join the union complained that its "examinations" were despotic.

By 1910, a year after Jacob Gordin's death, the trend toward an improved Yiddish theatre represented by Gordin's plays as well as those of such fellow "realists" as Leon Kobrin and Z. Libin, had exhausted itself. *Shund*, never truly defeated, came back more shamelessly than ever, and even such

---

the Schenley Theatre last evening to hear Boris Thomashefsky, the Yiddish star, play the part of Salman Putterknopp in *The Green Millionaire* that it stretched to the curb and was packed densely in the lobby long after the house was sold out. Fearing that windows would be broken and damage done to the theatre, the Superintendent sent a hurry call to the Oakland police station for five or six more officers. It was almost impossible for the ushers to handle the excited crowds, people who had only paid for standing room taking seats and others occupying the seats they could find, without regard to reservations, and refusing to move.

"The crowd was a picturesque one. Old people, happy and excited at the prospect of hearing the thespian idol of their race in their native tongue, and foreign women in quaintly draped scarfs and brilliant colors, accentuated its unusual character. . . . Boris Thomashefsky as the old Jewish coal and wood dealer was the very incarnation of the racial temperament—one could feel that even if Yiddish was as the language of another planet. Clever acting can be recognized by intuition, and the audience was proud of him, was sympathetic, and flurries of laughter and half-hushed exclamations of delight passed over it."

old-timers as Horowitz and Lateiner prospered again. Motifs of Jewish nationalism, stirred by the Kishinev pogrom and the rise of the Zionist movement, provided a new source of exploitation. Applause could be secured by ranting from the stage, "*A yid bin ikh, un a yid vel ikh blaybn* ("A Jew I am, and a Jew I will remain"). Thomashefsky grew wealthy out of a piece of sentimental claptrap called *Dos Pintele Yid*, a play he could always count on for retrieving losses suffered from an occasional venture on a Kobrin or Libin script. At a 1914 production of *The Polish Wedding* (*Di poylishe khasene*), chorus girls circulated in the theatre, distributing free pieces of cake. A hack named Isaac Zolatorevsky began churning out plays about prostitutes, gangsters, fallen women, and pious Jews, with titles like *White Slaves*, *The Sinner*, *Love for Sale*, and *Money, Love, and Shame*. To survive, Adler and Kessler also had to dip into *shund*.* And in their eagerness for profitable vehicles, some of the managers, especially Thomashefsky, began to "adapt" Broadway successes—though at this point the American stage was utterly trivial.

The persistence of *shund* came as a blow to those East Side intellectuals who had hoped that once and for all Gordin had raised the Yiddish theatre to a higher level. But while they attacked and deplored, only rarely did they ask whether *shund*, like its equivalents in all the popular arts, was intrinsic to the Yiddish theatre—perhaps, even, whether it evoked, in its own ways, some of the basic motifs of the Jewish imagination. Reviewing a Lateiner play in 1907, Cahan shrewdly called it a "music-hall skit stretched out over four acts," and made fun of its interweaving of "tragedy" and comic bits in rhymed couplets; but he did not stop to ask why *shund* was so deeply rooted in Yiddish theatre, or whether its persistence could be explained simply by pointing to the low cultural level of many immigrants.

A year later Lateiner's *Dos yidishe harts* ("The Jewish Heart") proved to be an enormous popular success, almost as great as *Dos pintele yid*. Lateiner counterposed two families, that of a simple Jewish innkeeper, Lemach, and that of a cultivated Romanian noblewoman, Madame Popesco. The plot, complicated beyond recapture, turns on the discovery that the hero, Jacob, a young painter in love with Lemach's daughter, Dina, is also the abandoned son of Madame Popesco, a fact she has long suppressed because she is living a false life. But when things become difficult for Jacob —one difficulty being the other son of Madame Popesco, Victor, who, as everyone in the audience must have grasped, is meant to stand for Esau— then Madame Popesco's "Jewish heart," that infinitely expansive organ,

---

* Abraham Cahan printed "An Open Letter to Jewish Actresses," pleading with them, as "honored ladies of the Yiddish stage, decent women and mothers," to avoid obscenities. "I am convinced that when you sing obscene songs or use filthy language you are pained. . . . Our stage takes liberties that you won't find in any other theatre in the world. Tell the Actor's Union that you refuse to sing filthy songs." The hilarity with which this suggestion must have been met by the hard-bitten characters who ran the actor's union is not hard to imagine.

drives her to speak out. At Jacob and Dina's wedding, she watches at a distance and finally expires from joy.

Together with this "tragic" motif, the play featured a good deal of comic byplay, mostly having to do with Lemach's efforts to assert control over his virago of a second wife. There are also songs, one of them sung by Dinah, which states the theme of the play in case, God forbid, someone in the theatre hasn't gotten it:

> No matter how much woe a Jew may suffer
> He always turns to his dear God who has not led him astray.
> He lives, survives; though troubles be great
> They lead him not from the path of righteousness.
> Any pain can be borne by him who has a Jewish heart.

Bad as the play is, it touches on a number of themes calculated to stir an immigrant audience to its depths: Jewish homelessness in a foreign land, the eternal sustenance of mother love, especially the Jewish variety, and so on. The theme of endurance is central to Yiddish culture, both the best and the worst of it, and what sophisticated readers find moving in the poetry of Leivick was vulgarized and parodied, yet in some sense also present, in the hack work of Lateiner. For whatever else *shund* may have been, it was not "escapist" in any obvious sense; it coarsened and corrupted, but it drove right to the center of "the Jewish heart." This was a perception that the Yiddish intellectuals, with their passion for enlightenment and their eagerness to create a culture on a level with those of Europe, could seldom allow themselves. They were too embattled within their own culture to allow their legitimate aesthetic distaste for *shund* to be complicated by a sociocultural grasp of its popular appeal.

A *Forward* writer calling himself Lead Pencil complained, for example, that

> the Jewish reader regards the written word as sacred and the theatre as trash. This is traditional with us: the first printed words in our history were religious writings, but the first Jewish theatre was merely the Purim play, with actors going from door to door and reciting their couplet: "Today is Purim and tomorrow it's gone/ Give us a penny and throw us out." It will take a long time before the Jews feel that theatre is a serious art.

What Lead Pencil said here was true enough, but as an explanation for the low state of Yiddish theatre it was a little self-serving. Yiddish literature could survive, insofar as it did, because it had the ardent support of a minority public, while the theatre necessarily had to depend on the masses for its sustenance. Even when Adler had played to half-empty houses during his early years because he insisted on producing Gordin, Andreyev, and Tolstoy, relatively large sums of money had been involved. The cultivated Yiddish minority either scorned the theatre outright or turned out to be too small for sustaining its worthier efforts. As a result the Yiddish theatre reflected, as it had to reflect, the crazily mixed levels and tastes of the immigrant masses. As the Yiddish poet Moshe Leib Halpern wrote:

> There was once a vulgarian who went to the synagogue on one corner of the street when he wanted to weep, and to a bawdyhouse on the other corner when he wanted to be gay. But once, when he wanted both to weep and be gay at the same time, he put up a theatre in the middle of the street that combined synagogue and bawdyhouse into one.

Yet what Halpern would not acknowledge was that the condition he deplored—a theatre of vulgar creativity—may have been true to the circumstances of immigrant life. The best qualities of Yiddish theatre came through, not when it aspired toward high culture, but when it spoke in its native voice. As long as both high and low brows accepted the simple division between *shund* and *literatur*—the first disreputable but vivid, and the second honorable but certain to lose money—Yiddish theatre was trapped. "The false identification of good drama with a species of good literature has merely [lent] life and popularity to *shund*. . . . For who wants to listen to a respectable bore when an interesting devil of a fellow is holding forth!"

When the *Forward* asked leading Yiddish actors in 1909 how their theatre might be improved, they answered with a range of banalities, deploring the lack of good playwrights now that Gordin was dead and the economic impossibility of staging serious plays if audiences did not respond. "Yiddish drama," said Kenni Liptzen, "is sinking lower and lower." Only Kessler spoke with candor: "*Shund* is more profitable. I must do plays that attract the public if I'm going to pay the rent." But "when I play trash it's like drinking castor oil." A few weeks later, when Sholem Asch came to America, he was greeted by an enthusiastic crowd at the Grand Theatre, where he made an appeal for a subsidized community theatre. Many speeches, as usual, were forthcoming, and committees too; but it all ended with nothing. Despite a "literary Thursday" now and then, Thomashefsky continued to prance on stage, Zolatorevsky to churn out his rubbish, and Kessler to take his castor oil.

Nothing revealed so sharply the limitations of the Yiddish theatre as its failure, two years earlier, to find a place for Sholom Aleichem, the great master of Yiddish literature, when he arrived in America hoping to earn his living by writing plays. Adler and Thomashefsky vied for his scripts, each offering the substantial advance of one thousand dollars; they began to prepare productions, Adler of a play about petty brokers in the old country, *Samuel Pasternak*, and Thomashefsky of a play about Jewish village musicians and singers, *Stempenyu*. Both opened on the same night in February 1907, and within two weeks both closed, depriving Yiddish theatre of its one possible genius.

The Yiddish press split sharply over the merits of the Sholom Aleichem plays, with the conservative *Tageblatt* and *Morning Journal* praising their evocation of folk life and the radical *Forward* and *Varheit* expressing discomfort over their lack of ideological militancy. Cahan in the *Forward* was particularly tiresome with literalistic criticisms of *Samuel Pasternak*, as if "realism" had become a kind of literary cell into which writers had to be confined for their own good. Sholom Aleichem, it is true, had not mastered theatrical techniques: he needed a little help in shaping an act or bringing characters on and off stage, and all his plays suffered from discursiveness, precisely the quality that came through most charmingly in his stories. Still, he was the only Yiddish writer of world stature, and the dialogue he wrote, whether for print or stage, was the pithiest in the language. Though professing great admiration for Sholom Aleichem, both Adler and Thomashefsky did not hesitate to tamper with his scripts, Adler "improving" dialogue and Thomashefsky introducing banal theatre lyrics into the folk milieu of *Stempenyu*. Only after Sholom Aleichem's death were some of his works successfully done on the Yiddish stage: it took a relatively sophisticated audience to appreciate the pure simplicities of his humor.

Ultimately, the problem of Yiddish theatre was a problem of the audience. There were immigrants flushed with the sentiments of Tolstoy and Turgenev, immigrants who had never before seen a stage production and responded to Adler and Kessler with naïve literalism, immigrants who found the very thought of theatre a desecration, and immigrants happy to sacrifice a meal in order to see their favorite on opening night. We have endless stories—and by now who can tell which are true?—about the ingenuous fervor of these audiences. Celia Adler writes that at a performance of *The Jewish King Lear* a man in the theatre, overcome by Jacob Adler's performance, rose from his seat, ran down the aisle and shouted, "To hell with your stingy daughter, Yankl! She has a stone, not a heart. Spit on her, Yankl, and come with me. My *yidene* [Jewess, wife] will feed you. Come, Yankl, may she choke, that rotten daughter of yours."

It was an unruly theatre. People munched fruit, cracked peanuts, greeted *landslayt*. A reader complained in the Yiddish press: "Audiences applaud at the wrong places, whereupon someone cries out, Order!, and then a second person yells, Order! to the first one, and a third, Order! to the second. You don't find this in any other theatre in the world." Probably because there was no such theatre anywhere else in the world, a theatre of the unwashed plebes rather than the decorous bourgeoisie. Carl Van Vechten, an American writer with a taste for slumming, found Yiddish audiences quarrelsome, avid, ill-mannered, and the last-minute rush for seats a "figurative biting, scratching, rough handling, accompanied with hard words." To work as an usher in these theatres required the wisdom of a Solomon.

What redeemed it all was the untutored passion of the audience, sometimes, recalls the stage designer Boris Aronson, "more exciting than the plays." Each star had his own *patriotn*, not the paid claque of opera, but pure-spirited fanatics who brought to the theatre an order of emotion other immigrants brought to religion or revolution.

Art and Trash

Nineteen-eighteen marks a turning point, the beginning of the second and last major upsurge of Yiddish theatre in America. Serious new playwrights, gifted new actors, ambitious repertory companies, efforts at coherent and even experimental productions, all appear now, lasting about a decade and then, by the early thirties, sliding into the final disintegration of Yiddish theatre in America.

What were the reasons for this second creative outburst? During the war years the immigrant Jewish community had prospered, settled into growing comfort, and begun to cultivate somewhat more refined tastes. There were children who brought back ideas from colleges, there were new immigrants who brought back ideas from Poland and Russia. By 1918 New York City had almost twenty Yiddish theatres, and a number of others were scattered across the main cities of the country. The prosperity in which at least some of these theatres found themselves meant that a corner might be found, a little money allotted, for serious plays. Younger actors like Jacob Ben Ami, Bertha Gersten, Maurice Schwartz, Muni Weisenfreund (Paul Muni), and Ludwig Satz began to take over major roles; if not quite so flamboyant as Adler or Kessler, and perhaps not so talented, they were certainly more disciplined and intent upon ensemble performance. Playwrights like Sholem Asch, David Pinski, Ossip Dymov, and Peretz Hirshbein had come over from Europe staking out artistic claims in the badlands of the American Yiddish theatre. Writers of varying gifts, they were all intent upon doing plays of merit. Some had found the doors of the professional Yiddish theatres closed to them and had worked, instead, with the many amateur groups that had sprung up in the immigrant communities. Such groups were either subsidized by fraternal organizations like the Workmen's Circle or consisted of enthusiasts who each chipped in a few dollars in order to mount their productions; they came to serve as a conscience, by no means always heeded, of the professional theatre.

Probably the most significant new factor was the gradual impact of a number of European theatrical companies. The renaissance of European theatre in the first two decades of the century left an imprint on the Yiddish theatre. Jacob Ben Ami and Peretz Hirshbein had formed a short-lived Yiddish company in Russia, after Hirshbein visited the Moscow Art Theatre and observed its scrupulous methods; by 1918 Ben Ami and Hirshbein, as well as others, tried to transplant some of the Moscow Theatre's central disciplines onto the Yiddish stage in America. Rudolph Schildkraut, a fine actor, brought from Europe some of the notions developed in the German experimental theatre, especially those of Otto Brahm. Max Reinhardt's famous Berlin theatre abandoned Brahm's ascetic style in favor of a sensuous theatre, "a big wedding cake" featuring lavish sets, copious music, elaborate staging—all of which were more congenial to the Yiddish theatre than the modernist styles appearing elsewhere in Europe. Toward the end of the First World War, a traveling east European company calling itself the Vilna Troupe went from Jewish town to town, bedraggled and penniless, producing plays in a style that might be called Yiddish Gothic—grotesque, shadowy, darkened. It scored a major success in 1919 with the debut of Ansky's *The Dybbuk,* and when an offshoot of the company came to New York five years later it offered *The Dybbuk* and Hirshbein's charming pastoral, *Green Fields.* The company was too offbeat and modernist to win the Yiddish audience, and most of its members returned to Europe; but a few, like Joseph Buloff, remained here, to work with Schwartz and, when they could scrape together a few dollars, start independent companies that offered plays for a year or two and collapsed. The Habima, organized in Moscow after the Russian Revolution, performed in Hebrew in a style of ecstatic stylization, or what one critic has called "mystic expressionism." This company came to New York in 1926, but, like the Vilna Troupe, failed to establish itself—though it did leave a mark on the experimental rim of the Yiddish theatre, especially the Artef (see p. 489). Even the American theatre, which Yiddish actors had scoffed at over the years, now began to show a few signs of liveliness, with the Provincetown Players and Washington Square Players gaining the attention of the more serious Yiddish directors.

It would be a mistake to suppose that precise lines of influence can be traced from any of the major European companies to the New York Yiddish theatre. The eclecticism of this theatre was so incorrigible that no European style could survive transplantation intact. What really mattered was not the theatrical ideology of the European companies as it might be transported to New York and sometimes mangled along the way; what mattered was the influx of sentiment concerning a "new" theatre, the feeling among young actors, directors, and writers that Yiddish theatre should share in the possibilities of their moment.

Hopes for such a development settled in 1918 on a company that Maurice Schwartz brought together at the Irving Place Theatre. A group of first-rate younger performers—Jacob Ben Ami, Celia Adler, Ludwig Satz, Bertha Gersten—came to work for Schwartz, lured by his promise of serious productions. When Ben Ami proposed doing Hirshbein's *A Secluded Corner* (*A farvorfn vinkl*) Schwartz was skeptical: it struck him as a mere *bikhl* (literally, little book, but used contemptuously about "literary" plays said to lack theatricality). Ben Ami insisted, took a pay cut in order to mount the production, and finally opened on November 16, 1918. Yiddish theatre historians regard this date as marking the start of their serious, or "art," theatre. The production was integrated in style, the actors spoke with purity and restraint, and the company avoided the egocentrism of the "star" system. Hirshbein's play was slight, but free of the bombast that had so often been the curse of Yiddish theatre. A bucolic comedy, it was set in the old-world countryside, where Jewish life seemed, insofar as Jewish life ever could seem, "natural."

For the sophisticated fraction of the Yiddish theatre public, all this came as a relief from Gordin's lumpy "problems" and coarse adaptations of European classics: a little like Synge after Galsworthy. The Yiddish and American reviews were excellent; Ludwig Lewisohn wrote that the company "is the noblest theatrical enterprise in New York." The play ran for fourteen weeks, very long for the Yiddish theatre, and was followed by productions of Hauptmann and two Yiddish writers, Pinski and Dymov.

Ben Ami represented something fresh in the Yiddish theatre, an actor-director completely dedicated to a vision of theatre as art. A colleague described him as "frail and reticent, with a touch of the mystic and the ascetic . . . a cultured, soulful player." Another Yiddish actor recalled Ben Ami, in a tone of respectful amusement, as one who "played with his shoulders." Allergic to compromise, Ben Ami broke from Schwartz and for two years, 1919–1920 and 1920–1921, led a group called the Jewish Art Theatre in productions of Hirshbein, Sholom Aleichem, Tolstoy, and Hauptmann that caused one critic, Clayton Hamilton, to say "the Yiddish theatre is now superior to the American. Yiddish theatre is aimed at art." But, alas, Ben Ami's group had a financial backer named Schnitzer, and Schnitzer had a wife with theatrical ambitions named Henrietta (whom Celia Adler derisively called the *balaboste*, or boss's wife). The company believed in rotating leads, Schnitzer in getting them for his wife, and soon Ben Ami was out and the company disbanded. Ben Ami went to the Broadway stage, where he was a notable success, though he tried several times in later years to revive, never effectively, a serious Yiddish company. In the seventies, an octogenerian, he was still acting in revivals of Yiddish theatre.

It was left to Maurice Schwartz—tougher in spirit if coarser in sensibility than Ben Ami—to build the one enduring repertory company in Yiddish. Over some thirty years, with interruptions now and then for recouping losses, Schwartz's Yiddish Art Theatre staged almost 150 productions, from *shund* to art, folksy genre pieces to "grotesque-cubist" experiments. Translations of Gorky, Schnitzler, Shaw, Molière, Toller, and Chekhov jostled the work of almost every significant Yiddish playwright.

Idealistic and crafty, imaginative and gross, pure in heart and a bruising "go-getter," Schwartz was simultaneously leading actor, stage director, play doctor, and manager. To keep his theatre alive over so many years was itself a triumph of will: he exploited actors, pilfered ideas from gentile directors, courted financial backers, entangled creditors in promises, used every device of modern publicity to win the Yiddish (and American) public, wrote, adapted, and butchered plays, and, to make up deficits, went on vaudeville tours in the United States and on Yiddish stock-company tours in Latin America.

A man of Rabelaisian energies and appetites, Schwartz wanted to put everything into theatre, loading his stage with the whole jumble of Yiddish cultural aspiration. He wanted to please the East Side intelligentsia while wooing the *alrightniks* from the outlying neighborhoods; he wanted to establish his reputation as a director comparable to Reinhardt and Vakhtangov and continue the tradition of Adler and Kessler, perhaps even Horowitz and Lateiner. "With his native shrewdness and mimetic faculties Schwartz grasped much that passes as a cultured man's equipment, although his training has been limited to the reading of classic plays and contact with cultured theatre-goers who visited him."

Schwartz had no conscious aesthetic program—or he had a dozen, which comes to the same thing. A "temple of art," such as Ben Ami and the intelligentsia dreamt of, he could not build: he was neither purist nor highbrow, and given the culture in which he had to work—it dictated that Yiddish theatre be a popular art or nothing—his energetic confusions were by no means a complete disadvantage. Schwartz yoked together all the conflicting impulses of Yiddish theatre and made of them an exuberant tension, sometimes brilliant, sometimes absurd. A Habima director, looking down his Hebraic nose, said of Schwartz: "The trouble was that he seldom followed a definite line in directing . . . several styles would sometimes be employed in one performance." This was true enough, and in some of Schwartz's more pretentious offerings, when he tried to show himself a master of *velt kultur* (world culture), the mixture of styles could be disastrous.

But eclecticism—as the aesthetic corollary of multilingualism, eternal wandering, and *galut*—was in the very nature of the Yiddish theatre. Ill-educated as he was, and therefore especially susceptible to the lures of alien culture, Schwartz understood in his bones that, finally, the kind of theatre he wanted to create could flourish only if it were rooted in Yiddish culture, in its deep if narrow soil, in the native, the indigenous, even the provincial. "Schwartz's greatest virtue," wrote a Yiddish critic, "is that he is not a spoiled intellectual, not a genteel youth avoiding conflicts. He is a common man who makes his own way. Common people built the Yiddish theatre, and common people will give it its content and significance. We hear the heavy breathing [of Schwartz's theatre] as it struggles to create. It reaches toward the heavens, but has dust on its shoes."

Schwartz the actor was as uneven as Schwartz the director. His gift was for unpolished comedy, his yearning for high classics. In the first he played with native ease and "an intuitive motor sense for impersonation"; in the second, he was simply a ham. Schwartz's adaptations of Sholom Aleichem were vivid, earthy, authentic, the first that succeeded in transposing the great humorist to the stage; but when he tried to do his own production of *The Dybbuk,* he was painfully heavy-handed, smothering it with scenery and circusing it out of its delicate beauty. Producing Leivick's *Rags,* one of the few serious plays about Jewish working-class life in America, Schwartz made a lucid piece of theatre. Producing Sholem Asch's *Sanctification of the Name* (*Kiddush hashem*), Schwartz became "a slave to spectacles and decorations": the play had forty-two speaking roles, mass scenes with fifty supernumeraries, elaborate sets, music, and choreography, as well as a fifty-six-page program.

Sometimes it all came together, Yiddish motifs and modern stagecraft. In 1926 Schwartz produced a stylized version of Goldfaden's old play *The Tenth Commandment,* for which Boris Aronson designed a brilliant expressionistic set. Abraham Cahan, faithful to his old love of "realism," found this production "a mishmash of repulsive noises, disgusting shrieks. One actor has two pairs of eyes, another three noses." The critic Alexander Mukdoyni, by contrast, wrote, "this is theatre in its purest and most refined form, a marvelous fusion of acting, daring sets, and gay, playful music." And the American reviewer John Mason Brown felt that Schwartz's production had "vast energy, a blatant, exciting kind of underscoring that is more familiar to Berlin than Broadway."*

In the thirties Schwartz scored his greatest commercial success with *Yoshe Kalb,* an adaptation of I. J. Singer's novel. About this play it is almost impossible to have a clear opinion at all, so hopelessly did it mix Schwartz's best and worst, his gift for sharply evoking Jewish traditionalism and his exploitation of Jewish sentimentalism. By now, in any case, Schwartz had completed most of his interesting work in the theatre; the remaining years, harder and harder to sustain financially, were given over to sluggish adaptations of social novels such as Asch's *Three Cities* and Singer's *The Brothers Ashkenazi* and to a growing mania for spectacle. If the earlier Schwartz had fancied himself a Yiddish Reinhardt, the later one showed unhappy resemblances to De Mille. The Yiddish Art Theatre formally disbanded in 1950, though Schwartz persisted in running about the world, performing here, producing there, still infatuated with greasepaint, floodlights, and the Yiddish word. "You always know," said Brooks Atkinson about Schwartz's theatre, "that you are not in a library."

At least as much could have been said for another significant company, the Communist-inspired Artef, which began to offer plays in 1928 and managed to survive for a decade. Its ideological narrowness apart, the Artef was a remarkable group. It recruited actors from the shops, training them night

---

* The testimony of qualified non-Jewish critics, who cannot be accused of parochial indulgence, is important here. James Agate, the English critic, reviewed a production of Andreyev's *Seven Who Were Hanged* which Schwartz brought to London: "The performance by these Yiddish players contains more great acting than I have ever seen on any stage in any place. . . . I do not propose to forget anything which happens in this play."

after night in stage techniques and both Yiddish and other dramatic literatures. It had a very gifted director, Benno Schneider, who had worked with Stanislavsky and Vakhtangov. Though it put on a number of straight agit-prop evenings, meant to fire the revolutionary sentiments of Yiddish-speaking workers, its best work had little to do with "socialist realism." A number of Artef plays used texts drawn from Mendele and Sholom Aleichem which tastefully, though now and then with some class-angling, re-created Yiddish classics. This was the "folk" side of Artef. A number of other plays drew upon the work of left-wing Yiddish writers like Moshe Nadir and Chaver Paver, as well as the Soviet Yiddish writers David Bergelson and Moshe Kulbak, and these were often done in a tensely stylized manner. This was the "modernist" side of Artef.

What seems remarkable about the company is not merely the high level of its work but that, finally, it responded more to aesthetic scruples than to political ideology. While the "cultural work" of the Communist-inspired groups in English was almost always middlebrow in character, the Artef functioned mainly as an avant-garde theatre, one of the very few Yiddish has ever known. The middle position having already been appropriated by the Schwartz company, Artef had no choice, if it was to establish its distinctiveness, but to take aesthetic risks. Though for a number of years one of the best companies in New York, Artef never managed to become part of the mainstream of Yiddish theatre. It succeeded far more readily in attracting English-speaking intellectuals than in establishing a permanent audience of the Yiddish masses, who seem to have found it too rigid politically and austere aesthetically.

A good many other attempts were made in the twenties and thirties to establish serious repertory companies, by Yiddish actors bravely banding together for a year or two and then having to retreat to commercial theatre; by Joseph Cutler, a Yiddish poet, and Jack Tworkow, a young painter, who in 1926 set up a brilliant puppet theatre in Yiddish; by the Yiddish branch of the Federal Theatre Project, which did some good work in the few years granted it. All failed.

The energies and gifts of Yiddish theatre in the twenties and thirties were by no means confined to the repertory companies. In the commercial theatres one could see actors of great talent, sometimes doing superb work, sometimes shaming their art, often both on the same evening. Ludwig Satz transformed Jewish comedy from traditional wordplay to a mime's body movement. Aaron Lebedeff, a lad with a shock of hair, polished boots, and embroidered shirt, would come prancing onto the stage, to dance and sing with a devil-may-care good nature: what the Russians, and the Jews after them, called a *molodiets*, a lively fellow who performs fine deeds. Samuel Goldenberg, Celia Adler, Lazar Freed, many others, were accomplished actors seldom able to fulfill themselves. Such players were trapped within the narrowing confines of a commercial theatre which, merely to survive, had increasingly to pander to a low order of taste. An entertainer like Lebedeff could still manage to seem fresh and good-spirited; but Satz, a sophisticated artist, suffered from self-contempt because of the roles he had to play and, like Kessler before him, would masochistically make still more debased as he went along.

Yet, all through the twenties and thirties, American theatre critics would hold up Yiddish theatre, or at least a portion of it, as a model of accomplishment and seriousness. In 1922 Gilbert Seldes wrote that Leivick's *Rags* had the "exceptional quality of infusing poetry into common speech—or perhaps more accurately, shaping common speech so that its poetry was not destroyed in utterance." He speculated as to why the Yiddish theatre could do plays so fine as Hirshbein's *Idle Inn* or Dymov's *Bronx Express*, far beyond the reach of Broadway. And Stark Young, the best theatre critic of the time, found in Yiddish acting "expressiveness of hands and eyes and shoulders . . . tremendous and inexhaustible vitality. . . . It has the realism of intense feeling, and a deep respect for that feeling. Its best effects come from a compulsive rendering of that intensity; and the beauty of these effects is a spiritual beauty, almost without appeal to the eye."

By the late thirties and the decades to follow, very little was left of the qualities that had excited Seldes and Young. Each year the audience shrank in size; those actors able to find a place for themselves on the American stage or in Hollywood were long gone; and the few stars who remained, like Menashe Skulnik and Molly Picon, often stooped to mere imitations of earlier plays, watering their scripts with English and exploiting sentiments of nostalgia.* One amateur group, the Folksbiene, survived through the decades on a subsidy from the Workmen's Circle; its productions, especially when including a great survivor like Joseph Buloff, were admirable; but to attend them was somewhat like visiting an animated museum.

For the Yiddish dramatists the situation had long been hopeless, and if it is true that there was always more talent on the stage than in the script, that must be laid to the failure of the Yiddish theatre to sustain its writers. One Yiddish scholar has published a study showing that the majority of plays written by the more esteemed playwrights were never given professional productions: "Hirshbein wrote forty-two plays in Yiddish, of which eight were staged. Pinski published fifty-six plays, and not more than ten were produced. . . . Leivick, in this regard, was the luckiest Yiddish dramatist, since of his twenty plays, twelve were done in professional theatres."

It does not seem likely that any large portion of Yiddish drama will survive the passing of the Yiddish theatre. A few plays still read well, offer-

---

* For some of the old-timers, especially those who had not been careful with their money, the final years were painful. Boris Thomashefsky, matinee idol for decades, was reduced to singing in a Second Avenue cabaret, competing with the noise of waiters and customers. "I won't give up," he said. "If I have no theatre, I'll appear at a cabaret."

ing possibilities for restaging in Yiddish or translation. Ansky's *The Dyb-buk*, most widely produced and acclaimed of Yiddish plays, touches upon the motifs by which a culture makes itself aware of possibilities for evil within its own norms of conduct, and then disciplines itself into a return to abstention. On the face of it a simple love story, the play dredges up, from the collective Jewish memory, a sense of the uncanny, the irrational, the awesome, everything not held in check by rabbinic discipline. It is a wonderful vehicle, built along a single line of fatality, with sharp transitions and strong climaxes—to read *The Dybbuk* is almost to see it played! Yet for all its brilliant darkness, it offered no path of development for the Yiddish theatre: it was a work sealed into the past, which could be imitated but not enlarged upon.

At the opposite pole of Yiddish drama, Hirshbein's *Green Fields* is one of the few plays that keeps its bloom over the years. A romantic-comic pastoral in which a pious young man is cozily absorbed into a not-so-pious rural Jewish community, the play charms through a relaxed acceptance of life. It does not strain toward high ethical or religio-mythic meanings; it balances form with matter lightly, content with its own pleasantness. Spontaneity, not exactly the most abundant of Jewish qualities, comes through *Green Fields* as an impulse rather than idea, so that in the happy ending, a little like a Shakespearean comedy in its balancing of couples, even the much-vaunted learning of the Jews gives way to deeper affections for land and air.

Other playwrights have made lasting contributions. The plays of Peretz, perhaps not for the stage, and those of Sholom Aleichem have an authenticity of their own. Leivick's dramas remain impressive, though some are clearly for the lamp and others are so entangled with Yiddishist motifs as to present difficulties for later readers or spectators. Asch's plays, like his novels, now seem heavy and overwrought, though perhaps still playable by unembarrassed actors for unembarrassed audiences.

An Art of Their Own

The position of the Yiddish theatre was always uneasy: it could never quite define its goals or values. Intellectuals kept hectoring it to satisfy one or another notion that usually derived from dogmas as to the historical responsibilities or immanent nature of Yiddish culture. After the First World War, the thought of older and more prestigious theatres in the gentile world kept nagging at those Yiddish theatre people who had some claims to artistry. Meanwhile, circumstances forced them to cater to audiences that neither did nor could share their interest in the latest experiments of the European or American theatre.

Jacob P. Adler stars in *Elischa* at the Grand Theatre.

Brown Brothers

The New York Public Library at Lincoln Center, Theater Collection

Jacob P. Adler,
idol of the Yiddish stage

Bertha Kalish, Yiddish actress

Courtesy of YIVO Institute for Jewish Research

Maurice Schwartz,
director of the Yiddish Art Theatre

tesy of YIVO Institute for Jewish Research

David Kessler, with Jenny Goldstein and Malvina Lobel, in a scene from
Lateiner's *Dos yidishe harts*, 1909

A scene from Abraham Blum's *Der yidisher general*

tesy of YIVO Institute for Jewish Research

Museum of the City of New York

Lazar Freed, Celia Adler, and Maurice Schwartz in Sholom Aleichem's *Stempenyu*,
produced by the Yiddish Art Theatre in 1929

Rudolph Schildkraut, Boris Thomashefsky, Ludwig Satz, and Regina Zuckerberg
in *The Three Little Businessmen*, 1924

An expressionist setting for *The Dybbuk*, 1927

e New York Public Library at Lincoln Center, Theater Collection

Courtesy of YIVO Institute for Jewish Research

Courtesy of YIVO Institute for Jewish Research

H. Leivick, Yiddish poet and playwright

Mani Leib, leader of *Di Yunge*

Courtesy of YIVO Institute for Jewish Research

Quigley Photographic Archives, Georgetown University

Moshe Leib Halpern, modernist poet

Anzia Yezierska, East Side daughter
and American novelist

Courtesy of George Burns

The Pee Wee Quartette, East Side troubadours

Al Jolson singing in blackface

Al Jolson, cantor
in the movie *Hollywood Cavalcade*

Iver Pictures

Culver Pictures

Culver Pictures

Sophie Tucker in a hat

Fanny Brice in the Ziegfeld Follies

Culver Pictures

Courtesy Whitney Museum of American Art

Max Weber, *Adoration of the Moon*, 1944

Courtesy Zabriskie Gallery

Abraham Walkowitz, *Sunday Afternoon*, 1905-1910

Collection of Chaim and Renee Gross; photo courtesy Forum Gallery

Raphael Soyer, *Dancing Lesson*, 1926

Smith College Museum of Art

Ben Shahn, *Sound in the Mulberry Trees*, 1948

City College scenes, clockwise, from top left: Morris Raphael Cohen lecturing; the lunchroom alcoves, center of radical politics; a student protest rally, 1934; students working in the library. Bottom left: a Communist student meeting in a New York park

Courtesy City College of New York

Courtesy of Grossinger's

The original Grossinger's, a seven-room farmhouse bought for $750 in 1914

Courtesy of Grossinger's

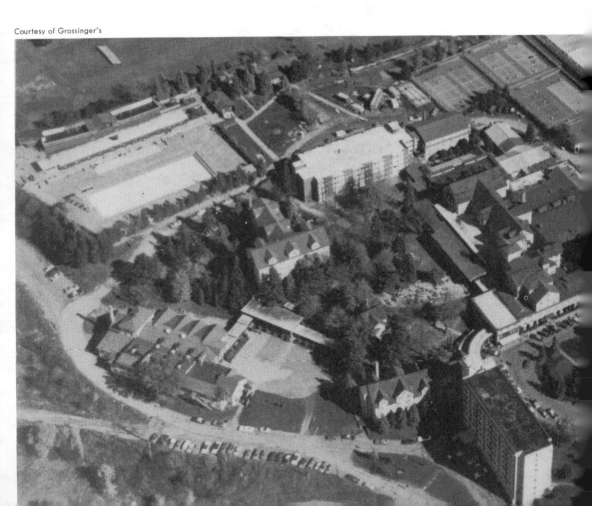

Courtesy of Grossinger's

The second Grossinger's, two miles from the farmhouse,
opened in 1925 and called the Ritz

Grossinger's in 1975, "complete with everything"

Zionist Archives and Library

Chaim Weizmann, first president of Israel, presents a Torah scroll
to President Harry S. Truman at the White House, May 25, 1948.

In the Yiddish theatre, the stage as spectacle, outburst, expression, was almost always more vital than dramatic text or program. Vast outpourings of creative energy made the performance of a Yiddish play an occasion for communal pleasure—the kind of pleasure that audiences took in seeing their experiences (or, more often, their memories) mirrored back to them in heightened form. But this outpouring of mimetic energy was so intimately related to folk sources and so little mediated by the cautions and indirections of high art, there was almost always an alloy of shoddiness running through the brilliance of performance.

For the more serious theatre people of the twenties and later, the problem was exasperating. While both they and the intellectuals might complain, for example, about the liberties that actors took with scripts, much too often it was precisely these liberties that brought the Yiddish theatre to life—especially with brilliant comics like Mogulesco and Satz. And while the serious theatre people might want to break away from historical pageant, folk legend, and provincial setting, insofar as the Yiddish writers and directors took this advice and turned toward "serious theatre," which often meant imitating Chekhov and Ibsen, they risked losing touch with the sources of Jewish creativity.

The central aesthetic question was this: to what extent is it profitable to think of Yiddish theatre in the terms commonly employed for sophisticated Western theatre? Obviously, to *some* extent, since there are continuities in all theatre. But to what extent did it make sense to apply the same order of expectations and criteria of judgment that one brought to the theatre of Shaw, Pirandello, and Hauptmann to the theatre of Goldfaden and Gordin? Or even Leivick and Hirshbein? Beyond such commonplaces as, say, the "universality" of the tragic, it turns out that a close examination would lead one to stress differences rather than similarities. The settings of Yiddish plays were extremely special in reference, as were their terms of emotional response (consider the distance between the Yiddish view of sentimentality and the French!) It was facts such as these that often reduced the more serious theatrical criticism in Yiddish to a species of nagging, in effect, a wish that Yiddish theatre were . . . not Yiddish theatre.* Any given complaint a Yiddish critic might make was likely to be accurate, yet the thrust of such criticism was not often helpful, since, insofar as Yiddish theatre people listened, it made them self-conscious and arty.

Yiddish theatre was an aesthetic medium that could best be appreciated either through a complete "inner" submission to its modes, such as its audiences achieved effortlessly, or through seeing it from a critical distance, not

---

* Not always, of course. When Alexander Mukdoyni published a study called "The Immigrant Drama," in which he noted that "Yiddish drama is still anchored to its European origins," and that with a few exceptions, such as Leivick's *Rags*, "there is no real Yiddish-American drama" dealing authoritatively with the life of the immigrants, he was making a significant critical observation. It was the virtue of this critic that, without accepting *shund* or indulging parochialism, he understood that Yiddish theatre could flourish only by drawing upon Jewish sources.

as an inferior replica of Western theatre but as a theatre indigenous to the Jewish experience—and, oddly enough, with some points of resemblance to Italian opera. For what counted in Yiddish theatre, as it counted in Italian opera, was the sheer display of virtuosity, a talent driving past its material in order to declare itself all the more vigorously. Hit the high C no matter what happens to the plot of the opera, do the bang-up scene where father banishes errant son no matter what happens to the story of the play. What counted, as perhaps it always must in popular art, was the exuberance of the occasion, available every evening as cast and audience joined in a magical interchange of pleasure. What counted was the virtuosity with which arche-typal characters were rendered: Jacob Adler as the towering, heartbroken father, Bertha Kalish as the steely Jewish heroine, Ludwig Satz as the clown, Aaron Lebedeff as the high-spirited rascal, Maurice Schwartz—well, as Maurice Schwartz.

There was a way of approaching both Yiddish theatre and Italian opera that only very simple or very sophisticated audiences could command. Whoever took seriously the plots of Italian opera would, as Dr. Johnson said of Samuel Richardson's plots, be tempted to hang himself; but if one saw these plots as residues of traditional romance or grandiose reflections of a culture's view of itself, they might make sense, if not in their details then in their larger rhythms. And much the same was true for the Yiddish plays, with their handful of worn and predictable plots.

The audiences cared more about expressiveness than coherence, more about moments of vision than organized themes. Yiddish theatre structured their responses in ways that brought a solace of recognition, sometimes a flash of illumination. It was a theatre spontaneously expressionistic, for it set as its goal not the scrutiny of personal relationships or the probing of per-sonal destinies, both of which have been dominant concerns of the modern and classical theatres of the West, but rather a mythic ordering of Jewish fate, whether through historical spectacle or family drama. Yiddish theatre cared for the common patterns of Jewish existence, its inner lines of forma-tion; it held up a mirror of recognition to its audiences—and they, for a good length of time, seemed almost to care less about what the mirror showed than about the mere fact that, in all its glitter, the mirror was there. As for what it did show, that was so strong and blunt that even the least-lettered of immigrants could gain pleasure and a primitive sense of definition by going to the theatre. The theatre was the art form that reached everyone in the immigrant world, collapsing distinctions between serious and popular, high and low art; and this inclusiveness came to be both its glory and its curse.

Take, for example, Gordin's *Mirele Efros*. By any ordinary standards it is a wantonly sentimental play, calculated to indulge aging spectators through its one-sided picture of generational conflict. The wisdom of its matriarch, Mirele, is blatantly asserted, and to a modern audience must seem hopelessly manipulative. Yet over the decades it has been one of the most successful Yiddish plays, and not merely because audiences have brought to it naïve expectations. In some deep way *Mirele Efros* spoke to the common Jewish perception, grounded in a sufficiency of historical experience, that the survival of a persecuted minority required an iron adherence to traditional patterns of family life. Mirele represents the conserving strength of the past, which alone has enabled the Jews to hold together in time. And audiences grasped this intuitively, just as Gordin had projected it intuitively.

But the Yiddish intellectuals could not quite see this, or wanted to see more than this. They had read Chekhov and Hauptmann, Ibsen and Schnitzler. They were troubled by the fact that Yiddish could boast of no modern drama to equal *Hedda Gabler* or *The Three Sisters*. They wanted a Yiddish drama that would be worthy of the European masters exploring bourgeois life, and nowhere could they find it. They failed to see that the troubles of middle-class life, the fantasies of a Nora or the meanderings of an Ivanov, could not take root in the Yiddish theatre because that order of life had not yet taken sufficient root among the immigrant Jews. The realist or naturalist drama that dominated late-nineteenth-century Europe would never thrive in the Yiddish theatre, as realism and naturalism did, to some extent, thrive in Yiddish literature.

No; the strength of Yiddish theatre was largely its own, an indigenous popular art. On the page most Yiddish drama seems hackneyed; on the stage it could overwhelm audiences, both Jewish and gentile, shattering aesthetic scruples and inhibitions. The strength of Yiddish theatre rested on such traditional folk materials as sentimental domestic drama, broad comedy, and symbolic versions of traditional legend. Ansky's *Dybbuk* and Leivick's *Golem* are works radically different in theatricality and literary value: the first is a "natural" for the theatre, the second a thoughtful closet drama; yet both rely on religious legend stylized to grotesque intensity.

It might be said, as indeed it often was, that Yiddish theatre could not thrive simply by returning to its indigenous sources; that the old folk themes and situations, the shrewd genre characterizations that were handed down, like mended clothes, from author to author were bound to wear out in the American setting; that some sort of leap was necessary, as the Vilna Troupe and Schwartz's Art Theatre and the Artef at their best undertook, from folk to cosmopolitan. But was there no possibility for bringing together the indigenous strengths of Yiddish theatre with the styles and experiments of modern drama? Perhaps; but only if there had been more time, only if there had been several generations that used Yiddish as their native tongue yet were also at home in Western culture. Had Yiddish culture survived with some measure of self-assurance, there might have appeared new playwrights spontaneously blending native and acquired motifs. But there was no time: a blink of history and it was all over.

Yiddish theatre had to work out its own terms of existence, mostly apart from and even in opposition to the theatres of Europe and America. It was a theatre of energy and emotion rather than refinement and nuance. It was a theatre blazing with the eloquence of its moment, and in the memories of a few the glow would remain.

CHAPTER FIFTEEN

The Scholar-Intellectuals

AT A TIME when the east European Jews were staggering through decades of immigrant deprivation, many German Jews, quicker to adapt to American circumstances, were establishing themselves economically and culturally. Some time would have to pass before this inequality of condition could be righted.

The east European Jewish immigrants had come from a culture more coherent but less cosmopolitan than that of the German Jews—a culture still in the grip of religious passions and far less ventilated by the Enlightenment. The scholarship of the east European Jews in such centers as Vilna, Saint Petersburg, and Warsaw, though beginning by the 1890's to succumb to secular temptations, still bore a heavy rabbinical and theological stamp. The official guardians of rabbinical culture looked upon Western thought with fear and loathing, and, as a result, the conflict in eastern Europe between faith and skepticism, between yeshiva commentary and rationalist historiography, took an especially dramatic form. The German Jews, by contrast, had worked out for themselves a reconciliation between their Judaism, which they saw strictly as a religion, and the styles of Western thought.

One result of this difference was that by 1900 the German Jews in America had created scholarly and cultural institutions decidedly more imposing than those of the east European immigrants. In 1875, under the guidance of Isaac M. Wise, wealthy German Jews set up the Hebrew Union College in Cincinnati, long to serve as a center of Judaic scholarship and a training college for Reform rabbis. Along similar lines, the Jewish Publication Society was formed in 1888 and the American Jewish Historical Society in 1892; while the Jewish Encyclopedia issued in the early 1900's an impressive compendium of *Wissenschaft des Judentums,* synthesized for the American reader and containing solid contributions by such scholars as Kaufmann Kohler, Richard Gottheil, Emil Hirsch, Cyrus Adler, and Louis Ginzberg. Both the Hebrew Union College and the Jewish Theological Seminary, founded in 1887 to train conservatively oriented rabbis, entered upon a period of productive scholarship: the former under the leadership of Kohler and the latter under Solomon Schechter, perhaps the most renowned Jewish scholar in Europe. Dropsie College, an institution devoted to Judaic scholarship, though not rabbinical in orientation, was set up in 1907. While the faculties of these institutions had some scholars with east European backgrounds, they drew mainly on the resources of German Jewry. "The rabbis and scholars trained in German methods," writes Joshua Trachtenberg in his survey of American Jewish scholarship,

> brought . . . a detachment from everyday interests and a dedication to learning as a sort of sacred abstraction which kept them aloof from the turbulently expanding community of American Jews. Thus, along with German academic emphasis on philology, wide erudition and proficiency in classical and Semitic languages, American Jewish learning tended to be "idealistic," minimizing if not excluding altogether social and economic forces; it was also apologetic, with a strong assimilationist tinge, in the interests of emancipation and integration in western society, and respectably middle class insofar as it had any social orientation whatever.

By comparison, the scholarly achievements of the east European Jews during the early years of the mass migration were meager. Mired in poverty and cut off from old-world roots, the yeshivas that were set up in several large American cities could neither match the standards of traditional rabbinical learning nor satisfy the intellectual needs of most Jews in the new world. The East Side had some scholarly figures like the admirable Alexander Harkavy, who assembled pioneer Yiddish-English and Yiddish-English-Hebrew dictionaries; but he was not a trained philologian and, in any case, had to spend much of his time on immediate tasks of popularization. As for the Hebraic scholars who drifted across from eastern Europe in the eighties and nineties, their lives were harder still: hopelessly isolated and without even the solace of sympathy from the immigrants themselves.

Only after the turn of the century did there begin to appear in America a group of scholar-intellectuals who worked in Yiddish, devoted themselves mainly to secular themes, and were oriented to the intellectual regeneration of the Yiddish-speaking masses. The conditions under which they lived and worked, both in eastern Europe and America, were sharply different from any we are likely to associate with the academic or intellectual life.

When secular-minded intellectuals began to appear in the east European Jewish community during the second half of the nineteenth century, its official leaders, rabbinical and otherwise, proved sharply hostile—and understandably so. For between the values of religious Orthodoxy and those of modern intellectuality there could be no lasting peace, only an occasional common defense against external enemies. Isaac Bashevis Singer, the Yiddish writer, describes his father's reaction upon discovering that he, Isaac, meant to become a secular writer:

> It was a great shock to my parents. They considered all the secular writers to be heretics, all unbelievers—they really were, too, most of them. To become a *literat* was to them almost as bad as becoming a *meshumed*, one who forsakes the faith. My father used to say that secular writers like Peretz were leading the Jews to heresy . . . he called Peretz's writing "sweetened poison," but poison nevertheless.

The ideological conflicts that tore the east European Jewish world in the last decades of the nineteenth century were enacted by men of intense convictions, men to whom disputes over the nature of Jewishness signified the future of the earth. The clash between fathers and sons that forms so powerful a theme in the work of nineteenth-century Russian and English writers seems mild in comparison with the crises—with their thunderings of anathema, their outcries against superstition, their wounds of loving combatants—that began to erupt among the east European Jews. For a youth in Lithuania or the Ukraine to choose a career as writer or intellectual meant not only to abandon family and home or run off to America: it meant a total wrenching of his psychic life. That may be one reason such decisions were often justified by a "total conversion" to socialist belief.

Once they abandoned Orthodoxy, there were two main possibilities for the young Jewish intellectuals. They could throw themselves into the Russian revolutionary movements, which usually led to a total repudiation of Jewish identity, or they could attach themselves to one or another political movement or cultural grouping within the secular Yiddish world. A few who broke away would come back repentant, shocked to discover that anti-Semitism was by no means absent from the Russian revolutionary movements or convinced that the idea of Jewish liberation through socialism was a mere utopian fantasy. Some brilliant young men—Trotsky, Martov, others —left the Jewish community forever. This meant, for the east European Jews, a major depletion of talent that would continue deep into the twentieth century and become especially acute during the later stages of the emigration to America. As for those aspiring young intellectuals who did remain within the Yiddish milieu, they continued to live under the shadow of their fathers and the faith of their fathers, even while trying to improvise some "essence" of Jewishness that might transcend religion or nationality and could survive in the secular world.

Where Should They Go?

The immediate situation of these intellectuals was both enviable and deplorable. Behind them they usually had a Jewish education as intense as it was parochial. The Bible remained a vibrant presence in their lives, yielding metaphors of drama, the substance of ethics, the music of poetry, and even worldly guidance; the Talmud and numerous attendent commentaries had trained them in the agilities of dialectic as well as standards of conduct; and Hebrew both as language and cultural resource was still available. By the late nineteenth century almost every Yiddish intellectual had also received a smattering of worldly education, either at Jewish schools or at the Russian and Polish schools they occasionally went to. A very few had even been allowed to enter Russian and German universities.

But if the Yiddish intellectuals were the direct heirs of a great tradition, they were also in the uncomfortable position of having to start almost from the beginning. Through a desire for collective renewal, sometimes through the sheer will to personal assertion, they were putting together the very terms of *Yiddishkeit*. The bounds and norms of Yiddish as a language had to be established each day; decisions had to be made as to the possibilities of Yiddish literature; and all this, in a "normal" culture the leisurely work of centuries, was here crowded into a few decades. Yiddish-writing intellectuals suffered ridicule not only within the Jewish world, but often among the intellectuals of surrounding cultures who smiled at the idea that a little Jew with earlocks, the son of a Vilna tailor, could have something valuable to say about Spinoza. It is hardly surprising that Yiddish intellectuals felt uneasy in relation to every possible milieu, their own almost as much as any other.

Many of the institutions we take for granted in Western culture were missing from the Jewish milieu: there were, for example, no Jewish symphony orchestras in Vilna, no Jewish art museums in Warsaw, though plenty of brilliant musicians and a few gifted artists. Two of the main settings for Western intellectuals, the university and bohemia, were rarely accessible to those writers and intellectuals who chose to remain with their fellow Jews. Because there were no modern universities in the east European Jewish world,* its secular scholarship had necessarily to be occasional and unsystematic, lacking in that richness of tradition which rabbinical scholar-

---

* There were, however, some institutions devoted to secular scholarship, such as the Historical Committee in Saint Petersburg, under the direction of the Jewish historian Simon Dubnow, and Baron David Günzburg's Institute of Oriental Studies.

ship could command. Young Jewish writers had either to attend gentile universities, bristling with enmity and alien concepts, or stumble along as autodidacts. That YIVO, the outstanding Yiddish center of learning, was not founded until 1925 in Vilna is a sign of how late it was before substantial institutions could be created within Yiddish culture.

As for bohemia, that classical setting for romantic and rebellious writers, only occasionally could cities like Warsaw, Kiev, and Vilna afford the social space or cultural ease. Yiddish literary and intellectual groups sprang up, of course, but the kinds of bohemia we have come to know in Paris, London, and New York, coherent neighborhoods in which writers and artists establish a distinctive milieu and improvise a deviant life style, were beyond the resources, perhaps beyond the imagining, of the east European Jews. Even in New York during the early years of this century, with its concentration of Yiddish writers, only the most fragile approximation of bohemia could be improvised—and none of the academy.

Not only were Yiddish-writing intellectuals in America too poor to venture on the programmatic poverty of bohemia, most of them still clung to the firm, even puritanical family patterns of Jewish tradition. For better or worse, these intellectuals were thrown in with the masses of their people, sharing their poverty, their work, their tenements. Nachman Syrkin, the ideological founder of Labor Zionism, lived on Charlotte Street in the east Bronx, a place of immigrant poverty; S. Niger, the leading Yiddish literary critic, lived in an equally modest section of Brooklyn. Such men neither could nor wished to experience the social estrangement that in western Europe and America has become a major fact of intellectual life.

In many areas of secular thought, the Yiddish scholar-intellectuals began to work without much of a sustaining tradition of their own. There had been some significant steps toward a secular Jewish historiography in the writings of east European scholars like Simon Dubnow, Meyer Balaban, and Israel Zinberg, yet it is significant that Dubnow wrote in Russian and Balaban in Polish and Hebrew, languages presumed to be more appropriate for scholarship than Yiddish. In disciplines such as sociology Yiddish was very weak and would remain so—in Europe because the very idea of sociology had just begun to be developed and could hardly be expected to take root quickly in Poland or Russia, and in America because the small number of Jews who did turn to sociological investigation received their training at American universities and wrote in English. By contrast, Yiddish literary criticism, being attached to a living body of creative work, had substantial achievements to its credit.

Their difficulties and handicaps notwithstanding, the Yiddish scholar-intellectuals enjoyed enormous spiritual advantages. They maintained a firm relationship with their people.* A close involvement in the Jewish experi-

* "The folk tradition in east European Jewish historiography," as Lucy Dawidowicz calls it, is a major example. "Critical study of east European Jewish history began at a comparatively late date, in the last decade of the 19th century, when Simon

ence shielded them from those sins of snobbism and indulgences of reaction, those postures of pseudo aristocratism, which have often marred Western culture. Lacking university and bohemia, publishing houses and foundations, they still managed to be heard. They transformed the Yiddish newspaper into a college of their own, struggling to articulate ideas and educate readers. They published their books by themselves, paying the printer out of their own pockets and selling a few copies at occasional lectures.

Disadvantages? To be sure. In reading the Yiddish scholar-intellectuals one often feels that, precisely because of their intimate relationship with their people, they felt obliged to start from scratch, explaining references that might more gracefully have been slid over, offering a quick historical review of the subject under discussion which an educated reader might find gratuitous or superficial. But against these difficulties, the Yiddish scholar-intellectuals, as men chosen for a task greater than themselves, were blessed with historical passion and ethical security.

The first major group of Yiddish intellectuals to establish themselves in America came during the early 1900's; others kept arriving until about the Second World War. In the earlier years the most prominent figures were Hayim Zhitlovsky, advocate of Yiddish cultural nationalism, and, flanking him as a friendly intellectual opponent, the theoretist of Labor Zionism, Nachman Syrkin, who lived in New York from 1908 until his death, in 1924. By persuasion Syrkin was not at all a Yiddishist, indeed, he was an early champion of a Hebraic revival; but wanting to bring the Labor Zionist message to the Jewish masses and having to earn his meager living by writing articles for the Yiddish press, he found himself using Yiddish a good deal more than he proposed to. In effect, he joined the Yiddish intelligentsia. Others came later, the literary critic Shmuel Niger in 1919, the political-cultural essayist Hayim Greenberg in 1924, the historian Jacob Shatzky in 1924, and Max Weinreich, a major scholar in Yiddish language and literature, in 1932.*

Dubnow decided to devote his life to the history of the Jews in Russia and Poland. Dubnow's first step was to collect basic raw data, primary source materials, and—a mammoth task—to construct from these a vast chronology of events in Russian Jewish history. To compensate for the lack of Jewish national or municipal archives, Dubnow started a movement for what may be described as 'folk' archives. He sparked an extraordinary popular movement among thousands of Jews in the Tsarist empire—university students as well as plain folk—who, following his guidance and instructions in *Voskhod*, a Russian Jewish periodical, accumulated for him huge amounts of documentary sources."

* At least a word should be said about one branch of Yiddish scholarship that has flourished in the United States and has come closest to meeting traditional academic expectations. Yiddish philology found an outstanding scholar in Judah A. Joffee, who had studied with Otto Jespersen and wrote notable works on old Yiddish language and literature. Other significant scholars in Yiddish linguistics include Yudel Mark, editor of the journal *Yidishe Shprakh*, and Nakhum Stutchkoff, who would publish in 1950 a valuable and comprehensive *Thesaurus of the Yiddish Language*. One possible reason for the high level of Yiddish linguistics is that scholars in this field were not as likely to be tempted by popularization as were Yiddish scholars in most other areas.

In outlook and style these men were notably different from both the German-Jewish and the American university-trained scholars, both of whom were devoted to the idea of academic detachment. Not, to be sure, that there was truth in the common notion, or prejudice, that Yiddish intellectuals were all autodidacts. Men like Zhitlovsky and Syrkin and, later, Greenberg and Weinreich had received solid training in Russian and German universities, some of them holding the Ph.D. They had published the customary monograph on a philosophical or historical theme and were absorbed in, sometimes overly fascinated by, Germanic philosophical speculation. Their work, even when dealing with strictly Jewish subjects, tends to be sprinkled with references to Kant, Hegel, and Spinoza—especially Spinoza, a figure endlessly fascinating to Jewish intellectuals who wish to maintain close ties with their native culture while establishing themselves in the Western intellectual tradition. Yet, as university men without universities, they had to carve out careers sharply different from the usual academic pattern.

Not only were they, as a rule, well trained in European universities, they were also spectacularly multilingual, writing and speaking readily in Yiddish, Hebrew, and Russian (or Polish), and also in at least one other European language, usually German. In America, with somewhat more difficulty, they picked up English, Greenberg learning to write it especially well. All of them were what a later generation would call *engagé*, committed to political-cultural movements within the Yiddish milieu and struggling to create a philosophical synthesis that would justify their sense of Jewish destiny. Usually this took the form of an effort to blend the socialist values they mostly took for granted with a national-cultural resurgence toward which they all aspired. Necessarily, they had to find outlets for their work which conventional academics might scorn, and, as intellectuals attached to Yiddish movements, they spent a good deal of their time on the lecture platform. Many of them, like Zhitlovsky, Syrkin, and Greenberg, became highly accomplished public speakers. Zhitlovsky and Syrkin would take regular national tours for their movement or for one of the fraternal orders like the Workmen's Circle, stopping a day or two in each city with a large immigrant population, speaking for their "party," the local Yiddishist group, and sometimes a *landsmanshaft*, and being entertained (or exhausted) by the leaders of the local Yiddish community, for whom the arrival of an intellectual from New York was an event causing much excitement.

One result of such commitments was that it proved hard for them to do sustained scholarly work—Syrkin, for example, would keep turning back to a history of the Jews that he was never able to finish. But if they paid for their role in the Yiddish community by falling victim to popularization, they also gained in cogency. Neither mere scholars nor mere intellectuals, they were really scholar-intellectuals whose work, though sometimes bruised by the passage of time, rarely seems "academic" in the unhappy sense of that term.

Poverty struck them as a natural condition. They earned their livings, insofar as they did, by lecture tours and by writing for the Yiddish press. Most of them preferred the *Day*, usually tolerant of intellectual material and less inclined than the *Forward* to demand that everything be flattened out for "the ordinary reader." Sometimes they wrote for Yiddish little magazines and party publications, though these could hardly bring in more than a few pennies. Niger lived by writing critical pieces for the Sunday edition of the *Day;* Greenberg by editing the *Yidisher Kemfer,* a Labor Zionist weekly. Coming later, Max Weinreich found a place in the American academy, first at Columbia and then at CCNY. To all of these men, modesty of circumstance seemed entirely proper, the way a Jewish intellectual ought to live.

Seen against the backdrop of American intellectual life, the concerns and styles of the immigrant Yiddish intellectuals might be regarded as somewhat provincial, cut off from the main currents of modern thought and culture. And it is true that the Yiddish intellectuals were so intensely absorbed in their own problems (as well as shy about approaching American writers), that they lived pretty much in a self-contained milieu. But to accept this view of them would be an unfair judgment. For the intellectuals who wrote in Yiddish were not at all confined to the limits of the immigrant milieu; they were part of an international culture, with strong centers in eastern Europe and growing outposts in both western Europe and Latin America. Debates concerning the relation between socialism and Zionism or the prospects for Yiddish culture might start on one continent but, if at all significant, quickly moved to another. A serious Yiddish intellectual living in a New York slum in 1910 or even 1925 was more likely than his American equivalent to know about new developments in Russian political thought and literature. He would regularly see the better Yiddish publications from eastern Europe, which paid increasing attention to the surrounding gentile cultures, and he would regularly meet with the intellectual celebrities—Shmarya Levin, Arkady Kremer, many others—who came from Poland or Russia to give public lectures in America or to press the claims of one or another Jewish political movement.

One of these visitors, Hayim Zhitlovsky, made a very strong impression when he first came to America, in 1904 (see p. 240). Settling here four years later, he established himself as a major figure among the East Side intelligentsia, though he could never have a fraction of the influence exerted by men like Abraham Cahan or Morris Hillquit among the mass of immigrants. Born in 1865 into a prosperous middle-class family, Zhitlovsky received a thorough European education, gaining a doctorate at the University of Berne in 1892. In his early youth he joined the surge of rebellious young Jews who abandoned both religion and folk to find fulfillment in the Russian revolutionary movement—in his case, not with the Marxist groups but with the populist Socialist Revolutionary party. "The Russian language and its literature," he would recall, "had turned us into Russians, flooding our spirits with Russian ideas, hopes, and aspirations." For a bright Jewish lad who had made an abrupt turn to secularism, there was not yet any figure in the Jewish world with the moral allure of a Tolstoy or a Turgenev, or even a Chernyshevsky. For people like himself and his friend S. Ansky, author of *The Dybbuk*, the fascination with gentile and peasant Russia was "profound and enveloping, and the road back [to Jewishness] very difficult." Later he came to think that if there had been in the 1870's a vital Yiddish culture, "our radical youth could more easily have taken the step from intellectual cosmopolitanism to national solidarity without having to make a detour into assimilationism."

For Zhitlovsky himself, the detour was brief. By 1885—Jewish intellectuals blossomed at an early age in Russia—he had worked his way to a rudimentary version of the idea that would control his entire intellectual experience: the Jews formed a nation regardless of whether they could claim a land of their own, they had a culture which found its demotic sources and strength in Yiddish, and their revival as a people depended on bringing together the socialist ideal and a national consciousness. Like the earlier Haskala enlighteners, Zhitlovsky at first turned to Yiddish because it was the only medium by which the common people, the mass of Jewish workers and petty bourgeoisie, could be reached. Utilitarian as this view of Yiddish might seem, it was for young Jewish intellectuals a kind of screen masking a deeper love for the whole culture of *Yiddishkeit*, a love, they felt, that had somehow to be justified by "higher" political or philosophical considerations.

In America Zhitlovsky spoke, wrote, and proselytized for his ideas with an astonishing energy. An attractive-looking figure, charming and witty on the platform, he exerted a sort of pedantic charisma on the "better" Yiddish audiences. Listening to Zhitlovsky could give one a sense of finally coming into direct relation with the deeper learning of Europe. He was never shy about invoking the names of the great philosophers and, whatever his faults, rarely indulged in the threadbare popularizing that was the bane of Yiddish cultural life. Taut with moral and intellectual passion, he had an omnivorous appetite for the verbal constructions and dialectic gymnastics of ideology—indeed, his whole intellectual career formed a careening through and past ideologies, from Russian populism at the start to fellow-traveling Stalinism at the end.

Zhitlovsky yoked almost every component of Yiddish thought into a grand eclecticism. His approach to traditional religion was more sophisticated by far than that of the late-nineteenth-century atheists: he analyzed Judaism in relation to the historical experience of the Jewish people, trying to separate supernaturalist faith from the ethical substance that had been intertwined with it, and recognizing the value of religious customs for both morality and discipline. He felt a strong kinship with the experience of *galut*, differentiating himself in this respect from the Zionists; yet he also recognized, here coming close to the Zionists, that centuries of oppression had severely damaged the European Jews. He insisted that they must discontinue their "parasitic" existence as traders, merchants, and *luftmenshn*, and, like the Zionists, urged that they become "productive workers," especially farmers. Proposing that the Jews return to the "prophetic outlook" which, he said, they had lost in the depths of the Middle Ages, Zhitlovsky insisted that a "progressive" nationalism need not come into conflict with internationalism—many of his polemical thrusts were directed against those Jewish radicals whose zealotry led them to deprecate Jewish national sentiment with a coarseness of spirit they would not have dared show in relation to any other national sentiment. The Jews, Zhitlovsky countered, must gain their rights not only as individual citizens but as a recognized national minority, and the culture they should develop was the culture they already had: plebeian, fraternal, deep rooted, in short, the culture of *Yiddishkeit*. He fought bitterly against all assimilationist trends, here joining hands with Zionists like Syrkin, for he believed that Yiddish was not merely a folk expression but served as the linguistic medium of the class struggle within the Jewish world. Grandiose and syncretic as Zhitlovsky's theorizing may have been, it had the immediate effect of enabling many antitraditionalists to remain within the Jewish framework.

Once, at a meeting arranged to discuss Jewish thought, Syrkin delighted his audience by describing the differences between himself and Zhitlovsky: "We have divided the world between us. Zhitlovsky takes everything that exists; I take everything that still does not exist. He has chosen the Yiddish which we have; I, the Hebrew which we do not have. He has chosen the diaspora which we have; I, the homeland which we still do not have."

The strength of Zhitlovsky's thought lay not in any particular idea or recommendation. His notion that Jews should become farmers was a piece of dogmatic willfulness with little relation to American realities. His insistence that Yiddish be the exclusive Jewish language meant cutting off millions of Jews throughout the world from his projected Jewish renaissance.* Zhitlovsky's strength lay in bringing together, perhaps in an impossible entanglement, almost all the major currents of Yiddish immigrant life: socialism *and* nationalism, universalism *and* resistance to assimilation, religious sentiment *and* modernist rationalism. Pull all these apart, give them the breath of life, and you have Yiddish culture. Paste them together in a synthesis abstract and dogmatic, and you have Zhitlovsky. What could not

---

* On this matter the Jewish historian Dubnow had justifiably argued: "History proves that if Jews had depended on only one language they would have vanished long ago. Even in ancient Palestine and the Eastern countries the people could not withstand language assimilation. Yiddish is dear to us, and it should be a cementing force, but it cannot serve as a base for our national culture. We dare not excommunicate millions of Jews who happen not to speak Yiddish."

survive as a theory nevertheless reflected in deep and authentic ways a common experience—indeed, helped significantly to mold it.

Zhitlovsky's prose lacks the lightness and muscularity of Peretz's or Hayim Greenberg's; there is "a touch of the library," to use a Yiddish phrase, in everything he writes, a certain self-conscious heaviness. But this vice is tied to a virtue. Throughout his career Zhitlovsky fought against the facile "popularizing" of Yiddish publicists, their tendency to shield half-baked ideas and half-absorbed knowledge by constantly invoking the need to "educate the masses." For many years there was a bitter battle on this issue between Zhitlovsky and Abraham Cahan. In an article published in the *Tsukunft* of 1910, entitled "Our Intellectuals," Cahan sneered at Zhitlov-sky's magazine *Naye Lebn* ("New Life") as an organ for "spiritual aristo-crats. . . . It would be better if Zhitlovsky could descend from his Talmudic-cerebral pedestal and speak to the masses. Zhitlovsky cares less about the spiritual state of his people than whether there are Yiddish books on the same 'unpopular' scientific subjects as those in world literature."

Zhitlovsky's reply was crushing. "Cahan doesn't seem to realize that in order to popularize one must first have knowledge." The articles in the Yiddish press, from the *Forward* to the *Varheit*, which try to popularize natural and social sciences, remarked Zhitlovsky, are full of errors—the *Varheit* informs its readers that the equator is at the center of the earth, the *Freie Arbeiter Shtime* transforms a maelstrom into a city, the *Forward* explains that aluminum is a kind of clay, and so on. "We must create an atmosphere which will provide the Jewish intellectual with as excellent fare as he obtains in other tongues. . . . Otherwise, he will abandon us, and leave us with nothing but *melamdim* [elementary-school teachers]." Zhitlovsky imagined Cahan approaching Karl Marx and saying to him, "Come, come, Karl—your style is too 'Talmudic.' In its present form it can only be under-stood by a handful of spiritual aristocrats. Let me fix it up for you." Insofar as Yiddish intellectual life attained substance and dignity, Zhitlovsky's insis-tence upon standards was decisive.

Dean of Critics

A very different kind of figure was Shmuel Niger (born Shmuel Charney), the major Yiddish literary critic of the twentieth century: far less ideological and far less given to public gestures than Zhitlovsky. Niger's work lay entirely within the bounds of Yiddish, as historian and critic of its literature, and his great strength was that he simply took for granted the viability of Yiddish, as critics in other languages take for granted the viabil-ity of their literatures. His work is therefore quite free of apologetics.

Yiddish literary criticism in the years before the First World War was rudimentary in character, often provincial and tendentious—the little that there was of it. The best Yiddish critic in eastern Europe, who used the pseudonym of Ba'al Makhshoves, had a genuine flair for placing the work of a writer like Mendele Mokher Sforim in its historical setting (see, e.g., the passage quoted on p. 14): he saw the life in and the life behind the work. But the idea that the work in its own right, and not simply as an index of Jewish opinion, might warrant close inspection had not yet penetrated very deeply in the Yiddish literary world. This is an idea that appears late in the life of a culture, and among Yiddish writers it would come into its own only after a certain exposure to European writing.

In 1908 there appeared in Vilna a magazine, *Literarishe Monatshriftn*, which put forward the view, striking for its moment, that literature should be treated as an end in itself and not as a device for educating the Jewish masses or advancing one or another Jewish ideology. A central figure on this journal was Niger, who had already attracted some notice with his youthful writings in behalf of the Socialist Territorialist movement (a small group proposing that the Jews create a homeland for themselves, but not on Palestinian soil). Losing interest in Jewish politics, Niger began to devote himself to writing criticism, even then notable for its seriousness and care, about the Yiddish literary works pouring out of both Europe and America. He was a confirmed Yiddishist, not as ideologue but as practicing writer; he was a secularist, but free of that crude religion-baiting which was then popular among radical Jewish youth; he wrote entirely about Yiddish literature, as if it were quite sufficient for absorbing the energies of a critic; he was intent upon establishing the worthiness of Yiddish writing in the life of the Jews, but he nevertheless tried honestly to see the novel or poem as a structure meriting intrinsic encounter and judgment. And he performed at least one other major service. He kept criticizing the tendency of the newly formed Yiddish intelligentsia to regard itself primarily as an agency for disseminating, and thereby watering down, European and/or Jewish culture to the masses. "The dissemination of culture," he wrote as early as 1908, "becomes the goal of an intelligentsia only when it despairs of its own creativity. . . . When intellectuals lose sight of their highest goal, cultural creativity, they become enamored of a surrogate goal, cultural dissemination." These casual sentences struck right to the central weakness of the Yiddish intelligentsia.

By the time he came to the United States, Niger was acknowledged throughout the Yiddish-speaking world as a major voice, and for the next thirty-five years, until his death in 1955, he would be the single most powerful figure in Yiddish letters. Most of his criticism was composed as weekly pieces for Yiddish newspapers, briefly for the *Forward* and over many years for the *Day*.

From a distance, an outsider might find it hard to understand why Niger should have so thoroughly dominated Yiddish literary life. His efforts at aesthetic theorizing, which culminated in a late volume entitled *Critics and Criticism,* were fairly commonplace—though, to his credit, he steadily resisted the social and national utilitarianism that spread across Yiddish culture, both during its formative years and in the later period when the dogma of "proletarian literature" was influential. His taste, even within the Yiddish framework, was conventional, rarely allowing him to be at ease with even mildly modernist writers. He was uneasy about the talented poets of *Di Yunge,* seldom coming to grips with the work of Moshe Leib Halpern or Mani Leib. For years he kept sparring with Jacob Glatstein, the most original Yiddish poet in America during the mid-twentieth century. While he knew the classical Russian writers and some of the German romantic poets, only seldom did he try systematically to compare Yiddish literature with the literature of Europe. His capacity for evaluation was limited and even in his own domain not always well grounded; he steadily overvalued the work of Sholem Asch, defending it even in later years when Asch's novels had lost their freshness.

Had Yiddish literature been able to enjoy anything like a normal development, had it not been compressed into a few fervent decades, Niger might well have been supplanted by more gifted critics. A few younger critics, like A. Tabachnik and B. Rivkin, had begun to show themselves more original in mind and more responsive to the details of a text. Rivkin spun brilliant theories about the function of Yiddish literature as a kind of surrogate for a nation striving but unable to come into being; Tabachnik devoted his career to an intense study of the poetry written by *Di Yunge,* displaying a gift for close analysis of texts that few Yiddish critics could match. And other critics came along—N. B. Minkoff, Shlomo Bickel, Jacob Glatstein—who in any particular instance might turn out a more penetrating essay than Niger.

Yet it was no mere accident, nor evidence of the low state of Yiddish literary culture, that for thirty-five years Niger commanded so eminent a position.* Appearing just after the early masters of modern Yiddish had done their work, Niger provided both readers and writers with a sense of precisely where they stood against the backdrop of their own history; and this was more important, because more sustaining, than refined analysis or authoritative evaluation. Niger provided a deep and secure knowledge of the place Yiddish literature held in the Jewish tradition. No one knew as well as

---

* For Niger personally, this was far from an unmixed blessing. A memoirist remarks: "Writers fawned on Niger and abused him; tried to bribe him, threatened him, tried to insinuate themselves into his good graces and insulted him. Their letters were sometimes twenty pages long; others, a big blank of paper with a single word: 'When?' 'Well?' 'Justice!'

"In the midst of this tumult Niger was terribly lonely. Only rarely did a colleague pay him a social visit, or inquire about his, Niger's, work, or ask him to come for a walk. Everyone who visited him wanted something for himself. He was looked upon as a sort of foundation. . . . He suffered from his loneliness. In public he was therefore always cold and correct, even with those colleagues whom he greatly admired."

he the complex of sources in the Jewish past—from homiletics to folklore, from Biblical phrase to Haskala tract—out of which Yiddish literature derived. In one of his best essays, "Yiddish Literature and the Woman Reader" (1919) he explored the provenance and social uses of Yiddish writing during the sixteenth and seventeenth centuries as no one had done before him. For both the comfort of the Yiddish writers and the assuagement of those Orthodox Jews who deplored the very idea of a secular Yiddish literature, he established the continuity between Jewish past and Yiddish word.

Perhaps because of his very limitations, Niger was the ideal link between the older Yiddish writers, those who had come to maturity before 1905, and their readers. He taught the Yiddish audience how to apprehend its masters, for he knew that only if an audience were created and tutored could the literature survive. Even if he overestimated Sholem Asch, he illuminated superbly Asch's reliance on the tradition of *kiddush hashem*, martyrdom in behalf of the sacred. The essay he wrote about the sweatshop short-story writer Z. Libin is not merely a portrait of a touching figure, it also evokes a whole aspect of immigrant culture:

> All of Libin's characters are very much like one another; only rarely is one of them individualized. But the circumstances of their life, the circumstances he does not cease to render, are those of a specific community at a given moment—the community in the epoch of the east European immigration to America. Whoever proposes to write the history of this community must look to Libin's work. And that is why even those of his stories that are too explicit to be artistic, even they constitute a kind of history. . . .
>
> Libin wrote *American* Yiddish ("*mama-tate un alle fier kinder zaynen bizi mitn pakn dem bundle*") . . . and with no one else is it as natural as with him. He writes as he talks, as everyone in his world talks. To polish his language would be as alien to him as to polish life.

Or consider this passage, in which he discusses Sholem Asch's early fiction about the east European *shtetl*:

> This was not the real *shtetl*, it was a legend about the *shtetl*, though a legend inspired by what the *shtetl* had once been in Poland. And precisely here was the main difference between Asch's and Peretz's romanticism. Peretz wanted to make reality out of legend, Asch legend out of reality. . . . Asch put into the Yiddish language the awakened energies and the strengthened belief of the Jewish community; his elevated tone did for Yiddish literature something like what belief in socialism and national renaissance did for the Jewish folk and intellectuals.

Niger's work is often somewhat ragged, betraying the limits of a critic who week after week has to turn out a piece for his paper. But in one book, a massive volume on Peretz, he did manage to compose a major work of criticism, delicately attuned to the nuances of his subject and providing not merely a full-scale account of a significant writer but also, in passing, a comprehensive introduction to the culture of east European *Yiddishkeit*:

Stylistically Peretz is modern. This can be seen in his brevity, his impatience, his nervousness. He was the first to lose that patience which writers and teachers have who are never in a hurry. His short, compressed sketches and stories . . . are without precedent in Jewish writing. Peretz brought impact and hurriedness into the structure of the Yiddish story; short-breathed, staccato, and aphoristic prose. The form, like the content, bore the mark of his modern, urbanized self.

There are critics who achieve eminence by rising above their culture, mastering and transforming it. Such a critic Yiddish has not yet had. But there are other kinds of critics, and Niger is one of these, who serve a literature by submitting to it, as faithful chronicler, expositor, and defender.

Given the fate of Yiddish literature, his work has become increasingly useful, indeed, indispensable. To those in the years ahead who may return to the half-forgotten texts of Yiddish, Niger's essays will prove a chronicle and guide, an authoritative historical and critical source, the voice of a culture as it speaks from day to day.

A Gifted Voice

Neither a zealous ideologue like Zhitlovsky nor a quiet scholar like Niger, Hayim Greenberg was probably the most gifted among the Yiddish intellectuals, certainly the one likely to seem most attractive to later generations of cultivated readers. Though active all his life in the Labor Zionist movement, and not merely as a journalist but also as a member of leading committees, Greenberg was the kind of figure who would be at home—well, almost at home—among modern intellectuals. His essays are marked by analytic dexterity, suave and mordant ironies, and an underthrust of self-doubt.

Born in 1897 in a Bessarabian *shtetl*, Greenberg became a *wunderkind* within the secular portion of east European Jewish life. At fifteen he was giving reports to Zionist gatherings and orations at illegal demonstrations. When the czar was overthrown, the young Greenberg taught Hebrew literature and Greek drama at the University of Kharkov; he had somehow picked up substantial fragments of Western and Hebraic learning. In his politics close to the Mensheviks, he tried to stay in Russia after the Bolshevik revolution, but the Lenin regime's harsh anti-Zionism made that impossible. Arrested several times for outspoken criticism and frustrated in his efforts to protect the Hebrew theatre, Habima, in Moscow, he left the country soured over "messianic socialism." In 1924 he arrived in America, where he spent the rest of his life as writer and editor, first of the *Yidisher*

Kemfer, the Labor Zionist weekly, and then of its English-language cousin, the *Jewish Frontier*.

Greenberg wrote easily and well in four languages—Russian, Hebrew, Yiddish, and English. Neither a doctrinal Hebraist nor a passionate Yiddishist, he kept a greater psychic distance from his culture than most other intellectuals still closely involved with the Jewish milieu. Essentially, he was a restless modern figure—sometimes his writing seems to consist of a musing for the walls, a turning and twisting that has little to do with any political movement, the kind of unsystematic virtuosity that has become a hallmark of modern intellectual life. Greenberg's Zionism, though it included a heavy quotient of organizational work, was not primarily organizational, and at some points he broke from the orthodoxies of his own commitment, as in his eloquent defense of *galut* (exile), written as a tacit polemic against those fellow Zionists who had fallen into the habit of sneering at this crucial arc of Jewish experience.

At once enthusiast and skeptic, public man and private intelligence, a creature of multiple moods and personae, Greenberg emerges finally as a *writer*, the kind who responds to his moment, receptive and caustic, oratorical and furtive. His interests were extremely wide, from the mystical components of Judaism to the relation between psychoanalysis and morality. Gandhi was an intellectual hero, yet one against whose misconceptions of the Jewish martyrdom in Europe he strongly argued. What matters most about his work is not the positions he took but the variety of his tone, the cut of his argument, the insight along the way. Here, for example, he speculates on the psychology of Sabbatianism in an essay paralleling Gershom Scholem's linkage of false messianism in the seventeenth and eighteenth centuries to a certain style of apocalyptic radicalism in our own:

> Sabbatai Zevi's mystically-heroic striving to bring about an absolute transformation in Jewish life was from the very start pregnant (if one may use such a simile) with a determination to depart from Judaism. His messianic mission which was fundamentally a mighty affirmation of Judaism, was, on its reverse side, a striving for the total negation of Judaism. . . . To *Galut* he declared in no uncertain terms: "I reject you." He challenged Jewish destiny to combat, and this declaration of war contained the logical conclusion never to revert to existing conditions. He must either rise above this fate, or descend below it, but under no circumstances would he remain face to face with it. *Galut* must be destroyed either by means of the complete liberation of Jewry, or as a result of its total extinction. This was the unconscious, but deeply rooted "logic" of Sabbatai Zevi's messianic career.

A harsher, more combative voice appears in the essay on Trotsky:

> If Trotsky and Stalin are typical of revolutionary salvationists, if those who undertake to redeem humanity bear within themselves such volcanos of hate, brutality, and criminality . . . then social redemption is a curse. Perhaps we should no longer laugh at the Jewish village woman who, when her husband

told her that the Messiah was about to come in a few days, exclaimed that the God who had saved us from Pharaoh and Haman . . . would have mercy and save us from the Messiah's hands.

And entirely characteristic is this bit of reflection, quoted from a conversation with the Hebrew poet Bialik, which takes a side glance at the wisdom of Sholom Aleichem's character Tevye:

> Tevye understood the mystery of rhythm. He understood that one must not be reconciled with a daughter who became an apostate, and that it was yet necessary from time to time to pass to a sphere of thought where "all these things aren't worth a wooden nickel," to immerse oneself in the atmosphere of universalism, so to speak. There is no contradiction between the two states. That is why I say that it is a kind of rhythm. Any Jew who is incapable of "ridding himself of his nationality" from time to time, and then returning to his roots, to his environment and its spirit, to his tribe if you please—such a Jew is a sick person.

A Disinterested Historian

If Greenberg partly resembles the kind of contemporary intellectual who finds himself drawn both to political commitment and philosophical skepticism, Jacob Shatzky, a gifted and prolific Yiddish historian, approaches the type of the disinterested scholar. Shatzky's major work, composed in America, was a three-volume history of the Jews of Warsaw, from their earliest appearance to their consolidation as a modern community in the nineteenth century; but he was a writer with a very wide range of interests, from the Haskala to psychoanalysis to the Yiddish theatre. The number of items in his bibliography comes to almost six hundred.

"I was born," wrote Shatzky in an autobiographical sketch,

> under the sign of Jewish history. . . . My father had a weakness for the funerals of those he thought of as "great Jews." . . . He believed one of the best Jewish educational methods was to make a child pay his last respects to the great. . . . I used to attach myself to every funeral procession that seemed important—according to the number of mourners. Often I did not even know who the deceased was, but hearing the eulogies at the cemetery, I felt that it was a privilege to be there in such lifeless proximity to the living past.

The child whose imagination was released by funerals became a precocious student who took his doctorate at the University of Warsaw in 1922 and five years later came to the United States, where he collaborated for many years in the work of YIVO and earned his living as librarian of the New York Psychiatric Institute. In one major respect, however, he was

different from the many other young Jewish intellectuals then maturing in
eastern Europe: he was not devoted to ideology and he had no connections
with any Jewish group or party. How unusual this was in the east European
Jewish milieu during the early years of this century has been made clear by
the Yiddish educator Leibush Lehrer:

> Among the Jewish intellectuals coming out of eastern Europe there was
> hardly one who did not identify with a ruling Jewish ideology. . . . In our
> lands of origin we had accumulated so much grief that there flared up in our
> imaginations messianic images of redemption. At the same time, however, the
> *Zeitgeist* was by now sufficiently worldly so that we were tempted to seek
> mundane paths to redemption. Consequently there grew up theories, slogans,
> organizations . . . breathing the spirit of messianism and offering schemes
> for hastening the moment when we would be redeemed. . . . [But] Shatzky
> did not identify himself with any of these communal outlooks; his great
> passion was to hunt out the facts about Jewish life in the past. In our ideo-
> logically dominated milieu, this was enough to make him seem very different.

Shatzky was one of the first Yiddish historians to assert programmatically the idea of an objective historiography; whatever the merits of this
view in general, it was especially valuable to Yiddish historical writing since
it encouraged attitudes of dispassionate self-scrutiny and self-criticism. In
practice, Shatzky did not always find it easy to live up to his creed, for his
temperament was fiery and polemical—Jewish historians need will of iron to
keep a critical distance from their materials. And as a lifelong Polophile,
Shatzky faced the additional problem of reconciling, if he could, his love for
Polish history and culture with the revelations he had to make in his work
about the centuries-long Polish treatment of the Jews.

Like other historians straining toward detachment, Shatzky reveals in
his *History of the Jews in Warsaw* a lively bias of temperament. His work is
best when he is massing and savoring details of social life; it then proceeds
out of a love for the texture of experience in its own right. In his *History*
Shatzky uses a range of sources—not merely the customary documents and
memoires but also popular folk sources and "subliterature," ranging from
kitchen romances to Hasidic tracts to women's prayer books—such as had
by no means become usual among Jewish historians. A cool irony tenses
some of his work, as in this description of the rise of a cultivated and
semiassimilated Jewish bourgeoisie in mid-nineteenth-century Poland:

> This kind of patron of Polish art and culture became . . . identified as the
> "progressive Israelite." A contemporary writer described the latter as one
> whose philosophy of life was to be esteemed by the respectable Poles without
> reaching the point where he would be completely estranged from the Jews.
> . . . The "progressive Israelite" collected Polish antiques in order to empha-
> size his Polishness. The greater the losses of his Polish publishing house, the
> more persuasive the evidence of his Polishness. . . . His Jewishness expressed
> itself in using his connections to promote philo-Semitic plays on the stage and

prevent the production of those hostile to the Jews. . . . Generally this Jewish patron supported music and opera, but left the ballet to the Polish aristocracy.

Eclectic in method and open in spirit, Shatzky also shows evidence in his work of a modern sociological sophistication, a trace of Marxist influence. Through an accumulation of evidence he demonstrates, for example, that by the first half of the nineteenth century there had developed a sizable group of Jewish artisans and craftsmen in Warsaw, thereby undermining the popular notion of Jewish "parasitism" and "unproductivity." In an excellent chapter on the Polish insurrection of 1831, he describes the complex interrelations among the social and cultural groupings within the Warsaw Jewish community as these were subjected to sudden upheaval by revolutionary Poland:

> The Jewish youth of Warsaw was stirred by the pathos of the democratic idea which the young [Polish] conspirators were advancing. True, the latter were doing this in a very cautious way, for they did not wish to provoke the older generation of Poles, which was very conservative in its outlook and was prepared to accept the idea of national freedom as long as that did not mean giving freedom to the peasants. . . . The young officers and students, those inclined to Jacobinism, debated these issues heatedly in Warsaw; the city was by now free of Russian spies, and it was no longer necessary to be cautious about what one said.

Jacob Shatzky brought to Yiddish scholarship in America the worldly restlessness of Warsaw; Max Weinreich, the intense thoroughness of Vilna. Born into a middle-class family in Latvia, Weinreich as a youth was very far from the meticulous professorial figure that he became in maturity. He began his journalistic career at the age of thirteen as a correspondent for a Yiddish Bundist paper in Vilna, and later, in his early twenties, edited a Bundist daily in Vilna. Gradually his interests began to change: he enrolled at the University of Marburg and in 1923 received a doctorate for a study in Yiddish linguistics. "Politics—the Bund, that is—[had] brought him to Yiddish, but Yiddish eventually displaced politics."

Vilna in the twenties was still a great center of Jewish religious and secular learning, and Weinreich, beginning his adult career as an instructor in the Yiddish Teachers Seminary, soon became one of the central figures of its secular intellectual life. In 1925, collaborating with a Yiddish linguist named Nakhum Shtif, Weinreich founded YIVO, or the Yiddish Scientific Institute, soon to become the major repository of Yiddish scholarship in the world. By now committed to a scholarship without apologetics, Weinreich nevertheless was motivated, like almost all of his intellectual contemporaries, by a passion for enlightenment, a sense of inescapable responsibility to the Yiddish-speaking Jews. As he wrote on a later occasion: "We want to fathom Jewish life with the methods of modern scholarship and whatever modern scholarship brings to light, we want to bring back to the Jewish masses."

Weinreich's energy was enormous, his sheer stubborness a major factor in maintaining YIVO through difficult years. In 1932 he left Vilna to teach for a time in America, and in 1940, when YIVO headquarters were transferred to New York, he again took over active direction of the institute. A genuine polymath, Weinreich wrote on linguistics, language, the history of literature, folklore, and history; one of his notable works is *Hitler's Professors* (1946), a study of the relation between German scholarship and the crimes of Nazism. Weinreich's main work, however, is the four-volume *History of the Yiddish Language*, in which linguistics is employed to illuminate the history of Ashkenazic, or east European, Jewry, to illustrate the rise and flowering of Ashkenazic Jewish culture, and to explore the socio-cultural relations between Jews and non-Jews. Tracing the gradual development of this culture as it first arose in the Middle Rhine valley more than a millennium ago and then gradually moved eastward across Europe, Weinreich saw its distinctiveness in freedom from "territorial connotations: geography, as it were, has been transformed into history."

A major theme in Weinreich's historical studies of Ashkenazic culture is its bilingualism, "two living languages, one that was immediate and the second mediated."

> A mediated language can be understood, can be quoted, can be sanctified, but people do not use it in their everyday life for communicating with one another or for expressing their feelings. You surely remember the anecdote of the Jewish lady who was in labor. Her first groan was in French "Mon Dieu!" then the second, in Russian, "Bozhe moy!," but when the doctor heard *"Got in himl,"* he knew that the real throes had begun. When the Hebrew language ceased to be unmediated, and that happened many centuries before Ashkenaz was born, its growth was affected: its chief accretion was no longer from below. Yet Hebrew in Ashkenaz survived in the hot-house of Yiddish for specific functions. . . .
>
> The term *loshn-koydesh*—the sacred tongue—suggests where to look for the division of functions between Ashkenaz's two languages. Some observant Jews will not utter the word *Shabes*, "the Sabbath," in the bath or toilet. They will say "the seventh." Yet we should not be misled into thinking that because the elder language is the sacred tongue, the other is the secular tongue. In traditional Ashkenaz, as Abraham Heschel put it so beautifully, Jews strove to introduce into each mundane act at least a trace of sanctity and, consequently, there was no utter mundaneness. There were only gradations of sanctity. . . . In the Latin schools [of the Middle Ages] students had to speak Latin exclusively even during recesses and were fined for uttering a word in the vernacular. With Jews, the whole of religious learning, from the *heder* for the youngest children through the yeshiva up to the casuistry of the greatest Talmudists, was conducted in Yiddish. . . . Through its function as a language of instruction, Yiddish became a medium of ex-

pression for a complicated juridical-moral philosophical conceptual world long before German, Polish, etc. became accepted media for similar purposes.

Among the Yiddish scholar-intellectuals, Weinreich came closest to being the kind of academic we customarily associate with the American university: toward the end of his career he taught at Columbia and City College. But apart from his academic work, Weinreich was a major figure within the Yiddish world. Even in the rapidly fragmenting milieu of Yiddish culture, he could assume a role more deeply integrated, carrying greater communal responsibility and status, than most American scholars so much as aspire to.

The scholar-intellectuals sketched here should be taken as no more than representative figures; there are others, a good number of them, nearly as distinguished as they.* At the time YIVO transferred its headquarters to New York, there was good reason to believe that Yiddish scholarship would remain productive and substantial; the quality of the work being undertaken seemed to be increasingly professional and precise. But in the several decades that followed it became painfully clear that the ranks were thinning. Once men like Niger, Shatzky, and Weinreich fell away, they simply could not be replaced. YIVO as an institution stabilized itself and even expanded, but what was missing, here as in all other branches of Yiddish cultural life, was that natural process of replacement which yields younger scholars and intellectuals for whom Yiddish would be not only their natural language but the signature of an encompassing way of life.

* A few names should be mentioned: Abraham Menes, historian and essayist; Abraham Koralnik, a charming belletrist; C. Bezalel Sherman, who brought modern sociological approaches into Yiddish; Jehiel Isaiah Trunk, essayist, notable for a study of Sholom Aleichem and a cultural history of the Warsaw Jews; Elias Tcherikower, historian of American Jewish labor; Jacob Mestel, drama critic and historian of the Yiddish theatre; Leibush Lehrer, educational theorist; Jacob Lestchinsky, economic historian; Philip Friedman, historian of the Holocaust.

CHAPTER SIXTEEN

The Yiddish Press

Everyone read a Yiddish paper, even those who knew little more than the *alef-bet*. There were seldom many books in the average immigrant's home, but the Yiddish paper came in every day. After dinner our family would leaf through it page by page, and sometimes my father would read some interesting items aloud. Not to take a paper was to confess you were a barbarian. For ordinary Jews who worked in the shops or ran little stores, the Yiddish paper was their main tie, perhaps their only tie, with the outside world.

These recollections may largely be true for the years after 1910, but they are not quite accurate with regard to earlier decades, when a penny for the paper was hard to come by. Later on, during the twenties and thirties, anyone who took a subway from Brooklyn or the Bronx on a weekday morning would see garment workers poring over copies of the *Forward* or the *Day*, both substantial dailies; and this was a cultural fact of some importance, signifying a step toward modern consciousness. But among the earlier immigrants, those who came toward the end of the nineteenth or start of the twentieth century, there were very few who brought with them the habit of reading papers. It is, after all, a habit fairly recent in the history of mankind, announcing a relationship with the external world and a sense of time as economic commodity which few old-country Jews either knew to exist or would have cared to acquire.

Reading a newspaper was something they had to learn in America, like putting coins into the streetcar box or sending female children to high school, and those who trained them in this habit were themselves immigrants who had first to learn that a newspaper is essential to urban life. In the course of learning this, the Jewish intelligentsia or semi-intelligentsia had to cleanse Yiddish of Germanic slang and *shtetl* quaintness in order to create a vocabulary of mundane transparency.

The first Yiddish papers in America, published in the seventies and eighties, were fragile weeklies, often irregular in appearance. Reflecting old-country rhythms and tonalities, the *Yidishe Tseitung* and the *Yidishe Post*, both started in 1870, concerned themselves mainly with communal and religious affairs. In 1874 Kasriel Sarasohn, later to become the first Yiddish "newspaper magnate," issued the *Yidishe Gazetn*, a conservative weekly sold or distributed mostly through grocery stores and butchershops. Gradually this paper struck roots in the immigrant milieu, appealing especially to those pious Jews who wanted to resist new-world influences. Like most of the ninety or so Yiddish papers that came out in various parts of the country before 1900, the *Yidishe Gazetn* served as a mixture of bulletin board for readers and testing ground for writers: the former could pick up scraps of news about synagogue and neighborhood, the latter express themselves through religio-moral reflections. In its language the *Yidishe Gazetn* fell somewhere between German and modern Yiddish, since "the *maskilim* journalists felt that to write in the sort of plain Yiddish the immigrant masses might easily understand would be 'uncivlized.' "

The radical Yiddish press established itself a few years later, in the late eighties and early nineties, with such weeklies as the socialist *Arbeiter Tseitung* and the anarchist *Freie Arbeiter Shtime* both starting in 1890. It was a point of honor for these papers to be more responsive to world events than the *Yidishe Gazetn*, and each in its own way contributed to the secularization of the Yiddish-speaking masses. The *Arbeiter Tseitung*, intent upon arousing unlettered workers, soon realized that it had to employ a simple Yiddish style, while the *Freie Arbeiter Shtime*, a shade more intellectual when it resumed publication in 1899 after a lapse of several years, proved admirably hospitable to literary work.

No matter what their ideology, the Yiddish papers of this era must be seen less as ventures in journalism than as outpourings of collective sentiment. They were deeply "internal" papers serving as voices in a communal dialogue—equivalent to immigrant gatherings over tea in the kitchen where people "talked things over." Those who read the Orthodox press took comfort from encountering familiar homilies, those who read the radical press found excitement in the novelties of secular agitation. Both wings of the

Yiddish press served most of all to persuade the immigrants that, even in the land of Columbus, they were not wholly lost. Orthodox and radical papers alike confirmed for their readers the sense that they counted for something. Hearing themselves talk, or reading their talk on newsprint, they knew they were alive. Chauvinist or Marxist rhetoric, letters from Europe tapping emotions of nostalgia, practical advice on making out in America, occasional reports of major events (circulation would jump whenever there was news of urgency, like the Dreyfus case or pogroms in Europe)—all helped the immigrant community maintain a precarious morale.

By the mid-nineties one Yiddish paper had achieved clear domination. The *Yidisher Tageblatt*, a daily offshoot of the *Yidishe Gazetn*, grew into a great blunderbuss of a paper, skillfully playing on the traditionalism of its readers and making the corruptions of gentile America into repeated occasions for verbal thunder. The *Tageblatt* bristled with attacks on socialist and atheist heresies, sometimes even trying to persuade its readers that the socialists, because they were "ungodly," served in effect as gentile missionaries. It raised as its slogan "Preserve the purity of the Jewish family"; it turned purple at the thought of radicals practicing free love and rabbis mentioning Christ in sermons; it raged with fury when the anarchists organized nose-thumbing Yom Kippur balls. But even as it kept urging immigrants "to maintain their most precious possession—religion," the *Tageblatt* did not hesitate to pick up some of the shoddier styles of American journalism—as, for that matter, would a great many other Yiddish papers in the years to come.

With Hearst in the lead and Pulitzer not far behind, the American press of the nineties was notoriously venal, and there was no reason to expect that Yiddish editors, whose livelihood depended on luring ill-educated people to part with a penny, would be able to resist the native models. They too splattered crime, sin, violence, and fabrication onto their pages—all with a Jewish twist and sometimes comical errors. For decades Yiddish journalists would tell the story of a Philadelphia Yiddish weekly which ran the headline "The Empress of China Has Come to America to Look for a Husband." The editor, Hayim Malitz, seeing a story on the shipping page of an American paper with the head "The Empress of China Arrived Yesterday on Her Maiden Voyage," took this to mean that China's virgin queen wanted a mate and then allowed his imagination to fill in the details.

News coverage in these early Yiddish papers was decidedly casual. Occasionally there would be a letter from eastern Europe, but most of the domestic material was simply lifted from German and English-language papers (a practice not exactly unknown even in the best day of Yiddish journalism). The *Volks Zeitung*, a German socialist daily printed in New York, was much admired by the radical Yiddish writers as a reservoir of truth and culture, and by the late nineties, when the *Arbeiter Tseitung* gave way to the daily *Ovend Blatt*, Yiddish journalists were known to squeeze a week's worth of news out of a single issue of the German paper.

An East Side newspaper office

Some Yiddish journalists, like John Paley, the editor of the *Tageblatt*, preferred to manufacture their own copy rather than borrow from others. One Chanukah day Paley, much less pious in person than in print, was enjoying a portion of fried oysters in his office. When a friendly Jewish peddler dropped in, Paley told the fellow he was eating Chanukah *latkes* (pancakes) and offered him some. After the peddler had eaten a few, Paley began to shout in mock horror that it was "unclean" food. Frightened and nauseated, the poor man threw up the contents of his stomach and had to be taken home, where he lay sick for several days. For Paley, however, the incident proved a source of good copy. In the next day's *Tageblatt* he concocted a story about a gang of anti-Semites who had caught a poor Jewish peddler on East Broadway and stuffed oysters down his throat until he died of suffocation.

Day after day, while his competitors stood by helplessly, Paley embroidered this tale. When the truth finally came out and the other papers were screaming with rage, Paley replied that the atheists were trying to ruin him. Soon he had other sensations to offer, tales of Jewish martyrdom, cleverness, and tears. During the Spanish-American War he dug up incidents from the Spanish Inquisition and printed them as if they had occurred only yesterday. The combination of Paley's inventiveness and the piety of his employer, Kasriel Sarasohn, brought journalistic success; by 1900 the *Tageblatt* circulation was said to have reached 100,000. In reality it was considerably less, though still larger than that of its competitors.

The character of early Yiddish journalism in America is nicely illuminated by a comparison that its historian, J. Chaiken, makes between two leading editors of the nineties, Philip Krantz and John Paley. Krantz was a refined intellectual, Paley a clever rogue. Krantz's socialist *Ovend Blatt* was dry, solemn, and little-read; Paley's Orthodox *Tageblatt* lively, careless, and popular. All his life Krantz would be a left-wing *maskil*, an "aesthetic, scholarly European" who was "a little too refined and intellectual to address himself to the raw immigrant workers." Writing in a laconic style, unlike the florid prose affected by his rivals, Krantz proposed "to give his readers what they needed, not what they wanted. At this point, however, the immigrant masses were still pretty much at the kindergarten level." Paley, by contrast,

> was a true son of his time. His cultural baggage was very light and his principles lighter still. . . . He synthesized *shtetl* religiosity with American sensationalism. His productivity was remarkable. Besides editorials and special articles, he usually wrote up most of the important news for the *Tageblatt* himself. If necessary, he could turn out a serialized novel. Sometimes he would vanish for days, off on a spree. Other times, if his editorial wasn't ready, he would reprint an antireligious diatribe from one of the radical papers and tack onto it an outraged headline: "What *chutzpa* the comrades have!"

Kindergarten and University

Reduced to simple journalistic terms, the problem now facing the Yiddish press, or at least its radical segment, was to find a way of blending the skills of a Paley with the rectitude of a Krantz. Was it possible to issue a daily paper in Yiddish that would nurture an intimate relationship with the masses while also trying seriously to raise their social and cultural awareness? Given the nature of journalism, this may have been a delusion, an effort to mix what cannot or should not be mixed. Yet the major venture in Yiddish journalism soon to be undertaken had as its premise precisely this idea: to be at once popular and serious, to entertain and educate, to combine kindergarten and university.

Not only was such a program attractive to young radical intellectuals like Abraham Cahan and Morris Hillquit, who thought of themselves as teachers on the East Side and students in the world at large; it also spoke to deeper needs within the immigrant community. By the mid-nineties the Jewish socialists had come to realize that the popularity of the *Tageblatt* was a barrier to their goal of political dominance on the East Side. To get past that barrier was not easy, to get past it by promoting the pallid and sectarian *Ovend Blatt* hopeless. As scholastic in its Marxism as Talmudic exegetes could be in their religion, the *Ovend Blatt* propagandized for a sterile brand of socialism, less a directive to popular struggle than a promise of ultimate redemption. It dismissed expressions of Jewish national feeling as "bourgeois," and with that overreaching zeal of cosmopolitan Jews who only yesterday were swaying in the yeshiva, it refused to join the agitation for Captain Dreyfus on the ground that he was an upper-class Jew, not an oppressed proletarian.

There were deeper reasons still for the forthcoming changes in Yiddish journalism. The Jewish unions, through the logic of their development, found themselves in sharper and sharper conflict with the De Leon leadership of the Socialist Labor party (see pp. 104–05). Though led by men who regarded themselves as socialists, the unions had to fight for immediate reforms which the De Leonists scorned, had to work out peaceable relations with nonsocialist union leaders whom the De Leonists abused, and had to respond with sympathy to the Jewish sentiments of their members, which the De Leonists dismissed. De Leon was an ideologue most comfortable in the seclusion of the sect, and as long as he practiced a kind of "dual unionism," that recurrent curse of the American left, his leadership could only be a disaster. The Jewish unions, by contrast, were a movement, mottled in doctrine but attuned to the needs of the workers. Between sect and movement there could be no peace, and by the late nineties the movement needed a voice of its own.

That voice was the *Jewish Daily Forward*, which started publication on April 22, 1897, and in a decade or so would become the largest Yiddish newspaper as well as a powerful institution in the Jewish immigrant world. From the outset it was a popular, social democratic paper, encompassing the widest range of Yiddish sensibility, from cheap sensationalism to high culture. Like a large enclosing mirror, the *Forward* reflected the whole of the world of Yiddish—its best, its worst, its most ingrown, its most outgoing, its soaring idealism, its crass materialism, everything.

Though its founders were still nominally in the Socialist Labor party, their efforts to set up a new Yiddish socialist daily free of the party's discipline clearly signified a forthcoming split. This split was inevitable: De Leon was intent on remaining within his little world, and the *Forward* people, led by Cahan and Louis Miller, were intent upon moving outward, a step or two closer to America. In a few years, as De Leon pronounced his anathema, the dissidents abandoned the SLP and united with a midwestern group led by Eugene Debs to form the Socialist party. Determined, meanwhile, that their paper should not fall prey to a party bureaucracy, the founders of the *Forward* avoided that evil by instituting another: personal control. After the first five or six years Cahan became the all but unchallenged ruler of the *Forward*, setting its policies, excluding critics from its staff and its pages, fixing its tone, and thereby becoming one of the two or three most influential men on the East Side.

What distinguished Abraham Cahan (1860–1951) was a highly personal intelligence, by no means reducible to the standard opinions of his milieu, and a rather grim and acrid temperament, as if all Jewish frustrations had come to rest on his soul. He could be narrow, philistine, and spiteful; his personal culture was limited; but when it came to apprehending the relations between the immigrant Jews and the world surrounding them, his mind was wonderfully keen. Distancing himself from his own involvements, he sensed and sometimes stated the overarching paradox of Yiddish culture in America: that the sooner it began to realize its visions, the sooner it would destroy them.

The beginnings of Cahan's life story are no different from those of other immigrants: born in a village near Vilna, raised by a father who ran a wretched little *heder*, and exposed in early youth to city life, which then led to immersion in Turgenev and Tolstoy, a loss of religious faith, conversion to radicalism, and near arrest during police roundups following the assassination of Alexander II. In 1882, a sallow and feverish youth, he landed in New York with forty rubles in his pocket "and the world's salvation in his soul." There followed the usual pains of adjustment, and then meetings, lectures, and speeches for the radical sects, studying English at night school, and writing pieces for the *Arbeiter Tseitung*.

In 1897, when the *Forward* was started, Cahan seemed a logical choice for editor, since he was both a fervent comrade and had shown a flair for writing propaganda. But once he took over the paper new ideas came into play, and many of his colleagues were badly upset. Cahan was determined to shake off the scholastic quarrels of Yiddish radicalism, and when contributors like Louis Miller and Michael Zametkin submitted polemics against their De Leonist rivals, he cut ruthlessly or refused to print them. He wanted a popular paper, not a party organ—a paper that the average Jew in the street could understand without preliminary courses in dialectics. And in a short time, though it is hard to say with what degree of self-awareness, he began to regard himself as a guide, perhaps *the* guide, for the masses of immigrants. His task, as he saw it, was simultaneously to educate them in Yiddish culture and tear them away from it in behalf of American fulfillment.

Eight months after starting the paper Cahan resigned as editor: he would either mold it according to an image clear in his mind or turn elsewhere. Unable to gain a free hand from his colleagues, he became an American journalist working for the *Commercial Advertiser*, a maverick paper edited by Lincoln Steffens. For nearly five years Cahan scoured the city, training himself as observer and reporter, writing vignettes, and penetrating American life as few writers on the East Side could. In 1902 he returned to the *Forward*, which had been ailing in his absence—and this time with powers that soon enabled him to establish himself as virtual dictator. The paper took on its characteristic mixture of *shund* and *literatur*, vulgarity and seriousness, a reaching down to immigrant narrowness and a reaching upward to Yiddish intelligence. More than an idea of journalism was at stake: Cahan saw his paper as embodying the potentialities and contradictions of the entire immigrant experience.

The kind of publicist who stands uneasily between masses and intellectuals, transmitting the sentiments of one to the other, he soon made himself into a Bonapartist arbiter of immigrant life. Many colleagues on the paper, and some Yiddish writers who wrote for it occasionally, suffered from the ruthlessness with which Cahan violated sensibilities in order to make the paper exactly what he wished. Under his editorship, the *Forward* would always have a monolithic narrowness, with even its inner variations of level and tone a function of his will.

Cahan himself was never quite sure whether he hoped to be a serious writer or a popular tribune, and precisely this ambivalence rendered him sensitive to the moods of the immigrant public. No Yiddish writer was as acute as he in grasping the desires of the Jews for spiritual gratification, material easement, and a way of life that might yoke the two. But what was most remarkable about Cahan was that this intuitive penetration of immigrant feelings depended not on any closeness to the masses, but rather on maintaining a psychic distance from them—for that matter, from the intelligentsia too. It seemed at times as if having been granted a dour vision of the final outcome of the whole Yiddish enterprise, Cahan took it as his special burden to carry through that vision to the end. Helping to lay the foundations for the immigrant Jewish culture, he worked mightily to undermine them: as if creation and disintegration were for him equally terms of fate.

We can hardly suppose that Cahan passed on to his friends such explicit notions. A man's life is never as neat as someone else's effort to define it. But if Cahan's writings rarely linger at a note of contemplativeness, almost everything about his character and behavior presupposes some brooding, half-suppressed stoicism, even fatalism, like that of a man who knows he has been stricken with an incurable disease yet stubbornly persists in his work.

Cahan was a gifted writer, more so in English, a language he never spoke with ease, than in Yiddish. In 1895 he published a novel called *Yekl*, a promising work that suffered from too close a rendering of immigrant dialect into English. The book caught the eye of William Dean Howells, who praised it and encouraged Cahan to pursue a literary career. In 1917 Cahan published *The Rise of David Levinsky*, a minor masterpiece of genre realism. Through a gritty accumulation of social detail, this book brings together a critique of the immigrant rush to success with a melancholy sense of how inevitable that rush was. Praised, and rightly so, for his English-language fiction, Cahan was one of the first Jewish writers in America for whom there lay open a choice between a career in English and a career in

Yiddish. When he chose the latter, it must surely have been with some feeling of sacrifice.

In Yiddish Cahan's most sustained work is a four-volume autobiography, priceless as historical record, distinguished at some points, but disappointing in its lack of personal reflectiveness. There is a certain Litvak dryness to Cahan's Yiddish, as there is to his memories, indeed to his very soul. He seems to have felt that to allow himself spontaneity of expression might threaten the role he had chosen as mentor of immigrants and guide into the new world.

Not even his most ardent admirers cared to suggest that Cahan was a likable man. He was often irritable and cranky, inordinately vain, seldom at ease. Adolph Held, for decades a close colleague, speaks highly in an unpublished manuscript of Cahan's gifts, yet has to acknowledge that he found Cahan intolerant and imperious, a sort of Bolshevik of the spirit—and this last phrase has a certain grim rightness, for Cahan, like the Bolsheviks, often behaved as if history were a secret ally granting him exclusive insight into its direction.

One biographer, Ronald Sanders, sees Cahan as a man who kept becoming more and more defensive, a hard-shelled man who after a time was besieged by confusions of value such as have become commonplace in our culture:

> Cahan, after a time of seemingly endless struggles . . . had [by 1910] lived out an American success story. He was a fifty-year-old smiling public man; his outer life had become the expression of two generations of Jewish immigrants. . . . Who could deny that this destiny was the projection of something that had risen from deep within himself? And yet something else remained locked within, as ineradicable as it was inexpressible, which insisted that all this activity, all this success, all this mastery of an American reality was false.

These lines come close to paraphrasing Cahan himself as he makes his farewell to David Levinsky: "Such is the tragedy of my success, such is the tragedy of my success!" Taking Levinsky's unhappiness as a projection of Cahan's guilt over his abandonment of youthful revolutionary fervor, Sanders quotes from an astonishing outburst that Cahan printed in a 1902 *Forward:*

> How terrible my life would be if . . . my idea did not continue to glow! My dear, my sacred idea! You are as young to me as I myself was twenty years ago; you give me light in my darkest moments, you give me a shred of self-respect when, in the humdrum course of things, I sometimes lost faith for a moment in my own decency. . . . Oh! But now I am a practical man; I am no longer a greenhorn. I sleep in peace and look peacefully upon the world. . . . I know that I am right in being like this, that twenty years ago I was too green, but nevertheless . . . I yearn for my greenness of old. *I yearn for my yearnings* of twenty years ago.

Reading this self-revelation, one comes to see a certain plausibility in the view that David Levinsky reflects Cahan's own feelings of inner dismay. "Levinsky's character was formed by hunger, and all his experiences contain as their common element, a core of permanent dissatisfaction. . . . Dissatisfaction has become an organic habit, a form which determines his apprehension of experience in general. . . . He is a man who cannot feel at home with his desires." Cahan-Levinsky emerges as a rigid and brittle figure whose abrasiveness of temper derives from the ordeals of his culture. A film of irritation coats the events of *The Rise of David Levinsky;* it is an irritation that encompasses Cahan's life as well.

Perhaps it is the irritation of a public figure who has resigned himself to the costs of his character and, with a deep unspoken certainty, knows that everything for which he strains, the achievement of his whole life, must end in ashes. His private self makes demands in behalf of ease, grace, and escape which his culture cannot satisfy; his public role traps him in an imperiousness of tone and repression of self which weary him all the more. Only in the theme of unfulfillment does his literary gift fulfill itself, yet all his life that gift is haunted by a foreboding of unfulfillment. "A man's conflicts," says Erik Erikson, "represent what he 'really' is."

A New Journalism

In its first five or six years the *Forward* set as a major goal breaking the *Tageblatt*'s hold on the Yiddish public. Scandals, sensations, and apparent slanders were among the weapons it used, and the *Tageblatt*, steered by the pugnacious Paley, was not slow to retaliate. The *Forward* charged in 1897 that the *Tageblatt*'s publisher, Sarasohn, was misappropriating funds entrusted to him for the relief of European Jews; two years later it proclaimed, with high glee, that Paley had once been (and perhaps still remained?) a *meshumed*, or convert to Christianity. In angry response, a band of *Tageblatt* supporters milled about the *Forward* office screaming "Lynch the *Forvetsniks*," but, as usual with Jewish quarrels, bones were not broken and blood was not shed. In 1903 the *Forward* caught the Sarasohn clan trying to wangle a deal with John Ahearn, the local Tammany boss, whereby a Sarasohn would be given a judicial nomination and the *Tageblatt* would discover the moral virtues of the Democratic party. How the *Forward* thumped with righteousness! And Sarasohn could only whimper in reply, "I just wanted to get a *jobele* for my brother. Is it against the law to do a brother a favor?" A still more violent battle, enlivened by mass meetings, speeches, and resolutions from unions and *landsmanshaftn*, was waged between the *Forward* and the *Tageblatt* over Jacob Gordin's early plays, with the former championing them as "realism" and the latter deploring them as calumnies against the Jewish people. Immigrants choked into the slums, struggling for bread and air, yet battling furiously over the value of theatrical "realism"!

The invective was choice. In the *Forward*, the *Tageblatt* regularly figured as "the conservative whore," Sarasohn and Paley as "the *yarmulke* and the crucifix." Paley, whose alleged Christianizing had not yet taught him to turn the other cheek, called the socialists "defilers of the Jewish family" and "wallowers in free love." Though its circulation was still smaller than that of the *Tageblatt,* the *Forward* succeeded by about 1903 or 1904 in establishing itself as the spokesman for anticlerical radicalism in the Jewish quarter and in winning a body of partisans to whom its word was sacred. An old socialist recalls that "in my home, the *Forward* was treated like the Bible. You didn't tear, cut or muddy the pages of the *Forward* any more than you did the Torah. In fact we boycotted a storekeeper who once wrapped two pounds of carp in pages of the *Forward*. For too many centuries barbarians had desecrated our word; we were not about to patronize a modern barbarian."

Once Cahan returned as editor, in 1902, the paper started to acquire its characteristic shape and tone. His first issue, dated March 16, made it clear that he meant to issue a paper intimate and breezy in voice, attached to the concerns of its readers, and utterly simple in diction. It would remain a socialist paper, with rashes of propaganda, but it would not be a party organ loaded with in-group polemics. Above all, it would turn a strong light—sometimes glaring, even lurid—on the immediate experiences of its readers, persuading them of the value and interest of their own affairs, right there on Hester and Henry streets. A lead piece, taken from something Cahan had first written for the *Commercial Advertiser* and headed "In Love with *Yidishe Kinder*," discussed the entanglements of intermarriage. Abraham Liessen, more clearly attuned to socialist interests, wrote about "*Protsentniks* in Sweatshops," attacking bosses who gave workers advances on pay and then deducted high interest. Cahan's lead editorial, entitled "Send Your Children to College if You Can, but Don't Let Them Become Disloyal to Their Parents," started off in a style that anyone able to read the simplest Yiddish would find accessible: "On Second Avenue at around eight o'clock every morning, one can see hundreds of Jewish boys from fourteen to eighteen or nineteen years old walking with books under their arms. They are walking uptown. . . . Their clothes are mostly poor and old, but their Jewish faces often . . . bear the stamp of lively, active minds."

These are Jewish college boys, children of immigrants. Cahan then described how Jewish parents sacrificed to send children to City College, how "an overeducated son of a poor family is sometimes ashamed of his father and mother," and how these generational clashes might be settled. On the last point he was a little vague.

Most heretical of all, Cahan began to curb the excesses of the Yiddish secularists, offering a concise description of "the three stages in the life of the freethinker" which must have irritated many of his friends: (1) when he passes a synagogue and gnashes his teeth; (2) when he passes a synagogue and smiles; (3) when he passes a synagogue and, though inclined to sigh because the world is still in a state of ignorance, nevertheless finds himself taking an interest in such moments, when men stand together immersed in a feeling that has nothing to do with the egoistic life." Yoking folk sentiment and radical fervor, Cahan established the distinctive formula of the *Forward*.

Over the years Cahan developed a staff which, though frequently restive, closely followed his journalistic prescriptions. At first there were the poet Morris Rosenfeld and the short-story writer Z. Libin writing folksy "human interest" pieces; Louis Miller, a sardonic polemicist; Benjamin Feigenbaum, who satisfied the older radicals with his agnostic compositions; the socialist poet Abraham Liessen, who wrote reflective essays on Jewish and cultural themes. Later Cahan added to his staff a number of gifted journalists: Hillel Rogoff, educated in America and the author of a popularized American history for *Forward* readers; Ben Zion Hoffman ("Tsivion"), a writer of sharp *feuilletons* specializing in fights with the Zionists; B. Kovner, who spun out a popular series called "Yente Telebende," about a henpecking wife and her henpecked husband. But the *Forward* was overwhelmingly Cahan's paper, its virtues and vices his virtues and vices. Those who could not bear Cahan went elsewhere.

Cahan's journalistic methods troubled the more doctrinaire radicals. Why, they began to mutter both in private and at meetings for the *Forward* Association, should they contribute their pennies and dimes to a paper that wasted a good part of its daily six pages on stories about criminal courts and the romantic meanderings of Jewish housewives? Because, answered Cahan, you want a paper the masses will read—otherwise, what's the use of all your socialist sermons? To which his critics answered, as part of a seemingly endless dialogue, that in the mishmash of his paper the socialist material tended to become merely ceremonial, lost in a welter of trivialities. Whereupon Cahan rebutted that the *Forward* somehow *was* managing to make more and more socialist converts. About this the critics had to remain mute, since Cahan was right, but they intimated darkly that his course would sooner or later take him away from orthodox socialism. And here it was they who were right.

Cahan outraged not only some of his comrades but also many Yiddish intellectuals.* That he banned potato Germanisms from his pages did not

---

* A thick volume could be put together of denunciations of Cahan by Yiddish writers and intellectuals. Leon Kobrin attacked him for vanity: "The more admiration he got, the more his sickly appetite grew." Isaac Hourwich attacked him for commercialism: "It is well known that as the *Forward* grew, the dollar became its God." Hayim Zhitlovsky attacked him for anti-intellectualism: "Cahan has made the *Forward* into a savage paper with the mind of a small child and the lusts of a grown scoundrel." Menakhem Boraisha attacked him for indifference to Yiddish: "He prepares gradually for that which in his opinion is inevitable—assimilation."
   In each of these accusations there was a strand of truth, but all of them failed to grasp the distinctive nature of Cahan's journalistic achievements. Cahan's vanity

bother them, but they were upset, as one of Cahan's supporters has put it, when he cut out "the flossy Hebrew words and phrases with which Yiddish writers often showed off their learning." The Yiddish writers would have angrily replied that "the flossy Hebrew words and phrases" represented the very heart of Jewish tradition, and to remove them from a Yiddish publication was culturally to deprive an already deprived public.

Weaving across the decades with a terrible bitterness, the conflict between Cahan and the Yiddish intelligentsia was partly due to a difference in perspective: he cared about journalism and they about literature. The Yiddishists wanted to make their culture and language into a lasting achievement, while for Cahan Yiddish was little more than a medium through which to reach the masses. It is only fair to add that, like the Haskala writers before him, Cahan began by thinking of Yiddish in this denatured way, but after a time the language seems to have won his heart, at least as much as anything could.

The Yiddish writers were trying to stabilize the language as a literary medium and create a literate—which is to say minority—public that would respond to their work; they wanted a pure vocabulary that, for a time, would be fenced off from alien intrusions. But Cahan held that Yiddish was whatever the Yiddish-speaking masses actually spoke. If *Forward* readers were absorbing into their speech a large number of English words, then the paper would have to absorb them too. Why should the German word for window, *fenster*, be considered acceptable Yiddish while *vinde* was not, even though more and more people on the East Side used *vinde* in their daily Yiddish speech? No fixed rules could be invoked here, only the pressures of spontaneous usage. "Boy," together with diminutives like *boyele, boychick*, and *boychickel*, became part of common speech, while "girl" did not—a girl remained, immaculately, a *meydele*. The word "kitchen" was absorbed into Yiddish, the word "table" not. Cahan simply followed and sometimes helped form common usage; and while this annoyed some of his contributors and alienated Yiddish literary people, it helped make the *Forward* a wonderfully readable paper.

Cahan pressed hard for his ideas. He instructed news writers not to translate English wire dispatches but to summarize them in their own Yiddish, a procedure that purchased vividness at the cost of accuracy. Adolph Held tells a story about an experience at the *Forward* during the First World War:

---

was a character flaw not exactly confined to him, either on the East Side or beyond. The *Forward*, when it was showing a profit, regularly contributed money to beleaguered trade unions, English-language socialist publications, and Jewish communal activities. If a part of the *Forward* showed the mind of a "small child," the other part was open to some of the best Yiddish writing of its time. And while Cahan did foresee the assimilation of the Jews in America, both his paper and his own work transcended the limits of assimilationist ideology.

When the war began I was the news editor. We used to write that one side had advanced ten kilometers and another retreated ten kilometers. One day Cahan came in and said to me, "Held, does your mother know what kilometers are?" I answered, "I doubt it, my father has to read the paper aloud to her." "All right," he said, "so when you write about kilometers and they come to that line, she can't go on any further. . . . From now on I'll come in every day and write a column of war news without all those hard words, so your mother can understand what is happening in the world."

The single greatest journalistic quality of the *Forward* was the sustained curiosity it brought to the life of its own people. In a later, more portentous age, this would have been called "the sociological imagination." Were Jewish children starting to take piano lessons? Were East Siders finding new occupations ranging from real estate to gangsterdom? Were lonely immigrant girls succumbing to the lure of suicide? Were *yentes* (busybodies) moving to West End Avenue and becoming "fancy ladies"? The *Forward* bustled to look into all these matters, for they told something important about the life of the immigrants. Nothing seemed too mundane for the *Forward* staff, and that may be one reason high-minded Yiddish critics often treated the paper with contempt.

The *Forward* wrote about Jewish prostitutes on Allen Street (and in Argentina too, whose white-slave trade was held in legendary fear by the immigrants). It conducted a contest among its readers about the meaning of *mazl* (you are invited to define the word yourself). It teased East Side restaurants that were tempted to feature non-Jewish dishes. It explained, not too solemnly, the mysteries of baseball to Jewish fathers. It proudly noted the increase of immigrant attendance at museums. It castigated garment bosses trying to roll back improvements in working conditions. It even gave instruction on the use of the handkerchief— for which Cahan was abused by his enemies, who said that Jews hadn't needed him to inform them about the fine points of hygiene. But Cahan stood his ground: he knew perfectly well that many Jews had gotten around to using handkerchiefs long before he was born, but he also knew that, in the chaos of the new world, they found reassurance in even the most rudimentary instruction.

Forward reportage was by no means always reliable. Its writers anticipated the faults of the "new journalism": assertion without evidence, subjective bias without factual control. Though many of them were gifted amateur sociologists, the *Forward* writers were sadly innocent in the uses of statistics. On balance, however, it is hard to think of another journalistic venture that has so comprehensively mirrored the life of an entire people.

If the *Forward* frequently verged on yellow journalism, it also played a large role in bringing to Yiddish readers the work of serious writers. Its labor coverage was extensive, though steadily slanted toward social democratic needs. Over the years it published serious essays by such European social democratic thinkers as Karl Kautsky, Léon Blum, Raphael Abramo-

In the office of the *Forward*

vitch, and Eduard Bernstein. After the First World War, when the paper
became prosperous,* Cahan would travel to Poland and, with a new tone of
largesse, import writers tempted by the fees he could offer. Some of the best
modern Yiddish writers, like Reisen and Asch, Schneour and Rosenfeld, and
the two Singers, published their fiction in the *Forward*. Never having abandoned his youthful attachment to "realism," Cahan seldom opened his pages
to the modernist tendency that arose in Yiddish literature during the
twenties. But by then a good many of the avant-garde Yiddish writers,
sharing the contempt for the popular media that was being expressed by

---

* This prosperity brought its embarrassments. In 1924 the *Forward* accepted advertisements from the Ford Motor Company, even though Henry Ford was an outspoken supporter of anti-Semitic publications. A sharp exchange of personal letters
between B. Charney Vladeck, the *Forward* business manager, and Louis Marshall
canvassed the issues at stake here. Vladeck, though visibly embarrassed, defended
the *Forward* on the ground that "it would be very poor policy on the part of the
Jews to boycott a product or refuse channels of publicity to a product because of
the views of the manufacturer." Marshall replied that the *Forward* "has the legal
right to refrain from publishing anything that it may desire. . . . It has consistently
refused to print the advertisements of political parties to which it is opposed. . . .
There was no possible justification on the part of the *Forward* to advance the
fortunes of Ford. . . . It knew that he had deliberately and maliciously assailed the
Jews."

their fellows in other languages, would not have cared to appear in the *Forward* anyway. In his treatment of the literary figures who adorned his paper, Cahan could be extremely capricious. His nastiness toward Jonah Rosenfeld, a gifted Yiddish story writer whom he kept on the *Forward* staff but whose work he frequently rejected, became a subject for gossip in Yiddish intellectual circles. In the 1928 files of a Yiddish little magazine, the *Feder*, one may still find a memorable excoriation of Cahan by S. Niger, the dean of Yiddish literary critics and usually a temperate man.

Tell Me, Dear Editor

Cahan's greatest, or at least most successful, journalistic stroke came in 1906. A year earlier a group of *Forward* writers, led by Louis Miller, had broken away to found their own daily, the *Varheit* ("Truth"). For a little while the *Varheit* gave the *Forward* a bad time; Miller was a free-swinging journalist who knew Cahan's foibles intimately and enjoyed teasing and tormenting his old friend. Looking for some novelty by means of which to snare ordinary Yiddish readers,* Miller began to publish a few letters that had come into his office expressing vague personal complaints. In Miller's fumbling effort Cahan saw the germ of an important idea that might satisfy his wish to make the *Forward* into a "true novel" by bringing into its pages the voices of the immigrant masses.

The device Cahan hit upon was the now-famous "Bintel Brief" ("Bundle of Letters") in which readers, many of them women, wrote about their problems and sought advice from the editor. Though the letters that began to come into the *Forward* were often semiliterate and required correction in grammar and spelling, some were composed with an astonishing directness and force. The feature was immediately popular, and when there were not quite enough letters "Cahan did not wait for spontaneous expressions of folk enthusiasm. He had witty writers set themselves to 'improving'

---

* Miller did come up with one feature that was highly popular on the East Side: a comic strip drawn by Samuel Zagat called "Gimpl Beinish, der Shadkhn" ("Gimpl Beinish, the Matchmaker"), which ran from 1912 to 1919. A little fellow in striped pants, frock coat, and top hat, with sharp beady eyes staring out of a bearded face, Gimpl kept trying to marry off one half the world to the other, finding candidates for love in the depth of his magic barrel. He would join a suffragette parade, visit military camps, scour the Catskill resorts in search of eligible boys and girls, and, more often than not, suffer humiliation for his pains. But Gimpl was endlessly good-natured, rather more so than the tart captions Miller wrote for Zagat's cartoons. An American poet, Aaron Kramer, later wrote a poem celebrating Gimpl, "who in yesterday's cartoon/ had miserably flopped,/ but, self propelled,/ was surely on the trail again. . . ." Gimpl still waits "for the slightest signal/ to tear loose from the microfilm of 1912/ and range the globe, self-propelled/ in search of prospects."

Gimpl introduces the young man for the daughter, but he prefers her mother

the letters that came in and prepare lengthy answers to the fictitious folk correspondents." Very soon, however, the "Bintel Brief" became a major institution of immigrant life, and far more letters came to the *Forward* than it could use.

The first item to appear in this new department ran in the January 20, 1906, issue. It is a mother's cry from the depths of immigrant life: "My boy, who's now the breadwinner in the family, is as deaf as the wall; he can't even hear his unhappy parents weep." The boy has bought a watch, which he adores and needs for work; a neighbor has stolen it, so that now the watch is at the pawnbroker's. Please, begs the writer, "mail the pawn ticket to me" and nothing more will be said. The letter ends with a sentence worthy of Zola: "Give me back my bread"—though we will never know, alas, whether the sentence was added by an imaginative *Forward* writer.

Much of the writing in the "Bintel Brief" was pedestrian, but it is remarkable how many passages of naïve poetry and stark eloquence survive. One writer "who has already lived half my years and . . . never had any peace," works as a janitor on Stanton Street, "where the sun is ashamed to shine." Another says, "I harnessed myself to the wagon of family life and pulled with all my strength. My wife was faithful and gave me a hand in pulling." A son leaving for America describes his mother's farewell: "There was no shaking of the alms box, you do that at funerals, and there was no gravedigging, but I put on the white shirt that was wet with my mother's tears and left." Another correspondent: "When does a worker go to Denver [the Jewish tubercular home]? When he has one foot in the grave!"

The range of themes in the "Bintel Brief" is very wide, far more than those which have become commonplace in advice-to-the-lovelorn columns. Complications of marriage and thwartings of love are of course present, since a good many immigrant Jews were romantic in temperament. A young woman writes of her horror at having been tricked into living with a man outside of marriage: "We're living together now for the eighth month and I feel as if I'm losing my mind. I can't stand his bass voice—it's as if a saw were rasping my bones." (With Anna Karenina, it was ears.) Another correspondent reports that "neighbors began to whisper that my wife was having an affair with our boarder, but I had no suspicion of her, whom I love as life itself." An abandoned wife cries out: "Max! The children and I now say farewell to you. You left us in terrible circumstances. You had no pity on us."

Hardly a subject but it troubles one or another correspondent. A man who has begun "to spit blood" often "thought of suicide, but my wife's great love for me and my weak character held me back." A barber announces his dismay at discovering that when he shaves his customers he fantasizes about cutting their throats. A worker in a raincoat factory growls with anger that a thirteen-year-old boy earning $2.50 a week is docked two cents when coming to work ten minutes late. An abandoned wife declares, "I will sell my children to people who will give them a home. I will sell them for bread, not money." A girl working in a factory, breadwinner for "eight souls," asks how to cope with a foreman who makes "vulgar advances." An immigrant without work in the 1908 depression bursts out: "Death is better than such a life. One goes about with strong hands, one wants to sell them for a piece of bread, and no one wants to buy." A worker confesses that during the cloakmakers' strike of 1910 he felt compelled to scab because he needed money to buy medicine for his sick wife: "Now my conscience bothers me. . . . I want to say here that I was always a good union man."

Manners and morals are recurrent interests. "Please help us decide who is right in the debate between friends: should a socialist and freethinker observe *yortsayt* [prayers for the dead]?" Many letters ask whether it is appropriate for "Americanized" immigrants to marry greenhorns. Others ask whether emancipated young people should marry in a synagogue just to please their parents. A "progressive cantor" wonders whether he has the moral right to continue in his profession even though he no longer believes in God. A housewife complains that her husband refuses to allow her to attend school two nights a week: is she unreasonable in her desires? A Jewish detective cannot find it in his heart to arrest a poor restaurant keeper who sells liquor without a license: is he violating his duty, dear Editor? A socialist asks whether a woman of his acquaintance, also of "advanced" views, is justified in requiring that her maid eat in the kitchen, apart from the family. A troubled immigrant confesses that "when I am absorbed in the Talmud I forget my loneliness and my room turns into a palace. I am considering going back to my remote Lithuanian town, there to bury myself in the Talmud, in a corner of the old *shul*, and live out my years. What is your advice?"

There are silly letters too. "The Unhappy Fool" writes that he loves "a fine girl" who has, however, "a flaw that keeps me from marrying her. . . . She has a dimple in her chin, and it is said that people who have this lose their first husband or wife." To which the *Forward* answers with unusual asperity: "The trouble is not that the girl has a dimple in her chin but that some people have a screw loose in their heads."

Very soon the "Bintel Brief" was the most popular feature in the *Forward*. Competitors tried to copy it, but without much success. Immigrants unable to write would come to the *Forward* office, asking that their "letters" be taken down. A new profession arose on the East Side, "Bintel Brief" scribes who for a few cents would compose letters for people too shy to write their own—most of these Cahan found too florid and cut up mercilessly. During the early years Cahan wrote most of the answers personally, finding himself in somewhat the same position Nathanael West would describe in *Miss Lonelyhearts*, a man flooded with the griefs of mankind. Mostly, his answers are admirable for their blend of shrewdness and humaneness. Cahan would draw miniature socialist lessons from the plight of his correspondents, but since he also grasped the immediacies of survival, he sincerely tried to ease their lot. He tells the socialists, yes, it's all right to marry in a synagogue, don't be so stiff-necked. He is a little more cautious about mixed marriages, an explosive subject in 1908, but he ventures to say that sometimes they work out. He pleads with his readers not to torment themselves with rigid formulas of conscience; he speaks for good sense, the value of manners in easing life. Confronted with problems beyond solution, he falls back on his own deep fatalism: *vos vet zayn, vet zayn*, what will be, will be.

Rivals and critics in the Yiddish world would always regard the "Bintel Brief" with contempt, seeing it as the ultimate proof of the *Forward*'s vulgarity. That there was vulgarity in the "Bintel Brief," to say nothing of sentimentalism, it would be pointless to deny. But most of the attacks were misdirected. The "Bintel Brief" served the immigrant world as a collective voice, an academy of manners and forum of opinion, a bulletin board on which to post news of missing husbands or errant wives, a medium of outcry and relief.

Even so unyielding a critic of the *Forward* as Hayim Zhitlovsky, who felt that indulgence of mass tastes was the curse of Yiddish culture, had to acknowledge that the "Bintel Brief"

> satisfied the need of the Jewish radical immigrants to extract some ethical lessons from their muddled experiences. . . . Sex and family problems had not yet been dealt with in Yiddish literature. In a moral crisis the ordinary man was bewildered and anguished. He had lost the old compass of tradi-tional religion, and now had to look to the foggy generalizations of Jewish radicalism and his new synagogue, the *Forward*. . . . Of course, it would have been better if the advice given in the "Bintel Brief" were more serious and on a higher intellectual level.

It was not only as a mirror to their own unexplored experiences that the "Bintel Brief" attracted the immigrants, it was also as a sort of handbook to those themes of romanticism which had just begun to make a shy entrance into Jewish life. The romantic sensibility, flooding Europe for over a cen-tury, had come late to the Jews. It had come with an overlay of Yiddish ethicism and a fringe of Russian high-mindedness. For the east European Jews, romantic love still seemed a daring idea, a fresh path to freedom, not yet turned treacherous by experiment and excess. For the intellectuals, romantic love could also figure as a variant of that higher morality to which free spirits might attach themselves. Not, of course, that the immigrant masses had such abstractions in mind when they read the "Bintel Brief"; to them it served as a source of gossip, advice, and admonition. But in many immigrant houses, the "Bintel Brief" would provide the occasion for a halt-ing discussion of the perennial problems of "men and women," gropings toward that philosophy of personal life which the decay of traditional cer-tainties had made urgent.

In later years the "Bintel Brief" would evoke embarrassment among those immigrants and children of immigrants who aspired toward cultural sophistication and found its pictures of raw experience hard to bear. But such feelings should not keep us from recognizing that if ever the immigrant world spoke directly from the heart, it was through the awkward passionate letters of the "Bintel Brief."

Voice of Immigrant Socialism

The socialism of the *Forward* was a loose, enfolding creed, with many virtues, many sins. If it showed little theoretical sophistication during the years before the First World War, pretty much the same was true for American socialism as a whole. The *Forward* looked for intellectual guidance to the Social Democratic parties of Europe, especially the German party of Bebel and Kautsky, with which it felt more at ease than with the populist fervor and sectarian rectitude that often characterized Debsian socialism in America. One problem the *Forward* could never overcome was that it tried to be a mass socialist paper in a country where there was no mass socialist movement; another, that it tried to yoke the conflicting impulses of its readers toward radical universalism and Jewish national feeling; still a third, that it could not help sharing the ambivalence of proletarian Jewish immigrants toward the American vision of success. Yet precisely insofar as it mirrored these problems and allowed itself to be torn by these contradictions, the *Forward* took on a unique role in the immigrant world, thereby gaining what might be called its Jewish authenticity.

As a sociopolitical force its greatest strength consisted in its close alliance with the Jewish trade unions, to which it frequently gave material help, valuable coverage, and even tactical advice. If one extreme of the paper gathered up *shund* and the other *literatur*, the vital center of the *Forward* lay in its intimate kinship with the immigrant working class. In the 1911 New York tailors' strike, for example, the offices of the *Forward* were converted into a strike headquarters and the staff of the paper placed at the service of the strike.

The socialism of the paper, though it might thin out toward pragmatic reform, also had the force of actuality: reportage of the cloakmakers' strikes, the Triangle fire, the growth and trials of the ILGWU, the struggles of workers in such cities as Philadelphia and Chicago (for which the *Forward* printed special editions), the electoral campaigns of Hillquit and London, the socialist opposition to the First World War, the imprisonment of Eugene Debs, and, later on, the red scares of the twenties, the rise of American Communism, the Sacco-Vanzetti case, and the re-emergence of the garment unions in the thirties. Never quite a party paper, the *Forward* spoke for a powerful segment of the immigrant community, those social democrats who had plunged into the work of building the Jewish unions.

Apart from criticism by left-wing socialists,* which never seriously hindered its growth, the first major political crisis for the *Forward* came during the war years, 1914–1918. At least in the early phase of the war, the

---

* At the 1913 New Haven convention of the Jewish Socialist Federation, a delegation was chosen to deliver a complaint to the editors of the *Forward* that it was neglecting to educate its readers in the spirit of socialism. Speaking for the Federation, Abe Sussman told the *Forward* Association: "As our press grew stronger, there were fewer and fewer Jewish socialists; the richer our press grew, the poorer in moral content become both the press and the movement." These charges created a furor among the *Forward* people, who rejected them as uncomradely, though acknowledging that improvements should be made in the paper's efforts at socialist education.

immigrant Jews, in common with most other ethnic communities in America, tended to see the war as a contest between Russian barbarism and German civilization. A reporter for the *Varheit*, strolling along East Broadway in 1914, heard nothing but curses against Czar Nicholas—testimony especially valuable since the *Varheit* was the only Yiddish paper to support the Allies.

Pro-German feeling spread across most of the Yiddish press. Cahan wrote in the *Forward* that "all civilized peoples sympathize with Germany, every victorious battle against Russia is a source of joy." While Russia had been spilling Jewish blood, Germany "since 1871 had made the greatest progress of all nations in science, in culture, and in the socialist labor movements." So widespread was this feeling that the *Varheit* was forced to change from a pro-Allied policy to one of neutrality.

With their well-earned pacifist impulses and their well-grounded suspicions of the major European powers, a good many immigrant Jews sympathized with those Americans who opposed the Wilsonian drift into the war.

> The *Forward* in the middle months of 1917 was faced with reconciling irreconcilables. As a socialist paper, it gave lip service to the Socialist Party's antiwar stand and the St. Louis resolution [passed at the party's convention in April 1917, it declared "unalterable opposition" to the war in the name of socialist internationalism]. But also, the *Forward* embraced the Russian revolutionary regime [which had overthrown the czar in February 1917]. The presence of the new Russia among the Allies made more credible their claim of waging a war for democracy. . . . Socialists with a burden of responsibility in public life were faced with particularly difficult decisions to reconcile their party views and public obligations.

As public pressure against dissidents kept increasing during the war, more was at stake for the *Forward* than an abstract "position." Its circulation had grown from 20,000 in 1900 to over 130,000 in 1918; it was not merely a socialist but also a Jewish paper; and, apart from a natural wish to preserve itself, the paper had to recognize that its difficulties in Washington affected not merely Jewish socialists but the Jewish community as well. Gradually, with a shrewd evasiveness, it eased away from the antiwar stand of the Socialist party, though never formally repudiating it. On October 5, 1917, the *Forward* nevertheless received a registered letter from the third assistant postmaster general asking it to show cause why its second-class mailing rights should not be revoked. The *Forward* turned in alarm, as east European Jews in trouble often found themselves turning, to Louis Marshall, the German-Jewish leader with an admirable record in support of civil liberties and immigrant rights. Marshall took the case but exacted a heavy price, asking Cahan for "a personal and confidential letter" which he could show the authorities in Washington as a sign that the *Forward* would observe the laws concerning the war and conscription. On October 14 "Cahan said, according to the front page report of the *Forward* . . . that though it would not renounce its convictions, the paper would desist from publishing them: 'Socialists obey the law even if they disagree with it.' "

An informal arrangement was then made whereby the *Forward* maintained its mailing rights and Marshall agreed to act as a sort of unofficial censor of its writings about the war. "He assured [Postmaster] Burleson that he 'carefully scrutinized the *Forward* daily and that Cahan strictly observed the pledge he had made.' "

In the eyes of the left-wing socialists this was a shameful retreat on a point of principle, but as Cahan saw it, he had saved the paper from harassment, perhaps destruction, at the hands of inflamed authorities. Now approaching a circulation of 200,000, the *Forward* could still support, as indeed it did, Socialist antiwar candidates and still come to the aid of Eugene Debs when he was arrested for criticizing the war. This, argued Cahan, counted for more than abstract reiteration of arguments aganst imperialist war. In any case, as a historian of this episode concludes, "Marshall's intercession had the effect of locating the *Forward* in the Jewish community more firmly than in the socialist community. This was actually the role Cahan had long ago selected for the *Forward*, though he might not have avowed it publicly to his comrades."

Another, more startling crisis in the political career of the *Forward*—and one that has often been thrust down "memory hole" by sympathetic historians of the paper—occurred a while after the seizure of power by the Bolsheviks in Russia. Like other socialists throughout the world, Cahan was roused to a pitch of enthusiasm in the early twenties, writing that the Bolshevik revolution constituted a socialist fulfillment of the democratic revolution that had overthrown the czar. It was quite as if Cahan now felt able to revive all those visions of the youth he had forsworn in the wry confession written on his fiftieth birthday.*

Cahan's opening editorial for 1922 hailed the Bolshevik regime as "the heroic defender of the highest human ideals." "There is no difference between the Socialist and Communist parties," he wrote a few weeks later, "and no reason why they should be separate—at least outside Russia." And perhaps his most remarkable defense of the Bolshevik dictatorship came in an article entitled "No Freedom of Speech in Russia: Is That Wrong?" which appeared in January 1922. Conceding that there was no freedom of

---

* In a memoir of Cahan written directly after his death, the Russian Menshevik leader Raphael Abramovitch recalls a meeting in Berlin in 1920. The two men embraced, but before Abramovitch could say a word Cahan burst out, "But you cannot write in the *Forward*." Why? Because "our line on Russia is entirely different from yours." When Abramovitch tried to tell Cahan about the political repressions enacted by the Bolshevik regime, Cahan raised his hands to his ears and shouted, "Don't destroy my illusions, I don't want to hear."

speech or elections in Russia, Cahan argued that "the fruit of the whole revolution would be . . . swept away if [the Bolsheviks] were to allow political freedom." They had done "wonderful things," they could not be "condemned" for their "suppression of the other parties" they were moving from "fanaticism" toward "reason and tolerance." And then he took another, more serious step in his argument: "The Soviet government suppressed the free word and the free vote even worse perhaps than was done by Czar Nicholas. . . . Well, everyone knows that's true. What of it? Russia is ruled by a dictatorship of the Communist party. . . . It's a necessity, and abolishing it would now constitute the greatest danger." In a sequel Cahan appeared to accept the complete Leninist rationale: though he "naturally" found it "very unpleasant" to confess that "a socialist party should powerfully restrict even for a brief period the political life of parties other than the governing one," this was "no great matter," since it was only temporary, "a transitional period . . . [which] is a historical necessity."

The debate over Bolshevism brought the *Forward* to a major crisis. It was not possible to keep these differences locked into the inner circles: polemical articles spilled across the pages of the paper.* Opposition to Cahan was led by Vladimir Medem, a leader of the Bund who had recently arrived from Poland and was acknowledged in all segments of the Jewish world as a figure of moral and intellectual authority. Medem launched a principled attack upon the enthusiasm so many Jewish socialists were displaying for the Bolshevik dictatorship, and he was especially sharp in the polemical assaults he directed against Cahan. Neither before nor since has Cahan been treated so roughly, even unceremoniously, in his own pages. Though other anti-Bolsheviks were briefly kept out of the *Forward* pages, Medem carried too much prestige to be treated that way. A dying man, he wrote scathingly about the Bolsheviks, attacking Lenin as a *kalter gazlen* (a cold-blooded thug). The worst apologists for the Bolshevik dictatorship, he wrote, are not those who deny it is violating socialist or democratic ethics, but those who say, "Yes, they are doing it and it's right." Arguing against Cahan's quasi-Leninist notion of a "transitional" dictatorship, Medem stated what would become the classical socialist critique of Bolshevism:

> This is the same revolutionary conceit which looks upon a cluster of "conscious ones" as the heroes who represent . . . the wise, the adept, the leaders. . . . The mass is nothing but inert material to be molded. If it balks at going along peacefully, then it must be dragged along forcibly. If the truth has no effect upon it, then lies must be employed.
>
> If a reversion to the Spanish Inquisition is necessary for the realization of socialism, then we can do without such a socialism.

---

* A group of six staff members resigned from the paper, aligning themselves with the Jewish Socialist Federation when it proposed to join the Communist International; one of them, Hillel Rogoff, came back to the *Forward* within a few months, not having ventured as far as Communism.

By the middle of 1922 Cahan began to retreat. He was upset by the trials of Mensheviks and Social Revolutionaries that were being staged by the Lenin regime. In autumn 1923, while traveling in Europe, he gained firsthand information about conditions in Soviet Russia, and upon his return took a view indistinguishable from that of Medem: "Russia has at present less freedom than it had in the earliest days of Romanov rule. . . . The world has never yet seen such a despotism." When Medem died, in January 1923, Cahan joined in the eulogies for the Bundist leader—but to acknowledge openly that he had been wrong and Medem right was more than he could then bring himself to do.

Once bitten, forever shy. The *Forward* became an intransigent critic of the Bolshevik regime and the Communist movement, one of the first publications in America to publish facts about Siberian concentration camps, which a good many liberal journals chose to neglect. In the eyes of some leftists, including for a time the followers of Norman Thomas, the *Forward* would even be excessive in its attacks on the Stalin regime; during the thirties it was not at all uncommon for liberals and leftists to compare the paper with the Hearst press because of "anti-Sovietism." In retrospect, it seems clear that the *Forward* performed a valuable service in its insistence upon the integral connection between socialism and democracy. Gradually, to be sure, its socialism faded into Sunday ceremonials, as the socialism of the garment-union leaders faded into pragmatic American politics. With the advent of Franklin Roosevelt's New Deal, the *Forward* became, in effect, an organ of Jewish liberal-labor opinion. Its opposition to Zionism also waned, and, like almost every other Jewish paper, it became a warm, though not uncritical, partisan of the new Jewish state.

A portrait of the *Forward* at the time of its greatest influence and prosperity has been left by Oswald Garrison Villard, the gifted liberal editor. Villard noted in 1922 that

> during the last ten years the *Forward* has earned one and a half million dollars, of which it has, after providing for its splendid up-to-date plant, donated $350,000 to union labor and to other causes for which it battles. Its assets today are worth more than one million dollars. . . . The *Forward* is often a most generous benefactor to struggling talent. There have been cases of foreign writers of promise coming to this country without means, who were not only at once placed on the salary-roll but were told that there was no compulsion upon them to write. Genius, in their cases, did not have to labor at all seasons; its product came when the spirit moved.

Villard went on to describe a typical issue:

> Its eight pages of eight columns each (28 or 32 pages on Sundays) offers a variegated bill of fare. Pictures, of course; occasional cartoons; little of crime (about two columns a day); often sensational matter . . . extraordinarily valuable letters from abroad, together with a great deal of Jewish and labor news, all with Hearst-like headlines. In one week in July 1922 it carried 24

columns of letters and cablegrams from its own correspondents (in eastern Europe). . . . In that same week it carried 154 columns of serious reading matter and 137 columns which can be termed "light matter," though this does not adequately describe it, for while the *Forward* writes down to its readers it is also printing today by far the best fiction and *belles lettres* of any newspaper in America.

For the next half-century the *Forward* remained the largest Yiddish daily in the world, hanging on through accumulated savings and by taking over the readership of lapsed rivals. As it slid into old age, the paper largely ceased being the voice of a distinct political tendency within the Yiddish-speaking world and came instead to speak for the whole of that world, or whatever remained of it.

Other Papers, Other Voices

It would be an exaggeration, but not an outrageous one, to say that the history of the Yiddish press in America consists of the *Forward* first and then all the others. Every Jewish political and cultural group felt obliged to have its own organ; independent entrepreneurs started a number of dailies, most lasting no more than a few years; but none could compete with the *Forward*. Now and then, political figures from the outside tried to penetrate the immigrant milieu by starting papers to gain the support of its voters or to reform them according to some preconception. In 1904 William Randolph Hearst, then still in his phase of populist demagogy, started a daily called the *Yidisher Amerikaner* in the hope of advancing his political ambitions; its nominal editor was one Jacob Pfeffer, over whom Hearst placed an Irish-American reporter to "keep an eye on things"; but the paper collapsed after several weeks, unable to sink roots in the culture it hoped to exploit.

Another, far more significant failure was the *Yidishe Velt* ("Jewish World"), which Louis Marshall set up in 1902 with the help of a phalanx of German-Jewish millionaires (Schiff, Warburg, Guggenheim, Lewisohn, Seligman, Lehman, Bloomingdale, etc.). Perhaps the ultimate presumption in the German-Jewish response to the east European Jews, this paper was started, wrote Marshall in his fund appeal, to be "everything that existing Yiddish newspapers are not, namely, clean, wholesome, religious in tone; the advocate of all that makes good citizenship, and so far as politics are concerned, absolutely independent." Never a man to mince words, Marshall assured his backers that "the people whom I represent are to have control of the newspaper and are to dictate its policy"—a sure guarantee of failure.

For editor Marshall chose Hirsh Masliansky, the Yiddish preacher, and for city editor Philip Krantz, the old socialist journalist. Though staffed by competent men, whose pay ($25 a week minimum) was the highest among Yiddish papers, the *Yidishe Velt* was a fiasco from the start. Its circulation never approached the 20,000 Marshall claimed, and in somewhat less than three years its backers lost over $100,000. The trouble was that its style was too bland for a public that liked its journalism highly seasoned; also, that it advocated "refinement" and gratitude to the *yahudim* (German Jews), which did not exactly endear it to the "uncouth masses." In politics, it propagandized for a civics-lesson "Americanism" and supported the municipal reformers of the Republican party, a group that never would learn to catch the ear of the East Side. Indifferent to Yiddish culture and insensitive to immigrant feelings, the paper came under merciless ridicule from its rivals, the Orthodox *Tageblatt* and the radical *Forward*, both of which, by contrast, sprang organically out of Jewish life. Marshall worked hard on the project, going so far as to learn Yiddish in order to direct his staff more effectively, but his hand was too heavy, his distance too great. At the end, he pleaded with his treasurer, "Let us get rid of this incubus as quickly as possible." Uptown was uptown, downtown downtown, and it would take another half-century in the warmth of affluence before the twain could meet.

Hundreds of Yiddish publications were started during the first two decades of the century—a few of the more interesting ones warrant mention. The *Yidisher Kemfer* ("Jewish Fighter"), a labor Zionist weekly begun in 1906 and still appearing in the 1970's, set a high intellectual tone. The theorist of socialist nationalism, Hayim Zhitlovsky, issued the *Naye Lebn* ("New Life") from 1908 to 1914 as an intellectual periodical. The poet Abraham Reisen edited the *Naye Land* ("New World," 1911–1912) and the *Literarishe Velt* ("Literary World," 1912–1913), cultural journals of some distinction. Under the editorship of Abraham Liessen, the *Tsukunft* ("Future," 1892–   ) became the leading Yiddish monthly, combining socialist reflection with literary breadth. The *Feder* ("Pen," 1919–1953) was a serious literary periodical which printed many of the Yiddish writers who preferred to avoid the dailies. And in a lighter vein, the *Groyser Kundes* ("Big Stick," 1909–1927) would smite each week the growing number of *alrightniks*, lambasting especially the *Forward* as "a fat *parvenu* who has deserted the principles of Karl Marx and defiled the holy temple of Yiddish journalism by becoming popular and yellow."

In the early twenties there were Yiddish dailies in Chicago, Philadelphia, Cleveland, and Montreal, all rather anemic in content and appearance, and unable to compete with the Yiddish papers of New York. Other papers came and went, like the *Tsayt*, a daily sponsored by the Labor Zionists, which struggled along for twenty months with a distinguished writer, David Pinski, as editor but was too elevated in tone and content for a broad readership—"It was like a face with perfect symmetrical features, but wholly without charm," recalled one of its sponsors. The Labor Zionists struggled desperately to keep the *Tsayt* alive. Their leaders went soliciting from house to house, such intellectuals as the Hebraist Nachman Syrkin and the Yiddishist Hayim Zhitlovsky joining in these chores; the considerable sum of $250,000 was collected; "but there was a limit to the capacity for sacrifice of the poor intellectuals and workers who constituted the movement." Syrkin's daughter, Marie, has noted wryly the phases of decline in the life of a paper like the *Tsayt*, and not of that paper alone: "The first was to alarm all adherents and urge further sacrifices. Then all editorial members of the staff slashed their 'salaries'; the only persons exempt from this process were generally the true proletarians, such as the printers, who were protected by unions and brooked no nonsense. The final stage, before the inevitable demise, was characterized by a complete absence of salaries, even slashed ones."

For the Yiddish press as a whole, the decade between the First World War and the Great Depression was the most prosperous. The *Forward* enjoyed a circulation of over 200,000. The *Morgen Zhurnal* ("Morning Journal," 1901–1953), a decent but dull conservative paper with 80,000 readers, supported the Republican party and appealed to Orthodox readers somewhat more literate than those who took the *Tageblatt*. Each morning it would print as many as four to six pages of classified advertisements, ranging from want ads to matrimonials. During the peak of the labor season, its advertising revenues would rise to $3,000 an issue, and in the twenties its annual profit reached between $100,000 and $200,000. The *Tog* ("Day"), started in 1914 as a liberal, nonparty paper leaning toward Zionism, became a respected institution in Yiddish life, second in circulation only to the *Forward*. Toward the end of the First World War, in order to speed news about the fate of Jews stranded in eastern Europe, there was founded the first Yiddish press service, the Jewish Telegraphic Agency, which expanded and professionalized the foreign coverage of the Yiddish press—for immigrants always a matter of acute interest.

The Time of the Day

By modern American standards, say, those of the New York *Times* and Washington *Post*, the most satisfactory Yiddish paper was the *Day*. It came at a time when some immigrant Jews were beginning to move beyond stale battles between Orthodox and secularist Jews; it sought a greater freedom for diverse opinions than could be found in the other papers; it provided news with reasonable objectivity; and it used a "medium" Yiddish, free of old-country meanderings but also not quite so sparse and "Americanized" as that of the *Forward*. In its early years the *Day* appealed to the more literate segments of the Yiddish public, those that cared for the Yiddish tradition but were moving away from fixed ideological stances. In 1918 it took over

Louis Miller's *Varheit*, an erratic sheet that had wandered from left social-ism to left Tammanyism; the merger provided the once-fiery Miller with a roost for his declining years and the *Day* with a wider base of readers. Staking out a middle position—liberal but not radical, respectful toward religion but not pious, friendly to Zionism but not tied to any faction—the *Day* faithfully reflected the gradual fading of ideological passions in immi-grant Jewish life.

Eclectic by necessity, it lined up for its more serious pages intellectual figures like the Zionist theoretician Syrkin, the nationalist-Yiddishist Zhit-lovsky, the littérateur Abraham Koralnik, and a range of Yiddish writers from Joseph Opatashu to Peretz Hirshbein. Its cultural department was for many years the best in the Yiddish press, with S. Niger's weekly articles offering an authoritative, scholarly gloss on Yiddish literature. (All Yiddish papers tried to provide more or less serious reviews of literature and theatre; their coverage of art and music, perhaps because these were of less interest to their readers, ranged from dilettantish to invisible.) The single most distinguished literary contribution of the *Day* was its serial publication from 1922 through 1927 of a Yiddish version of the Bible by the poet Yehoash.

Forced, like every paper, to search for a wider audience, the *Day* gradually made concessions to popular tastes, never quite in the sensational-istic way of the *Forward* but quite enough to irritate the Yiddish intelli-gentsia. Though its column "Mener un Froyn" ("Men and Women") could never compete with the *Forward*'s "Bintel Brief," it offered other attrac-tions to ordinary readers. Joel Slonim, in his spare time a Yiddish poet, wrote highly charged crime reportage for the *Day*. Slonim brought a new rhythm to Yiddish journalism: rapid, staccato sentences, without embellish-ment, as "punchy" as if written for the *Daily News*. He would mix portraits of veteran Irish gangsters with sketches of Hasidim, pieces about fighters like Jack Dempsey with articles about a rich Chicago girl, Jewish of course, who married a "baron" of the underworld and at the wedding had to pay off twenty-five of his former sweethearts. As no other Yiddish reporter, Slonim knew his way around the underworld and city hall. Flanking his crime pieces were such favorites as Jean Jaffe, the first major woman re-porter on the Yiddish press, who traveled around the world, describing places like India and Japan for readers who might be a little foggy as to where they were, joining a group of Yemenite Jews as they fled from Aden to Palestine, and doing pieces for the woman's page; Lazer Borodulin, who provided a weekly compost of science information;* and Henokh Acker-

* Borodulin was also the first, perhaps the last, author of science fiction in Yiddish. In 1929 he published a book about the search of a Yiddish reporter for a scientist named Berger who had perfected a death ray and vanished with a red-haired girl across the Sambatyon River, where, legend has it, live the *royte yidelekh*, or the tribe of missing "red Jews." The land of these *royte yidelekh* is run by "antigravity magnets," but, in accord with Jewish legend, the Sambatyon "rested all day on the Sabbath."

man, described by a colleague as "a frustrated poet," who specialized in "Amazing Stories of Real Life," written with a rich quotient of tears (also real names and addresses attached): "He Found His Wife's Picture in a Strange Man's House—and This Revealed a Remarkable Story"; "A Story About a Poor Doctor, His Beautiful Wife, Her Wealthy Stepfather—and a Meeting in a Hospital." Toward the end of his career, Ackerman, running dry of material and/or invention, began to rewrite his earlier stories—how many kinds of Jewish suffering can there be?—but his readers, blessed with long memories, sent in letters of indignant complaint.

Perhaps the most valuable property the *Day* ever had was Sarah Bronstein Smith, queen of the *shundroman* (soap-opera serial). Arriving in the United States at the age of fifteen, she worked for a while in a sweatshop, made her literary debut in the *Forward* in 1908, and became a reporter for the *Morning Journal* later that year. When the *Day* started publication, she soon joined its staff and remained with it for decades. Tone-deaf to Yiddish, wonderfully humorless, yet with an eye that quickly got to the heart of the lurid, Mrs. Smith turned out quick sketches of courtroom scenes, later collecting them in a book called *Ver iz shuldig?* ("Who Is Guilty?"), a monotone of horrors about a mother strangling her offspring, an engineer killing his wife because she mocks his taste in music, a madam crying out to the court, "You punish me in public and kiss me in private." Graduating to serials, Mrs. Smith published at least a dozen of them in the *Day*, as well as hundreds of shorter fictions, all spiced, sentimental, and ardently moralistic.

A typical serial, *Di froy in keytn* ("Woman in Chains") tells the story of Frieda Sherman-Gilbert, who, after five years of marriage, feels trapped: "He has grown cold to her." Frieda leaves Eddie in search of "a new life," and Eddie, while sending her ten dollars a week to feed the kids, also starts looking for that scarce commodity. After sufficient tribulations, Frieda gains success as a playwright, yet all turns to ashes in her mouth when she learns that Eddie is sick. She rushes off to him, and there is a hospital reconciliation. Notable moments in this work include Frieda's reflection that most of the women she knows buy their husbands supper in a delicatessen yet are "worshiped by them," while she "prepares a good meal every night but all I get from my husband is a grunt." Mrs. Smith, evidently abreast of modernist literature, knew that such matters as sexual malaise could excite readers to whom it was still an embarrassing subject: "Frieda was terrified of his embraces. The last few years she tried to avoid lovemaking. At night she would curl up tight so as not to touch or awaken him." At the end, "the clear blue sky brought them peace. Gratefully, his weak fingers tried to press hers." Like many such productions, Mrs. Smith's serials touched upon genuine problems and yearnings in the lives of her readers. Over the years she remained a steady feature of the *Day*, no doubt attracting far more readers than those who cared to follow Zhitlovsky on the dialectics of culture or Niger on literary trends.

A sense of the *Day* as a newspaper, indeed, of the Yiddish press as a whole, may be gained by glancing at the contents of three issues from different years:

November 15, 1914

Lead story: the Leo Frank case in Georgia, a young Jewish man accused of murder (later to be lynched), reported with reasonable objectivity. Straight news about the European war. Shorter items about Jewish workers trying to organize their own bank, plans for expanding a Brownsville Talmud Torah, and so on. A full page ad for Ruppert's beer, stressing its "digestive and nutritive value." Editorial on helping war-stranded Jews in Russia. Article by Zhitlovsky, "The war is really a struggle between German militarism and Russian czarism. Whoever wins, it will be a disaster; whoever loses, a cause for rejoicing." (This was not the line of the *Day*, but writers like Zhitlovsky and the ex-anarchist Zolatoroff were given considerable freedom.) A poem by Moshe Leib Halpern. A translation of Zola, "The War at the Mill." A chapter from the *shundroman Der royter sod* ("The Red Secret"). A human-interest page: "She Can't Be a Teacher Because She Is a Mother." A regular feature, "Ziftsn fun der alter heym" ("Sighs from the Old Country"), in which readers send in letters they have received from European relatives about pogroms and suffering. Some jokes and classified ads.

January 19, 1920

Front-page stories on efforts to expel Socialists from New York State Assembly, and political news in Europe. A Copenhagen correspondent writes that Gorky, Lenin, and Luncharsky have set up a committee "to combat anti-Semitism in the Soviet Union." Flu epidemic in Chicago. News from the front in the Russian civil war. Editorial on Clemenceau's fall in France. Feature articles by Isaac Hourwich on Lloyd George and the Irish problem, Abraham Koralnik on his travels in America. The human-interest page: "Why Jews Hate Apostates." The *shundroman*: Leon Kobrin's *The Awakening*, about Annie, in love with a gentile boy, but Rabbi Bernstein persuades her to break off, and though she takes piano lessons, she remains restless. *Feuilletons*, humor, ads.

January 6, 1935

Main headline on the Lindbergh kidnap trial. Other news about plea from Polish Jews for help, Roosevelt's conference with congressional leaders on jobs. Editorial: "Roosevelt is All Talk and No Action." Feature articles include Zhitlovsky on religion and Communism in Poland, Borodulin on the black widow spider ("the most dangerous of all"), Koralnik celebrating an anniversary of a novel by Mendele, Niger reviewing the collected stories of the immigrant Yiddish writer Libin. On the women's page Jean Jaffe talks about how to lose weight, false eyelashes, new types of plastic tablecloths, and Dina Jones (obviously a pseudonym) discusses the new fashions. The usual serials, community news, labor reports, and ads for Ex-Lax, corsets, the French lines, and so on.

The *Day*, which came to an end in 1971 because of a steady loss of readers, was never so brilliant a paper as the *Forward*, but neither was it ever as scandalous. From a study of the *Forward* one could extract an impressionistic, not always reliable, but wonderfully rich portrait of immigrant life. Hardly so from the *Day*, which was more respectable, timid, and bourgeois. But as the years went on, the differences between the papers narrowed, each finding it necessary to move a little closer to the other. When the *Day* collapsed, most of its readers turned to the *Forward*: the ideological disagreements had gradually faded, and, in any case, the *Forward* was now the only remaining Yiddish daily.

Writing to the End

By early 1974 the *Forward* decided, as most of its readers had many years earlier, that it was time to move. East Broadway was no longer the thoroughfare of the Yiddish intelligentsia, it was a street where aging staff members felt uncomfortable, even fearful. The plan was to join with other Yiddish-speaking groups, like the Workmen's Circle, to set up a new center in mid-Manhattan. Meanwhile, the *Forward* continued to be edited from the ninth floor of 175 East Broadway, a shabby place with little cubicles in which the staff members write their pieces. On the tenth floor is the composing room, where some fourteen or fifteen linotype and Ludlow machines eject Yiddish type and elderly compositors make up the pages.

In the flush years when Abraham Cahan edited the paper, half a century ago, the *Forward* had as many as seventy-five regular staff members; later, when Hillel Rogoff took over, there were about forty. Now there are twenty-two, not all in the best of health or able to put in a full day's work. Still, the paper gets written and printed: on weekdays eight pages, on Fridays twelve to sixteen, on Sundays twenty to twenty-four. It does not appear on Saturdays, says its editor, Simon Weber, simply because there is no longer enough strength to do the job.

Filling up even eight pages with readable material is hard. Each man knows his task: writing editorials, covering the Jewish trade unions, reviewing the occasional Yiddish play, collecting news items about the fraternal societies. The newsroom, which has teletype machines from United Press International and the Jewish Telegraphic Agency, is staffed by three regulars and headed by Meyer Shtiker, an experienced journalist who is also a gifted Yiddish poet and translator of T. S. Eliot. These men are responsible for the front and back pages of the paper, and they know just how to take an English-language dispatch and boil it down into a concise Yiddish item. To a reader accustomed to the generosity, or verbosity, of the New York *Times*, the *Forward*'s news coverage must seem skimpy, but the gist of things does get printed and other portions of the news are discussed in the feature articles. On Sundays there is a weekly summary, done with reasonable skill. Except when Jewish passions are deeply involved, as with warfare in the Middle East, the *Forward* news coverage is objective in content and tone.

The remaining six pages consist of advertisements (increasingly hard to get); a regular section of labor news (by no means as acute as it once was and too often, now, mere publicity for Jewish union leaders); theatre and movie reviews (undistinguished); several serial fictions, ranging from old-style *shund* to the brilliant work of Isaac Bashevis Singer, who keeps sending in stories in a neat Yiddish script across half-sheets of paper. The "Bintel Brief" still appears each day, more of a habit than a vital feature. Editorials are taken seriously at the *Forward* and are apparently still scanned for political guidance by at least some of its readers; each morning Weber and his assistant, David Mattes, discuss which subjects are appropriate and which position to take.

Most of the paper—this has always been true of Yiddish journalism—consists of feature articles, about two columns in length, or thirteen to fourteen hundred words. Weber estimates that with his enlarged Friday and Sunday editions he needs about seventy-five such pieces a week. That all of even most of these should be of high quality is clearly impossible, and both editors and staff members, whose sense of irony has not been dulled by the passage of the years, admit that a fair portion of what gets printed is poor stuff and would never have been accepted twenty-five or thirty years ago. But there is no choice: talent, scarce, grows scarcer each year.

Some features are done by outside contributors. Mordche Shtrigler, an astonishingly prolific writer who also edits (and writes most of) the weekly *Yidisher Kemfer*, sends three pieces a week to the *Forward*, often dealing with Yiddish language, Jewish traditions, and the like, topics about which he is learned. Joseph Mlotek runs a weekly page called "Pearls of Yiddish Poetry," in which he reprints forgotten Yiddish verse, some of it sent in by readers whose memories have been stirred. Chaim Grade, a distinguished Yiddish poet and novelist, contributes a piece of fiction each Sunday—he shifted to the *Forward* when the *Day* ceased to publish. And there is a good deal of correspondence from abroad: Paris, London, Buenos Aires, and of course Israel.

Like most Yiddish periodicals, the *Forward* has largely abandoned its earlier political identity—whatever appears in its pages about socialism is likely to be reminiscence or ceremonial. Sheer necessity has transformed it into a general Yiddish paper that must satisfy the needs of the entire spectrum of Yiddish readers. And the one concern all of them share is Israel. The *Forward* has two regular correspondents in Israel, as well as a number of occasional contributors. One correspondent, M. Tsanin, is a writer of some force and independence who does not hesitate to criticize the Israeli leadership, though of course from a pro-Israeli perspective. Complaints occasionally come from readers, but Weber prints Tsanin because "he is intelligent and writes fluent Yiddish."

The paper claims a bit more than fifty thousand readers, most of them elderly, some middle-aged, very few young. Each year the circulation drops by a predictable fraction, and within perhaps seven or eight years the gains that followed the closing of the *Day* will have been lost. It is not uncommon for the *Forward* to receive a letter in English from a son or daughter asking that a subscription be canceled because an aging parent can no longer see well enough to read the paper. No one pretends that the paper is still what it used to be: it is neither as good nor as bad, neither as brilliant nor as cheap. The readers continue to be loyal, perhaps because the mere sight of Yiddish in print brings them pleasure and reassurance, and more and more of them send in their forty dollars a year for mail subscriptions to California and Florida. By now the paper runs on a deficit, but the *Forward* Association's careful investments over the years have yielded enough returns to make up the losses.

How long can this go on? To hear that question over and over again must weary the *Forward* writers, yet they remain courteous when it is asked. It is, after all, the question of their lives. To make one's way around the ninth floor on East Broadway, from Weber's office to Shtiker's newsroom to the cubicle in which Isaac Metzker writes up his reports of Jewish social agencies, is to meet with the same sense of reaching an end, the same wry yet mutedly urgent replies, and even the same remark that everyone attributes to Abraham Cahan: that the death of the Yiddish press will come not from a lack of readers but from a lack of writers. And so, no doubt, it will be.

4

DISPERSION

CHAPTER SEVENTEEN

Journeys Outward

THE DISPERSION of the immigrant Jews began the very day they started shaping themselves into a community. In the act of creating their own subculture lay the certainty of sharing a later dispersion. This did not mean ceasing to be a Jew or to identify with Jewish interests; it did not even mean ceasing to live among Jews. It meant, simply, moving away. Moving away from immigrant neighborhoods in which Yiddish still prevailed; moving away from parents whose will to success could unnerve the most successful sons and daughters; moving to "another kind" of Jewish neighborhood, more pleasing in its physical look and allowing a larger area of personal space; and moving toward new social arrangements: the calm of a suburb, the comfort of affluence, the novelty of bohemia.

All this, which it had set into motion through its own will, the East Side watched with an uneasy pride. It was unable, in any case, to stop or impede these changes. For the stronger the immigrant culture felt itself to be, the more certain became the flight of its offspring.

Some of them, talented and articulate, fled toward various arenas of American culture, coming to represent or anticipate the trends of immigrant life. Our interest, in the pages that follow, is not to provide histories, even in miniature, of the American Jewish entertainers, or the American Jewish painters, or the American Jewish novelists and intellectuals; it is to trace a curve of their journeys in the hope of illuminating the larger motions of immigrant dispersion.

Entertainers and Popular Artists

In every gang of kids spilling onto the Jewish streets of 1900 or 1905—kids whose mothers hoped they would grow up to become manufacturers, accountants, and doctors—there was bound to be one who dreamed of "breaking in" with a comic act or vaudeville troupe. It was a desire that often left him uneasy: try explaining to immigrant parents that their darling son wants to become a "bum" who cracks jokes in gentile theatres!

So he kept to the streets, where he could evade the nagging of his parents and enjoy the bubbling of immigrant life. He didn't care for school, though he was bright enough, and he didn't read much, preferring to nurture his own fantasies. What he wanted was to get moving while his limbs were agile and his appetites sharp.

He traveled light. Jewish woes, ideals, inhibitions seem to have left him untroubled. To sweat in a garment shop, even as a boss, or shout oneself hoarse on a soapbox: that was how the older Jews dribbled away their lives. He had other ideas. The world was an arena for pleasure, with its theatres, money, and women, and meanwhile, since he had to keep living in the slums, he practiced his routines, watched the professionals in the theatres,* and made the streets his stage.

The proliferation of entertainers—comics, singers, dancers—in the immigrant and other Jewish neighborhoods is a remarkable fact. There are the famous or once-famous names: Al Jolson, George Jessel, Eddie Cantor, Sophie Tucker, Fanny Brice, Ben Blue, Jack Benny, George Burns, George Sidney, Milton Berle, Ted Lewis, Bennie Fields, many others. And there are the hundreds who played the small towns, the ratty theatres, the Orpheum circuit, the Catskills, the smelly houses in Brooklyn and the Bronx.

How are we to explain this explosion of popular talent among the immigrant Jews? The immediate Yiddish past offered some models—the *badkhn*, the jester, the fiddler, the stage comedian—but while providing sources of material, these figures were not nearly so consequential in old-country Jewish life as the entertainers were to become in America. Some-

---

* "I went to all the shows, no charge," said Eddie Cantor. "I'd just hang around till intermission, then the crowds would come out and I'd go in. I never saw the first act of anything."

thing must have happened in the American ghettos to spring new gifts or release old ones.

One clue, simple but not to be underestimated, is that by the early 1900's a good portion of the theatrical business in New York, and some of it beyond, had fallen into Jewish hands: first the Klaw and Erlanger "syndicate," which had rationalized the booking system and tied up scores of theatres throughout the country, and then the new dynasty of the Schubert brothers, east European Jews with a coarse hunger for success and few scruples in their climb to reach it, who competed with "the syndicate" while also forming alliances with parts of it. In vaudeville the powerful Orpheum circuit was in Jewish hands, and two Jewish furriers named Marcus Loew and Adolph Zukor, together with Joseph and Nicholas Schenck—all to become major figures in the Hollywood film industry—started a people's Vaudeville Circuit in 1909, consisting of two theatres in Brooklyn and two in New Jersey.

These were years in which vaudeville was enormously popular, a major form of American entertainment always needing replenished talent or whatever rough approximations could be passed off on the smaller towns. Because many of the booking agents and stage managers were themselves Jews, an Eddie Cantor or Fanny Brice trying to break into show business didn't have to worry about prejudice.* Besides, the people who would be auditioning them didn't care whether Cantor was a Jew or a Buddhist, Brice an agnostic or a Presbyterian, just as long as they could "put across" a song and tell a funny story. The easygoing cynicism prevailing in this milieu had certain moral advantages: it brushed aside claims of rank and looked only for the immediate promise of talent. Just as blacks would later turn to baseball and basketball knowing that here at least their skin color counted for less than their skills, so in the early 1900's young Jews broke into vaudeville because here too people asked not, who are you? but, what can you do? It was a roughneck sort of egalitarianism, with little concern for those who might go under, but at best it gave people a chance to show their gifts.

There must have been other, deeper reasons for the Jewish plunge into entertainment, though about these we can only speculate. Among the "common," unlearned Jews who came to America, energies were released at least as much as among the learned—and not only energies, but ambitions and yearnings. Between the careers of Al Jolson, singing "Mammy" in blackface, and Morris Raphael Cohen, lecturing on Spinoza, parallels can be drawn

---

* Or about the little dodges Jews took for granted other Jews had to use. "One afternoon we were interviewing the leader of a Hawaiian band we wanted to book. . . . I [A. J. Balaban] ardently wished to present this foreign novelty but the price was too high. The leader, in very hesitant, broken English tried to impress us with the enormous investment he had in the men of this orchestra brought so far from their homeland. . . . I took a long chance and threw a question at him. 'Kennst redin Yiddish?' (Can you speak Jewish?) 'Geviss,' he answered just as quickly and in a natural New Yorker's tone, without a trace of an Hawaiian accent. We quickly came to terms, complimenting him on his ability to impersonate."

which neither might care to notice but which time has made clear: drives toward perfection of work and ackowledgement in the world. What the intellectually ambitious Jews looked for in the schools, others were finding in the streets.

The streets are crucial. Forming each day a great fair of Jewish life, they became the training ground for Jewish actors, comics, and singers. You mimicked the hoity-toity Irish teacher who recited Browning in high school, you mocked the snarling rabbi who bored you in Hebrew school, and it made your friends hop with glee. Especially if you were a little fellow and not so good at stickball, you could gain attention by comic bits, sassy songs, crazy antics, dirty stories. If your father was a cantor—Al Jolson's was; so were George Gershwin's, the songwriter Harold Arlen's, and Eddie Cantor's (part time)—you could imitate and parody his chanting, as if uncertain which might come in more handy, the imitating or the parodying.

Ill-lettered Jews, those condescended to in Yiddish as *di proste*, had been held in check too long by the repressiveness of old-world moralism and the system of "respect" for learning. Now, in America, it was their turn—still more, the turn of their sons and daughters. Full of sap, excited by the sheer volume of street noise, letting loose sexual curiosities beyond the clamp of Jewish shame, these kids became taxicab drivers, bookies, hoofers, comics, sometimes prize fighters. A long-contained vulgarity, which had already come to form a vital portion of Yiddish culture in eastern Europe as a challenge to rabbinic denial and *shtetl* smugness, now broke through the skin of immigrant life. It was a vulgarity in both senses: as the urgent, juicy thrust of desire, intent upon seizing life by the throat, and as the cheap, corner-of-the-mouth retailing of Yiddish obscenities. It may be easy to separate these kinds of vulgarity when talking about them, but in life it was not. The budding comics and entertainers, eager to make "the big time" and impatient with customary refinements of taste, were ready to employ either kind of vulgarity—since they were themselves a compound of both—in order to hold an audience, first on the stoops and sidewalks, later in vaudeville and legitimate theatres.

In his teens George Burns started the Pee Wee Quartette with three other Jewish boys, singing in back yards and saloons and afterward passing the hat. "We rotated the job of hat passer because we didn't trust each other." At Hamilton Fish Park, "where all the great buck [tap] dancers started," Burns would watch the kids showing each other steps "and wish I could do it." George Jessel was brought by his grandfather Simon Schwartz to a lodge meeting, where he sang, before an audience sipping tea and gossiping, "Every Morn I Bring Thee Violets" and "I'm Afraid to Go Home in the Dark." Fanny Brice ran her first show in a shed on St. Marks Avenue in Brooklyn, charging a penny admission. When she had accumulated twenty pennies, she draped a shawl over her head, proclaiming she was an old Jewish lady alone on a bridge at midnight with a hungry baby, and started wailing that she had no money for milk or coal. It was all in the Jewish tradition, with generous tears. Al Jolson, often hungry as a boy, would go to a Bowery restaurant called McGirk's, sing "Rosie, You Are My Posie," and win a free meal from the owner. For a good many of the Jewish entertainers, there was an intermediate stop between the streets and the theaters—working in the summers at Jewish hotels in the Catskills as a "social director" or in a modest touring company, where they could sharpen their jokes and spill into pungent, or vulgar, Yiddishisms. The "Borsht Belt" would later serve numerous comedians as a kind of minor-league training for major success.

Joe Sulzer, later Smith in the Smith and Dale comedy team, grew up on the East Side during the 1890's and in his deep old age would remember the neighborhood as the matrix of almost all his work:

> A colored fellow used to come and dance on our street. It was called buck dancing. He had sand and threw it on the sidewalk and danced. The sound of the sand and the shuffle of his feet fascinated me and I would try to dance like him. It made me feel I wanted to go on the stage. I was then seven years old. I kept practicing dancing, and I also used to practice juggling—a fork and a knife and an apple over my bed.
>
> Later on, I'd go to the Gaiety Museum, where Dave Posner was the manager. There were freaks there, and I used to run errands for them . . . get them coffee and stuff. The freaks included a fire-eater, a strong man, two giant sisters, a big-lipped Ubangi, midgets, and a fat woman. I loved to hang around there.
>
> I kept practicing dancing. I could do little steps but couldn't do a break. When you can break, you can improvise. At nine I borrowed my brother's long pants and went to the Broadway Theatre on the Bowery. I'd try to imitate what I saw. I kept it up, going to different shows.
>
> When I was fourteen, I met my partner, Dale, on Delancey Street. At the time he was Marks and I was Sulzer. He could dance and I had already sung at the University Street Settlement, so the two of us started hanging around together.
>
> We'd pick up routines from the street. Charlie was real good at it. He'd see a guy with a watermelon and before you know it, he'd be doing funny things with that watermelon. We stayed out as long as we wanted. Even if I was away a couple of nights, no one knew the difference. There were thirteen of us in the family!
>
> Later on, Charlie and I would go to Tony Pastor's on Fourteenth Street and watch the acts. Our favorites were Montgomery and Stone. They were big at the time. We got some patter from them, blackened up, and tried out our stuff in front of a shoeshine parlor on Delancey Street. Soon this guy comes over and says, "Hey, you wanna do a stag?" This was in 1899. I says, sure, OK, and we do it. I guess you might say this was our first break.

Of all the stars-to-be, Eddie Cantor was the one who made the richest use of the Jewish streets. With an urchin's spontaneity he thought up pranks and miniature skits, collecting a crowd on Henry Street for the sheer pleasure of it; sometimes he would "hang myself from the street lamps to make the kids laugh"; at P.S. 177 he sang "My Mariuch She Took-a de Steamboat" for a playground concert. Sent to a camp for poor children at Surprise Lake, Eddie recited "The Traitor's Deathbed" and "The Soul of the Violin," meaning to be intensely dramatic, but through his grimaces and rolling of eyes, evoking mere laughter. That was the point in his career where he switched from tragedian to comedian. And when his first big chance came, it was also on the streets: Roy Arthur of nearby Jefferson Street had gotten a job with a team of jugglers and after strolling over one afternoon to watch Eddie do his bit on Henry Street, he told Eddie to drop in at his agent next week for a tryout.

The Jolsons, Burnses, and Brices worked very hard to learn their craft, but when it came to ordinary jobs, what their parents would have called honest work, they were not so reliable. When George Burns got a job at the Borgenicht and Kornreich dress factory, he was fired because he entertained the girl operators at lunchtime with songs and dances. Hopelessly "fresh," Eddie Cantor "didn't seem to fit in" when he went to work as a shipping clerk. "I was always trying to be funny, even in the midst of such grave matters as mailing market letters and hanging clothes." One day the boss yelled, "Get that pop-eyed guy outta here!" A few Jewish entertainers drifted to the edge of delinquency in their adolescence, Fanny Brice shoplifting, George Burns doing errands for a saloon run by a gangster called "Big Puss" (who once asked for help with a job of murder, which George prudently declined), and Eddie Cantor teaming up with some street gangs. But these people were not really cut out for crime. What they wanted was adventure, excitement, changes of scene, rapidity of experience. In their rebellion against the respectability of immigrant Jewish life, they brushed for a moment or two against its delinquent depths, but their sights were elsewhere.

Wheedling auditions through stubbornness and luck, they began to perform for money. At fifteen Groucho Marx answered an ad saying a boy singer was wanted in a vaudeville act, at four dollars a week; he went to the address given, was met by a "hook-nosed, middle-aged man in a blue kimono, wearing just a touch of lipstick on his thin lips," who went by the name of Robin Larong. Hired because he sang "Love Me and the World Is Mine" to Larong's satisfaction, Groucho rehearsed with him for two weeks on a tenement roof, went off on a disastrous two-week tour, and then was left stranded in a small Michigan town. But he hardly cared: he was now an actor. George Burns's Pee Wee Quartette was

> booked for amateur night at the Cannon Street picture house . . . we were torn between being thrilled to death and scared to death, not of the audience, but of the men in the front row whose job it was to get you off the stage if you laid an egg. They didn't use a hook the way most theatres did then; they

used a long pole with a hoop on the end. They would drop this over you like
a butterfly net and drag you off the footlights.

Sophie Tucker had one of her first engagements at a "little ten-cent theatre
owned by Lowe, Zucker, and Schenck at 116th Street and Lenox Avenue.
. . . All they showed was a one-reel slapstick comedy and me in blackface
for the ten afternoon shows, and whiteface for the ten night shows. Twenty
shows a day for a salary of twenty dollars a week." Eddie Cantor arranged
with a pal "to play at weddings, bar mitzvahs, club socials, local theatricals.
. . . Joe Welch's line always served as a handy opening. It appeared funny
for a young boy with a beard to shake his head gravely and say, 'If I had my
life to live over again I wouldn't be born.' " Becoming a professional trouper
meant an endless grind of touring, at least for those who got beyond the
semiprofessional class. At thirteen Walter Winchell, tenor of the "Imperial
Trio" ("The Little Men with Big Voices") barnstormed across the country
for months, learning "how to dodge the authorities hunting for child performers, how to make his meal allowance stretch, how to save on rent by
sharing a room with a girl performer on the same circuit." For a Jewish boy
or girl from New York it meant discovering a whole new way of living,
indeed, a whole new country.

Cheerfully eclectic, untroubled by "artistic" notions or rigid conventions, ready to take a crack at whatever they could get to do, the young
Jewish entertainers filched a little here and patched a little there, only
gradually coming toward a style or styles of their own. They did "Dutch"
(German) dialect routines, Irish imitations, Yiddish parodies, blackface,
slapstick, sentimental ballads, standard hoofing, a little ragtime. By the turn
of the century there was an established tradition of "Hebe" comedians (see
p. 401), most of whom had simply appropriated the earlier modes of
"Dutch" humor. Growing up in an immigrant neighborhood made one
familiar with a fine variety of accents, so that the young entertainers coming
out of the East Side or its equivalents were prepared for the kinds of ethnic
humor popular in American vaudeville during the early years of the century. But Yiddish didn't really come into its own as a source of humor—
sometimes of smut—until the generation of Jolson, Tucker, and Jessel.
Sophie Tucker knew that in certain theatres, year after year, she could
always bring down the house by ending her act with "My Yiddishe Mama."
One evening Eddie Cantor found that an English routine had fallen completely flat at an East Side performance simply because the audience didn't
know English; the next night he put the whole thing into Yiddish and won
"shouts of approval."

The eclecticism of the aspiring Jewish entertainers, their readiness to
try "almost anything," was particularly striking in the career of the songwriter Irving Berlin. In 1909 he wrote "Sadie Salome" (a song about a
Jewish girl who left her "happy home," went on stage, and was implored by
her sweetheart Mose, "Don't do that dance, I tell you Sadie/ That's not a

bus'ness for a lady!/' Most e'rybody knows/ That I'm your loving Mose/ Oy, oy, oy, oy—where is your clothes?") That same year he also wrote "I Wish That You Was My Gal, Molly," with an Irish motif; "Dorando," a topical song in Italian dialect; and "Oh! How That German Could Love." In 1910 he published "Colored Romeo," a mock-black song; "Yiddishe Eyes"; "Yiddle on Your Fiddle (Play Some Ragtime)"; and "Good-Bye Becky Cohen." Becky's boyfriend says he's going off to war and Becky replies: "what, fight for nothing/ Where's the percentage in that?/ No, you better mind your store/ Let McCarthy go to war." And "Yiddishe Eyes" has for its chorus:

> Oy, oy, oy, those Yiddishe eyes, Benny had those Yiddishe eyes,
> That shone so bright with an Israel light:
> Eyes that could tell a diamond in the night.
> Oy, oy, oy, those Yiddishe eyes, Benny had those Yiddishe eyes,
> He took a look in her bankbook with his Yiddishe eyes.

Some of these songs, which later generations might find troubling, were beamed to Jewish audiences. "A sure-fire hit in Jewish neighborhoods," writes Carrie Balaban in her reminiscences about the early years of vaudeville, "was 'Nathan, Nathan, Tell Me Vot Are You Vaitin', Nathan." While Yiddish theatre usually found its richest materials in the Jewish past, the American Jewish entertainers were more at ease with their immediate moment: courting in broken English, poking fun at accents, acquiescing, a little mindlessly, in the common notions about sharp business practices among Jews. (Forty-five years later Irving Berlin wrote in a letter to Groucho Marx, "there are some songs I would be tempted to pay you not to do," since, he said, they would no longer be taken in the spirit in which they had been written.)

Even as this generation of performers was unmistakably Jewish and defined itself at least in part through the cultural symbols and references of Yiddish, much of its early success was gained from acts done in blackface. A considerable tradition of blackface entertainment preceded the rise of the Jewish performers, but by about 1910 they had taken it over almost entirely, making it one of their specialties and endowing it with a flavor of their own. Irving Berlin scored his first success as a songwriter with a blackface tune, "Alexander's Ragtime Band"; Al Jolson made blackface recital the foundation of a spectacular career, mostly on stage and then in the movies; Sophie Tucker was billed as the "World-Renowned Coon Shouter" or, in a more refined version, "Manipulator of Coon Melodies"; Eddie Cantor "played Salome (still in blackface)," combining racial impersonation with a veiled transvestite burlesque; George Burns "had seen Jolson and I figured if he was a hit with a big wide mouth, I'd be a riot with a bigger one"; George Jessel toured for a long time, sometimes together with Cantor, in a blackface routine. Later, when Al Jolson made *The Jazz Singer*, the first American talking picture, he brought together—for him, a quite natural thing to do—Yiddish shmaltz and blackface sentiment in a story about a successful American singer, son of a cantor, who returns to the East Side to chant the Kol Nidre while his father lies dying.

Perhaps it was no more than shrewd opportunism, an eagerness to give audiences exactly what they seemed to want, which led so many Jewish entertainers to work in blackface; but it is hard to resist the impression that some deeper affinity was also at work. Ronald Sanders, in a fine study, has suggested that blackface provided "a kind of Jewish musical fulfillment" through a strain of "ethnic pastiche." When they took over the conventions of ethnic mimicry, the Jewish performers transformed it into something emotionally richer and more humane. Black became a mask for Jewish expressiveness, with one woe speaking through the voice of another. Irving Berlin inserted Yiddishisms into songs deriving from "coon song" conventions; Sophie Tucker "started interpolating Jewish words in some of my songs, just to give the audience a kick"; George Gershwin, more subtly, blended Yiddish folk tunes and black melodies into a blue union. (Gershwin's biographer, Isaac Goldberg, found a musical kinship between the "Negro blue note" and the "blue note" of Hasidic chant. Put Yiddish and black together, he wrote, "and they spell Al Jolson.") "The great American tradition of ethnic pastiche," continues Sanders, "had by now [c. 1910] become a Jewish specialty. . . . Pastiche is a gift of peoples who live in culturally ambivalent situations."

Blacking their faces seems to have enabled the Jewish performers to reach a spontaneity and assertiveness in the declaration of their Jewish selves. ("Was this the only way Al Jolson could have gotten his intense Jewish shmaltz across to general audiences?") The blackface persona, bringing a freedom of the anonymous and forbidden, could become so powerful a force that sometimes the entertainer felt a need to make it clear that it was only a persona. After one of her stomping exhibitions in blackface, Sophie Tucker would peel off a glove and wave to the crowd "to show I was a white girl." A surprised gasp would rise from the audience, then a howl of laughter, as if in tribute to all that impersonation could dredge up.

Some routines used strictly Jewish motifs. Fanny Brice would come out as Madame Du Barry, gorgeously attired and waving her fan, and then declaim with a thick Yiddish accent: "I'm a bad voman, but I'm demm good company." (Fanny, by the way, had to learn the Yiddish accent that became her trademark; she grew up not knowing the language.) Smith and Dale had a bit in their "Dr. Kronkeit" skit, done more with Jewish inflection than Yiddish accent:

SMITH: I would like to read you the Cash of the Light Brigade.
DALE: Charge, charge!
SMITH: Okay, I'll give you credit.

In the Follies of 1928 Eddie Cantor played a Jewish aviator from Newark whose plane was called "Mosquito—the Spirit of New Jersey." Quizzed by Major Brown as to the "principal aviators of 1927," he answered,

> "Well—Chamberlin, Levine, Ruth Elder, Levine, Commander Byrd, Levine—"
> "Who else?"
> "Did I mention Levine?"
> "What's your name, anyway?"
> "Ginsberg."
> "First name?"
> "Gregory."
> "Gregory Ginsberg! Is that your right name?"
> "My right name is Levy."
> "Why did you change it?"
> "Well, I was in the South, around the Mississippi, during the floods and I read headlines in the papers that they were going to blow up all the *levees*."

George Jessel wrote a sketch called "Mama in the Box":

> I enter the upstairs box of the theatre, accompanied by my stage mother with shawl, funny hat, etc. I explain to her that this is a celebrated French drama that we are going to see.
> "But," she asked, "how will I understand it?"
> I tell her that I will translate it to the audience in English and she replies: "But English I don't understand much either."
> Then I promise to translate it for her into Yiddish, so that each time an actor on the stage says something in French I give a funny translation in English for the rest of the audience and in . . . Yiddish to my mother.
> Mother doesn't quite understand the action of the play. She eats apples, gets into arguments with persons in the box, causes much consternation among the players on the stage. The leading man stops the action of the play, says something excitedly to her in French. I translate it to my mother. She insults him in Yiddish and he returns the insult in Yiddish. The whole cast joins in and the curtain falls.

Such material, amusing and mildly pointed, was used by most of the Jewish entertainers who came to prominence in the first few decades of the century. It suggests, as does the record of their lives, that for them Jewishness was cause neither for self-denying shame nor ethical nail-biting. It would be an exaggeration to say that they were oblivious to that sense of the problematic which has been so deeply ingrained in Jewish experience; what they did was to take the elements of Jewish self-consciousness and transform—sometimes reduce—them into set-piece jokes and routines. In Jessel's skit the climax of the French actors speaking Yiddish became, in its way, a commentary as sharp as those made by many serious writers about the entanglements of "Jewish identity." But while often shrewd and intelligent, the Jewish entertainers were seldom reflective—the very pace at which they lived, the compulsiveness with which they worked, made reflection unlikely.

Rarely if ever did they deny being Jewish; rarely turn down requests to do Jewish benefits. They would declare themselves "proud to be a Jew" in much the same aggressively uncomplicated spirit that they would declare themselves "proud to be an American." But what it meant to be a Jew, or for that matter an American, they seldom bothered about.*

They were sentimental Jews: Sophie Tucker was apparently as moved by her innumerable renditions of "My Yiddishe Mama" as her audience was. They were nostalgic Jews: Jolson, Jessel, and Cantor, meeting once in San Francisco, decided the best way to celebrate was to have dinner in a kosher restaurant. They were defensive Jews: Cantor took more ribbing than he should have from Will Rogers and W. C. Fields about his reluctance to eat ham and pork, and while this evidently hurt his feelings, he accepted such things as unavoidable in the American setting.

Thrown together, the Jewish entertainers felt at ease in a way they never could with gentile colleagues. Cantor and Jessel once shared a show at Loew's Paradise in the Bronx—it was like coming home. People crowded into the theatre out of "loyalty . . . for a couple of local boys who'd made good. Some of the women brought us homemade soup. (They left it at the stage door!)"

These Jewish entertainers were seldom self-conscious about Yiddish dialect humor, probably because they felt no doubts about their good will. Rarely packing much satiric thrust, they wanted to amuse, not attack, to please, not preach.** To think seriously about their public roles was beyond their capacity, or at least their inclination. Pushing hard for a dollar yet quick to turn soft over a colleague's misfortune, they lived as if the casual street values they had picked up as adolescents were enough to carry them through life. Confronted with anti-Semitism or even a hint that their skits bore troubling implications (some dialect stories could be nasty, especially the Max Mefoofsky anecdotes printed by Walter Winchell in his gossip column), they would have made a staunch defense, with their fists as well as their mouths. But only rarely does one find, at least in the public record, an

* Jack Benny was one of the few Jewish comedians of this generation who did not use explicit Jewish materials or a style of delivery with strong Yiddish or immigrant components. It was as if he remained untouched—perhaps because he did not come from New York—by the influences which had shaped the work of his contemporaries. Or, in some complicated and repressed way, did his routine of endlessly repeated stinginess and his parodies of violin playing touch on certain "racial" sentiments?

** As if criticizing this earlier generation of Jewish performers, Lenny Bruce would do a skit in the fifties about Jews getting into show business. The Jews, he said, had a "hip boss, the Egyptian" in charge of the Pyramids, whom they were forever trying to charm. Tough as he was, the Egyptian finally succumbed: "I mean," he said, "it's an *art* with them. Let's go watch a Jew be charming. Hey! Jew! Do that charming bit for us." Pretty soon "the Jew gets into show business . . . he's making the images" and charming the gentiles. This sly story has points of similarity with the attacks Zionist spokesmen used to make earlier in the century on "Diaspora psychology."

expression of feeling as persuasive as Fanny Brice's remark, "I never did a Jewish song that would offend the race. . . . I wasn't standing apart, making fun. . . . I *was* the race."

The distinctiveness of these entertainers, if it can be isolated at all, seldom appeared in their opinions, and not even in their use of Jewish materials; it came through most vividly in the rhythm and tone of their work, the pulsation of their nerves, the unfolding of what we call "personality." Jolson's large-gestured sentimentalism, Jessel's gritty wisecracking, Brice's *yente* grandeur, Cantor's frantic shakiness: all these were spin-offs from immigrant experience. More important still was the almost hysterical frenzy with which many of them worked, their need to perform under the highest possible pressure, as if still heeding the Jewish folk view that for a Jew to succeed he must do things twice as well, or as hard, as a gentile. Warned once that she was ruining her vocal chords through overwork, Sophie Tucker screamed with laughter: "These are no vocal chords, kid, these are bands of steel."

The critic Gilbert Seldes, writing in the twenties, observed in Jolson and Brice qualities of "daemonic" abandon and heat. Calling them "possessed," he went on to remark:

> In addition to being more or less a Christian country, America is a Protestant community and a business organization—and none of these units is peculiarly prolific in the creation of daemonic individuals. [Jolson and Brice] gave something to America which America lacks and loves—both are out of the dominant class. Possibly this accounts for their fine carelessness about our superstitions of politeness and gentility . . . [and their] contempt for artificial notions of propriety.

It was on the American stage that the turbulent "cutting loose" and "breaking out" of the street Jews won its earliest recognition—a "cutting loose" and "breaking out" in which the Jewish entertainers showed an affinity with those black entertainers who, somewhat earlier, had taken the role of the "daemonic."

The "daemonic" spirit that Gilbert Seldes had praised would persist into the work of the Marx Brothers, but with a new and more complex character. Greatly helped by the scripts of S. J. Perelman and, later, George S. Kaufman, the Marx Brothers split open the conventions of stage entertainment into extremes of social satire and chaotic farce; they were no longer so obsessed as earlier Jewish entertainers had been with simply pleasing the audience; they sought, instead, to spin it helplessly, dizzily away from standard expectations of coherence.

Perelman, a writer whose work links the humor of the Marx Brothers with the fiction of Nathanael West, was a master of canny inconsequence, wild puns, and the stolid parodying of clichés. Toward the pretensions of the world he adopted a strategy of ruthless deflation, something common enough among satirists, but here taken a step further, toward a demolition of the idea of order itself. This could lead to silliness, as it led to surrealism, but even silliness, the Marx Brothers showed, had a point. In their films the disassembled world is treated with total disrespect, an attitude close to the traditional feeling among Jews that the whole elaborate structure of gentile power is merely trivial. The gleeful nihilism of the Marx Brothers made a shamble of things, reducing their field of operations to approximately what a certain sort of East Side skeptic had always thought the world to be: *ash un porukh*, ashes and dust.

At the very time the Marx Brothers were sharpening their humor—in effect, releasing hostilities of a scope the Jolson-Cantor group never dared to acknowledge—there was also starting a process of "de-Semitization" in the popular arts. In 1944 Ben Hecht noticed "the almost complete disappearance of the Jew from American fiction, stage, and movies." Eight years later Henry Popkin put together a bundle of evidence showing that in the popular arts "the Jew" had become "the little man who isn't there. This . . . originates not in hate, but in a misguided benevolence—or fear; its name is *sha-sha* . . . [and its source] is Hitler. When Hitler forced Americans to take anti-Semitism seriously, it was apparently felt that the most eloquent reply that could be made was a dead silence."

The examples that Popkin gave were at once amusing and disturbing. In the paperback reprint of Irving Shulman's popular novel *The Amboy Dukes*, characters named Goldfarb and Semmel in the original edition became Abbot and Saunders. In the paperback reprint of Jerome Weidman's *I Can Get It for You Wholesale*, Meyer Babushkin became Michael Babbin, and Pulvermacher became Pulsifer. Walter Winchell dropped the Mefoofsky stories and began campaigning righteously against dialect humor. The Jewish comedians fell upon hard days, everyone seemed so touchy—and the talented Lou Holtz had to go off the air because he, of all people, was accused of being anti-Semitic. In the movies the great retreat began in the mid-thirties, with veteran actors who had done Jewish roles—George Sidney, Harry Green, Gregory Ratoff, George E. Stone—unable to find work.

> The comic villain of George S. Kaufman's *The Butter and Egg Man*, a character named Lehman, retained his original name when the play was filmed under its own title in 1928 and as *The Tenderfoot* in 1934; but in 1937, when the play became *Dance, Charlie, Dance* he was named Morgan, and in 1940, when the play had another metamorphosis as *An Angel from Texas* he became Allen. . . . When *The Front Page* was filmed in 1931 the Governor's befuddled emissary kept the name he had in the original play—Irving Pincus; in the second movie version, *His Girl Friday*, he was called Joe Pettibone. When Clifford Odets's *Golden Boy* was filmed the boxing promoter Roxie Gottlieb became Roxie Lewis. . . .
>
> Even plays and novels telling stories of Jewish life were "de-Semitized." In John Howard Lawson's *Success Story*, filmed in 1934 as *Success At Any Price*, Ginsburg became Martin and Glassman became Griswold, with Doug-

las Fairbanks Jr. and Colleen Moore acting these leading roles, which had been played on Broadway by Luther and Stella Adler. . . . When Irwin Shaw's parable of tyranny and revolt, *The Gentle People*, was filmed under the title *Out of the Fog*, the Jewish tailor Goodman turned into an Irish tailor named Goodwin.

In *Having Wonderful Time*, based on Arthur Kober's play, the Catskill vacationers became [gentiles] . . . Stern became Shaw, Kessler became Kirkland, Aaronson was Armbruster, Sam Rappaport was Emil Beatty. . . .

Not that in the decades of Hitler and the Second World War, "de-Semitization" was, or could be, total. In 1934 Al Jolson made a movie, *Wonder Bar*, with snatches of Yiddish; Milt Gross kept doing his cartoons with heavy dialect and linguistic mangling; Groucho Marx, in *Animal Crackers*, sang "My name is Captain Spalding, the African explorer" and added in a stage whisper, "Did someone call me *shnorer?*"; in 1937 the songwriter Sammy Cahn translated the Yiddish song "Bei mir bist du sheyn" for the Andrews Sisters, who made it a hit in English and sometimes sang it in Yiddish, following a transliteration; "The Goldbergs" became a popular television serial. But the tone changed. Sam Levenson—amiable, unthreatening, a soft suburban sage—was highly successful as a Jewish storyteller and, in keeping with the constrained spirit of the moment, refused to tell stories about "the little Jew" (apparently favoring large ones). He piously added that he kept his work within the "great Hebrew-Christian tradition"—though at its sharpest Yiddish humor had dealt blows to both "Hebrew" and "Christian." Understandable as such blandness may have been in those dreadful years, the result was a kind of self-censorship, replete with "good will" and poor humor.

As American culture turned toward a philo-Semitic phase after the Second World War, everything changed again. New Jewish comedians sprang up, mostly sons and grandsons of immigrants, *shpritzing* one-liners with a willed abandon and in a mishmash of English and Yiddish. Some seventy-five to one hundred Yiddish words, by no means the most elegant, broke into American speech through the offices of comedians like Buddy Hackett, Jack E. Leonard, and Sid Caesar; it soon became possible to witness the bizarre spectacle of television shows presumably aimed at the heartland of America being peppered with Yiddishisms. By 1965 another chronicler of mass culture, Wallace Markfield, was noting exactly the opposite of what Henry Popkin had described in the fifties: now the Jewish motif, and especially Yiddish, were everywhere in our popular entertainments.

> Turn to any TV variety show, await the stand-up comic, and chances are good that he'll come on with accents and gestures and usages whose origins are directly traceable to the Borscht Belt by way of the East European *shtetl* and the corner candy store. His material is a million light years removed from the old-style Bob Hope-type monologue. . . . It is involuted, curvilinear, ironic, more parable than patter. . . .

Among the more memorable moments [of Jack Carter, Jan Murray, and Jackie Miles]:

"Kildare? This is Dr. Gillespie. Do you know what you did this morning, you young whelp? You performed an appedectomy with a *milkhidik* scalpel!"

"Simba, those jungle drums are driving me mad. . . . What are they saying—what, what, what?" "They say, 'You no have to be Jewish to enjoy Levy's bread!' "

Perhaps the boldest, most compulsive user and misuser of Yiddish was Sid Caesar, whose take-offs on foreign films included: (1) a Nipponese romance starring *gantse mishpokhe* (whole family, whole kit and kaboodle, whole sick crew), *gehakte leber* (chopped liver), and *shmate* (rag); (2) a chunk of Neopolitan naturalism loaded with lines like, "Whos wearin' my *gatkes?*" (long underwear); and (3) a Gallic romp set in a *boîte* named *La Fligl* (The Chicken Wing).

We are getting, on TV situation comedies, Indians behaving like members of the Shmohawk tribe, abstract painters named Schmeer, Chinese valets mixing batters of *kreplakh*, private eyes calling themselves shamuses, Russian spies pausing for "a nice glass tea."

What were these comedians doing with their systematic flaunting of Yiddish at a time when among Jews themselves the language was falling into disuse? In the past, employed by a Jolson or a Cantor, Yiddish had served as a kind of secret sign, a gleeful or desperate wave to the folks back home by a performer who liked it to be known that he was still a Jewish boy faithful to the old plebeian ways and the bracing street vulgarisms. (In the seventies, this would be repeated and parodied by Mel Brooks in the movie *Blazing Saddles,* where an Indian chief bursts into pure Yiddish—now no longer an inside joke but a major boast.) Waving to the folks back home, reassuring them or oneself that one was still what one had been born, remained an important function of the "Yiddishization of American humor." But more was at stake. The outbursts of Yiddish reflected the rise of a large and affluent middle-class Jewish audience in the big cities, which could now share with the comics a display of precisely the "Jewish vulgarity" earlier generations had been so intent upon keeping under wraps: there was pleasure of a sort in both performer and audience signaling, *it's no longer necessary to be careful.* At the same time, these audiences could be tickled with nostalgic—or, what finally came to the same thing, coarse antinostalgic—references: *it's no longer necessary to be defensive.* Just as Sophie Tucker had known that a Yiddish verse was always good for tears in Brooklyn or the Bronx, so the stand-up comics of the fifties and sixties knew they might milk a laugh out of a snarling return to Jewish mothers and other shared embarrassments. Embarrassment was an important element in this humor, as it had been in the humor of Jewish entertainers thirty or forty years ago; but now it became more needling, less innocent, given to malice and savage abrasions—the self-contempt of Jews embarrassed not so much about the culture from which they had emerged (or, as some felt, escaped) but about the shame they could still feel at their own ethnic denials and evasions. Using a term from the Yiddish vernacular like *gatkes*, Sid Caesar was making fun, in a fairly harsh way, of the impulse shared by many second-generation Jews to hide the "low" or "inelegant" aspects of their past from gentiles—and, indeed, from themselves. But in doing this, he was also expressing a certain disdain for gentiles who, without having the faintest notion of what *gatkes* might mean, still tuned in and laughed at Sid Caesar's comedy routines.

If embarrassment played a strong role in the work of the Jewish comics during the fifties and sixties, contempt was at least as important. Yiddish seems to have served these comedians, often men of acute self-consciousness, as a way of dissociating themselves from the very scene they were intent upon conquering—a rough splatter of Yiddish could become a way of suggesting that they knew they were in the service of unworthy ends, that the whole business of Hollywood, theatres, night clubs, success, and money was finally *dreck*. Their stage and screen bilingualism refracted a moral duality, spilling contempt on Jews, themselves not least of all, for being inauthentic and on gentiles for rewarding them. Often grating on the ears of those who really knew and loved the language, this outburst of Yiddish spoke of cultural loss, not return; it marked an end, not a renewal.

From the earlier anxiety to please—to please at all costs: self-denial, self-effacement, self-exhaustion—the humor of the Jewish entertainers moved, through the passage of generations, toward a rasping aggressiveness, an arrogant declaration of a despised Jewishness. Does the world regard us as vulgar? Very well, we will give it a bellyful of vulgarity. Do our parents despair of our ineptitude? Very well, we will proclaim it a badge of honor. Reflecting and exploiting the psychic uncertainties of the sons and grandsons of immigrants, the Jewish humor of the fifties and sixties spoke most painfully about the difficulties of overextended adolescence, the sense of disablement by parents who loved too much and demanded too much. From such dilemmas, and the embarrassments they spawned, some Jewish comics wove fantasies of loathing, which could bring a big-city audience with many middle-class Jews to shocked laughter because it uncovered a kinship in the forbidden. Much of this humor stemmed from the culture of immigrant streets, and, in an article about Lenny Bruce, Albert Goldman offered a strong description of its transmutation:

> He is . . . a genuine folk artist who stands in a relation to the lower-middle-class adolescent Jewish life of New York not unlike that of Charlie Parker to the Negroes of Harlem. And like Parker, he derives his strength from having totally available to himself—and then being able to articulate—attitudes, ideas, images, fragments of experience so endemic to a culture that they scarcely ever come to conscious awareness. . . .

Bruce . . . grew up as part of the adolescent "underground" that exists beneath the lower-middle-class gentility of such Brooklyn neighborhoods as Bensonhurst, Borough Park, and Brighton Beach. Adolescent defiance is scarcely unique, but the group of which Bruce was a part acted out its anger not only by rubbing shoulders with the socially outlawed (pushers, prostitutes, loafers, show-business types, Negro jazzmen) but also through staging sessions of ritualistic parody in which they vented their contempt for the life around them. . . . It was in this "home-cooking" school that Bruce learned how to free-associate on his feet, and it was here also that he trained himself in the technique of the *shpritz*—the spontaneous satire that gathers momentum and energy as it goes along, spiraling finally into the exhilarating anarchy of total freedom from inhibition.

"Total freedom from inhibition" (not exactly a modest program for the children of immigrants, or anyone else for that matter) went well enough with a self-mocking persuasion that one is something of a *shlemiel*. As a possible mirror to the self, the *shlemiel* has a deep attractiveness at every point of our existence, for surely everyone holds a deep persuasion—and with sufficient basis, too—that he or she is indeed a *shlemiel*. In the work of the Jewish comics flourishing in the fifties and sixties, the *shlemiel* became the other self of the free-floating ranter. The *shlemiel* as available Jewish archetype—and which Jewish mother had not at some point imprinted on the skull of her son that, in the light of the suffering she had expended on him and the demands she rightly made of him, he was nothing but a *shlemiel* —took a savage turn in the routines of Lenny Bruce and, usually, a sweet one in those of Woody Allen. Just as the political comic Mort Sahl was the M.C. whose wisecracks had been elevated to social consciousness, so Woody Allen was a reincarnated Menashe Skulnik, quintessential *shlemiel* of the Yiddish theatre, but now a college graduate acquainted with the thought of Freud and recent numbers of *Commentary*. His humor deriving partly from, or at least seeming similar to, the absurdities of Perelman, Woody Allen exploited the parochial helplessness of Jewish sons, their feelings of sexual feebleness and worldly incapacity; but he did this with an undertone of wistfulness and affection that marked him off from most other Jewish comedians of his moment.*

* Allen also had a gift for deflating the wisdom of authority, as in his parodies of the Hasidic tales:

A man who could not marry off his ugly daughter visited Rabbi Shimmel of Cracow. "My heart is heavy," he told the Rev [*sic*], "because God has given me an ugly daughter."

"How ugly?" the Seer asked.

"If she were lying on a plate with a herring, you wouldn't be able to tell the difference."

The Seer of Cracow thought for a long time and finally asked, "What kind of herring?"

The man, taken aback by this query, thought quickly and said, "Er— Bismarck."

"Too bad," the Rabbi said. "If it was Maatjes, she'd have a better chance."

The momentum of fury which had been gathering in the work of some Jewish performers—comic simulations, but sometimes real fury—came to a head in the work of Lenny Bruce, a performer intent upon leaping out of performance, a prophet corrupted who ranted against corruption, a lacerated nihilist at once brilliant and debased. Bruce had an astonishing gift for getting to the more tender portions of our cultural shame, prodding and pricking them into red inflammation. He broke past the genteel falsities of social concord, he undermined the necessary surface of social manners. What the Marx Brothers had done as surreal fantasy, shrewdly keeping in the realm of play, Bruce came to do with deadly intent: he wanted to lay waste the world, while pleading, when it yanked him before its courts, that he was just a man of constructive purpose, "a Jew before this court." At the end, as his act became an action, his fantasy a delirium, and his prophecy a mere fix, it all collapsed into cold literalism.

Few Jewish performers, perhaps none at all, could be so ruthless as Bruce in his exorcism of the liberal pieties to which, one supposes, he kept a residual loyalty to the end. At a time when efforts to shock produced little but boredom, Bruce did retain the power to shock, in part because he was not, like, say, Norman Mailer, good-natured beneath it all or still infatuated with high art and reputation. Bruce's Goldwater skit was a relatively mild but funny variation on Jewish delusions and gentile nightmares:

> Not many Jews feel hostility toward Goldwater because he is Jewish and changed his religion. See, *all* Jews did that. I'm Leonard Alfred Schneider, not Lenny Bruce. I'm Lenny Bruce legally, but it was a pain in the ass, man. A lot of dues.
>
> So dig. Goldwater lives in Arizona. He did a switch, man. He says, *"Frig it.* I'll *keep* my name and I'll change my *religion."* That was his bit.
>
> That's weird, you know? Finally we have a man in—that's going to be Goldwater's last step: gets in, gets before the T.V. cameras for the acceptance speech, and *he rips off the mask and you see the big nose and the semitic look and the spittle coming out and* [Goldwater screaming vindictively] "YAHA-HAHAAAAAA! WE'LL BURN ALL THE CHURCHES!"

More ominous, genuinely frightening, was his skit about Christ and the Jews:

> . . . you and I know what a Jew is—*One Who Killed Our Lord.* I don't know if we got much press on that in Illinois—we did this about two thousand years ago—two thousand years of Polack kids whacking the shit out of us coming home from school. Dear, dear. And although there should be a statute of limitations for that crime, it seems that those who neither have the actions nor the gait of Christians, pagans or not, will bust us out, unrelenting dues, for another deuce.
>
> And I really searched it out, why we pay the dues. Why do you keep breaking our balls for this crime?
>
> "Why, Jew, because you skirt the issue. You blame it on the Roman soldiers."

Alright. I'll clear the air once and for all, and confess. Yes, we did it.
I did it, my family. I found a note in my basement. It said:
'We killed him.
    signed,
       Morty.'
And a lot of people say to me,
"Why did you kill Christ?"
"I dunno . . . it was one of those parties, got out of hand, you know."
We killed him because he didn't want to become a doctor, that's why
we killed him.

Having stored up a bellyful of Jewish humiliation, Bruce cast it back
onto his audiences. The laughter he won was a nervous laughter, tingling
with masochism; it was like the laughter of convicts caught in a scheme to
escape. Humor of this kind bears a heavy weight of destruction; in Jewish
hands, more likely self-destruction, for it proceeds from a brilliance that
corrodes the world faster than, even in imagination, it can remake it. A
corrupt ascetic is a man undone. Bruce remained a creature of show biz,
addicted to values he despised, complicit at the "upper" levels of his life in
the corruption of the big time and yielding at the "lower" levels to the lure
of drugs and chaos. Toward the end, his performances sputtered out in dry
rage, quasi-legal ramblings against district attorneys who were persecuting
him. He became a *magid* (preacher) without a message, a martyr without a
cause. He fell back, deeply back, into a Jewish past that neither he nor his
audiences could know much about—a reborn Sabbatai as stand-up comic.

The circle seemed complete: from the Jewish performers intent on
pleasing at all costs, battling their way out of the immigrant streets and into
the world of pleasure and money, to the Jewish performers sputtering
stored-up resentments, assaulting friend and foe, grinding into the bleakness
of a shrunken messianism. "I cannot relate my own griefs," said Heine,
"without the thing becoming comic."

Painters and Sculptors

For no one could the course of immigrant dispersion have been more
problematic than for those Jewish artists who began working on the East
Side, or similar neighborhoods in American cities, slightly before and after
1900. The personal experiences of these young people were not very different from those of other sons and daughters growing up in Jewish families.
They too came from poor and working-class homes; they too had to break a
path toward an identity, or at least mode of existence, in America. But by
choosing to become painters and sculptors they assumed new kinds of
burdens. In a very few years they would have to turn from the insularity of

their families and their neighborhoods to the strange, sometimes rather frightening world of art. For the more adventuresome among them, this often meant a journey to Paris, the site of artistic modernism—just as Soutine and Chagall, a few years later, would go from town or *shtetl* to Paris. Emerging from a culture in which the very conception of visual art was still frail, the apprentice painters and sculptors of the immigrant milieu had to make a leap across both geography and history in order to test, perhaps fulfill, their talents.

Even the least lettered immigrant Jew had some sense of the writer as a cultural figure who was supposed to merit respect; rarely did he have a similar sense of the artist. Most Jewish immigrants, to be sure, had little direct engagement with literature or music, yet these fell within what might be called their "boundaries of respect." But the life of the painter they could rarely envisage as a career for their children; it evoked pitfalls rather than honors; it represented a leap into the gentile unknown, and about such leaps their experience advised a certain skepticism.

Maurice Sterne, as a child in a small Baltic town, showed an early interest in drawing, but soon learned that "the graphic arts had absolutely no place in our lives. Religious Jews took very seriously the Biblical injunction against 'graven' images, and I was badly punished one day by the rabbi . . . for drawing his picture on the ground with a stick." Within his family there were differences of attitude toward the boy's talent: his sister, on a visit to Moscow, took him to see the Tretiakoff Gallery, while his parents, indifferent to his "burning desire" to become an artist, sent him to a trade school. "Every moment I could, I spent in drawing and I gave very little attention to the teachers who tried to make me a locksmith." When the family came to America, in 1889, young Sterne, though still only fourteen, "put on the drab factory apron of the Jewish immigrant," and worked first as a tobacco stripper, then in a bronze factory, and later "in a flag factory on the lower West Side."

Jo Davidson, born on the East Side, would remember "strange sour smells, drab unpainted walls, and moving—we were always moving," like thousands of other families in flight from rent bills. "We were exceedingly poor and often didn't have enough to eat." To the elder Davidson it seemed outrageous that his son should dream of becoming an artist, for that meant being "a loafer, a perpetual pauper, an absolutely useless person." Nor were the Davidsons alone in holding this attitude.

Jacob Epstein's family, more prosperous, was also more sophisticated. While his parents "did not approve of all that I did, they saw that I had what might be called a special bent. My turning to sculpture was to them [nevertheless] mysterious." They did not actively discourage him, it was just that they "could not understand how I could make a living by Art." Abraham Walkowitz's mother ran a newspaper stand on Delancey Street, and as a boy he had to help sell papers in the afternoons—a life half an inch from subsistence and hardly the sort to encourage a career in art. William Gropper's father was indigent, and the family depended on his mother's dressmaking at home. "Gropper's first working experience was carrying bundles of cloth home from the lofts for his mother to sew at night. At fourteen he left P.S. 171 and began working twelve hours a day, six days a week, for $5.00 and nothing more for overtime." Arnold Friedman, fatherless at five, worked with his mother "in one of those wretched little East Side grocery stores open at all hours and giving their customers home service besides. . . . In his early teens, he became a wage earner, working at the Produce Exchange." Ben-Zion, coming to America in his late teens, worked as dishwasher and Hebrew teacher, both about equally lucrative. William Zorach and Ben Shahn were trained in their youth as lithographers, considered a rather "good" trade. The few decades between them in age made for a sharp difference in condition, Zorach suffering extreme poverty while Shahn could even attend college for a while.

There were some happy exceptions to this pattern of cultural incomprehension and parental hostility. The son of a poor Brooklyn tailor, Max Weber met with no resistance when he decided to become an artist; he dropped out of Boys High after a restless year and talked his way into Pratt Institute even though he lacked the formal requirements. The Soyers—Raphael, Moses, and Isaac—were luckier still. Their father was a Hebrew writer in the provincial Russian town of Borisoglebsk, but far from sharing the contempt for art of the fathers of Soutine and Chagall, Abraham Soyer encouraged his children to draw and make paper cutouts. "He adorned his own dwelling . . . with small reproductions of old masterworks, and he told [his sons] about Michelangelo, Raphael and Rembrandt." Guided by this sensitive father, himself learning to taste the pleasure of worldly culture, the Soyers had even visited a few museums before reaching America.

To become an artist, the young Jewish aspirant had to possess exceptional strength of will, a stubborn insistence that he would go his own way whether or not his family approved. The biographies of American Jewish artists share this one point of similarity: almost all of them turned to drawing and painting in their early years and then, some natural gift released, were determined to strike out in a direction barely known to their culture—quite as if they had decided to make up for those hundreds of years which separated the east European Jews from the art of the West. And most of them were fortunate in encountering teachers in America who would have felt it an utter disgrace to care about such low considerations as social origin, accent, or race. Indeed, a good many of the native American artists who taught these Jewish boys were roused to tender sympathies.

For his first instruction Jacob Epstein went to the Art Students League, as did Arnold Friedman, who agonized for three months before working up enough nerve to apply for admission. Friedman had as his teacher Robert Henri, one of "the Eight," a group of painters who briefly came together out of a common desire to break past the academicism reigning in the American art world during the early 1900's. "Warm, thoughtful, severely honest yet kind," Henri urged his students to depict, as Friedman often would, the immediacy of their surroundings. Whatever its ultimate value to twentieth-century painters, Henri's advice that they should look for beauty or poetry even in the most sordid of urban settings was clearly liberating to young men still held fast by the slums. Morris Kantor was also a student of Henri, as was William Gropper, who worked under him at the Ferrer School, an anarchist-sponsored institution started in 1911. Henri and George Bellows taught there without pay, coming on Sundays to inspect the work of the students and to offer them encouragement and advice. Max Weber was equally fortunate, studying at Pratt with Arthur Wesley Dow, an enlightened teacher who had spent years abroad with the Orientalist Fenollosa and had become an expert in the art of Japan and China.

Hyman Bloom and Jack Levine, both growing up some years later in Boston, met a young artist named Harold Zimmerman, who introduced them to Professor Denman Ross of the Harvard fine arts department. A lively teacher, Zimmerman opened the two boys to what Bloom would later call "the possibilities of the imagination"; a generous man, Ross subsidized them with a stipend of twelve dollars a week so that they could study full time. Zimmerman and Ross took them to museums and galleries: "The European tradition was not something ripe for rejection, but a precious discovery. . . . For [students like Bloom and Levine] the past was new too." As it would be for all the young Jewish artists during the first few decades of the century.

(Arriving in Florence at four in the morning during the spring of 1907, Max Weber left his bags at the station and went immediately to look at the Duomo and Giotto's tower. "I was alone except for a few early-morning worshipers in the Duomo. It all looked strangely beautiful in the light of early dawn, but it was not strange to me for I had met it in Arthur Dow's class in Brooklyn. '*There it is*,' I said, and I opened my heart to it as a dear friend who had come back after years of absence.")

Perhaps the most remarkable place of instruction for Jewish art students was itself a Jewish institution: the Educational Alliance. By the early 1880's the Alliance (see pp. 229–35) was offering art classes twice a week in sessions lasting from one to two hours; these continued until 1905, when the problems of mass immigration became so severe, the Alliance decided to cut down its expenditures on such "luxuries" as art instruction. Among those who taught in the pre-1905 classes were Jerome Meyers, a painter who did soft-grained vignettes of the East Side, Henry McBride, an art critic, and Abraham Walkowitz, one of the most talented painters to come out of immigrant Jewish life. "There were lapses between jobs," Jo Davidson has remembered, "and when they came I would . . . go to the afternoon drawing class of the Educational Alliance." At fifteen Jacob Epstein helped the

Alliance organize one of its art shows. In 1895 it held an enormous month-long exhibit, perhaps the same one at which Epstein worked, and a total of 105,710 persons came! In 1917 the Alliance reopened its art school, enlisting over the years such teachers as Chaim Gross and Moses Soyer. The more enlightened Jewish unions, like the ILGWU and the Amalgamated, provided some money to set up a "Workers Art Traveling Scholarship" for talented pupils—it enabled a few to go directly from East Broadway to Montparnasse. Peter Blume, who began to study at the Alliance in 1921, when he was fifteen, shared a class with Gross and the Soyers; he would recall that they met "advanced students and artists [at the Alliance], some of whom were working in the manner of Cézanne and El Greco, others of whom were Constructivists and Futurists. We were not isolated . . . we hounded the art galleries. . . . The Alliance brought me in contact with a sense of high seriousness. . . . Time was not given to us to waste—we bought it with hard work." Moses Soyer would write that the Alliance art students

> were allowed to come and go as they wished, for most of them were poor and had to work. Ostrowsky [the director of the school] accorded them absolute freedom of expression. . . . A communal spirit pervaded the school. In summertime we would go *en masse* to Woodstock to do watercolors. . . . One of the most remarkable things about the school was perhaps its models. They were the people who made up the teeming East Side. After painting for years the eternal nude, male or female, against the eternally gray school wall, it was a relief and almost a rediscovery to face a bearded, Rembrandtesque Hebrew patriarch, a jolly Italian woman, a pregnant gypsy, or a wistful Negro child.

The roster of Alliance Art School alumni is notable: Ben Shahn, Saul Baizerman, Leonard Baskin, Adolf Gottlieb, Louise Nevelson, Barnett Newman, Mark Rothko, Louis Schanker, others. "Many of these got additional training at institutions 'uptown,' but it was only logical for ghetto boys and girls to seek places for study first in their own neighborhood, to save time and carfare they could ill afford, aand to avoid being embarrassed by their Yiddish accents, poor clothing, foreign names and manner."

All of this, when placed against the background of immigrant life, is surely astonishing. How, one wonders, did so keen an interest suddenly appear among even a small minority of immigrant Jews in painting and sculpture? Part of the answer may be that while few east European Jews had ever been able to visit museums or look at paintings and sculpture, reports had spread through the Yiddish papers and by word of mouth concerning successful Jewish artists in Russia. In its hunger to absorb Western culture, the secularized portion of east European Jewry was prepared for the idea of art before it could encounter art itself. There were already a number of famous Jewish artists in Russia during the last few decades of the nineteenth century, figures like Isaac Levitan the landscape painter and Mark Antokolski the sculptor. If most *shtetl* and even urban Jews had no

real idea of what such men were doing, the network of clan gossip was
efficient enough for word to get around that "we" now had painters honored in Moscow and Saint Petersburg quite as "we" had writers and musicians.* Growing up in Vitebsk, Chagall studied with a Jewish painter named
Pen; in Saint Petersburg there was a distinguished Jewish art teacher named
Bakstin. These were isolated figures, but given the cultural eagerness and self-
consciousness pervading the east European Jewish world, they were all the
more likely to be noticed.

And there was more Jewish art in eastern Europe than is commonly
supposed. By now we are familiar with decorative elements on Torah cur-
tains, candlesticks, spice boxes, prayer shawls, Chanukah lamps, and other
ritual objects; less widely known is the fact that, the second commandment
notwithstanding, there was also a simple representational art in illustrated
Haggadahs used for Passover services. In the wooden synagogues the east
European Jews had developed a style of building that could have its own
austere beauty—a beauty of poverty. All of this, it may be supposed, had
some effect on at least a minority of immigrants, obliquely preparing them
for later encounters with Western art.

Other influences made themselves felt through cultural pressures and
frictions. The German Jews in America had been purchasing art for several
decades, such men as the department-store magnate Benjamin Altman acquiring notable collections of paintings. In sponsoring the Educational Alliance as an agency to bring the higher things of life to their east European
cousins, the German Jews felt it desirable that, together with religious instruction, sewing groups, lessons in hygiene, and courses in Greek thought,
there also be some art classes. And however much they might grumble, the
East Side immigrants knew that what the German Jews were offering them
was something they wanted.

Yet the primary source of their interest in art, as in every other area of
culture, must surely be traced to the immigrant Jews themselves. Like a
tightly gathered spring trembling with unused force, their life had been held
in for centuries. Once settled in America and past the initial traumas, they
released the energies of generations, and with those energies, a hunger to
taste and acquire the goods of this world: money and culture, power and
spirit. It was entirely possible for an immigrant father to look balefully on
his son's desire to become an artist, even to think that *shmiren* pictures was a

---

* The proliferation of musical prodigies is legendary. Sholom Aleichem tells a story
of being approached one summer by a wildly excited man who said his son was
"another Paganini." Sholom Aleichem immediately turned impresario and arranged
a private concert. "The boy violinist made his first appearance before his first audience in bare feet, the pockets of his trousers bulging with nuts which he had been
offered . . . before coming to the concert. He performed masterfully," and the
audience contributed money so that he could go to western Europe for instruction.
The boy's name was Mischa Elman—and there were scores of other, would-be
Mischa Elmans.

dubious or unworthy occupation, and yet to want his children to learn about art, to go to museums, to try their hands at drawing, indeed, to take in "everything." And when the Alliance, a few blocks away, held one of its art shows displaying the work of those errant Jewish boys, this same immigrant father might venture to drop in. It didn't hurt to look.

Newcomers to the experience of art, the Jewish painters were late-comers to the world of art. The American artists from whom they had much to learn were, as it turned out, estimable but rather minor figures—that, indeed, was one of the things they had to learn from them. Writing about the more original and innovative American artists during the first years of the century—"Prendergast, Hartley, Marin, Weber, Davis, Maurer, Demuth"—the art historian Meyer Schapiro says that "none was of the stature of the great European innovators. It is not because they are imitators of the Europeans; they are unmistakable personalities, with their own savor, but their work does not seem to us as far-reaching as that of the pioneers abroad. There is no Melville or Whitman or James among our painters." A somewhat sharper view of these American artists is advanced by Hilton Kramer: "This first generation of painters who undertook, at the turn of the century, to cast their native experience in a radical pictorial mode of foreign origin, suffered all the well-known afflictions of provincial aspirants to cos-mopolitan achievement. . . . These artists could scarcely hope for a place in the front rank of the European *avant-garde* from which they drew their inspiration."

That the American artists to whom the Jewish neophytes went for instruction were themselves minor figures became clear in the course of apprenticeship, so that the bolder among the apprentices came to feel that the only solution for their problems was to leapfrog across American art directly to Paris. They would leave behind the narrowness of the immigrant subculture, they would discard whatever frail ties they might have with American artistic conventions, they would move straight to the heart of the new. Max Weber, having saved two hundred dollars after two years of teaching at a Duluth normal school, went to Paris in 1905 at the age of twenty-five; became a friend of Matisse, Derain, Vlaminck, and Picasso; took in the Cézanne exhibition at the Salon in 1906 ("as soon as I saw Cézanne's pictures, they gripped me at once and forever"); and found in the venerable Henri Rousseau a mentor and guardian. For a boy who had grown up in the slum streets of Williamsburg, this transformation was nothing less than extraordinary. It helps explain both Weber's role as a pioneer modern-ist in American art, quite in advance of many native painters who were more rooted than he in native traditions, and the flitting eclecticism one remarks in his work, a quality of always assimilating and never having quite assimilated, a style of the eager, even brilliant impersonator. Following Weber a year later to Paris was Abraham Walkowitz, who studied at the

Académie Julian and immersed himself in the work of Cézanne, Matisse, and Rousseau. Less striking a figure than Weber, Walkowitz now seems a painter more individual and recalcitrant. He learned from the modernist masters but held to his own manner, a somewhat shy and somber ruminativeness, with muted colors and tones in the depiction of city scenes and a stubborn return to the contours and sensuality of the human body, for a Jewish artist as "revolutionary" in its way as Weber's discipleship to the Paris school. Others followed Weber and Walkowitz to Paris, Moses Soyer, for example, arriving in the mid-twenties with the help of a scholarship from the Workmen's Circle.* That seems almost like an emblem of our whole story: a Yiddish organization enables a young artist to go to Paris, thereby multiplying the risks that he will disengage himself from the cultural values that form its reason for existence.

Perhaps, then, because they started from "nowhere," without the blessings or burdens of an overpowering artistic tradition, some of the Jewish painters in America could speed past the earnest limits of American art and move to the center of modernism. "The introduction of modern art in this country . . . has depended largely on the foreign-born or their immediate descendants. Its point of entry was the port of New York. . . . Among the first artists to absorb the modern ideas were Max Weber, Abraham Walkowitz, Jacob Epstein, Joseph Stella, and Gaston Lachaise, all (except Epstein) foreign-born." And especially important as a center for advanced art at this time was Alfred Stieglitz's "291" gallery, in which a number of the Jewish artists first displayed their work.

Some of the Jewish painters used Jewish subjects and settings in their work from the very start, but for others, especially a modernist like Weber, it was necessary first to absorb the experiments of the Paris school and then return to Jewish themes. In 1917 there occurs a major change in Weber's work: he ceases to be a radical innovator, or disciple of the radical innovators, and begins to "paint poetic themes with a [Jewish] religious undertone. His former variety of subjects gives way to a simple range, more human and more expressive of racial character." It was as if there were now a need to resist, or more likely, slow the cultural metamorphosis that had been necessary for becoming an advanced artist at all. Whether one regards this as a retreat from the avant-garde, a return to native sources, or both, it was a strongly felt decision. Somewhat earlier, Weber began printing some Yiddish poetry and essays in *Shriftn*, an irregular anthology put out by *Di Yunge* (see p. 428); one of these poems, an incantatory celebration of

---

* But in the fifteen or twenty years that separate the journeys to Paris of Weber and Walkowitz from those of Soyer and Shahn there is an important difference. By the time the latter two arrived in Paris, during the twenties, there was already a group of Jewish painters, most of them emigrants from eastern Europe, living there, to whom young Jewish-American artists naturally gravitated. For Weber and Walkowitz the journey was more risky, and it is therefore all the more remarkable that they quickly found their way to the most advanced artists in Paris.

New York, juxtaposed references to the Jewish East Side and "the great city of cubistic forms." In the early twenties *Shriftn* brought together, for the first time, Yiddish writers and Jewish artists, including in its pages prints, drawings, and woodcuts by Walkowitz, Weber, and others—as well as some reproductions of Boris Aronson's expressionist sets for Yiddish theater.

At least for a time, Jewish settings, symbols, and subjects played an important role in the work of the artists emerging from the immigrant milieu. Most of them would have agreed with Walkowitz that "art has nothing to do with imitation of objects, art has its own life"; but, insofar as they produced representational or semirepresentational works, they were naturally drawn to the materials they knew best and that stirred them most deeply. Walkowitz did a series of subdued cityscapes—*The Park, The Lake, Bathers, Rutgers Square*—in which he asserted his own tonality as an artist, at once contemplative and sensuous, through the depiction of characteristic immigrant moments. Weber painted more exotic Jewish figures—*Hasidic Dancers, The Rabbi, Talmudists, Invocation*—in a style yoking together elements of abstraction with a frenzied Jewish lyricism. Ben Shahn, even before doing his Haggadah illustrations in a manner influenced by Chagall and Rouault, did some semirealistic paintings in which Jewish iconography floats about like detached atoms: East Side scenes like *New York* and *Sound in the Mulberry Tree*. Hyman Bloom portrayed rabbinical figures and Jack Levine Biblical figures, in expressionist styles that brought together romantic and gothic feelings. The Soyers painted genre pictures, sadly immigrant in atmosphere, of Jewish apartments, members of their family, unemployment offices. In the work of these and many other painters there was an abundance of Jewish materials and references, but almost nothing in the way of a common style or method.

One or two efforts were made during these years to hold the Jewish artists together as a group, perhaps a sign that they were drifting farther and farther apart. In 1915 a teacher named John Weichsel organized the People's Art Guild, which issued a manifesto in English and Yiddish declaring that "a number of Jewish painters and sculptors have decided to organize themselves into an association." Reaching a membership of three hundred, at least some of it non-Jewish, this group arranged during its two years of activity some fifty art shows, the largest one at the *Forward* building in May 1917. Walkowitz was the artist most frequently featured in these shows. The one at the *Forward* was a tremendous success, the Yiddish writer David Ignatow remembering that "the crowds who came to the opening were so great, it became necessary to call the police. . . . Our poet, Moshe Leib Halpern, who was scheduled to speak at the opening ceremony, could enter the hall only by climbing through a window."

In the mid-twenties two Yiddish-speaking painters, Benjamin Kopman and Jennings Tofel, then working in a romantic and somewhat "mystical" style, organized the Jewish Art Center on the East Side. Raphael Soyer, who came to one or two of its gatherings, has described it a little unkindly as "inbred . . . proud, touchy, self-conscious and pretentious in its Jewishness." Such groups were fated to a brief existence. When Jewish artists like Soutine, Zucker, and Blatas drew together in Paris after the First World War, they were trying to relieve their loneliness as exiles, and what they formed was a community of aspirants and *luftmenshn*. But the Jewish artists in New York were at home here, at least as much as they could be anywhere, and the efforts to band them together seem to have been little more than sidings along a journey they had no choice but to take.

That the East Side, or its paler equivalents, had a strong effect on the early years of the Jewish artists, we may suppose to be certain. But whether or how it affected their work itself is another question. The Jewish immigrant milieu, and behind it, the world of the east European Jews, had very little to offer by way of a commanding tradition in painting and sculpture. Available traditions in the various arts devoted to synagogue ornamentation were completely insufficient for establishing a distinctive Jewish style in painting, sculpture, and architecture; they might, at best, offer iconographic or ornamental motifs. From the immigrant milieu, a young painter like Walkowitz or a sculptor like Zorach could derive an intense cultural ambition, a "burning desire" (to recall Maurice Sterne's words) for distinguishing or expressing himself; but that ambition was necessarily generalized and, with regard to the substance of his work, had little directive power. He was cast adrift, and had no choice but to hunt, improvise, impersonate, and learn from the outer world. For the young Jewish painters who began to work soon after the turn of the century, it was often the Ashcan school that provided the first major stimulus. From it they derived the persuasion that the world in which they lived, the very world they might want to abandon, formed an appropriate setting for works of art. From it they also derived a tone of social sincerity, the effort to render honestly, without false heightening or rosiness, the textures of the urban scene. And perhaps they also derived a range of coloring, somewhat subdued and moderate.

In this art, "which might be called East Side realism," writes Harold Rosenberg,

> quantities of paintings and sculptures were done by Jews of old men with beards, grandmothers sitting in front of tenements on Essex Street, people going to Synagogue, street ceremonies of dedicating a Torah. . . . If one were to judge by subject matter, this is as legitimately Jewish art as the painting of Christian subjects is Christian art. But though art may be characterized in terms of subject matter, subject matter does not characterize it as art. . . . To grasp the feeling of a work, one must look beyond its subject to the style in which it is painted. Style, not subject matter or theme, will determine whether or not paintings should be considered "Jewish" or placed in some other category.

To speak of an artistic style in terms of a defining culture is to speak of a rather lengthy process in which influences settle and cohere, traditions are slowly formed, and a chain of kinships and associations is gradually created. Precisely all this was absent and, indeed, impossible in the immigrant milieu. To become a painter was in a crucial sense to cut oneself off from the Jewish community, certainly to a greater extent than was true for the Jewish writers, who if they did not continue in a direct line from Yiddish literature were nonetheless influenced by it in ways they could not always know. To become an avant-garde painter meant to become an avant-garde Jew: a figure apart, perhaps torn away, undertaking a journey of dispersion more radical than that of most other Jews. Jewish subjects could be returned to, as in some instances they were—but returned to after, and perhaps only after, the Jewish artists had gone through the experience, at once alienating and liberating, of an apprenticeship as "universal" painters.

The question that has troubled many critics and a few artists—is there a distinctive contemporary Jewish art?—must, it would seem, be settled in the negative. Yet one wants not so much to argue against this judgment as to hesitate a little and equivocate a little more, since it is hard to believe that the immigrant experience did not have some significant effect on the work of the American Jewish artists. The paintings of the Soyer brothers, for example, may indeed be stylistically derived from modern French art, but anyone looking at a group of pictures by Raphael Soyer is not likely to feel about them—as one would about a group of pictures by Bonnard or Matisse —that they come out of, or evoke, a sense of pleasure at being in comfortable relation with the external world. Soyer's pictures reflect a certain heaviness of milieu, a sense of being ill at ease in the world, the immigrant's feeling of not being "at home"—and the same can perhaps be said about other immigrant Jewish painters.* There is a painting by Soyer called *Dancing Class,* which shows in the foreground two rather awkward young people trying to dance while in the rear some elderly figures, obviously parents, are dozing off in their chairs. It would be idle to speak here of a Jewish style, since the formal means employed by Soyer are not distinctively "Jewish"; yet the picture communicates something about the immigrant experience through more than its declared subject. The postures of its figures are bent, a little fearful and clumsy; these immigrant postures, held through the decades, seem now to be shaping the very contours of the picture; and not to be aware of this is probably to miss something of the picture's aura.

More than subject, less than style, is at stake here. One wants to speak of

---

* By the early years of the century, Hilton Kramer has remarked after reading the above lines, it was only among French painters that there could still be found "a sense of pleasure at being in comfortable relation with the external world." In the work of such northern and central European expressionists as Edvard Munch, Oskar Kokoschka, and Egon Schiele there is present a pervasive feeling of anxiety and alienation, and it may be this feeling which drew a good many Jewish painters, in both Europe and America, toward expressionism.

"aura," "tone," "posture," "inflection"—all admittedly vague and difficult terms, yet pointing to a felt reality: that the dichotomy between subject and style which allows for neat categorizing is not quite as definitive as those who make it would like to believe, and that there are intermediate pictorial elements, ways of drawing figures and setting in backgrounds, which touch on both subject and style and cannot readily be disposed of through either category. Some tonality of "Jewishness" may therefore inhere in Soyer's picture, just as some tonality may inhere in Walkowitz's cityscapes (perhaps more than in Weber's rabbis). This tonality manifests itself in the postures of figures, the contours of physiognomy (Weber seems to have believed there was a distinctive Jewish face), the persistence of subject and setting, and a characteristic feeling, slightly awkward and given to pathos.

Writing about Chagall's Biblical drawings, Meyer Schapiro has used the term "Jewish Gothic" as a way of indicating the folkloristic and expressionistic distortions, yoking motifs from indigenous past and cosmopolitan present, which he finds in Chagall's work. The claim being suggested here is that the way a Jewish painter handles his Jewish setting may be significantly different from the way a gentile painter might approach the same setting. By contrast, a picture by Raphael Soyer depicting a Jewish family at Friday-night dinner has been called "a French painting" by Harold Rosenberg, and in style it is evidently that; but there may also be some point, a gain in perception, if we think of it as a French painting with a Jewish aura such as could not come from the brush of a French painter. "A golden glow as of chicken soup," writes Rosenberg, "permeates the picture"—exactly, and that is not a French glow.

The whole problem is likely to seem more interesting to the historian of Jewish life than to the historian of modern painting. For at a certain point we may stop asking, is there a Jewish art? and instead ask, why do we feel inclined to trouble with the question of Jewish art at all? And we may then discover that a strong motive for asking both questions is not so much an effort to "place" certain works of art but a fear that among artists from the immigrant quarter the process of dispersion has been so terrifyingly rapid that it foreshadows a similar fate for others.

Once beyond the representational, the "Jewishness" of art by Jewish painters becomes an all but meaningless question, dissolved as it now is into the categories of the modern. At this point, writes Harold Rosenberg as a critical defender of modernism,

> the activity of Jewish artists has risen to a new level. Instead of continuing in the masquerade of conforming to the model of the American painter by acquiring the mannerisms of European art, American Jewish artists . . . began to assert their individual relation to art in an independent and personal way. Artists like Rothko, Newman, Gottlieb, Nevelson, Guston, Lassaw, Rivers, Steinberg and many others helped to inaugurate a genuine American art by creating as individuals. This work inspired by the will to identity has

constituted a new art by Jews which, though not a Jewish art, is a profound Jewish expression. . . . To be engaged with the esthetics of self has liberated the Jew as artist by eliminating his need to ask himself whether a Jewish art exists or can exist.

For these painters, in any case, the course of dispersion has been virtually complete. Jewish by birth and sometimes commitment, they have produced an art which cannot be described in any but the universal terms of modernism. Within slightly more than half a century, the Jewish immigrant milieu had yielded some distinguished painters and sculptors, but at the stringent cost that evidence of its sensibility was to be increasingly removed from their work.

The American Jewish Novelists

Out of the immigrant milieu there came pouring a torrent of memoir, fiction, and autobiography, ranging from the cheap hokum of ethnic self-indulgence to serious works of art. Written in English but often with Yiddish tonalities unconsciously preserved or deliberately imported, these writings mirrored the yearnings of nostalgia, the tyrannies of memory, the powerful measures of loss. They formed a portion of American literature, but in voice, assumption, even style, broke off on a tangent from the main lines of native tradition. Most of this writing turned out to be of small literary value, the very urgencies behind its compostion hardening into narrowness of scene, parochial return, and mere defense. A handful of novels, stories, and poems may live.

Let us call this body of writing a regional literature—after all, the immigrant neighborhoods formed a kind of region. The writing of American Jews about the immigrant milieu can then be seen as regional in that it focuses on a contained locale; regional in that it displays curious or exotic local customs for the inspection of readers whose ways until recently have been assumed to constitute a norm; regional in that it comes to us as a burst of literary consciousness resulting from the encounter between an alien group, racing toward assimilation yet half persuaded it is unassimilable, and the host culture of the country.

So regarded, the writing of American Jews in the twentieth century comes to fit into the general movement of American literary history: as an absorbing of local-immigrant experiences into a national culture that has always defined itself not as fixed but as becoming. And what it has become is to a large extent what it has absorbed from alien intruders.

If we now see the work of writers like Henry Roth, Daniel Fuchs, Saul Bellow, Delmore Schwartz, and Bernard Malamud as a version of American regionalism, it may be useful to compare it with southern writing, the other main regionalism of this century. In both instances, a subculture finds its voice and its passion at exactly the moment that it approaches disintegration. This is a moment of high self-consciousness, and to its writers it offers a number of advantages. It offers them an inescapable subject: the judgment, affection, and hatred they bring to bear upon the remembered world in which they grew up, and the costs exacted in the process of tearing themselves away.* It offers the emotional strength that comes from traditional styles of conduct—honor for the South, "chosenness" for the Jews—which the writers struggle to regain, escape, overcome, while finding through this very struggle their gift of tongue. It offers the vibration of old stories retold, whether by aging Confederate soldiers or skullcapped grandfathers recalling the fright of the czars. It offers the lure of nostalgia, a recapture of moments felt to be greater and more heroic than the present, all now entangled with a will toward violent denial of the past. It offers the rhythm of exhaustion, a way of life coming to its end and measured in its tragic fullness, from which there often follows—as if theme were turning treacherously upon imagination—a plague of sterility in the writers themselves. And it offers a heritage of words, a wonderful rich mess of language, for the southern writers everything from Ciceronian courtroom rhetoric to the corrupt vividness of redneck speech, and for the Jewish writers everything from the high gravity of Yiddish declamation to the gutter sparklings of the street. "To be the child of immigrants from Eastern Europe," wrote Delmore Schwartz,

> is in itself a special kind of experience; and an important one to an author. He has heard two languages through childhood, the one spoken with ease at home, and the other spoken with ease in the streets and at school, but spoken poorly at home. . . . To an author, and especially to a poet, [this double experience of language] may give a heightened sensitivity to language, a sense of idiom, and a sense of how much expresses itself through colloquialism. But it also produces in some a fear of mispronunciation; a hesitation in speech; and a sharpened focus upon the characters of the parents.

At a crucial point the comparison between southern and Jewish writing breaks down; much of the value in making the comparison is that it should. It breaks down at the point where we leave the formal parallels in the relationship between receding cultures and obsessed writers and proceed to examine the content of each culture. The culture of the South, whatever its corruptions or idiosyncrasies, has been a Christian culture, and not all the rivers of blood shed in the Civil War can finally separate it from the culture of the North. The culture of the Jews, no matter how comfortably nestled

* Writing in 1944 that "the young Jewish writers of today are the children of immigrants, and as such—not completely integrated in society and yet not wholly foreign to it—they enjoy a critical advantage over the life that surrounds them," Isaac Rosenfeld was echoing similar statements by Allen Tate about the situation of southern writers.

into crevices of American society, remains fundamentally apart: at odds with, perhaps even alien to, the host culture, at least insofar as being Christians or Jews still affects our lives. And it does affect our lives, it affects them deeply, despite the fading of religious persuasions.

At least since the Diaspora, the Jews have been multilingual, as price or reward of *galut*, reflecting their uncomfortable condition through the simultaneous use and then merging of alien and native languages. Even more significant is what Max Weinreich has called "internal bilingualism" (see p. 516), the development in the Ashkenazic Jewish community of "two *living* languages, one that was immediate [Yiddish] and the second mediated [Hebrew]." This internal bilingualism can be seen as having had, very roughly, two stages: the first, lasting some centuries, in which Hebrew and Yiddish coexisted as unequal partners, with Hebrew accorded social and moral primacy; and the second, starting in the nineteenth century, in which Yiddish asserted itself not merely as a language but as token of a way of life that came to signify a new phase in Jewish history. Seen from the vantage point of fifty or a hundred years hence, the Yiddish phase may well be judged as a time in which the unity of the Jewish people was shattered; seen from our own moment, the Yiddish phase strikes one as a flowering of mind, energy, culture. In any case, Yiddish signifies here not merely a language but a whole era in cultural history, first in eastern Europe and then, for a few decades, in the United States.

With this Jewish tradition in its fullness most American Jewish writers have had only a slight and problematic relationship—indeed, a torn and deprived relationship. The migration to America all but destroyed the internal bilingualism of Jewish life and thereby the historical complexities and religious balances that had contained it. Insofar as the work of the American Jewish writers bears a relationship to the Jewish past, it is mostly mediated through the historical phase of Yiddish, one that itself represents a major break within—and perhaps from—the tradition. But even the relationship of these writers to the culture of Yiddish, source and root of their early experience, is marked by rupture, break, dissociation, by a will to flee, and, once and for all, be done with. So that in speaking here of the line of Jewish sensibility which can still be found in the work of these writers, we should be clear that we are not in the presence of rich organic continuities, a tradition gathering and encompassing. Whatever these writers have gained from native American culture and the culture of international modernism— a great deal, of course—the Jewish side of their experience came to be fragmented. If, as J. V. Cunningham tells us, a literary tradition constitutes "a principle of order . . . which directs and determines the selection of the materials that enter into a work," then for the American Jewish writers the tradition of the Jews has figured more and more as lapsed rather than available possibilities. Knowing as much, the best of them have made this their central theme: the experience of loss as impetus to self-renewal.

But even a lapsed tradition, even fragments of the past that have been brushed aside, even cultural associations that float in the atmosphere waiting to be sheltered, all have a way of infiltrating the work of the American Jewish writers. The internal bilingualism of Hebrew and Yiddish is replaced by a precarious substitute, a half-internal and half-external bilingualism of Englished Yiddish and Yiddished English, from which there sometimes arises a new and astonishing American prose style.* Tradition broken and crippled still displays enormous power over those most eager to shake it off. And tradition seemingly discarded can survive underground for a generation and then, through channels hard to locate, surface in the work of writers who may not be aware of what is shaping their consciousness. *Tradition as discontinuity*—this is the central fact in the cultural experience of the American Jewish writers.

Though structured according to the narrative strategies of modernism —James Joyce is a shaping presence throughout the book—Henry Roth's *Call It Sleep* draws its substance, the whole unfolding of socioethnic detail, from the Jewish immigrant experience. The sensibility of Genya, its superb womanly heroine, can hardly be grasped by a reader unaware of the way late-nineteenth-century Russian romanticism swept over the cultivated segments of east European Jewry and roused among them yearnings they could hardly name. More important is Walter Allen's observation that while the six-year-old protagonist of *Call It Sleep*, David Schearl, and his street friends use a ghastly mutilated English, his parents talk in Yiddish, which Roth renders not in the ugly patois that so often disfigures this sort of fiction but in "a remarkably pure English, the English of people of cultivation."

This acute observation needs to be amended only by remarking that the English in which Roth renders the Yiddish speech of his adult characters is not merely "pure," it is also a little strange and offbeat in rhythm. Genya tells her boy: "Aren't you just a pair of eyes and ears! You see, you hear, you remember, but when will you know? . . . And no kiss? . . . There! Savory, thrifty lips!" The last phrase may seem a bit "poetic" in English, but translate it into Yiddish—*Na! Geshmake, karge lipelakh!*—and it rings exactly right, beautifully idiomatic. Roth here continues the Jewish tradition of bilingualism, but in a strangely surreptitious way, by writing portions of his book in one language and expecting that some readers will be able to *hear* it in another.

---

* This style, copied, vulgarized, and parodied by a good many American Jewish writers, does not always meet with the approval of native American writers who appoint themselves defenders of the purity of the English language. Katherine Anne Porter, though not mentioning individual writers, has attacked "a curious kind of argot, more or less originating in New York, a deadly mixture of academic, guttersnipe, gangster, fake-Yiddish, and dull old worn out dirty words—an appalling bankruptcy in language, as if [these writers] hate English and are trying to destroy it." Less charitable is Gore Vidal, complaining in a Mayflower voice that "with each generation American prose grows worse, reflecting confused thinking, poor education, and the incomplete assimilation of immigrant English into the old language."

In Abraham Cahan's *The Rise of David Levinsky,* a distinguished novel of immigrant Jewish life also set in the years before the First World War, we have a book that is linguistically impoverished yet can move one as a gaunt emanation of the entire immigrant myth. Cahan's novel shows no particular "influence" of Yiddish literature, for it makes no sense to speak in such terms about a book that might have been written in either language, Yiddish or English, and translated, with some felicity, either way. Cahan was not one of the sons turning back to the Yiddish world, he was completely in and of it, a major intellectual figure on the East Side. He. wrote novels in English out of a sense of historical fatalism, not to look back at the confinements of the immigrant milieu but rather to look out from them. He mastered English sufficiently to outline, in a sparse and flavorless prose, the central immigrant story of success/disappointment—indeed, with regard to the immigrant experience his book has a mythic comprehensiveness such as *The Great Gatsby* has for native American experience. But Cahan might as well have written in Yiddish, a language in which he also lacked verbal resources. He arose out of the immigrant culture at the point where it was shuffling together remnants of Yiddish and fragments of English, or at the point, perhaps, where it really had no language at all. From this condition of loss, this negation of Jewish bilingualism, he made a remarkable book.

Both of these novels, the best we have portraying the earlier immigrant years, gain their strength from authenticity of knowledge, a deep, unspoken immersion. *Call It Sleep* is most notable as a summoning of detail, *The Rise of David Levinsky* as a contour of experience. Roth's novel patiently enters and then wholly exhausts the immigrant milieu—it scrutinizes norms and aberrations of behavior with an almost unnerving intensity, yet also manages to keep a good measure of distance. Roth is caught up with the phobic and dangerously overwrought little boy through whom he surveys the immigrant world; but he is also very far from that world, a disciple of modern literature who has earned detachment from his own sources and griefs.

Transposed Yiddish and Joycean constructions; David Schearl's uncorrected apprehensions of the East Side, a mixture of stony realism and ecstatic phantasmagoria; and the discipline of a man who, in re-creating the experience of a boy he once was, cuts himself off forever from that boy—this nervous union of perspectives is not only the ground of the book's artistry, it is also the term of survival for a serious writer breaking away from immigrant Jewish life. The whole experience is here, rendered with a luxuriant fullness: quarrelsome grownups, marauding toughs, experiments in voyeurism and precocious sex, dark tenements with rat-infested cellars, the oppressive comedy of Hebrew school where children learn to torment an enraged rabbi, and, above all, the beauty of his mother, tall and pale, glowing with feminine grace and chastened sexuality, that sexuality always present in the Jewish world but rarely acknowledged. A writer possessed by his materials, driven by a need to recapture the world of his youth, does not choose his setting: it chooses him. And here it chooses him through the purity of discovery and terror which forms the boy's vision, through the warmth of a mother whose lap is heaven, through the strange accents and rasping consonants of that *other* language, the speech of childhood repressed and recaptured.

Equally authentic, Cahan's book seems dry, frugal, the work of a parsimonious imagination, reflecting that aspect of immigrant sensibility which was self-denying before the good things of the world and persuaded that the gifts of sensuality are not for Jews, no matter what they say or think about them. *The Rise of David Levinsky* moves one through its rhythm of conception, as if it were a fable enclosing the lives of all immigrants, successful and failed—a fable salvaged from the innocence of frustration. Muted in its puzzlements and hungers, this story of a successful businessman to whom life remains as incoherent at the end as at the start, releases the deepest of immigrant emotions, beneath faith, ideology, or rhetoric.

The claustrophobic actuality of Roth's and Cahan's books carries over into a trilogy—*Summer in Williamsburg, Homage to Blenholt, Low Company*—that Daniel Fuchs wrote in the thirties as a *comédie humaine* of Brooklyn immigrant life. Set in a gray slum at the foot of the Williamsburg Bridge, Fuchs's novels take the immigrant story a generation further, to the American-born sons and daughters growing up in the early thirties, ready to flee their parents but without purpose or possibility. The cramped life of the slums is to be decisive, even traumatic, in shaping Fuchs' work. There can hardly have been another American writer, except perhaps James T. Farrell, whose image of life has been so tightly bound by his adolescent years, whose entire creative effort is so painful a struggle to come to terms with memory and its costs, yet whose achievement, in the bruised serenity that shines through his best work, seems finally much more than the growl or whimper which a young writer brings to his unhappiness.

If it makes sense to speak of American Jewish writing as a regional literature, Fuchs is one of the most regional—even provincial—among these writers. Rarely does his horizon extend beyond the slum: it is there that he finds his truth and his sadness. All of Fuchs's novels are dominated by a sense of place as it grasps a man's life and breaks him to its limits. *Summer in Williamsburg* may seem at first like still another study of an unhappy, sensitive youth, but it soon becomes clear that Fuchs is not merely prey to a dilemma, he is actively developing a novelistic idea. And that idea is the way the power of environment, the tyranny of conditions, can take over a life.

The power of the Jewish past fades, there is hardly even a conscious rejection of it; all that remains in these novels is the children of the immigrants, scurrying through Williamsburg streets, seeking ways of escape and avenues of pleasure but soon learning that escape is unlikely and pleasure brief. And that, insists Fuchs with a quiet but self-tormenting passion, is the law of Williamsburg life. From first to last he is obsessed with this single theme: escape and trap. At the end of *Summer in Williamsburg* the central figure sadly reflects on what he sees about him:

That was the choice . . . Papraval [his uncle, a racketeer] or his father. Papraval, smoking cigars, piled up money and glowed with sweat and happiness, while his father sat with his feet on the windowsill in the dimness of a Williamsburg flat. . . . He was heading in his father's direction. . . . Look at him, Philip said, he's old, he's skinny, and all he has after all the years is a cigarette and a window.

What Fuchs brings to the immigrant experience is a wry and disenchanted tenderness,* perhaps because he possesses that capacity for accepting the "given," that stoicism which, like an underground river, winds through both Jewish faith and Jewish rebellion. It is not exactly love for his world or his people that is at stake here, but something that for a writer like Fuchs is more important: a total absorption in his materials, so that his rendered world creates an illusion of coming not from craft or contrivance but from some deeper, shared necessity.

Fuchs's best book, *Homage to Blenholt*, releases a gift for exuberant comedy, a sweetly mocking play with Jewish daydreams. Untroubled by the vice of abstraction, Fuchs is the most novelistic of all the American Jewish novelists. No theories concerning the destiny of the Jews weigh upon his books; he seems quite indifferent to those modern notions which transform Jewish characters into agents of the human condition, symbols of estrangement, heroes of consciousness. He writes about quite unremarkable people, Jews in the slums, neither larger nor smaller than life; he writes as a young man enjoying the discovery of his mimetic powers but also as an older man, Jewish to the marrow, who is never able to forget the essential sadness of things. Two generations speak through his work, that of the father, the ridiculed "Mr. Fumfotch," and that of the son, a Brooklyn Harold Lloyd aflame with dreams of grandeur. Moving past ideologies as if some blessing of fate had made them invisible, Fuchs is closer to such Yiddish storytellers as Sholom Aleichem than are most of the later, more intellectualized American Jewish writers, since for him, too, the life of the Jews is a sufficient subject, a universe unto itself. The past has been lost, the future seems inaccessible, but the immigrant present encloses everything: a cigarette and a window.

In the short stories of Delmore Schwartz there is a further evocation—sometimes brilliant, sometimes merely claustral—of the clash between first- and second-generation American Jews. The gap between them in Schwartz's stories is considerably greater than in Fuchs's novels, since now the leading actors are often intellectuals or would-be intellectuals. Nowhere else has the comic hopelessness and pathos of this conflict been rendered so well as in Schwartz's early stories, nor has anyone written so very much from the "inside" about the ambivalence of the intellectual sons.

Schwartz's most remarkable story, "In Dreams Begin Responsibilities,"

* Writing about Clifford Odets's plays, Harold Clurman speaks of his "tenement tenderness." It is a fine phrase, suggesting that gentleness of feeling sometimes shared by fellow victims.

rests on a brilliant device for rendering the chasm between generations. A young man watches a film of his own parents' courtship, but when he tries to shout a warning against the dreadful mistake they are about to enter, an usher in the theater sternly warns him that he cannot interfere. Time recaptured does not mean that life can be changed. In "America, America," a deeply considered story, the young writer Shenandoah Fish listens to his mother tell a story about the decline of a Jewish family. It is precisely the kind of story that could easily evoke standard feelings of contempt for middle-class Jewish life and standard self-regard in behalf of cultivated alienation; but while sharing these feelings, and recognizing that he cannot abandon them even if he would, Shenandoah Fish also suffers a revelation of how smugly he has looked upon the experiences described by his mother and how unearned has been the "irony and contempt" that he had shown it. It is this doubleness of perspective, a humane readiness to see both link and distance between generations, which helps to make this story so rich a portrait of immigrant life.

> He reflected on his separation from these people [the immigrant Jews], and he reflected that in every sense he was removed from them by thousands of miles, or by a generation. . . . Whatever he wrote as an author did not enter the lives of these people, who should have been his genuine relatives and friends, for he had been surrounded by their lives since the day of his birth, and in an important sense, even before then. . . . The lower middle-class of Shenandoah's parents had engendered perversions of its own nature, children full of contempt for everything important to their parents.

Schwartz soon perfected a style of his own: sardonic in its rumination, verbally awkward, full of ironic apothegms and burlesque sententiousness, wavering between self-comfort and self-attack, ready to take the risks of seeking through narratives some precarious fraction of wisdom. The tags that dot his early stories and poems—"America, America," "a youthful author of promise," "we carry our fathers on our backs," "let your conscience be your bride," "doesn't your father know what he is doing?"— seem like joking emblems of the cultural predicaments of an entire generation.

Schwartz taught his readers, other intellectuals and perhaps mostly other Jewish intellectuals, to accept the dignity of their self-consciousness. His tone was deflated, as if it were looking over its shoulder to see whether it was being followed by rhetoric. His prose seemed to be composed of several speech layers: the singsong, slightly pompous intonations of Jewish immigrants educated in night schools, the affectionate mockery of that speech by American-born sons, its abstraction into the jargon of city intellectuals, and finally, the whole body of this language flattened into a style of uneasiness, an antirhetoric.

In his later stories Schwartz saw the distance between generations as good-humored comedy, fixing upon the way the grandchildren of Jewish immigrants could appropriate the traditional roles of American innocence, supremely confident that through a mere unfolding of personal charm they could reach success, goodness, and fulfillment. The theme of such stories as "Successful Love" and "An American Fairy Tale" could be described as the irrelevance of the very enlightenment for which the immigrant Jews had struggled so desperately, but which their children simply pass by, amiably indifferent to, and even tolerant of, their parents' earnest obsolescence.

In the pleasures they take in comedy, Fuchs, Schwartz, and Saul Bellow share certain qualities as writers, but in their underlying feelings for the world they are radically different. Fuchs is locked into the resignations of the immigrant moment, Schwartz takes as his point of approach the incomprehensions between generations, while Bellow keeps struggling for some understanding, no matter how fragmentary, of the whole mysterious ordeal of Jewishness. Among all the American Jewish writers he draws upon the richest Jewish culture, which in the circumstances may simply mean that he knows enough to surmise the extent of our dispossession. His relation to Yiddish is easy and authoritative, though by no means sentimental. If there are similarities between his con men and stoop philosophers, loose on the froth of modern society, and that archetypal Jewish *luftmensh*, Sholom Aleichem's Menachem Mendel, it is at least plausible to suppose that the relationship forms a direct influence and is not the mere by-blow of cultural propinquity. Almost alone among his contemporaries, Bellow seems to be consciously drawing upon the immigrant tradition, as well as whatever portions of the older European Jewish tradition may have survived in the settings of his youth—and, what is more, he wishes to filter these experiences through a sophisticated historical consciousness. His fast talkers, of whom Dr. Tamkin in *Seize the Day* is perhaps the fastest, not only speak for that "wildly eclectic world of semi-enlightenment and semi-literacy which constitutes the modern mass mind when it expresses itself in ideas"; they could be regarded as the offspring of certain real-life figures who have appeared in the pages of this book, spreaders of enlightenment, lecturers and speakers with total programs, the Barondesses and Feigenbaums. In another of Bellow's novels, the protagonist, Augie March, ruefully asks himself, "Why did I always have to fall among theoreticians!"—almost as if he were asking, "Why did I have to be born among immigrant Jews!"

Bellow has made of certain second-generation Jewish neighborhoods— the Chicago West Side, the Upper West Side of New York—his own created province or regional locale, almost as much as Wessex is Hardy's and Yoknapatawpha Faulkner's. The Upper West Side is a grimy place, at once unfit for human habitation and the scene of what must be called an advanced civilization. It is ugly, filthy, dangerous; its streets are crammed with the flotsam of humanity; yet here too are stately refugees, stuffy reformers, literary intellectuals, eager Puerto Ricans, and Jews haunted by memories of sweatshops and concentration camps. In this menagerie of integration, anomie, and good feeling, people still manage to live. That is Bellow's emphasis—people live. In the Upper West Side, as Bellow sees it, the continuities of ordinary living, neither a triumph nor mere disaster, coexist somehow with the raspy notional foolishness our culture casts off like smoke. The Upper West Side becomes transformed in Bellow's fiction into a principle of sorts, a mixture of health and sickness exemplifying our condition. Would it be excessive to say that this principle draws some of its energies from the Jewish tradition, the immigrant past? What, asks the quintessential *shlemiel* Tommy Wilhelm (born Velvel), what is man's real business in life, if not "to carry his peculiar burden, to feel shame and impotence, to taste those quelled tears. . . . Maybe the making of mistakes expressed the very purpose of his life and the essence of his being here."

Bellow's style draws upon Yiddish, not so much through borrowed diction as through underlying intonation and rhythm. The jabbing interchange of ironies, the intimate vulgarities, the blend of sardonic and sentimental which characterizes Yiddish speech, all are lassoed into Bellow's English: so that what emerges is not an exploitation of folk memory but a vibrant linguistic transmutation. Here is Maurice Venice, one of Bellow's *luftmenshn*, speaking:

> Finally, finally I got her number and phoned her and said, "This is Maurice Venice, scout for Kaskaskia Films." So right away she says, "Yah, so's your old lady." Well, when I saw I wasn't getting nowhere with her I said to her, "Well, miss, I don't blame you. You're a very beautiful thing and must have a dozen admirers after you all the time, boy friends who like to call and pull your leg and give a tease. But as I happen to be a very busy fellow and don't have the time to horse around or argue, I tell you what to do. Here's my number, and here's the number of Kaskaskia Distributors Inc. Ask them who am I, Maurice Venice. The scout." She did it. A little while later she phoned me back, all apologies and excuses, but I didn't want to embarrass her and get off on the wrong foot with an artist. . . . Because I seldom am wrong about talent. If I see it, it's there.

Sometimes Bellow turns, in his own voice, to that sharp, nervous prose American Jewish writers have made their own, a prose that depends upon the heightening and tensing of urban speech rhythms:

> Fair-haired hippopotamus!—that was how he looked to himself. He saw a big round face, a wide, flourishing red mouth, stump teeth. And the hat, too; and the cigar, too. I should have done labor all my life, he reflected. Hard honest labor all my life, he reflected. Hard honest labor that tires you out and makes you sleep. I'd have worked off my energy and felt better. Instead, I had to distinguish myself—yet.

Bellow has brought to completion the first major new style in American prose fiction since those of Hemingway and Faulkner: a mingling of high-flown intellectual bravado with racy-tough street Jewishness, all in a comic rhetoric that keeps turning its head back toward Yiddish even as it keeps racing away from it. And throughout his work there is a half-mocking voice, self-reflexive and self-puncturing, so that his relation to the materials of immigrant life always remains quizzical and probing, like the relationship established by the Yiddish master I. L. Peretz in those of his stories employing Hasidic motifs.

Seen against the crumbling of Yiddish culture, Bernard Malamud is the most enigmatic, even mysterious, of American Jewish writers. In his best stories he writes as if, through some miraculous salvage, the ethos of Yiddish has become an intimate possession. At such moments, something happens in his stories that one cannot pretend to explain: Malamud not only draws upon Jewish figures and themes, not only evokes traditional Jewish sentiments regarding humaneness and suffering, he also writes what can only be called the Yiddish story in English. There is something uncanny about this, leading to a greater respect for the idea of transmigration of souls. Malamud can grind a character to earth; but in his best stories there is a hard and bitter kind of pity, a wry affection preferable to the wet gestures of love, which makes him seem a grandson—but a grandson without visible line of descent—of the best Yiddish writers. For, as far as one can tell, he does not work out of an assured personal relation to Yiddish culture; he seems to have reached out for the *idea* of it rather than to possess its substance. Perhaps the moral is that for those who wait, the magic barrel will be refilled.

In his failures, the connection with the past is not made, and instead there is a willed, inflated Jewishness, a sentimentalizing of Yiddish sentimentalism, which he takes out of its homely setting and endows with a false vibrato. For this Malamud, Jewishness seems a program rather than an experience.

But a story like "The Magic Barrel" seems in its characters, its ethos, its unembarrassed yielding to melodrama, like an extended finger of Yiddish literature moving not from left to right but from right to left. Here the question of influence becomes acutely provoking, and one wonders whether Malamud knew, or how precisely he knew, that he was employing standard materials of Yiddish culture. The matchmaker, or *shadkhn*, is a stereotypic Yiddish figure: slightly comic, slightly sad, at the edge of destitution. When Sholom Aleichem's Menakhem Mendel is down and out in Russia, his schemes for making millions having come to nought, he falls back upon being a matchmaker. In Yiddish theatre, for instance in an old warhorse of a play like Ossip Dymov's *Yoshke Musikant*, the matchmaker is a comic stand-by, dressed in opulent shabbiness and never more than a shade from pathos. During the years 1912–1919 one of the most popular features in the American Yiddish press was a comic strip drawn by Samuel Zagat called *Gimpl Beinish*, a ne'er-do-well matchmaker suffering constant humiliation (see pp. 533–34).

Did Malamud know of such materials? Had they reached him directly, or, what seems more likely, did he hear conversations at home about a newspaper read, a play atteaded? Perhaps there was a direct influence, the result of inner knowledge, but it seems more likely that such figures and motifs of the past, lost for a time in the silence of cultural repression, came to him (as Yiddish critics like to say) "through the air," particles of culture floating about, still charged with meaning and potent enough to be reshaped in American fiction.

Among the more consequential American Jewish writers Philip Roth was perhaps the first for whom the Jewish tradition yielded little moral or imaginative sustenance. Reading his first collection of stories, *Goodbye, Columbus*, one might have supposed that this gifted writer was continuing in the tradition of Jewish self-criticism and satire—a substantial tradition extending in Yiddish from Mendele Mokher Sforim to Isaac Bashevis Singer and in English from Cahan to Bellow and Malamud. In these writers the assault upon Jewish philistinism and the mockery of Jewish social pretensions is both familiar and unrelenting. But as Roth continued to publish, it became clear that despite his use of Jewish settings and his acerbity of tone, he was not really part of that tradition—it yielded him no terms of criticism or value. Indeed, his importance in the development of American Jewish writing was that, finally, he seemed to be cut off from any Jewish tradition.

A few of Roth's early stories constitute powerful criticisms of Jewish middle-class vulgarity, but it would be hard to show that these criticisms proceed from a firmly held cluster of Jewish norms or even memories. Roth's cultural role has been to reflect not merely the deracination—he would perhaps say detachment—of younger American Jews but also the irritation that some younger American Jews have brought to their Jewishness. It is as if he were the captive of the very cultural setting against which he rails. And by the time he began to write, it took no particular emotional courage or freshness of insight to launch attacks on middle-class suburbia: that had become fairly standard among American Jewish writers, indeed American writers of all kinds.

In a fine story like "Defender of the Faith," Roth's uncomfortable awareness that he comes at the end of a line serves to lend ironic thrust and moral complication to his work: there, the inner entanglement with Jewish solidarity and Jewish deceits is used not to satisfy chic tastes but to explore the dangers which any tradition, even the best tradition, presents to flawed human beings. Never a writer deeply absorbed in human experience for its own sake, and always impatient to mobilize his fictions in behalf of scoring a point, Roth was nevertheless able in some early stories to vent an impressive fury against the world that made him. But afterward, all that he could summon in his querulous denials of what the Jewish past had denied him was a thin-lipped animus against Jewish woes, Jewish mothers, Jewish sentiments,

Jewish aggrandizements. He was reduced to a sterile humor, what in Yiddish is called *kvetching*. This could sometimes be very funny, as in his assemblage of skits called *Portnoy's Complaint*, but too often it dropped into a mere wail for release from the claims of Jewish distinctiveness and burdens, so that, out of nothingness, the Rothian protagonist could create himself anew as "a human being." Who, born a Jew in the twentieth century, has been so lofty in spirit as never to have shared this fantasy? But who, born a Jew in the twentieth century, has been so deluded as to stay with this fantasy for more than a few moments?

In the sixties Roth's brittleness of sensibility achieved a moment of representativeness. The applause he won from liberated readers, also bored with endless talk about "the Jewish heritage" (for whom it was not always distinguishable from their mothers' whining), reflected the point at which the underground springs of both Yiddish culture and the immigrant experience had finally dried up.

The imaginative sustenance that Yiddish culture and the immigrant experience could give to American Jewish writers rarely depended on their awareness or acknowledgement of its presence. Often, it took the form of hidden links of attitude and value. At the least, it could provide a social milieu seen as representing moral rigidity, ingrown provincialism, and immigrant bias, from all of which young literary protagonists would then take off in search of freedom and autonomy. It hardly mattered how the background of Yiddish served in the fiction of American Jewish writers, just as long as it was still *there*, the starting point from which writers could move on private journeys of spirit. But once that Yiddish world began to crumble, once it no longer offered its silent buttress to the imaginaton, these writers had sooner or later to enter a state of crisis. They began to face problems like those which Yiddish writers faced after the Holocaust: what remains for a novelist once the world of his youth has been destroyed, that world which overwhelms his every page even though, and perhaps just because, he is turning away from it?

For the American Jewish writers there remained of course America, but as a subject for fiction, America, as many of them discovered, is very large, very slippery, very abstract, very recalcitrant. Can it really be said that any of these writers have thus far grasped a portion of the larger American experience with the authority they have shown in writing about immigrant Jewish experience?

Even in its fading the Yiddish past asserted a claim to power; its very absence came to be a kind of revenge.

The New York Intellectuals

> . . . a unique type of human being, the "Jewish intellectual," who springs from the tradition of the *talmud hakhem,* the lifelong student. For two thousand years the main energies of Jewish communities in various parts of the world have gone into the mass production of intellectuals.
> —Harold Rosenberg

The "mass production of intellectuals" did not come to a halt during the most difficult years of the migration to America, but it necessarily had to take new and uncertain forms. One or two distinguished figures, like Morris Raphael Cohen, moved directly from the East Side to the American academy, and there were some men, like David Blaustein, Isaac Hourwich, and Paul Abelson, not quite first-rate minds but accomplished and serious, who served now and then as the East Side's English-language spokesmen in the American community. But for the most part, the immigrant Jews were still trying to replenish their own resources of talent and mind, hoping to contain these within the perimeter of a self-sufficient culture. That this effort was doomed to failure everyone knows by now—the mere presence of City College as a training school for bright and ambitious Jewish boys meant that insofar as the East Side produced English-speaking intellectuals it would have to lose most of them to the outer world.

A few decades would pass, however, before there could appear a group of second-generation Jewish intellectuals drawn mainly from the immigrant quarters, who proposed to define themselves as autonomous minds concerned mainly with problems beyond the immigrant, perhaps beyond the Jewish horizon. Not until the thirties did this really happen, though there were of course accomplished Jewish writers on the American scene in earlier years. By the end of the First World War and then into the twenties, writers like Ludwig Lewisohn and Waldo Frank, sons of German-Jewish families, had become influential in American literary life, though their relation to East Side culture tended to be one of amiable distance. (Lewisohn showed an interest in Yiddish theater, and later, after becoming a Zionist, did some translating from the Yiddish.) Another gifted literary intellectual who began to work in the twenties, Louis Kronenberger, also came from a German-Jewish family and had no strong or first-hand knowledge of immigrant culture. During the twenties there appeared an influential group of Jewish writers—or writers of Jewish descent—associated with the *New Yorker,* the theatrical world, and the Algonquin Hotel in New York. "Broadway intellectuals," someone has called them: they included such figures as George S. Kaufman, Moss Hart, Dorothy Parker, S. N. Behrman, and George Jean Nathan. In the middle twenties, at the opposite pole of sensibility, a number of young Jewish writers like Joseph Freeman, Michael

Gold, Bertram Wolfe, and Will Herberg made their debut as spokesmen for American Communism. By the early thirties a very considerable number of intellectuals, many of them Jewish, would be turning leftward. Far smaller but intellectually notable was the group of Jewish writers, Lionel Trilling among them, who were drawn to the *Menorah Journal*, an English-language magazine that tried to evoke the cultural richness of the Jewish past. And the Zionist movement produced some keen English-speaking intellectuals, especially, in later years, men like Maurice Samuel and Ben Halpern.

Yet none of these groups or individuals can be said to have constituted a major tendency in, or emerging out of, the immigrant milieu. They were distinguished cousins, important precursors, or solitary figures, seldom closely related by birth or even denial to the immigrant culture. The first major group to come out of immigrant life, small though it would always be, was that generation of literary and political writers who have come to be called "the New York intellectuals."* This group of critics, essayists, and journalists—the early ones included Philip Rahv, William Phillips, Meyer Schapiro, Paul Goodman, Harold Rosenberg, Sidney Hook, and Lionel Abel—first appeared as anti-Stalinist radicals in the mid-thirties, though some had been briefly connected with the Communist movement a few years earlier. They then persisted, less a group than a scatter of semirelated individuals, through some extreme self-transformations into the mid-seventies. Their role in American cultural life, surely overestimated in recent years, remains a problematic one; but that they represented an important trend among second-generation immigrant Jews, turning away from the setting of their birth and speeding toward modernist culture, seems beyond dispute.

The New York intellectuals comprised the first group of Jewish writers to come out of the immigrant milieu who did not crucially define themselves through a relationship to memories of Jewishness. They were the first generation of Jewish writers for whom the recall of an immigrant childhood seems not to have been unshakable. They sought to declare themselves through a stringency of will, breaking clean from the immediate past and becoming autonomous men of the mind. If this severance from immigrant experiences and Jewish roots would later come to seem a little suspect, the point needs nevertheless to be emphasized that when the New York intellectuals began to cohere as a political-literary tendency around *Partisan Review* in the thirties, Jewishness as idea or sentiment played only a minor, barely acknowledged role in their thought. (Apart, that is, from a bitter awareness that no matter what their cultural or political program, the sheer fact that they had recently emerged from immigrant families meant that their group still *had* to be seen within the context of American Jewish life.)

---

* An awkward phrase, but by now, part of common usage. It is simply a shorthand for what might otherwise be spelled out as "the intellectuals of New York who began to appear in the thirties, most of whom were Jewish."

Energy was released, and with that energy a range of ambitions from the pure to the coarse. What made Sammy run was partly that his father and his father's father had been bound hand and foot. And in all the New York intellectuals there was, there had to be, a fraction of Sammy. All were driven by a thrust of striving, an unspoken conviction that lost time had now to be regained.

The youthful immigrant experiences recalled by Alfred Kazin in his lyrical autobiography are, apart from distinctive outcroppings of temperament, more or less typical of the experience of many New York intellectuals. But Kazin's affectionate stress on the Jewish sources of his sensibility seem mainly the judgment of retrospect, a recognition in the fifties and sixties that no matter how hard you might try to shake off your past, it would still cling to your speech, gestures, skin, and nose; still shape, with a thousand subtle movements, the way you did your work and raised your children. In the thirties, however, the reigning notion was quite the opposite. Precisely the idea of discarding the past, breaking away from families, traditions, and memories excited the New York intellectuals—the idea of a fresh start, or self-creation, which, depending on one's perspective of the moment, can be seen as either an idea drawn from American tradition or Jewish heresy. The New York intellectuals meant to declare themselves citizens of the world, and that succeeding, perhaps become writers of this country.

Upon its sons and daughters the immigrant Jews branded marks of separateness while inciting dreams of universalism. They taught their children both to conquer the gentile world and to be conquered by it. The values controlling Jewish immigrant life by the twenties and thirties were mostly secular, radical, and universalist, and while these were often served by a parochial vocabulary, they nonetheless bore within them elements of European culture. Even as they were moving out of the constricted immigrant milieu, the New York intellectuals were being prepared by it for the tasks they would set themselves in the outer world. They were being prepared for the intellectual vocation as one of assertiveness, speculation, and free wheeling; for the strategic maneuvers of *a vanguard*, at this point almost a vanguard in the abstract, since there were no ranks in the rear; and for a union of politics and culture, with the politics radical and the culture modernist. The idea of such a union had its sources partly in the secular Jewish tradition, where hopes had risen for bringing together socialist politics and nineteenth-century humanist culture; now it was to receive a fulfillment beyond national or ethnic limits.

That the literary avant-garde and political left were not really comfortable partners would become evident with the passage of time; in Europe it already had. But during the years when the New York intellectuals began to publish in *Partisan Review* and *Commentary* there was a feeling in the air that a union of *the advanced*—critical consciousness and political conscience —was the need of the moment. To resort to a term of Renato Poggioli, the

New York writers constituted not so much an intellectual elite as an intelligentsia in the European sense, that is, "an intellectual order from the lower ranks . . . created by those who were rejected by other classes; an intellectual order whose function was not so much cultural as political."

The history of the West in the last century offers many instances in which Jewish intellectuals played a major role in the development of political radicalism; but almost always this occurred within sizable movements, for which intellectuals served as spokesmen, propagandists, and functionaries. In New York, by contrast, the intellectuals had no choice, if they were to retain their integrity, but to begin with a dissociation from Stalinism, the only significant "left" movement in the country. What for European writers like Koestler, Silone, and Malraux would be the end of a road was here the beginning.

In a fairly short time, then, the New York intellectuals found that the meeting of political and cultural ideas which had stirred them to excitement could also leave them stranded and distressed. Radicalism, in both its daily practice and ethical bias, proved inhospitable to certain aspects of literary modernism. Literary modernism, especially that strand drawing upon European patrician outlooks, often had a way of cavalierly dismissing the world of daily existence, which to the New York writers, hopelessly and forever plebeian, remained intensely absorbing. Literary modernism could sometimes align itself with reactionary movements, an embarrassing fact that required either complicated explanations or complicated dissociations. In the dispute that raged among literary people over awarding the Bollingen Prize to Ezra Pound in 1949, the New York intellectuals, or most of them, lined up in opposition to the view that an aesthetic celebration could be made for Pound's poetry in which no crucial account had to be taken of its anti-Semitism. Some of the New York intellectuals argued that Pound's anti-Semitic views were so appalling intrinsically that they could not bring themselves to honor his poetry, distinguished as it might be. Others argued that the moral ugliness of the passages in which Pound slandered the Jews gravely marred the poetry as poetry. Still others argued, in the words of Clement Greenberg, that even a favorable aesthetic judgment of Pound's poetry need not be taken as decisive, since it implied the questionable corollary of "an absolute acceptance of the autonomy not only of art but of every separate field of human activity." Serious literary issues were raised by all of these arguments, but in each instance, it now seems clear, being Jewish could make a crucial difference in how one responded to something like the Pound affair. One could try to suppress as "a remnant of nationalism" the deep affront which Pound's anti-Semitism gave, but at a certain point there came the invigorating thought that there was no good reason whatever to suppress such feelings.

As their initial enthusiasms wilted and they became more and more aware of difficulties, the New York writers discovered that their relationship to literary modernism was less authoritative and more ambiguous than they had liked to suppose. The great battles for Joyce, Proust, and Eliot had been fought in the twenties and mostly won; now, while clashes with entrenched philistinism might still occur, these were mostly mopping-up operations. The New York intellectuals came toward the end of the modernist experience, just as they came at what may yet have to be judged the end of the radical experience, and as they certainly came at the end of the immigrant Jewish experience. One quick way of describing their situation, a cause of both their feverish brilliance and recurrent instability, is to say that *they came late.*

During the thirties and forties their radicalism was anxious and problematic, as for serious people it had to be; and a few moments after it was adopted, it began to decay. The crisis of socialism was world-wide, profound, and the only way for a radical to avoid that crisis was to bury oneself in a left-wing sect. By 1936, when the anti-Stalinist *Partisan Review*, was begun, its central figures—Rahv, Phillips, Hook—had shed whatever sympathies they once felt for Stalinism, but the hope that they could work up another ideological system, some cleansed version of Marxism, was doomed to failure. Some gravitated for a short time toward Trotskyism, but apart from admiration for Trotsky's personal qualities and dialectical prowess, they found little satisfaction there: no version of orthodox Marxism could retain a hold on intellectuals who had gone through the trauma of abandoning the Leninist world view and had experienced the depths to which the politics of this century, most notably through totalitarianism, called into question Marxist categories. From now on, the comforts of system would have to be relinquished.

If, in a final reckoning, the radicalism of the New York intellectuals lacked strong political foundation or ideological support, it played a major role in their development. It represented a moment of fervor, a reality or illusion of engagement, a youth tensed with assurance: so that the repetition of at least some of the ideological styles of immigrant Jewish socialism became, paradoxically, a way of breaking out of the confinements of immigrant Jewish life. And their radicalism gave the New York intellectuals a distinctive character as a group: a flair for polemic, a taste for the grand generalization, an impatience with what they regarded (often parochially) as parochial scholarship, an internationalist outlook, and a tacit belief in the unity—even if a unity beyond immediate reach—of the intellectual vocation. Here, too, they may not have been quite so far from their grandfathers as they supposed.

The New York writers, and most notably *Partisan Review*, helped complete the process of internationalizing American culture, somewhat as the immigrant Jewish painters helped bring the styles of the Paris school to American art. What the Russians and Poles would later call "cosmopolitanism" was lent a touch of glamour by the New York writers. *Partisan Review* was the first journal in which it was not merely respectable but a matter of pride to print one of T. S. Eliot's *Four Quartets* side by side with Marxist criticism—and even a few reviews of Sholom Aleichem and Peretz. Not only did the magazine break down the polar rigidities of hard-line Marxists and hard-line nativists; it also sanctioned the idea, perhaps the most powerful cultural idea of the last half-century, that there existed an all but incomparable generation of modern masters who in a terrible age represented the highest possibilities of the imagination. A new sensibility was therefore forged by this group of young Jewish writers, a mixture of root-less radicalism with a desanctified admiration for figures like Joyce, Eliot, Kafka. Bored by the apparent parochialism of native American culture, the sons of the immigrant Jews helped break down the whole idea, no longer so enabling for our writers, that there was a peculiar grace or virtue in the "Americanness" of American literature.

By the forties perhaps, but certainly by the fifties, a good many New York intellectuals began to express sentiments of uneasiness about the ulti-mate fate of cultural modernism. Coming toward the end of its greatness, they had to puzzle over the irony of its success. It was no longer a literature of opposition, and thereby began the metamorphosis signifying its slow death—since, whatever else it may be, cultural modernism must define itself in terms of opposition to prevailing institutions and norms. Critical essays on writers like D. H. Lawrence began to appear, asking what to make of his call for "blood consciousness," what one's true response could be to his notions of the leader cult. Later there would be a notable essay by Lionel Trilling in which he acknowledged mixed feelings toward the modernist writers, and then a cutting attack by Philip Rahv on Jean Genet, that perverse genius in whose fiction the compositional resources of modernism seem all but severed from its moral, indeed, its human resources.

By the end of the Second World War, the New York intellectuals had reached a point of severe crisis, though as frequently happens at such moments, they themselves felt they were entering a phase of enlarged influ-ence. Everything that had kept them going—the vision of socialism, the defense and exploration of literary modernism, the assault on the debase-ments of mass culture, their distinctive brand of socioliterary criticism—now came into question. A sharp turn followed into uncertainty, fashion, and social accommodation. American culture, seemingly at peace with a society of affluence, opened up to these intellectuals for the first time; suddenly, writers who had seen themselves as a beleaguered minority faced the problems of responding to public rewards. The academy became hospi-table to free-lance intellectuals, the literary journals more so. A benign philo-Semitism, the consequence of some shudders over the Holocaust, settled over the culture for a decade or two.

A time of conservatism in the nation as a whole, the fifties marked a notable turn toward conservatism, more as temper than idea, among the New York intellectuals. The left-wing anti-Stalinism which had been their sign of distinctiveness hardened into an anti-Communism which drove some intellectuals to become surreptitious accomplices of the Cold War. A legitimate revulsion against Bolshevism led to a casual dismissal of socialism. A warranted respect for the values of democracy became entangled with impatience, sometimes contempt for radicalism.

During the McCarthy years, the New York intellectuals did not entirely cover themselves with glory. *Commentary*, by now a major Jewish magazine, was inclined under Elliot E. Cohen's editorship to minimize the McCarthyite threat and preferred, instead, to attack the delusions of those liberals, many of them Jewish, who saw no parallel threat from Stalinism. Most of the New York intellectuals were of course opposed to McCarthyism and spoke vigorously in opposition, yet it was clear that there had been a significant decline in their radicalism and an equivalent growth in their readiness to look upon American society, not only its democracy but its capitalism also, as a reasonably good arrangement.

In these years there began that series of quick gyrations of opinion, interest, and outlook which would mark intellectual life at mid-century. In place of the avant-garde idea we now had the *style of fashion*, though to suggest a mere replacement may be too simple, since fashion has often shadowed the avant-garde as a kind of dandified double. Some intellectuals turned to a weekend of religion, some to a semester of existentialism, some to a holiday of Jewishness without faith or knowledge, some to a season of genteel conservatism. Leslie Fiedler, no doubt by design, seemed to go through more of such episodes than anyone else: even his admirers could not always be certain whether he was *davening* or doing a rain dance. These twists and turns were lively, and they could all seem harmless if only one could learn to look upon intellectual life as a variety of play, like potsie or king of the hill. What seemed troubling, however, was not this or that fashion, but the dynamic of fashion itself, the ruthlessness with which, to remain in fashion, fashion had to keep devouring itself.

It would be unfair to give the impression that the fifteen years after the war were without significant growth or work. Together with the turn toward conservative acquiescence, there were serious and valuable achievements. The emphasis upon complexity of thought which characterized intellectual life during these years could be used as a rationale for conservatism, and perhaps even arose from the turn toward conservatism; but in truth, the lapsed radicalism of earlier years *had* proved to be simplistic, the world of "late" capitalism *was* perplexing, and for serious people complexity *is* a positive value. Even the few intellectuals who resisted the dominant temper of the fifties underwent during these years significant changes in their political outlooks and styles of thought. Not all was waste; the increasing sophistication and complication of mind was a genuine gain.

Meanwhile, the world seemed to be opening up, with all its charms, seductions, and falsities. In the thirties the life of the New York writers had been confined: the little magazine as island, the radical sect as cave. Partly they were recapitulating the pattern of immigrant Jewish experience: an ingathering of the flock in order to break out into the world. Once it became clear that waiting for the revolution might turn out to be steady work and that the United States would neither soon veer to fascism nor sink into depression, the intellectuals had little choice but to live within (which didn't necessarily mean become partisans of) the existing society.

There was money to be had from publishers, no great amounts, but more than in the past. There were jobs in the universities, even for those without advanced degrees. Some writers began to discover that publishing a story in the *New Yorker* or *Esquire* was not a sure ticket to Satan; others to see that the academy, while perhaps less exciting than the Village, wasn't invariably a graveyard for intellect and might even provide a shelter in which serious people could perform honorable work. This dispersion involved losses, but usually there was nothing sinister about it.

What brought about these changes? Partly ideological adaptation, a feeling that capitalist society was here to stay and there wasn't much point in maintaining a radical position or posture. Partly the sly workings of prosperity. But also a loosening of the society itself, the start of that process which only now is in full swing—the remarkable absorptiveness of modern society, its readiness to abandon traditional precepts for a moment of excitement, its growing permissiveness toward social criticism, perhaps out of indifference, or security, or even tolerance.

In the sixties well-placed young professors and radical students would denounce the "success," sometimes the "sellout," of the New York Jewish intellectuals. Their attitude reminds one a little of George Orwell's remark about wartime France: only a Pétain could afford the luxury of asceticism, ordinary people had to live by the necessities of materialism. But really, when you come to think of it, what did this "success" of the intellectuals amount to? A decent or a good job, a chance to earn extra money by working hard, and in the case of a few, like Trilling and Kazin, some fame beyond New York—rewards most European intellectuals would take for granted, so paltry would they seem. For the New York writers who lived through the thirties expecting never to have a job at all, a regular pay check might be remarkable; but in the American scale of things it was very modest indeed. And what the "leftist" prigs of the sixties failed to understand—or perhaps understood only too well—was that the "success" with which they kept scaring themselves was simply one of the possibilities of adult life, a possibility, like failure, heavy with moral risks and disappointment. The whole business: debts, overwork, varicose veins, alimony, drinking, quarrels, hemorrhoids, depletion, the recognition that one might not prove to be another T. S. Eliot, but also some good things, some lessons learned, some "rags of time" salvaged and precious.

Here and there one could find petty greed or huckstering, now and again a drop into opportunism; but to make much of this would be foolish.

Common clay, the New York writers had their share of common ambition. What drove them, and sometimes drove them crazy, was not, however, the quest for money, nor even a chance to "mix" with White House residents; it was finally, when all the trivia of existence were brushed aside, a gnawing ambition to write something, even three pages, that might live.

The Jewish intellectuals should have regarded their entry into the outer world as utterly commonplace, at least if they kept faith with the warnings of Stendhal and Balzac that one must always hold a portion of the self forever beyond the world's reach. Few of them made much money on books and articles. Few approached any centers of power, and precisely the buzz of gossip attending the one or two sometimes invited to a party beyond the well-surveyed limits of the West Side showed how confined their life still was. What seems most remarkable in retrospect is the innocence behind the assumption, sometimes held by the New York writers themselves with a nervous mixture of guilt and glee, that whatever recognition they won was cause for either preening or embarrassment. For all their gloss of sophistication, they had not really moved very far into the world. The immigrant milk was still on their lips.

In their published work during these years, the New York intellectuals developed a characteristic style of exposition and polemic. Let us call it the style of brilliance. The kind of essay they wrote was likely to be wide ranging in reference, linking notions about literature and politics, sometimes announcing itself as a study of a writer or literary group but usually taut with a pressure to "go beyond" its subject, toward some encompassing moral or social observation. It is a kind of writing highly self-conscious in mode, with an unashamed vibration of bravura and display. Nervous, strewn with knotty or flashy phrases, impatient with transitions and other concessions to dullness, willfully calling attention to itself as a form or at least an outcry, fond of rapid twists, taking pleasure in dispute, dialectic, dazzle— such, at its best or most noticeable, was the essay cultivated by the Jewish intellectuals. In most of these essays there was a sense of *tournament*, the writer as gymnast with one eye on other rings, or as skilled infighter juggling knives of dialectic. Polemics were harsh, often rude. And audiences nurtured, or spoiled, on this kind of performance, learned not to form settled judgments about a dispute until all sides had registered their blows: surprise was always a possible reward.

This style may have brought new life to the American essay, but in contemporary audiences it often evoked a strong distaste and even fear. "Ordinary" readers could be left with the fretful sense that they were not "in," the beauties of polemic racing past their sluggish eye. Old-line academics, quite as if they had just crawled out of *The Dunciad*, enjoyed dismissing the New York critics as "unsound." And for some younger souls, the cliffs of dialectic seemed too steep. Seymour Krim has left a poignant account of his disablement before "the overcerebral, Europeanish, sterilely citified, pretentiously alienated" New York intellectuals. Resentful at the fate which drove them to compare themselves with "the overcerebral, etc., etc.," Krim writes that he and his friends "were often tortured and unappeasably bitter about being the offspring of this unhappily unique-ingrown-screwed-up breed." Similar complaints could be heard from other writers and would-be writers who felt that New York intellectualism threatened their vital powers.

At its best the style of brilliance reflected a certain view of the intellectual life: free-lance dash, peacock strut, daring hypothesis, knockabout synthesis. For better or worse it was radically different from the accepted modes of scholarly publishing and middlebrow journalism. It celebrated the idea of the intellectual as antispecialist, or as a writer whose speciality was the lack of a speciality: the writer as dilettante-connoisseur, *luftmensh* of the mind, roamer among theories. But it was a style which also lent itself with peculiar ease to a stifling mimicry and decadence. Sometimes it seemed as if any sophomore, indeed any parrot, could learn to write a scintillating *Partisan* review, so thoroughly could manner consume matter. In the fifties the cult of brilliance became a sign that writers were offering not their work or ideas but their personae as content; and this was but a step or two away from the exhibitionism of the sixties. Brilliance could be a sign of intellect unmoored: the less assurance, the more pyrotechnics, as if it were still necessary to "make an impression" on the external world.

Meanwhile, as no one quite forgot, they were still Jews, not entirely committed and rarely believing Jews, but Jews shaken by the terror of their time. And this simple, inescapable fact counted for more in their work and their lives than any of them would have supposed two or three decades earlier. Here one Jewish intellectual speaks:

> We were living directly after the Holocaust of the European Jews. We might scorn our origins; we might crush America with discoveries of ardor; we might change our names. But we knew that but for an accident of geography we might also now be bars of soap. At least some of us could not help feeling that in our earlier claims to have shaken off all ethnic distinctiveness there had been something else, something shaming. Our Jewishness might have no clear religious or national content, it might be helpless before the criticism of believers; but Jews we were, like it or not, and liked or not.
>
> To recognize that we were living after one of the greatest and least explicable catastrophes of human history, and one for which we could not claim to have adequately prepared ourselves either as intellectuals or human beings, brought a new rush of feelings, mostly unarticulated and hidden beneath the scrim of consciousness. It brought a low-charged but nagging guilt, a quiet remorse. Sartre's brilliant essay on authentic and inauthentic Jews left a strong mark. Hannah Arendt's book on totalitarianism had an equally strong impact, mostly because it offered a coherent theory, or at least a coherent picture, of the concentration camp universe. We could no longer escape the conviction that, blessing or curse, Jewishness was an integral part of our life.

CHAPTER EIGHTEEN

At Ease in America?

THE OUTWARD journeys of these four groups can be seen as flanking actions to a great transformation in the life of the immigrant Jews. Events set into motion at the turn of the century reached their climax some fifty years later: the majority of east European Jewish immigrants were no longer shopworkers but now earned their living through middle- and occasionally upperclass occupations. By the fifties a substantial Jewish working class could still be found in New York City, but, within the Jewish community as a whole, the proletarian segment kept shrinking in both absolute size and relative weight.

For the immigrant Jews this transformation represented a major social ascent, without parallel for speed or range in any other immigrant group. Writing in 1955, Nathan Glazer offered a cogent summary:

> In the 1930's about half of those American Jews who were still immigrants [mostly east European] were still workers; only a slightly larger proportion of the second generation were clerks, office workers, salesmen and the like. However, the fifteen years of prosperity from the end of the thirties to the mid-fifties have wrought great changes, and created the Jewish community

we know today. The effect of these changes has been to raise the east European Jews—the immigrants of 1880–1923, their children and grandchildren—more or less to the level previously achieved by the German Jews.

What Jewish thinkers at the turn of the century had viewed as the badly distorted occupational structure of Diaspora Jewry (a working class confined to light industries, almost no farmers, an insufficiency of "productive labor," a disproportionate concentration in petty trade, etc.) turned out to be much more attuned to the occupational structure of the industrial or postindustrial countries. This was due partly to changes in the Jewish occupational structure itself, but mostly to rapid advances in these countries from labor-intensive to labor-saving production, from small-scale farming to large-scale agricultural industries, and from a manual labor force in primary production to one increasingly assigned to service, distribution, managerial, and intellectual or semi-intellectual tasks. By the middle of the century it no longer seemed so "abnormal" that few Jews were farmers or that they crowded the professions. And those Jewish political and cultural movements which had rested their expectations on the survival of a strong Jewish proletariat—movements such as Labor Zionism, socialism, and even segments of Yiddishism—found that their "social base" was approaching dissolution.

Statistical data on the social changes among American Jews (whom we may take to be all but indistinguishable from the east European immigrants and their offspring) is not nearly so complete as it should be. But we have enough to allow some conclusions, inferences, and qualifications.

During the years between the two world wars, the proportion of American Jews employed in middle-class vocations rose significantly. Gradually, they also changed the kinds of middle-class vocations to which they turned, with a declining proportion of Jews in manufacturing, and a rising proportion in trade, clerical services, public agencies, and the professions.

In 1940, according to estimates by Jacob Lestchinsky, some 50 percent of employed American Jews were in trade, as compared with 21 percent of the general population; 28 percent were in industry, as compared with 32 percent of the general population; and 10 percent were in the professions, as compared with 7 percent of the general population.

Later statistics show these trends to persist. Over 55 percent of the Jews employed in the United States, according to the 1957 government religious census, were "professionals and technical" and "managers, officials and proprietors," as compared with slightly over 23 percent for Americans as a whole. By the mid-sixties, according to the combined results of four Gallup polls, the total of Jewish blue-collar workers had dropped to 18.2 percent of employed Jews, as compared with the 22.2 percent estimated by the government religious census of 1957. The Jewish working class kept shrinking from year to year. These polls further indicated that the total of professional and semiprofessional workers among Jews was almost twice as high as among non-Jews (27.6 percent as against 14 percent), while the percentage of Jews who were businessmen and executives had declined a little, showing "clearly the tendency of the younger generation to prefer the professions to business."

Further occupational changes were noted in a 1972 paper by the distinguished economist Simon Kuznets, who proposed the following estimates of Jewish occupational structure for the late sixties:

> Given . . . the general upward movement of the share of the professional-technical occupations, a share by 1970 [for American Jews] of well over 30 percent, and perhaps close to 35 percent, would be plausible. The share of the combined clerical and sales group would show relatively little movement, and could perhaps be kept at its 1957 level of about 22 percent. The share of total blue-collar labor, which was also 22 percent in 1957, must surely have declined with the declining weight of the foreign-born, and could reasonably be set at about 15 percent. The share of the managerial-proprietorship group . . . would be 28 percent, compared with 35 percent in 1957. . . . More important, within this managerial-proprietors group, the share of salaried managers and officials in total nonfarm male employed labor force must have risen, perhaps by a couple of percentage points. These plausible conjectures suggest that the professional-technical and managerial groups may have come to dominate the occupational structure of the Jewish male labor force, accounting for well over 40 percent of the total (in the late sixties) and approaching a 50 percent mark in the near future—a gain at the expense largely of blue-collar occupations and individual proprietorships.*

This picture of a community largely moving into middle-class status can be rounded out with a few quick demographic strokes: a birth rate below that of the general population, leading in effect to zero population growth among American Jews; a drop in the proportion of Jews within the American population from 3.7 percent in the twenties to less than 3 percent by the seventies; an extremely high rate of Jewish youth attending college (estimated at more than 80 percent); a tendency, because of higher education, changing occupations, lower levels of self-employment, and weakening family ties, for Jews to move from the major centers of Jewish population— that is, away from the Northeast and toward the West and South. (Between 1930 and 1968, the proportion of American Jews living in the western region increased from under 5 percent to 13 percent.) There was a parallel

* Kuznets's estimates were largely confirmed in a paper published in 1972 by Fred Massarik and Alvin Chenkin, which draws upon a 1971 group of surveys of American Jewry. For males over twenty-five in the labor force, this study showed a proportion of technical and professional workers of 41 percent and 29 percent respectively, compared with Kuznets's esitmates of 35 percent and 35 percent—the totals agreed, but not the distribution (which may, however, have been due to the fact that the Massarik-Chenkin study limited itself to those twenty-five and over). The Massarik-Chenkin report showed the clerical and sales group among Jews at 17.5 percent; craftsmen and operatives (blue-collar workers) at 9.5 percent; service workers and laborers at 1.5 percent; unknown, 1.7 percent. Again the results were in substantial harmony with the Kuznets estimates.

movement from the cities both to the suburbs and, a bit later, to small towns beyond the suburbs.*

Only in New York City is there a significant divergence from the over-all trend of American Jews to move into the middle class. The reasons are familiar: a higher proportion of immigrants, both early and recent, than in other Jewish communities; a larger number of Orthodox Jews, who have traditionally been concentrated in lower economic groups; a long history of working-class occupations in the garment trades; and the fact that even a city like New York can support only so many professional and business people.

A 1963–1964 study at Columbia University indicates that among native-born Jews in New York City the largest group consisted of professionals and technical workers (31 percent), which is twice as large as among first-generation Jews and nearly twice as large as the average in the city. But there was still a considerable minority of blue-collar Jewish workers in New York City, 16.2 percent among the native-born Jews and 46.5 percent among the foreign-born. Even in this rather sizable component of Jewish blue-collar workers, however, many of its members were employed in skilled occupations (e.g., garment cutters), with only a very few Jews working as laborers, service workers, or unskilled and semiskilled factory hands.

Notable as the over-all socioeconomic improvement of the American Jews had been, there were important qualifications to be made. Very few Jews occupied positions of genuine power within the corporate economy; few held major posts as executives in basic industries; most of those listed as businessmen and managers owned or were employed in small businesses. "In the great banks, insurance companies, public utilities, railroads, and corporation head offices that are located in New York, and in the Wall Street law firms, few Jews are to be found. An American Jewish Committee study of graduates of the Harvard Business School shows that the non-Jewish graduates proportionately outnumber Jewish graduates in executive positions in the leading American corporations by better than 30 to 1."

Disguised or half-disguised policies of social exclusion served to keep all but a handful of Jews away from the centers of economic power in the United States.

> Big business is no longer conducted in the firm's office but rather over whiskey and soda in some high-ranking club. The chance of promotability at the executive level is to no small degree dependent on the individual's ability to be accepted in such circles. Social discrimination at this level has a definite influence on Jewish economic patterns. A large company will be

---

* In 1931, 47.6 percent of Chicago's Jews were concentrated on the West Side. According to 1958 estimates, only 5.5 percent remained in that area of the city, a decline from an estimated 131,000 to 12,000 persons. By contrast, the North Side of Chicago had increased its Jewish population from 56,000 persons in 1931 to 127,000 in 1958, or from 20 to 57.7 percent of the total. In 1958 an estimated 62,000 of the Chicago area's 282,000 Jews were living in the suburbs.

doubly hesitant in appointing a Jew to any position. This necessitates his affiliation to various social clubs, which in many cases either do not accept Jewish members or maintain a fixed quota for them. The Anti-Defamation League of the B'nai B'rith reported in 1967 that a nation-wide survey taken in 1966 of 1,152 city and country clubs showed that 665 of them discriminated against Jews (513 barred Jews completely and 152 used a quota system). The same clubs had been surveyed in 1962 and during the intervening years there had been a drop in discrimination of only 4 percent.

A further qualification to the economic improvement of the American Jews had to do with the minority still trapped in poverty. Precisely who these Jews were or how many there were, no one knew for certain. A blend of complacence and shame kept them from receiving adequate attention either within or beyond the Jewish community. Mostly, they consisted of aging workers who had to subsist on pensions, recent immigrants who had yet to find a secure place for themselves, members of Orthodox congregations huddled in neglected areas, and those persons from all groups who succumb in the struggles of a competitive society. An estimate of the early seventies placed the number of Jewish poor in the United States at between 350,000 and twice that amount—by no means a small group when one remembers that the entire Jewish population of the country hovers around six million. One concentration of poor Jews could be found in Miami Beach, a city usually identified with affluent excess: "South Beach [an area of Miami Beach] people have an average annual income [in the late sixties] of $2,460. Thousands are living on less than $28 a week for rent and food. Of more than 40,000 people clustered there, 80 percent are over 65 and 85 percent are Jews."

Statistics for the early sixties, when a family of four was said to require an income of about nine thousand dollars in order to have a "decent" existence, indicate that considerable proportions of the Jewish population in major cities had to make do with smaller amounts. Among the foreign-born Jews in New York City 12.9 percent of the families had an income of less than three thousand dollars in 1963; 8 percent in Boston in 1965; 21.6 percent in Rochester in 1957; 9.5 percent in New Jersey in 1960. In Philadelphia 20.7 percent of all Jewish families earned less than five thousand dollars a year in 1966, and in Milwaukee, 22 percent in 1964. These figures, derived from communal surveys, require some caution in interpretation: aging families, often reduced to two members and therefore requiring smaller incomes than the nine thousand dollars specified as the "decent" minimum, may also have received support from adult children and been able to fall back upon savings. Nevertheless, pockets of Jews, especially the aged immigrants, continued to live in poverty.*

* And some lived in circumstances of humiliation, especially those among the sick and aged who were forced to spend their final years in nursing homes. During the mid-seventies there were revelations of scandal about the New York nursing

The Suburbs: New Ways to Live

Transported suddenly into unfamiliar suburbs, the second- and third-generation Jews—some of them children and grandchildren of those immigrants who had been left behind in poverty—began to look for new ways to live. From the very start, their experience was marked by a strain of self-consciousness. They were reaching toward ease and comfort, while wanting also to retain fragments of their Jewish past. They were eager to appropriate the amenities their educations had taught them to value, while hoping to shake off parochial stigmas and embrace a new largesse of spirit and style. They moved far enough into the pleasures of assimilation almost to feel ready for the pleasures of nostalgia.

But since they were, after all, Jews, many of them seem to have had some awareness of the oddity or the humor of their condition: they who had grown up in streets filled with immigrant noises were now buying private homes with plots of grass, lawn mowers, weed killers, and station wagons. And as they moved into the suburbs step by ambitious step, their journey was studied and overstudied by sociologists, psychiatrists, novelists, and journalists, themselves often Jewish, and all intent upon squeezing out solemn conclusions or easy ridicule. The one thing that could be said with any assurance about this journey to the suburbs is that it was seldom begun or completed with much ease.

Jewish suburbanites themselves kept discussing over and over again the social migration they had undertaken, inviting one another to exchange impressions over "coffee and Danish" (itself a sign they were far from wanting to obliterate their cultural past). They discussed this experience in the temples and community centers, which, for the first time, many felt obliged to join. They read articles and books claiming to sketch the suburban silhouette. A nagging sort of historical consciousness attended their entrance into the suburban middle class—just enough, at times, to induce introspection and embarrassment.

Adaptations had to be made to a new order of life: learning how to take care of a lawn and cope with a "garden shop," fixing correctly the tonalities of suburban social life, discovering those softenings of opinion and voice that might be needed at a local school meeting, and finding the kinds of people with whom more could be shared than the accident of proximity. There were pleasures too, mild but genuine. It was good to bask in a luxury

---

homes—mistreatment, callousness, profiteering. Some owners and managers of these homes were people who had established themselves as prominent "figures" in the Jewish community. It was, no doubt, inevitable that Jews share in the moral failures of American society; but for anyone to whom the tradition which this book tries to evoke is still alive, such revelations are bound to be painful.

of space, as if all the elements in one's field of vision had been expanded. It was pleasant "to walk on your own earth and feel your own green grass and plan your own mysteries of birth and bloom and death. Only in our wildest dreams, the ones we didn't tell each other, did we include the ownership of broad acres, half acres, quarter acres."

Part of the reason for moving to the suburbs had been a wish to get away from those constricting "old Jewish neighborhoods"—sometimes, from the people who lived in them—yet one of the first consequences was to force upon the new suburbanites major problems in self-definition. Living on Ocean Parkway in Brooklyn or Moshulu Parkway in the Bronx meant yielding all one's senses to a Jewish ambience; living on Manhattan's West Side meant immersion in an ethnic mix which, soon enough, broke down into ethnic pockets. But moving into the suburbs required that people decide whether or not they wanted to declare themselves as Jews. At first everyone seemed amiable and anonymous, young and shiny, not stamped with an encrusted ethnicity. But that was just the trouble, since merely to surrender to the ways of suburbia was in effect a declaration about what one wanted to be. "The young Jews who moved to Park Forest [a suburb near Chicago]," wrote Herbert Gans in 1957,

> were probably neither more nor less identified with and concerned about Judaism and Jewishness than their friends who remained in Chicago. But in Park Forest they found they could no longer live as before. In the city they had lived so much *with* Jews that there was little need to worry about living *as* Jews. But in Park Forest their neighbors were as likely as not to be not Jewish, and the latter's proximity made them conscious of the difference, all the more so as they felt that these neighbors saw and treated them *as* Jews.

One of the first things the newly suburban Jews did was to seek out other Jews. (There were exceptions, of course: an estimated 20 to 30 percent of the Jewish population in the suburbs avoided any sort of Jewish identification.) At least some of them must have been alive to the irony that they were going to escape from "old-fashioned Jewishness." perhaps from Jewishness entirely, but would escape together, as Jews, comforted by the presence of other, also-escaping Jews.

The inner tone and structure of Jewish life underwent major changes during this shift from city to suburb. Whatever spoke too emphatically of traditional ways in religious practice, or too stridently of traditional ideologies in Yiddish secular life, was left behind. A few Yiddish groups, like the Workmen's Circle, did try to adapt themselves to the new setting, and in some of the plainer suburbs, like certain towns on Long Island, succeeded in establishing a foothold. But most immigrant institutions held little appeal for the new suburbanites—they were at once too keen in memory and too inharmonious with present desires. Only after life in the suburbs had settled into a measure of stability could they speak openly of their Yiddish origins and memories, giving vent to those feelings of affection they had found it prudent to suppress.

The central Jewish institution of the suburbs turned out to be the temple, modernized, bland, affluent, well staffed, sumptuously built (though seldom with architectural distinction). A place of many purposes, it combined house of worship, community center, Sunday school, social hall, and hangout for the young. The rabbi, an efficient manager of communal affairs and arbiter of clashing social and religious styles, spoke English well, dispensed a smattering of "modern psychology," offered book reviews in the guise of sermons, and cultivated a public image strikingly different from the poor, bedraggled rabbi of the old immigrant *shul*. If also a man of some principle, the suburban rabbi would bemoan in private, and at rabbinical gatherings, the low religious state of his members, their lack of Jewish knowledge and indifference to religious practice.

Except for the High Holy Days, attendance at services was low—indeed, there was some truth to the charge that the suburban temple had become little more than a secularized community center with religious attachments, featuring social events, lectures, Israeli fund drives, athletic contests, clubs, and so on. It was a place where both traditional Jewish faith and traditional Jewish skepticism had lost their cutting edge. Neither having really triumphed over the other, both gradually melted into a low-pressured and undemanding religiosity that stressed good works, liberal ethics, Jewish responsibility. For those Jews with an inclination to self-scrutiny, the temple could hardly be a very satisfying place; yet if they lived in the suburbs it was often the only available focus for even a minimal Jewish identification.

In its religious practices, the suburban temple tended to wear down the differences among Jewish denominations. Usually Reform or Conservative in name, it drifted into what one writer has nicely called "east European Reform," a mixture of Reform permissiveness toward religious observance at home and semi-Conservative ceremonials, Hebrew reading, and singing at the services. This bland eclecticism, like a clouded mirror, reflected the ambivalence of suburban Jews toward both themselves and their past. They desired to create themselves anew, without the "narrowness" and "heaviness" of spirit they associated with the parochial life of their parents; but they felt reluctant to abandon precisely these tokens of the past, since without them, they feared, their lives would have no historical substance, nothing to characterize them but the latest house they had bought or the most recent vote they had cast.

The authors of a study of "Crestwood Heights," a suburb near a large Canadian city, neatly caught this conflict of Jewish desires:

> The Jewish family recently arrived from an area of first or second settlement must decide whether or not to send the children to the Orthodox synagogue, now away downtown. Or perhaps the father must renounce position in the Orthodox fold for mere participation in the "more liberal" Reform syna-

gogue, a step which can hardly be taken without a twist of the heart. Or it may be that the emancipated Jew, resident for some period in cosmopolitan Crestwood Heights, may suddenly feel that he wants his children to learn "what it means to be a Jew," heir of an ancient and a great tradition. Then back into the modern decor of a Crestwood Heights home come the Star of David and the candelabra, the Menorah and the quiet prayer of kerchiefed wife before the lighted candles, the full circle of the family around the table each Friday night. The break has been made by the parents only to be healed again by the children. And so the inexorable cycle continues—Orthodoxy, complete renunciation, return to a revised version of an ancient religion, one which can more readily be reconciled with the over-all ideals of Crestwood Heights.

What might be called "the suburban Jewish compromise" revealed itself most graphically in the desire of second- and third-generation Jews, themselves rarely synagogue attenders, to provide Jewish education for their children. For the adults, growing up Jewish had been in the very nature of things, well beyond choice. For their children, the suburbs opened the possibility of an uncharted existence, and while a minority of suburbanites welcomed this as confirmation of having become "fully human," the majority saw it as a threat of deracination and wanted their children at least to "feel Jewish." "The parents themselves," wrote Herbert Gans, "sought to escape involvement in the community's specifically Jewish religious and cultural institutions even though they did look to their fellow Jews . . . for their friendships and informal social life. A Jewish community from which adults excluded themselves, and whose institutions functioned almost solely for children, was something new. . . . [It was] a child-oriented Jewish community."

One of the better suburban studies elicited responses from Jews as to why they continued to practice at least some of the religious rituals, and these responses lend support to Gans's analysis:

> Rituals are good for children. If you want them to be Jewish, you need customs to preserve it.

> I observe the holidays to please my sons, who learn about them at Sunday school.

> I observe these practices out of habit. All the people I know observe them. They're the convenient ones—they don't interfere with anything else.

And, with a somewhat mordant candor:

> I don't want my children to get too much religious training—just enough to know what religion they're not observing. After all, if gentiles know about it, so should Jews.

Jewish education at afternoon or Sunday schools had seldom been able to avoid the curse of superficiality, but in the suburban congregations, where the motives for starting it were badly muddled to begin with, the probability of failure was especially high. Writing in the mid-fifties, a serious Jewish educator, Dr. L. H. Grunebaum, sketched a gloomy picture. At least 80 percent of the parents affiliated with a large and prosperous Westchester congregation do "little more than send [their] children to [the Sunday] school." Why do they bother to do even that much? Out of nostalgia, family habit, indecision regarding religious belief. "Yet, surely one of the decisive factors is the social life of suburban parents and children. . . . Nearly everyone has some religious affiliation. Most children go to some Sunday school. Jewish children will find that many of their gentile friendships gradually become more and more attenuated." So, in time, the sensitive Jewish parent sees that "if he wants his child to become a soundly and smoothly integrated participant in suburban life, he had better join a congregation and send his child to Sunday school." The consequences were evoked by Dr. Grunebaum with an admirable candor:

> [In the suburban Jewish home] interest in the Jewish tradition has withered, ceremonies are not adhered to; the basic skills of prayer have been lost; their relationship to God bothers few people. . . . Hebrew is unknown. . . .
> The children . . . suffer from a kind of mild schizophrenia. *Here* are the rabbi, director, cantor and teachers; *there* are the parents. . . . *Here* is supernaturalism, prayer, the Ten Commandments, Jewish customs and ceremonies. *There* is science, atomic facts, sex and Mickey Spillane, Americans ways and values. . . . So it comes about that the attempt to make children more secure as members of the Jewish community has in many cases the opposite result. Uncertainty and insecurity are increased and the children's suspicion of adult hypocrisy is strengthened because the traditions, customs and beliefs of the religious school are at complete variance with home life.

Let us suppose that Gans and Grunebaum, with the impatience of intellectuals, overstated their case, and let us grant what is probably true, that in the years after they wrote there occurred an improvement in the spiritual tone of the Jewish suburbs, a certain growth in refinement and restraint. What nevertheless seems impossible to deny is the prevalence of confusion and flaccidity, a going-through of religious and ethnic motions that had largely lost their earlier charge of meaning and now yielded only modest satisfactions.

There was another measure, however, applied by social scientists who were interested in the development of Jewish life in America but had no particular ties—or had given up their ties—with the immigrant past. For intelligent observers like Nathan Glazer and Marshall Sklare, what was most remarkable about the suburbs in which Jews congregated was the persistent attachment to "Jewish identity," however vague and hard to define that sentiment might be. Studying the midwestern Jewish suburbanites of "Lakeville," Marshall Sklare provided evidence for this approach. In "Lakeville" Reform Judaism became increasingly traditional in character; there was almost no conversion to other faiths; and the sense of Jewish involvement, even if pedestrian, remained fairly strong. True, Sklare's "Lakeville" respondents defined Judaism in moralistic rather than sacramental terms—"the religious man is distinguished not by his observance of rituals but by the scrupulousness of his ethical behavior." But the actuality of their lives extended beyond a nebulous "Jewish humanitarianism"; it meant joining temples, contributing heavily to Jewish causes (especially support of Israel), sending children to Sunday schools, and an expressed concern to ward off intermarriage. "We find that Jewish commitment—no matter how defined, and we discover from [Sklare's study] that it is often defined as nothing more than the *acceptance* of Jewish identity, no matter how *that* is defined —stands at as high a level as it has ever stood in the modern world." Seeing this as a cause for reassurance required—at least if one started from a traditional Jewish outlook, either religious or secular—a rather sharp scaling down of expectations.

To what extent, then, did the culture of the east European Jewish immigrants leave a significant imprint on the lives of their children and grandchildren? By its very nature, this question cannot be answered with any exactness, the experience of the second- and third-generation Jews, especially those in the suburbs, being unfinished and still open to unpredictable mutations. But a serious answer would surely recognize the presence of deep continuities between the East Side and Long Island, immigrant neighborhood and Americanized suburb.

Cultures are slow to die; when they do, they bequeath large deposits of custom and value to their successors; and sometimes they survive long after their more self-conscious members suppose them to have vanished. A great many suburban Jews no longer spoke Yiddish, a growing number did not understand it, some failed to appreciate the magnitude of their loss; but their deepest inclinations of conduct, bias, manner, style, intonation, all bore heavy signs of immigrant shaping. What Jewish suburbanites took to be "a good life," the kinds of vocations to which they hoped to lead their children, their sense of appropriate conduct within a family, the ideas capable of winning their respect, the moral appeals to which they remained open, their modes of argument, their fondness for pacific conduct, their views of respectability and delinquency—all showed the strains of immigrant Yiddish culture, usually blurred, sometimes buried, but still at work. Like their parents, many were still enamored of that mystery called "education," still awestruck by the goods of culture. Most Jewish suburbanites retained the strong, rather conservative feeling for the family they had acquired in the homes of their parents. (Having become more cosmopolitan, they could not live entirely by that conservative feeling—promiscuity and divorce were problems for them, as for non-Jewish suburbanites; but the persuasion that precious values inhere in family life survived among them, if only as a prod to guilt.) Like their counterparts in the cities, the suburban Jews remained a crucial segment of the cultural audience in America: the operagoers, the ballet supporters, the book buyers. If Jewish socialism had almost vanished, it took on a second, less impassioned life in the liberalism prevailing among suburban Jews. And the tradition of *tsedaka*—charity, in the larger sense of communal responsibility—remained powerful, lashing the suburban (and urban) Jews to feats of self-taxation that could not be matched in any other American community. Settled into the modest comforts of private life, they could still be roused, time after time, to the claims of public responsibility.

The suburban Jews were tied to the immigrant past in still another way. During the sixties, when the New Left became a significant force in the American universities, a good many of its leading figures—Mark Rudd, Abbie Hoffman, Jerry Rubin—came from Jewish homes. Too often mistaking the limited wealth of garment manufacturers in Westchester and Long Island for the summits of bourgeois power, such young people turned with fury against their middle-class parents. They refused, on principle, to consider the experience, the sufferings, of the older generation, for they were sick and tired of stories about immigrant ordeals which, as they saw it, masked present-day privilege and indifference. A few of these young people, driving themselves to ideological excess, became enemies of Israel, which they saw as an accomplice of Western imperialism; proclaiming themselves Trotskyists or Maoists or Weathermen, they collected funds for Al Fatah, the Palestinian terrorist movement. Exasperating such a posture may have been, and insufferable too, but was it really without precedent in the immigrant world? Was there not a line of continuity, however faint, between the Jewish anarchists of the 1880's who had ostentatiously held Yom Kippur balls and the Jewish New Leftists of the 1960's who aligned themselves with the Arabs? Was there not a long-standing tradition of violent dissociation, postures of self-hatred, and contempt for one's fathers? In new circumstances, of course, everything took on new forms, but behind these new forms it was always possible to detect the materials of the past.

Among Jewish intellectuals and semi-intellectuals, as well as the more sophisticated children of the suburbs, it became a commonplace to disparage the suburban Jews as philistine and vulgar—part of what Michael Harrington has called "the folk-rock faith . . . in the essential vapidity of suburban life," with "charcoal cooking as one of the most powerful symbols of what is wrong with Mom and Dad." In books, lectures, and articles there were frequent sneers at "bagel and lox" Jewishness. Of philistinism there was of course plenty in the Jewish suburban communities, though one would be hard put to show there was any more of it than in Yiddish-speaking immigrant neighborhoods or, for that matter, in American society as a whole. Those who loftily dismissed "bagel and lox" Jewishness failed or preferred not to grasp that certain pinched qualities of suburban Jewish life—residual attachments to foods, a few customs, and a garbled Yiddish phrase—might signify not merely self-serving nostalgia but also blocked yearnings for elements of the past that seemed spiritually vital. The suburban Jews had come upon the scene at a moment when Jewish culture in America no longer possessed its earlier assurance and vigor; they lived with whatever remnants of their youthful experience they could salvage; and "bagels and lox" (not to be sneered at in their own right!) were part of what they still had left, tokens of the past to which they clung partly because it reminded them of all that was gone.

There was also in suburban Jewish life a distinct alloy of vulgarity: the lavish *bar mitzvahs* with mountains of paté and fountains of champagne, the weddings that resembled movie premières, the country clubs edging into gentile snobbish, the stuffed tastelessness of expensive homes, the vacations at the Fountainebleau in Miami or Grossinger's in the Catskills. All these were partly the display of newly affluent people whose tastes would surely improve as they grew easier with their money—indeed, one problem of suburban life was that as vulgarity decreased, it might be replaced by a kind of prefabricated blandness. But, in part, too, the vulgarity of the suburbs derived from the early immigrant neighborhoods themselves. A cool-headed rabbi spoke about this during the fifties:

> If you look at the current phenomenon historically, you can find a lot to explain it. These new [community] centers, by and large, are sponsored by persons whose main experience with Jewish tradition, if they had any at all, was very likely to have been in the storefront *heders* in the Bronx and Brooklyn. Sometimes I think that the square boxes they now put up commemorate their origins, so to speak. Having become wealthy, they enlarge and shine up the tiny, grubby cube in which they used to prepare for Bar Mitzvah. However that is, you've got to admit that these centers are an improvement. They represent a striving to arrive, in Rockefeller Center terms, all marble and bronze, that is really touching. The catering is certainly more dignified, less commercial, than the kind of thing that went on in the lofts of Tremont and Pitkin Avenues. . . . After all, you can't expect them to build on the model of the Touro Synagogue, which itself had its own tradition.
>
> Let's be a bit realistic—how can one be a purist in these matters? If you're going to have Jewishness of any sort in this country, you've got to start somewhere, preferably with familiar, easy-to-swallow things, even the near-pagan spectacles of Bar and Bas Mitzvah and operetta-like weddings, the forms of male and female Rotarianism, and the athletic competitions.

One reason this description was useful lay in the fact that its author recognized that vulgarity didn't suddenly spring into being the day Jews began moving into the suburbs. By placing the problem in a historical context, he undercut the temptation to easy postures of superiority. There had been plenty of vulgarity in the immigrant streets: how could there not be? There was plenty of vulgarity in American life as a whole, and it was by no means wholly unlike that of the Jewish suburbs. Indeed, it is a question whether the life of any society would be bearable without some alloy of vulgarity, if only as a relief from idealisms both authentic and false.

Still, there may be some truth in the view often expressed by older Yiddishists and younger intellectuals that something about the vulgarity of the suburb was more troubling than the immigrant variety. Suburban vulgarity tended to be more pretentious and *arriviste*, less rooted in the strenuous detail of a folk culture; the immigrant kind was probably more spontaneous and innocent, certainly freer of the vices of snobbism. Middle-class vulgarity draws upon material surplus, while that of the poor is a way of coping with material scarcity. At best, however, these are analytical distinctions, and between the two kinds or phases of vulgarity, especially as they intertwined in a social experience of more than half a century, there were surely deep ties. The garment manufacturer who made his son's *bar mitzvah* into an extravagant display may have been influenced by memories of earlier occasions on Tremont Avenue in the Bronx or Eastern Parkway in Brooklyn.

The life of second- and third-generation Jews in the suburbs was not, as a rule, marked by a distinguished culture, nor was it notable for spiritual intensities; but it had strong elements of humaneness and social decency as well as, now and again, a touching self-doubt. If there was a decline from the passions that had enriched immigrant life, there was also an easing of the deprivations that had scarred it. In any case, the risk in comparing immigrant with suburban society was to set off the supposed best of one against the acknowledged worst of the other.

Open to substantial criticism, the suburban Jewish communities that began to flourish at mid-century were still far from fixed as a social enterprise. Changes, perhaps large-scale changes, were certain to come. Meanwhile, a little understanding of the forces that had made the Jewish suburbs what they were might encourage some tolerance and affection.

Into the Public Realm

If religious faith had been hollowed out in the life of many younger American Jews and the culture of their immigrant parents had become a memory to be dismissed or merely indulged, there was still one major avenue for the release of the tradition of *menshlichkeit*—humaneness, responsibility—which they retained from their youth. The intensities of internal Jewish life were now gradually diffused into American public affairs. American Jews, from the twenties onward and into the seventies, were largely committed to a politics of liberalism, both in the narrow sense of voting for the New Deal wing of the Democratic party and in the larger sense of favoring an internationalist foreign policy, a strong defense of civil liberties, active social legislation in behalf of deprived groups, and special public efforts to help American blacks. This political-ethical commitment was clearly expressed in every presidential election since at least 1936.

In 1936, the Twenty-fourth Ward in Chicago was probably the most Jewish ward in the nation. There Roosevelt received 96 percent of the vote. Elsewhere Jews were not as solidly Democratic. Four years later, Jewish wards in Boston and assembly districts in New York showed an appreciable increase in Democratic strength. Over 90 percent of the Jews in New York County's Seventeenth Assembly District cast ballots for F.D.R. In 1944 Jewish Democratic strength increased still further. In Boston's Jewish Fourteenth Ward, more than 95 percent of the Jewish votes cast went to Roosevelt.

The results of national sample surveys conducted by the American Institute of Public Opinion and by the National Opinion Research Center show that more than 90 out of every 100 Jews voted Democratic in 1940 and 1944. . . .

Jewish Democratic strength diminished in 1948, but the combined Truman-[Henry] Wallace vote was almost as high in Jewish wards and assembly districts as it had been for F.D.R. in 1944. The Wallace vote was essentially Democratic. . . .

Although 1948 was a year when most Democrats could be sharply separated from Republicans by status characteristics, Jewish voters could not be so simply divided. The most radical candidate, Wallace, won the votes of many well-educated upper-middle-class Jews who had heretofore voted for Franklin Roosevelt, but the Republicans gained very little over 1944.

In 1952, all segments of Truman-Wallace strength except Negroes shifted somewhat to Eisenhower. But analysis of aggregate returns from Jewish areas and the results of national surveys show that the Jewish defection was slight indeed. . . .

According to the results of American Institute of Public Opinion surveys in 1944, the Jews were the only high economic status group to look with favor on governmental guarantees against economic insecurity. The results show that 53.8 percent of the Jewish business and professional men were for such government guarantees, as compared to an average of about 20 percent for non-Jews in these same occupations.

Other survey evidence showed that, even though there were proportionately fewer Jewish manual laborers than in any other religious denomination, a higher proportion of Jews than of any other group wanted to give more power and influence to working people. While 58.8 percent of the Jews wanted [to do this], only 31.1 percent of the Congregationalists, 37.1 percent of the Presbyterians, and 34.7 percent of the Episcopalians—the other high occupational status groups—agreed.

According to 1952 surveys [on issues concerning civil liberties, congressional investigating committees, federal security programs, etc.], the opinions of Jews were at variance with those of the rest of the population. Gallup and Roper public opinion polls found the Jews more hostile to Joe McCarthy, less disturbed by charges of Democratic tolerance of communism in government, and more zealous in defending nonconformity than Catholics and Protestants.

When one came to think of it, the Jewish commitment to liberalism was a remarkable fact. The Jews were the only ethnic community in the United States in which significant numbers of people, while or after rising in socioeconomic condition, did not seem to change their political loyalties. And this alignment with liberalism characterized the politics of American Jews even when it seemed to threaten the immediate interests of some or many of them. Nor is it a secret that the number of Jews active in liberal, radical, protest, and civil-libertarian movements has been highly disproportionate.* Traditional and inherited sentiments within the Jewish community played a stronger role than perceptions of a new standing in the American class structure.

The commitment to liberalism was based on at least two factors: the once-powerful tradition of secular Jewish socialism, now fading but still felt and remembered, and sometimes affecting younger people who did not know the historical forces that were acting upon them, and the premise, shared by Jews in the West for perhaps two centuries, that Jewish interests and, indeed, survival were best served by an open, secular society promoting liberal values and tolerating a diversity of religious groups.**

It was only natural, in these circumstances, to wonder whether the persistent liberalism of American Jews might be a case of ideological lag. Would they not sooner or later "catch up" with their improved social condition by turning toward a more conservative politics? By the sixties there were a number of seemingly plausible reasons for expecting the American Jews—even though many of them were still alive to remembered voices of immigrant parents and grandparents—slowly to turn toward the right.

Disenchantment over Communist anti-Semitism in eastern Europe was a shattering experience for a good many of the older, Yiddish-speaking "pro-

---

* In the larger cities and some suburbs near New York, Los Angeles, and Chicago there also survived into the fifties groups of Jewish "progressive" sympathizers, heirs of the Popular Front, sometimes still attached to the Soviet Union but more often inclined to evade or suppress what had by then become known about Stalinism. Often English-speaking professionals and middle-class people, they were especially active in the cause of Julius and Ethel Rosenberg, who had been convicted and executed in the fifties as spies of the Soviet Union but whom they regarded as innocent martyrs to Cold War persecution. A good many individuals with this political outlook remained in the Jewish milieu; but once the news came out of the murder of a large number of Yiddish writers in the Soviet Union in 1952, and once the reports of anti-Semitism in the Soviet Union and Poland became so persistent that they could not be dismissed as mere slander, the organized "progressive" tendency within the American Jewish world shrank to relative insignificance.

** During the sixties some Jewish New Leftists tried to ground their politics in "the prophetic tradition," with the hope thereby of staking out a claim to Jewish legitimacy. These efforts ignored the complex diversity of Jewish history since the Diaspora, as indeed before then. With enough wrenching one could find "ancestors" in the Jewish past for almost any opinion. If one wanted a "Jewish justification" for liberalism or radicalism, the honest course was to provide it in terms of the present situation rather than trying to enlist prophets no longer in a position to speak for themselves.

gressives," as also for the younger, English-speaking ones. If this did not lead directly to conservative ideas, it certainly encouraged conservative moods. Intensifying such responses was the flirtation of portions of the New Left with Arab terrorism: it takes no great powers of imagination to conjure up the feelings of most Jews when they read about Jewish students—a handful, but a visible handful—collecting funds for Al Fatah! And among Jews who had never been near the radical milieu, Soviet anti-Semitism often brought about a generalized revulsion from all forms of leftist or even liberal thought.

Perhaps a deeper cause, though one impossible to measure, was a growing feeling that Jewish life in America was by now reasonably secure, or at least as secure as Jewish life ever could be anywhere. Some observers consequently expected that in time there would follow a gradual decline in the felt urgency of American Jews to transcend their own, "narrow" class interests and respond to universalist moral appeals. Rightly or wrongly—this argument went—many Jews were now inclined to feel more and more "at home" in the United States; the messianic strand in Jewish life (despite a remarkable new outburst through the New Left) seemed to be dimming; and thereby the conclusion might be reached that Jews should start enjoying the luxury of responding to political events "like ordinary Americans," that is, in accord with their individual or class interests.*

A study of the 1972 presidential election indicates that, despite an estimated drop of about 15 to 17 percent in Jewish support for the Democrats, the Jews were second only to blacks in voting for McGovern. "Jews voted

---

* The electoral evidence was inconclusive. A turning point in Jewish political responses is said to have occurred in 1966, when a estimated 55 percent of New York's Jews, according to a sample poll of Brooklyn voters, voted against Mayor John Lindsay's newly created Civilian Review Board. Proponents of the Civilian Review Board considered it a channel through which blacks and Puerto Ricans might register complaints against police brutality; opponents saw it as a device initiated by well-to-do white liberals for weakening police authority in a city already plagued by high crime rates. Among the Jews in the Brooklyn poll, highly educated professionals overwhelmingly supported the review board, while poorly educated lower-class Jewish workers strongly opposed it—in part, no doubt, because the latter, forced to remain in deteriorating neighborhoods, felt much more endangered by crime. Whether this referendum was really a decisive test of Jewish liberalism remains an open question, since many of the lower-class Jews who voted against the review board were also supporters of liberal social welfare measures in federal and state politics.

Mayoralty elections in Los Angeles, Minneapolis, and Philadelphia indicated voter swings to the right during the late sixties and at least partial Jewish support for this trend. In the 1969 New York mayoral election, two right wingers, Mario Procaccino and John Marchi, got three votes for every two given John Lindsay—and New York, of course, is a heavily Jewish city. In 1971, the reactionary Frank Rizzo became mayor of Philadelphia, and a study of that election indicates that, again, the Jewish vote split along class lines, with lower-income groups largely supporting Rizzo and upper-income groups going for his liberal Republican opponent. The Jews did not elect Rizzo; whites *in toto* voted around two to one for him, whereas Jews divided about fifty-fifty between Rizzo and his opponent. "But that was not good enough for those who expected Jews—*and Jews alone*—to remain unaffected by the law and order issue."

more for the Democrat and less for the Republican than any other body of white voters—Protestants, Catholics, businessmen, farmers, workers; even professors; even students. Moreover, McGovern did better with the more prosperous Jews than with the less. East and West, North and South, the McGovern share of the Jewish votes cast was between 60 and 70 percent, and the Nixon share between 30 and 40 percent." There was a rise in the number of registered Jewish voters, as also of all registered voters, who chose not to cast ballots in the 1972 presidential election—perhaps a signal of distaste for both candidates. "In 1972 the many non-voting Jews cast a significant vote for the third candidate, Neither—neither McGovern nor Nixon. Of all registered Jewish voters, about 25 percent voted for Nixon."

But again it was not entirely clear that this vote signified a clear shift by American Jews toward the right. There were possible grounds for a shift of Jewish voters away from McGovern which might not preclude a later return to supporting the Democratic party. McGovern's alleged "isolationism," the preference some Israeli leaders indicated for Nixon, the large-scale defection of trade unions from the Democratic candidate, the "radical" tax proposals advanced by McGovern at the start of his campaign, the presence among his supporters of chic celebrities who were associated in the minds of many Jews with the political tone of the Lindsay administration in New York City—all of these counted as contributing factors. What no one quite knew was the relative weights to assign to each.

One difficulty has to do with the term "liberal." It is a term with no single meaning, only a cluster of imprecise and at times contradictory suggestions. Perhaps, while the majority of American Jews did remain committed to liberalism during the decades after the Second World War, it was to a liberalism increasingly "moderate" and a bit more conservative. The general commitment to liberalism continued, especially among Jewish professionals and middle-class people, but the intensity with which it was held and the readiness to expend energy and accept inconvenience in its behalf may slowly have declined. Among plebeian Jews, especially those unable to escape decaying and dangerous urban neighborhoods, there was a trend toward a split politics: support for the kinds of economic reforms introduced by the New Deal but hostility to social innovations associated with the upheavals of the sixties.

A convenient symbol of this partial running down of energies was Abe Beame's election in 1974 as the first Jewish mayor of New York City. Beame's father, Philip, a paper cutter, had been a socialist who used to take Abe to meetings. "That was Eugene Debs, and that group," Abe Beame would recall. "You listen as a kid, and so much stays with you." But what did stay with him? Not radical or populist fervor, nor reforming zeal; perhaps a residual sense of social decency strained to manageable dimensions.

Yet it would be a mistake to suppose that the liberal outlook has vanished among American Jews. There are factors in Jewish life which encourage the persistence of liberalism. Were the tradition of social activism to be abandoned or seriously weakened, one result would be a very severe crisis of identity among nonreligious yet "Jewish" Jews, especially those who keep a foothold in organizational life. For the Orthodox nothing is finally crucial except an unbreakable tie with God: that defines them as Jews. But for many others, from Conservative rabbis to socialist intellectuals, being Jewish, though surely not reducible to social idealism, unavoidably carries a crucial measure of social idealism. Remove that measure and the problem of Jewish distinctiveness must become increasingly acute, since there would be one reason fewer for feeling that, despite embarrassments at self-definition, Jews in America still have a tradition uniquely their own and contributions to the society distinctively their own. For some time to come, then, a somewhat mellowed liberalism seems likely to retain the loyalties of large numbers of American Jews.

While inner social and economic transformations of the American Jews were obviously important in shaping their new consciousness, a number of historical events and problems, not necessarily touching their immediate lives, would have been acknowledged by most Jews to be of still greater urgency: the Holocaust, the formation of the state of Israel, and the question of anti-Semitism.

The Holocaust and After

During the postwar years the life of American Jews was inherently "schizoid." At home: improvements in social and economic conditions, a growing sense of ease, comfort, security. Abroad: the greatest horror in the history of mankind, the destruction of six million Jews for reasons no mind could fathom, no intuition penetrate. How were these two elements of Jewish experience to be reconciled? The only honest answer was that they could not be: it was a division which anyone who retained even the faintest sense of Jewish identity would have to live with as best he could.

One possible response to the Holocaust was an outpouring of rhetoric; but while there were the inevitable meetings, memorials, and manifestoes, for once the Jewish mania for speech was subdued. "Even an outcry," wrote the Yiddish poet Aaron Zeitlin, "is now a lie, even tears are mere literature, even prayers are false." Jewish scholars patiently accumulated historical data concerning the Holocaust, driven by a kind of clenched meticulousness to scrape together every last, unbearable fact. And there was a quantity of literary effort, most of it doomed to a failure of mere language—though the Yiddish poems of Jacob Glatstein, approaching their subject almost by stealth, spoke of emotions after the killing: mordant, resigned, hushed.

But what could the Holocaust mean for ordinary Jews, the sons and daughters of immigrants who neither made speeches nor wrote poems, the kinds of people who had but recently improved their life and were now trying to find some frail comforts while still persuaded that they lived under a sentence of unique destiny? or the kinds of people who wanted to pass on to their children some sense of that destiny, if only they knew the words? They did not speak much about it, since they no more knew what to say than did the poets. Some Jewish intellectuals, supposing there must always be words appropriate for each experience, were inclined to conclude that ordinary Jews were forgetting the Holocaust—did they not continue to go about the usual business of life through the usual days of the year?

We have no certain knowledge about such matters. Yet anyone possessing even a casual acquaintance with American Jews—including the half-Jews, quarter-Jews, and anti-Jews—is not likely to believe they had forgotten the Holocaust. Perhaps they had driven their memories deeper beneath the surface of consciousness than was quite seemly. Perhaps they had tried, with an understandable if inexcusable yearning, to shield their children from encountering this dread beyond description. But forgotten they had not. Those few who still knew Yiddish might say, after an old proverb, that they wanted the Jews to survive *oyf tselokhes*, out of spite, which is perhaps a sardonic equivalent of the view put forward by the theologian Emil Fackenheim that Jews must not give Hitler posthumous victories.

Memories of the Holocaust pressed deep into the consciousness of Jews, all, or almost all, making them feel that whatever being a Jew meant, it required of them that they try to remain Jews. This was in part a matter of fear; somewhat more, a matter of need; but most of all, a matter of honor. Beyond that, any pretense of explaining the Holocaust, any theory as to its causes, was bound to crumble into inconsequence, a mere trifling with categories in face of the unspeakable. There was nothing to do but remember, and that was best done in silence, alone.

Israel and the American Jews

The emergence of the state of Israel had, among its numerous effects, one that was barely noticed at the time: it sped the dissolution of the ideologies that had prevailed among immigrant Jews. Old disputes between socialists and Zionists now lapsed into mere habits of recall or were dropped entirely (except for a small group of Bundists, refugees from occupied Poland, who clung tenaciously to their socialist internationalism while also, with some justice, criticizing the new Jewish state for insensitivity toward Yiddish).

How one responded to Israel had no necessary connection with past views about Zionist ideology. One could believe that Zionism had been mistaken in crucial respects yet support the state founded by the Zionists.

For the American Zionists, Israel brought a condition of permanent crisis. They were reduced to a society of sympathizers from afar; they were taunted by David Ben Gurion, Israel's first premier, for failing to undertake *Aliyah,* or settlement in Israel (given their convictions, what could they answer?); and in time they were accorded less attention by Israeli emissaries than those wealthy non-Zionist Jews whose help was urgently needed. The reaction of most American Jews, whether immigrant or native-born, was to show their solidarity with Israel less as a fulfillment of the Zionist or any other idea than as a vibrant historical reality, the place where survivors of the Holocaust and other Jews in flight could make a life for themselves.

Israel brought other changes to the Diaspora Jews. "For the first time in generations a code word for Jew is no longer the medieval 'wandering Jew' or 'rootless cosmopolitan' but the 'Zionist,' the individual fiercely rooted in his soil—exactly the opposite of the former stigma." The mere fact that Israel existed—that it beckoned, implored, demanded—meant that second- and third-generation Jews were being prodded into decisions of commitment or refusal. A new consciousness of what being a Jew might mean was thereby released. And with that new consciousness, a new morale. For non-religious Jews, Israel became the chief alternative to assimilation. Even the enemies of the Jews had to acknowledge radical transformations of tone: hostile cartoons depicting the snub-nosed Moshe Dayan as a hook-nosed warrior testified to an utterly novel image of the Jew—novel, at least, in the modern era. Some Jews, both religious and radical, were by no means happy with this image, but that did not gainsay its power.

There were also new difficulties. Problems of crisscrossing, perhaps conflicting, loyalties could not be kept hushed. The authority of Israel within the baroquely structured milieu of organized American Jewry became enormous, sometimes decisive, and despite the moderately leftist tilt of the Israeli government, its impact upon American Jews was necessarily conservative. For insofar as it constituted a state determined to preserve itself, Israel found it necessary to take a "pragmatic" stand toward international arrangements of power, and in practice this often meant a large degree of dependence upon American military help—which, in turn, brought about public statements and relationships that caused liberal Jews in America to feel troubled. Some of the more reflective Zionist leaders had to recognize the probability of an inherent clash between the state of Israel and a universalistic movement attached to it. Yet even those American Jews uneasy before the growth of Israeli prestige—which often favored within the American Jewish milieu professional fund-raisers and *nouveaux riches**—

---

* Judah Shapiro, a leader of American Labor Zionism, noted as the two major consequences for American Zionism of its close identification with Israel: "1. pragmatism and consensus replaced ideology and polemic; 2. the instrumentality for raising funds also became the arbiter for the allocation of funds; philosophies and programs became beneficiaries and pleaders; fund raisers and large contributors became governors and leaders."

had also to recognize that, simply becuase it was a state, Israel could do things no private agency ever had been able to. Israel could rescue persecuted Jews from northern Africa, it could bring to trial Adolf Eichmann, it could provide shelter for disaffected Russian Jews.

Among the more thoughtful figures within the Jewish community there was much discussion of still another consequence of the formation of Israel. To what extent had the emergence of the new state undermined the traditional Jewish concept of *galut* (Hebrew) or *golus* (Yiddish), terms signifying exile and alienness? One view affirmed that once the Jews had a state to which they could "return," the concept of *galut* was removed from the "plane of a tragically imposed necessity and reduced . . . to a matter of deliberate choice," since now, for the first time in two millenniums "Jews living outside [of Israel] do so of their own free will. . . . The concept of *galut* is impossible once it becomes a mere function of an *individual* choice; a Jew who simply declines to return to a restored and reconstituted Zion is obviously not suffering the pangs of exile." For others, the concept of *galut* had acquired over the centuries a significance much richer than that of enforced separation from Zion; it had become a term encompassing the moral and cultural substance of two thousand years of Jewish life ("The time has come for us to proclaim the enduring legitimacy of the Diaspora on a spiritual level.") These opinions, in all their refinements and nuances, were more than exercises in dialectic; they were agitated reflections of a continued search for self-definition.

If a major consequence of the emergence of Israel upon American Jews was to strengthen their own sense of worth, there was another, somewhat paradoxical one: it enabled them to postpone that inner reconsideration of "Jewishness" which the American condition required. For the minority of fervent believers, being Jewish was not a problem; only the search for ways adequately to sustain the faith was a problem. But for the majority of American Jews who regarded themselves as either secular or indifferent, the question of what it meant to remain a Jew grew increasingly difficult. Less and less could "Jewishness" be described as a common culture, the substance of shared immigrant life. With a fair display of logic, some Jews concluded that, since they were not religious and had passed beyond the boundary of *Yiddishkeit*, their "Jewishness" was not central to their lives, it was a mere accident of birth, and while they did not propose to cringe in shame, neither did they have much taste for parochial assertions. They preferred to see themselves as good Americans, or good liberals, or good human beings.

But for many, perhaps most, of the sons and daughters of the immigrants, difficulty in defining their "Jewishness" did not for a moment call into question the actuality of their Jewish experience. They knew they had been shaped by a common past; they feared they might have to face common dangers; they suspected they shared a common fate. These problems in self-perception led to peculiarly nervous discussions about "who is a Jew?"—

though, in fact, almost everyone knew quite well whether or not he was one.

Almost all Jews agreed that Israel had to be helped, nurtured, and kept alive. Some felt this with a kindled passion, others with uncertainty, still others with embarrassment; but except for tiny sects of ideologues fringing the far right and far left, all believed that the survival of Israel was a necessity. Helping Israel thereby became a major communal activity among American Jews, undertaken with the usual range of styles from reflectiveness to busyness. But if one could establish oneself as a Jew by "working for Israel," then one might put aside those irksome spiritual and metaphysical problems life was now imposing on all nonreligious Jews. This was neither an unworthy nor a dishonorable evasion—first comes survival and then definition. But it left a growing mound of intellectual debts which sooner or later would have to be paid.

A Fear Beyond Escaping

Haunted by the demons of modern history, most of the immigrants and many of their children kept a fear, somewhere in their minds, that anti-Semitism might again become a serious problem in America. By mid-century, it was often less an actual fear than a persuasion that they *should* keep this fear, all past experience warranting alertness even if there was no immediate reason for anxiety. There had been several waves of anti-Semitic sentiment in the American past, and it took no special gifts of discernment for Jews to be aware that it remained a presence, usually latent but sometimes erupting into nastiness. The social anti-Semitism of the early decades of the century, relatively bluff and "good-natured," had been accepted by most immigrants as part of the way things were; the anti-Semitism of the twenties and early thirties, sustained first by Henry Ford's money and broadcast later by the radio priest, Father Coughlin, had been more frightening because more directly political. For fifteen or twenty years after the Second World War the Jews breathed a little more easily in America—these were the years that one Jewish leader called "the Golden Age," perhaps the result of a widespread shame once word of the Holocaust reached the American people. Something of major importance occurred at this time: anti-Semitism ceased to be respectable, it could no longer be declared openly by public men or business leaders, it had to be tucked away in private clubs, locker rooms, bars. During these years public anti-Semitism was mostly the work of cranks, fundamentalist ranters, and other agents of malaise. But in the society as a whole, it was no longer good form to make sneering references to "hooked noses," or to use the word "Jew" as a verb meaning to bargain.

Yet none of this, in the feelings of most Jews, warranted a lowering of their guard. There were still just enough occasional incidents—a synagogue desecrated here, a case of gross discrimination there—to keep alive that sense of precariousness which had long ago become an essential part of Jewish consciousness. And then, in the sixties, there began to appear a new problem, anti-Semitism among black militants. For immigrant Jews often still living in semipoverty next to black neighborhoods, this signified that if there was a threat to Jewish security it came mostly from below: from urban blacks who in the schools, a few industries, and some unions were pressing to undo Jewish positions and accomplishments—pressing, especially, to undermine the merit eystem that had made possible those Jewish positions and accomplishments.

For decades American blacks had served, through bitter circumstance, as a kind of buffer for American Jews. So long as native hatreds were taken out primarily on blacks, they were less likely to be taken out on Jews. If Jews have been the great obsession of Christianity, blacks have been the great obsession of Americans. As long as this condition obtained, both organized and spontaneous haters could concentrate their attention on the blacks and only secondarily on the Jews.

Had the Jews felt themselves to be part of "the white majority" and followed a mere crude calculus of self-interest, they might have joined other whites in holding down the blacks. Some Jews did, of course, in the South and elsewhere; but the majority felt themselves to be allies of the blacks, occasionally active and more often passive—and at times just about the only reliable allies the blacks had. Smarting under prejudice themselves and often committed to universalistic and radical goals, Jews contributed heavily to the leadership of the civil rights movement in the early sixties. Jews who had "made it" set out to help blacks who had not. Heavy contributors to the revolution of rising expectations, Jews were, in the aftermath, occasional victims of declining expectations.

If only in retrospect, one can understand why there occurred—had to occur, perhaps—the turning of activist blacks against Jewish or, for that matter, white gentile allies. Black militants often felt that Jews in or near the civil rights movement were patronizing in their attitudes, tending to assume, especially if they had fixed leftist ideologies, that it was they who had the word and it was their task to "train" the feckless blacks. Who can estimate how much validity there was to this black response? What is not in question is its intensity. The achievement of autonomy meant that there would have to be some irksome jostling of friends, and in general, despite bruised feelings, Jews active in the civil rights cause came to understand this. What they could not tolerate was the fringe of blacks who pushed a legitimate need to be on their own into a repetition of coarse anti-Semitic slogans.

Meanwhile, there were developments in American society which brought new conflicts between black and Jewish communities. Southern blacks poured into the northern cities, where they soon ran up against a complex of unsolved problems: the backlash of adjacent ethnic groups, the sociocultural traumas of adjusting to urban life, the economic hardships of the ghetto, and, perhaps most of all, the shock of discovering that they remained a group still discriminated against, still suffering internal disruption and pathology, still overwhelmed by the heritage of centuries of oppression. At this point in the spectacular collapse of spectacular expectations, the civil rights coalition came apart and black nationalism grew stronger. Stronger in subjective expressiveness than objective results, the "black revolution" expelled whites from its ranks. Very often that meant Jews.

How widespread the flare-up of anti-Semitism was within the black community, no one knew exactly. Some studies indicate that there was less of it among blacks than among white gentiles. That some Jews, and especially Jewish "defense" organizations, exaggerated the depth and range of this black anti-Semitism seems probable. But it is beyond question that anti-Semitism had shown itself openly along the more "radical" fringes of black nationalism, especially among the Black Panthers.

It is crucial to note here that even in the mid-twentieth century many American Jews, certainly a good many of those who came out of the east European immigrant world, still *felt* like losers. Being able to buy a home, or move into a suburb, or send kids to college could not quickly dissolve that feeling. Black antagonism—whether deep rooted or, as seems more probable, the verbal upchuck of fringe groups—was linked in their minds with a possible resurgence of global anti-Semitism and the visible enmity of Arabs toward Israel. And who could easily separate, in such reactions, justified alarm from "paranoid" excess?

Aggravating such fears were problems of social friction between adjacent black and Jewish communities, the latter often composed of older people no longer much inclined to an articulate liberalism and mostly concerned with group survival and personal safety. Jews, like other whites, tended now to link the problem of crime to the problem of the blacks. That much of the crime among black youth was related to rage following upon the discovery that the revolution of rising expectations would not be rapidly followed by a revolution of rising gratifications; that most of the victims of black crimes were themselves black; that, in some distorted way, even the ability to release their rage in antisocial acts indicated a gradual phychic freeing of blacks from earlier postures of submissiveness; that pathologies in the black community constituted a price for historical injustice such as no other group in America had ever had to suffer—all this was true. But it provided no immediate answer to the retired Jewish garment worker or aging shopkeeper in Crown Heights or the northeast Bronx who was frightened of being mugged. One result was the rise within Jewish neighborhoods of demagogic types like Jerry Birbach, who inflamed every sensitive Jewish nerve in a 1972 struggle over integrated housing in Queens.

There were younger Jews, brought up in a moment of relative tolerance, who grew impatient with the rooted fears of their parents and critical of those Jewish organizations which kept sounding the alarm against even the most trivial anti-Semitic incidents. Trying hard to be evenhanded, such younger Jews would say that they remembered from their youth outbursts of antigentile feeling by their parents, contempt for churches and *goyim*—and why were these any better in principle than hatred of Jews by gentiles?

In principle, of course, they were not. But the evenhandedness of such younger Jews almost always missed the point, as did their ridicule of Jewish "overreaction" to the threat of anti-Semitism. For behind the words they remembered having heard in their childhood—fear and disdain of the *goyim* —lay an all but endless collective experience. And those who retained a historical sense, something fairly uncommon among the American young, could understand and even sympathize with the "overreaction" of the masses of Jews.

Nor did this "overreaction" derive solely from personal or collective memories. The persuasion that anti-Semitism, virulent or mild, was a constant in the Western world had settled deep into Jewish awareness. Not many Jews could or dared bring it to speech, but many Jews seemed persuaded that as long as Christianity survived, so must anti-Semitism. The "tradition of the curse" which Christianity had traditionally placed upon those Jews who refused to follow Jesus had become integral to the mythology of our culture, handed down from generation to generation. Joel Carmichael has vividly detailed this process:

> What makes anti-Semitism unique, and uniquely linked to Christianity as such, is the dramatic element of mystical satanism that is the only way specifically Christian thought can explain the historic existence of the Jewish people since the Crucifixion. For if the drama of Christianity is to retain its magnetism, if personal salvation via the redemptive Crucifixion, with or without the intervention of a Church, is to remain a potent symbol for the Christian masses, the Jews constitute an alien, repugnant, and profoundly indigestible element in the world.

To say all this was not to insist that anti-Semitism had always to manifest itself with constant intensity. "Perhaps it is best regarded as a latent sore spot in Christian society, flaring up under contributory pressures or infections. Jews may accordingly have simply to go on coping with anti-Semitism tactically, just as, in fact, they have always done."

Not many Jews could have said all this as well as Carmichael, but many of them, one hazards, shared a similar sense of things. They were held by a well-earned sense of historical realism beyond the grasp of those sons and daughters who wished to believe that the exile had come to an end, the lion had lain down with the lamb, and a mere two or three decades after the Holocaust Jews could suppose themselves to be living in sufficient safety.*

The Immigrant Survivors

And the immigrants themselves? The aging men and women reaching the end of their lives on a diminished East Side, in Queens or the Bronx, Miami or Los Angeles, those for whom Yiddish was still their natural, sometimes their only language?

Through prodigies of will, the declining number of people still devoted to Yiddish continued to speak, write, and publish. In relation to the possible audience, the quantity of Yiddish publication was astonishing, far beyond what any economic calculus might warrant. Distinguished writers like Isaac Bashevis Singer and Chaim Grade issued novels in Yiddish; poets like Rachel Korn and Eliezer Greenberg, reaching in their late years a plateau of "serene plainness," would send out a volume of verse to a friend here, a reader there; lesser writers published their books privately, with little prospect of seeing them reach more than a few score of people.

The *Tsukunft*, only a little older than most of its readers, continued to appear as a monthly, somewhat fallen from its days of early glory but from time to time printing an item of distinction. From her East Side apartment, and whenever she could gather enough material and money, the fine lyric poet Kadia Molodowsky put out a little magazine, *Sviva*, devoted to poetry and belles-lettres. From Tel Aviv came the *Goldene Keyt*, a quarterly of letters under the editorship of Abraham Sutzkever, a Holocaust survivor—this was perhaps the best of Yiddish magazines. From Buenos Aires there was a series of coarsely printed but valuable reissues of Yiddish writers. In its years of decline Yiddish culture was more than ever an international culture, a fraternity of survivors scattered across the globe.

Political weeklies and monthlies sponsored by the dwindling Yiddish political groups kept coming out of New York. There were the *Yidisher Kemfer*, the labor Zionist weekly; *Unzer Tsayt*, the monthly Bundist journal; the *Vecker*, voice of the right-wing Jewish Social Democrats; and others. Quarreling with one another, they maintained a skeleton of community; printing in their back pages a steady array of death notices, they witnessed the culmination of their years.

* In 1965 the Vatican Council finally declared that Jews were not to be blamed for the crucifixion of Jesus. It was a long-needed and long delayed statement and, no doubt, would yield considerable benefits to the cause of humaneness; but remembering the historical record of the Church on this matter, and its role during the Holocaust, it was not always possible, mere flesh being what it is, to avoid the reaction of that caustic immigrant who said, "*A sheynem dank aykh,*" which, roughly translated, means "Thanks a lot."

None of these gallant efforts could stem the course of change. Except in small, isolated clusters of Jews who for religious or ideological reasons deliberately tried to keep themselves apart from the world, there was no longer any community in which young people were brought up to speak Yiddish as their first, their native tongue.* The Yiddishists kept trying to find a toehold in the future, sponsoring high-school classes in Yiddish, college courses in Yiddish literature (often in translation), reading circles of adults wishing to reconnect with their past, and at YIVO, that indispensable center of Yiddish scholarly work, a graduate program for Jewish secular culture and history. But the mere fact that the surviving Yiddishists could find encouragement in such small-scale efforts showed how bleak their prospects really were. A culture can thrive only when rooted in a living language, only when that language is used spontaneously, organically, by a people in its daily life. But with each passing year that was less true of Yiddish.

Institutions of the immigrant milieu survived, some through mere stubbornness, others through inertia, and still others through a rechanneled usefulness. The Educational Alliance, no longer a predominantly Jewish institution, now served blacks and Puerto Ricans as well. The HIAS helped Russian Jews who had fled from Soviet anti-Semitism to find jobs and homes in America. The Workmen's Circle registered a modest gain in membership during the seventies, perhaps because it was the only large organization still devoted to Yiddish culture and therefore a natural home for those who still felt an attachment to it.

The most powerful institutions still led by immigrant survivors were the garment unions. Pragmatists in their old age, concerned with day-to-day struggles and mostly indifferent to ideology, the veterans of Jewish labor held on, still canny at the arts of consolidating power, still shrewd at negotiating with employers in an industry forever depressed and unstable, and still proud of traditions and achievements they remembered. In some of the Jewish or once-Jewish unions, notably the Amalgamated Clothing Workers, a younger, transitional leadership took over in the early seventies. Replacing the old immigrant leaders were middle-aged technicians, Jewish lawyers and negotiators who worked well for the unions but rarely had any personal experience in the shops or the Yiddish milieu. In about a decade these new men, rising to the top in the ILGWU as well as the Amalgamated, would themselves probably be replaced, in some places by Italians and in New York by blacks and Puerto Ricans.

For the Jewish leaders, the garment unions had fallen on painful days. These unions were wealthy, powerful, and influential; but with the sharp

---

* The "small, isolated clusters" were mainly Hasidim in Brooklyn and elsewhere, who maintained a tight inner structure, a high morale, and a strict religious outlook. For the secular Yiddishists who had struggled for decades to preserve the language they loved, it seemed a bitter irony that only among their pious opponents within ʳʰe Jewish world was this effort meeting with much success.

changes in their ethnic composition, the elderly leaders felt increasingly isolated and beleaguered. A chasm of values, language, style, premises, all separated them from their own members, some 80 percent of whom were black and Puerto Rican women little inclined to take an interest in union affairs. The Jewish leaders who had once seen themselves as the vanguard of unionism were now subject to needling attacks by left-wing journalists insisting that the ruling group in the ILGWU was a racist autocracy. The black and Puerto Rican workers seldom actively rebelled against the Jewish leadership and seldom became active members or showed much potential for leadership. Those of the Jewish veterans who did not just shrug helplessly, as if they had no choice but to accept a bad turn from history, found themselves bewildered. Their security in office was not endangered, but their political self-esteem was—it is hard, even in comfort, to outlive one's hour.

The thousands of new members in the garment unions had no connection with the great tradition of Jewish unionism. Sweatshops were, for them, not in the past but in the present, and union triumphs were something that came, if they came at all, from on high. "They are aware of that which touches their present: that a good many of them are poorly skilled and low-paid and that, often, they do not understand the language of the men who represent them." Outside critics and a few of the newer union members charged that the ILGWU deliberately kept blacks and Puerto Ricans away from leadership; the union answered that most of these new members showed no interest, and that women members cared more about getting home after work than sitting around for union meetings. There were no blacks on the general executive board of the ILGWU and only one Puerto Rican; the union replied that it did not believe in tokenism, and that as soon as black and Puerto Rican leaders emerged, they would receive proper recognition. "But first they must be trained."

Were the ILGWU leaders, as the more extreme critics charged, deliberately keeping blacks and Puerto Ricans away from the better jobs and power within the union? Given their background, convictions, and shrewd sense of what is necessary in union life, very few ILGWU leaders could have been supposed to be guilty in this sense. But was it possible that, because of uneasy suspicions regarding people with whom they had little in common, the Jewish leaders were sometimes guilty of patronizing or unconsciously overlooking the interests of these members? It was entirely possible.

Harsh accusations of discrimination and angry countercharges of union-baiting flew across the garment center. Black groups like the NAACP kept repeating their accusations, and the ILGWU kept replying, more and more angrily, that the black organizations were trying to make political capital out of a situation that, while difficult, was steadily improving. Like the clashes between black and Jewish urban neighborhoods which pitted the very poor against the poor or nearly poor, these problems seemed beyond immediate solution. Leaders proud of their records within the union movement and seeing themselves as guardians of a great tradition could not be expected simply to step aside on demand. They had their convictions and their needs. But to newly articulate groups all this might seem an irrelevance of the past. In time, no doubt, the situation would resolve itself through a transfer of authority, but meanwhile the costs were high on both sides. Whatever the justice of particular accusations or the truth of particular replies, the saddest part of the story is that at the end such troubles had to arise at all.

By the late sixties or early seventies there were perhaps a quarter of a million poor Jews living in New York City alone, and some twenty thousand of them still on the East Side, in old tenements and modest housing projects. For many of these aging immigrants, not having enough coins to buy the food they wanted was a problem in quite the same way that it was for other, better-publicized groups. Still worse was the sense of abandonment, "left behind and left alone," in neighborhoods that seemed frightening, *were* frightening. On Delancey near Essex, buildings that had started to decay half a century ago stood next to synagogues long closed up—"windows are shattered, doors are boarded with random widths of warped wood, Hebrew letters are covered by Puerto Rican posters and announcements of wrestling matches. Garbage and glass lie in the streets, on the steps, in the narrow alleys that separate buildings."

Old Jewish ladies still come to the Educational Alliance, where it is safe and clean, and they can "hear beautiful stories and sing songs and hear lectures." Yet one complains, "I was robbed in the toilet of my rent money and Medicaid card. I applied for a new card nine weeks ago. I'm still waiting. . . . We senior citizens are treated like little children." An old man nearby speaks with a heavy Yiddish accent: "We used to sleep in the park, even in the nighttime. It was safe then. Now they rob you even in the park."

It is hardest for those who were "active," those who held the banners of causes and movements, veterans of union organization who can be found in Penn South, the ILGWU co-operative houses in the Chelsea area of Manhattan, where they rent moderately priced apartments that are comfortable and air-conditioned. Jacob, a retired union organizer, who had once gone to the Soviet Union and come back disenchanted, sputters with inchoate anger at all he sees about him. His wife, Sophie, five years younger and still working as an operator in a garment shop, speaks of their life:

> I'm not retired yet. Jacob is. It's difficult for him. There's not enough to do. So he's angry. And I'm not sure he knows why. He spends a good deal of time reading. A lot of newspapers. All the retired people in this co-op read newspapers and magazines. A great deal. By me, it's a disease. . . . It's too difficult to understand the world now. There are no sides that we can take.
>   Jacob and I don't have the problems that some of our friends have. I'm

still working. That's what makes the difference. I tell myself it's a lot better than it used to be for old people. At least, with social security and union retirement, you have a little dignity, a little independence. You're not a horse, to fall down and die in the shop.

They stick it out, the people like Jacob and Sophie; they have a determination to see life through, a strange mixture of sentiment and pluck. In any case, as a neighbor remarks, "it is not from society that they feel estranged, it is from their own pasts. And they are not so much confused as disappointed. For this is it. This is all there is. Penn South, with all its limitatons, is as close as they have come to the commonwealth of their dreams."

Many retired immigrants get by respectably, with their Social Security, union pensions, savings, and help from children. In Brighton Beach or Van Cortlandt Park, along South Beach in Miami, they stroll out on sunny days, the women in their neat print dresses and the men in their short-sleeved shirts. They read the *Forward*, since, agree with it or not, there's no other Yiddish newspaper left; they talk, sometimes boast a little, about their children; they rehearse their lives, nurture their memories; they head for the parks to sit in the sun; some still go to the inevitable meetings and lectures, whatever remains of the local Zionist group or Workmen's Circle branch, coming together on a Sunday afternoon because it is easier and safer than on a midweek night.

(In *Tell Me a Riddle*, Tillie Olsen's harrowing story about immigrant life, husband and wife, married for forty-seven years, burst into fierce battle as they sense the ending of their time. It is as if the stored-up quarrels are all that, finally, they have to offer each other. The wife lies sick with cancer: "Light she grew, like a bird, and, like a bird, sound bubbled in her throat while the body fluttered in agony. . . . 'Aah, Mrs. Miserable,' he said as if she could hear, 'all your life working, and now in bed you lie, servants to tend, you do not even need to call to be tended, and still you work. Such hard work it is to die? Such hard work?' ")

The old Jewish stoicism, perhaps the thickest remaining sediment of immigrant life, sees them through, insofar as anything can. They still believe strongly in family life, in the unspoken connections of sharing; they are romantic but without the romantic vocabulary (which may be what enables them to remain romantic). They become, as Jews will, hypochondriacal, discussing their symptoms as if counting assets, but even about this they can summon some of the old sarcasm, those bitter thrusts which Yiddish endlessly allows. The world interests them intensely, though they are frank, with one another, to admit they often find it beyond comprehension: not much has turned out as they thought, except perhaps their own endurance as immigrant Jews who have lived to see their fruit and are not sure what to make of its taste. Survivors through will and sacrifice, they are still here.

Epilogue:
Questions upon Questions

Through the work of almost every east European Jewish thinker at the turn of the century there keeps recurring a powerful motif: that the Jews, by some act of heroic transformation, must achieve for themselves "a normal life." What the coming of the Messiah had been for Orthodoxy, the dream of "a normal life" became in the secularized messianism which took hold of the modern Jewish imagination. "Next year in Jerusalem" was replaced by programs for building the New Jerusalem, and "the Jew dancing on the brink of a miracle" by Jews determined to make their own miracles. Socialists, Zionists, communalists, Yiddishists, territorialists, nationalists, even some religionists: for all of these "a normal life" became the substance of a transfigured messianic yearning. If messianism had meant for the traditional Jew "a life lived in deferment," his modern offspring grew intoxicated with the drug of hope. The crooked course of Jewish history, wonderful as some of its secret corners and byways had been, now had to be straightened out; the Jews would have to be made ready for productive labor, social integration, modern culture, perhaps nationhood; and at long last, no longer pariahs or wanderers, they would live like other peoples.

As we say on Yom Kippur, the Lord decides who will ride on horse-
back and who will crawl on foot. The main thing is—hope! A Jew
must always hope, must never lose hope. And in the meantime, what
if we waste away to a shadow? For that we are Jews—the Chosen
People, the envy and admiration of the world.
                              —Sholom Aleichem's Tevye the Dairyman

This desire for "a normal life" climaxed the experience of centuries. It was a wish to break out of a humiliating passivity, and, by joining ranks with other peoples in a world of order and rationality, to assume an active historical role. Almost every fresh impulse in Jewish life—the turn to secular politics, the blossoming of Yiddish culture, the mass migration to America, the rediscovery of national sentiment—testified to the intensity with which this desire was held. But it was a sign of a shared difficulty, perhaps of an "inherent" Jewish difficulty, that almost every strand of Jewish opinion acknowledged that the Jews could not gain "a normal life" in any normal way: not through personal striving, not through individual sobriety or collective efforts, not through any of the paths available to other peoples.

"A normal life" for a people whose whole history, by the standards of the external world, had been strikingly abnormal, could therefore be regarded as reachable only through extraordinary measures: through programs, upheavals, shattering transformations of a political-ethical character. True, there were still religious Jews who believed that so long as the Jews remained in *galut* "abnormal life" was appropriate, that is, normal; they looked with disapproval upon any attempt "to press for the End," let alone attain messianic goals through mundane action; they placed their faith in God and were prepared to wait. But waiting was precisely what the most energetic young Jews proposed no longer to do.

Did it then occur to the Jewish ideologues that achieving "a normal life" through the kinds of "abnormal" exertions they felt constrained to advocate might in turn lead to new varieties of Jewish "abnormality"? Surely it must have, since they were intelligent people; perhaps they had no choice but to shrug that dilemma away as one that later generations would have to face. Or did the Jewish ideologues recognize that the idea of "a normal life" may have been, for Jews, unacceptable and even unrealistic? No doubt this too occurred to them and in moments of irony they must have reflected that the urgency with which every branch of Jewish opinion strained toward the chimera of "a normal life" gave sufficient indication that the old Jewish "abnormality" continued to reign. And then, of course, there was a possibility which few of the Jewish ideologues could really take into public account, since it seemed likely to induce the very resignation they were pledged to resist—the possibility that for Jews to remain Jews it might be better not to worry about anything so improbable as "a normal life," since it would have to be purchased at too high a cost in self-laceration and self-denial. Perhaps the essence of being a Jew meant to live forever in a state of expectation for that which would not come.

America—the full significance of which no Jewish thinker could yet take into account—imposed its own decision. Once past initial barriers, the Jews were allowed an entry into social and economic life on terms more favorable than any they had dreamed of. But America exacted a price. Not that it "demanded" that the immigrant Jews repudiate their past, their religion, or their culture; nor that it "insisted" they give up the marks of their spiritual distinctiveness. American society, by its very nature, simply made it all but impossible for the culture of Yiddish to survive. It set for the east European Jews a trap or lure of the most pleasant kind. It allowed the Jews a life far more "normal" than anything their most visionary programs had foreseen, and all that it asked—it did not even ask, it merely rendered easy and persuasive—was that the Jews surrender their collective self. This surrender did not occur dramatically, at a moment of high tension. It took place gradually, almost imperceptibly, and with benefits so large and tangible that it would long remain a question for legitimate debate whether Jews should have tried to resist the process of absorption. That they could have succeeded, hardly anyone supposed.

In part, they did resist. They chose to reject a complete self-obliteration, the shameful fate of dissolving into anonymity. The "end of the Jewish people" which Georges Friedmann had foreseen or feared in his striking book did not come, nor is it likely to come in the near future. Jews in America would remain Jews; their institutions would survive, flourish, and multiply; their religion would be kept alive by a phalanx of sentinels, and it could be chosen by anyone, Jewish or not, who was drawn to its promise. But very little of what had held the immigrant Jews together—the fabric of their ways, the bond of common tradition, the sharing of language—was able to survive much beyond a century.

> *Jewry is not merely a question of faith, it is above all a question of the practice of a way of life in a community conditioned by faith.*
> —Franz Kafka

Nor is the question, at this point, whether the Jews gained or lost as a result of their transformation in America. Most of them never thought much about it, or if they did, it was with the shrug of resignation their fathers had taught them. Many of them felt it was just as well to be done with the old Yiddish ways, the bent backs and excited voices and psychic stigmas. The Zionists and Hebraists felt this at first with delight and then with a twinge of regret; the affluent and bourgeois with the conviction (who could argue against it?) that things had become better in America, far better; and ordinary folk with some sense of loss or depletion, which might signify no more than a readiness to yield to the spirit of the time and all that it certified as inevitable. The immigrant Jews had gained immeasurably and lost immeasurably. Who is able to cast a final balance, we hardly know.

Insofar as they chose still to regard themselves as Jews, even if nonreligious Jews, they were left with a nagging problem in self-perception, a crisis of identity, as it came to be called, which seems beyond solution or removal, except perhaps through a full return to religious faith or a complete abandonment of Jewish identification. They had achieved "a normal life" in America and, for those with any taste for self-scrutiny, it was a life permanently beset by the question: who am I and why do I so declare myself? To live with this problem in a state of useful discontent was perhaps what it now meant to be a Jew. And in bearing the troubles of an unfixed identity, they had finally entered the American condition.

> *Before his death, Rabbi Zusya said, "In the coming world, they will not ask me: 'Why were you not Moses?' They will ask me: 'Why were you not Zusya?' "*
>
> —Hasidic tale

Since being a Jew in any affirmative sense was no longer settled by the mere fact of having been born one, there remained a seemingly endless number of gradations in the choice of identity. (But was identity something one could *choose?*) "If there were a Jewish community in the old sense, with Jewish identity established beyond question by one's membership in that community," wrote a leading Jewish intellectual, "to be anything less than a total Jew would be an individual aberration. Such, however, is plainly not the case with us, when Jewish identity is so much a matter of acts of the will and intellect. Since it is a matter of seeking one's identity within an open community, the perspective of the [Jewish] semi-outsider has its validity." For such a fractional Jew "may be identified by his history, by the presence of the Jewish past within him. He is a Jew in that his experience contains the possibility of linking himself with the collective and individual experience of earlier Jews."

The cultural life of the East Side and its paler equivalents throughout America might seem provincial to Jewish sons and daughters eager to escape the grip of their parents, might seem so even to the parents themselves, but in reality it was an *international* culture, with concentrations on four continents and its main centers in eastern Europe and America.

When immigrant Jews spoke of *menshlichkeit* as the norm by which they hoped to guide their ethical life, they were not merely invoking the values of a small people trying to find a rationale for its powerlessness; nor were they merely calling upon the richness of a national-religious tradition that derived from the oldest monotheism in Western culture; they were also bringing into play a version—only partly absorbed, sometimes distorted, but also often refined—of nineteenth-century European humanism. With their quick and brittle receptivity, the east European Jews had been enormously open, at least by the last few decades of the nineteenth century, to Enlightenment ideas and values. In all of Europe no one else responded with greater enthusiasm than did many of the younger Jews to appeals for universalism and progress, concord between nations and the brotherhood of man. And if circumstances kept them from trying to put into practice the politics of liberalism, many of them were nevertheless eager to accept its norms. It is no accident that the state of Israel, at the very moment of its creation, took on essential features of a Western parliamentary system, in good part because most of its founders were east European Jews who had been deeply affected by the ideas of the Enlightenment.

Many east European Jews were ready to become, as some did, "good Europeans," the kind of civilized men who meant to rise above mere nationalism in a fellowship of liberal culture. The east European Jewish intelligentsia, both the portion that remained in Europe and the portion that came to America, wanted somehow to unite the moral strengths of its own tradition with the new values of democratic humanism. Inward-looking as was the culture of *Yiddishkeit* in Europe, and inward-gathering as at first it had to be in America, it held fast to the premise that modern Jews could be faithful to their own traditions while becoming citizens of the world. The culture of *Yiddishkeit*, or at least its "advanced" secular portion, set itself the goal of yoking the provincial and the universal. The noblest ideas and values of nineteenth-century Europe would find a home in Yiddish, and Yiddish voices like Sholom Aleichem and Peretz would find a home in the world. History, of course, was to destroy this hope, history mainly in the form of twentieth-century totalitarianism; given the deeply inlaid anti-Semitism of the Christian tradition, perhaps this hope was always a delusion.

The culture of the Jews in *galut*—or in homely Yiddish, the culture of the *golus*-Jew—was largely ignored and dismissed by the gentile world: that was only to be expected. It was also sneered at by many Jews themselves, who could not really believe that anything "fine" or "high" could come out of those wretched *shtetlakh* and those grimy East Side streets. Both Zionists and assimilationists, those who wanted to assert a new Jewish identity and those who wanted to escape it entirely, would find the memory of Yiddish culture a source of embarrassment, though words of justice were spoken at least once, by the brilliant Zionist writer Hayim Greenberg in an essay he wrote in 1945 criticizing his comrades for the disdain they showed toward Diaspora Jewry:

> Bialik once said: "A people has as much sky over its head as it has ground under its feet." I frequently used to quote this aphorism, and it always made a great impression on people not close to us. I still think . . . that there is much truth in this statement—but not the full and absolute truth that is valid everywhere and at all times in the life of a people. Even when he made this

statement Bialik knew, far better than those against whom he directed it, that for some two thousand years Jews had not a square inch of ground under their feet but much sky over their heads. . . . A skyless people could not have created the Talmud and the Midrashim, Kabbala and Messianic movements, the Shulhan Arikh and Hasidism.

Jewish traditionalists might say, of course, that it was not really necessary for Jews to seek moral or cultural renewal in any alien sources, since renewal could be found abundantly within the Jewish past itself. Perhaps so. But the actuality was that a great many Jews, both in eastern Europe and America, were not content to remain with traditonal ways; they turned with a feverish eagerness to liberalism, tolerance, science, progress, secularism, socialism. They took intellectual flame at the moment when their own tradition came into an abrasive but vital relation with the ideas of modern Europe.

There is a Jewish reading, encouraged by Orthodoxy, that would now see the whole experience of *Yiddishkeit* as still another in a long series—spread across the millenniums—of Jewish flights into alien cultures that could end only in adulteration and self-denial. This extreme view comes into conflict with the fondness for Yiddish, even Yiddish secular culture, which many Orthodox Jews have felt; deep down, they can hardly suppose it represented no more than a first step toward apostasy. But a more complex version of this view is available: that, for all its impressive qualities and achievements, the culture of Yiddish necessarily had to drift toward a self-dissolution, that it could not, by itself, sustain Jewish life for very long. Secularism, cosmopolitanism, a diffused this-worldly messianism, while rendering momentarily brilliant the surfaces of Jewish life, could all be seen as threats to ultimate Jewish survival. Even the state of Israel, because primarily secular in character, could be seen as a threat to ultimate Jewish survival, bringing a measure of security to Jews yet draining off their religious and spiritual experience. But such arguments, even if touching on significant realities, were finally directed against the course of history itself: against those developments in Jewish life which had made inevitable the breakdown of religious hegemony and the rise of secular outlooks.

In any case, by the middle of the twentieth century, the Yiddish past could no longer serve most Jews in the United States as a sufficient base for a vital culture or a revival of Jewish feeling. And less because of any inherent deficiencies in that past than the sheer brutality of historical circumstances. For only a dwindling number of the children and grandchildren of the immigrants could the memory of Yiddish still yield a point of definition, a tremor of value.

> *As a little bit of musk fills an entire house, so the least influence of Judaism overflows all of one's life.*
> —Ossip Mandelstam

Much of the East Side is beyond recall, and must remain so. There is nothing glamorous about poverty, nothing admirable about deprivation, nothing enviable about suffering. Whole areas of human possibility and pleasure were blocked off by the immigrant milieu, in part because it needed the repressions of discipline, in part because it derived from a traditon of severity, in part because it had to cope with material want. And the toll in self-denial was often very high. Human beings should not have to live with the enforced austerities that many Jewish immigrants accepted as their lot. Life ought to be freer, more playful, more spontaneous than the immigrants usually could or knew how to make it.

Yet, even while registering these impressions, one suspects they do not get to the heart of the matter. There were strengths, great strengths peculiar to the immigrant Jewish milieu: a rich and complicated ethic that remains embodied in the code of *menshlichkeit*, a readiness to live for ideals beyond the clamor of self, a sense of plebeian fraternity, an ability to forge a community of moral order even while remaining subject to a society of social disorder, and a persuasion that human existence is a deeply serious matter for which all of us are finally accountable. Not that these strengths were unique to the immigrant Jews or that there is any reason to suppose they might not survive the immigrant milieu; but for many children and grandchildren of the East Side, it was through this world that one first came to glimpse a life worthy of the idea of man.

We cannot be our fathers, we cannot live like our mothers, but we may look to their experience for images of rectitude and purities of devotion. It is the single commanding power of the Yiddish tradition that it seems immediately and insistently to thrust before us the most fundamental questions of human existence: how shall we live? What are the norms by which we can make judgments of the "good life"? Which modes of conduct may enable us to establish a genuine community?

You can hold back from the suffering of the world, you have free permission to do so, and it is in accordance with your nature, but perhaps this very holding back is the one suffering you could have avoided.
—Franz Kafka

Among all immigrant groups, not only the Jewish, a certain mode of apologia creeps into their self-considerations. They "point with pride" to the contributions they have made to American society: writers, baseball players, musicians, night-club comedians, millionaires, radicals, physicists, politicians. Behind such apologia lies an unspoken assumption that a court of native American opinion has the right to pass final judgment, deciding whether or not immigrant cultures merit acceptance and respect.

While the east European immigrant Jews can claim an abundant share of such "contributions," their very readiness to indulge such claims may be a kind of self-denigration, a failure of dignity. For, by a more serious measure, their greatest contribution has been less what America has accepted than what it has resisted: such distinctive traits of the modern Jewish spirit at its best as an eager restlessness, a moral anxiety, an openness to novelty, a hunger for dialectic, a refusal of contentment, an ironic criticism of all fixed opinions.

The messianic impulse of secular Jewishness may finally have reached a point of exhaustion by the mid-twentieth century. I doubt it; but if so, Jewish life can be expected to enter an entirely new and unpredictable phase. A good portion of what was best in Jewish life, as also what was worst, derived from this secularized messianism as it passed on from generation to generation, sometimes all but snuffed out and at other times suddenly flaring up violently. The intense moral seriousness of Jewish life was shadowed by a streak of madness, the purity of messianic yearning by an apocalyptic frenzy. Nor was it always possible to tell the two of them apart. Struggling with one another like the good and bad angels of Jewish religious myth, they made their way into the immigrant streets and then even to suburbs extending like faint replicas of those streets.

Brushing past questions of what was "normal" or "abnormal," the immigrant Jews created a life that was necessarily marked by both. They found a way, for a time, of linking the high moral fervor they had brought with them and the hope for social betterment America aroused in them. Perhaps the union of the two was the closest to "a normal life" that Jews could reach.

We need not overvalue the immigrant Jewish experience in order to feel a lasting gratitude for having been part of it. A sense of natural piety toward one's origins can live side by side with a spirit of critical detachment. We take pleasure in having been related to those self-educated workers, those sustaining women, those almost-forgotten writers and speakers devoted to excitements of controversy and thought.

The story of the immigrant Jews is all but done. Like all stories of human striving, it ought to be complete, with its beginning and its end, at rest in fulfillment and at ease with failure. A story is the essential unit of our life, offering the magical imperatives of "so it began" and "so it came to an end." A story encompasses us, justifies our stay, prepares our leaving. Here, in these pages, is the story of the Jews, bedraggled and inspired, who came from eastern Europe. Let us now praise obscure men.

Acknowledgments

Reference Notes

Glossary of Yiddish Terms

Bibliographical Notes

Index

Acknowledgments

Throughout the years during which this book was written, I have been privileged to have as my main English-language researcher Kenneth Libo, whom I first met when he was a graduate student at the City University of New York. I have never, in many years of literary work, encountered anyone with so remarkable a capacity for precise and imaginative probing into historical materials. Kenneth Libo has given himself to this project with great generosity; he has not only done prodigies of research, but has been a sharp and persistent critic of early drafts. He also provided a preliminary version of a major portion of Chapter Five. I am grateful to him as researcher, colleague, and friend.

Yiddish-language research for this book has been done primarily by Ada Fogel and Gershon Friedlin. A devoted Yiddishist, Ada Fogel brought to her task an intimate knowledge of the Yiddish milieu, much patience, and a readiness to tax her eyes over microfilms of old Yiddish papers. Gershon Friedlin, a lively connoisseur of Jewish matters, was the ideal man for finding just the right Yiddish quotation, just the right incident or anecdote in books and publications all but forgotten. I have learned from both and am grateful to both.

Let me also thank a number of graduate students at the City University of New York who undertook, on a more transient basis, a variety of research tasks: Mildred Goldczer, Arlene Kirsh, Mirra Rafalowicz, Elizabeth Pierson, Robert Nelson, David Bensman, Marcia Fox, and Pennina Petruk.

A portion of the material in this book is drawn from interviews with people, famous and obscure, who lived through the experience of the immigrant Jews. The interviews with Jewish trade unionists were conducted by Bernard Rosenberg and Harry Silverstein; full texts of these are available at YIVO. Other interviews, with residents of old-age homes, vaudeville actors, politicians, and so on, were conducted by Kenneth Libo, and still others by the author.

Since this book represents a culmination or synthesis of much of my earlier work, I have found myself occasionally borrowing—more often, adapting—a few paragraphs from various of my writings. In Chapters One and Thirteen I have taken material from the introductions, written jointly by Eliezer Greenberg and myself, to *A Treasury of Yiddish Stories* and *A Treasury of Yiddish Poetry*. In the section on dual unionism in Chapter Ten, I have adapted some material from *The American Communist Party: A Critical History* by Lewis Coser and myself. In Chapter Seventeen, the section on the American Jewish novelists draws in part upon earlier essays on Saul Bellow and Philip Roth which appear in *The Critical Point,* and the section on New York intellectuals upon my essay "The New York Intellectuals," which appears in *Decline of the New.*

In undertaking so large and wide-ranging a book, it has been not only unavoidable but entirely appropriate that I should draw upon the work of many scholars. These are all variously acknowledged in the notes and bibliography, but one requires special mention here as well: Moses Rischin's *The Promised City,* a pioneering work of scholarship with regard to the east European Jews.

It is a pleasure to acknowledge a debt to Jacob Epstein, who, as a young artist, provided illustrations in 1902 for Hutchins Hapgood's *The Spirit of the Ghetto,* some of which have been reproduced in this book; and to Mrs. Samuel Zagat for permission to reproduce a panel from her husband's Yiddish-language comic strip, *Gimpl Beinish.*

Two institutions have been especially helpful in enabling me to complete the years of research and writing that have gone into this book. The City University of New York provided aid on several occasions, and I find myself thinking with an especial warmth of gratitude to the past and present presidents of its Graduate Center, Mina Rees and Harold Proshansky. And then there is YIVO, that blessed repository of Yiddish learning and historical materials, without which this book would simply not have been possible—especially its indefatigable and splendid librarian, Dina Abramovich.

Several friends have read portions of this book and offered valuable criticisms. Eliezer Greenberg, my friend and teacher in Yiddish literature, read Chapter Eight; Harold Clurman, Chapter Fourteen; Lucy Dawidowicz, Chapter Fifteen; Ronald Sanders, the section on popular entertainers; and Hilton Kramer and Meyer Schapiro, the section on American Jewish artists. In writing this book I have thought of Meyer Schapiro as my ideal audience: there can be no greater satisfaction than to satisfy his intellectual and scholarly standards—or even to approach them.

A number of institutions have provided grants which enabled me to take semesters off from teaching in order to work on this book: the Guggenheim and Rockefeller foundations. My thanks to them. And my thanks to two smaller, Jewish foundations—the Atran Foundation and the Chanin Foundation—which provided help for the research.

Finally, a word of gratitude to the godfather of this book, William B. Goodman, an editor of rectitude and insight, who provided help, encouragement, and patience. He is well named. I owe a special debt as well to Ronne Peltzman, who undertook the difficult task of copy editing this book with skill and wit.

Reference Notes

The notes are grouped according to the sections within each chapter. Unless otherwise specified, place of publication for books listed is New York.

The following abbreviations are used in the notes below:

AJA	*American Jewish Archives*
AJHQ	*American Jewish Historical Quarterly*
AJHS	*Publications, American Jewish Historical Society*
AJYB	*American Jewish Year Book*
For.	*Jewish Daily Forward*
JSS	*Jewish Social Studies*
USS Reports	*University Settlement Society Reports*
YIVO Annual	*YIVO Annual of Jewish Social Science*

CHAPTER ONE

"trickle of Jewish emigration": Salo Baron, *The Russian Jew Under Tsars and Soviets*, 1964, pp. 87–88. Herzen quote: Alexander Herzen, *My Past and Thoughts*, vol. 1, 1968, pp. 219–20. Nicholas's decree: Lucy Dawidowicz, *The Golden Tradition: Jewish Life and Thought in Eastern Europe*, 1967, p. 30.

The World of the Shtetl

"visit to a *heder*": quoted in Louis Greenberg, *The Jews in Russia*, vol. 1, New Haven, 1944, p. 57. "Jewish school in Vitebsk": quoted in Baron, p. 142. "beginnings of Jewish proletariat": Ezra Mendelsohn, *The Class Struggle in the Pale*, 1970, pp. 1–26. "jumble of wooden houses": Maurice Samuel, *The World of Sholom Aleichem*, 1943, pp. 26–27. "Bible a daily newspaper," *ibid*. Berlin quote: Isaiah Berlin, *Chaim Weizmann*, 1958, p. 17. Heschel quote: Abraham Heschel, *The Earth Is the Lord's*, 1950, p. 51. "Jewish poverty . . . kind of marvel": Ba'al Makhshoves, "Mendele, Grandfather of Yiddish Literature," in Irving Howe and Eliezer Greenberg, *Voices from the Yiddish*, Ann Arbor, 1972, pp. 36–37.

Ferment and Enlightenment

"absolute negation of *Galut*": Hayim Greenberg, *Selected Essays*, vol. 2, 1964, p. 94. "Zionists chose to revolutionize": Dawidowicz, p. 54. Dubnow quote: Simon Dubnow, *Nationalism and History: Essays on Old and New Judaism*, ed. Koppel S. Pinson, Philadelphia, 1958, p. 333. "single-handed a Jewish nineteenth century": Jacob Glatstein, "Peretz and the Jewish Nineteenth Century," in Howe and Greenberg, p. 53.

The Start of Social Change

"armor for Jewish people": Hayim Zhitlovsky, "Moses Hess—Socialist, Philosopher, Jew," in Howe and Greenberg, p. 179. "50 percent of Jewish population": Baron, pp. 65, 113–14. "rural Jews . . . employment in cities": Mendelsohn, p. 4. Kautsky quote: Mendelsohn, p. 1. Vilna 1892 petition: Yefim Yeshurin, ed.,

Vilna, a zamelbukh gevidmet der shtot vilna, 1935, p. 133. Bund report, 1896: L. Greenberg, vol. 2, p. 142. Liessen on workers' struggle: Mendelsohn, pp. 59–60. "Kremer and Gozhanskii": *ibid.*, p. 60. Moses "the Binder": *ibid.*, p. 39. young artisan describes: *ibid.*, p. 38. Minsk labor militant: *ibid.*, p. 46. Levin quote: *ibid.*, p. 33. Daitch quote: Baron, p. 166. (These experiences also documented in Baron, pp. 166ff.; L. Greenberg, vol. 1, pp. 148–50; vol. 2, pp. 57, 162.)

The Prospect of America

Russky Evrei and Mandelstam: L. Greenberg, vol. 2, pp. 62–63. "a form of demonopathy": Baron, pp. 174–75.

CHAPTER TWO

"motives similar . . . first to last": Maldwyn Jones, *American Immigration,* Chicago, 1961, p. 4. pioneers of Am Olam: Mark Wischnitzer, *To Dwell in Safety,* Philadelphia, 1948, p. 210. Price diary, 1882: "The Memoir of Dr. George M. Price," *AJHS,* December 1950, p. 101. "America . . . everybody's mouth": Mary Antin, *From Plotzk to Boston,* Boston, 1899, p. 12. "Where do you travel?": Chune Gottesfeld, *Tales of the Old World and the New,* 1964, p. 100.

Crossing into Europe

refugees in Brody, 1882: Zosa Szajkowski, "How the Mass Migration to America Began," *JSS,* October 1942, pp. 295–97. "German Jewish community . . . brunt of tidal wave"; "Orderly migration"; Nathan quote: Wischnitzer, pp. 100, 95, 99. Netter correspondence, 1881: Elias Tcherikower, "Jewish Immigrants to the United States, 1881–1900," *YIVO Annual,* 1951, p. 159. Netter to Paris, 1882: Szajkowski, *passim.* America "most civilized region": Zosa Szajkowski, "Materialn vegen der yidisher emigratsie kayn amerika," *YIVO Bleter,* vol. 19, 1942, p. 277. "Impossible accept": Szajkowski, "How the Mass Migration to America Began," p. 297. "Strangely enough, American Jewry": Wischnitzer, p. 40. Myer S. Isaacs quote: Max Kohler, "The Board of Delegates of American Israelites, 1859–1878," *AJHS,* vol. 29, 1925, p. 101. "A statistical account of expenditures": Esther Panitz, "The Polarity of Jewish Attitudes Toward Immigration," *AJHQ,* December 1963, pp. 114–15. Julius Goldman quote: *ibid.*, p. 121. Romanian decrees: Joseph Kissman, *Shtudyes tsu der geshikhte fun rumenishe yidn in 19tn un onheyb 20stn yorhundert,* 1944, ch. 2. fusgeyer: Joseph Kissman, "The Immigration of Rumanian Jews up to 1914," *YIVO Annual,* 1947–48, pp. 163–64. "Song of the *Fusgeyer*": Zosa Szajkowski, "Jewish Immigration Policy in the Period of the Rumanian 'Exodus' 1899–1903," *JSS,* January 1951, pp. 59–60. "After the speeches": Jacob Finkelstein, "Zikhroynes fun a fusgeyer fun rumania kayn amerika," *YIVO Bleter,* vol. 26, September–October 1945, p. 108, *passim.*

The Lure of America

"Even an imaginative American": Marcus Ravage, *An American in the Making,* 1917, p. 31. Stanislaw Mozrowski: quoted in Willard A. Heaps, *The Story of Ellis Island,* 1967, pp. 22–23. "In the evening": Ravage, pp. 51, 55. "A person gone to America": *ibid.*, p. 10. Couza anecdote: *ibid.*, p. 18. "I remember . . . a book": Gregory Weinstein, *The Ardent Eighties,* 1928, pp. 6–7. Hebrew periodicals, *"Bank Wechsel"*: Sanford Ragins, "The Image of America in Two East European Hebrew Periodicals," *AJA,* November 1965, *passim.* Price booklet:

Moses Rischin, *The Promised City: New York's Jews, 1870–1914*, Cambridge, Mass., 1962, p. 33.

From Border to Port

"We were to leave the train": Abraham Cahan, *The Education of Abraham Cahan*, ed. Leon Stein, Philadelphia, 1969, p. 199. "The crowd was told": C. Davidson, *Out of Endless Yearnings: A Memoir of Israel Davidson*, 1946, p. 14. "In a great lonely field": Antin, pp. 174–75. "Two weeks within high brick walls": *ibid.*, p. 177. Diederich report, 1903: *Special Consular Reports, Emigration to the United States*, vol. 30, Dept. of Commerce and Labor, 1904, p. 50. "People tell them": Sholom Aleichem, "Off for the Golden Land," *Jewish Immigration Bulletin*, February 1917, p. 10. "a whole array of vocations": Lloyd Gartner, *The Jewish Immigrant in England, 1870–1914*, London, 1960, p. 34. Alter incident: Davidson, p. 15. Bremen emigrants: *Special Consular Reports*, pp. 47–51. "as though for wedding feast": Israel Kasovich, *The Days of Our Years*, 1929, p. 172. steerage cost, 1903: *Special Consular Reports*, pp. 14, 17.

The Ordeal of Steerage

Handlin description: Oscar Handlin, *The Uprooted*, Boston, 1951, pp. 61–62. "We were huddled together": Morris Raphael Cohen, *A Dreamer's Journey*, Boston, 1949, p. 61. "The sky was blue": manuscript autobiography, YIVO, no. 89. "On board the ship": Kasovich, pp. 172–73. "steerage never changes. . . . irate emigrants": Edward Steiner, *On the Trail of the Immigrant*, 1906, quoted in Heaps, pp. 36–38. congressional committee on steerage conditions: *Report of the United States Immigration Commission*, vol. 37, 1911, p. 15.

At Ellis Island

"The day of the emigrant's arrival": Stephen Graham, *With Poor Immigrants*, 1914, p. 41. Castle Garden "perfect farce": Ann Novotny, *Strangers at the Door*, Riverside, Conn., 1971, p. 23. Ward's Island riots: Edward Corsi, *In the Shadow of Liberty: The Story of Ellis Island*, 1935, p. 61. "There is Ellis Island": Samuel B. Frommer, "Ellis Island: A Giant Sieve," *Jewish Immigration Bulletin*, January 1917, p. 16. veteran inspector: Corsi, p. 73. "contagious and loathsome diseases," etc.: Heaps, p. 76. third doctor: Arthur Henry, "Among the Immigrants," *Scribner's*, March 1901, p. 302. "line of male immigrants": *Despatch from H. M. Ambassador at Washington Reporting on Conditions at Ellis Island Immigration Station*, England, 1923 (N.Y. Public Library, SEB, p.v. 184, 11). "Our Jews love to get tangled up": *For.*, 18 March 1910. "During the year 1907": Henry Pratt Fairchild, *Immigration: A World Movement and Its American Significance*, 1933, pp. 190–91. "immigration officials . . . not always as humane": Corsi, p. 264. "Jewish nose": *Report of the United States Immigration Commission: Dictionary of Races or Peoples*, vol. 4, 1911, p. 74. La Guardia quote: Fiorello La Guardia, *The Making of an Insurgent*, 1948, p. 64.

A Work of Goodness

HEAS colonies: N.Y. *Times*, 8 August 1882. HEAS treatment, Ward's Island: N.Y. *Times*, 15 October 1882. HIAS bulletin, English translation: John Foster Carr, *Guide to the United States for the Jewish Immigrant*, 1912, p. 7. HIAS employment bureau: *First Annual Report*, HIAS, 1909. HIAS and Russian peasants: Mark Wischnitzer, *Visas to Freedom*, Cleveland, 1956, pp. 45–46.

Aronoff case: Edith Abbott, *Immigration: Select Documents and Case Records*, Chicago, 1924, pp. 319–32.

"Hordes" of Aliens

"heirs of all time": Herman Melville, *Redburn*, 1849, ch. 33. Henry George quote: John Higham, *Strangers in the Land*, New Brunswick, N.J., 1955, p. 42. "It was not difficult for this early generation": *ibid.*, p. 39. "The tremendous immigration influx of 1882": *ibid.*, p. 46. Kopeloff, strikebreaking: I. Kopeloff, *Amol in amerika*, Warsaw, 1928, pp. 48–64.

Open Door—and Closed

literacy proposals and immigration legislation: Roy Garris, *Immigration Restriction*, 1926, ch. 4. Marshall on immigration: Charles Reznikoff, ed., *Louis Marshall: Champion of Liberty*, Philadelphia, 1957, pp. 139, 113. Marshall letter, 1905: *ibid.*, p. 111. Williams to T. Roosevelt: Esther Panitz, "In Defense of the Jewish Immigrant (1891–1924)," *AJHQ*, September 1965, p. 60. *For.* on immigration disputes: *For.*, 7 July 1909, 14 July 1909, 2 August 1909, and throughout remainder of year.

The Jews Who Came

Weber and Kempster report: Louis Greenberg, *The Jews in Russia*, vol. 2, New Haven, 1944, p. 74. Jewish migration, families: Samuel Joseph, *Jewish Immigration to the United States, 1881–1910*, 1914, pp. 126–29. Jewish migration, occupational characteristics: Liebmann Hersch, "International Migration of the Jews," *International Migrations*, vol. 2, 1931, pp. 490, 496, 501, 504, 507. "I am a tailor": Benjamin Erdberg, interview, Hebrew Home for the Aged, New York, July 1970. Litwin dispatch: *For.*, 2 September 1909. "When Mother saw me copying": Darwin Hecht, *This Is My Life*, 1963, pp. 24–25. remark of a Jewish historian: Bernard D. Weinryb, "Jewish Immigration and Accommodation to America," *AJHS*, May–June 1957, p. 391. "On the average of 1,000 Jews": Hersch, pp. 480–81. "A powerful storm-wind ripped": manuscript autobiography, YIVO, no. 117.

CHAPTER THREE

opening composite sketch drawn from: C. Davidson, *Out of Endless Yearnings: A Memoir of Israel Davidson*, 1946, p. 17; Marcus Ravage, *An American in the Making*, 1917, p. 69; Israel Kasovich, *The Days of Our Years*, 1929, p. 274; Boris Bogen, *Born a Jew*, 1930, p. 36; Max Gordon, *Max Gordon Presents*, 1963, p. 6; Gregory Weinstein, *The Ardent Eighties*, 1928, p. 13; Abraham Cahan, *The Education of Abraham Cahan*, ed. Leon Stein, Philadelphia, 1969, p. 219; Ravage, p. 63; Samuel Rosenblatt, *Yossele Rosenblatt: The Story of His Life as Told by His Son*, 1954, p. 110; Mary Antin, *The Promised Land*, Boston, 1912, p. 185; Edward Steiner, *On the Trail of the Immigrant*, 1906, p. 52.

The First Shock

"A few Jewish families": Cahan, pp. 219–20. *"ulitza"*: Hirsh Masliansky, *Zikhroynes: fertsik yor lebn un kemfn*, 1924, p. 192. overcrowding, 1883: *Report of the United States Immigration Commission*, vol. 15, 1911, pp. 476–77. "Curse you, emigration": Cahan, quoted in Elias Tcherikower, ed., *Geshikhte fun der yidisher arbeter-bavegung in di fareynikte shtatn*, vol. 1, 1943, p. 273.

"A Gray, Stone World"

"The need to adjust": C. Bezalel Sherman, *The Jew Within American Society*, Detroit, 1960, pp. 122–23. "able to skip": *ibid.* "first immigrant generation":

B. Rivkin, *Di grunt-tendentsn fun yidisher literatur in amerika*, 1948, p. 55. "overcome with longing": Kasovich, pp. 277–78. "more poetry, more music": Abraham Cahan, *The Rise of David Levinsky*, 1917, p. 459. "forgets . . . his place of birth": Eliezer Greenberg, *Moshe Leib Halpern in ram fun zayn dor*, 1942, p. 26. "more than 3,000 Russian-Jewish immigrants": Tcherikower, vol. 1, pp. 245–46. "gray, stone world": Leon Kobrin, *Mayne fuftsik yor in amerika*, Buenos Aires, 1955, p. 304. "new and alien people": quoted in E. Greenberg, p. 29. Benequit quote: I. Benequit, *Durkhgelebt un durkhgetrakht*, vol. 1, 1934, p. 37. "The Jewish neighborhood": Lloyd Gartner, "The Jews of New York's East Side, 1890–1893," *AJHS*, March 1964, p. 267. Schiff and missionaries: David Max Eichhorn, "A History of Christian Attempts to Convert Jews of the United States and Canada," dissertation, Hebrew Union College, 1947. a scare story: *For.*, 24 May 1899.

A New Tempo, A New Way
"Physical exhaustion": Harry [Hillel] Rogoff, *An East Side Epic: The Life and Times of Meyer London*, 1930, p. 5. "I had occasion": Morris Raphael Cohen, *A Dreamer's Journey*, Boston, 1949, p. 66. "only one friend": Ephraim Lisitzky, *In the Grip of Cross Currents*, 1959, p. 20. "Stop it!": *ibid.*, p. 174. Hebrew writer: quoted in Aaron Antonovsky, *The Early Jewish Labor Movement in the United States* (English condensation of Tcherikower), 1961, p. 138. Hebrew parodies: Israel Davidson, *Parody in Jewish Literature*, 1907, pp. 98–105; also S. Niger, "Yiddish Culture in the United States," in *The Jewish People, Past and Present*, vol. 4, 1955, p. 306. "immigrant . . . disappointed": Ravage, pp. 61, 79. immigrants' struggle for existence: David Blaustein, "The People of the East Side Before Emigration and After Immigration," *USS Reports*, 1904, p. 77.

Peddling and Sewing
"you become a peddler": Tcherikower, vol. 1, p. 237. Witcowsky memoir: quoted, Harry Golden, *Forgotten Pioneer*, 1963, pp. 46, 52, 55. Oyzer Blaustein quote: Tcherikower, vol. 1, p. 248. Weinstein quote: *ibid.*, p. 249. "The next day": Kasovich, p. 177. "Abraham the butcher": I. Raboy, *Iz gekumen a yid kayn amerika*, 1944, p. 218. "I made six dollars": Benequit, vol. 1, p. 51. Students of Jewish immigration: Antonovsky, p. 156. "The Jewish contractor": quoted in *ibid.*, pp. 163–64. "ride up half a mile": Jacob Riis, *How the Other Half Lives*, 1890, p. 108. "when the weather permits": quoted in Louis Levine, *The Women's Garment Workers*, 1924, p. 19. "The boss of the shop": quoted in Sherman, p. 163. "The contractor approached": quoted in *ibid.*, p. 164. "tuberculosis seems": quoted in Antonovsky, p. 171. factory inspector, 1899: *ibid.*, p. 171. garment factories, 1885: Jacob Lestchinsky: "The Economic and Social Development of American Jewry," in *The Jewish People, Past and Present*, vol. 4, 1955, pp. 81ff. "early class struggles": quoted in Sylvia Kopald and Ben Selekman, "The Epic of the Needle Trades," *Menorah Journal*, October 1928, p. 229. "In the 'inside' shops": Levine, pp. 20–21. wages, 1880's: *ibid.*, p. 22. depression, 1893: J. M. Budish and George Soule, *The New Unionism in the Clothing Industry*, 1920, p. 23. "Mannis was heartsick": Raboy, pp. 64–65.

Going to the Land
"In free America": Abraham Menes, "The Am Oylom Movement," *YIVO Annual*, 1949, p. 16. Minsk group: *ibid.*, p. 19. "Land was free": *ibid.*, p. 22. Sicily Island: Gabriel Davidson, *Our Jewish Farmers and the Story of the Jewish Agricultural Society*, 1943, p. 212. "our daily schedule": quoted in Menes, pp. 30–31.

Cahan quote: *ibid.*, p. 33. Charles K. Davis: unpublished diary, in American Jewish Archives, Cincinnati, quoted with permission.

In the Tenements

"Big Flat" and investigator's reports: *43rd Annual Report*, New York Association for Improving the Conditions of the Poor, 1886, pp. 43–52. "The cantor rehearses": quoted in Antonovsky, p. 119. "Not everyone was equally poor": S. P. Schonfeld, *Zikhroynes fun a shriftzetser*, 1946, p. 41. *Ner Hamaaravi:* Shlomo Noble, "The Image of the Jew in Hebrew and Yiddish Literature in America, 1870–1900," *YIVO Annual*, 1954, p. 89. Veiller quote: Lawrence Veiller, "Tenement House Reform in New York City, 1834–1900," in Robert W. De Forest and Lawrence Veiller, *The Tenement House Problem*, vol. 1, 1903, p. 115. "no richly-fed men": N.Y. *Times*, 13 September 1894. Judge Steckler: William P. McLoughlin, "Evictions in New York Tenement Houses," *Arena*, December 1892.

The Implacability of Gentleness

early life: R. L. Duffus, *Lillian Wald, Neighbor and Crusader*, 1938, pp. 1–32. "Within half an hour": Lillian Wald, *The House on Henry Street*, 1915, pp. 6–7. Lavinia Duck quote: Duffus, p. 39. "I came with . . . little program": *ibid.*, p. 55. Her tasks were endless, etc.: *ibid.*, pp. 42–46. letters to Jacob Schiff and case notes: N.Y. Public Library, Lillian Wald collection. "little Louie": Helena Huntington Smith, "Rampant but Respectable," *New Yorker*, 14 December 1929, p. 33. N.Y. *Press* quote: Duffus, p. 90. Riis quote: Jacob Riis, "Personals," *Survey*, 26 July 1913, pp. 551–52. "implacability of gentleness": Arthur Schlesinger, Jr., *The Crisis of the Old Order, 1919–1933*, Boston, 1956, p. 25.

A Chaos in Hebrew

synagogues, Hebrew teachers, 1890: Baron de Hirsch survey, see Gartner, *passim*. Rabbi Moses Weinberger: in Lloyd Gartner, *Jewish Education in the United States*, 1969, p. 104. "The teachers were . . . well grounded": Masliansky, p. 204.

Dislocation and Pathology

"vices . . . mostly Americanized Jews": Isaac Max Rubinow, "The Jewish Question in New York City, 1902–1903," ed. Leo Shpall, *AJHS*, December 1959, p. 115. Mazet Committee testimony: *Report of the Special Committee of the Assembly Appointed to Investigate the Public Offices and Departments of the City of New York and the Counties Therein Included*, vol. 1, Albany, 1900, p. 1895. Riordan: *ibid.*, p. 2029. Lena Myers: N.Y. *World*, 23 April 1896. "On sunshiny days": Michael Gold, *Jews Without Money*, 1930, p. 15. "flesh trade": *For.*, 10 January 1898. "Jews constitute six percent": Abraham Cahan, "The Russian Jew in America," *Atlantic Monthly*, July 1898, p. 137. grand jury on "so-called divorces": N.Y. *Times*, 25 December 1890. Jews and crimes of violence: William McAdoo, *Guarding a Great City*, Chicago, 1906, pp. 148, 155. police and court records, 1898: W. S. Andrews, "A Study of the East Side Courts," *USS Reports*, 1900, pp. 22–29. scholarly survey: Tully Neumann, "The Jews in Crime in New York City, 1900–1914," master's thesis, Yeshiva University, 1970. "Shapiro murders Liberman": *For.*, 22 November 1897. "Wants to be a hero": *For.*, 8 October 1897. "Adler's family": *For.*, 29 January 1898. *"babke"*: *For.*, 9

November 1897. "bride to shame": *For.*, 14 March 1898. Shrek, Saks: *For.*, 3 September 1897. Rothstein: Leo Katcher, *The Big Bankroll: The Life and Times of Arnold Rothstein*, 1958, *passim*. "Mother" Mandelbaum: Herbert Asbury, *Gangs of New York*, 1937, p. 217. Smith-Dreyfus marriage: N.Y. *Herald*, 22 December 1892.

Voices of the Left

"we were scabs": I. Kopeloff, *Amol in amerika*, Warsaw, 1928, p. 54. Cahan's first and second lectures: Cahan, *Education of Abraham Cahan*, pp. 237–38. Weinstein quote: Antonovsky, p. 206. Most's "Catechism": *ibid.*, p. 221. "teachings of the three": *ibid.*, p. 208. "Quotations pour out": Jacob Merison, "Der ershter peryod fun der anarkhistisher bavegung," quoted in *ibid.*, p. 224. "the religious question": *ibid.*, p. 246. "For me . . . disbelief": Morris Winchevsky, *Gezamelte verk*, vol. 9, 1927, pp. 155–57, quoted in *ibid.*, p. 248. "I do not believe in religion": Alexander Berkman, *Prison Memoirs of an Anarchist*, 1912, pp. 15–16. "Grand Yom Kippur ball": N.Y. *Sun*, 24 September 1890. "war against God": Kopeloff, p. 275. "one man is guiltier": Marie Ganz, *Rebels: Into Anarchy—and Out Again*, 1920, pp. 187–88. Goldman quote: *Mother Earth*, April 1910, quoted in Charles Madison, "Anarchism in the United States," *Journal of the History of Ideas*, January 1945, p. 62. "obsessed by one idea": Abraham Menes, "The East Side and the Jewish Labor Movement," in Irving Howe and Eliezer Greenberg, *Voices from the Yiddish*, Ann Arbor, 1972, p. 204. "union of cleaners": Bernard Weinstein, *Di yidishe yunyons in amerika*, 1929, pp. 491–94. cloakmakers' strikes 1885: N.Y. *Times*, 20 August 1885. "strike of the knee-pants makers": *For.*, 18 March, 1898. "family organization": *Yidishe Folkstseitung*, 2 July 1886. "I want more light": *ibid.*, 17 September 1886. "For intellectual stimulus": Cohen, pp. 72–73. Cahan on "sweatshop hands" and "religion": quoted in Charles Bernheimer, ed., *The Russian Jew in the United States*, Philadelphia, 1905, p. 40. a *mishna* class: Cahan, "The Russian Jew in the United States," p. 139. Cahan on fanaticism: *For.*, 22 April 1911. "pleasure to die": Michael Aaronson, *Morning Journal*, 16 April 1959. "Barondess looked like a brother": Joseph Rumshinsky, *Klangen fun mayn lebn*, 1944, p. 560. "In accursed Russia": Kobrin, pp. 326–27.

CHAPTER FOUR

"It cannot be denied": Elias Tcherikower, ed., *Geshikhte fun der yidisher arbeter-bavegung in di fareynikte shtatn*, vol. 1, 1943, p. 282. Thernstrom quote: Stephan Thernstrom, *The Other Bostonians: Poverty and Progress in the American Metropolis, 1880–1970*, Cambridge, Mass., 1973, ch. 7.

An Early Combat

non-Jewish account: "Riot in the Ghetto," *Collier's*, 16 August 1902. "more than even Jewish patience": *For.*, 30 July 1902. "Nobody ever talked about inequality": *For.*, 2 August 1902. An unpleasant side effect: *For.*, 19 September 1905. Ladies Anti-Beef Trust Association, etc.: *For.*, 15 May 1902. A scene at court: *For.*, 15 June 1902. Cohen paper-box factory strike: William English Walling, "A Children's Strike on the East Side," *Charities*, 24 December 1904, p. 305. Liessen on Kishinev: *For.*, 20 May 1903. "The Americans promise not to hinder": *For.*, 31 May, 1903. Niger on Kishinev: S. Niger, "Yiddish Culture," in *The Jewish People, Past and Present*, vol. 4, 1955, p. 305. "Are We Safe in America?": *For.*, 16 June 1903.

New Tastes, New Styles
oysesn: *For.*, 14 July 1903. vacations: *For.*, 30 June 1904. Victrolas: *For.*, 9 May 1904. piano lessons: *For.*, 16 October 1904. Canal Street, 1903: Tcherikower, p. 252. "formation of a well-to-do class": Charles Bernheimer, ed., *The Russian Jew in the United States*, Philadelphia, 1905, p. 105. clerks of East Side: *For.*, 2 March 1906. English on East Side: David Blaustein, "The Child of the Immigrant," *American Hebrew*, 22 December 1905, p. 159. "you could recognize a greenhorn": *For.*, 20 January 1905. Hapgood on immigrant customs: Hutchins Hapgood, *The Spirit of the Ghetto*, 1902, p. 33. East Side stores on Sabbath: *For.*, 4 February 1906. working papers: *For.*, 8 July 1911. Hebrew Free Loan Society: Bernheimer, p. 71. Ladies Fuel and Aid Society: Sophie Ruskay, *Horsecars and Cobblestones*, 1948, p. 46. "Mother had been collecting": Elizabeth Stern, *My Mother and I*, 1917, p. 106. Hebrew printers: H. Frank, "Ekonomishe organizatsies fun yidishn mitelshtand in di fareynikte shtatn," *YIVO Bleter*, vol. 15, 1940, pp. 103–23. Libin quote: *For.*, 10 June 1909.

Spreading Across the City
Harlem "a Jewish city": *For.*, 31 July 1910. Yossele Rosenblatt: Samuel Rosenblatt, *Yossele Rosenblatt: The Story of His Life as Told by His Son*, 1954, p. 100. "The Jewish presence is strong": *For.*, 8 August 1905. Brownsville as village: Dr. M. Raisen, quoted in Tcherikower, p. 252. number of Jews in Brownsville: Alter F. Landesman, *Brownsville*, 1969, p. 95. "Only yesterday everybody laughed": *For.*, 3 December 1903. boarders in New York and Brooklyn: Charles Bernheimer, "Rent Strikes and Crowded Neighborhoods," *Outlook*, vol. 88, 1908, p. 128. Bronx, 1903: *For.*, 20 February 1903. Bennett on Bronx: Arnold Bennett, *Your United States*, 1912, pp. 189–90.

An Experiment in Community
Jewish criminals: Theodore A. Bingham, "Foreign Criminals in New York," *North American Review*, September 1908, pp. 383–94. "it did not fulfill its founders' goals": Arthur Goren, *New York Jews and the Quest for Community*, 1970, p. 247. Kaplan quote: *ibid.*, p. 248.

The Failure of the Banks
"they would try to prevent": M. Aronson, *Morning Journal*, 7 October 1951. Jacob "brought his money": I. Raboy, *Iz gekumen a yid kayn amerika*, 1944, p. 230. Yarmulowsky and Mandel "not in satisfactory condition": N.Y. *Times*, 4 August 1914. Kobre ad: *For.*, 11 August 1914.

Beginnings of a Bourgeoisie
alrightnik: Abraham Cahan, *The Education of Abraham Cahan*, ed. Leon Stein, Philadelphia, 1969, p. 488. Cahan sketches: *For.*, 5 January 1907, 4 February 1907, 9 October 1906. "Several well-known firms": Florence Richards, *The Ready-to-Wear Industry*, 1950, p. 10. Garment industry, 1900 to 1912: Ben Selekman, *The Clothing and Textile Industries of New York*, 1929, p. 54. rich immigrants: Burton Hendricks, "The Great Jewish Invasion," *McClure's*, January 1907, p. 307. Glazer quote: Nathan Glazer, "The American Jew and the Attainment of Middle-Class Rank," in Marshall Sklare, ed., *The Jews: Social Patterns of an American Group*, Glencoe, Ill., 1958, p. 140. "The second generation": William English Walling, "What the People of the Lower East Side Do," *USS Reports*, 1904, pp. 84–85. Boston denominations: Thernstrom.

What the Census Shows

Statistics used in this section are taken from a forthcoming book by Herbert Gutman, *Afro-Americans and Their Families, During and After Enslavement, 1750–1930,* scheduled for publication in spring 1976. Professor Gutman kindly allowed me to use this material in advance of his own book, and I am grateful to him.

A Slow Improvement

Douglas and Rees statistics: Paul Douglas, *Real Wages in the United States,* Boston, 1930, pp. 265, 264; Albert Rees, *Real Wages in Manufacturing, 1890–1914,* Princeton, N.J., 1961, pp. 3–6, 126, *passim.* Pope study: Jesse Pope, *The Clothing Industry in New York,* Columbia, Mo., 1905, pp. 56–57. Dyche quote: Louis Levine, *The Women's Garment Workers,* 1924, p. 175.

CHAPTER FIVE

1908 census: "The Menace of Crowded Cities," *World's Work,* vol. 16, 1908, p. 10270. Manhattan apartments: *Report of New York City Commission on Congestion of Population,* 1911, pp. 110–11. "a region . . . neglected": Gordon Atkins, "Health, Housing and Poverty in New York City, 1865–1898," dissertation, Columbia University, 1948, p. 78. suicide problem: Charles Bernheimer, ed., *The Russian Jew in the United States,* Philadelphia, 1905, pp. 291ff. tuberculosis, 1906: Maurice Fishberg, *Tuberculosis Among the Jews,* 1908, p. 14. death rate, TB, immigrant Jews compared with native-born: Samuel Goldsmith, "The Jewish Tuberculosis, Some 'National' Aspects of the Problem," *Jewish Social Service Quarterly,* May 1924, p. 29; also *American Israelite,* 15 October 1908. Denver poem: *Hatikvah,* May 1924. Jewish disease rates, pneumonia, diphtheria, etc.: John S. Billings, *Vital Statistics of New York & Brooklyn,* Washington, D.C., 1894, p. 164. Walton House, Irish immigrants: Oscar Aaronson, "My Generation," unpublished memoir, 1939, p. 8. Riis to Wald: quoted in Rhoda Huff, *America's Immigrants,* 1967, p. 99. "one hopeless form of tenement construction": Jacob Riis, *The Battle with the Slums,* 1902, pp. 102–03. dumbbell tenements: N.Y. *Times,* 16 May 1879. building on the East Side, 1900: Roy Lubove, *The Progressives and the Slums,* Pittsburgh, 1962, pp. 257–72.

Working in the Shops

Baron de Hirsch survey, 1890: Lloyd Gartner, "The Jews of New York's East Side, 1890–1893," *AJHS,* March 1964, pp. 264–75. statistics on "Russian-born" workers, 1900: *Report of the United States Immigration Commission,* vol. 1, 1911, pp. 827, 836. Jewish work force, garment industry: "Cloak and Suit," *Fortune,* June 1930, p. 96. growth of garment industry, 1889–99: Leo Wolman, "Garment Industries," *Encyclopedia of Social Sciences,* vol. 6, 1931, p. 575. "bridal set": Harry Lang, "62," *Biography of a Union,* 1940, p. 25. clothing industry, 1900, 1914: *U.S. Census of Manufactures,* 1900, 1914. Baxter, Chatham streets: William M. Bobo, *Glimpses of the New York City by a South Carolinian,* Charleston, S.C., 1852, quoted in Egal Feldman, "Jews in the Early Growth of New York City's Men's Clothing Trade," *AJA,* April 1960, p. 6. ads for clothing, 1863: Judith Greenfield, "The Role of the Jew in the Development of the Clothing Industry in the U.S.," *YIVO Annual,* vol. 11, 1947–48, p. 181. thirty-nine tasks same garment: Jesse Pope, *The Clothing Industry in New York,* Columbia, Mo., 1905, p. 70. "As a rule, it takes 10 persons": *U.S. Census of Manufactures*, 1900, p. 301. shop conditions, 1911: Dr. George M. Price, "A General Survey of the Sanitary Conditions of the Shops in the Cloak Industry," *First Annual Report of the Joint Board of Sanitary Control in the Cloak, Suit & Skirt Industry of Greater New York*, 1911, p. 42. "janitor's apartment": *ibid.*, p. 68. "adequate flushing": *ibid.*, p. 64. evils of contractor system: quoted in *ibid.* marginal boss: Jacob Riis, *How the Other Half Lives*, 1890, pp. 125–26. tenement house work: Pauline Goldmark, *Survey*, 15 April 1911, p. 114. average wage, 1914: Earl Strong, *The Amalgamated Clothing Workers of America*, Grinnell, Ia., 1940, p. 3. average wage, 1930: "Cloak and Suit," *Fortune*, June 1930, p. 94. contractors went under: Wolman, p. 579.

Rising in the World

　　Borgenicht recalled: Louis Borgenicht, *The Happiest Man*, 1942, p. 62. further quotes from Borgenicht, pp. 90, 103, 239, 264. Jewish cigar makers: *Encyclopedia Judaica*, vol. 12, 1971, p. 1085. butcher workers: Joseph Belsky, *I the Union*, 1953, p. 21. "We are knocked out": *Sixteenth Annual Report, New York Bureau of Labor Statistics*, Albany, 1898, pp. 1046, 1051. Jewish building workers, 1913: William Haber, *Industrial Relations in the Building Industry*, Cambridge, Mass., 1930, p. 299. UHT locals: *Jewish Communal Register*, 1918, pp. 700–12. conditions, butcher workers: Belsky, pp. 7–9. bakery workers: *New York State Preliminary Report of the Factory Investigating Commission*, 1912, pp. 209, 211. cigar industry conditions: Meyer Jacobstein, *The Tobacco Industry in the United States*, 1907, pp. 146–51. improved conditions postwar: Leo Grebler, *Housing Market Behavior in a Declining Area*, 1952, p. 227.

Ways to Make a Living

　　East Side shops: *For.*, 5 December 1915, 27 May 1916, 7 July 1916. professionals, 1907: *Encyclopedia Judaica*, vol. 12, p. 1085. occupational survey, 1913: unpublished survey of New York Kehilla, *AJA*. "First they became lessees": Burton Hendricks, "The Great Jewish Invasion," *McClure's*, January 1907, p. 317. Carl Laemmele: John Drinkwater, *The Life and Times of Carl Laemmele*, 1931, pp. 3–48. By 1910 . . . young businessmen: Norman Zierold, *The Moguls*, 1969, *passim*. Jewish employment, 1900, clerks and salesmen: Simon Kuznets, "Economic Structure and Life of the Jews," in Louis Finkelstein, ed., *The Jews*, 3rd ed., vol. 2, 1960, p. 1639. Jews in civil service: Burton Hendricks, "The Jewish Invasion of New York," *McClure's*, March 1913, pp. 138–41. Jewish professionals "hundreds": Bernheimer, p. 107; also, Nathan Goldberg, "Occupational Patterns of American Jews," *Jewish Review*, April 1945, pp. 3–23. Jews in teaching: George Cohen, *The Jews in the Making of America*, Boston, 1924, pp. 140–42. medical-school graduates: Jacob Goldberg, "Jews in U.S. Medicine," *Harofe Haviri* [Hebrew], 1939, p. 42, cited in Jacob Lestchinsky, "The Economic and Social Development of American Jewry," in *The Jewish People, Past and Present*, vol. 4, 1955, p. 84.

CHAPTER SIX

　　table manners: *For.*, 21 July 1903. Zalkin-Lipsky story: Marie Ganz, *Rebels: Into Anarchy—and Out Again*, 1920, p. 8.

At the Heart of the Family

　　"Privacy in the home": Samuel Chotzinoff, *A Lost Paradise*, 1955, p. 81. "three boarders": *For.*, 8 August 1904. "youth . . . studying Virgil": Paul Abelson, "The East Side Home," *USS Reports*, 1897, p. 29. "Janitors aren't born": *For.*, 11 June 1914. *landslayt* in kitchen: Sophie Ruskay, *Horsecars and Cobble- stones*, 1948, p. 22. "private Coney Island": Zero Mostel, interview, 12 April 1973. "My mother worked": Alfred Kazin, *A Walker in the City*, 1951, pp. 66–67. "She was nervous, clever": Bernard Horwich, *My First Eighty Years*, Chicago, 1939, pp. 8–10. "In our home": Elizabeth Stern [Mrs. Leah Morton], *I Am a Woman and a Jew*, 1926, p. 28. "They were able": Richard D. Brown, "Two Baltic Families Who Came to America: The Jacobsons and the Krushaks," *AJA*, April 1972, p. 49. fat meat: Maurice Hindus, *Green Worlds*, 1938, p. 89. "Some time ago": *For.*, 30 January 1903. Genya–David: Henry Roth, *Call It Sleep*, 1962 ed., p. 18. mother's resourcefulness: Chotzinoff, p. 137.

Boarders, Desertion, Generational Conflict

"Each boarder paid": Samuel Cohen, *Transplanted*, 1937, p. 119. "My wife took in": *For.*, 9 March 1903. UHC records, 1903–04: Solomon Lowenstein, "Jewish Desertions," *Jewish Charities*, February 1905. fifty-four cases: *Charities and the Commons*, 26 May 1906. 561 cases in 1912: *For.*, 20 June 1921. missing persons: *For.*, 4 September 1910. Baranov on desertion: *For.*, 25 February 1910. "We called upon the old religion": Morris Raphael Cohen, *A Dreamer's Journey*, Boston, 1949, p. 98. "daughter of Babylon": Anzia Yezierska, *Red Ribbon on a White Horse*, 1950, p. 33. Sammy running: Budd Schulberg, *What Makes Sammy Run?*, 1941, p. 237. "abyss of many generations": Lincoln Steffens, *Autobiography*, 1931, p. 89. "[immigrant Jews] . . . were nobodies": Arthur Goldhaft, *The Golden Egg*, 1957, p. 28. " 'Stop! You–you–' ": Eddie Cantor, *My Life Is in Your Hands*, 1928, p. 50. Cahan on sports: *For.*, 6 August 1903. Brownsville childhood: William Poster, " 'Twas a Dark Night in Brownsville," *Commentary*, May 1950, p. 466. Liessen on Jewish youth: *For.*, 10 July 1910.

The Inner World of the Landsmanshaft

Except as specified below, the material quoted in this section comes from *Di yidishe landsmanshaftn fun New York*, a WPA study, 1938. "Died Too Far Uptown," "When He Fails to Pay": N.Y. *Times*, 6 August 1896. *landslayt* street corners: *For.*, 18 January 1906. *landslayt* cafés: *For.*, 17 January 1914. "society doctor": Dr. Samuel Silverberg, interview, 12 March 1972. Baron on cemeteries: quoted in C. Bezalel Sherman, *The Jew Within American Society*, Detroit, 1960, p. 155. number of *landsmanshaftn:* Jacob Lestchinsky, "The Economic and Social Development of American Jewry," in *The Jewish People, Past and Present*, vol. 4, 1955, p. 64. *yizkor bikher:* Philip Friedman, "Di landsmanshaftn-literatur in di fareynikte shtatn," *Jewish Book Annual*, no. 10, 1951.

Shul, *Rabbi, and Cantor*

"The Orthodox Jewish faith": Abraham Cahan, *The Rise of David Levinsky*, 1917, p. 110. "Many . . . irreligious immigrants": N.Y. *Evening Post*, 7 September 1896, quoted in Rudolf Glanz, "Jewish Social Conditions as Seen by the Muck- rakers," *YIVO Annual*, vol. 9, 1954, p. 326. Forsyth Street synagogue: Charles Bernheimer, ed., *The Russian Jew in the United States*, Philadelphia, 1905, p. 150. Golden Rule Hall: Richard Wheatley, "The Jews in New York City," *Century*, January 1892, p. 337. "At least 100 men": Chotzinoff, p. 203. "To look at this whispering": N.Y. *Evening Post*, 11 April 1895, quoted in Glanz. "The net pro- ceeds": N.Y. *Evening Post*, 25 September 1897, quoted in *ibid.*, p. 327. Yossele

Rosenblatt in Harlem: Samuel Rosenblatt, *Yossele Rosenblatt, The Story of His Life as Told by His Son,* 1954, p. 110. "rabbi . . . superfluous burden": Peter Wiernik, *History of the Jews in America,* 1931, p. 284. *kashruth* struggles: Rabbi Abraham Karp, "New York Chooses a Chief Rabbi," *AJHS,* March 1955, p. 162. Rabbi Vidrowitz: *ibid.,* p. 174. "unrealistic to expect": *ibid.,* pp. 182–83.

Versions of Belief
    number of synagogues, 1881, 1890: J. R. Rosenbloom, "The American Jewish Community," in B. Menkus, ed., *Meet the American Jew,* Nashville, 1963, pp. 8–10. "residual Orthodox": Charles Liebman, "Orthodoxy in American Jewish Life," *AJYB,* 1965, pp. 31, 34. "*yeshivot* . . . of the old type": Arthur Hertzberg, "The American Jew and His Religion," in Oscar Janowsky, ed., *The American Jew,* Philadelphia, 1964, p. 113. Orthodox synagogues under assault: David Stein, "East Side Chronicle," *Jewish Life,* January–February 1966, p. 31. Rabbi Wise: *ibid.,* pp. 31–32. "without melody or emotion": *ibid.,* p. 33. Young Israel innovations: Lucy Dawidowicz, "From Past to Past," *Conservative Judaism,* Winter 1968, p. 26. "refused to defer": Liebman, p. 59. origins of Conservative Judaism: Moshe Davis, *The Emergence of Conservative Judaism,* Philadelphia, 1963, *passim.* "organic historical development": Theodore Friedman, "Jewish Tradition in 20th Century America: The Conservative Approach," in Theodore Friedman and Robert Gordis, eds., *Jewish Life in America,* 1955, p. 39. What such Conservative thinkers: Hertzberg, p. 111. Schechter quote: Solomon Schechter, *Studies in Judaism,* First Series, Philadelphia, 1938, pp. xvii–xix. "practical difficulties of reconciling": Liebman, pp. 44–45. Orthodoxy "functioned as a cultural constant": Marshall Sklare, *Conservative Judaism,* 2nd ed., 1972, pp. 44–45. "merely a stopover for Jews?": T. Friedman, p. 52.

From Heder to Secular School
    "earnest, medieval men": Alexander Dushkin, *Jewish Education in New York,* 1918, p. 67. *melamed* as victim: Arthur Hertzberg, "Seventy Years of Jewish Education," *Judaism,* October 1952, p. 362. Dolitsky on *melamed:* quoted in Ephraim Lisitzky, *In the Grip of Cross Currents,* 1959, p. 167. "May your skull be dark": Roth. "Pip's education": Charles Dickens, *Great Expectations,* ch. 10. "Running through Friedkin's mind": Joseph Opatashu, *Hibru,* Vilna, 1928, pp. 8–9. man with "straggly grey beard": Goldhaft, p. 71. "Jews Neglect Jewish Education": *Tageblatt,* 24 February 1908. Kaplan and Cronson survey: Oscar Janowsky, "Jewish Education," in Janowsky, ed., *The American Jew,* p. 129. salaries of Jewish teachers: *ibid.,* p. 129. Hebrew school for girls, 1905: Leo Honor, "Jewish Elementary Education in the United States, 1901–1950," *AJHS,* September 1952, p. 10. yeshiva lockout: *Tageblatt,* 6 May 1908. "raise our children": Shlomo Berkowitch, "Tanes un manes tsum yidishn shulveyzn," *Yidish,* 19 November 1932.

Dreamers of a Nation
    Hoveve Zion breakup: Judd Teller, "Zionism, Israel, and American Jewry," in Janowsky, ed., *The American Jew,* p. 306. Zionism before 1914: Rufus Learsi, *Fulfillment: The Epic Story of Zionism,* 1951, pp. 148–49. "The Zionist office": quoted in Marnin Feinstein, *American Zionism, 1884–1904,* 1965, p. 283. "vulgar acculturation": Abraham G. Duker, "The Impact of Zionism on American Jewry," in Friedman and Gordis, p. 307. Zeff speech: quoted in Feinstein, p. 169. *Macca-*

bean quote: Naomi W. Cohen, "The *Maccabean*'s Message: A Study in American Zionism until World War I," *JSS*, July 1956, p. 163. Brandeis on Zionism: quoted in Melvin I. Urofsky, "Zionism: An American Experience," *AJHQ*, March 1974, p. 224.

A Bit of Fun on the East Side

East Side saloons: F. H. McLean, "Bowery Amusements," *USS Reports*, 1899, p. 14. "winter picnic-grounds": John M. Oskison, "Public Halls of the East Side," *USS Reports*, 1899, p. 38. dancing-school scandals: S. P. Schonfeld, *Zikhroynes fun a shriftzetser*, 1946, p. 45. "unbridled . . . dances": *For.*, 9 May 1902. Bernstein's Dancing School: George Burns, *I Love Her, That's Why*, 1955, pp. 51–53. "New Irving Hall": Oskison, p. 39. "19 different posters": Belle Mead, "The Social Pleasures of East Side Jews," master's essay, Columbia University, 1904, p. 5. *poyern balln:* M. Aronson, *Morning Journal*, 10 November 1949. gardens: James Smith, "Back Yard Gardening," *USS Reports*, 1899, p. 25. "On hot summer nights": Chotzinoff, p. 174. tour of parks: *For.*, 17 August 1910. commissioner of parks vs. Jews: *For.*, 31 July 1910. decorum in parks: *For.*, 29 June 1908. Yiddish music halls: Paul Klapper, "The Yiddish Music Hall," *USS Reports*, n.d. (1905–07?), pp. 19–22. "music halls . . . shut down": *For.*, 24 May 1908. "Everybody loves the movies": *For.*, 28 July 1914. "for entertainment we would walk": Sarah Mindel, interview, Hebrew Home for the Aged, New York, July 1970. Tammany ferryboat trip: Chotzinoff, pp. 159–60. socialist picnics: Abraham Cahan, *The Education of Abraham Cahan*, ed. Leon Stein, Philadelphia, 1969, p. 398. Bronx Park: Michael Gold, *Jews Without Money*, 1930, p. 110.

Up into the Catskills

As early as 1890, etc.: Alf Evers, *The Catskills*, 1972, *passim*. a veteran hotel-keeper: Alex Wittenberg, interview, June 1972. "it was given added muscle": Evers, p. 677. Ellenville *Journal* quoted: *ibid.*, p. 682. Evergreen, Park House ads: *For.*, summer issues, 1904, 1906. Rolnick at Liberty: Joseph Rolnick, *Zikhroynes*, 1954, p. 171. "It is a pleasure to breathe": *For.*, 9 August 1904.

Matchmakers, Weddings, Funerals

"shocked father": Lillian Wald, *The House on Henry Street*, 1915, p. 216. Kramer article: *For.*, 30 April, 1916. Louis Rubin matchmaker: Meyer Berger, "Bearded Cupid," *New Yorker*, 11 June 1938. "From the butcher": I. Raboy, "Di khasene," in *Ikh dertsayl*, 1920, pp. 119–20. recollections of weddings: Louis Green, Sarah Mindel, Mr. Blum, Mrs. Schwartz, interviews, Hebrew Home for the Aged, New York, July 1970. Victoria Hall: *For.*, 3 July 1900, 3 July 1903. "aristocrats and radicals": Schonfeld, p. 55. funeral costs: N.Y. *Evening World*, 6 May 1897. "the tenement of the corpse": Michael Gold, "East Side Memories," *American Mercury*, September 1929, pp. 95–96. "a horrible wailing": Marcus Ravage, *An American in the Making*, 1917, p. 260.

CHAPTER SEVEN

"many intelligent people": *For.*, 3 January 1910. "Jewish young people": *For.*, 18 November 1904. Zhitlovsky: quoted in George Wolfe, "Notes on American Yiddish," *American Mercury*, August 1933, p. 478. Yiddish words in English: H. L. Mencken, *The American Language*, 4th ed., 1965; supplement 2, 1967, p. 634; supplement 1, 1966, p. 434. *affodern, oysayd, oysgen:* J. H. Neumann, "Notes on American Yiddish," *Journal of English and Germanic Philology*, vol. 37, 1938, pp. 403–21; also Julius Rothenberg, "Some American Idioms from the Yiddish," *American Speech*, February 1943, pp. 43–45; A. A. Roback, "You Speak Yiddish, Too," *Better English*, February 1938, p. 53. Weinreich: *For.*, 5 October 1930. "The night school": Boris Bogen, *Born a Jew*, 1930, p. 45. "If our teacher had met us": Edward Steiner, *From Alien to Citizen*, 1914, p. 78. "immigrants will be pushed": Samuel Strook, "The Night Schools and the Immigrant," *Jewish Immigration Bulletin*, August–September 1916, p. 6. bakers' union classes: *For.*, 24 September 1917. "It may be questioned": Paul Abelson, "The Education of the Immigrant," *Journal of Social Science*, September 1906, p. 165.

"Americanizing" the Greenhorns

"slovenly in dress": *Jewish Messenger*, 25 September 1891, p. 4. historian friendly to Alliance: S. P. Rudens, "A Half-Century of Community Service: The Story of the New York Educational Alliance," *AJYB*, 1944, pp. 73–86. "importance of physical training": *First Annual Report*, Ed. Alliance, 1893. Committee on Moral Culture: Louis Marshall, 8 November 1899, in American Jewish Archives, Cincinnati. Marshall to Samuel Greenbaum letter, 3 February 1919, quoted in Lucy Dawidowicz, "*The Jewish World:* A Study in Contrasts," *JSS*, April 1963, p. 110. "spirit was not mute": Rudens, p. 74. classes "sparsely attended": *Eleventh Annual Report*, Ed. Alliance, 1903. "My class was composed": Sam Franko, *Chords and Discords*, 1938, p. 127. one of Franko's students: Samuel Chotzinoff, *Day's at the Morn*, 1964, p. 87. "synagogues in dance halls": *Nineteenth Annual Report*, Ed. Alliance, 1911. "It is a discouraging fact": Bernard Ernst, "East Side Boys and Manual Labor," report to Ed. Alliance, 1902. Educational League: *American Hebrew*, 15 June 1900, p. 155. Gordin's sketch: Jacob Gordin, "Di volteter fun der ist sayd," in *Yakov Gordins eyn-akters*, 1917, pp. 28–44. "leaders of the East Side": Boris Bogen, *Jewish Philanthropy*, 1917, p. 233. Zero Mostel: interview, 12 April 1973. "While it was still dark": Joseph Rolnick, *Zikhroynes*, 1954, p. 200. "We were 'Americanized' ": Eugene Lyons, *Assignment in Utopia*, 1937, pp. 4–5. Cohen recollection: Morris Raphael Cohen, *A Dreamer's Journey*, Boston, 1949, p. 280.

A Visit to the Cafés

Keidansky material: Bernard Richards, *Discourses of Keidansky*, 1903, pp. 199–209. Trotsky at Monopole: Louis Waldman, *Labor Lawyer*, 1944, pp. 63–64. Miklos violin: Chotzinoff, p. 228. "cafés were kept going": Judd Teller, "Yiddish Literature and American Jews," *Commentary*, July 1954, p. 32. "hall bedroom": Charles Bernheimer, ed., *The Russian Jew in the United States*, Philadelphia, 1905, pp. 225–26.

A Passion for Lectures

lectures, 1897 through 1915: *For.*, *passim*. Ravage in shirt factory: Marcus Ravage, *An American in the Making*, 1917, pp. 147–48. Gorky speaking: *ibid.* " 'balls' bearing no resemblance": Marie Syrkin, *Nachman Syrkin, Socialist Zionist*, 1961, p. 137. "intoxicating joy": Ravage, p. 148. Hillquit speech: Morris Hillquit, *Loose Leaves from a Busy Life*, 1934, p. 80. Chattanooga lecture: S. Almazov *Pearl, Mit dem vort tsum folk*, 1947, pp. 83–89. Zhitlovsky lectures: David Shub, *Fun di amolike yorn*, 1970, pp. 87–88. the Syrkins: Syrkin, pp. 138, 142. Wykoff on lectures: Ravage, p. 174. Cahan on Feigenbaum: *For.*, 11 November 1932. Singer on Feigenbaum: *For.*, 12 November 1932. antireligious diatribes: Shub, p. 62. Cahan on Feigenbaum's first lecture: *ibid.* "Our Jehovah showed": Benjamin Feigenbaum, "Der yuahover kharakter fun dem altn yidishn got," *Tsukunft*, February 1894.

The Self-Educated Worker
Litwin article: *For.*, 15 February 1904; see also *For.*, 25 October 1904. Cherry Street tenements: Hillquit, p. 8. the Mayer family: John Cournos, *Autobiography*, 1935, pp. 156–57. Wolfe's drugstore: C. Davidson, *Out of Endless Yearnings: A Memoir of Israel Davidson*, 1946, p. 26. Warschauer's tea-house: Ravage, p. 155. Katz's music store: Chotzinoff, p. 133. Walkowitz: *For.*, 4 November 1917. Lewisohn Stadium: Melekh Epstein, *Pages from a Colorful Life*, Miami, 1971, p. 59. Cahan on education: *For.*, 23 April 1903. "We know workers": *For.*, 15 February 1904. "Sometimes I think my life": David Goldenbloom, manuscript memoir.

Fathers and Sons
"Each new wanderer": Abraham Cahan, *The Education of Abraham Cahan*, ed. Leon Stein, Philadelphia, 1969, p. 196. A tenement worker says: J. L. Steffens, "Schloma, the Daughter of Schmul," *Chap Book*, vol. 5, 1896, p. 128. Asch quote: Sholem Asch, *Hayim Lederers tsurikumen*, Warsaw, 1930, p. 37. "severe conflict": manuscript autobiography, YIVO, no. 1. "Of culture in my house": Max Gordon, *Max Gordon Presents*, 1963, p. 11. "In Russia the father": Hutchins Hapgood, *The Spirit of the Ghetto*, 1902, p. 34. "While yet a child": *ibid.*, p. 37. "One morning my father": Arthur Goldhaft, *The Golden Egg*, 1957, p. 78. "It was not for myself": Alfred Kazin, *A Walker in the City*, 1951, pp. 21–22. "My Father Sits": Jerome Weidman, "My Father Sits in the Dark," in *My Father Sits in the Dark and Other Selected Stories*, 1961.

CHAPTER EIGHT
"streets were ours": Irving Howe, unpublished memoir. "diet of kippered herring": Eddie Cantor, *My Life Is in Your Hands*, 1928, p. 21. "on one corner": Anzia Yezierska, *Red Ribbon on a White Horse*, 1950, p. 101. "boy . . . looking brown": Cantor, p. 31. "washing away our sins": Dr. Herman Welkowitz, interview, Hebrew Home for the Aged, New York, July 1970. Allen Street: Louis Waldman, *Labor Lawyer*, 1944, p. 27. Sammy Aaronson: Sammy Aaronson, *As High as My Heart*, 1957, p. 18. "I played hooky": Harry Golden, *The Right Time*, 1969, p. 49. close to being a bum: Cantor, pp. 47–62. "We'd go to play ball": Louis Green, interview, Hebrew Home for the Aged, New York, July 1970. Jewish boys competitive: Charles H. Warner, "Tendencies in East Side Boy's Clubs," *USS Reports*, 1901, p. 43. "separation of boys and girls": Sophie Ruskay, *Horsecars and Cobblestones*, 1948, pp. 41–42. "maybe five dollars": Marie Ganz, *Rebels: Into Anarchy—and Out Again*, 1920, p. 56. Henry Klein's story: Henry Klein, *My Last Fifty Years*, 1935, p. 10.

Parents and Children
"We push our children": *For.*, 20 January 1911. "piano in front room": *For.*, 6 July 1903. "Alter, Alter": Arthur Goldhaft, *The Golden Egg*, 1957, p. 122. East Side, no privacy: Yezierska, p. 110. "There never seemed": Irving Howe, "A Memoir of the Thirties," in *Steady Work*, 1966, p. 355.

Delinquents and Gangs

"upwards of 300 boys and girls": Louis Marshall to Nathaniel Elsberg, 25 February 1902, in American Jewish Archives, Cincinnati. children's courts: *For.*, 18 April 1904. drive children out?: *For.*, 18 April 1904. Younker quote: "Jewish Delinquent Children," *Charities*, 26 May 1906. "Mr. Ordway": minutes, Social, Educational and Improvement Club. pickpockets: Frederick King, "Influences in Street Life," *USS Reports*, 1900, p. 31. Rough schools of experience: *ibid.*

Girls in the Ghetto

"fear of young women": Lillian Wald, *The House on Henry Street*, 1915, p. 203. Council of Jewish Women: Rebecca Kohut, *His Father's House*, New Haven, 1938, p. 254. "So I got a place": Rose Schneiderman, "A Cap Maker's Story," *Independent*, 27 April 1905, p. 936. "When a grown girl": *For.*, 8 September 1905. Hannah's blouse: Samuel Chotzinoff, *A Lost Paradise*, 1955, p. 173. Chernyshevsky: *ibid.*, p. 83. One such young woman: Elizabeth Stern, *My Mother and I*, 1917, pp. 84–87. Yezierska's jobs: Anzia Yezierska, "America and I," *Scribner's*, February 1922. "I am a Russian Jewess": Anzia Yezierska, *Salome of the Tenements*, 1923, p. 65. "While I was struggling," "What is it I hear," "struck by the radiance": Anzia Yezierska, *Red Ribbon on a White Horse*, 1950, pp. 31, 93, 216. "wanted a room": Stern, pp. 99–100.

Going to School

Kelly quotes: Myra Kelly, *Little Citizens*, 1904, pp. 56, 87, 125, 126. "When teacher called out": Ruskay, pp. 30–31. Davidson letter: C. Davidson, *Out of Endless Yearnings: A Memoir of Israel Davidson*, 1946, p. 23. "densely puzzled and pondering": Kelly, p. 237. Jewish pupils "mentally alert": Selma Berrol, "Immigrants at School, 1898–1914," dissertation, City University of New York, 1967, p. 61. school principal quoted: Edward Ross, *The Old World in the New*, 1914, p. 159. "mental arithmetic": Jacob Riis, *How the Other Half Lives*, 1890, p. 84. study of Jewish teachers: Isaac Rosengarten, "The Jewish Teacher in the New York Public Schools," *Jewish Forum*, July 1918, pp. 3–14. "What a struggle": Mary Antin, *The Promised Land*, Boston, 1912, p. 210. "At the age of five": Irving Howe, "The Lost Young Intellectual," *Commentary*, September 1947, p. 364.

Jewish Children, American Schools

school figures, 1905: Charles Bernheimer, ed., *The Russian Jew in the United States*, Philadelphia, 1905, p. 185. Jewish groups vis-à-vis Board of Ed.: Berrol, p. 52; *Tageblatt*, 25 September 1908. historian of New York education: Berrol, pp. 53–54. "Respect for age": David Blaustein, *Memoirs*, ed. Miriam Blaustein, 1913, p. 61. "other characteristics," Jewish students: David Snedden, *Civic Education*, Yonkers, N.Y., 1922, pp. 291–92. 1907 syllabus: Board of Superintendents, New York, *Syllabus for C Classes*, 1907. C, D, E classes: Board of Superintendents, New York, *Report*, 1912. study of laggard students, 1908: L. P. Ayers, *Laggards in Our Schools*, 1909, pp. 106–07.

Immigrants and the Gary Plan

Julia Richman, Yom Kippur: *For.*, 12 February 1911. school curriculum examined: *For.*, 21 December 1912. "discarded the old progressive tenet": Diane Ravitch, *The Great School Wars, New York City, 1805–1973*, 1974, p. 198. "banish the imported Gary system," "our boys and girls": quoted in *ibid.*, pp. 217, 223.

City College: Toward a Higher Life

1878 Greek-letter societies: Moses Rischin, *The Promised City: New York's Jews, 1870–1914,* Cambridge, Mass., 1962, p. 261. *Free Press, College Mercury,* Prof. Anthon: S. Willis Rudy, *The College of the City of New York: A History, 1847–1947,* 1949, pp. 178–79. Baruch remembrance: *Alumnus,* October 1953. "Rigid discipline": Morris Raphael Cohen, *A Dreamer's Journey,* Boston, 1949, p. 90. Hershkopf memoir: *Alumnus,* October 1948. "drawing lesson": Davidson, p. 29. passionate alcoves: Meyer Liben, "CCNY—a Memoir," *Commentary,* September 1965, p. 65. "My principal characteristic": Lenore Cohen Rosenfield, *Portrait of a Philosopher: Morris R. Cohen in Life & Letters,* 1962, p. 5. "Am too conceited": *ibid.,* p. 12. youthful socialism: Cohen, p. 98. probing, combative style: Liben, p. 65. "He never let us down": *ibid.* Richard Morris: quoted in Rosenfield, p. 96. "I could not feel": Cohen, p. 151. "none of the vitality": *ibid.,* p. 270.

CHAPTER NINE

Liessen, 1902: quoted in I. S. Hertz, *Di yidishe sotsialistishe bavegung in amerika,* 1954, p. 84. Chicago comrade: *ibid.,* p. 89. "socialist branches": *ibid.,* p. 96. Winchevsky quote: *ibid.,* p. 86.

Early Weaknesses

"The Jew's conception": *Report of the United States Industrial Commission,* vol. 15, 1901, p. 319. Beatrice Webb: Selig Pearlman, "Jewish-American Unionism, Its Birth Pangs and Contributions to the General American Labor Movement," *AJHS,* June 1952, p. 305. Chicago witness, Hertz, p. 95. Feigenbaum, antinationalist: Bernard Bloom, "Yiddish-Speaking Socialists in America," *AJA,* April 1960, p. 61. Zametkin: Hertz, p. 102. "We will consider": *ibid.,* p. 94. "To be national": K. Frumin, "Natsional oder natsionalistish?" *Tsukunft,* February 1904, p. 98. "What special demands": editorial, *Tsukunft,* December 1908, p. 768. Vladeck memoir: B. Charney Vladeck papers, Tamiment Library, New York University. early Bund: David Shub, *Fun di amolike yorn,* 1970, pp. 314–21. "Everything in America": Hertz, p. 124. "grine" and "gele": *ibid.,* p. 127. Hillquit resolution: quoted in Ira Kipnis, *The American Socialist Movement, 1897–1912,* 1952, p. 284.

The Girls and the Men

Braff: Louis Levine, *The Women's Garment Workers,* 1924, pp. 103–07. high-school student: *ibid.,* p. 108. "Some of us cried": Abraham Rosenberg, *Di klokmakher un zeyere yunyons,* 1920, p. 182. tailors' Local 9: Rosenberg, quoted in Levine, p. 141. Dyche: *ibid.* UHT: Hertz, p. 129. UHT conflict with AFL: Melvin Dubofsky, "Organized Labor and the Immigrant in New York City, 1900–1918," *Labor History,* April 1961, p. 188. "hopes . . . wane": Levine, p. 143. working conditions, shirtwaist: *ibid.,* p. 174. "Our organizing": *ibid.,* p. 148. Clara Lemlich: *ibid.,* p. 154. "old Jewish oath": *ibid.* "no mere accident": Morris Hillquit papers, Wisconsin Historical Society, and Tamiment Library, New York University. Magistrate Olmstead: Levine, p. 159. Bernard Shaw: *ibid.* "Into the foreground": *ibid.,* p. 157. N.Y. *Sun* reporter: McAlister Coleman, "All of Which I Saw," *Progressive,* May 1950, p. 25. shirtwaist and cloakmakers' strikes: Levine, p. 168. Local 1: Hyman Berman, "The Cloakmakers Strike of 1910," in Joseph Blau, ed., *Essays on Jewish Life and Thought,* 1959, p. 65. "Wherever cloakmakers gathered": Rosenberg, p. 192. collecting money: Berman, p. 82. "About two o'clock": Rosenberg, p. 208. "Every hall": Levine, p. 182. "preferential union shop": Berman, p. 80. "scab shop": *ibid.* "Everywhere men and women": Rosenberg, p. 250. "a common . . . background": Will Herberg, "The Jewish Labor Movement in the United States," *AJYB*, 1952, pp. 19–20. Jewish manufacturers: Julius Henry Cohen, *Law and Order in Industry*, 1916, p. 15. "How do we reconcile": Hyman Berman, "A Cursory View of the Jewish Labor Movement: An Historiographical Survey," *AJHS*, December 1962, p. 80. Schaffner's response to strike: Matthew Josephson, *Sidney Hillman: Statesman of American Labor*, 1952, p. 53.

The Triangle Shirt Fire
    reporter at fire: Leon Stein, *The Triangle Fire*, Philadelphia, 1962, pp. 20–21. Schneiderman: N.Y. *Times*, 12 May 1911.

The Jewish Working Class
    "frightened people": Louis Painken, interview, May 1971. old-time leftist: Paul Novick, interview, 7 June 1971. "the decisive role": Abraham Menes, "The East Side and the Jewish Labor Movement," in Irving Howe and Eliezer Greenberg, *Voices from the Yiddish*, Ann Arbor, 1972, p. 204. Sam Schaeffer letter: quoted in Ray Stannard Baker, "The Rise of the Tailors," *McClure's*, vol. 24, 1904–05, p. 128. furriers' strike, 1912: Philip S. Foner, *The Fur and Leather Workers Union*, Newark, 1950, p. 46. Zimmerman on 1914 atmosphere: interview, 26 March 1971. "East Side waited for . . . paradise": M. Aronson, *Morning Journal*, 10 November 1949. "Jewish labor in the American Jewish community": Herberg, p. 29. "success in America": Nathan Glazer, "The American Jew and the Attainment of Middle-Class Rank," in Marshall Sklare, ed., *The Jews: Social Patterns of an American Group*, Glencoe, Ill., 1958, pp. 142, 144. aging Jewish unionist: Abe Zwerlin, interview, 17 March 1971.

The Socialist Upsurge
    Debs speaking: *For.*, 14 October 1908. "Socialist Sunday school": A. McClure, *Leadership of the New America*, 1916, p. 191. Workmen's Circle: Arthur Gorenstein, "A Portrait of Ethnic Politics," *AJHQ*, March 1961, pp. 205–06. "During the campaign weeks": Harry [Hillel] Rogoff, *An East Side Epic: The Life and Work of Meyer London*, 1930, p. 16. registered voters, East Side: Moses Rischin, *The Promised City: New York's Jews, 1870–1914*, Cambridge, Mass., 1962, p. 231. "Our Exile . . . neglect": *For.*, 9 November 1908. "great Socialist propagandist": S. P. Schonfeld, *Zikhroynes fun a shriftzetser*, 1946, p. 53. 1908 campaign: N.Y. *Times*, 26 October 1908. Hillquit at 1908 rally: N.Y. *Evening Call*, 12 September 1908, quoted in Gorenstein, p. 211. Jewish Socialists unique: Gorenstein, p. 212. *Tageblatt* on Hillquit: *Tageblatt*, 26 October 1908. "Jewish quarter . . immigration": Gorenstein, p. 218. Boudin quote: *ibid.*, p. 224. "London's election": Melekh Epstein, *Jewish Labor in the United States*, vol. 1, 1969, pp. 359–60. London at Madison Square Garden: Rogoff, p. 60. London's daughter: quoted in Melekh Epstein, *Profiles of Eleven*, Detroit, 1965, p. 167. leader of fur workers: Isidore Cohen, quoted in Rogoff, pp. 49–50. London in Congress: *ibid.*, p. 69. Brooklyn branch and Ludwig Lore: Nathan Fine, *Labor and Farmer Parties in the United States*, 1928, p. 337. London on Zionism: Epstein, *Profiles of Eleven*, p. 181. "One evening I was to speak": Morris Hillquit, *Loose Leaves from a Busy Life*, 1934, p. 188. Barondess attack: Zosa Szajkowski, "The Jews and New York

City's Mayoralty Election of 1917," *JSS*, October 1970, p. 288. Marshall attack: *ibid.*, p. 291. Untermeyer attack: Epstein, *Profiles of Eleven*, p. 212. "singular genius of Mr. Hillquit": N.Y. *Times*, 2 November 1917. *American Hebrew:* quoted in Szajkowski, p. 298. *American Jewish Chronicle:* quoted in *ibid.*, "A Jewish multimillionaire": *For.*, 4 November 1917. Hillquit vote: Daniel Bell, *Marxian Socialism in the United States*, Princeton, N.J., 1967, p. 103. breakdown of city-wide returns: Szajkowski, p. 300.

The Meaning of Jewish Socialism

"laboratory and training-ground": Herberg, p. 65. "garment workers . . . Americanized": Benjamin Stolberg, *Tailor's Progress*, 1944, p. 157. "most fervent Socialist agitators": Herberg, p. 28. "In the course of winning": Ben Seligman, "The American Tailor," *Contemporary Jewish Record*, December 1944, p. 597.

CHAPTER TEN

Tageblatt on Russian Revolution: *Tageblatt*, 18 November 1917. Olgin on Lenin: *For.*, 18 November 1917. Jews returning to Russia: Zosa Szajkowski, *Jews, War and Communism*, 1972, p. 292. "A Chicago Yiddish daily": *ibid.*, p. 285. Henry Street demonstration: *For.*, 10 July 1917. Cahan on Yiddish culture: *For.*, 23 March 1917. "Former Prisoners": *For.*, 15 July 1917. Litwin quote: *For.*, 4 May 1917. "The Socialist picture": Daniel Bell, *Marxian Socialism in the United States*, Princeton, N.J., 1967, p. 116. Hillquit quoted: *ibid.* "first fights breaking out": Louis Waldman, *Labor Lawyer*, 1944, pp. 67–68. Hillquit "a Babbitt": Leon Trotsky, *My Life*, 1930, pp. 274–75. "The majority of the branches": *For.*, 29 May 1919. Olgin quoted: Melekh Epstein, *The Jew and Communism, 1919–1941*, 1959, p. 72. Salutsky quoted: *ibid.* "We are not an organ": *ibid.*, p. 94. Krantz: *ibid.*, p. 96. "guns of . . . Bolshevik soldiers": Vladimir Medem, "On Terror," *Dissent*, Spring 1975. Olgin, "I want to go": Epstein, p. 99. Goldman from Russia: Szajkowski, pp. 301–02. Medem in 1921: Vladimir Medem, "Notitsen fun a grinem," *Tsukunft*, July 1921.

Civil War in the Garment Center

(Several paragraphs in this section have been adapted from Irving Howe and Lewis Coser, *The American Communist Party: A Critical History*, Boston, 1957.)

"In Norfolk, Virginia": Irving Howe and Lewis Coser, *The American Communist Party: A Critical History*, Boston, 1957, p. 224. Zimmerman recollection: Charles Zimmerman, interview, 26 March 1971. "There was much in the union": Will Herberg, "The Jewish Labor Movement in the United States," *AJYB*, 1952, pp. 19–20. "A machine was built": Melekh Epstein, *Jewish Labor in the United States*, vol. 2, 1969, p. 128. Hillquit speech: *Proceedings*, ILGWU 17th Convention, 1924, p. 115. Hillquit speech four years later: *Proceedings*, ILGWU 19th Convention, 1928, p. 108. A writer close to garment unions: J. B. S. Hardman, "The Needle Trade Unions: A Labor Movement at 50," *Social Research*, Autumn 1950, pp. 345–46.

Dual Unions—and the Furriers

"In May 1912 Israel Gold": Philip S. Foner, *The Fur and Leather Workers Union*, Newark, 1950, pp. 73–74. Zimmerman quoted on Gold: Epstein, *Jewish Labor*, p. 175.

A Network of Culture

Moses and Pharaoh: *Freiheit,* 13 April 1922. "yearly antireligious demonstration": *Freiheit,* 14 September 1933. aim of IWO schools: Kalmon Marmor, *Funk,* 14 September 1930. children in thirty-six bungalows: Epstein, *Jew and Communism,* p. 260. Olgin speech: *Proceedings,* Communist party, N.Y. State Convention, 1938. Detroit IKUF: *Yidishe Kultur,* January 1950. description, Workers Club: Epstein, *Jew and Communism,* p. 208. "culturists" vs. "proletarians": *Funken,* October 1933, p. 14. Midwest meeting, fellow traveler: *For.,* 10 December 1939. *Kemfer* on Hitler-Stalin pact: *Yidisher Kemfer,* 3 November 1939, 12 September 1939. Communist leaflets: *Yidisher Kemfer,* 3 November 1939. boycott, Nazi Germany: *For.,* 19 November 1939.

Recovery, Growth, Adaptation

"the traditional habits": Herberg, p. 45. "renewed vigor . . . unions": *ibid.,* p. 472. strike, 1933: Benjamin Stolberg, *Tailor's Progress,* 1944, p. 211. Amalgamated growth: Matthew Josephson, *Sidney Hillman, Statesman of American Labor,* 1952, p. 365. Dubinsky rise: Stolberg, p. 213. Dubinsky as a boy: J. C. Rich, "David Dubinsky: The Young Years," *Labor History,* Spring 1968, pp. 5-13. in Siberia: Waclaw Solski, "The Schooling of David Dubinsky," *Commentary,* August 1949, pp. 142-45. "not over-fastidious": McAlister Coleman, "The Rise of David Dubinsky," *Nation,* 14 May 1938, p. 538. "Our enemies . . . dancing": A. H. Raskin, "Dubinsky: Herald of Change," *Labor History,* Spring 1968, p. 23. "used to take tickets": *ibid.,* p. 22. "the term 'Jewish labor movement' ": Herberg, p. 56. Internally, the Jewish unions: Joel Seidman, *The Needle Trades,* 1942, pp. 43-49. Membership in Jewish unions, 1951: Herberg, p. 62. ethnic changes, Local 22: Will Herberg, "Old-Timers and Newcomers," *Jewish Frontier,* November 1953, p. 24. "feeling of embitterment": *ibid.,* p. 27. attitudes to newcomers: *ibid.,* p. 29.

From Politics to Sentiment

"member of the Workmen's Circle spends his time": Judah Shapiro, *The Friendly Society,* 1970, p. 33. Vladeck quote: *ibid.,* p. 47.

CHAPTER ELEVEN

William Howard Taft: *Tageblatt,* 19 June 1908. Jews, presidential voting: Lawrence Fuchs, "American Jews and the Presidential Vote," in Lawrence Fuchs, ed., *American Ethnic Politics,* 1968, pp. 52-53. gangster on reform: M. R. Werner, *Tammany Hall,* 1928, p. 144. campaign, 1904: Moses Rischin, *The Promised City: New York's Jews, 1870-1914,* Cambridge, Mass., 1962, p. 229. Plunkitt, "like everlastin' rocks": quoted in Werner, p. viii. Irish traditions: Daniel Moynihan, in Daniel Moynihan and Nathan Glazer, *Beyond the Melting Pot,* 1963, pp. 224-25. Irish nationalist activity: William Shannon, *The American Irish,* 1963, p. 134. "All there is in life": *ibid.,* p. 78. "I seen my opportunities": Werner, p. xii. "I hate Purity": Mr. Pile, in Anthony Trollope, *Ralph the Heir,* 1871. dough day: Samuel Ornitz, *Haunch, Paunch and Jowl,* 1923, p. 178. Plunkitt's day: William Riordan, *Plunkitt of Tammany Hall,* 1905, pp. 167-83. "politician who steals": quoted in Werner, p. 298. "The Alderman": Jane Addams, "Why the Ward Boss Rules," *Outlook,* vol. 58, 1899, pp. 879-81.

Getting on with Tammany

Engel portrait: Mary Simkhovitch, *Neighborhood*, 1938, p. 65. "Traffic in votes": Abraham Cahan, *The Rise of David Levinsky*, 1917, pp. 132–33. George election: Gustavus Myers, *The History of Tammany Hall*, 1901, p. 323; also Arthur Silver, "Jews in the Political Life of New York City, 1865–1897," D.H.L. dissertation, Yeshiva University, 1954. "Jew in Exile": *Tageblatt*, 7 June 1908. *Tammany Times* quotes: 13 September 1897. Samuel Koenig, etc.: Arthur Mann, *La Guardia: A Fighter Against His Times*, Philadelphia, 1959, p. 51. Eighth Assembly District votes: *Nation*, 1 December 1904. "On a hot night": S. L. Blumenson, "The Politicians," *Commentary*, March 1956, pp. 13–14. Henry Schimmel material: interviews, May–June 1973. "likable rascal": Louis Eisenstein, *A Stripe of Tammany's Tiger*, 1966, p. 22. Sulzer and Levy: *ibid.*, p. 23. young men in Tammany clubs: Charles Bernheimer, ed., *The Russian Jew in the United States*, Philadelphia, 1905, p. 259. Louis Lefkowitz: interview, 14 May 1973. Eisenstein quotes, Eisenstein, pp. 3, 15, 16, 17, 65, 58, 47, 18, 214.

The Jews and the Irish

Schimmel quotes: interviews, May–June 1973. Ahearn-Dickstein: Eisenstein, p. 67–68. Knickerbocker Club: Dorothy Waring, *American Defender*, 1953, p. 34. "amiable and solvent Jew": Sol Bloom, *The Autobiography of Sol Bloom*, 1948, p. 200. Sirovich: Richard Boyer, "Boy Orator Grows Older," *New Yorker*, 5 November 1938, p. 27. Shorenstein: Edward Costikyan, *Behind Closed Doors*, 1968, pp. 325–26. Rankin diatribes: Emanuel Celler, *You Never Leave Brooklyn*, 1953, p. 177.

Maneuvering Within the City

"Low Invades": N.Y. *Sun*, 13 October 1897. Blaustein protests: N.Y. *Times*, 17 November 1900. Jews and Board of Ed.: N.Y. *Times*, 25 December 1906. Barondess correspondence, 17 December 1906, 2 April 1908, 2 February 1910, 9 September 1911, 23 October 1911, 3 November 1911, 12 January 1912, all in Barondess papers, N.Y. Public Library. Frank-La Guardia: Mann, p. 155. La Guardia wisecrack: *ibid.*, p. 157. mayoral campaign, 1933: Arthur Mann, *La Guardia Comes to Power*, Philadelphia, 1965, p. 116. McKee: *ibid.*, p. 114. McKee and Jews. *ibid.*, p. 116. Tammany Law Committee: George Backer, interview, 8 June 1973. Jewish appointments: Theodore Lowi, *At the Pleasure of the Mayor*, 1964, p. 41.

Low Roads, High Roads

Rosenthal: Andy Logan, *Against the Evidence*, 1970, p. 53. "bosses and outlaw elements": *ibid.*, p. 17. Morgenthau on Wilson: Henry Morgenthau, *All in a Life-Time*, 1923, p. 131. Brandeis, 1912: Yonathan Shapiro, "American Jews in Politics: The Case of Louis D. Brandeis," *AJHQ*, December 1965, p. 203. "Brandeis had come home": Ben Halpern, "Brandeis' Way to Zionism," *Midstream*, October 1971, p. 13. Brandeis's social philosophy: Stuart Geller, "Why Did Louis D. Brandeis Choose Zionism?" *AJHQ*, June 1973, p. 400. Lippmann quote: Matthew Josephson, *Al Smith: Hero of the Cities*, Boston, 1969, p. x. "When tough, heavy-set": Eddie Cantor, *My Life Is in Your Hands*, 1928, p. 44. Smith and Tammany: Henry Pringle, *Alfred E. Smith: A Critical Study*, 1927, p. 150. "Settlement workers": Henry Moskowitz, "New York's East Side as a Political Barometer," *Outlook*, 27 February 1918, p. 325. Smith and Schneiderman: Josephson, p. 291. "highbrows and crackpots": Pringle, p. 73. Smith's old cronies: *ibid.*, p. 72. Tammany song: Josephson, p. 285. Moskowitz's "ambition": *ibid.*, p. 303. Smith speech to WUL: Pringle, p. 67. "greatest brain": N.Y. *Times,* 3 January 1933. "Powerful Tammany leaders": Frank Graham, *Al Smith, American,* 1945, p. 135. "From the moment she": Vincent Sheean, *Personal History,* 1935, pp. 323–24. "Belle . . . kept Smith liberal": Gerard Swope, quoted in Josephson, p. 444. footnote on refugees: David Wyman, *Paper Walls,* Amherst, Mass., 1968, pp. 209, 211; Henry L. Feingold, *The Politics of Rescue,* New Brunswick, N.J., 1970, pp. 302, 305. "Brooklyn precincts": Samuel Lubell, *The Future of American Politics,* 1952, p. 207.

CHAPTER TWELVE

"Hebrew immigrants obstructing": N.Y. *Tribune,* 13 June 1882. "clambering upon every wheel": N.Y. *Tribune,* 6 August 1882. "filthy . . . habits": N.Y. *Tribune,* 4 September 1882. bathing habits: N.Y. *Herald,* 23 June 1882. "strangers to soap": N.Y. *Tribune,* 20 June 1882. "much thievishness": N.Y. *Times,* 19 June 1892. "Some . . . immigration": *Nation,* 5 February 1891. "Money is their God": Jacob Riis, *How the Other Half Lives,* 1890, p. 107. Jewish peddler, pawnbroker, Ikey, etc.: Oscar Handlin, "American Views of the Jew at the Opening of the 20th Century," *AJHS,* June 1951, *passim.*

The Native Reformers

Bishop Potter to East Side: George Hodges, *Henry Codman Potter,* 1915, pp. 282–83. Potter to Schiff: in American Jewish Archives, Cincinnati. reformers' gentility: Moses Rischin, *The Promised City: New York's Jews, 1870–1914,* Cambridge, Mass., 1962, p. 196. municipal campaign, 1890: Robert Muccigrosso, "The City Reform Club," *New-York Historical Society Quarterly,* July 1968, p. 249. municipal campaign, 1897: Gerald Kurland, "The Amateur in Politics," *New-York Historical Society Quarterly,* October 1969. Coit and truckman: James Paulding, *Charles B. Stover,* 1938, p. 171. Wald on Stover: quoted in *ibid.*, p. 132. Chapman on Stover: *ibid.*, p. 185. "a special affinity": *ibid.*, p. 118. "Loyalty to East Side": *ibid.*, p. 120.

Stage, Song, and Comic Strip

Frank Bush: Stephen Bloore, "The Jew in American Dramatic Literature," *AJHS,* June 1951, p. 345; also Douglas Gilbert, *American Vaudeville,* 1940, pp. 72–73, 288. contemporary reviewer: Allen Dale, in David Warfield papers, Performing Arts Research Center, N.Y. Public Library at Lincoln Center. "Whirl-i-Gig": Felix Isman, *Weber and Fields,* 1924, p. 258. Lillian Russell: *ibid.* Belasco on noses: Warfield papers. Warfield on "Hebrew race": *ibid.* Bush's song: Gilbert, p. 288. "Levinsky at the Wedding": *ibid.*, p. 291. "rich, creamy, lime-lighted": Warfield papers. Mawruss and Abe: Montague Glass, *Abe and Mawruss,* 1911, pp. 250, 283. "we take the greatest care": N.Y. *Review,* 21 February 1914.

From Henry Adams to Henry James

"four-hundred-and-fifty thousand Jews": Harold Dean Cater, ed., *Henry Adams and His Friends: A Collection of His Unpublished Letters,* Boston, 1947, p. 583. "every money-lender": W. C. Ford, ed., *Letters of Henry Adams, 1892–1918,* Boston, 1938, pp. 110–11. "Not a Polish Jew": Henry Adams, *The Education of Henry Adams,* 1918, ch. 16. "burden of guilt": Miriam Beard, quoted in Edward Saveth, *American Historians and European Immigrants,* 1948, p. 84.

Howells quotes: William Dean Howells, *Impressions and Experiences*, 1896, pp. 56, 57. H. G. Wells: H. G. Wells, *The Future in America*, 1906, pp. 148–50. Ellis Island, "the Yiddish world": Henry James, *The American Scene*, ed. Irving Howe, reprint, 1967, pp. 131–38. "In my lingerings": Hutchins Hapgood, *A Victorian in the Modern World*, 1939, p. 142. East Side "helps you to see": quoted in Moses Rischin, Introduction to Hutchins Hapgood, *The Spirit of the Ghetto*, reprint, Cambridge, Mass., 1967, p. xxv.

Legal Rights, Social Rebuffs

Schiff to Potter: American Jewish Archives, Cincinnati. "native Americans threw": John Higham, *Strangers in the Land*, New Brunswick, N.J., 1955, p. 161. educator, 1909: quoted in Milton Gordon, *Assimilation in American Life*, 1964, p. 98. Woodrow Wilson: quoted in *ibid.*, p. 101. Yale and Princeton: Norman Hapgood, "Jews and College Life," *Harper's Weekly*, 15 January 1916, p. 54. CCNY fraternity: S. Willis Rudy, *The College of the City of New York: A History, 1847–1947*, 1949, p. 294. Harvard, 1922: quoted in Stephen Steinberg, *The Academic Melting Pot*, 1973, pp. 21–28. President Lowell: N.Y. *Times*, 17 June 1922, 16 January 1923. university quotas: Steinberg, ch. 1. Lewisohn incident: Ludwig Lewisohn, *Upstream*, 1926, p. 143. "given up graduate study": Lionel Trilling, "Young in the Thirties," *Commentary*, May 1966, p. 47. "Democracy will be": quoted in Gordon, pp. 140–41. infusion of alien cultures: *ibid.* "cooperative of cultural diversities": Horace Kallen, "Democracy vs. the Melting Pot," *Nation*, 18 February and 25 February 1915.

CHAPTER THIRTEEN

Kobrin on Yiddish masters: Elias Schulman, *Geshikhte fun der yidisher literatur in amerika, 1870–1900*, 1943, p. 109. *Arbeiter Tseitung* quote: *ibid.*, pp. 104–05. "A huge mass of potential Yiddish readers": B. Rivkin, *Di grunt-tendentsn fun yidisher literatur in amerika*, 1948, pp. 53–54. "Poems and stories": *ibid.*, p. 54. "It was hardly an accident": N. B. Minkoff, *Pionern fun yidisher poezie in amerika*, vol. 1, 1956, p. 14.

Sweatshop Writers

Winchevsky verses trans. by Aaron Kramer. Edelstadt verses trans. by Aaron Kramer. Rosenfeld verses trans. by Aaron Kramer. Winchevsky compared with Rosenfeld: A. Tabachnik, *Dikhter un dikhtung*, 1949, pp. 14–15, 19. Kobrin remembering Rosenfeld: Leon Kobrin, *Mayne fuftsik yor in amerika*, reprint, 1966, pp. 32, 36. Libin, "dark, thin": Hutchins Hapgood, *The Spirit of the Ghetto*, 1902, p. 202. "My muse": quoted in S. Niger, *Dertsayler un romanistn*, 1946, p. 206.

Poets of Yiddishkeit

Exchange between Peretz and Winchevsky: S. Niger, *I. L. Peretz*, Buenos Aires, 1952, p. 185. Yehoash verse trans. by Marie Syrkin. Reisen verses trans. by John Hollander. "If every record": Irving Howe, "Journey of a Poet," *Commentary*, January 1972, p. 77. an "evening" for Reisen: Moshe Nadir, *Teg fun mayne teg*, 1935, pp. 150–51. poets following Reisen: Rivkin, p. 34.

The Rise of Di Yunge

"Most deeply satisfying to us": Reuben Iceland, *Fun unzer friling*, 1954, p. 46. Mani Leib verses trans. by Marie Syrkin, John Hollander. relation of *Di Yunge* to American literature: Janet Hadda, "Di haspue fun amerika oyf der yidisher literatur," *YIVO Bleter*, vol. 44, 1973, pp. 248–51. "Sentimentality had to be": Joseph Opatashu, "Yiddish Literature in the United States," in Irving Howe and Eliezer Greenberg, *Voices from the Yiddish*, Ann Arbor, 1972, p. 311. "We suffer from an epidemic": Zisha Landau, "Far'n kuvit fun vort," *Inzel*, March 1925, p. 3. critical attack on *Di Yunge*: L. Feinberg, *Vokh*, 21 March 1930, pp. 13, 15. "majority of *Di Yunge*": Iceland, p. 191.

Three Yiddish Poets

Mani Leib verses trans. by John Hollander, Marie Syrkin, Nathan Halper. Leivick verses trans. by Cynthia Ozick. Leivick recollection: Howe and Greenberg, *Treasury of Yiddish Poetry*, p. 37. Halpern verses trans. by John Hollander, Nathan Halper. Halpern quotes: Charles Madison, *Yiddish Literature*, 1968, p. 303. Isaac Bloom quote: Eliezer Greenberg, *Moshe Leib Halpern in ram fun zayn dor*, 1942, p. 25. what saved him from chaos: *ibid.*, p. 45. "The most ordinary ignoramus": Halpern letter to M. Olgin, *Freiheit*, 16 July 1922, quoted in *ibid.*, p. 70. Schwartz verses trans. by Irving Howe.

The Modernist Poets

Yiddish poet, who is he?: Jacob Glatstein, "A shnel-loyf iber der yidisher poezie," *In Zikh*, January 1920, pp. 19–28. "We introspectivists": *In Zikh*, February 1920, pp. 63–69. "For us there does not": *ibid.*

Literary Life on the East Side

Sholom Aleichem in Yiddish press: Marie Waife-Goldberg, *My Father Sholom Aleichem*, 1968, p. 290. When Sholom Aleichem settled in New York: *ibid.*, ch. 17. "collaborate on a crazy poem": Nadir, p. 179. "I was hired": *ibid.*, pp. 220–21. "All the authors got": I. Chaiken, *Yidishe bleter in amerika*, 1946, p. 342.

Yiddish Fiction in America

"The secretary took tiny soft steps": Joseph Opatashu, *Hibru*, Vilna, 1928, pp. 9–13. "Where are you now": Zalman Schneour, *Noah Pandre*, London, 1936. Sholom Aleichem to Opatashu: quoted in Madison, p. 328. attacks on Sholem Asch: Niger, *Dertsayler*, pp. 320ff. "It is entirely untrue": *Yidishe Kultur*, no. 16, 1942. Greenberg rebuke: *Yidisher Kemfer*, 18 February 1944. "Jewish readers and writers": Niger, *Dertsayler*, p. 497. theme of Jesus: *ibid.*, pp. 496, 498. Soloviev's belief: James Billington, *The Icon and the Axe*, 1966, pp. 466–67.

After the Holocaust

"The tendencies characteristic": S. Niger, quoted in Howe and Greenberg, *Treasury of Yiddish Poetry*, p. 52. Zeitlin verses trans. by Robert Friend. Molodowsky verses trans. by Irving Howe, Adrienne Rich. "The more modern our poetry," A. Tabachnik, "Tradition and Revolt in Yiddish Poetry," in Howe and Greenberg, *Voices from the Yiddish*, p. 295. Glatstein verses trans. by Marie Syrkin, Nathan Halper.

CHAPTER FOURTEEN

"high-church impressiveness," "protocol of . . . Passover": David Lifson, *The Yiddish Theatre in America*, 1965, p. 19. *The Sorceress*: Marvin Seiger, "A History of the Yiddish Theatre in New York from 1882 to 1892," dissertation, University of Indiana, 1960, p. 176. Thomashefsky anecdote: Boris Thomashefsky,

Teyater shriftn, 1908, pp. 5–22. early Yiddish companies: B. Gorin, *Di geshikhte fun yidishn teyater*, vol. 2, 1918, p. 30. "Almost all the music": Joseph Rumshinsky, *Klangen fun mayn lebn*, 1944, p. 389. *Yidishe Gazeten:* cited in Seiger, pp. 196–204.

The Vital Hacks

"Judith and Holofernus": Edward King, *Joseph Zalmoneh*, 1893, p. 54. "occasionally an actor": Gorin, p. 27. Horowitz on Gordin: quoted in Leon Kobrin, *Erinerungen fun a yidishn dramaturg*, vol. 1, 1925, pp. 23–25. "strolling along East Broadway": Abraham Cahan, *The Education of Abraham Cahan*, ed. Leon Stein, Philadelphia, 1969, p. 385. (In Cahan's text, it is David Kessler who is named, but the description is obviously inappropriate for Kessler. I am assuming that Cahan made a slip of the pen and actually had Adler in mind.) "clowns and comedians": Kobrin, pp. 23–25. actor's entrance: Gorin, pp. 85, 102–03. Thomashefsky performance: S. L. Blumenson, "The Golden Age of Thomashefsky," *Commentary*, April 1952, p. 346. "closing scene": *Yidishe Gazeten*, 20 February 1885. "a tragical-musical melodrama" through "The end comes": Philadelphia *Record*, 31 October 1891. *Romeo and Juliet*: N.Y. *Post*, 23 May 1903. Pinski quoted: David Pinski, "The Yiddish Theatre," *Jewish Communal Register of New York, 1917–18*, 1918, p. 576. expert in Elizabethan literature: Prof. Gerald Pinciss, personal communication, 24 February 1974.

Time of the Players

"I was curious": quoted in Zalme Zilberzweig, ed., *Lexikon fun yidishn teyater*, 1931, col. 394. Adler's *Siberia* speech: Kobrin, pp. 122–23. Cahan on *Siberia:* quoted in Ronald Sanders, *The Downtown Jews*, 1969, p. 307. Years later Cahan: Abraham Cahan, *Bleter fun mayn lebn*, vol. 3, 1926–31, p. 189. Hester Street onto stage: Kobrin, p. 25. "folksy didacticism": Jacob Mestel, *Unzer teyater*, 1943, p. 65. Gordin on drama: quoted in Jacob Shatzky, "Briv tsu un fun Yakov Gordinen," *YIVO Bleter*, vol. 38, 1954, p. 311. "Russian spirit": Hutchins Hapgood, *The Spirit of the Ghetto*, 1902, p. 168. Huzdak: Sanders, p. 315. "David Masheles is told": *ibid.*, p. 311. "Jewish immigrant . . . transfiguration": Lifson, p. 78. Pinski on Gordin: Zilberzweig, *Lexikon*, col. 444. "A Yiddish star": Joseph Buloff, interview, April 1973. "remarkable sincerity": Hapgood, p. 137. "realism with a little extra": Harold Clurman, interview, March 1972. "behind the curtain": *ibid.*

A Theatre of Festival

Mrs. Thomashefsky: quoted in Charles Madison, "The Yiddish Theatre," *Poet Lore*, Winter 1921, p. 513. Kobrin remembered: Kobrin, vol. 2, pp. 54–55. Sholem Asch: *For.*, 2 April 1926. "Adler prepared himself": Hayim Ehrenreich, *For.*, 2 April 1926. critic quoted Adler: Henry Tyrrell, "Jacob Adler–the Bowery Garrick," *Theatre Magazine*, November 1902, p. 20. Yiddish critic praised: B. Gorin, "Shylock," *Teyater Zhurnal*, 15 December 1901. *Times* reviewer: N.Y. *Times*, 20 May 1903. Isadora Duncan: Kobrin, vol. 2, p. 69. Barrymore: Rumshinsky, p. 389. *Nature, Man, and Animal:* Kobrin, vol. 2, p. 67. Adler in hospital: Zilberzweig, *Lexikon*, p. 22. Playing once in Baltimore: Rumshinsky, pp. 427–28. Adler, London restaurant: Sholem Asch, *For.*, 2 April 1926. Dinah Feinman recollection: Celia Adler, *Celia Adler dertsaylt*, vol. 1, 1959, p. 5. Adler funeral: *For.*, 2 April 1926. Clurman on Kessler: Harold Clurman, "Ida Kaminska and the Yiddish Theatre," *Midstream*, January 1968, p. 54. "He broke a toothpick":

Kobrin, vol. 1, p. 224. Mogulesco: *ibid.*, vol. 2, p. 11. Mogulesco's last role: *ibid.*, pp. 28–29. Liptzen: Clurman, p. 55. Kalish: Rumshinsky, p. 399. Sarah Adler: Clurman, p. 55. Kessler's theatre advertisement: *Day*, 18–22 November 1914. star's role: Mestel, p. 40. Yiddish *Doll's House:* B. Gorin, "Yiddish Theatre in New York," *Theatre Magazine*, January 1902. Thomashefsky in Pittsburgh: Pittsburgh *Dispatch*, 13 May 1915. "something of a rascal": Clurman interview. actors' union statement: *For.*, 1 January 1900. union "examinations": Herman Yablokov, *Arum der velt mitn yidishn teyater*, 1968, pp. 545–46. *Polish Wedding: Day*, 7 November 1914. Zolatorevsky plays: Lifson, p. 255. Cahan "Open Letter": *For.*, 23 September 1917. Cahan review of Lateiner: *For.*, 23 September 1907. Lead Pencil: *For.*, 4 May 1917. "there . . . was a vulgarian": *Freiheit*, 7 April 1922. *shund* and *literatur:* Samuel Grossman, "Five Years of the Yiddish Art Theatre," *Menorah Journal*, August 1923, p. 204. Liptzen and Kessler quoted: *For.*, 25 December 1909. Asch appeal: *For.*, 6 January 1910. Sholom Aleichem in theatre: Marie Waife-Goldberg, *My Father, Sholom Aleichem*, 1968, pp. 209–20. Adler performance, *Jewish King Lear:* Celia Adler, p. 173. "Audiences applaud": *For.*, 5 February 1903. Carl Van Vechten: quoted in Lifson, p. 170. Boris Aronson: quoted in *ibid.*, p. 178.

Art and Trash

Reinhardt's theatre: Clurman interview. Habima "mystic expressionism": Heinz Politzer, "Habima in New York," *Commentary*, July 1948, p. 153. Lewisohn review: *Nation*, 13 December 1919. Ben Ami "frail aand reticent": Grossman, p. 206. "played with shoulders": Buloff interview. "Yiddish theatre . . . superior": Lifson, p. 416. Schwartz's "native shrewdness": Grossman, p. 205. Habima director: Raiken Ben-Ari, *Habima*, 1957, p. 201. "Schwartz's greatest virtue": Alexander Mukdoyni, *Teyater*, 1927, p. 135. Schwartz the actor: Grossman, p. 205. Schwartz's *Dybbuk: ibid.*, p. 209. "slave to spectacles": Adler, p. 621. "theatre in its purest . . . form": *Morning Journal*, 19 November 1926. Cahan on *Tenth Commandment: For.*, 19 November 1926. "vast energy, a blatant exciting kind": John Mason Brown, "The Gamut of Style," *Theatre Arts Monthly*, February 1927, pp. 86–100. James Agate testifies: James Agate, *Red Letter Nights*, London, 1944, pp. 111–12. Atkinson on Schwartz: N.Y. *Times*, 30 November 1947. Seldes on *Rags:* Gilbert Seldes, "Jewish Plays and Jew-Plays in New York," *Menorah Journal*, August 1922, pp. 236–40. Stark Young, Yiddish acting: *New Republic*, 4 January 1922. Thomashefsky at cabaret: *For.*, 10 July 1939. Yiddish playwrights unproduced: Jacob Shatzky, "Di yidishe drame," *Jewish Book Annual*, vol. 10, 1951–52, *passim.*

An Art of Their Own

"Yiddish drama still anchored": Alexander Mukdoyni, "Di emigrantishe drame," *YIVO Yorbukh fun omoptayl*, 1938, pp. 254–77.

CHAPTER FIFTEEN

"rabbis and scholars": Joshua Trachtenberg, "American Jewish Scholarship," *The Jewish People: Past and Present*, vol. 4, 1955, p. 413. I. B. Singer quoted: Joel Blocker and Richard Elman, "An Interview with Isaac Bashevis Singer," *Commentary*, November 1963, p. 368.

Where Should They Go?

"folk tradition in . . . Jewish historiography": Lucy Dawidowicz, "Toward a History of the Holocaust," *Commentary*, April 1967, p. 51. "The Russian language": Hayim Zhitlovsky, *Zikhroynes fun mayn lebn*, vol. 1, 1935, p. 220. fascination with gentile: *ibid.* "our radical youth": *ibid.* Syrkin-Zhitlovsky story: Marie Syrkin, *Nachman Syrkin, Socialist Zionist*, 1960, p. 158. "History proves": quoted in Saul Goodman, *Traditsye un banayung*, 1967, p. 158. Cahan article: Abraham Cahan, "Unzer intelligents," *Tsukunft*, January–February 1910. Zhitlovsky reply: Hayim Zhitlovsky: "A pur verter vegn intelligents un am haaretsn," *Naye Lebn*, March–June 1910.

Dean of Critics
"dissemination of culture": quoted in N. B. Minkoff, *Zeks yidishe kritiker*, Buenos Aires, 1954, p. 294. "Writers fawned on Niger": Solomon Simon, "Der perzenlikhkayt Shmuel Niger," in Saul Goodman, ed., *Yorbukh gevidmet Shmuel Niger*, 1968, p. 62. Niger on Libin: S. Niger, *Dertsayler un romanistn*, 1946, pp. 212, 214. on early Sholem Asch: *ibid.*, p. 334. on Peretz: *ibid.*, p. 171.

A Gifted Voice
"Sabbatai Zevi": Hayim Greenberg, *The Inner Eye*, vol. 2, 1964, pp. 94–95. on Trotsky: *ibid.*, p. 237. conversation with Bialik: *ibid.*, p. 218.

A Disinterested Historian
"I was born": Jacob Shatzky, "Balance Sheet of a Jewish Historian," in Lucy Dawidowicz, *The Golden Tradition: Jewish Life and Thought in Eastern Europe*, 1967, p. 264. "Among the Jewish intellectuals": Leibush Lehrer, "Yankev Shatski, der mensh un zayn verk," in E. Lifschutz, ed., *Shatski bukh*, 1958, p. 45. "This kind of patron": Jacob Shatzky, *Geshikhte fun yidn in varshe*, vol. 2, 1947–53, pp. 168–69. "The Jewish youth": *ibid.*, vol. 1, p. 307. "Politics—the Bund": Lucy Dawidowicz, "Max Weinreich (1894–1969): The Scholarship of Yiddish," *AJYB*, 1969, pp. 59–68. "We want to fathom": quoted in *ibid.*, p. 63. "A mediated language": Max Weinreich, "Internal Bilingualism in Ashkenaz," in Irving Howe and Eliezer Greenberg, *Voices from the Yiddish*, Ann Arbor, 1972, p. 281.

CHAPTER SIXTEEN
"Everyone read": Irving Howe, unpublished memoir. "*maskilim* journalists": I. Chaiken, "75 yor yidishe presse in amerika," *Jewish Book Annual*, vol. 3, 1944–45, p. 6. *Tageblatt* bristled: Elias Schulman, *Geshikhte fun der yidisher literatur in amerika, 1870–1900*, 1943, p. 46. "maintain . . . most precious possession": Gedaliah Bublik, "*Di Tageblatt* un ortodoksishen yidishkeit," in I. Chaiken, *Yidishe bleter in amerika*, 1946, p. 80. Paley's treatment of Spanish-American War: *ibid.*, pp. 109–11. Paley, "true son": *ibid.*, pp. 114–19.

Kindergarten and University
the *Ovend Blatt*: Jacob Rich, "Seventy Years of the Jewish Daily *Forward*," *For.*, English supp., 14 May 1967. Cahan landing in New York: Ernest Poole, "Abraham Cahan," *Outlook*, 28 October 1911. Adolph Held on Cahan: interview, YIVO, 23 May 1964. Sanders on Cahan: Ronald Sanders, *The Downtown Jews*, 1969, pp. 391–92. "How terrible my life": quoted in *ibid.*, p. 270. "Levinsky's character": Isaac Rosenfeld, "Land of the Sad," in *An Age of Enormity*, 1962, p. 276.

A New Journalism
"Lynch the *Forvetsniks*": *For.*, 6 July 1899. Sarasohn-Ahearn: *For.*, 30 September 1903. Sarasohn whimper: *For.*, 2 November 1903. An old socialist recalls:

Gus Tyler, "Looking Back at the *Forward*," *New York*, 1 May 1972. "On Second Avenue," "three stages": quoted in Sanders, pp. 257–60. Kobrin attack: Leon Kobrin, *Mayne fuftsik yor in amerika*, Buenos Aires, 1955, p. 53. Hourwich attack: *Naye Lebn*, June 1909, p. 24. Zhitlovsky attack: quoted in *Yidishe vokhnshrift*, 1 March 1912, p. 196. Boraisha attack: *Vokh*, 31 January 1930. "flossy Hebrew words": Rich. "When the war began": Held interview. Vladeck-Marshall correspondence: in American Jewish Archives, Cincinnati, quoted with permission. Jonah Rosenfeld incident: B. Z. Goldberg, "Ab. Cahan, der historisher emes," *Yidishe Kultur*, October 1951, February 1952. "memorable excoriation": S. Niger, "Gele kritik," *Feder*, May–June 1928, p. 78.

Tell Me, Dear Editor

"Cahan did not wait": Chaiken, *Yidishe bleter*, p. 191. "Bintel Brief" letters taken from *For.*, 1899–1914; also Isaac Metzker, ed., *A Bintel Brief*, 1971, *passim*. so unyielding a critic: Hayim Zhitlovsky, *Gezamelte shriftn*, vol. 10, 1919, pp. 96–97.

Voice of Immigrant Socialism

tailors' strike, 1911: Abraham Menes, "The Jewish Labor Movement," *The Jewish People, Past and Present*, vol. 4, 1955, p. 372. Jewish Socialist Federation, 1913: I. S. Hertz, *Di yidishe sotsialistishe bavegung in amerika*, 1954, pp. 142–43. reporter strolling, 1914: *Varheit*, 29 July 1914, quoted in Joseph Rappaport, "The American Yiddish Press and the European Conflict in 1914," *JSS*, July 1957, p. 115. Cahan on war: *For.*, 7 August 1914, 28 August 1914. "*Forward* in . . . 1917": Lucy Dawidowicz, "Louis Marshall and the *Jewish Daily Forward*," *Essays for Max Weinreich*, The Hague, 1964, p. 35. *Forward* and Post Office, Marshall's role, etc.: *ibid*. memoir of Cahan: Raphael Abramovitch, *For.*, 5 September 1951. Cahan on Bolsheviks: *For.*, 1 January 1922, 14 February 1922. Cahan on freedom and Bolshevik Russia: *For.*, 18 January 1922. Cahan's Leninist rationale: *For.*, 24 January 1922. Medem reply: letter of Raphael Abramovitch, *For.*, 17 February 1922. Lenin as *gazlen*: Vladimir Medem, *Fun mayn lebn*, vol. 1, 1923, p. 291. Medem on Bolshevism: *For.*, 15 April 1922; see also *For.*, 17 March 1922, 16 August 1922. Medem material: Sam Portnoy, "V. Medem's polemik mitn *forverts*," *Unzer Tsayt*, September 1973, pp. 34–37; Sam Portnoy, "V. Medem's letster-gerangel," *Unzer Tsayt*, October 1973, pp. 27–29. Cahan back from Europe: *For.*, 10 November 1923. "during the last ten years," a typical issue: Oswald Garrison Villard, "America's Most Interesting Daily," *Nation*, 27 September 1922, pp. 301–02.

Other Papers, Other Voices

Yidisher Amerikaner: Chaiken, *Yidishe bleter*, p. 324. *Yidishe Velt*: Lucy Dawidowicz, "Louis Marshall's Yiddish Newspaper, *The Jewish World*–a Study in Contrasts," *JSS*, April 1963, pp. 102–32. Yiddish journals: Philip Rubin, "The Yiddish Press," *American Mercury*, March 1927, p. 345. the *Tsayt*: I. Kopeloff, *Amol un shpeter*, 1932, p. 324. "The first was to alarm": Marie Syrkin, *Nachman Syrkin, Socialist Zionist*, 1961, pp. 206–07.

The Time of the Day

Slonim pieces: *Day*, January 1920, *passim*. science fiction: Lazer Borodulin, *Oyf yener zayt sambatyon*, 1929, p. 38. Ackerman stories: *Day*, 16 August 1942, 30 August 1942. *shundromanen*: Sarah B. Smith, *Ver iz shuldig?*, 1919, p. 60. Frieda Sherman-Gilbert: Sarah B. Smith, *Di froy in keytn*, 1919, pp. 10, 19, 115.

CHAPTER SEVENTEEN

Entertainers and Popular Artists

"I went to all the shows": Eddie Cantor, *Take My Life*, 1957, p. 16. syndicate: Jerry Stagg, *The Schubert Brothers*, 1968, ch. 1. little dodges Jews took: Carrie Balaban, *Continuous Performance*, 1964, p. 47. "We rotated the job": George Burns, *I Love Her, That's Why*, 1955, p. 6. Hamilton Fish Park: *ibid.*, p. 13. "Every Morn I Bring": George Jessel, *So Help Me*, 1934, p. 8. Fanny's first show: Norman Katkov, *The Fabulous Fanny*, 1953, p. 8. Al Jolson: Michael Freeland, *Jolson*, 1972, p. 30. Smith narrative: Joe Smith, interview, 12 June 1974. urchin's spontaneity: Eddie Cantor, *My Life Is in Your Hands*, 1928, p. 48. "hang myself": Cantor, *Take My Life*, p. 13. "My Mariuch": *ibid.*, pp. 55–56. Surprise Lake, Jefferson Street: Cantor, *My Life Is in Your Hands*, pp. 34, 116. Burns fired: Burns, p. 37. "always trying to be funny": Cantor, *My Life Is in Your Hands*, p. 71. Marx-Larong: Groucho Marx, *Groucho and Me*, 1973, pp. 57–63. "amateur night": Burns, p. 10. "little ten-cent theatre": Sophie Tucker, *Some of These Days*, 1945, p. 38. "play at weddings": Cantor, *My Life Is in Your Hands*, p. 75. Imperial Trio: Bob Thomas, *Winchell*, 1971, p. 19. "shouts of approval": Cantor, *My Life Is in Your Hands*, p. 76. "A sure-fire hit": Balaban, p. 30. Berlin to Marx: quoted in Dave Jay, *The Irving Berlin Songography, 1907–1966*, New Rochelle, N.Y., 1969, p. 171. "Coon Melodies": Tucker, p. 33. "played Salome": Cantor, *Take My Life*, p. 67. "had seen Jolson": Burns, p. 44. "ethnic pastiche": Ronald Sanders, "Jewish Composers and the American Popular Song," in Douglas Villiers, ed., *Next Year in Jerusalem* (tent. title; scheduled for publication, 1976). "started interpolating Jewish": Tucker, pp. 40–41. blue notes: Isaac Goldberg, *George Gershwin*, 1931, p. 41. "was this the only way?": Sanders. peel off a glove: Tucker, p. 35. Dr. Kronkeit: Smith interview. Follies, 1928: Cantor, *My Life Is in Your Hands*, pp. 188–89. "Mama in the Box": Jessel, p. 60. Loew's Paradise: Cantor, *Take My Life*, p. 205. Bruce skit: *The Essential Lenny Bruce*, ed. John Cohen, 1967, p. 50. "I never did a Jewish song": Katkov, p. 205. "bands of steel": quoted in Cantor, *Take My Life*, p. 33. Jolson and Brice "possessed": George Seldes, *The Seven Lively Arts*, 1924, pp. 75–82. Hecht, 1944: Ben Hecht, *A Guide for the Bedeviled*, 1944, p. 207. "the little man who": Henry Popkin, "The Vanishing Jew of Our Popular Culture," *Commentary*, July 1952, p. 46. "comic villain": *ibid.*, pp. 51, 52, 53. Sammy Cahn: "American Confetti," N.Y. *Post*, 2 March 1974. Levenson quoted: Popkin, p. 50. "Turn to any TV variety show": Wallace Markfield, "The Yiddishization of American Humor," *Esquire*, October 1965, pp. 114–15. "a genuine folk artist": Albert Goldman, "The Comedy of Lenny Bruce," *Commentary*, October 1963, p. 314. Hasidic parody: Woody Allen, *Getting Even*, 1972, p. 54. "a Jew before this court": Albert Goldman, *Ladies and Gentlemen, Lenny Bruce!!*, 1974, p. 503. Goldwater skit: *The Essential Lenny Bruce* p. 88. Christ skit: *ibid.*, pp. 40–41.

Painters and Sculptors

"graphic arts had . . . no place": Maurice Sterne, *Shadow and Light: The Life, Friends, and Opinions of Maurice Sterne*, 1965, p. 7. "Every moment": *ibid.*, p. 19. "strange sour smells": Jo Davidson, *Between Sittings*, 1951, p. 11. parents "did not approve": Jacob Epstein, *An Autobiography*, London, 1963, pp. 6–7. "Gropper's first working": August L. Freundlich, "William Gropper Retrospect,"

Los Angeles, 1968, p. 11, quoted in Alfred Werner, "Ghetto Graduates," *American Art Journal*, November 1973, p. 75. "East Side grocery": William Schack, "The Ordeal of Arnold Friedman, Painter," *Commentary*, January 1950, p. 40. Ben-Zion: Alfred Werner, "Ben-Zion, Jewish Painter," *Midstream*, November 1973, p. 31. "He adorned his dwelling": Alfred Werner, *Moses Soyer*, 1970, p. 22. "Warm, thoughtful": Moses Soyer, "Recollections of a Student," Ed. Alliance Art School Retrospective, 1963. Ferrer School: Lillian Symes and Travers Clement, *Rebel America*, 1934, p. 278. Zimmerman and Ross: Frederick S. Wight, *Hyman Bloom*, Boston, 1954, p. 2. Duomo and Giotto: Lloyd Goodrich, *Max Weber*, 1940, p. 9. "lapses between jobs": Davidson, p. 8. exhibit, 1895: Alexander Dobkind, "The History of the Art School," Ed. Alliance Art School Retrospective, 1963. Blume on Alliance: Peter Blume Retrospective, Kennedy Galleries, March 1968. Soyer on Alliance: Soyer. "Many of these": Werner, "Ghetto Graduates," p. 76. "another Paganini": Marie Waife-Goldberg, *My Father Sholom Aleichem*, 1968, pp. 141–42. "none was of the stature": Meyer Schapiro, "Rebellion in Art," in Daniel Aaron, ed., *America in Crisis*, 1952, p. 225. "first generation of painters": Hilton Kramer, *The Age of the Avant-Garde*, 1973, p. 278. Weber on Cézanne: Sheldon Clyde Schoneberg, "Max Weber," in Joseph Gaer, *The Best of Recall*, # 2, 1967, p. 133. "introduction of modern art": Schapiro, p. 228. changes in Weber's style: Goodrich, p. 40. Weber poems: *Shriftn*, Spring 1910. People's Art Guild: M. Sawin, "A. Walkowitz, the Years at 291: 1912–1917," master's thesis, Columbia University, 1967. Ignatow: quoted in *ibid*. Jewish Art Center: Raphael Soyer, *Self-Revealment*, 1969, pp. 51–52. "East Side realism": Harold Rosenberg, "Is There a Jewish Art?" *Commentary*, July 1966, p. 58. "golden glow": *ibid*. "activity of Jewish artists": *ibid*., p. 60.

The American Jewish Novelists

"young Jewish writers": Isaac Rosenfeld, "Under Forty," *Contemporary Jewish Record*, February 1944, p. 35. "To be the child of immigrants": Delmore Schwartz, "Under Forty," *ibid*., p. 12. "internal bilingualism": Max Weinreich, "Internal Bilingualism in Ashkenaz," in Irving Howe and Eliezer Greenberg, *Voices from the Yiddish*, Ann Arbor, 1972, p. 281. "a principle of order": J. V. Cunningham, *Tradition and Poetic Structure*, Denver, 1960, p. 19. "a curious kind of argot": Katherine Anne Porter, "A Country and Some People I Love," *Harper's*, September 1965, p. 68. "with each generation": Gore Vidal, "Literary Gangsters," *Commentary*, March 1970, p. 62. "a remarkably pure English": Walter Allen, Afterword to Henry Roth, *Call It Sleep*, 1962 ed. Genya tells her boy: Roth, *Call It Sleep*. "That was the choice": Daniel Fuchs, *Summer in Williamsburg*, 1934. "tenement tenderness": Harold Clurman, *The Divine Pastime*, 1974, p. 236. "He reflected on his separation": Delmore Schwartz, "America, America," in *The World Is a Wedding*, 1948. "wildly eclectic world": Richard Chase, "The Adventures of Saul Bellow," in Irving Malin, *Saul Bellow and His Critics*, 1967, p. 31. Maurice Venice: Saul Bellow, *Seize the Day*, 1956. "Fair-haired hippopotamus!": *ibid*.

The New York Intellectuals

"unique type": Harold Rosenberg, *Discovering the Present*, Chicago, 1973, p. 280. idea of intelligentsia: Renato Poggioli, *The Idea of the Avant Garde*, Cambridge, Mass., 1968, p. 86. Greenberg on Pound: Clement Greenberg, "The

Pound Case," *Partisan Review*, May 1949, pp. 515–16. "We were living directly": Irving Howe, "The New York Intellectuals," in *Decline of the New*, 1970, pp. 244–45.

CHAPTER EIGHTEEN

"In the 1930's about half": Nathan Glazer, "Social Characteristics of American Jews, 1654–1954," *AJYB*, 1955, pp. 3–41. occupational statistics, 1940: Jacob Lestchinsky, "The Economic Development of the Jews in the United States," *The Jewish People, Past and Present*, vol. 1, 1946, p. 399. Over 55 percent of the Jews: Yisrael Ellman, "The Economic Structure and Characteristics of American Jewry," *Dispersion and Unity*, no. 11, Jerusalem, 1970, p. 103. Gallup poll results: *ibid.*, p. 104. "Given . . . the general upward movement": Simon Kuznets, "Economic Structure of U.S. Jewry: Recent Trends," unpublished manuscript, 1972, quoted by courtesy of author. "estimates . . . largely confirmed": Fred Massarik and Alvin Chenkin, "United States National Jewish Population Study: A First Report," *AJYB*, 1973, pp. 264–309. Chicago Jews, population shifts: Sidney Goldstein, "American Jewry: A Demographic Analysis," *AJYB*, 1971. N.Y.C. divergences: Ellman, p. 114. Columbia University study: J. Elinson, D. W. Haberman, C. Gell, *Ethnic and Educational Data on Adults in New York City, 1963–1964*, 1967, pp. 45–52. "In the great banks": Daniel Moynihan and Nathan Glazer, *Beyond the Melting Pot*, Cambridge, Mass., 1963, p. 149. "Big business no longer conducted": Ellman, p. 129. estimate, poor Jews: Bertram Gold, Introduction to Dorothy Rabinowitz, *The Other Jews*, 1972, p. 6. South Beach: Mel Ziegler, "Jewish Poverty Among Jewish Affluence," *Jewish Digest*, March 1969, pp. 9–12. income estimates, sixties: Ellman, p. 127.

The Suburbs: New Ways to Live

"walk on your own earth": Harry Gersh, "The New Suburbanites of the '50s," *Commentary*, March 1954, p. 215. "young Jews . . . Park Forest": Herbert Gans, "Progress of a Suburban Jewish Community," *Commentary*, February 1957, p. 120. "east European Reform": *ibid.*, p. 115. Crestwood Heights: John B. Seeley, R. Alexander Sim, Elizabeth W. Loosley, *Crestwood Heights*, 1956, p. 212. "The parents themselves": Gans, p. 113. religious rituals: Judith Kramer and Seymour Levantman, *Children of the Gilded Ghetto*, New Haven, 1961, pp. 160–61. Dr. Grunebaum quotes: Theodore Fraenkel, "Suburban Jewish Sunday School," *Commentary*, June 1958, p. 490. "Lakeville": Marshall Sklare, *Jewish Identity on the Suburban Frontier*, 1967, p. 89. "Jewish commitment . . . identity": Nathan Glazer, "A Jewish Community," *Commentary*, August 1968, p. 67. "folk-rock faith": Michael Harrington, "Naked City," *Partisan Review*, Summer 1968, p. 456. cool-headed rabbi: quoted in Morris Friedman, "New Jewish Community in Formation," *Commentary*, January 1955, p. 45.

Into the Public Realm

"In 1936, the Twenty-fourth Ward" through "According to 1952 surveys": Lawrence Fuchs, "American Jews and the Presidential Vote," in Lawrence Fuchs, ed., *American Ethnic Politics*, 1968, pp. 53–55, 70–72. electoral evidence inconclusive: David Abbot, Louis H. Gold, Edward T. Rogowsky, *Police, Politics and Race*, 1969, p. 7. Rizzo election: Henry Cohen and Garry Sandrow, *Philadelphia Chooses a Mayor*, 1972, p. 9. "Jews voted more": Milton Himmelfarb, "The

Jewish Vote (Again)," *Commentary*, June 1963, p. 81. "That was Eugene Debs": Robert Daley, "The Realism of Abe Beame," N.Y. *Times Magazine*, 18 November 1973.

Israel and the American Jews

"For the first time in generations": Marie Syrkin, "How Israel Affects American Jewry," *Midstream*, May 1973, p. 29. "pragmatism and consensus": Judah Shapiro, "The Assignment Was the Future," *Jewish Frontier*, December 1972. *galut:* Joel Carmichael, "The Meaning of *Galut* in America Today," *Midstream*, March 1963, p. 11. "legitimacy of the Diaspora": Gerson Cohen, "The Meaning of Israel in the Perspective of History," *Conservative Judaism*, Spring 1973, p. 8.

A Fear Beyond Escaping

"What makes anti-Semitism unique": Carmichael. "Perhaps it is best regarded": *ibid.*

The Immigrant Survivors

"They are aware": Dorothy Rabinowitz, "The Case of the ILGWU," *Dissent*, Winter 1972, p. 87. "first they must be trained": *ibid.* Delancey and Essex: Mark Effron, "Left Behind, Left Alone," *National Jewish Monthly*, April 1974, p. 16. "hear beautiful stories": *ibid.*, p. 14. Sophie and Jacob: Leonard Kriegel, "Silent in the Supermarket," *Dissent*, Winter 1972, pp. 91–99.

EPILOGUE

"dancing on the brink of a miracle": Harold Rosenberg, *Discovering the Present*, Chicago, 1973, p. 256. "a life lived in deferment": Gershom Scholem, *The Messianic Idea in Judaism*, 1971, p. 35. "If there were a Jewish community": Rosenberg, p. 268. "Bialik once said": Hayim Greenberg, "Golus-Jew," in Irving Howe and Eliezer Greenberg, *Voices from the Yiddish*, 1972, p. 271.

Glossary of Yiddish Terms

di alte heym   the old country

badkhn   wedding bard

berye   highly efficient housewife

bikhl   a small book; also used among Yiddish theatrical people to refer to a script

brith   circumcision ceremony

chutzpa   vast impudence, excess of gall

daytshmerish   a version of Yiddish rendered heavy and pompous through an excess of Germanisms

dorf   village

edelkeit   refinement, nobility of feeling

finsternish   darkness

folksmasn   literally, folk masses; the common people

freylakhs   happiness, fun; also, a happy dance

frum   pious

galut   exile

halla   twisted white bread used for the Sabbath

Haskala   movement for Jewish enlightenment which arose in Germany and eastern Europe in the eighteenth and nineteenth centuries

hazan   cantor

heder   elementary Hebrew school

herem   excommunication

intelligentn   intellectuals

kaddish   prayer for the dead

kapote   long coat

kashruth   Jewish dietary code

khasene   wedding

khokhme   wisdom, cleverness

khupe   wedding canopy

khurbn   Holocaust

dos kleyne menshele   the little man; often used as a designation for the ordinary person, the ordinary Jew

landsman (pl. *landslayt*)   one who comes from the same town in the old country

landsmanshaft   society of immigrants from the same town or region in the old country

luftmenshn   literally, people of the air; those who live without visible means of support

makher   busybody, operator

magid   preacher

maskil   learned man

masn   the masses

melamed   elementary Hebrew teacher

mensh   man; used as a term of approbation for someone possessing qualities of humaneness and responsibility

meshumed   apostate

meydel   girl

minyan   quorum of ten males for religious services

mishna   the oral law which forms the basis of the Talmud

mitzvah (pl. *mitzvot*)   good deed

oyf tselokhes   out of spite

pilpul   dialectic

di proste   the unlettered, the vulgar

pushke   tin box, often used for charitable collections

shabes   the Sabbath

shadkhn   matchmaker

sheyn   pretty

shive   period of mourning for the dead

shlemiel   a bumbling, luckless creature

shleper   literally, a dragger; one who procrastinates

shnorer   beggar; also, miser

shokhet   ritual slaughterer

shtetl   Jewish town

shul   synagogue

shund   trash

takhles   final outcome, the end of it all, fate

talit (pl. *taleysim*)   prayer shawl

treyf   unkosher, defiled

tsadik   spiritual leader, holy man

tsedaka   charity

tsimes   dessert or stew; also used colloquially to suggest making a fuss

yarmulke   skullcap

yente   female busybody

yikhes   status

yortsayt   observance of the anniversary of a death

Bibliographical Notes

The Reference Notes constitute the sources upon which I have drawn in writing this book; it would be pointless to reprint all of them here. The citations that follow are intended as a listing and description of major sources, and as a guide for serious readers wishing to explore the subject further.

PRIMARY SOURCES

Yiddish is essential. The files of the *Jewish Daily Forward* provide an incomparable reservoir of material—reportorial, impressionistic, sociological, polemical—concerning the immigrant Jewish experience. Like other Yiddish papers, the *Forward* is not always reliable, especially with regard to economic matters; but it is endlessly interesting. We have gone through its files, day by day, for at least the first twenty years of publication and somewhat less closely for later years. The files of other Yiddish papers, especially the *Tageblatt* and the *Day*, have also been consulted systematically.

Yiddish magazines are valuable, most of all the *Tsukunft*, which provides a monthly record of thought within the immigrant community, especially its socialist segment. Also valuable and consulted were the files of the *Yidisher Kemfer*, the Labor Zionist weekly; the *Arbeiter Tseitung*, the early radical paper; the *Naye Lebn*, an intellectual-literary journal; and a range of literary magazines—*Literatur, Shriftn*, the *Inzel, In Zikh, Getseltn*, etc. An informal bibliography of such journals appears in Chaper Sixteen.

The memoir literature in Yiddish is quite rich, and the interested student should consult E. Lifschutz, *Bibliography of American and Canadian Memoirs and Autobiographies in Yiddish, Hebrew and English*, a YIVO publication, 1970. Among the best of these are memoirs by S. Almazov, I. Benequit, Bernard Weinstein, Boris Thomashefsky, Hirsh Masliansky, Leon Kobrin, I. Kopeloff, Israel Kasovich, Joseph Rolnick, Joseph Rumshinsky, Abraham Rosenberg, and S. P. Schonfeld. Titles of their books appear in the Reference Notes, or at appropriate points in this bibliography.

YIVO, the indispensable center for Yiddish studies, also houses numerous collections of documents, clippings, and manuscript autobiographies pertaining to the immigrant experience. The Jewish Labor Bund, at the Atran Center in New York City, has a useful collection of material about the Jewish labor movements in eastern Europe and the United States.

Primary sources in English include several valuable collections: the Morris Hillquit papers, now fully microfilmed at the Tamiment Library, New York University; the Joseph Barondess letterbooks and scrapbooks, New York Public Library; the B. Charney Vladeck papers, Tamiment Library; the newspaper and miscellaneous scrapbooks at the American Jewish Historical Society at Brandeis University; the Jacob Riis newspaper clipping collection at the City College of

New York. The Lillian Wald collection, NYPL, is thin. All have been consulted, as have the extensive holdings of the American Jewish Archives in Cincinnati. Useful memoirs can also be found at the Oral History Project, Columbia University.

Government documents, though not conveniently arranged for the purposes of this study, were frequently useful, especially the Industrial Commission reports of 1900–02, and the Immigration Commission reports, 1907–11. Material on wages, working conditions, etc., can also be found in the reports of the New York State Bureau of Statistics of Labor. The minutes of the New York City Board of Education have been consulted.

Various institutions of the immigrant community—HIAS, the Educational Alliance, the Bund, the ILGWU—have archives that contain useful material, though some of these organizations were careless, especially in the earlier years, about preserving records. Many such collections are now being stored at YIVO.

The English-language press for the last two decades of the nineteenth and the first several of the twentieth century is a necessary, if sometimes frustrating, source. The New York *Times* and the *Commercial Advertiser* paid attention, sometimes in a condescending way, to the immigrant Jews. The New York *World* provided rather close coverage of labor activities. The *American Hebrew,* a weekly reflecting German-Jewish opinions, should be consulted regularly. Also important is the *Jewish Communal Register of New York City 1917–1918,* issued by the Kehilla in 1918.

SECONDARY SOURCES

Elias Tcherikower, ed., *Geshikhte fun der yidisher arbeter-bavegung in di fareynikte shtatn,* 2 vols., 1943 and 1945, is a storehouse of Yiddish material about immigrant life, especially in the late nineteenth century. These volumes have been issued in a condensed English version by Aaron Antonovsky as *The Early Jewish Labor Movement in the United States,* 1961. Other Yiddish secondary sources appear below, topic by topic.

The most valuable synoptic study in English is Moses Rischin, *The Promised City: New York's Jews, 1870–1914,* Cambridge, Mass, 1962, meticulously researched, a foundation for all subsequent work in this area. Hutchins Hapgood, *The Spirit of the Ghetto,* 1902, is a classic, radiant in its sympathies. A basic source, Abraham Cahan's memoirs, *Bleter fun mayn lebn,* 5 vols., 1926–31, is now being translated; the opening volumes have appeared as *The Education of Abraham Cahan,* ed. Leon Stein, Philadelphia, 1969. Ronald Sanders's *The Downtown Jews,* 1969, has good material, with intelligent observations, on the Yiddish theatre and the Jewish labor movement.

YIVO publications, over the years, contain authoritative, specialized studies. *YIVO Bleter,* occasional volumes of miscellaneous studies, are rich in materials about immigrant Jews; some of these have been translated for the *YIVO Annual.* Another regular publication that periodically contains authoritative scholarship on immigrant Jewish life is the *American Jewish Year Book.*

The memoir literature in English is extremely uneven, but several superior volumes merit close attention. Perhaps the single most valuable memoir wonderfully rich in evoking the details of East Side life—is Samuel Chotzinoff, *A Lost*

Paradise, 1955. Also highly recommended are the following: Morris Raphael Cohen, *A Dreamer's Journey*, Boston, 1949, especially good for the 1890's; Morris Hillquit, *Loose Leaves from a Busy Life*, 1934, for its portraiture of the Jewish Socialist milieu; Marcus Ravage, *An American in the Making*, 1917, a serious and reflective work; Bernard Horwich, *My First Eighty Years*, Chicago, 1939; Alfred Kazin, *A Walker in the City*, 1951, a lovely portrait of growing up in an immigrant home; Ephraim Lisitzky, *In the Grip of Cross Currents*, 1959; Sophie Ruskay, *Horsecars and Cobblestones*, 1948, especially good on childhood; Elizabeth Stern, *My Mother and I*, 1917, revealing in regard to family life; Gregory Weinstein, *The Ardent Eighties*, 1928, a major source for the early years; Anzia Yezierska, *Red Ribbon on a White Horse*, 1950, a poignant memoir of a woman's struggle for articulation; Louis Borgenicht, *The Happiest Man*, 1942, extremely valuable for material on Jewish garment manufacturers; and Harry Golden, *The Right Time*, 1969, full of social detail.

A number of miscellanies contain useful articles on various aspects of immigrant Jewish life. Those which most merit consultation are: Oscar Janowsky, ed., *The American Jew*, Philadelphia, 1964; Theodore Friedman and Robert Gordis, eds., *Jewish Life in America*, 1955; Louis Finkelstein, *The Jews*, 3rd ed., 2 vols., 1960; and *The Jewish People, Past and Present*, vol. 4, 1955. An early but still very valuable volume of this kind is Charles Bernheimer, ed., *The Russian Jew in the United States*, Philadelphia, 1905.

The remaining citations are arranged according to topic.

EASTERN EUROPE

The single most authoritative historical work is Salo Baron, *The Russian Jew Under Tsars and Soviets*, 1964. Lucy Dawidowicz's lengthy introduction to her anthology of east European Jewish thought, *The Golden Tradition*, 1967, is a first-rate work of synthesis. Ezra Mendelsohn's *The Class Struggle in the Pale*, 1970, contains fresh materials. Abraham Heschel's *The Earth Is the Lord's*, 1950, is a historical rhapsody presenting the *shtetl* in ideal terms; it should be read together with the more realistic critical essays by Ba'al Makhshoves and Abraham Ain in Irving Howe and Eliezer Greenberg, *Voices from the Yiddish*, Ann Arbor, 1972. Though popular and widely used, Mark Zborowski and Elizabeth Herzog, *Life Is with People*, 1952, requires much caution: it is saccharine and static.

THE JOURNEY ACROSS

Almost every memoir in Yiddish or English contains some vivid passages about the Atlantic crossing. Among the best are those in Mary Antin, *From Plotzk to Boston*, Boston, 1899; Marcus Ravage, *An American in the Making*, 1917; and Abraham Cahan, *The Education of Abraham Cahan*, ed. Leon Stein, Philadelphia, 1969. Oscar Handlin, *The Uprooted*, Boston, 1951, is rich in historical insights about the immigrant upheaval. Edward Steiner, *On the Trail of the Immigrant*, 1906, a contemporary study, should be consulted, as should the reports of the Immigration Commission.

Mark Wischnitzer, *To Dwell in Safety*, Philadelphia, 1948, and his *Visas to Freedom*, Cleveland, 1956, are useful standard studies. Samuel Joseph, *Jewish Immigration to the United States, 1881–1910*, 1914, contains much factual material, as does the careful work of Liebmann Hersch, "International Migration of the

Jews," *International Migrations*, vol. 2, 1931. Among the specialized studies the following should be consulted: Zosa Szajkowski, "How the Mass Migration to America Began," *Jewish Social Studies*, October 1942 (all of Szajkowski's monographs contain rich accumulations of material); Esther Panitz, "The Polarity of Jewish Attitudes Toward Immigration," *American Jewish Historical Quarterly*, December 1963; Joseph Kissman, "The Immigration of Rumanian Jews Up to 1914," *YIVO Annual*, vols. 2–3, 1947–48; and Jacob Finkelstein, "Zikhroynes fun a fusgeyer fun rumania kayn amerika," *YIVO Bleter*, vol. 26, September–October 1945. On Ellis Island there is not yet an authoritative study. Consult Willard A. Heaps, *The Story of Ellis Island*, 1967; Ann Novotny, *Strangers at the Door*, Riverside, Conn., 1971; and Edward Corsi, *In the Shadow of Liberty*, 1935.

THE EARLY YEARS, 1881–1900

For this period, English-language sources are scarce and thin. Perhaps the best are Gregory Weinstein, *The Ardent Eighties*, 1928; Israel Kasovich, *The Days of Our Years*, 1929; Morris Raphael Cohen, *A Dreamer's Journey*, Boston, 1949; and Abraham Cahan, *The Education of Abraham Cahan*, ed. Leon Stein, Philadelphia, 1969. Cahan's novel *The Rise of David Levinsky*, 1917, with strong elements of the memoir, is indispensable.

The Yiddish memoirs are much richer for these early years: especially valuable are those by Leon Kobrin, I. Benequit, S. P. Schonfeld, I. Kopeloff, Hirsh Masliansky, and Bernard Weinstein. The compendium of studies edited by Elias Tcherikower, *Geshikhte fun der yidisher arbeter-bavegung in di fareynikte shtatn*, vols. 1 and 2, 1943 and 1945, is a very rich source. Also valuable are B. Rivkin's *Di grunt-tendentsn fun yidisher literatur in amerika*, 1948; Jacob Riis, *How the Other Half Lives*, 1890; the Yiddish fiction of I. Raboy; Lillian Wald, *The House on Henry Street*, 1915; and the periodic reports of the University Settlement Society, sometimes tinged with a little condescension but usually sympathetic and keen.

The most valuable material for this period remains in Yiddish: the memoirs and the press of the time.

SLUM AND SHOP

There is no single comprehensive study of slum conditions on the East Side, though Jacob Riis's early studies, *How the Other Half Lives*, 1890, and *The Battle With the Slums*, 1902, are still indispensable. Roy Lubove, *The Progressives and the Slums*, Pittsburgh, 1962, should be looked into; also, Gordon Atkins, "Health, Housing and Poverty in New York City, 1865–1898," a 1948 Columbia University dissertation. Charles Bernheimer, ed., *The Russian Jew in the United States*, Philadelphia, 1905, has useful material on this matter, as has Moses Rischin, *The Promised City*, Cambridge, Mass., 1962.

Shop conditions, mostly in the early garment industry, are well described in Jesse Pope, *The Clothing Industry in New York*, Columbia, Mo., 1905, as also in Egal Feldman, "Jews in the Early Growth of New York City's Men's Clothing Trade," *AJA*, April 1960, and Judith Greenfield, "The Role of the Jew in the Development of the Clothing Industry in the U.S.," *YIVO Annual*, vol. 11, 1947–48. Tcherikower, *Geshikhte fun der yidisher arbeter-bavegung*, has essential material scattered through its pages. All the histories of Jewish trade unions contain material on this theme, especially the best of them, Louis Levine, *The Women's*

Garment Workers, 1924. But here too it is necessary to work one's way through the Yiddish press, the memoirs in Yiddish and English, and the secondary literature.

On the economic conditions of immigrant workers in the years between 1900 and 1920 we have no definitive studies—indeed, the weakest side of the scholarship concerning immigrant Jewish life is that dealing with economic conditions and business history. See, however, Simon Kuznets, "Economic Structure and Life of the Jews," in Louis Finkelstein, ed., *The Jews*, 3rd ed., vol. 2, 1960, and Nathan Goldberg, "Occupational Patterns of American Jews," *Jewish Review*, April 1945.

SOCIAL LIFE, MANNERS, EAST SIDE WAYS

About all these absorbing topics, which form the substance of Chapters Six through Eight, there are few comprehensive efforts at synthesis. The interested student is advised to go through the Reference Notes under each topical heading. A few remarks, however: Samuel Chotzinoff, *A Lost Paradise*, 1955, is a wonderfully evocative book, perhaps the richest of its kind in English; it ought to be reprinted. The University Settlement Society Reporters are especially good in these areas. It is worth consulting the files of such magazines as *World's Work* and *The Survey* for occasional material in this area. For the *landsmanshaftn*, the 1938 WPA compendium, *Di yidishe landsmanshaftn fun New York*, requires careful reading. Rudolf Glanz, "Jewel Social Conditions as Seen by the Muckrakers," *YIVO Annual*, vol. 9, 1954, is a handy compilation. On religion in the immigrant milieu, Charles Leibman, "Orthodoxy in American Jewish Life," *AJYB*, 1965, is authoritative. See also, as especially helpful, Lucy Dawidowicz, "From Past to Past," *Conservative Judaism*, Winter 1968; Theodore Friedman, "Jewish Tradition in 20th Century America: The Conservative Approach," in Theodore Friedman and Robert Gordis, eds., *Jewish Life in America*, 1955; Moshe Davis, *The Emergence of Conservative Judaism*, Philadelphia, 1963; aand Marshall Sklare, *Conservative Judaism*, 2nd ed., 1972.

On Jewish education, Alexander Dushkin, *Jewish Education in New York*, 1918, is helpful for the early years. Arthur Hertzberg, "Seventy Years of Jewish Education," *Judaism*, October 1952, is a serious overview, as is Oscar Janowsky, "Jewish Education," in Oscar Janowsky, ed., *The American Jew*, 1964.

On Zionism, all the work cited in the Reference Notes are essential.

On the Jewish passion for self-education, Marcus Ravage, *An American in the Making*, 1917, is especially suggestive.

For a study of Jewish schoolchildren, see Selma Berrol, "Immigrants at School, 1898-1914," a 1967 City University of New York dissertation. Myra Kelly's *Little Citizens*, 1904, is piquant and necessary. Diane Ravitch, *The Great School Wars, New York City, 1805-1973*, 1974, contains authoritative material touching on this sphere.

The literature on City College is very suggestive, especially Meyer Liben, "CCNY—a Memoir," *Commentary*, September 1965; and Morris Raphael Cohen, *A Dreamer's Journey*, Boston, 1949.

JEWISH LABOR, JEWISH SOCIALISM

The primary Yiddish sources include I. S. Hertz, *Di yidishe sotsialistishe bavegung in amerika*, 1954, careful and thorough; Tcherikower, *Geshikhte fun der yidisher arbeter-bavegung*, a basic source; Herz Burgin, *Geshikhte fun der yidisher arbeter-bavegung*, 1915, dated but necessary; David Shub, *Fun di amolike yorn*, 1970, a lively memoir; the two indispensable books by Bernard Weinstein, *Di yidishe yunyons in amerika*, 1929, and *Fertsik yor in der yidisher arbeter-bavegung*, 1924; and Abraham Rosenberg's crucial memoir, *Di klokmakher un zeyere yunyons*, 1920.

The single best analytical statement on the Jewish labor movement, agree with it or not, is Will Herberg, "The Jewish Labor Movement in the United States," *AJYB*, 1952. Louis Levine's *The Women's Garment Workers*, 1924, though dated, is a very fine book. Useful studies include: Melvin Dubofsky, "Organized Labor and the Immigrant in New York City, 1900–1918," *Labor History*, April 1961; Hyman Berman, "The Cloakmakers Strike of 1910," in Joseph Blau, ed., *Essays on Jewish Life and Thought*, 1959; Abraham Menes, "The East Side and the Jewish Labor Movement," in Irving Howe and Eliezer Greenberg, *Voices from the Yiddish*, Ann Arbor, 1972; Arthur Gorenstein, "A Portrait of Ethnic Politics," *AJHS*, March 1961; and Zosa Szajkowski, "The Jews and New York City's Mayoralty Election of 1917," *JSS*, October 1970. For general background see Daniel Bell, *Marxian Socialism in the United States*, Princeton, N.J., 1967; Melekh Epstein, *Jewish Labor in the United States*, 1969 (written by a veteran Jewish leftist, rich in materials, but requiring caution with regard to details); Leon Stein, *The Triangle Fire*, Philadelphia, 1962; Joel Seidman, *The Needle Trades*, 1942; and Matthew Josephson, *Sidney Hillman: Statesman of American Labor*, 1952.

COMMUNISM, BREAKUP OF THE LEFT

Again, the Yiddish sources are indispensable, especially the files of the social democratic *Forward* and the Communist *Freiheit*. Melekh Epstein, *The Jew and Communism, 1919–1941*, 1959 (see comment on his other book, paragraph above); Zosa Szajkowski, *Jews, War and Communism*, 1972; and Irving Howe and Lewis Coser, *The American Communist Party: A Critical History*, Boston, 1957, contain background material on the Yiddish-speaking Communists. Judah Shapiro, *The Friendly Society*, 1970, is a brief history of the Workmen's Circle.

AMERICAN POLITICS

The literature in this area is limited in range and depth; much work remains to be done (e.g., a thorough study of the relation between Jews and Tammany Hall). Arthur Silver, "Jews in the Political Life of New York City, 1865–1897," is a factually detailed dissertation, Yeshiva University, 1954. William Shannon, *The American Irish*, 1963, is a fine book suggesting parallels. Daniel Moynihan and Nathan Glazer, *Beyond the Melting Pot*, Cambridge, Mass., 1963, has good pages on this subject. The two histories of Tammany Hall—Gustavus Myers, *The History of Tammany Hall*, 1901, and M. R. Werner, *Tammany Hall*, 1928—are anecdotal, vivid, but insufficient. A serious student of the early years would want to leaf through the files of the *Tammany Times*. There is good material in Matthew Josephson, *Al Smith: Hero of the Cities*, Boston, 1969, and Arthur Mann, *La Guardia: A Fighter Against His Times*, Philadelphia, 1959. Theodore Lowi, *At the Pleasure of the Mayor*, 1964, has a sophisticated treatment of patronage. And wonderfully self-revealing is the autobiography of a lifelong Tammany hanger-on: Louis Eisenstein, *A Stripe of Tammany's Tiger*, 1966.

For the administration of Franklin Roosevelt and the Jewish refugees, see two solid books: David Wyman, *Paper Walls*, Amherst, Mass., 1968, and Henry L. Feingold, *The Politics of Rescue*, New Brunswick, N.J., 1970.

AMERICAN RESPONSES
Most of the material has been culled from sources listed in the notes, but helpful secondary studies include: Oscar Handlin, "American Views of the Jew at the Opening of the 20th Century," *AJHS*, June 1951 (richly documented); Douglas Gilbert, *American Vaudeville*, 1940; Edward Saveth, *American Historians and European Immigrants*, 1948; Milton Gordon, *Assimilation in American Life*, 1964; and Stephen Steinberg, *The Academic Melting Pot*, 1973.

YIDDISH LITERATURE
Important studies in Yiddish include: Elias Schulman, *Geshikhte fun der yidisher literatur in amerika, 1870–1900*, 1943 (good on the late nineteenth century, for journalism as well as literature); B. Rivkin, *Di grunt-tendentsn fun yidisher literatur in amerika*, 1948 (acute theorizing on the social role of Yiddish writing); N. B. Minkoff, *Pionern fun yidisher poezie in amerika*, vol. 1, 1956 (sympathetic portraits of the sweatshop writers); A. Tabachnik, *Dikhter un dikhtung*, 1949 (first-rate criticism on *Di Yunge* poets); Reuben Iceland, *Fun unzer friling*, 1954 (a vivid memoir by a theoretician of *Di Yunge*); Eliezer Greenberg, *Moshe Leib Halpern in ram fun zayn dor*, 1942 (an excellent study of a major Yiddish poet in America, with many references to larger literary developments); and S. Niger, *Dertsayler un romanistn*, 1946 (authoritative essays on earlier Yiddish writers in America).

In English, see the introductions to the anthologies by Irving Howe and Eliezer Greenberg, *A Treasury of Yiddish Stories*, 1954; *A Treasury of Yiddish Poetry*, 1969; and *Voices from the Yiddish*, Ann Arbor, 1972. See also Charles Madison, *Yiddish Literature*, 1968.

YIDDISH THEATRE
The fundamental text for the early period is B. Gorin, *Di geshikhte fun yidishn teyater*, 1918. A useful study of the early period, relying on Gorin, is Marvin Seiger, "A History of the Yiddish Theatre in New York from 1882 to 1892," a University of Indiana dissertation, 1960. David Lifson, *The Yiddish Theatre in America*, 1965, the standard English-language survey, must be used with caution: it is ill-organized and uneven in quality.

A number of memoirs in Yiddish are extremely valuable: Leon Kobrin, *Erinerungen fun a yidishn dramaturg*, 1925; Boris Thomashefsky, *Teyater shriftn*, 1908; Celia Adler, *Celia Adler dertsaylt*, 1959; and Joseph Rumshinsky, *Klangen fun mayn lebn*, 1944. Ronald Sanders, *The Downtown Jews*, 1969, is good on Yiddish theatre. Hutchins Hapgood, *The Spirit of the Ghetto*, 1902, contains a vivid contemporary account. The criticism of Alexander Mukdoyni, *Teyater*, 1927, and Jacob Mestel, *Unzer teyater*, 1943, should be consulted. An especially helpful article is Samuel Grossman, "Five Years of the Yiddish Art Theatre," *Menorah Journal*, August 1923. Stark Young, perhaps the best drama critic writing in America during the time the Yiddish theatre flourished, has some very fine short appreciations, *Immortal Shadows*, 1948. Zalme Zilberzweig, ed., *Lexikon fun yidishn teyater*, 1931, is a storehouse of material.

YIDDISH SCHOLARSHIP

The student who commands Yiddish should consult Hayim Zhitlovsky, *Zikhroynes fun mayn lebn*, 1935; Saul Goodman, ed., *Yorbukh gevidmet Shmuel Niger*, 1968; indeed, the writings of Niger, Weinreich, Shatzky, and many others, which yield knowledge and pleasure. In English, Joshua Trachtenberg, "American Jewish Scholarship," *The Jewish People: Past and Present*, 1955, is a responsible survey. Dawidowicz, *The Golden Tradition*, 1967, and Howe and Greenberg, *Voices from the Yiddish*, contain representative selections from Yiddish scholars, essayists, polemicists, and memoirists. Hayim Greenberg's essays, *The Inner Eye*, 2 vols., 1964, should be read for their intellectual keenness.

THE YIDDISH PRESS

There is no substitute for going through the papers themselves. I. Chaiken, *Yidishe bleter in amerika*, 1946, is the standard survey. Elias Schulman, *Geshikhte fun der yidisher literatur in amerika, 1870–1900*, has material on the early press. Sanders, *The Downtown Jews*, is abundant on this matter.

JEWISH ENTERTAINERS AND POPULAR ARTISTS

The popular biographies and autobiographies, often ghostwritten, must be ploughed through for valuable materials that can be found together with trivia and puffery. Ronald Sanders, "Jewish Composers and the American Popular Song," in Douglas Villiers, ed., *Next Year in Jerusalem*, scheduled for publication in 1976, is suggestive. Henry Popkin, "The Vanishing Jew of Our Popular Culture," *Commentary*, July 1952; Wallace Markfield, "The Yiddishization of American Humor," *Esquire*, October 1965; and Albert Goldman, "The Comedy of Lenny Bruce," *Commentary*, October 1963, all merit consultation.

PAINTERS AND SCULPTORS

Alfred Werner, "Ghetto Graduates," *American Art Journal*, November 1973, is a reliable survey. Harold Rosenberg, "Is There a Jewish Art?" *Commentary*, July 1966, is a brilliant discussion. Most of the material has to be gathered from specialized monographs, catalogues, etc.

JEWS IN CONTEMPORARY AMERICA

The literature on this subject is vast, and no pretense is made here of even beginning to mention the important items. Below are a few that were especially helpful in the writing of this book: Nathan Glazer, "Social Characteristics of American Jews, 1654–1954," *AJYB*, 1955, as also his *American Judaism*, 2nd ed., Chicago, 1972, for sophisticated treatments of Jewish social and economic positions; C. Bezalel Sherman, *The Jew Within American Society*, Detroit, 1960, a sociological study paying special attention to the east European immigrants; Sidney Goldstein, "American Jewry: A Demographic Analysis," *AJYB*, 1971, perhaps the best study of its kind; and Yisrael Ellman, "The Economic Structure and Characteristics of American Jewry," *Dispersion and Unity*, no. 11, Jerusalem, 1970, a useful summary of the literature.

On suburban life, see Herbert Gans, "Progress of a Suburban Jewish Community," *Commentary*, February 1957, a very acute article; John B. Seeley, R. Alexander Sim, Elizabeth W. Loosley, *Crestwood Heights*, 1956, one of the first and still most stimulating of the suburban studies; and two other basic studies, Judith Kramer and Seymour Levantman, *Children of the Gilded Ghetto*, New Haven, 1961, and Marshall Sklare, *Jewish Identity on the Suburban Frontier*, 1967.

On Jews in politics, see Lawrence Fuchs, "American Jews and the Presidential Vote," in Lawrence Fuchs, ed., *American Ethnic Politics*, 1968, and the provocative essays of Milton Himmelfarb in his *The Jews of Modernity*, 1973. As with a good many other topics touched upon in these pages, much remains to be done with this one.

(Continued from copyright page)

Movement in the United States" by Will Herberg, published in *American Jewish Year Book*, and *The Education of Abraham Cahan* by Abraham Cahan, edited by Leon Stein, both copyright by The Jewish Publication Society of America; Macmillan Publishing Co., Inc., for *The Russian Jew Under Tsars and Soviets* by Salo Baron, copyright © Salo W. Baron 1964, and *A Dreamer's Journey* by Morris Raphael Cohen, copyright 1949 by The Free Press; *Midstream* for "The Meaning of *Galut* in America Today" by Joel Carmichael; *The Nation* for "The Rise of David Dubinsky" by McAlister Coleman, and "America's Most Interesting Daily" by Oswald Garrison Villard; *The National Jewish Monthly* for "Left Behind, Left Alone" by Mark Effron; Robert Speller and Sons, Publishers, Inc., for *A Stripe of Tammany's Tiger* by Louis Eisenstein and Elliot Rosenberg; The Seabury Press, Inc., for *The Story of Ellis Island* by Willard A. Heaps, copyright © 1967 by Willard A. Heaps; *Social Research* for "The Needle Trade Unions: A Labor Movement at 50" by J. B. S. Hardman; United Hebrew Trades Publications for *Di yidishe yunyons in amerika* by Bernard Weinstein; The University of Michigan Press for *Voices from the Yiddish* by Irving Howe and Eliezer Greenberg; Vanguard Press, Inc., for *An East Side Epic: The Life and Work of Meyer London* by Harry Rogoff, copyright 1930 by the Vanguard Press, copyright © renewed 1957 by Harry Rogoff; The Viking Press, Inc., for *The Women's Garment Workers* by Louis Levine, copyright 1924 by the International Ladies Garment Workers Union; Wayne State University Press for *The Jew Within American Society* by C. Bezalel Sherman, copyright © 1960 by the Wayne State University Press; Yale University Press for *The Jews in Russia*, vol. 1, by Louis Greenberg; Yiddisher Kultur Farband for *Di grunt-tendentsn fun yidisher literatur in amerika* by B. Rivkin; YIVO Institute for Jewish Research for *The Early Jewish Labor Movement in the United States* by Aaron Antonovsky, "The Am Oylom Movement" by Abraham Menes, published in *YIVO Annual*, and *Geshikhte fun der yidisher arbeter-bavegung in di fareynikte shtatn*, vol. 1, edited by Elias Tcherikower. George Burns kindly gave permission to quote from his book *I Love Her, That's Why*.

Index